OFFICIAL ACCOUNT
OF THE MILITARY OPERATIONS

IN

CHINA 1900-1901

BY

MAJOR E. W. M. NORIE
ASSISTANT-QUARTERMASTER-GENERAL
FOR INTELLIGENCE
BRITISH CONTINGENT,
CHINA FIELD FORCE

The Naval & Military Press Ltd

Published by
The Naval & Military Press Ltd
5 Riverside, Brambleside, Bellbrook
Industrial Estate, Uckfield, East Sussex,
TN22 1QQ England

Tel: +44 (0) 1825 749494
Fax: +44 (0) 1825 765701

www.naval-military-press.com
www.nmarchive.com

In reprinting in facsimile from the original, any imperfections are inevitably reproduced and the quality may fall short of modern type and cartographic standards.

PREFACE.

This official account of the military operations in China, 1900-01, was originally compiled by Major E. W. M. Norie, who was Assistant-Quartermaster-General for Intelligence on the Staff of the British Contingent, China Field Force. It has, however, been subjected to considerable revision and editing in the Intelligence Department, and has also been amplified by the incorporation of several reports which Major Norie had not included.

The account commences with the rise of the Boxer Secret Society, and the outbreak of hostilities against foreigners in the northern provinces, and extends over the period of actual military operations for the relief of the Foreign Legations in Peking up to the conclusion of peace, and the consequent withdrawal of the greater part of the allied forces from China.

The information given has been obtained from all official reports and publications bearing on the subject, and from unofficial diaries and descriptions of various incidents of the campaign.

         W. G. NICHOLSON,
Intelligence Department,   D.G.M.I.
 War Office,
  12*th September*, 1903.

CONTENTS.

CHAPTER I.
Events which led up to the War	PAGE 1

CHAPTER II.
Development of the situation at Tien-tsin and Capture of the Taku Forts - - - - - 8

CHAPTER III.
Relief of Tien-tsin - - - - - 17

CHAPTER IV.
The Peking Relief Column under Vice-Admiral Sir E. H. Seymour 23

CHAPTER V.
Defence of the Settlements at Tien-tsin and Capture of the Native City - - - - - 31

CHAPTER VI.
Despatch of the British Contingent — China Expeditionary Force—from India - - - - 42

CHAPTER VII.
Advance of the Allies from Tien-tsin; Actions of Pei-ts'ang and Yang-tsun; Relief of the Legations and Occupation of Peking - - - - - 51

CHAPTER VIII.
Siege of the Legations - - - - - 71

CHAPTER IX.
Progress of Events in and around Peking up to the end of September 1900 - - - - 89

CHAPTER X.

Course of Events in North China preceding Negotiations for Peace - - - - - - - 100

CHAPTER XI.

Course of Events in other parts of China - - - 108

CHAPTER XII.

Occupation of Shan-hai-kuan and Ching-wang-tao, and Arrangements for the repair and working of the Railway from Shan-hai-kuan to Peking - - - - 120

CHAPTER XIII.

Punitive Expedition to Pao-ting fu - - - 129

CHAPTER XIV.

Military Operations up to the end of December, 1900 - - 137

CHAPTER XV.

Military Operations from the Commencement of 1901 up to the Conclusion of the Campaign - - - - 143

CHAPTER XVI.

Negotiations for Peace, resulting in the withdrawal from China of the bulk of the Foreign Contingents, and the Return to Power of the Chinese Government - - - - 157

APPENDICES.

APPENDIX A.
PAGE
Despatches relating to the operations in China - - - 171

APPENDIX B.
Amalgamated Scheme for the despatch of an Expeditionary Force to China, as finally approved by the Government of India - - - - - - - - 349

APPENDIX B. 1.
Detail of the China Expeditionary Force - - - - 386

APPENDIX B. 2.
Field Service Clothing supplied to troops and followers - 396

APPENDIX C.
Return of Stores provided from England and Canada for the China Expedition - - - - - - 400

APPENDIX D.
Detail of Troops, Animals, Guns, &c., embarked - - 406

APPENDIX E.
Transport by Sea of the China Expeditionary Force from India to China - - - - - - - 426

APPENDIX F.
Standing Orders of the China Expeditionary Force - - 431

APPENDIX G.

Report on the working of the Commissariat Department of the China Expeditionary Force - - - - - 443

APPENDIX H.

Report on the Transport operations of the China Expeditionary Force - - - - - - 448

APPENDIX I.

Medical arrangements for the China Expeditionary Force - 451

APPENDIX J.

Medical History of the Campaign - - - - 462

APPENDIX K.

Accommodation of the Troops of the China Expeditionary Force during the Winter of 1900-1901 - - - 472

APPENDIX L.

Veterinary Notes on Fittings of Transports and Management of Horses on board ship - - - - - 474

APPENDIX M.

Report on the working of the Army Veterinary Department with the China Expeditionary Force - - - 477

APPENDIX N.

Report on Signalling, China Expeditionary Force - - - 481

APPENDIX O.

Police Administration of the British Quarter of the Chinese City, Peking - - - - - - 483

APPENDIX P.

Ultimatum of the Foreign Admirals demanding the Surrender of the Taku Forts - - - - - - 489

APPENDIX Q.

Imperial Edicts, &c., relating to the Boxer Movement - - 490

APPENDIX R.

Imperial Decrees giving effect to the Terms of Peace - - 499

APPENDIX S.

Return of the Troops from China on the reduction of the China Expeditionary Force - - - - - 509

INDEX - - - - - - 510

MAPS AND PLANS.

			PAGE
1.	Sketch illustrating capture of the Taku Forts, 17th June 1900	to face	16
2.	Attack on Tien-tsin City, 13th and 14th July 1900	,,	40
3.	Sketch of action at Pei-ts'ang, 5th August 1900	,,	58
4.	Sketch of action at Yang-tsun, 6th August 1900	,,	60
5.	Relief of the Legations, 14th August 1900	,,	68
6.	Peking, 14th, 15th and 16th August 1900	,,	70
7.	Relief of the Pei-t'ang, 16th August 1900	,,	70
8.	Defence of the Legations, Peking, 20th June to 14th August 1900	,,	88
9.	Sketch Map of Peking showing areas administered by the Powers after first occupation	,,	92
10.	Administration map of Peking after the departure of the Americans and Russians	,,	156
11.	General map of the area covered by the operations	front pocket	
12.	General Plan of Ching-wang-tao	rear pocket	
13.	Sketch map of Country around Ching-wang-tao	,,	,,
14.	Rough sketch of Shan-hai-kuan and surrounding country	,,	,,
15.	Plan of Tong-shan	,,	,,

CHAPTER I.

EVENTS WHICH LED UP TO THE WAR.

Before proceeding to describe the series of military events which culminated in the relief of the Foreign Legations in Peking and the occupation of the capital of China by the contingents of the Allied Powers, it may be of interest to give some account of the rise and spread of the Boxer movement.

The real origin of the *I-ho-ch'uan*, or "Fists of Patriotic Union," commonly known under the title of "Boxers," is difficult to trace, for whereas some authorities assert that it was the outcome of the cession of Kiao-chou to the Germans, and had for its object the defence of the province of Shan-tung against the invasion of the foreigner, others maintain that it is really an old society, which the general state of unrest had brought to life again. Whatever its origin, it is now a matter of history that the obscure society, which in the beginning might have been easily suppressed, grew rapidly into a vast and dangerous association of brigands, which the Government soon found beyond its powers to control.

For centuries past the Chinese empire has been a hotbed of secret societies, of which some are confessedly political and anti-dynastic, while others are of a more harmless nature, and were originally founded with the object of mutual protection of their members either against the illegal exactions of unjust officials or the depredations of robber bands. In most cases, however, the original object has been lost sight of, and the societies, by the gradual introduction of bad characters in search of protection, have become dangerous to the Government and to society at large. So much has this been recognised, and such is the dread in which they are held by the officials, that all secret societies throughout the empire are forbidden by law, and strenuous endeavours are made to suppress them.

One of the oldest and most widespread of the secret societies is the *Ko-lao-hui*, or Society of the "Elder Brother," which at first was founded with the object of mutual protection for its members against the exactions of the mandarins, but has now become anti-Manchu and hostile to the reigning dynasty. An offshoot of the parent society is the *Ta-tao-hui*, or "Big Knife Society," which has its head-quarters in Ho-nan, and is said to be violently anti-foreign, and especially anti-Catholic. When the Boxers first came into prominence they were supposed to be this *Ta-tao-hui*, but it now appears that they were a distinct and separate society, though no doubt many *Ta-tao-hui* and other secret society men joined their ranks.

In China, as elsewhere, an air of mystery as to its proceedings appears to be recognised as a valuable asset to a secret society for obtaining recruits to the cause, and the professors and teachers of the Boxer cult were not behindhand in laying claim to direct inspiration from the gods and the possession of supernatural powers. They declared that the gods had appeared to assemblies of their members, and announced that the rain would be withheld till the telegraph lines and railways were totally destroyed and the foreign devils driven from the land, but that, when this was successfully accomplished, the fruitful seasons and timely rains would return. Moreover, they were not to fight alone, for when the appointed time arrived myriads of spirit soldiers would descend to earth and fight in the ranks of the faithful protectors of the religion against the foreigners. By the use of hypnotism, which appears to have been employed by their experts with great success, or by the choice of epileptic subjects, the people beheld men thrown into a state of trance, under the effects of which they gave utterance to strange sayings, which were translated by the Boxer teachers into messages from the gods to suit the occasion.

The training of the novices was entrusted to "professors," all of whom came from the Shan-tung province. It consisted of drills and severe athletic exercises, and also of religious rites and the worship of certain gods, among which were Kuan-ti, the god of war, and the fat, laughing Buddha. Women were also admitted to the ranks, and became most enthusiastic supporters of the movement.

When the course of training was completed, and the initiation was finished, the full-fledged "Boxer" was declared to be invulnerable to wounds inflicted by any sort of weapon, and instances are known of Boxers inviting Chinese soldiers to fire at them at point blank range, fully convinced that no harm would befall them. That the result was immediately fatal was easily accounted for by the Boxer professors, who asserted that the subject was not fully initiated or was deficient in faith, and the people, usually so hard to convince on any subject outside their knowledge, appeared to be quite ready to accept this unsatisfactory explanation.

The whole scheme of the Boxer movement was craftily conceived. Knowing the aversion of the Government to all secret societies, the leaders were careful to profess great loyalty towards the Throne, and adopted as their motto the words "Exalt the dynasty and destroy the foreigners." Furthermore, they had gained the favour of Yu-hsien, the rabidly anti-foreign Governor of the Shan-tung province, who, though he probably had no faith in their pretensions to supernatural gifts, thought he saw a chance of carrying out his designs against the foreigners through their agency.

The Boxers rapidly increased in numbers. The mysterious powers, which their teachers professed to confer on their followers, appealed to the imagination of the young men and boys of the country, who flocked to join their ranks, while the prospect of rapine and loot attracted all the ruffians within a wide radius.

The rising was further helped by natural causes. For two years past there had been great scarcity of rain, resulting in the failure of crops, and, as has been already said, the Boxers proclaimed that this state of things was due to the influence of the foreigner, and that until he was removed the rain would be withheld. In the Shan-hsi province, where the foreigners had made surveys and opened mines, the outlook was particularly bad, and great scarcity prevailed, resulting in famine and suffering. The Boxer teaching was therefore readily believed by the superstitious Chinese. Boxer professors appeared everywhere, and each village had its band of youths, who practised the Boxer exercises and rites, whereby they were to become invulnerable to foreign bullets, donned the Boxer uniform, and armed themselves with swords and spears; firearms and all such heathenish devices being at first discarded as of foreign invention, and therefore contrary to their beliefs.

With an eye to pleasing the people, the Boxers declared their aim to be the destruction of the Roman Catholic priests and converts, and their first attack was upon a Roman Catholic chapel at Li-lien-yuan, in Shan-tung, where a temple had formerly stood which had been purchased by the Catholics and replaced by a chapel.

In March 1899 the French Minister obtained from the Chinese government a decree whereby all Roman Catholic priests were given official rank in their districts, but were debarred from interfering in the magisterial courts. This conferred considerable power on the priests, which was not shared by the Protestant missionaries, and it would appear that it was often used to shield the wrong-doer simply because he was a convert. The Catholic converts are very numerous in North China, and, presuming on the protection afforded them by the priests, they frequently treated their unconverted compatriots in a high-handed manner, which gradually resulted in their being cordially hated by the country people.

The Chinese are really very tolerant towards foreign creeds, as is shown by the presence of alien religions throughout the empire for many hundreds of years, but it was quite another thing when they often found it impossible to obtain justice against a fellow Chinaman simply because he had adopted a new belief.

The prospect of balancing accounts with the converts and with their protectors the priests, through the agency of the Boxers, was therefore by no means displeasing to the unregenerate Celestial, who happened to have a grudge against any of the community.

Accordingly, the early attacks of the Boxers were directed against the Catholic converts, many of whom had their houses burnt and possessions confiscated, while a few were killed. From being unchecked the desire for violence grew, and very soon the Protestant converts shared the same fate as the Catholics; all were " secondary devils," and only less obnoxious than the pure foreigner.

At first the Boxers confined their operations to Shan-tung, but towards the end of 1899 they spread into the southern part of Chi-li, where the persecution of the Christians also commenced. The foreign Ministers and missionaries had for some time been anxiously watching the growth of the organisation, when the news reached Peking that an English missionary, Mr. Brooks, had been murdered by Boxers in Northern Shan-tung on the last day of the year 1899.

The British Minister at once demanded the execution of the murderers, the punishment of the officials concerned, and the suppression of the obnoxious society; but how were these demands carried out by the Chinese Government? The two men who actually committed the murder were beheaded; some of the lesser officials were reprimanded; and Yu-hsien, ex-Governor of Shan-tung and head patron of the Boxers, was ordered to Peking, having been succeeded in office by General Yuan Shih-k'ai. At the capital he was received with honour and with special marks of favour by the Empress-Dowager, being shortly afterwards appointed to the Governorship of the neighbouring province of Shan-hsi, where he had ample opportunity of fostering the Boxer movement. An edict was indeed published ordering the suppression of seditious societies, but pointing out that all societies were not harmful. In fact, the whole decree was so worded as to exonerate the Boxers from blame and encourage them to persevere.

Yuan Shih-k'ai, the new Governor of Shan-tung, had a difficult task to perform. He was fully alive to the fact that the Boxer movement was calculated to land the empire in war with the foreign Powers, with defeat as the inevitable result, but, while opposed to the dangerous society, he had to appear to be in sympathy with the Court which encouraged it. He therefore steered a middle course, and while remaining loyal to the government, maintained order in his province, and it is to his credit that throughout the troubles the missionaries in Shan-tung were protected, and were all assisted to escape to places of safety.

Very different was the state of affairs in the neighbouring provinces of Chi-li and Shan-hsi. The officials had been informed that the government was favourably disposed towards the Boxers, who were not to be treated harshly. Compelled, therefore, at first to tolerate the society, they soon found themselves powerless to restrain it, and a reign of terror began. With unchecked power to do harm and free indulgence in lawlessness, the desire for looting and violence increased, and terrible tales of outrage, committed on Protestant and Catholic converts alike, began to arrive at Peking from the south, and these reports showed that the Boxer movement was spreading steadily northwards towards the capital, till it was certain that Boxers were training and recruiting close to its walls.

Gaining courage as their numbers increased, the Boxers openly defied and terrorised the provincial officials, and spread devastation through the land. They professed to be able to "smell out" converts or others who had foreign sympathies, and any who offended them or whose wealth they coveted, was straightway accused on one or other of these grounds and promptly murdered. Thus, a commander in Tung Fû-hsiang's army who attempted to argue with a band of Boxers in one of the main streets of Peking was at once accused of being a friend of foreigners, and was dragged off his horse and butchered. It was only natural, therefore, that the officials avoided all interference with the Boxers, who had thus unrestrained liberty to commit any outrage they pleased.

In the meantime the foreign Ministers were vainly demanding the suppression of the rising, being put off with assurances by the Tsung-li Yamen that troops were being sent to restore order. Unfortunately the Court was divided into two factions, and of these the ignorant anti-foreign Manchu faction was in the ascendant, and sympathised with and encouraged the Boxers. The more enlightened party, which was chiefly composed of the high Chinese officials, was fully persuaded of the danger into which the empire was drifting, and constantly voiced their opinions in the State councils; but the opposition was too strong for them, and easily overruled their advice.

Yü-lu, the Viceroy of Chi-li, had recognised the necessity of keeping the Boxers in check, but on the 22nd May 1900, a party of his cavalry was ambushed at Lai-shui and destroyed.

Fresh reports were constantly arriving of attacks on Chinese Christians, and the London Mission chapel at Kung-tsun, 40 miles south-west of Peking, was destroyed.

On the 19th May 1900, Père Favier, the Roman Catholic Bishop of Peking, whose experience of the Chinese is unrivalled, and whose sources of information through the Roman Catholic converts are very extensive, reported to the French Minister that he considered the situation to be extremely serious. In the district of Pao-ting fu numerous Christians had been murdered, and the persecution of converts was daily drawing nearer to the capital. The movement was aimed against all Europeans, and not only against the foreign religion, as was clearly set forth on the Boxer banners. Père Favier further stated that the rising would spread to Peking, where first the churches and then the Legations would be attacked. The city was full of anti-foreign placards, and new ones were appearing every day. In fact, the movement was very similar to that in Tien-tsin in 1870, when the same threats were used and the same warnings given and disregarded, with most lamentable results. Père Favier also asked for guards to be sent to protect the Pei-t'ang cathedral, which is the Roman Catholic headquarters in Peking.

This warning was communicated by M. Pichon to his colleagues, and, emanating from such a source, was not to be disregarded. The Ministers accordingly addressed another strong note to the Tsung-li Yamen demanding the suppression of the Boxers and the restoration of order. The Tsung-li Yamen professed to be taking all means in their power to suppress the rising, and assured the Ministers that the safety of the Legations would be the especial care of the Chinese Government, who regarded the Boxers as rebels and outlaws.

While however the Tsung-li Yamen was giving these assurances to the foreign Ministers, the Manchu party, notably Kang-yi, was doing all in its power to encourage the Boxers and assure them of the favour of the Empress Dowager.

On the 28th May the Boxers burnt Feng-tai railway station, and tore up part of the line, which however was quickly repaired. The Ministers now considered that the situation in Peking had become critical and telegraphed to Tien-tsin for armed guards for the Legations. These were forthwith despatched, and, to the number of 337 men, reached the capital without opposition on the 31st May.

The Boxers had also begun to destroy the railway at Pao-ting fu, and the European railway employés left that place on the 29th May by river for Tien-tsin. They were, however, pursued and attacked by Boxers, and four of their number were killed.

On the 1st June two English missionaries, Messrs. Robinson and Norman, were attacked at Yung-ch'ing-hsien, 40 miles south of Peking. The Church of England Mission was burnt and Mr. Robinson was pursued and at once cut down, but Mr. Norman, having been taken prisoner, was not murdered till the following day, having in the meantime been subjected to most inhuman tortures.

In the meanwhile Tung Fu-hsiang's Kan-su troops, wild, undisciplined, anti-foreign Mohammedans, who had been removed from the neighbourhood of Peking at the instance of the foreign Ministers during the winter of 1898-99, were ordered back to the capital and immediately fraternised with the Boxers.

On the 7th June General Nieh's troops, who had been protecting the railway line from Tien-tsin to Peking, were ordered to return to their camps at Lu-tai, but they remained in the neighbourhood of Yangtsun for several days.

All communication between the Legations and the outside world was by this time cut off, and the Boxers were soon openly drilling in Peking itself. On the 9th, Tung Fu-hsiang's troops entered the capital and with them came hosts of Boxers, who, in the uniform of their society, and armed with swords and spears, boldly paraded the streets, declaring that their mission was to exterminate the foreigners.

On the 11th June the Japanese Chancellor, Mr. Sugiyama, was murdered by Tung Fu-hsiang's troops at the Yung-ting mên, or south gate of the Chinese city. A tardy decree was published the following day to the effect that the Empress Dowager was grieved at the occurrence, which was the work of outlaws, though it was well known throughout Peking to have been done by regular troops.

On the 13th June the Boxers first attacked the Legations, and on the same day commenced their wholesale massacre of Chinese Christians.

CHAPTER II.

Development of the situation at Tien-tsin and the capture of the Taku Forts.

While the situation at Peking was becoming critical, as related in the preceding chapter, the state of affairs in other parts of Chi-li was also causing great anxiety. The Viceroy, Yü-lu, was apparently doing his best to maintain order, but the same rumours which reached the Legations in Peking were also current in Tien-tsin and along the railway at Tong-shan, Pei-tai-ho and Shan-hai-kuan, and the greatest anxiety was felt as to what was to be the outcome of the Boxer rising in the interior. The demeanour of the natives was also unsatisfactory and there was a general feeling of unrest and insecurity.

At Wei-hai-wei also a restless spirit was observable amongst the people in the ceded territory, and this was undoubtedly due to the spread of the Boxer movement in other parts of the Shan-tung province. Boxer emissaries were spreading reports as to our intentions towards the people, and saying that, in addition to the land tax, they would have to pay duties on all kinds of property, even including their women, and were inciting them to resist the foreigner. The villagers began to hold meetings and to form societies for purposes of drill, and seditious feeling spread rapidly.

Notice of a large meeting proposed to be held in March having reached the Commissioner, the Chinese Regiment was sent to disperse and, if possible, disarm it. The meeting was taken by surprise and disarmed after very slight resistance, and its leaders brought into Wei-hai-wei and placed in prison. There was no further trouble till the arrival of the Chinese Commissioners for the delimitation of the boundary. They held a secret meeting in the city of Wei-hai-wei, at which resistance to British authority and collection of taxes was preached, and false information given to the people as to the intentions of the British Boundary Commissioners. Full information as to what occurred at the meeting was obtained through soldiers of the Chinese Regiment who had been sent to attend it dressed as ordinary villagers.

The Chinese Commissioners did all they could to delay the starting of work on the delimitation and were finally told that the British Commissioners would start work on a certain date and that they could accompany them or not, as they pleased. They did accompany them and the work began.

Their conduct still continued very suspicious and unsatisfactory, and on the 3rd of May 1900 they flatly declined to proceed any further with the delimitation. The matter was reported to the Commissioner of Wei-hai-wei who, strengthened the escort of the British Commissioners by two more companies of the Chinese Regiment, and directed them to proceed with their work with or without the presence of the Chinese Commissioners.

The survey portion of the Commission under Major Penrose, R.E., escorted by a small detachment of the Chinese Regiment, was suddenly attacked on the 5th of May by a badly armed force of about 1,500 Chinese, and a fierce fight ensued in which Major Penrose was severely, and Captain Pereira and four men of the escort were slightly wounded. The Chinese were only driven off when reinforcements, in the shape of a company of the Chinese Regiment, under Lieutenant-Colonel Bower, arrived on the scene, and on retiring they left twenty dead bodies on the field.

The following day a large force of Chinese attacked a party of sixty men of the Chinese Regiment under Captain Watson, and fought for two hours before being driven off with loss. On this occasion the Chinese were armed with rifles, and even had a small cannon. There were no casualties in the British force.

The villagers now turned against the Chinese Commissioners, who took refuge in a village near the boundary. At the request of Yuan Shih-ka'i, the Governor of Shan-tung, a force consisting of a few Royal Marines and a detachment of the Chinese Regiment was sent to effect their release, and brought them back to Wei-hai-wei. They were thence returned to Chefoo, and the demarcation was completed by the British on the 17th May without further opposition.

In the meanwhile the anxiety at Tien-tsin was increasing, and grave rumours of attacks on Chinese christians were daily received, while it was reported that the anti-foreign movement was spreading and steadily drawing nearer to the settlement.

At last. on the 28th May, railway communication with Peking was cut off, the railway station and workshops at Feng-tai, the important junction between the Tien-tsin—Peking and Lu-han railways, were reported to be in flames, and the Boxers were said to have torn up part of the line. This news was immediately followed by requests from the Ministers at Peking for the despatch of armed guards to the capital to defend the Legations.

On the 30th H.M.S. "Hermione" and "Brisk" were joined at Taku by the "Orlando" and "Algerine," and a force of marines and seamen was at once disembarked. Three officers, Captains B. M. Strouts, L. S. T. Halliday, and E. Wray, all of the R.M.L.I., and seventy-six men proceeded to Peking, and one hundred and four men to Tien-tsin. The breach in the railway had been repaired, and the whole of the Legation guards of Great Britain, America, Italy, Russia, France, and Japan, to the number of 337 men, arrived safely at Peking on the 31st May. The German and Austrian guards followed later on the 3rd June. On the same day the "Centurion" and "Whiting" left Wei-hai-wei for Taku, being shortly afterwards followed by the "Endymion" and "Fame," and by the 4th June twenty-four men-of-war, of different nationalities, were collected in the anchorage off the mouth of the Pei-ho.

Admiral Sir E. Seymour, Naval Commander-in-Chief of the China Station, telegraphed to Sir Claude MacDonald on the 1st June that he was prepared to land a further force of 200 men, if their services were required, but on the 2nd June received a reply that, since the arrival of the Legation guards on the 31st, affairs in the capital were much quieter.

Sir Claude MacDonald had invited Admiral Seymour to visit Peking again, he having been there the previous month, but this the latter was unable to do, and on the 3rd June he proceeded to Tien-tsin to discuss the situation with the British consul, and afterwards returned by river to his flagship.

On the 4th June a gun and gun's crew were despatched from the "Centurion" to Tien-tsin to strengthen the defence of the settlement, and the following day a force of one hundred men was sent to H.M.S. "Algerine" in the mouth of the river, so as to be ready for immediate landing should its services be required. The anchorage for ships off Taku is some 13 miles from the shore, from which it is separated by a bar, which can only be crossed when the tide is nearly full, even by steamers of light draught, thus great delay is liable to occur in communicating with the land.

On the 5th orders were sent to H.M.S. "Humber" at Wei-hai-wei to embark a detachment of Marines from the garrison there and proceed to Pei-tai-ho and bring away several Europeans who were known to be there. On the 10th June a party of fifty men under Lieutenant C. D. Roper, of H.M.S. "Aurora," was sent from Tien-tsin to Tong-shan to protect European lives and the valuable railway workshops and mines at that place. There they remained till the 16th, when, the position becoming untenable, they withdrew to Pei-tai-ho and, on the 21st, embarked, with all the other Europeans, in the "Humber" for Taku.

Pei-tai-ho is a watering place not far from Shan-hai-kuan, where at this period several British subjects were living, and many of the employés on the railway, driven from their posts by the spread of the anti-foreign movement, had retired to it for safety. It contained much property of value in the shape of houses, &c., but, as troops could not be spared for its defence, this had all to be abandoned, and the place was shortly afterwards burnt to the ground by the Chinese. However, there was no loss of life among the Europeans, as they had all been removed to places of safety.

On the 6th June, in response to a request from the British Consul, fifty seamen were sent up to reinforce the guards at Tien-tsin. Seventy-five Marines of H.M.S. "Centurion," under Major Johnstone, R.M.L.I., were also sent, but they were intended for Peking, should the British Minister require their services, he having asked if this number could be spared, without stating if he required them immediately or not. These latter did not, however, get beyond Tien-tsin, and joined Sir Edward Seymour's force on 10th June.

On the same date it was agreed, at a meeting of the senior naval officers, that, in the event of communication with Peking being cut off, an international force of sufficient strength would be at once despatched to re-open it.

On the 7th June H.M.S. "Aurora" joined the fleet off Taku, and reports were received that General Nieh's troops had fought a successful engagement against the Boxers, in which a large number of the latter had been killed. This success was not so gratifying to the Court at Peking, and General Nieh was severely censured for his vigorous measures, and his troops, which had been employed in guarding the railway, were ordered to return to their camps at Lu-tai.

The state of affairs continued to be very grave, and constant rumours arrived of Boxer outrages in the neighbourhood of Tien-tsin, while the railway was reported to be damaged at several points. The general situation, however, remained unchanged until the night of the 9th June, when Admiral Seymour received a telegram from the British Minister informing him that unless the Europeans in Peking were at once enabled to withdraw to the coast, their retirement at a later date would be impossible. This information was immediately communicated to all the other naval commanders, and their co-operation was asked for, while preparations were made to despatch all the British forces available. These latter were sent ashore in the "Fame" and "Whiting," and in a tug, and by 6 a.m. on the 10th June they were entrained at Tang-ku, the first train reaching Tien-tsin at 7.30 a.m. Here it remained two hours, while the Admiral paid a visit to the British Consul.

Captain E. H. Bayly, of H.M.S. "Aurora," with the greater part of the force landed from that ship, was left at Tien-tsin to take command of the British contingent there.

About 9.30 a.m. a start was made for Peking. The train, containing 300 British, 112 Americans, 28 Austrians, and 40 Italians —total 480 men, all under command of Admiral Sir E. Seymour —proceeded without difficulty till 3.30 p.m. Near Yang-tsun a large camp of General Nieh's troops was passed, but a few miles before reaching the next station, Lo-fa, the line was found to be damaged, and a halt had to be made for the night.

Two more trains joined here, bringing up the total force to 915 British (62 officers, 640 seamen, and 213 marines), 25 Austrians, 40 Italians, 100 French, 450 Germans, 54 Japanese, 112 Americans, and 112 Russians—total 1,808 officers and men.

Next morning, the 11th June, the trains proceeded to Lo-fa, and here a fourth train joined them, containing 200 Russians and 58 French, bringing up the total to 2,066 officers and men.

The advance was continued to Lang-fang, which was reached on 12th June, large repairs being required to the permanent way before that place could be approached, and after 15th June communication with Tien-tsin was interrupted, the Chinese having destroyed the railway in rear of the trains.

Affairs at Tien-tsin had now reached a critical stage.

On the 11th June the Chinese began to leave the settlement and close their shops. A reinforcement of 150 British arrived from Tang-ku, and these were fol'owed on the 13th by a force of about 1,700 Russians, with cavalry and guns. After the departure of the relief column for Peking the Chinese authorities did all in their power to prevent the despatch of reinforcements by rail, and large and threatening mobs collected at the railway station and attempted to obstruct work. Trains were, however, despatched until the 14th, when the destruction of the line rendered their running impossible.

On the departure of Sir Edward Seymour with the relieving column, the command of the British forces devolved on Rear-Admiral Bruce, who arrived at Taku in H.M.S. " Barfleur " on the 11th June.

During the night of the 14th news was received that all the available rolling stock had been sent up the line towards Lu-tai to bring down a large garrison of Chinese troops to Tang-ku, with the object of occupying the Taku forts in strength.

A council of the international naval commanders was at once summoned to discuss the situation, and, as it was obviously imperative to guard against the possibility of communication with Tien-tsin being cut off, orders were sent to the various gunboats lying in the river to prevent the removal of rolling-stock from Tang-ku, and oppose the advance of Chinese troops on that place, using force if necessary. It was further decided that, if the Chinese attempted to occupy Tang-ku, it would be necessary to destroy the Taku forts, and thus secure the entrance to the Pei-ho and the means of landing troops.

On the night of the 15th information arrived that the Chinese were placing electric mines in the channel of the Pei-ho, that the forts were being provisioned, and that reinforcements had reached the South Fort by land. A second council was consequently held on the forenoon of the 16th, the result of which was that an intimation was sent to the Viceroy of Chi-li at Tien-tsin, and also to the commandant of the Taku forts, that, as the action of the Chinese authorities constituted a grave menace to the safety of the allied troops further up the river at Tien-tsin and on the march to Peking, the naval commanders had decided to temporarily occupy the Taku forts. Further, that it was desirable that this occupation might be peacefully effected, by the Chinese handing over the forts to the Allies before 2 a.m. on the 17th June, but that if they had not done so by the hour named the forts would be occupied by force.

At the same time the necessary orders were issued to the captains of the allied ships in the river, and preparations were made for carrying out the operation, landing parties of the different nations being sent in during the afternoon.

The British landing party, under Commander C. Cradock, of H.M.S. " Alacrity," reached the " Algerine " about 6 p.m.

on the 16th, and he and Commander R. H. J. Stewart of the "Algèrine" at once went on board the Russian ship "Bobr" to attend a conference of the allied captains, when it was decided that if the forts had not surrendered before that hour, the bombardment would commence at 4 a.m. on the 17th, by which time the different vessels were to be in the following positions: opposite the North-West Fort the British "Algerine," immediately above her the German "Iltis," and above her, again, the Russian ships "Bobr," "Koreytz," and "Gilyak," and the French gunboat "Lion." The American "Monocacy" was to remain at Tang-ku to guard the railway and assist the various landing parties, who, with the exception of the British, were to march from that place to a rendezvous on the military road, which runs along the left bank of the river to the forts, where the British landing party would join them at a certain hour.

It had been arranged that after the necessary bombardment had been carried out the North-West Fort should first be attacked, and then the North Fort, both of which are on the left bank of the river. After they had been captured the long string of South Forts, on the right bank, would be dealt with. Commander Stewart also directed Lieutenant and Commander R. Keyes, of H.M.S. "Fame," to take the "Whiting" under his command and seize at 1.30 a.m. four Chinese torpedo-boat destroyers, which were moored alongside their Government yard, so that they should not interfere with the passage of the "Iltis" and "Lion" to their allotted positions.

At 12.50 a.m., when all the ships except the "Iltis" and "Lion" were in position and the British landing party was on the upper deck of the "Algerine" ready to land, the Chinese suddenly opened an almost simultaneous and heavy fire from all the forts, which was immediately replied to by the allied ships. The landing party was at once put into the boats, so as to clear the "Algerine's" decks, and by 2.30 a.m. the men were all ashore, without having suffered any casualties, and immediately joined the contingents of the other powers.

Commander Cradock now took command of the entire force, which consisted of :—

	Officers.	Men.	Total.
British	23	298	321
Germans	3	130	133
Japanese	4	240	244
Russians	2	157	159
Italians	1	24	25
Austrians	2	20	22
*Total	35	869	904

* The United States forces did not take an active part in the operations at Taku, their Admiral considering that he could not co-operate without the approval of his Government being first obtained.

At 2.45 a.m. the advance commenced, with half the British, and the Italians, Germans, and Japanese in the front line, and the rest of the British, the Russians, and Austrians in support. The ground for 1,000 yards in front of the North-West Fort is perfectly flat, hard mud, without a vestige of cover, and the fort is surrounded by a moat, crossed opposite the gate on the west face by a bridge. The troops were advancing against the north face of the fort, with their right resting on the river bank, and the plan of action was as follows: The firing line was to advance in skirmishing order to within 50 yards of the north face, then close to the right, and, swinging round the north-west corner down the military road, was to charge over the bridge and storm the west gate.

At about 2.45 a.m. the fire of the ships on the North-West Fort ceased, to allow of the assault being carried out, but, as the troops approached, it soon became evident that owing to the darkness the fort had suffered very little damage, and was practically intact, with all its guns still in action. Under these circumstances Commander Cradock, in consultation with the other commanding officers, decided to halt and get the troops under cover of a bend of the river until the fort was further reduced. At the same time information was sent back to the ships as to the condition of affairs, and, as it was now daylight, fire was immediately reopened from the "Algerine" and "Iltis" with such good effect that by 4.30 a.m. the guns of the fort were practically silenced, though two field guns again came into action when the attack was renewed.

The second advance was in different formation to the first, for when the rest of the troops retired under cover of the river bank, the men of the "Alacrity" and "Endymion" had remained 300 yards to the front, protected by a small rise in the ground. When the attack recommenced they were joined by the Russians extending their line to the left, while the Italians came in on their right between them and the river, the remainder of the British and allied forces being close up in support. The Russians subsequently inclined away to the left to threaten the east face of the fort and the Chinese right rear.

On nearing the fort the charge was sounded, and the British closed to their right as previously arranged, but the Japanese doubled up from the supports in column of route along the road, and a race ensued between them and the British for the west gate, the two nations scaling the defences together. Commander Hattori, of the Japanese Navy, was among the first up the parapet, and turning to assist Commander Cradock, was immediately afterwards shot dead. The gate of the inner fort was quickly forced and the capture of the place was thus completed.

The North Fort was next attacked, but offered very slight resistance, and the British and German gunners were each able to turn and work one of the fort's guns on the still active artillery of the South Forts across the river.

While these events had been taking place on shore, the ships in the river, having opened the way for the land assault on the

North-West Fort by silencing its guns, were preparing to engage the South Forts on the other bank. At 5 a.m. a prearranged signal was hoisted on the "Algerine," and repeated by the other vessels, and at 5.30 the little fleet, with the exception of the "Gilyak," which had a compartment full of water and could not move, weighed anchor and moved down stream into a new position opposite the South Forts, being heavily engaged with the Chinese artillery all the way, and suffering considerable loss. Indeed it was at this period that nearly all the British casualties occurred.

At 6.20 a.m. the "Algerine" anchored, and the "Iltis," which was following close behind, passed on ahead and anchored close in front, the remaining ships being some distance astern. The fire from the South Fort was at this time extremely heavy, but, from the ships being close under them, most of the shells flew harmlessly overhead. At about 6.55 a.m. a magazine inside the Chinese forts blew up, and this seems to have completed the discomfiture of the defenders, as their fire from this point almost entirely ceased, and at 7.10 a.m. the fire from the ships was also discontinued, and the forts were occupied without further opposition.

During the operations the British casualties amounted to 1 man killed and 2 officers and 13 men wounded.

The ship which suffered most was the Russian "Gilyak," which had 10 men killed, and 2 officers and 47 men wounded. She was disabled by a shot which severed one of her steampipes, and most of her casualties were caused by a shell, which penetrated one of her smaller magazines and exploded some charges in it.

The German "Iltis," which was fought throughout the action with conspicuous gallantry, lost her gunner and 7 men killed, while her captain and about 30 men were wounded.

The French "Lion" had one man killed.

The Russian "Koreytz" had two officers and several men killed and wounded.

The Russian "Bobr" had no casualties.

At the same time that the reduction of the forts was taking place, Lieutenant R. Keyes, in command of H.M.S. "Fame," had, in conjunction with H.M.S. "Whiting," successfully carried out the boarding and capture of the four Chinese torpedo-boat destroyers lying at their Government wharf between Taku and Tang-ku.

Having reconnoitred their position beforehand, Lieutenant Keyes found that the four boats were moored head and stern in single line along the southern bank, and arranged that, in attacking them, the "Fame" should lead, followed at a distance of about a cable and a half, the distance between the furthest up-stream destroyer and the second from her, by the "Whiting," and that each vessel would tow a whaler with a boarding-party of 12 men under a lieutenant. The "Fame" and her whaler were to tackle the two up-stream destroyers, while the "Whiting" and her whaler boarded the other two. Keeping well out in the stream as if to pass them, as soon as the "Fame" was opposite the furthest up-stream boat, and the "Whiting" opposite the third up-stream boat, they sheered in and laid a boarding party alongside each destroyer, the whalers boarding the boats next astern to those boarded by the "Fame" and "Whiting."

Immediately the bombardment commenced, this operation was carried out, and met with complete success. Very little resistance was made by the Chinese crews, and, after the exchange of a few shots, they were driven overboard or below hatches, there being no casualties on our side. The cables were then slipped, and the prizes towed to a safer anchorage at Tang-ku, valuable assistance being rendered at this time by two boats of the Tien-tsin Tug and Lighter Company, under Mr. Macrae, which took two of the prizes in tow, and by 5 a.m. they were securely berthed at Tang-ku.

While towing one of the prizes up-stream, the "Whiting" received a 5-inch shot in her hull just forward of the engine room bulkhead on the starboard side, which passed through a coal-bunker, did considerable damage to tubes, and put No. 4 boiler out of action, but caused no further damage.

Rear-Admiral Bruce only retained one of these destroyers, which was re-named the "Taku." The other three were handed over to the German, French, and Russian Admirals respectively.

One of the tugs now reported that it was bound up-river with despatches and stores for Tien-tsin, but that the Chinese crew were afraid to pass the Chinese fort of Hsin-ch'eng about twelve miles above Taku. The "Fame" and "Whiting," therefore, escorted it past the fort, which appeared to be unoccupied, as no opposition was offered, and afterwards returned to Taku.

The occupation of Taku was now complete. The landing stages and the terminus of the railway were in the hands of the Allies, and easy communication between the ships and the shore permanently secured.

The North-West Fort was occupied by the British, the North Fort by the Japanese, and the South Fort by the Germans and Russians.

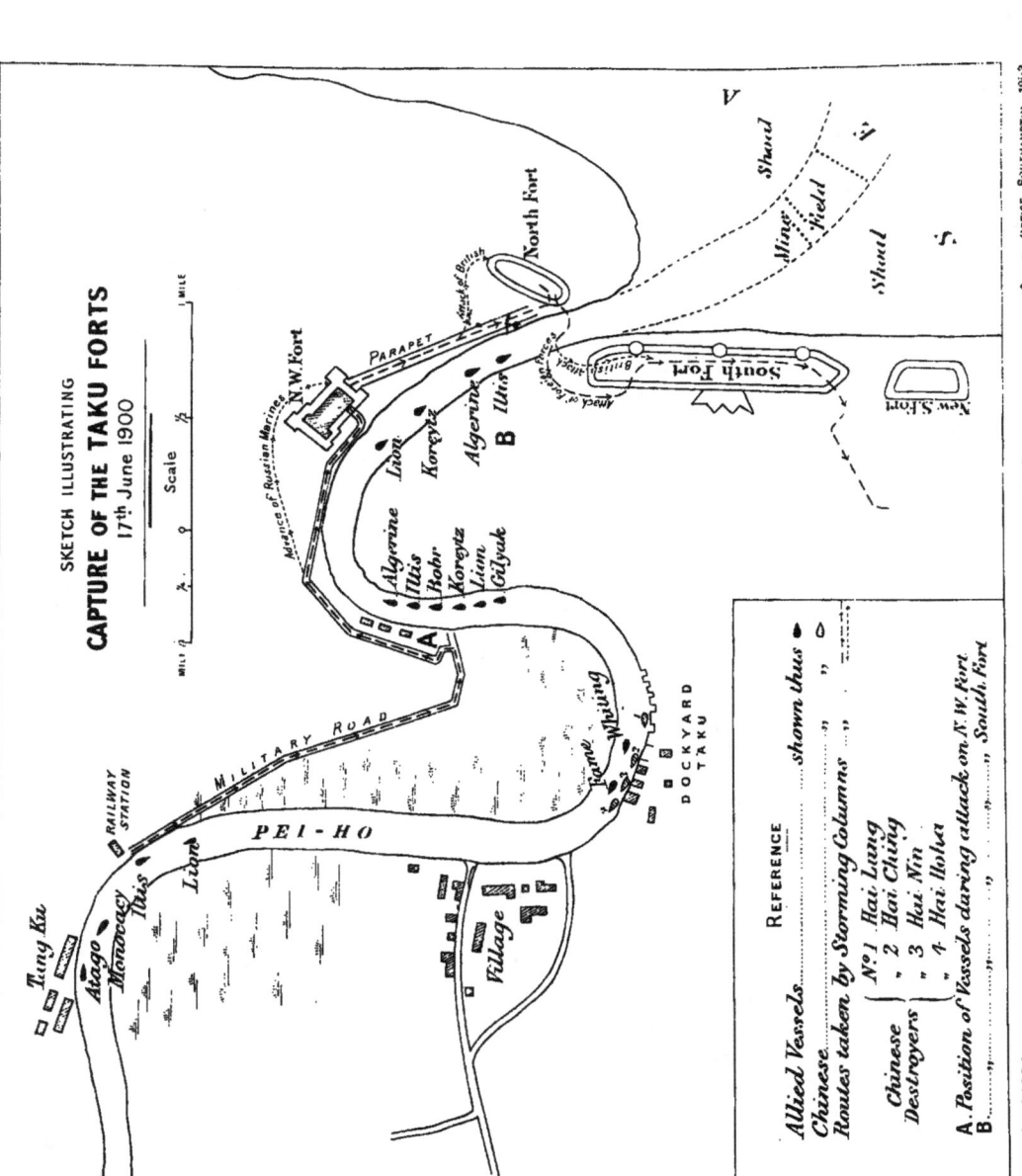

CHAPTER III.

Relief of Tien-tsin.*

The position at Tien-tsin was now grave. After the departure of the Relief Column under Admiral Seymour, Captain E. H. Bayly, of H.M.S. "Aurora," remained in command of the small British garrison of 393 men.

The total garrison of Tien-tsin at this period was approximately as follows:—

Austrians	50
British	393
French	50
Germans	110
Italians	40
Japanese	50
Russians	1,800
United States	43
Total	2,536

The Boxers were drawing closer to the settlement and becoming more daring. On the 14th June the railway to the north was torn up, and on the 16th repairs had to be commenced within half a mile of the station. On the 15th some mission houses in the French settlement and the Roman Catholic Cathedral in the native city were burnt, and telegraphic communication with Taku was interrupted, but the Viceroy was reported to be still doing his best to protect foreigners. A searchlight train patrolled the line between Tien-tsin and Tang-ku all night, and a guard of 200 Russians occupied the station of Chün-liang-ch'eng, half-way between these two places.

On the 16th June the Boxers made their first attack on the Tien-tsin settlements, and set fire to several stores and houses before they were driven out. They also attacked the Russians at the railway station, and a train sent down towards Tang-ku was fired on by the forts and compelled to return to Tien-tsin.

On the 17th a body of Chinese troops opened fire on a party which had gone out to drive off some Boxers who were wrecking the railway. They were soon put to flight, without loss on our side, but several skirmishes took place during the day, and the

---

* *See* also Admiral Seymour's despatch in Appendix A.

Chinese commenced the bombardment of the settlements from the native city.

It also became necessary to capture the Chinese Military College, a large building opposite to and commanding the British settlement, and this was done by a party of the Allies, including 48 British Marines, under command of Major Luke, R.M.L.I. The place was stormed, the guns found in it were destroyed, and as the building could not be held, it was burnt down. The Chinese had offered considerable resistance, but the British loss amounted to only one man killed, and one officer (Major Luke) and four men wounded.

The next morning it was found that communication with Tang-ku by rail was completely cut off, and a party, which had started by train for Chün-liang-ch'eng in the morning, found the track torn up, and had to return to Tien-tsin after being engaged with the enemy. It was, however, in time to assist, by a flank attack, in repulsing an advance by the Chinese in force upon the railway station, which was held by the Russians, supported by two British companies under Commander Beatty.

The fighting throughout the day had been continuous and severe.

On the 19th the Chinese recommenced their attack, and brought up two field guns to the railway embankment opposite the British Concession, with which they opened fire on the settlement. It being necessary to dislodge or capture these guns, Commander Beatty crossed the river with three companies of seamen, and manœuvred to within 200 or 300 yards of them. The Russians were expected to co-operate in this attack from the railway station, but, while the British party was awaiting their arrival, a large force of Chinese suddenly appeared on the right flank, and, from the shelter of a mud wall, poured in a heavy fire, which wounded Commander Beatty, Lieutenants Powell and Stirling, Midshipman Donaldson, and 11 men. Mr. Donaldson afterwards died of his wounds. The force had consequently to fall back without effecting the capture of the guns, but their range having been obtained by a 9-pr. gun, which had been brought up to the Bund outside the British consulate, the Chinese shortly afterwards withdrew them. Lieutenant Wright, who was directing the fire of the British gun from the roof of the consulate, was dangerously wounded by one of the enemy's shells.

On the same day Mr. J. Watts of the Tien-tsin Volunteer Corps, who possessed a thorough knowledge of the country, undertook to carry despatches to Taku, with which place communication had been entirely cut off. Leaving Tien-tsin at 9.30 p.m. with a guard of only three Cossacks, he succeeded in getting safely through and delivered his despatches, after a most hazardous night ride of over 30 miles, through a country swarming with Boxers and Chinese troops.

The next two days were comparatively quiet in Tien-tsin; the Chinese only indulging in small attacks and skirmishes, and making no general assault. The bombardment of the settlements, however, went on continuously.

On the 22nd, European troops were seen in the far distance advancing from the direction of Tang-ku. These were the first of the relieving force, and it is now necessary to turn back a little and see what was being done to reinforce the allied troops in North China.

On the 4th June the Ministers of Great Britain, Austria, France, Germany, Italy, Japan, Russia, and the United States had telegraphed from Peking to their respective Governments, and reported that at any time the Legations in the capital might be besieged, with railway and telegraphic communication cut off. They also suggested that instructions might be issued to the officers in command of the various squadrons at Taku, to be in readiness to take concerted measures for their relief, if such action became necessary.

On the 6th June Admiral Seymour suggested that troops should be sent to Tien-tsin from Hongkong, and offered H.M.S. "Terrible" for their transport, and on the 8th instructions were sent from the Secretary of State for War to the General Officers Commanding at Hongkong and Singapore to send all troops which could be spared from their commands to Chi-li, should their services be required by Admiral Seymour, promising at the same time that troops so withdrawn would be replaced from India.

On the 10th June it was reported that a force of 600 French marines and 400 seamen had left Marseilles for Taku, and on the 11th the Russians landed 1,746 men with four guns, cavalry, and transport, at Taku, which force proceeded to Tien-tsin on the 13th.

On the 12th June the Government of India was asked to be prepared to replace the troops withdrawn from Hongkong and Singapore by native regiments from India, and the same day Admiral Seymour telegraphed to the General Officer Commanding, Hongkong, to send up all available troops to Taku in H.M.S. "Terrible" and on the 14th and 17th the following force left Hongkong under command of Major Morris, Royal Welsh Fusiliers:—

Corps.	Officers.	Men.
Hongkong Artillery	6	147
2nd Battalion Royal Welsh Fusiliers	7	318
Hongkong Regiment	2	301
Royal Engineers	1	33
Departmental details	6	36
Total	22	735

Also four 2·5 inch R.M.L. guns of 400 lbs. with 800 rounds of ammunition, and four Maxims 303 inch with 10,000 rounds per gun.

On the 18th June the Russians landed about 1,200 more troops at Taku with Major-General Stessel in chief command. On the 19th Admiral Bruce requested Colonel Dorward, commanding at Wei-hai-wei, to send 200 men of the Chinese Regiment, and any available Royal Engineers, to Taku as soon as possible, and this force with one officer and 10 men of the Royal Engineers, under command of Lieut.-Colonel H. Bower, 1st Chinese Regiment, reached Tang-ku on the 22nd and immediately disembarked.

On the 21st Colonel Dorward was appointed to the temporary command of the troops in North China, with the rank of Brigadier-General, and proceeded to Taku from Wei-hai-wei on the 23rd.

At 5 a.m. on the 21st June Commander Cradock with a detachment of 150 seamen left the North-West Fort at Taku for Tien-tsin, and the same day H.M.S. "Terrible" arrived with the first detachment of troops from Hongkong, consisting of 382 officers and men. These were at once landed and next morning proceeded by rail to overtake the party under Commander Cradock.

In the meanwhile a strong force of Russians, with a party of about 150 Americans and a few Italians, had gone on ahead to attempt the relief of Tien-tsin, but had fallen into an ambush and been forced to retire, and were at this time somewhere in the neighbourhood of the railhead near Chün-liang-ch'eng.

Later in the day of the 22nd, after the detachment under Major Morris had left Taku, Lieut.-Colonel Bower with ten officers and 192 men of the Chinese Regiment, one officer and 10 men Royal Engineers, and a 12-pr. gun and gun detachment from H.M.S. "Terrible," proceeded by train to the railhead along with a party of Russians, who, however, detrained before the railhead was reached. On reaching the railhead, some ten miles from Tien-tsin, Lieut.-Colonel Bower found the British detachments under Major Morris and Commander Cradock halted there, and heard that Major-General Stessel, with about 1,200 men, was encamped some distance further up the line, and that it was intended to renew the attempt to relieve Tien-tsin on the following morning. The relieving force started accordingly from the railhead at daybreak on the 23rd, but Lieut.-Colonel Bower's party, having been unable to unload their 12-pr. gun from the train in the dark, could not accompany it.

In the advance the Russians moved along the railway and to the right of it, the British, Americans, and Italians being to the left of the line. About six miles from Tien-tsin the enemy were encountered, and the force came under a heavy fire, but the advance was pressed steadily forward until the last bridge before entering the settlement was reached. At this point the Chinese offered considerable resistance, but were finally dislodged by a 3-pr. field gun lent by the Americans, assisted by the artillery of the Russian column on the right flank, and soon after noon the relieving force marched into Tien-tsin. The British casualties during the advance amounted to two men killed and five wounded. The Russian force encamped on the left bank of the Pei-ho opposite the British settlement; the remainder of the force proceeded into the Foreign settlements.

On the 24th June Lieut.-Colonel Bower, who had been joined by about 170 men of the Hongkong Regiment, after leaving a guard of 40 men of the latter corps and 100 men of the Chinese Regiment at the railhead to protect the line and stores, pressed forward to Tien-tsin with the rest of his force, the 12-pr. gun and a large quantity of ammunition. A company of seamen with a 12-pr. gun from H.M.S. "Terrible," under Lieutenant J. Drummond, also joined up. The work of dragging the gun along the heavy roads was very severe, and here the men of the Chinese Regiment proved of the greatest assistance, but it was not till 9.30 p.m. that the party reached the settlement, after a most trying and arduous march.

In the meanwhile news had reached Tien-tsin that Admiral Seymour's column was holding the Hsi-ku armoury, a few miles to the north of the native city, but, being encumbered with sick and wounded, required assistance to bring them in. Arrangements were at once made by Captain Bayly with the Russian General for the despatch of troops to their relief, and at midnight the force, consisting of 1,900 men, of whom 1,000 men and two guns were Russians and 600 British, rendezvoused on the left bank of the river. The whole were under the command of Colonel Shirinsky of the Russian army, and, after a night march, they arrived with little difficulty about 7 a.m. on the 25th opposite the armoury.

At this time the garrison of Tien-tsin amounted to about 4,500 troops, of whom some 3,000 were Russian and 983 British. The casualties in the British naval force since the 10th June amounted to one officer and six men killed and seven officers and 45 men wounded.

On the 25th the "Terrible's" 12-pr. came into action against the Western Arsenal and set it on fire, and later it was placed in position on the river bank, and succeeded in silencing the gun or guns in the Chinese city, which had been bombarding the settlements.

On the same day Brigadier-General Dorward landed at Tang-ku and proceeded, with some Hongkong Artillery and a party of the Hongkong Regiment, to the railhead, where he found a large accumulation of stores belonging to all the different nationalities, and everything in great confusion. He at once gave orders that all stores should be cleared away to the camp close by, and thus greatly facilitated the detraining and movement of troops, and, in order to see it properly done, he remained at the railhead till the afternoon of the following day, when he marched with the Hongkong Artillery to Tien-tsin, where Admiral Seymour's column, together with the relieving force sent to its assistance, had arrived that morning.

The same morning Lieutenant Keyes proceeded up the Pei-ho from Taku with H.M.S. "Fame," to reconnoitre, and if possible destroy, the Hsin-ch'eng fort, which commanded the navigation of the river at a point some twelve miles from its mouth. The place was found deserted and the British force of 32 men entered it without opposition. Square in plan, it mounted six 15 c.m. Krupp B.L. guns at the four corners, the north-east and south-east corners, which commanded the approaches by river and road from Taku, mounting two guns each. If the fort had been properly held it would have been very difficult to take, while, as the guns were in excellent order, any attempt to force the passage of the river would have been attended with great risk.

The party quickly disabled the six guns by smashing the carriages with guncotton, and, having blown up the magazine, which contained some fifty tons of gunpowder, returned to Taku.

The relief of Tien-tsin was now complete and the communications of the settlement with the sea permanently assured. Fresh troops were constantly arriving, and, on the 26th June, Rear-Admiral Bruce estimated that, in addition to the 2,300 British, the following foreign forces had landed at Taku :—

German	1,340
American	335
Russian	3,735
Japanese	3,752
Austrian	26
Italian	138
French	421
Total	9,747

Making a total of about 12,000 troops in all.

CHAPTER IV.

THE PEKING RELIEF COLUMN UNDER VICE-ADMIRAL SIR E. H. SEYMOUR.

It is now necessary to go back a fortnight and describe the operations of the relief column, in their gallant attempt to relieve Peking. As stated on page 11 the entire force of over 2,000 men, transported in four trains, had concentrated at Lo-fa station, some 28 miles from Tien-tsin, on the 11th June, and had, so far, met with no active opposition from the Chinese, though their advance had been delayed by the damaged state of the permanent way.

To protect the line a guard of thirty men, afterwards increased to sixty, under command of an officer, was left at Lo-fa, and the rest of the force continued its advance towards Lang-fang. It was intended to leave guards at various other points on the railway as the force advanced towards Peking. In the evening, at a point about three miles short of Lang-fang, the first body of Boxers was encountered. They had attempted unsuccessfully to cut off an advanced party sent forward to repair the line, and now advanced in skirmishing order to attack No. 1 train, but were quickly driven off with the loss of about thirty-five of their number killed.

The following morning, after the line had been repaired, the whole of the trains reached Lang-fang safely, but it was found that the damage to the line ahead was very serious and was evidently being done by bodies of men working in front of the column at no great distance, as it appeared to have been very recently carried out. In order to drive off these line-wreckers and if possible occupy the next railway station at An-ting, about thirteen miles further on towards Peking, Lieutenant A. G. Smith, of H.M.S. "Aurora," with a party of 3 officers and 44 men, was sent forward along the railway, while the rest of the force halted at Lang-fang to repair the permanent way, bridges, &c.

By the following morning, the 13th June, Lieutenant Smith had occupied a village on the railway some miles in the direction of An-ting, and here his party was attacked three times in succession by Boxers, who were however driven off without much difficulty, and with a loss of about fifteen of their number killed. At 10.30 a.m. a force of about 450 Boxers made a most determined attack on the village, charging in line with great courage and enthusiasm. After a sharp fight they also were driven off with the loss of about 150 killed, and the attack was not renewed. As the British force was now running short of ammunition, Lieutenant Smith decided to retire, and rejoined the main body at Lang-fang at 2.30 p.m. The same afternoon Major Johnstone, R.M.L.I., with a party of sixty men, was despatched towards An-ting to protect the railway, but after proceeding a few miles he found that it had been completely torn up for a distance of about a mile, and that all the sleepers had been carried away. His party also was attacked by Boxers in a village near the line, but drove them off with a loss of about twenty-five killed, there being no casualties among the British force. As there appeared no prospect of effecting anything, the party returned to Lang-fang on the evening of the 14th.

The same morning a large force of Boxers made a most determined attack on Lang-fang station. They advanced to close quarters under cover of a deserted village, which was occupied by a picket of five Italians, who however had apparently been surprised and overpowered before they could give the alarm, their dead bodies being afterwards recovered. The Boxers advanced with the greatest courage against No. 1 train, which was drawn up beside a well, where most of the men were busy drawing water. In spite of a withering fire, some of the Boxers actually reached the train before they were killed, but eventually they were driven off with the loss of about 100 dead.

The same afternoon, about 5.30 p.m., a messenger arrived on a trolly from Lo-fa station, and reported that the guard at that place was being attacked by a strong force of Boxers. Sir E. Seymour at once proceeded with one of the trains to its relief, but on arrival found that the fighting was practically over, and that the Boxers were in retreat. The reinforcements were able to inflict some loss upon them as they retired, and they left about 100 killed on the field. The British had two seamen wounded, one of whom died shortly afterwards.

All this time strenuous efforts were being made to repair the line beyond Lang-fang, but the progress was slow, and on the 15th it was reported that the line between Lo-fa and Yang-tsun had again been seriously damaged. Three considerable bodies of Boxers had been observed moving about in the neighbourhood of Lo-fa station, and an attack was expected, but they eventually moved off, with the intention, it was supposed, of destroying the railway at some point towards Tien-tsin. Further inspection on the morning of the 16th revealed the fact that communication with Tien-tsin had been cut off, and No. 1 train was at once sent back to repair the line, and eventually reached Yang-tsun on the morning of the 17th. Here it was found that the railway station had been destroyed and the line onward towards Tien-tsin completely wrecked, communication with that place being rendered impossible.

Sir E. Seymour had by this time decided that it would probably be impossible to relieve Peking by way of the railway, and that it might be necessary to use the alternative river route. Owing to the delay involved in effecting repairs to the line, provisions were running short, and there was also a scarcity of ammunition. As the railway beyond Lang-fang was almost certainly destroyed beyond possibility of repair, some other means of transport would be needed, and this was not available. Communication with the base at Tien-tsin was cut off, and nothing was known of what had been taking place there since the 13th. For the above reasons Admiral Seymour determined to withdraw the trains from Lang-fang and Lo-fa to Yang-tsun, and orders to this effect were despatched on the 17th.

Some days previously he had sent orders to Tien-tsin for the despatch of junks, provisions and ammunition to Yang-tsun, with a view of establishing a base there for a river column to Tung-chou, from which point Peking could be reached by a march of thirteen miles. But so overrun was the intervening country with Boxers and hostile Chinese, that not one of his messengers got through to Tien-tsin, and even if they had it would have been impossible to carry out the Admiral's orders, as Tien-tsin itself was in a state of siege and the reaches of the river above the Foreign settlements were in the hands of the Chinese.

No. 3 train returned to Yang-tsun from Lo-fa on the afternoon of the 18th June, and in the evening Nos. 2 and 4 trains arrived from Lang-fang. Before starting they had been unexpectedly attacked at Lang-fang by a very strong force of about 5,000 men, including cavalry. The assailants, in addition to the Boxers, included in their ranks a large number of regular Chinese troops, armed with magazine rifles of the latest pattern. Banners captured from them showed that they belonged to the Kan-su force commanded by General Tung Fu-hsiang, which had been recalled by the Chinese Court from Chi-chou to the capital.

It is of interest to note that this first attack by Imperial troops on the relieving force of the allies, took place on the 18th June, the day after the capture of the Taku forts.

The enemy attacked in front and on both flanks, pouring in a heavy fire on the allied forces advancing to engage them. The fighting was severe, and the Chinese were repulsed with heavy loss. They rallied, however, when they saw our troops withdrawing towards the trains, and made a second fierce attack, in which they were again beaten off with even heavier loss than before, leaving over 400 dead behind them. The allied forces had 6 men killed and 48 wounded.

The question now arose as to what was to be done next. The force was running short of supplies, the advance by rail on Peking was proved to be impracticable, and junks were not available to transport the troops by river. Endeavours had been made to procure supplies from the town of Yang-tsun, but, probably owing to fear of the Boxers on the part of the Chinese, these negotiations had fallen through.

On the 19th June a conference of the officers commanding the detachments of the various nationalities was held, and it was decided that, as it was impossible to retire by the railway, the trains should be abandoned and the force would withdraw to Tien-tsin along the left bank of the Pei-ho, the wounded and such stores as were necessary being conveyed on junks, four of which had been seized by the Germans on the previous day, their crews having been surprised in the act of removing sleepers and rails from the line.

Preparations were at once made and by 3 p.m. the retirement began, but, owing to the difficulty of navigating the junks, only 2½ miles had been covered before darkness set in. A 6-pounder Q.F. gun of H.M.S. "Centurion" had to be thrown overboard to enable the junk carrying it to be floated.

The march was continued in the early morning of the 20th, but the progress was very slow on account of the junks, and the Chinese appearing in front had to be driven out of each successive village before the column could pass through. The enemy proved to be incapable of withstanding a bayonet charge, the cheers of the men as they advanced to the attack effectually dispersing them before coming to close quarters. In the afternoon the Chinese brought a 1-pounder Q.F. gun into action, and, though it did little damage, it greatly harassed the march. After fighting all day the troops halted for the night, having covered only about 8 miles.

The next day, the 21st, the march was resumed, and continued resistance was experienced from the enemy, who brought a field gun into action in addition to the 1-pounder Q.F. gun. The field gun was however quickly dislodged by the fire of the Allies, but was again brought into action on various occasions throughout the day. Village after village had to be captured by assault, and also the town of Pei-ts'ang, which is the principal place between Yang-tsun and Tien-tsin. Finally, about 6 p.m., it was found that the Chinese were holding a very strong position across the line of retreat, from which it was impossible to dislodge them during daylight, and it was accordingly decided that the force should halt for rest and food, and that after midnight they should advance by a night march. Owing to the continuous opposition the progress during the day had been very slow, only 6 miles being covered. During the day Captain J. R. Jellicoe, of H.M.S. "Centurion," was dangerously wounded while leading his men at the storming of one of the villages.

At 1 a.m. on the 22nd June the force started again, the field and machine guns having been placed on a junk, which had been captured the previous day. It, however, shortly afterwards filled and sank, and only the Maxims were saved. During the march fires were seen at one or two places, evidently signalling the advance, but no opposition was met with till after the first mile and a half had been, covered, when a heavy fire was suddenly opened by the enemy from a village directly in front of, and about 200 yards from, the advanced guard. The British marines quickly carried the position by a bayonet charge, and the advance continued without further opposition, until, as the day was breaking, about 4 a.m., the head of the column found itself opposite what proved to be the Imperial armoury at Hsi-ku, situated on the right bank of the river. Two unarmed Chinese soldiers came out of a house and apparently wanted to speak, so a halt was made to hear what they had to say, which was merely to ask who the troops were and where they were going. The reply given seemed to satisfy them. They then walked quietly back to the house, but scarcely were they under cover when a heavy gun and rifle fire was opened on the Allies from the armoury, at close range, just across the river. Luckily cover was close at hand in a village and behind the river embankment, and the main body was still in rear ; but the junks with the wounded were carried down by the current, and the two that were leading suffered from a severe fire, five men being killed before the junks could be towed up again and put under shelter.

Rifle fire was directed against the enemy's guns in the armoury, and several of the men working them were shot. At the same time Major Johnstone, R.M.L.I., with a party of 100 marines and seamen, crossed the river a little higher up than, and out of sight of, the enemy's position. They advanced under cover of a village to within 150 yards of the north corner of the armoury, and from there charged with a cheer into the works, which were soon abandoned by the Chinese. A German detachment also crossed lower down the river and captured several guns, and they with the British detachment quickly cleared the armoury grounds.

The Chinese, however, did not intend to give up the position without a struggle, and in the afternoon made a most determined attempt to retake it. Having prepared the way by a heavy shell fire, they advanced to the assault, and were only driven back after having suffered very heavy loss. It was afterwards ascertained that their strength amounted to about 8,000 men The allies also suffered severely, and Commander Bucholtz, of the Imperial German Navy, was killed. The main body of the forces and the wounded had now crossed the river and occupied quarters in the armoury, which was put in a state of defence. An attempt was also made to communicate with the garrison at Tien-tsin, and for this purpose a party of 100 marines, under command of Captains R. O'M. Doig and H. T. R. Lloyd, R.M.L.I., recrossed the river in the evening and attempted to reach the settlements, under cover of darkness, by a circuitous route to the northwards along the railway. Mr. A. Currie, of the Imperial Chinese Railway, offered his services as guide, and the railway was safely reached ; but here opposition was at once encountered, alarm bugles sounded in various directions, and the Chinese opened a heavy fire. The country which the small force would have had to cross is extremely broken and almost impassable by night, and, after suffering the loss of four of its number, the party had to withdraw again to the armoury.

The necessity of procuring assistance from Tien-tsin was very urgent, as the further advance in that direction by junk was impossible, on account of the Chinese forts lower down the river. There was, however, no other means of transport available, and the wounded, now aggregating the large number of 230, would have had to be carried by the troops, which would have occupied all the men available, leaving none to guard the column from attack.

The question of supplies was also a serious one, as these were running low, but this cause of anxiety was removed by the discovery on the 23rd June of a large quantity of rice in one of the buildings in the armoury and also of immense supplies of guns, arms, and ammunition, and war material of the latest pattern. Affairs now assumed quite a different complexion, and it was evident that if necessary the force could hold out for several days, but the placing of the wounded under proper treatment was still of the first importance, and several messengers had already been despatched with the hope of getting news of the situation through to Tien-tsin. The intervening country was, however, so closely watched that they all appear to have been captured, and none of them reached the settlement.

At daylight on the 23rd the Chinese again made an unsuccessful attempt to retake the armoury, and the engagement continued until 8 a.m., when they were finally driven off. There had been several fresh casualties among the allied troops and Captain Beyts, R.M.A., of H.M.S. "Centurion," was killed.

Several of the Chinese guns found in the armoury were now mounted on the defences, and the beleaguered force assumed the offensive by bombarding a Boxer position near the armoury and a Chinese fort lower down the river. This had an excellent effect, as the enemy gave little more trouble, and their attempts to retake the place entirely ceased. A wounded Chinese soldier, brought in on the following day, reported that the troops, which were those of General Nieh's command, were much discouraged by their want of success, as they had attacked the armoury in great strength and had been badly beaten.

Relief was now near at hand. One of the Chinese messengers, sent out on the 23rd, had at last managed to get through to Tien-tsin, and had given an account of the position of the relief force. He had been captured by the Boxers and tied up to a tree, but, as he managed to destroy his message before he was taken, they could find nothing incriminating about him, and he was finally released, and made his way with great difficulty through the allied lines into the settlement.

Early on the morning of the 25th of June one of the guns in the Chinese fort down the river was seen to be firing in the direction of Tien-tsin, and to create a diversion fire was opened on it from two guns in the armoury, with the desired effect. About 6 a.m. European troops were reported to be in sight, and an hour later the relieving force, under Colonel Shirinsky, arrived opposite the armoury on the left bank of the river.

Preparations were now made to evacuate the armoury, which had afforded such opportune shelter to the hard-pressed column. In the afternoon all the wounded were transported across the river, and were followed later by the whole of the force, which bivouacked on the left bank for the night. Arrangements were also made to destroy the supplies of warlike stores, the value of which was estimated at three and a half million sterling.

Subsequent events proved that the occupation of this place might have been of great advantage to the Allies. On the other hand, its retention was not considered feasible by the authorities on the spot, who were in the best position to judge, and at 3 a.m. on the 26th of June the retirement on Tien-tsin commenced. When the troops moved off Lieutenant E. G. Lowther-Crofton and Mr. C. Davidge, torpedo gunner, of H.M.S. "Centurion," remained behind to set fire to the storehouses in the Armoury. Fires were lit in five separate places, and the destruction of the place appeared to be fairly complete. After finishing their work the officers rejoined the main body, which arrived safely in the settlement about 9 a.m.

The composition of the force which attempted the relief of the Legations at Peking was as follows :—

—	Officers.	Men.	Guns.	Under Command of
Austrians	1	24	-	Lieut. Prochasca.
British	62	640 seamen 213 marines	1 6-pr. Hotchkiss Q.F. 3 9-pr. M.L. 2 ·45 Maxims. 6 ·45 Nordenfelts.	Vice-Adm. Sir E. R. Seymour.
French	7	151	1 field gun	Capt. Morelles.
German	23	427	2 Maxims	Capt. von Usedom.
Italian	2	38	1 Maxim	Lieut. Sirianni.
Japanese	2	52	-	Capt. Mori.
Russian	7	305	1 field gun	Comdr. Chagkin.
United States	6	106	1 13-pr. 1 Colt automatic.	Capt. B. H. McCalla.
Total	110	1,956 2,066	19	

All the officers in command were naval officers.

The total casualties of the force amounted to:—

	Officers.		Men.	
	Killed.	Wounded.	Killed.	Wounded.
Austrian	—	—	1	1
British seamen	—	8	15	66*
„ marines	1	—	14	23*
French	—	—	1	10
German	1	6	11	56
Italian	—	—	5	3
Japanese	—	—	2	3
Russian	—	4	10	23
United States	—	2	4	25
Total	2	20	63	210

Total casualties - - - - - - 295.

Total British casualties - - - - 127.

* Two of these men subsequently died of their wounds.

CHAPTER V.

DEFENCE OF THE SETTLEMENTS AT TIEN-TSIN AND CAPTURE OF THE NATIVE CITY.

After the return of the Peking relief column the allied forces, concentrated in Tien-tsin, acted for some time strictly on the defensive. Admiral Seymour describes the place at this date, the 26th June, as presenting a very desolate appearance. The railway station wrecked; the huts of the labouring, but hostile, Chinese, all round the settlements, burnt down to prevent the enemy taking cover in them; the houses in the settlement mostly showing the effects of the heavy bombardment, many of them unoccupied and closed, and some burnt by incendiaries; the streets barricaded with bales of wool, rice, &c.; and trade entirely suspended, both in the settlements and on the river.

For the safety of the railway it was considered necessary to drive the Chinese out of the large Eastern Arsenal, which lies about a mile and a half to the north-east of the railway station. Arrangements were accordingly made for a combined attack to be carried out on the 27th June. The Russians attempted to carry the place by assault on the 27th, and, on being brought to a stand by the Chinese rifle fire, were obliged to send in urgent requests for assistance. Reinforcements, consisting of a British naval detachment with a twelve-pounder gun, and some American and German troops, were immediately hurried up, but as no one understood clearly what was required considerable confusion ensued, and there were several casualties among the reinforcing troops. Two companies of the Chinese Regiment were then brought up to protect the left flank, which was threatened by attack from a large body of Chinese, and the assault having been pressed home on the north-west and south-west corners of the arsenal, the place was eventually captured and the Chinese driven out. The British casualties in this action amounted to seven men killed and two officers and nineteen men wounded.

The Russians formally took over charge of the arsenal for the benefit of the united allied forces, but subsequently appropriated and removed practically the whole of the valuable stores and machinery for their own use.

On the following day it was suggested by the Russian General that an attack on the eastern part of the native town, lying outside the walled city, might result in the capture of the Chi-li Viceroy in his Yamen, but, as the undertaking would have involved much fighting in narrow and tortuous streets, with no sufficiently important advantage to be gained, the idea was given up.

On the same day a messenger reached Tien-tsin with the following despatch from Sir Robert Hart, dated Peking, 8 a.m.,

24th June: "Our case is desperate, come at once." Any attempt to relieve Peking at this time was, however, out of the question, as the available allied troops were fully occupied in guarding Taku, Tang-ku, and Tien-tsin, and the lines of communication between these places.

On the 29th the Consular body at Tien-tsin handed over the control of affairs to the military commanders. Vice-Admiral Alexieff arrived at Taku the following day, and assumed supreme command of the Russian forces, and, at a meeting of the senior naval officers at Taku on the same date, it was decided that, as the expected reinforcements to the allied troops in the near future would only raise their strength to about 20,000 men, the immediate relief of Peking was not to be contemplated.

The exact strength of the various contingents in the Chi-li province was reported on this date to be as follows:—

	Officers.	Men.
Austrian	12	127
British	184	1,700
French	17	387
German	44	1,300
Italian	7	131
Japanese	119	3,709
Russian	117	5,817
United States	20	329
Total	520	13,500

with 53 field guns and 36 machine guns.

An important political event which occurred on the 28th June, and which throws a strong light on the attitude of the Chinese Government towards the Allied Powers, who believed that they were assisting that government to suppress the Boxer movement and restore order in North China, was the despatch from Pao-ting fu of the following Imperial Edict from the Court at Peking to all the Viceroys and Governors in Central and Southern China.

It was worded as follows: " Whereas open war has broken " out between China and the Foreign Powers, and the " Boxer Society round Tien-tsin and throughout Chi-li, co-" operating with the Imperial troops, have been victorious, " we have already issued Decrees praising their bravery. These " loyal people are to be found throughout the empire, and all " Governors and Viceroys, if they can raise forces from their " number, can rely on them to oppose the insolence of the " foreigners with the greatest success. The high provincial " authorities shall therefore memorialise immediately regarding " their plans of campaign. The Viceroys of the Yang-tse and " coast provinces are hereby commanded to use their most " strenuous endeavours to put these instructions into effect."

This was, in effect, an open declaration of war against the Allied Powers by the Chinese Government, but most of the

Viceroys and Governors concerned chose to consider that it came from Prince Tuan, whom they declared to be a rebel. They therefore decided not to obey it.

The greatest credit is due to Chang Chih-tung and Liu K'un-yi, the Viceroys at Wu-chang and Nanking respectively, who, at great personal risk, maintained order in the Yang-tse provinces throughout this critical period. The Viceroy at Hang-chou alone refused to accept the responsibility, and the state of lawlessness and unrest, caused by the preaching of Boxer emissaries, resulted in the murder of certain missionaries in the western part of Che-kiang province.

In Tien-tsin the condition of affairs remained unchanged. There was constant "sniping" on the settlements from the native houses on the outskirts, which necessitated the despatch of troops to drive out the enemy and destroy the buildings that sheltered them. The Chinese were busily employed in mounting fresh guns at various points, and it was reported that reinforcements of troops were daily arriving in the native city.

It is impossible to say what the actual strength of the enemy's troops was at any particular period, but according to reliable information obtained by the British Consul it was as follows at the beginning of June :—

13,000 under General Nieh, about Tien-tsin, Lutai, &c.
10,000 under Tung-lu, south of Peking.
6,000 under Tung-fuhsiang, east of Peking.
12,000 under Sung-Ching at Shan-hai-kuan.
2,200 under Ma at Ho-kien-fu.
1,000 under Hsin-Cheng, besides the hordes of Boxers.

The greater number of these were concentrated at Tien-tsin by the end of June.

Wet weather prevailed, and the Allies were engaged in strengthening their defences and repelling attacks on the railway station. After an attack on this point on the 2nd July the Russians refused to defend it any longer, and it was afterwards held by contingents of about one hundred men each from the British, French, and Japanese forces.

On the 3rd July a heavy shell fire was opened on the settlements and Russian camp from guns posted in the forts in the native city, and from a new battery to the north-east on the railway. The bombardment was resumed on the following morning, and a demonstration was also made towards the Western Arsenal, but it was kept at a distance by the guns in the British settlement.

Apparently this move was only intended to draw off the allied troops to the right bank of the river, as in the afternoon the Chinese made a most determined attack on the railway station, which lasted for about two hours. Under cover of pouring rain and thick mist, and an accurate and heavy shell fire from several guns, they got to close quarters and the fighting was stubborn. Reinforcements, consisting of 100 British bluejackets and the Chinese Regiment, were quickly on the spot, and the Chinese were eventually beaten off, leaving about fifty of their number dead on the field. Considering the intensity and accuracy of the enemy's fire the casualties among the British troops were surprisingly few, only three men of the Chinese Regiment being wounded.

On the same day two additional 12-pr. guns were received from H.M.S. "Terrible," and two 9-pr. Krupp guns from the forts at Taku. These brought up the numbers of the British guns to three 12-prs., two 9-pr. M.L. field guns, two 9-pr. Krupps, and three 6-pr. Hotchkiss. The Russians had eight field guns and three mountain batteries.

The Chinese mounted four more guns at the south gate of the city, and the British placed another 12-pr. at the woollen mills on the south-west of the settlement. Desultory shelling and continuous sniping went on from day to day, and on the 6th the Chinese opened fire at short range, from a gun they had mounted unobserved among some ruined houses near the French settlement. As this gun was doing considerable damage a detachment was sent out, under command of Major Bruce of the Chinese Regiment, to locate and, if possible, capture it. Unfortunately, it was discovered to be on the opposite bank of the river, and as there were no means of getting across, the party had to retire. In the afternoon a second attempt was made to silence this gun, a 9-pr. being brought up to engage it. The enemy, however, were on this occasion prepared for the attack, and opened such a heavy and well-aimed fire on the party that it was found impossible to bring the 9-pr. into action, and, in the subsequent retirement, the small British force suffered severely. Midshipman F. Esdaile, of H.M.S. "Barfleur," was killed, Major Bruce was dangerously wounded, and four seamen, and five men of the Chinese Regiment, were also wounded.

On the 7th the settlements were heavily bombarded in the forenoon, the enemy's guns being answered by the fire of the allies. The shells which burst in a house occupied by the men of H.M.S. "Centurion" killed three and wounded four of their number.

A reconnaissance by the Japanese cavalry towards the south-west revealed the presence of a strong force in that direction, and, as they were apparently working round with the idea of cutting communication between Tien-tsin and Taku by river, a scheme was prepared for a combined attack on the 9th to drive them out of their position, and, if possible, seize the Western Arsenal. The capture of the arsenal had become necessary, as the Chinese had mounted three fresh guns there during the night of the 7th, which enfiladed the British 12-pr. battery at the Woollen Mills, and seriously interfered with its action.

Accordingly, before daylight on the 9th July, a force of 1,000 Japanese, including three troops of cavalry, four mountain guns, and a detachment of engineers; 950 British, including 400 seamen and marines, two companies Royal Welsh Fusiliers, two companies Chinese Regiment, and 50 men of the Hongkong

Regiment; 150 Americans, and 400 Russians, moved out at 3 a.m. from the British settlement, by the Taku Gate, towards the south. The operations were planned by Major-General Fukushima of the Japanese army, and it had been arranged between him and Brigadier-General Dorward that he was to command the whole allied force. As the Russians, however, declined to serve under a Japanese officer, he only commanded his own men, and General Dorward commanded the rest of the force.

After proceeding about a mile and a half due south the force wheeled to the west, and half a mile further on deployed. The Japanese were on the left, with their cavalry covering their outer flank. Next to them were the British, with the Naval Brigade in support, and the Russian detachment in reserve, and on the right, with an interval between them and the British, were the Americans, who had been directed to move under cover of the mud parapet which encircles Tien-tsin direct on the Western Arsenal, timing their advance by the march of the main body.

The first objective was the village of Hei-niu-chuang, which was held by the enemy, and, the fire of their guns having been quickly silenced, the line advanced to the assault. On the extreme left the Japanese carried a village held by about 400 Chinese, and the Japanese cavalry, getting in among them, killed about 200 and captured four small Krupp guns. The position having been taken the line again changed front, facing the West Arsenal, about a mile and a half distant across a wide ditch. Under cover of the fire of the allied guns the Japanese engineers quickly threw a bridge over the ditch, by which the force crossed, and the advance was at once continued in open order. The Americans and a few Japanese scouts were the first to reach the arsenal, when it was found that the Chinese had withdrawn, and the place was so battered by shell fire and so exposed to fire from the south wall of the native city, that its occupation by the Allies was decided to be undesirable. Accordingly, after having destroyed several Chinese houses in the vicinity, which might have afforded shelter to the enemy's "snipers," and having blown up the bridge over the canal, which connected the arsenal with the native city, the force withdrew to the settlements, which were reached about 10.30 a.m.

The British casualties were two men killed and seven wounded; those of the Japanese four officers and 33 men killed and wounded; the Chinese loss was estimated at about 350 killed.

On the 10th July the artillery of the defence was further strengthened by the arrival of two 4-inch guns and one 4·7-inch gun from the British fleet at Taku.

On the same day a scheme was arranged for a general assault on the native city of Tien-tsin, to take place on the 12th. At the request of the Russian General this attack was postponed till the 13th July.

At the same time another enterprise was set on foot by the Russians, who proposed to attack the Chinese artillery position on the railway, to the north-east of the settlement, the fire from which had been doing a great deal of damage to the houses in the foreign concessions for some time past. They proposed to cross the Lu-tai canal, which ran in front of the batteries, by pontoons, but the operation had finally to be abandoned, as the construction of the pontoon bridge was found to be impracticable.

It seemed almost possible that the Chinese had received information of this intended attack, as early in the morning of the 11th, at the moment when the troops taking part in the enterprise would have been safely out of the way, the enemy suddenly made a most determined attack on the railway station. The mixed guard of three hundred men was quickly reinforced, but the enemy fought with the greatest courage for about four hours before they were finally driven off. Several of them actually got into our defences before they were killed, and many were shot within a few yards of them. They suffered severely, and the casualties among the Allies were also heavy, amounting to about 150 men killed and wounded. The British had three men killed and ten wounded, but the French and Japanese casualties were far greater, owing chiefly to the former bringing up their reinforcements into the firing line in close formation, and the latter leaving their defences to deliver a counter attack.

In the meantime reinforcements had been constantly arriving in Tien-tsin, and the garrison now amounted to 12,170 men. The officers and men of H.M.S. "Centurion" were therefore sent back to their ship, as it was considered that their services could now be spared, and on the 12th July Vice-Admiral Sir E. H. Seymour and his staff also returned to the flagship at Taku.

Nothing of importance occurred on this date, but a large body of Chinese troops were seen marching into the native city from the north-west.

Preparations were now made to carry out the assault on the native city. The city is rectangular in shape and was enclosed by massive walls about 30 feet in height, pierced by four gates, one in the centre of each of the four sides. Outside the walls ran a wet ditch, and suburbs of native houses lie outside the city on all sides. The country to the south is fairly open, there being a belt of houses near the wall, beyond which only a few scattered clumps of houses interrupt the view, though the ground is much cut up with ponds and excavations. The mud parapet which encircles the city is on the south side, about 2,000 yards from the south wall, and the western arsenal lies just inside it. The suburbs on the south-east, east, north, and west are very extensive, and are compactly built with narrow, tortuous streets. About 350 yards to the north of the city runs the Huai-ho or Grand Canal, and 300 yards to the east is the Pei-ho, into which the Huai-ho flows. The city was therefore very strong for defence.

The plan of operations decided upon was as follows :—The

American, British, French, and Japanese troops were to attack the south face of the city from the direction of the mud parapet, the South Gate being the main objective. At the same time a force of Russians and Germans with a few French were to attack the batteries north-east of the city, and to co-operate from that side. As the latter force had further to go, it was arranged that it should move off so as to deliver its attack at 10 a.m. on the 13th, while the southern force was to begin operations as early in the morning as possible, so as to draw off the enemy in that direction. Owing to unforeseen circumstances, however, the Russian attack was checked, and therefore did little to assist the assault on the South Gate, though it was eventually carried out successfully.

The southern force moved out from the settlements at about 3.30 a.m. in three columns. On the right were the French, 900 strong, under Colonel Pelacot. They were to follow the mud parapet and march towards the Western Arsenal. In the centre were the Japanese, 1,500 strong, under Brigadier-General Fukushima. They were to march parallel with the French, about 500 yards from the mud parapet. On the left were the Americans, 900 strong, and the British, 800 strong, including a naval force of 300, and also 30 Austrians, all under the command of Brigadier-General Dorward. They were to move parallel to, and about 500 yards from, the Japanese. Beyond the Anglo-American column was a detachment of 150 Japanese cavalry covering the left flank, and watching the movements of the enemy in that direction. They moved out to the racecourse, supported by a battalion of Japanese infantry, who afterwards rejoined their main body. As the advance progressed the right column was checked at a bridge about a quarter of a mile from the arsenal, which was swept by the enemy's fire from the city wall. The left column was also slightly delayed by having to clear parties of the enemy out of some villages on its line of march, and when the centre column arrived at the road leading to the arsenal and the South Gate the left column was about a quarter of a mile in rear. The Japanese, however, quickly cleared the Chinese out of the arsenal, and the left column moving forward occupied the mud parapet further to the west. The troops were now in position along the mud embankment facing the southern side of the city, the French as before on the right, the Japanese in the centre, and the British and Americans on the left.

At 5.30 a.m. the bombardment of the city commenced. In the British concession one 4-inch, three 12-pounder, and a few field and boat guns came into action, all being manned and worked by the Naval Brigade. These were assisted by the fire of three 3·2-inch American guns, four British mountain guns, six small French guns, and 18 mountain guns of the Japanese artillery, which had come into position round the arsenal and behind the mud parapet.

About 7.15 a.m. the advance of the infantry commenced. The Japanese in the centre directed, and marched on the South

Gate, but advancing hurriedly they caused the Americans and British on their left to come under very heavy fire in trying to keep their position. General Fukushima also asked for support to be sent to the left of his line, and General Dorward sent up the 9th U.S. Infantry for this duty. At the same time a detachment of the Hongkong regiment, with two Maxims, was posted on the mud parapet to keep off a hostile force of about 1,500 infantry and cavalry, which was threatening an attack from the west.

As the attack developed the Japanese firing line extended much further to the left than was expected, and the British and American troops were forced close up to the suburbs, outside the south-west corner of the city wall, from which a very heavy fire was opened on them. They, however, succeeded in maintaining their position throughout the day.

The reserves now advanced to the shelter of the mud parapet, and the guns moved inside to a closer range, from whence they continued the bombardment of the South Gate. The Chinese, in addition to their numerous guns inside and north-east of the city, had brought eight guns into action in a fort about $1\frac{1}{4}$ miles west of the West Gate, and a large force of the enemy was visible in that direction, though kept at a distance by the the detachment of the Hongkong Regiment which had been specially detailed for that duty.

The French in their advance had come under heavy fire, had failed to extend for the right attack, and were broken up into small parties which were sheltering in the houses along the road to the South Gate. The 9th U.S. Infantry had also lost their way, and had got into an exposed position near the French concession, on the right of the Japanese, and had suffered heavily, the commanding officer, Colonel Liscum, being mortally wounded. General Dorward at once ordered up a hundred men of the Naval Brigade, under Lieut. Phillimore, to their assistance, and sent in to the settlement for two companies of the Chinese regiment with stretchers. On their arrival they were sent forward, under command of Major Pereira, to the American position, and succeeded in bringing away a large number of wounded under a heavy fire, Major Pereira himself being wounded. As it was now reported that the Americans and the men of the Naval Brigade, who had gone to reinforce them, had got into a fairly good position, with sufficient cover, they were ordered to remain were they were, and thus protected the Japanese right flank. Subsequently word was sent back that the Americans were running short of ammunition, and Captain Ollivant, with a party of the Chinese Regiment, was sent forward with a fresh supply. The troops got their ammunition, but Captain Ollivant and several men were killed.

All this time the practice of the naval guns, directed by Captain Bayly and Lieutenant Drummond, R.N., had been most excellent and had been of the greatest assistance to the infantry in keeping down the enemy's rifle fire from the wall;

but about 1 p.m. General Dorward received a note from the Chief Staff Officer of the Japanese troops requesting that all artillery fire might cease, as the Japanese had effected an entrance into the city. This request was at once complied with, and a general advance of the troops to support the assault on the city commenced. The report however of the Japanese having got inside was untrue, and the advancing lines came under a heavy and well-directed fire from the walls, which increased in intensity as they got closer. Ultimately the mistake was discovered and the troops, after losing heavily, had to take cover in the buildings along the ditch at close range from the city wall.

The Japanese engineers had intended to blow in the South Gate and had advanced to carry out their object with the greatest gallantry. On approaching the gate, however, they had come under such a terrific fire from the wall and the buildings in front of it, and had lost so heavily, that they were obliged to retire.

The artillery was again ordered to open fire, and this enabled the troops to maintain their advanced position until nightfall.

Towards evening information was received from the Japanese cavalry that bodies of the enemy were moving round, the left and threatening an attack on the rear. To meet this new development it was necessary to withdraw the Royal Welsh Fusiliers, under Captain Gwynne, and the 6th U.S. Marines, under Major Waller, from their advanced position on the extreme left of the line. This necessitated their crossing a considerable area of fire-swept ground, but, by concentrating the fire of the naval guns on the enemy's position opposite our left, the movement was successfully carried out, and the troops reached the mud parapet with little loss. The fire of the guns was now turned on the Chinese barricades opposite our right flank, to enable the 9th U.S. Infantry, under Major Jesse Lee, and the British naval detachment to withdraw. This was a more difficult manœuvre, as the troops were in such close touch with the enemy that they were liable to be struck by the shells from our naval guns, and were also exposed to the enemy's fire at short range. However, they not only succeeded in working their way back to the mud parapet with slight loss, but also brought back with them a considerable number of dead and wounded.

Dispositions were now made for protecting the flanks and rear of the force and the troops remained in position for the night, food and water being sent out to them from the settlement.

About 3 a.m. on the 14th July the Japanese engineers crossed the ditch, by a bridge they had constructed in the night, and succeeded in blowing in the South Gate, and after an hour's fighting in the streets the city was in possession of the Allies.

The British fought their way from the South out through the North Gate, and in the canal beyond captured one hundred and eighty junks and a stern-wheeler, which proved very useful for transport in the subsequent advance on Peking. A detachment also captured the west fort, and in it the eight guns which had been replying to our artillery throughout the previous day.

The Russians had also at length been successful in their attack on the Chinese positions to the north-east, and having routed the enemy captured eleven of their guns.

About midday the large fort to the north-east of the city was captured by a party of Japanese, who had advanced from the railway station, and the occupation being now complete, the city was divided up for purposes of administration into four quarters, garrisoned respectively by American, British, French, and Japanese detachments.

The losses of the Allies during the fighting of the 13th and 14th July were as follows :—

	Total Casualties.
British : 2 officers and 17 men killed and 3 officers and 78 men wounded - - -	100
American : 1 officer and 30 men killed, 3 officers and 108 men wounded - - -	142
French : about 110 killed and wounded -	110
Austrian : 5 men wounded - - -	5
Japanese : 5 officers and 105 men killed and 13 officers and 279 men wounded - -	402
Russians : about 120 killed and wounded - -	120
Total casualties - - - -	879

The Chinese had lost heavily and had fled thoroughly demoralised. Their principal leader, General Nieh, was reported to have been killed by the bursting of a shell on the 11th. The Viceroy Yu-lu had fled from Tien-tsin the same day, and had been followed on the 13th by the next two senior military commanders, Generals Sung and Ma.

The Russians occupied the Chinese forts and fortified camps on the left bank of the Pei-ho and also the Hsi-ku armoury, in which it was discovered that there was still a considerable quantity of warlike material—guns, rifles and ammunition, which had not been destroyed when the Peking relief column abandoned the place. It was arranged by the allied commanders with Vice-Admiral Alexieff, that the Russians should guard these stores for the common advantage of the Allied Powers, but, as in the case of the Eastern Arsenal, they subsequently appropriated almost the whole amount.

A hitch also occurred in the scheme for occupying the native city, as the French commander, though his troops had not been particularly prominent in the fighting on the 13th, claimed half the city on the plea that his men were among the first to enter it. It was eventually arranged that the French should occupy the north-west quarter, the British the south-west quarter, the Japanese the north-east quarter, and the Americans the south-east quarter. This arrangement was put in force on the 17th, and the work of removing the corpses and improving the sanitation of the town, which was urgently needed, was at once taken in hand.

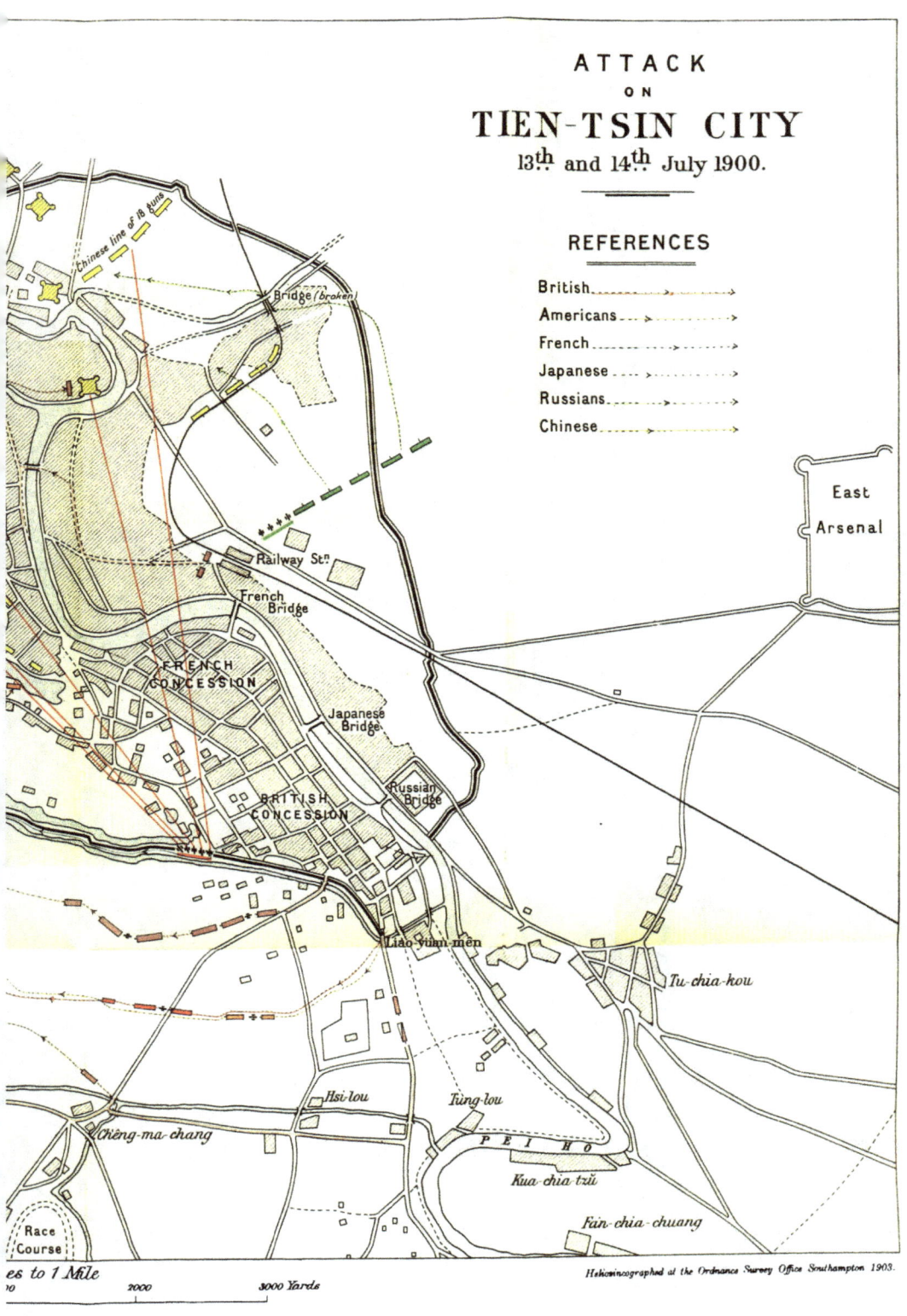

On the 16th a conference of the naval commanders assembled at Taku under the presidency of Sir E. H. Seymour, and it was decided that the railway from Tang-ku to Tien-tsin should be handed over to the care of the Russians, for the mutual benefit of the Allies, and with the stipulation that it should be given back to the former administration, as soon as military requirements would allow of this being done.

On the 17th it was decided that the governorship of Tien-tsin city should be vested in a triumvirate of representatives of the three nations most directly interested in China : Great Britain, represented by Lieutenant-Colonel Bower ; Russia, by Colonel Wogack ; and Japan, by Colonel Aoki.

On the 18th July the first reinforcements from India, consisting of half of the 7th Bengal Infantry Regiment, reached Tien-tsin. These were followed shortly afterwards by the rest of the regiment, the headquarters and 135 men of the Royal Welsh Fusiliers, a wing of the 24th Punjab Infantry, and the 12th Battery, Royal Field Artillery ; and, on the 25th July, Sir Alfred Gaselee and the Head Quarters Staff of the British contingent of the China Expeditionary Force arrived at Taku.

News had reached Tien-tsin of the destruction of the Manchurian Railway north and south of Mukden, and a message from Sir Claude MacDonald dated the 4th July had been received, in which he said that the Legations in Peking could still hold out for ten days or a fortnight, unless the Chinese attacked with determination, in which case the defence could not last for more than four or five days. Great anxiety was therefore felt as to the fate of the Europeans in the capital.

CHAPTER VI.

Despatch of the British Contingent—China Expeditionary Force—from India.*

The outbreak of the anti-foreigner movement in North China, and the spread of the Boxers towards Peking, as reported by telegram, had been watched with great interest in India.

On the 12th June 1900 the Secretary of State for India telegraphed to Lord Curzon that it might be necessary to send the troops in garrison at Singapore and Hongkong on service to North China, and inquired if the Indian Government would be prepared to replace the troops, so withdrawn, by regiments from India.

To this message the Viceroy replied that the Indian Government would undertake to replace the garrisons at Singapore and Hongkong by native troops from India if required, and was also prepared, if further developments rendered the employment of additional troops necessary, to furnish a force from India of one horse-artillery battery, one native mountain battery, two native cavalry regiments, four battalions of native infantry, and a company of sappers and miners, for operations in China.

On the 14th June all the available troops at Hongkong had been despatched to Taku at the request of Sir E. Seymour, and on the 16th the Secretary of State telegraphed to the Viceroy asking for the immediate despatch of troops to Singapore and Hongkong to replace those withdrawn. The 7th Regiment of Bengal Infantry, and 1st Regiment of Sikh Infantry, were in consequence ordered to be in readiness to proceed to China.

On the 18th June the Secretary of State again wired that the position of affairs at Peking and Tien-tsin was now very grave, and requested that the Government of India would take up the necessary steamer transport, and arrange for the immediate despatch of an expeditionary force to China, consisting of one battery of horse or field artillery, one regiment of native cavalry, three battalions of native infantry, and one company of sappers and miners, with land transport. This force to be in addition to the two native infantry battalions already ordered to proceed on garrison duty to Singapore and Hongkong.

Orders were immediately issued from Simla to the Director of the Royal Indian Marine at Bombay to take up the necessary shipping and suggest ports of embarkation. At the same

---

* See Appendices B, C, D, E, and L for further details regarding the despatch of this force.

time the following troops were warned for service in China: 12th Battery, R.F.A., with R.-7 ammunition column unit; 1st Bengal Lancers; 1st Madras Pioneers; 22nd Bombay Infantry; and 24th Punjab Infantry. Orders were also issued that all the troops were to be armed with ·303-inch Lee-Metford rifles and carbines. They were to be accompanied by the necessary medical establishment, ordnance reserves and engineer field-park, and were to take with them their obligatory regimental mule transport and mobilisation equipment. R.-7 ammunition column unit was ordered to be equipped with pole-draught waggons and harness, and eight special signalling units from British infantry battalions in the Madras and Bombay commands were detailed to accompany the force.

Brigadier-General Sir Alfred Gaselee, K.C.B., A.D.C., was selected to command the expedition, and Colonel E. G. Barrow, C.B., was appointed second in command, and infantry brigadier. As it was found impossible to spare more mule transport from India, two coolie corps, each of a strength of one thousand men, were ordered to be recruited in the Punjab. It was afterwards proposed to despatch four additional corps, making six in all, but eventually only two more of similar strength were sent. None of these coolies were ever used in China for carrying loads, for which work they were originally intended, but a number of them were employed in various ways. They did not prove a very useful addition to the force, and most of them were shortly afterwards sent back to India.

The experiment was also tried of enlisting Japanese coolies for transport work, and five hundred of them arrived at Taku from Kobe about the 11th July. They, however, were not found to be a success, as, though strong and hardy, they were not amenable to discipline, and gave considerable trouble, and they were soon sent back to Japan.

On the 22nd June Lord Curzon telegraphed to the Secretary of State for India, asking to be informed if there was any probability of more troops being required for China. On the same day Lord George Hamilton replied that, as the situation in Chi-li was becoming more and more serious, Her Majesty's Government considered it desirable to increase the force from India to a strength of 10,000 native soldiers, including another cavalry regiment, more sappers and miners, and, if possible, another battery. At the same time the Home Government undertook to deliver in India by the 1st October four fresh battalions of British infantry.

To this increase of force the Viceroy agreed, but informed the Secretary of State that inquiries were being made as to the practicability of the country in North China at that time of year for cavalry and artillery. If the reply on this subject was favourable, he proposed to send a brigade of three native cavalry regiments instead of the two asked for, and a horse artillery battery. If, on the other hand, the country was reported to be unsuited for the action of mounted troops, the two additional cavalry regiments and the horse artillery battery would not be despatched till the end of the rainy season in Chi-li.

The remainder of the force would be organised in two brigades, each of four native infantry battalions, exclusive of the two battalions for garrison duty at Hongkong and Singapore; and divisional troops, consisting of one field artillery battery, one regiment of native cavalry, one pioneer battalion, and three sapper companies.

With regard to the despatch to India of four battalions of British infantry from England, Lord Curzon said that the Indian Government would prefer the return of the Indian Contingent from South Africa, especially the infantry and artillery.

To make up the eleven infantry battalions required by the above scheme, the following additional six regiments were directed to embark at Bombay, their obligatory transport being despatched from Calcutta :—2nd Regiment of Bengal Infantry ; 14th Sikhs ; 1st Battalion, 4th Gurkha Rifles ; 3rd Regiment of Madras Infantry ; 26th and 30th Regiments of Bombay Infantry. It was afterwards decided that the obligatory transport of each unit should be despatched in the same steamer as the troops to which it belonged, so that the corps should arrive at their destination complete, and this arrangement was in every case carried out.

In view of the increased strength of the force, the temporary rank of Major-General, with the local rank of Lieutenant-General, was conferred on Sir Alfred Gaselee, and Brigadier-General E. G. Barrow was appointed Chief of the Staff, with the local rank of Major-General, it being intended that, if the necessity arose, he should succeed General Gaselee in chief command.

Sir Alfred Gaselee was also appointed to the chief command of all Imperial British troops in North China, and orders were received from England, that, as the cost of the expedition was to be borne by the Imperial Treasury, the direction of operations would be undertaken by the Home Government, which would issue its instructions through the Secretary of State for India.

The force was organised as follows :—

1st Brigade.

Under command of Brigadier-General Sir NORMAN STEWART, Bart.

7th Rajput Regiment of Bengal Infantry.
26th Baluchistan Regiment of Bombay Infantry.
1st Regiment of Sikh Infantry.
24th Regiment of Punjab Infantry.
Two Native Field Hospitals.
One Supply Column.

2nd Brigade.

Under command of Brigadier-General O'Moore Creagh, V.C.

2nd Rajput Regiment of Bengal Infantry.
14th Sikh Regiment of Bengal Infantry.
1st Battalion, 4th Gurkha Rifles.
30th Regiment of Bombay Infantry (3rd Baluch Battalion).
Two Native Field Hospitals.
One Supply Column.

Divisional Troops.

12th Battery, Royal Field Artillery.
R.-7 Ammunition Column Unit.
1st Regiment of Bengal Lancers.
1st Regiment of Madras Pioneers.
No. 4 Company Bengal Sappers and Miners.
No. 3 ,, Queen's Own Madras Sappers and Miners.
No. 2 ,, Bombay Sappers and Miners.
Eight Special Signalling Units of British Infantry.
One section of a British Field Hospital.
One Native Field Hospital.
One Supply Column.

Garrison Troops, Hongkong.

3rd Regiment of Madras Infantry.
22nd Regiment of Bombay Infantry.

A hospital ship was authorised to carry invalids between China and India.

Wei-hai-wei had been selected by the War Office as the base for the troops in North China, and Colonel Lorne Campbell was appointed Commandant of the base, with the local rank of Brigadier-General.

Five British officers were attached to the force for duty with Chinese transport, to be organised locally, and a number of Special Service officers were appointed later for duty at the Treaty Ports.

The despatch of the expedition was pressed forward with all haste and the first detachment to leave India for North China was the left wing of the 7th Bengal Infantry, which sailed from Calcutta in the British India s.s. "Nerbudda", on the 25th June, and arrived at Taku on the 17th July. It was followed on the 29th June by the right wing of the regiment, in the s.s. "Palamcotta," and after that date an almost continuous stream of transports carried away troops and stores, from Calcutta, Bombay, Madras, Karachi and Rangoon, right up to the middle of September.

At first great difficulty in the fitting out of the transports at Calcutta was caused by the abnormal heat at the end of June and the beginning of July. Several cases of heat-stroke occurred among the native workmen, and the Chinese carpenters for some days refused to work at all.

The non-arrival on their expected dates of some of the vessels chartered, and unforeseen extensive repairs found necessary in others, to fit them for the accommodation of troops, also caused delay in their despatch. However, by hard work and good management, the loss of time thus involved was very slight, and very little alteration had to be made in the original dates of sailings.

Before embarking from Calcutta each Infantry battalion received one ·303-inch Maxim gun with 30,000 rounds of ammunition. Of the latter 4,000 rounds were carried on the gun, 2,200 were in regimental charge, and the remainder was deposited in the Ordnance Field Park. To work the guns, detachments were selected from the regiments, and trained under officers during the voyage. In addition to this armament ten ·303-inch Maxims, with pack-transport mountings, were sent out from England to Wei-hai-wei for the use of the China Expeditionary Force, and arrangements were also made to supply twenty pom-poms, to be delivered within the next three months, provided the personnel to work them could be furnished from India. Four pom-poms were also sent to China from South Africa.

As there was not a sufficient amount of ·303-inch ammunition available in India to supply the force, two million rounds were sent out from England, and a second consignment of two million rounds was despatched at a later date, when the strength of the force was subsequently increased by two additional brigades.

Arrangements were made, by the Secretary of State for India, for the supply of fodder from Australia, various articles of warm clothing from England and Canada, and coffee-shop stores, hospital comforts, &c. from England.

Twenty thousand tons of Japanese coal were stored at Hongkong, for the use of the transports carrying the force.

On the 3rd July Sir Alfred Gaselee embarked at Calcutta with his staff on board the s.s. "Zebenghla." Singapore was reached on the 10th July, the transport remaining outside the harbour only long enough to take off despatches, and then proceeding to Hongkong, where it arrived on the 15th July.

A general feeling of gloom hung over the port, as a message had just been received from Shanghai, which stated that there could no longer be any doubt that the Legations at Peking had fallen, and that all the Europeans there had perished at the hands of the Boxers. This mischievous lie was embellished with circumstantial details, and, like many similar inventions of the Press, should never have been published.

General Gaselee remained at Hongkong three days, as there were a number of questions to be discussed and settled with the Governor, Sir Henry Blake, and General Gascoigne, commanding the troops. On the 17th July the Viceroy Li Hung-chang arrived at Hongkong from Canton on his way to Shanghai, and had an interview with the Governor, at which Generals Gaselee,

Gascoigne, and Barrow were present. On the 18th the "Zebenghla" left Hongkong for the north, but on the 21st was stopped at sea by H.M.S. "Bonaventure," which took off Sir Alfred Gaselee and General Barrow to Shanghai, to confer with the local authorities on measures for the proper defence of the port, &c. As a result of his visit General Gaselee gave it as his opinion that the minimum garrison, which would suffice for the defence of Shanghai, would be 3,000 men, and considered that a suitable force for the purpose would consist of a battery of artillery, a native cavalry regiment, a brigade of native infantry, and a company of sappers and miners. The Second Brigade of the China Expeditionary Force was consequently diverted to Shanghai, where it remained throughout the subsequent operations in North China.

The "Zebenghla" arrived at Wei-hai-wei on the 22nd July, and Generals Gaselee and Barrow rejoined her there on the 24th. The same afternoon she left for Taku, which was reached about 2 p.m. on the following day.

In the meantime, on the 5th July, the Secretary of State for India telegraphed to the Viceroy that four 6-inch breech-loading howitzers, two 9·45-inch howitzers and four 4·7-inch quick-firing guns, on travelling carriages, with personnel and 500 rounds per piece, would shortly be despatched to North China from South Africa. This heavy ordnance with 15 officers and 305 men of the Royal Garrison Artillery, under command of Colonel Perrott, R.A., left Capetown for Hongkong on the 23rd July. To draw these guns 1,304 siege-train bullocks were sent to Wei-hai-wei from India, but long before the guns arrived, Peking had been captured by the Allies and the fighting was practically at an end. The guns remained at Wei-hai-wei, and the siege-train bullocks were sold by auction.

On the 7th July "C" battery, Royal Horse Artillery, R.-2 Ammunition Column Unit, the 16th Regiment of Bengal Lancers, and the 3rd Regiment of Bombay Cavalry were warned for service in China, and Brigadier-General G. L. R. Richardson, C.B., C.I.E. was appointed to command the Cavalry Brigade.

Khan Bahadur Dhanjibhoy, of Rawal Pindi, offered to provide nine ambulance tongas with twenty horses, the necessary personnel, and twelve months' supply of repairing material, for service with the Cavalry Brigade in China, and this offer the Secretary of State for India accepted.

On the 12th July it was announced from England that a Balloon Section would be sent to China.

On the 13th July and following days the undermentiond additional corps were warned for service in China. The 45th, 48th, and 52nd batteries of Royal Field Artillery; 1st battalion, Scottish Rifles; 2nd battalion, Royal Inniskilling Fusiliers; 1st battalion, Royal Highlanders; 1st battalion, Shropshire Light Infantry; 6th regiment of Bengal Infantry; 20th Punjab Regiment of Bengal Infantry; and 34th Punjab Regiment of Bengal Infantry (Pioneers).

On the 19th July the Viceroy informed the Secretary of State for India that a second division, consisting half of British troops and half of native troops, was held in readiness for despatch to China should their services be required. At the same time he pointed out that the British troops could only be spared from India if they could promptly be replaced from elsewhere. Unfortunately this was not found to be possible, and the British infantry brigade was consequently not sent to China.

On the same date the Maharajah Scindia of Gwalior offered to equip and maintain a hospital ship, at a cost of twenty lakhs, and present it to the British Government for the use of the China Expeditionary Force, and this offer was accepted by Her Majesty and acknowledged in terms of high appreciation.

The Maharajah eventually selected the s.s. "Zayathla" for the above purpose, and after being refitted and renamed the "Gwalior," it sailed on its first trip from Calcutta on the 23rd September, and subsequently rendered most valuable service to the Expeditionary Force.

On the 16th July Sir Alfred Gaselee and General Gascoigne had recommended that the Hongkong Regiment should be employed in North China, its place at Hongkong being taken by a third native infantry battalion from India. The Viceroy of India agreed to supply the battalion required, but requested that sanction should be given to the Indian Government to raise three new native battalions at Imperial expense, to replace those sent for garrison duty to China. He desired that these battalions should not be considered special corps for colonial service only, but should form part of the Indian army; the Indian Government being liable to be called upon to supply regiments, when required, of a strength of 800 men each, for periods of three years of foreign service, on special terms. To these suggestions Her Majesty's Government assented.

On the 20th July orders were issued for the despatch of a survey party to China, and the following day a detachment of mounted sappers was sanctioned with the force.

Owing to the appearance of cholera among the 14th Sikhs their departure had to be countermanded, and the 34th Pioneers were detailed to replace them temporarily in the 2nd Brigade. When the 14th Sikhs should be able to rejoin, the 34th Pioneers were to become the third battalion for garrison duty at Hongkong, in place of the Hongkong Regiment ordered to North China, but the regiment was promised that, in the event of a second division being sent to China, they would take their place in it.

On the 25th the American hospital ship "Maine," which had been working in connexion with the British forces in South Africa, was placed at the disposal of the Indian Government, for service in China, by the Atlantic Transport Company and the Committee of American ladies. As the British contingent was already provided with two hospital ships, the "Gwalior" and the "Carthage," which were ample for its requirements, the

"Maine" was principally used by the United States contingent of the allied force.

On the 2nd August orders were issued for the immediate despatch of a third native infantry brigade from India to China, which was composed as follows :—

3RD BRIGADE.

Under command of Brigadier-General A. J. F. REID, C.B.
    6th Regiment of Bengal Infantry.
    4th Regiment of Punjab Infantry.
    20th Regiment of Punjab Infantry.
    5th Infantry Regiment, Hyderabad Contingent.
    Two Native Field Hospitals.
    One Supply Column.

The last-named battalion was ordered on arrival at Hongkong to take the place of the 34th Pioneers in the garrison of the port, when the latter regiment would rejoin the 3rd Brigade.

Just previous to its departure for China an outbreak of cholera occurred in " C " battery, Royal Horse Artillery, which necessitated its detention at Mhow. " B " battery, Royal Horse Artillery, was consequently detailed to replace it in the expeditionary force, and, after having exchanged its 12-pr. equipment for 15-pr. equipment, it sailed from Calcutta for China on the 13th August. The Cavalry Brigade was therefore composed as follows :—

CAVALRY BRIGADE.

Under command of Brigadier-General G.L.R. RICHARDSON, C.B., C.I.E.
    " B " Battery, Royal Horse Artillery.
    R.-2 Ammunition Column Unit.
    1st Regiment of Bengal Lancers.
    16th   "   "   "   "
    3rd   "   " Bombay Cavalry.
    One Section of a British Field Hospital.
    Two Sections of a Native Field Hospital.
    One Supply Column.

On the 6th August the despatch of a fourth native infantry brigade to China was ordered, which was composed as follows :—

4TH BRIGADE.

Under command of Brigadier-General, J. T. CUMMINS, D.S.O.
    28th Regiment } of Madras Infantry.
    31st Regiment }
    Ulwar Infantry Battalion   } Imperial Service
    Bikanir Camel Corps (dismounted) }   Troops.
    Two Native Field Hospitals.
    One Supply Column.

To this brigade were attached :—
  1st Regiment of Jhodpur Lancers ⎱ Imperial Service
  Maler Kotla Sappers (one company) ⎰   Troops.
  Two Sections of a Native Field Hospital.

and orders were issued that all the above troops were to be armed with ·303-inch Lee-Metford weapons, as in the case of the other brigades.

Two special signalling units, one British and one native, were attached to both the 3rd and 4th Brigades.

On the 29th August the Government of India gave orders for the organisation, equipment and despatch of a Remount Depôt of 250 horses from Calcutta to Hongkong, at which latter place it was established. It was intended for the supply of remounts to the artillery and cavalry of the British force.

The embarkation of the whole of the troops belonging to the British contingent of the China Expeditionary Force was completed by the departure of the Ulwar Infantry from Calcutta in the ss. "Ludhiana" and "Landaura" on the 14th September 1900; and on the 9th October the movement of the three additional batteries of Royal Field Artillery and the four British infantry battalions, which had been warned for service in China in the middle of July, was finally countermanded.

As all the existing telegraph lines on the mainland of China were in the hands of the Chinese, including that from Shanghai to Chih-fu, the British Consuls at these places represented that, as the Chinese could not be relied upon to forward messages, a submarine cable should be laid from Shanghai to Taku via Wei-hai-wei, to ensure rapid communication between the troops in Chih-li and the outside world. This suggestion was acted upon and the cable was joined up to Taku on the 4th September. Pending its completion a ship was chartered and employed in carrying messages from Taku to the telegraph line at Chemulpho.

On the 8th August Australia sent a contribution to the Imperial forces assembling in China, in the shape of a Naval Brigade, consisting of 200 men from Victoria and 300 from New South Wales. The Brigade embarked at Sydney in the transport "Falamas," and arrived at Taku on 9th September.

The men were employed on shore, part at Tien-tsin and part (the New South Wales contingent) formed the garrison of Peking after the 8th October.

Besides the Naval Brigade, the South Australian cruiser "Protector" was employed for some time in the Gulf of Pechili, where her services were most useful. She returned to Australia on the 2nd November.

CHAPTER VII.

Advance of the Allies from Tien-tsin; Actions of Pei-ts'ang and Yang-tsun; Relief of the Legations and Occupation of Peking.

Before proceeding from Taku to Tien-tsin, General Gaselee and his Chief of the Staff attended a conference of the admirals and senior naval officers of the Allied Powers, on board H.M.S. "Barfleur," on the forenoon of the 26th July. He immediately afterwards proceeded to Sin-ho, which lies about three miles above Tang-ku, on the left bank of the river, and which had been selected as the landing-place for the British troops and stores. This place was connected by a branch line with the railway from Tang-ku to Tien-tsin, and arrangements had been made with the Russian railway officials to run two trains, of 15 vehicles each, daily from Sin-ho to Tien-tsin, one starting in the morning and the other in the evening. By filling the trucks three-quarters full with kit and stores and allowing the men to sit on the top, the troops were quickly transferred to Tien-tsin with all their baggage complete, as they arrived from the transports. The largest trucks were capable of carrying 19 horses or 24 mules.

Having inspected the arrangements at Sin-ho and given such orders as were necessary, General Gaselee proceeded to Tien-tsin by river, and arrived there at 8.30 a.m. on the 27th.

Since the capture of the native city on the 14th July, everything in and around Tien-tsin had been perfectly quiet. The French Concession was in ruins, but the British Concession had not suffered nearly so much, though most of the houses were more or less damaged by shell fire, and, owing to the flight of the Chinese employed in the settlements, the place was extremely insanitary. To prevent an outbreak of sickness among the troops immediate steps had to be taken to improve matters.

The all-important business now was the immediate relief of the Legations in Peking, though this view was not shared by all the Allies. On the 10th of August the Russian Minister of War stated that the advance of the allied forces on Peking was impracticable for two or three weeks, though four days earlier, on the 6th, effective opposition to the advance of the troops on the part of the Chinese had been finally crushed at the battle of Yang-tsun.

On his arrival at Tien-tsin, General Gaselee at once examined the question of the possibility of rescuing the Europeans in Peking, and represented to the commanding officers of the allied forces that, since their own position at Tien-tsin was perfectly assured and a large number of troops were already concentrated at that point, it would be a lasting disgrace to their arms if their fellow-countrymen in the Legations were now allowed to perish, without every endeavour being made to rescue them.

The latest news from Peking was more than three weeks old, and caused the gravest anxiety, as the British Minister then stated that, under favourable circumstances, he did not consider that the hard-pressed garrison could hold out more than two or three weeks. It was therefore possible that the catastrophe had already happened, and it was perfectly certain that if any attempt at rescue was to succeed, it must be made at once, and that prompt action was of paramount importance.

There were two other reasons for an early advance. The rainy season which had so far held off might at any time set in, and a few heavy storms would render the country impassable. Secondly, the Chinese forces, which, after the capture of Tien-tsin, had scattered in a demoralised condition, were now beginning to collect again, and a considerable body was known to be in position barring the road to the capital. They had cut the river banks with a view to flooding the low-lying country, and every day the inundations were spreading; while their defensive works were increasing in strength, and fresh reinforcements were arriving to oppose the Allies.

At first the allied commanders were disinclined to agree with General Gaselee's views. They considered that the march on Peking could not commence before the middle of August at the earliest. Major-General Chaffee, commanding the troops of the United States, wished to await the arrival of his artillery, which was shortly expected; while Lieut.-General Yamaguchi, commanding the Japanese troops, considered the force too small for the attempt. The Allies had expected General Gaselee to arrive with a force of some 10,000 men, whereas, owing to the 2nd Brigade having been deflected to Shanghai, he had less than 4,000 available for the advance, and could expect no increase to his strength for some weeks. The Russian General Stessel appeared to be chiefly concerned with the progress of affairs in Manchuria, and consequently averse to withdrawing Russian troops from the neighbourhood of the coast.

On the 1st August Lieut.-General Liniévitch arrived in Tien-tsin and took over command of the Russian forces from General Stessel. He at first expressed himself as opposed to the forward move, on the plea that the troops then available were insufficient to make success a certainty, and that a reverse would do incalculable harm and could not be risked. He asked for two days to consider the situation, and then agreed to co-operate.

In the expectation that the British contingent would number 10,000 troops, the Japanese had arranged that their own contingent should consist of about 6,000 men, and had made all their plans on this basis. Their junks could only carry about nine days' supplies for the above number, and their small land supply column was only capable of carrying one extra day's rations. With three days in regimental charge, this gave supplies for 6,000 men for 13 days. Much credit is due to them, that when it was found that the British could only furnish about 3,000 men, the deficit was made up from the Japanese forces, who responded most loyally to the call, though at great inconvenience.

With transport sufficient only for the requirements of 6,000 men, the Japanese undertook to advance with double that number to Peking, and to attempt to make up the deficiencies in food and transport from the country as they advanced. By capturing several junks at Yang-tsun they were able to reorganise their river transport, but the land supply column could not be increased, with the result that a great deal of extra work was thrown upon it, and, in spite of daily double journeys, the troops had occasionally to go without food, picking up what they could in the villages. When Tung-chou was reached immense quantities of rice were captured in the town, and no further difficulty in feeding their troops was experienced.

At the beginning of August the northernmost outpost of the allies was in the Hsi-ku armoury, which was held by the Russians. From this point a considerable force of Chinese could be seen busily entrenching itself about a mile to the north, between the river and the railway, the bridges of which had been destroyed. Their principal camp was visible near the village of Pei-ts'ang, about five miles from Hsi-ku, and they seemed to be particularly active on the railway embankment, just north of the broken fifth bridge from the Tien-tsin railway station.

It was, however, impossible to determine the exact form or extent of their position, on account of the high crops, which completely covered the flat plain, and prevented observation, even by mounted men. The horses of the 1st Bengal Lancers had just come off board ship, and as yet were hardly fit for reconnaissance work, so were given a rest preparatory to the forward movement on Peking. Russian and Japanese patrols had been searching the country on both banks of the river, and had frequently been fired on from villages, or by riflemen concealed in the crops, without, however, being able to ascertain much of the enemy's disposition or strength.

With a view to clearing up the situation and obtaining further information on these points, the Japanese undertook a reconnaissance in force on the morning of the 30th July. The Japanese force, which was accompanied by Lieut.-General Yamaguchi and his staff, consisted of one brigade of six battalions, one battery of six 7-pr. mountain guns, firing black powder, and one squadron of cavalry. General Gaselee, Major-General Norman Stewart, commanding the 1st Brigade, and some officers of their respective staffs watched the operation.

The Japanese rendezvoused, at 4 a.m., at the Hung-ch'iao or Red Bridge, north of Tien-tsin city, and, leaving two battalions in reserve near the bridge, advanced parallel to the river, along the right bank, to the village of Ting-tzu-ku, just north of the Hsi-ku armoury. A short distance beyond this point, at about 6 a.m., they came in contact with the Chinese, who were holding a small house on the main road. From this the Japanese expelled them, and then found that the main Chinese position was in the village of Mun-chia-chuang, on the opposite bank of the river, from which a heavy fire opened.

About 7 a.m, the Japanese passed a company across the river at Ting-tzu-ku, which occupied the village of Tien-chih, but then found their further progress barred by a deep unfordable watercut, extending east from the Pei-ho to the broken fifth bridge on the railway, the opposite bank being strongly held by the Chinese, protected by entrenchments.

It was now evidently impossible to get nearer the Chinese, and the reconnaissance resolved itself into an action in which the Japanese suffered pretty severely, their white uniforms and close formations rendering them particularly conspicuous. It was accordingly decided to withdraw the troops, and the retirement began about 12 noon. The object of the reconnaissance, which was to uncover the Chinese right and ascertain if they had bodies of troops on the right bank, had only been partially successful.

The apex of their position, covered by the river and the unfordable cut mentioned above, had been disclosed, and the cavalry had penetrated some distance up the right bank, but had failed to discover the entrenched position, which the Chinese had prepared some distance further back. On the extreme left the Japanese had advanced to a powder magazine, about three miles west of the river, and had cleared out a few of the enemy, but found no other troops in that direction.

It was now quite certain that the Chinese were in strong force in the neighbourhood of Pei-ts'ang, and, at a conference of the General Officers, held on the 3rd August, it was decided to drive them out of their position on the 5th August, and to advance as far as Yang-tsun, where the railway, river, and road routes to Peking converge. Pending the success of the preliminary operations, the question of a further advance towards the capital was left in abeyance.

The strength of the allied force available for the march on Peking was, in round numbers, as follows :—

	Men.	Guns.
Japanese	10,000	24
Russians	4,000	16
British	3,000	12
Americans	2,000	6
French	800	12
Germans	200	—
Austrians ⎱ Italians ⎰	100	—
Total	20,100	70

The first objective was the Chinese position at Pei-ts'ang, which it was intended to attack on the morning of the 5th August. From native information it had been ascertained that considerable reinforcements of troops and stores had been arriving from the direction of the Grand Canal, while the powder magazine, discovered by the Japanese on the 30th July, was reported to be now strongly held by the enemy, and connected with Pei-ts'ang by a line of entrenchments. This information was subsequently proved to be correct.

The plan agreed upon was that the Japanese, British, and United States troops should operate on the right bank of the Pei-ho, so as to turn the Chinese right flank, while the remainder of the Allies threatened their left on the left bank of the river. It was further agreed with the Japanese and American generals that the attack on the right bank should take the form of a turning movement from the embankment, which runs from Hsi-ku village towards the powder magazine, the Japanese leading, with the British and Americans following in succession.

In pursuance of the above agreement, the British force, composed of the following troops, moved out of the settlement on the afternoon of the 4th, and bivouacked to the south of the embankment, a short distance west of Hsi-ku village.

Unit.	Men.	Guns.
Naval Brigade	—	4
Royal Marine Light Infantry	300	—
12th Battery, R.F.A.	—	6
Hongkong Artillery	—	⎰ 2 ⎱ 4 Maxims.
Detachment, R.E.	—	—
Royal Welsh Fusiliers	300	—
1st Bengal Lancers	400	—
7th Bengal Infantry	500	—
24th Punjab Infantry	300	—
1st Sikh Infantry	500	—
Hongkong Regiment	100	—
Chinese Regiment	100	—

The British were followed by the Americans, who bivouacked on their right rear in the direction of the armoury.

During the night the Japanese marched past the British bivouac, and moved straight to their assigned position on the extreme left, so as to be in readiness to attack the powder magazine before dawn.

Before describing the forward march of the relieving force on Peking, it is necessary, for the proper appreciation of the operations, to refer to the abnormal climatic conditions of the year 1900. Both it and the previous year had been exceedingly dry—in fact, years of famine, in which the rains had failed; and it was greatly due to this circumstance that the rapid advance was possible. Had the ordinary conditions prevailed, it is impossible to say to what extent the progress of the column would have been affected, but it is quite certain that the difficulties of the Allies would have been infinitely greater than they were, and the advantages in favour of the Chinese would have been relatively increased.

It is of interest to notice that the year 1860 was also a dry year.

In an average year the rains in July and August are very heavy, especially in the hills to the north and west of the Chi-li plain, and the water, pouring into the rivers from countless tributaries, causes them to overflow their banks and inundate the whole of the flat country between Peking and the coast. The Hun-ho, in particular, discharges a flood of water through its left bank, which transforms the country south of the Hunting Park, as far east as Ma-tou and Ho-hsi-wu, into a vast swamp, out of which the railway, the villages, and the embankments alone stand high and dry.

The country to the east of the Pei-ho is in a similar condition in time of flood. The surplus water is carried off in the direction of the Pei-tang-ho by canals, and these, overflowing their banks, also inundate large tracts. All communication, except by boat or along the few raised roads and the railway, becomes impossible, for, even where the water is shallow, the low-lying unmetalled roads are quickly churned into deep mud, and become unfit for traffic. Under these conditions the only line of advance for the relieving force would have been by boats on the river, and along the narrow raised roads on its banks, which, however, were out of repair and breached in several places, and much time would have been lost in making them passable. The advantages to the Chinese in opposing an advance on such a narrow front are too obvious to require comment. The railway had been destroyed, and its sixty-five bridges between Tien-tsin and Peking had been broken, so it could have been of but little use as an alternative line.

By great good fortune the actual conditions were entirely different. The country was not inundated; the actions of Pei-ts'ang and Yang-tsun were fought over ground which, in an ordinary year, would have been covered with water; the columns throughout the advance marched on a broad front and the transport moved freely by the cross-country roads, seldom using the embankments; incommoded not by mud, but by the excessive heat and blinding dust, which, if it did not stop the onward march, was still extremely trying to men and animals alike.

The Chinese were fully alive to the advantages which a flooded country would have conferred upon them, and must have anxiously hoped for rain during the three weeks, which elapsed between the fall of Tien-tsin and the commencement of the march of the Allies. They made one attempt to flood the country by cutting the river bank in front of the Pei-ts'ang position, as has been already mentioned, and the water from this cut spread out to the east of the railway into a very extensive inundation, which effectually checked the progress of the Russian and French infantry on the 5th August, and prevented them from taking any part in the battle of Pei-ts'ang. It also afforded an idea of what the difficulties to the advance would have been if the whole country had been under water.

Surprise was expressed that the Chinese had not tried flooding the country on a large scale, but there were at least two reasons why this was not done. The Chinese themselves were largely dependent on boat transport for carrying their supplies, and the drawing off of the water to any great extent would have rendered the river unnavigable. Secondly, though the military might wish to flood the country, the peasants objected to it, on account of the damage to their crops, and, in the absence of a commander strong enough to enforce his orders, they would probably have prevented its being done.

After their defeat at Yang-tsun the flight of the Chinese was so disorganised, and the advance of the Allies in pursuit so rapid, that it prevented any further attempt to cut the river banks, though something of the sort was undoubtedly comtemplated at Ho-hsi-wu.

This subject has been dealt with at considerable length, as it is a most important point, and must not be lost sight of in considering possible plans of operations in the future over the same ground.

To return to the battle of Pei-ts'ang. By 1 a.m. on the morning of the 5th August the Japanese troops had assembled at their rendezvous, and the right wing, consisting of the 41st regiment of infantry, two batteries of artillery, and a squadron of cavalry, moved forward on the villages of Ting-tzu-ku and Tang-chia-wan.

About 1.30 a.m. the left wing, consisting of the 21st brigade of infantry, four batteries of artillery and the rest of the 5th Cavalry Regiment, with a company of Engineers, began to advance along the embankment towards the powder magazine, and came in contact with the Chinese about 2 a.m. The enemy were very strongly entrenched, and supported by artillery fire, and so stubborn was their defence that the powder magazine was not captured until about 4.30. a.m. The Japanese fought chiefly with the bayonet, and the losses were heavy on both sides.

In the meanwhile a battalion of Japanese infantry had worked round the left of the magazine and captured Kan-chia-ju after a sharp fight. Liu-chia-pei, about a mile west of the magazine, was also occupied and held by a battalion, to protect the left flank from attack from the west and south, while the Japanese and British cavalry watched the country to the north-west.

About 4. a.m. dawn began to break, and soon afterwards the two batteries of the Japanese right wing came into action on the embankment and opened fire on Tang-chia-wan. The Chinese, however, had got the range of the embankment accurately, and several casualties occurred from their shell and rifle fire.

About the same time the infantry of the Japanese right wing became engaged with the enemy, who were entrenched in a wood to the south-west of Tang-chia-wan, where sharp fighting had occurred in the reconnaissance of the 30th July. The fighting was very fierce, but the Japanese gradually gained ground, and by about 5.30 a.m. had occupied both Tang-chia-wan and Hsin-chuang, a village lying a little further to the north.

In the meanwhile the British troops were moving north between the two wings of the Japanese, and the Americans, further to the east, were supporting the Japanese in Tang-chia-wan along the main road. The British naval guns were also bombarding the enemy's position from a point on the right bank of the Pei-ho, just north of the Hsi-ku armoury, but, as it was extremely difficult to follow the movements of the troops in the high crops, their fire was confined to the Chinese entrenchments along the railway embankment, and in the neighbourhood of Pei-ts'ang. The French and Russian batteries also shelled the enemy from the left bank.

About 5 a.m. the batteries of the Japanese left wing came into action against Ma-chang from a point about half a mile north of the magazine, and soon afterwards the Japanese artillery of the right wing and the British field battery joined in from the west of Tang-chia-wan.

The Chinese now fell back to their second entrenched position, which ran west from the river bank, to the south of Pei-ts'ang, in the direction of Kan-chia-ju, but from this they were soon expelled, and Wang-chuang was captured by the Japanese about 8.30 a.m., the enemy falling back on Pei-ts'ang, while many fled to the north up the right bank. About 10.30 a.m. the boat bridge at Pei-ts'ang was captured, and the Chinese, finding their right flank turned, began to withdraw sullenly towards Yang-tsun by the left bank, between the river and the railway, being shelled in their retirement by the 12th Battery R.F.A. with some effect.

As it was impossible to transport the guns and troops rapidly across the boat bridge, an attempt was made to advance on Yang-tsun by the right bank, but after proceeding about half a mile a deep swamp was met with, stretching far to the west, in which the horses sank to their girths. Further on, to the north of the village of Niu-chuang, was a deep unfordable stream, and, as advance in this direction was proved to be impossible until

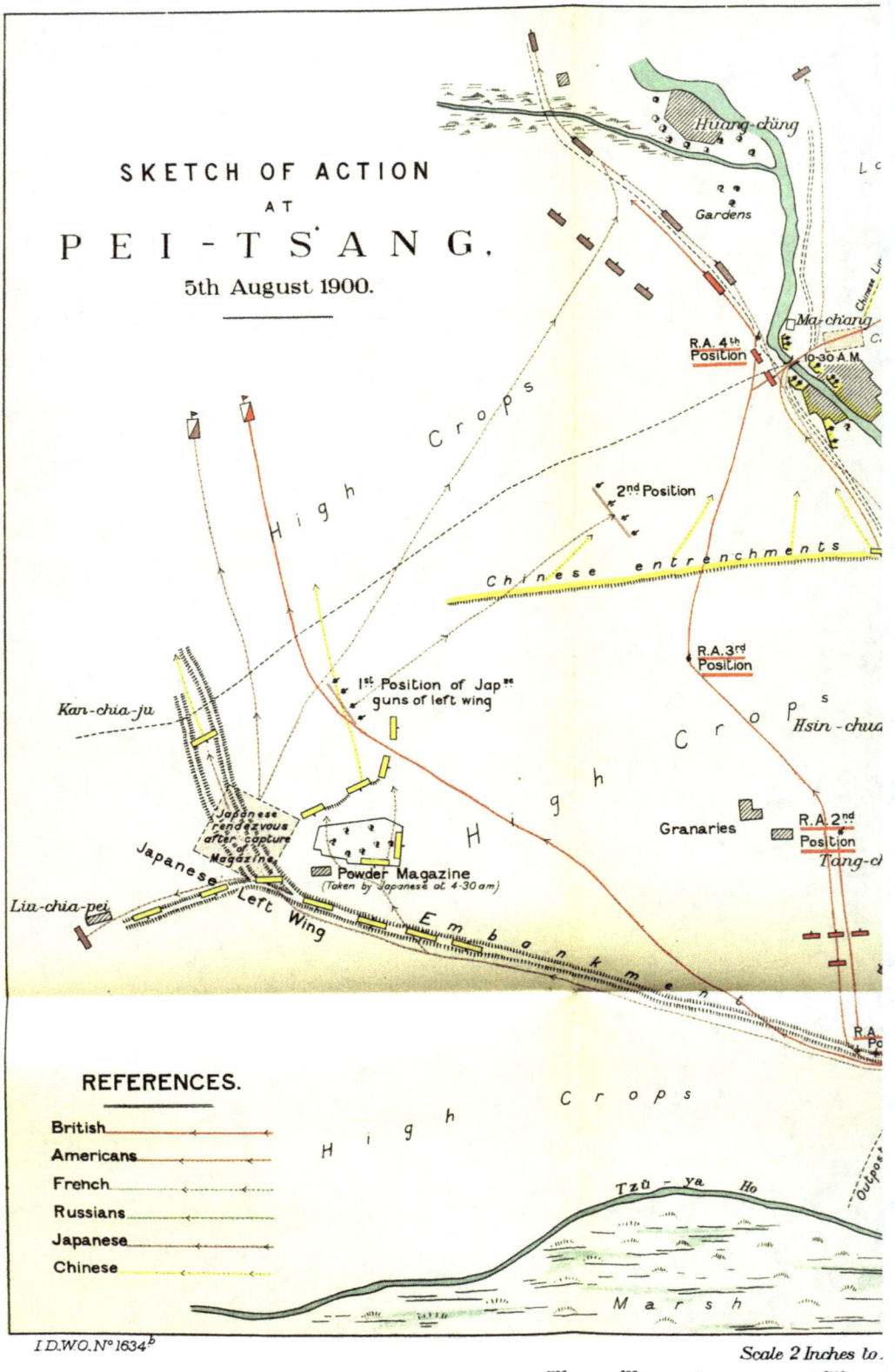

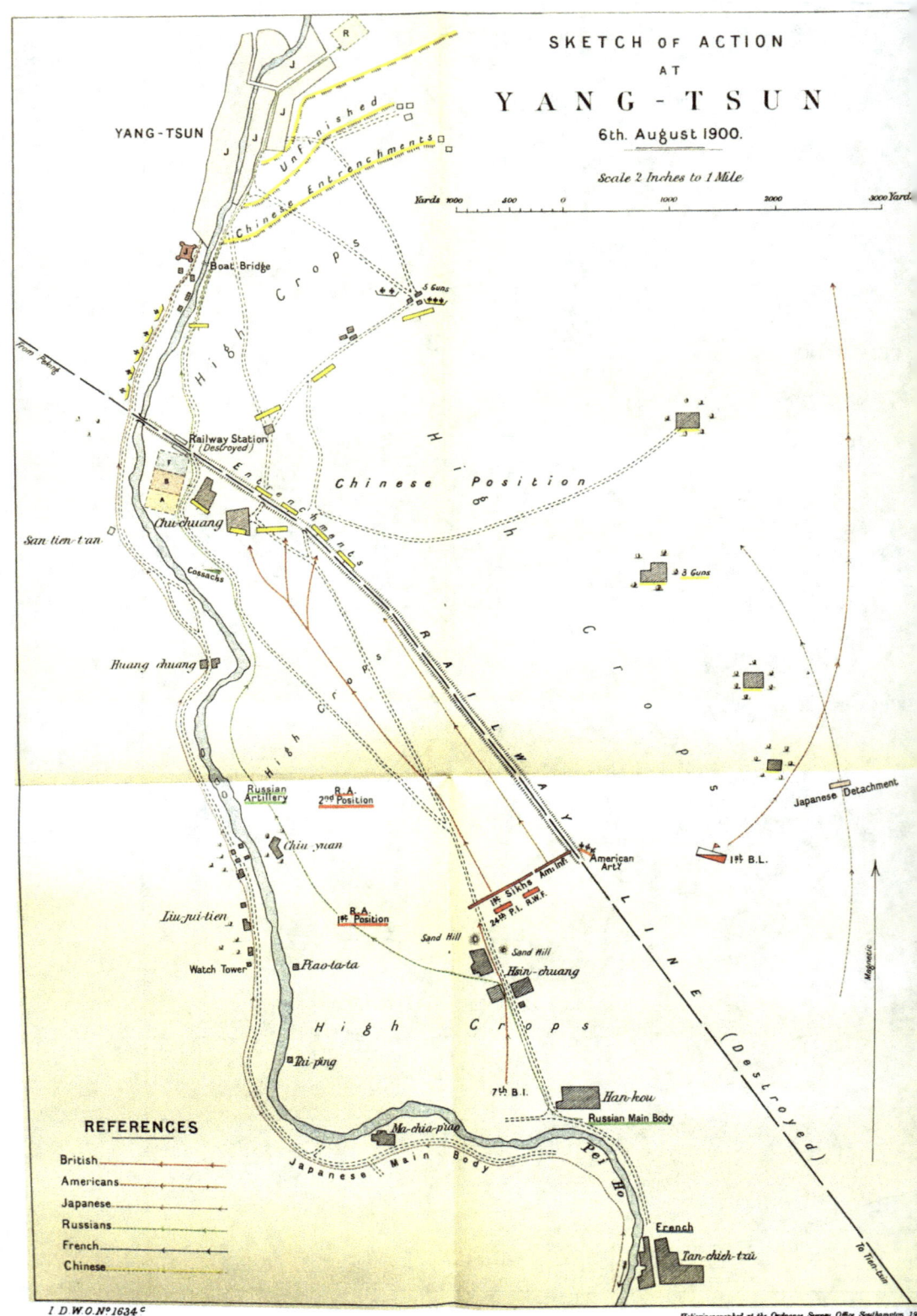

the road had been repaired, the attempt was abandoned, and it was decided to halt at Pei-ts'ang for the night, outposts being thrown out to the north. The heat had been intense and the troops had been on the move for about twelve hours.

On the left bank the Russians and French had been stopped by the inundations and had taken no part in the fighting.

During the day the Japanese casualties amounted to over 300 killed and wounded. The British lost 26 killed and wounded, while the other Allies reported no casualties.

It was impossible to estimate the Chinese losses accurately, but they left over 300 dead on the field, and it was reported by spies that more than 500 wounded had been removed up-stream in junks. As a result of their defeat large numbers deserted, and the "yings," or camps, were reported to have dwindled from 500 to about 200 men each.

As will be seen from the above account the Japanese monopolised all the fighting, and carried the enemy's positions in succession with the greatest gallantry. It was however almost impossible to get a very clear idea of the various phases of the fight, as the high crops and the morning mist greatly restricted the view in every direction.

On the 6th August the march on Yang-tsun was resumed at 6 a.m. The main body of the Japanese advanced by the right bank of the river, while the rest of the Allies and a detachment of Japanese marched on the left bank. The British were the last to start, but the progress of the Russians and French was so slow that they were soon passed by our troops, and the order of march arranged itself into the British on the left next the river, with the Americans on the right between them and the railway, while the Japanese detachment was still further to the east beyond the railway. The Russians and French were some distance in rear of the British.

At about 10 a.m. the head of the column reached the village of Hsin-chuang, about three miles south of the railway bridge over the Pei-ho, near Yang-tsun, and from two small sandhills, immediately to the north of the village, an excellent view of the enemy's position was obtained. It stretched along the high railway embankment, with its right resting on the village of Chu-chuang, south-east of the big railway bridge, while the extreme left was in some villages considerably to the east of the railway line. It was afterwards found that they had also constructed lines of entrenchments on the low ground in front of the embankment, but these could not at first be seen on account of the crops.

Before the action commenced a body of Cossacks came in contact with the Chinese near Chu-chuang, and drew a heavy fire. They were dismounted in a dry watercourse near the village, and there they remained, unwilling to advance or retire, until the position was captured.

About 11 a.m. the Russian and French infantry began to arrive, and dispositions for the attack were shortly afterwards made.

The British extended to the right of the road leading straight from the sandhills to Chu-chuang, with the Americans on their right towards the railway embankment. The left of the road was intended for the Russians and French, who, however, never came into line. The British cavalry moved out to the right flank, as did the American artillery, which came into action to the east of the railway. The British and Russian guns occupied positions on the left flank, the latter echeloned in rear of the former.

The British advance was in widely extended lines of skirmishers, the 1st Sikhs leading, supported by the Royal Welsh Fusiliers and the 24th Punjab Infantry, and it was noticeable how quickly the khaki uniforms blended with the crops and became difficult to distinguish. The blue shirts of the Americans, who kept in much closer formation, and often in groups, were, on the other hand, very conspicuous, and this fact no doubt accounted for their numerous casualties, as, though the British troops carried the position, their casualties in killed and wounded only amounted to about half those among the United States troops.

About 2,000 yards from the enemy's entrenchments the troops came under a very heavy shell and rifle fire, but the attack was pressed steadily forward, and the position was carried without a check. The Chinese, who were well covered by their earthworks, had probably not suffered very heavily, and effected their retreat on the town of Yang-tsun, which lay about a mile and a half further to the north. This place was afterwards found to be very strongly entrenched, but the enemy made no attempt to hold it. The bulk of their forces crossed by two boat bridges to the right bank of the river, and retired, utterly demoralised, towards Peking, while a considerable number fled north along the left bank.

They managed to withdraw most of their guns, which had been kept well retired and out of reach of the advancing Allies.

During the attack the rifle fire of the Chinese, though heavy, had been wild, but their guns had got the range accurately, and dropped their shells right among the advancing infantry, without, however, inflicting much loss.

The British casualties amounted to six men killed; one died of sunstroke; Lieutenant Costello, 24th Punjab Infantry, and 37 men were wounded; total, 45. The Americans had about 80 casualties, including many cases of sunstroke.

The British and American troops halted at the railway. The heat was intense, and the troops suffered much in consequence.

The Russians arrived at the embankment near the railway bridge about an hour later, and shortly afterwards moved forward towards the town, and took up their quarters to the north of it. The French remained with the British and Americans on the river bank near the railway bridge.

In the meanwhile the Japanese on the extreme right, who, owing to their position, had taken no part in the assault, marched straight on to Yang-tsun, and occupied the town at about 2.30 p.m., without meeting with any opposition.

Their main body, in its advance along the right bank of the river, had been delayed by having to construct bridges over the streams and cuts in the road, and did not reach Yang-tsun till about 6 p.m.

The railway all the way from Tien-tsin had been wrecked, the rails, sleepers, fish-plates, &c., had all been torn up and removed. The railway station was a total ruin, but the large girder bridge over the Pei-ho had suffered little damage, the girders at the shore end, on the right bank, only having been slightly displaced. Had the Chinese succeeded in destroying the bridge, the girders, lying in the stream below, would have rendered the onward progress of the junks carrying our supplies almost impossible.

On the 7th August the whole force halted for the day at Yang-tsun. The Japanese sent forward a covering party of one regiment of infantry, a squadron of cavalry, two batteries of artillery, and a company of engineers, up the right bank of the river to Nan-tsai-tsun, which place they occupied after a slight skirmish with the enemy.

A conference of the allied Generals was held during the day, and it was decided that, as the resistance of the Chinese had apparently been broken, the advance on Peking should at once be vigorously pushed on, without giving the enemy time to recover themselves. They were now thoroughly demoralised, and said to be suffering greatly from the heat. Yü-lu, the viceroy of Chi-li province, was said to have committed suicide the previous day, after witnessing the defeat of his troops, though another report stated that he had been killed by a fragment of one of our shells.

It was further arranged at the conference that in the onward march the troops would move in the following order: Japanese, Russians, Americans, British. The French, having no transport, were to remain for the present and garrison Yang-tsun, being supported by detachments of 150 men each from the British, Japanese, and American forces. The Japanese and Russians were to take it in turns to supply one battalion as a right flank guard on the left bank of the Pei-ho, and the British, Russian, and Japanese cavalry were to act together in covering the front of the whole force, under the orders of the commander of the Japanese cavalry.

It had been found that the water in the wells, contrary to expectation, was excellent, cold, and clear, while that from the Pei-ho was full of sand and mud, and took a long time to settle. The troops generally used well-water throughout the advance, and no ill-effects were experienced.

On the 7th the water in the Pei-ho had suddenly fallen about 18 inches, and this had delayed the arrival of the junks carrying the Russian supplies, and in consequence they were not ready to start next morning.

At 4 a.m. on the 8th the Japanese moved off, followed by the Americans. The British marched at 7 a.m., and reached their bivouac on the bank of the river at Nan-tsai-tsun about 11 a.m. The heat was intense, and marching through the high crops exceedingly trying. The Japanese occupied the villages, as they continued to do throughout the march on the capital, and the Americans bivouacked alongside of the British. Most of the junks came up in the course of the day, and the Russians arrived in the evening.

In the afternoon a native Christian arrived in the Japanese camp with letters from the Legations in Peking, which stated that the Europeans there were still holding out successfully, and had provisions up to the 16th. He also brought a cypher message to General Gaselee from Sir Claude MacDonald, recommending him to attack Peking from the south and endeavour to effect an entrance into the Tartar City by the Sluice Gate under the wall, to the south of the Legation Quarter.

On the 9th the advance was continued to Ho-hsi-wu, the British marching again at 7 a.m., in rear of the other contingents. The distance is only 11 miles, but the march was an extremely trying one on account of the intense heat and stifling dust. The progress was also very slow from continual checks in front. Many of the Americans were prostrated by the heat, owing, it was thought, to their head-dress not being sufficient protection from the powerful sun, but even the natives of India suffered considerably.

The Japanese were again in front, and on nearing Ho-hsi-wu found the place occupied by the enemy. The Chinese were quickly driven out and pursued as far as Ma-tou, the troops occupying Mu-chang for the night. Near Ho-hsi-wu a squadron of the 1st Bengal Lancers came in contact with a force of about 300 Chinese cavalry, who turned out to be part of General Ma Yü-kun's troops, as the banners captured from them bore his name. Owing to the high crops, cavalry action was difficult, but about 40 Chinese were killed, our own troops having only two men wounded.

The British column did not reach Ho-hsi-wu till late in the afternoon, and bivouacked on the right bank of the river, just south of the village. A deep cut had been dug through the right bank, apparently with the idea of flooding the country, but the rapid advance of the Japanese had interrupted the work before it could be completed.

A temple near the camp was found to contain a very large quantity of gunpowder, and this had to be carefully guarded till the column had marched forward on the next day.

After our experience on the 9th it was decided that the infantry would not march the following day until the evening. The cavalry and artillery, however, went on at 10.30 a.m., but, taking the wrong road, got into deep sand and lost several horses from exhaustion.

During the 10th most of the junks arrived and the sappers were busy constructing a post, as it had been decided to leave a guard at this point. About 4.30 p.m., the infantry started, but it was still so hot that a long halt was made after the first mile. About 6.30 p.m., when the column was about two and a half miles from Ho-hsi-wu, the temple containing the gunpowder was blown up by the Engineers under Major Scott-Moncrieff, the C.R.E., who had remained behind for the purpose. It was a wonderful sight and spread an immense cloud over the sky, the explosion being heard and felt at a very great distance, though no damage resulted to any member of the allied force.

Two companies of French troops with a battery of light guns had rejoined the force at Ho-hsi-wu, in order to participate in the entry into Peking.

Ma-tou was reached about 2.30 a.m. on the 11th. Later in the morning the Japanese advanced to Chang-chia-wan, followed by the Russians. On nearing that place their advance guard was fired on by the Chinese, and after a smart fight, which lasted about an hour, the enemy were driven out of their position, leaving about 40 dead on the field. The Japanese then pressed forward and were again fired at from the village of Kao-chia-chuang, which they captured after a slight resistance, and advanced to another village about a mile further on, when they found themselves within 3,000 yards of the walled city of Tung-chou. Chinese troops were visible on and in front of the walls, and a Japanese battery came into action and shelled the town for a short time, without drawing any reply.

The British marched at 5.30 p.m. preceded by the Americans. The march was an easy one and Chang-chia-wan was reached before midnight. The place is low-lying and marshy and the water supply is bad.

On the morning of the 12th August the Japanese moved forward in the early morning, on the south-east and south-west gates of Tung-chou, and blew them in respectively at 3.30 a.m. and 4.30 a.m., but, on entering, it was found that the whole of the Chinese troops had retired towards Peking during the night. This afforded a further proof of their demoralisation. Tung-chou is a large city with high massive walls, only pierced by six strong gates, and is therefore very defensible against an enemy unprovided with heavy ordnance, but there was no attempt at defence and no sign of troops anywhere in the neighbourhood.

The Japanese occupied the town. The British took up their quarters on the river bank to the south-east, where is the landing place for the junks. The Russians and Americans bivouacked near the south-west gate. A temple close to the British quarters was found to contain a very large supply of gunpowder, which had to be carefully guarded until it could be destroyed.

In the afternoon a conference of the British, American, Russian, and Japanese Generals was held, at which it was decided that the troops should halt at Tung-chou on the 13th, while reconnaissances were made to examine the country towards Peking. On the 14th the combined force was to move forward to a position outside the walls of Peking, ready to assault the city on the morning of the following day, viz., the 15th August. The British, American and Japanese Generals were anxious to attack on the 14th, but, in deference to the wishes of General Liniévitch, who expressed his inability to move earlier, the attack was postponed to the 15th.

The forward movement on the city was to be made in the following order. The Japanese to march along the paved road from Tung-chou towards the Chih-ho mên, or eastern gate of the Tartar City; the Russians by roads north of the Japanese on the Tung-chih mên, or north gate, on the eastern side of the Tartar City; the Americans by the road along the south bank of the canal from Tung-chou to Peking, on the Tung-pien mên, or north-east gate of the Chinese City; and the British by roads further to the south on the left of the Americans, on the Sha-huo mên, or east gate of the Chinese City.

It must be explained that the Tartar City is nearly square in plan, and is surrounded by a very massive wall about 50 feet in height, crenellated at the top and pierced by nine gates, two in each of the north, east and west sides and three in the south wall, which separates it from the Chinese City. The latter is roughly rectangular in shape, and is also surrounded by a wall, less massive than that of the Tartar City and about 30 feet in height. The Chinese City has seven gates, two of which are on the west and two on the east sides and three on the south side. When a Chinaman living in the Tartar City goes into the Chinese City he calls it " going outside the city."

From this description it is evident that a force entering the Chinese City is still outside the Tartar City, and, as the Legations are all inside the latter, a second operation would be necessary before access to them could be gained.

In accordance with the above agreement reconnoitring parties moved forward on the morning of the 13th. The British detachment, consisting of the 1st Bengal Lancers and 7th Rajputs, advanced to the village of Pan-pu-tien-erh, about three miles from the Sha-huo mên, and occupied a walled enclosure round a temple. The Americans were near the British on their right and the Japanese were at Ting-fu village on the paved road. Their cavalry reconnoitred towards Peking, where they reported that there was little sign of activity on the walls.

During the night of the 13th—14th heavy firing was heard in the direction of Peking, and this was supposed to be an attack by the Chinese, either on some of the allied outposts, or upon the Legations.

It was subsequently discovered that the Russians had passed the Japanese in the darkness, and had attacked the Tung-pien mên, the gate allotted to the Americans. They apparently succeeded in getting on to the wall of the Chinese City, in the neighbourhood of the gate, without any opposition, but had failed in their further advance along the foot of the south wall of the Tartar

City, and, meeting with a heavy fire from the Tartar wall, had had to retire and seek shelter in the suburbs.

The British troops at Tung-chou hearing the heavy firing in front fell in about 2 a.m. and marched towards Peking. Soon after 6 a.m. the Japanese advanced troops, at the urgent appeal of the Russians for support, attacked the Chih-ho mên, near which place their main body arrived about 9 a.m., and, as the gate was very strongly held, the Japanese commander decided to bombard it and the Tung-chih mên, before attempting to storm them. Accordingly 54 guns were brought up into position, and opened fire on the two gates and the wall between them.

About 2 p.m. another attempt was made to blow in the Chih-ho mên, but the party was driven back, and it was then decided to wait till dusk before making any further attempt, when a simultaneous assault was to be made on both the Tung-chih mên and Chih-ho mên. With this object in view the 21st infantry regiment and a company of engineers moved off from the rendezvous of the Japanese main body, to the east of Chih-ho mên, and marched towards the Tung-chih mên.

While these events were happening on the right, the British cavalry had left their bivouac in the early morning, and reconnoitred towards the Sha-huo mên, but were stopped by rifle fire from the crops. They then moved to their right and got in touch with the Americans on the canal.

About 7 a.m. the main body of the United States troops began to come up, and about 8 a.m. the British, who had had furthest to march, also arrived. After a rest the American and British columns moved slowly forward towards their respective gates, meeting with very little opposition. On arrival at the Tung-pien mên about 12.30 p.m., the Americans found the Russian column taking cover in the houses outside the city. Bringing up their artillery they soon succeeded in breaking in the gate and entered the Chinese City, about the same time as the British arrived at the Sha-huo mên. The latter gate, being found practically undefended, was quickly broken open and the troops streamed into the town.

The British column marched steadily west, meeting with very little opposition, until it arrived at the cross roads about half a mile south of the Ha-ta mên of the Tartar City, where a short halt was made to enable the straggling and exhausted column to close up. A good deal of firing could be heard in the north-east corner of the Chinese City, where the Americans were evidently engaged. The 1st Bengal Lancers and 24th Punjab Infantry were now ordered to march straight to the Temple of Heaven, in the surrounding parks of which General Gaselee intended to quarter the bulk of the British troops. At the same time a portion of the 7th Bengal Infantry was detached towards the Ha-ta mên, to cover the right flank of the column in its advance, and to get in touch, if possible, with the Americans. The remainder of the troops continued their advance westwards, towards the middle of the Chinese City.

Through the Legation Quarter runs a broad water channel, which in time of heavy rain carries off the surplus water from the Tartar City, through an opening in the Tartar City wall called the Sluice Gate. It was known from Sir Claude MacDonald's cypher message that the portion of the city wall, on both sides of the Sluice Gate, was in possession of the Legation troops at the time when the message was despatched, and it was expected that, if they were still holding out, a comparatively easy entrance could be effected into the Legations through this gate. Great anxiety was, however, felt as to the fate of the defenders, for it was now guessed that much of the heavy firing heard during the previous night must have been directed against the Legations, presumably in a last desperate attempt by the Chinese to overwhelm them before succour arrived. Of the result of this attack nothing was known.

On reaching a point about due south of the Sluice Gate, General Gaselee, with some of his staff officers and about 70 men of the 1st Sikhs and 7th Bengal Infantry, turned north and marched through the narrow and tortuous lanes, until the edge of the moat outside the Tartar City wall was reached. From this point the British, American, and Russian flags could be seen floating on the wall about 200 yards to the west, and the troops raised a cheer, which was answered by a spluttering fire from the wall and the guard towers over the Ha-ta mên. A signal-man then appeared near the foot of the American flag, and sent the message "Come up Sluice Street by the water," and on moving towards him the troops soon caught sight of the arch of the Sluice Gate, under the part of the wall on which he was standing.

Doubling across the moat, under an ill-aimed fusillade, the party was soon under cover in the sluice ditch. Further progress was barred by two strong gratings of upright timbers, but, with the help of Chinese converts inside, a few of the bars were quickly displaced, and about 2.40 p.m. the first of the relieving force found themselves passing through the British and Russian Legations, amid cheering crowds of European and Chinese refugees.

Preparations were at once made to drive off the Chinese, who still kept up a heavy fire on the Legations, the noise from the bullets striking the roofs and walls being at times quite deafening, though, from the height of the defences, the danger was comparatively slight. A party of the 1st Sikh escort, under Major T. E. Scott, D.S.O., moved out, through the defences on the western face of the British Legation, to drive the enemy out of the houses on that side, while the detachment of the 7th Bengal Infantry, under Major Vaughan, which had also entered the Tartar City by the Sluice Gate, relieved the Legation troops on duty on the defences.

In the meanwhile the main column, consisting of the 12th Battery R.F.A., the Maxim detachments, the Royal Welsh

Fusiliers, and the 1st Sikhs, had continued its advance on the Ch'ien mên, or great central gate in the south wall of the Tartar City. This they were preparing to assault when a small body of American marines, belonging to the Legation Guard, advanced along the wall and seized the main guard-house over the gate. At the same time our troops got in by the gate below, and two of the Maxims came into action. The Chinese made a plucky charge, but were repulsed and driven out of the houses between the Ch'ien mên and the Legation Quarter, suffering heavily in their retirement. Eventually two guns of the 12th Battery R.F.A. and the 1st Sikhs marched into the British Legation, and the rest of the main column retired to the Temple of Heaven, where they took up their quarters for the night.

On nearing the Temple of Heaven it was seen that the Yung-ting mên, or southern gate of the Chinese City, was still held by the enemy's troops. These were promptly driven out with considerable loss, and the gate was seized and occupied by a British detachment.

About 4.30 p.m. General Chaffee arrived at the Legations by the Sluice Gate, and the Ch'ien mên was occupied by the United States troops. The Russian detachments, found by the Americans at the Tung-pien mên, entered the Chinese City with them, and, moving west, followed the British troops into the Tartar City by the Ch'ien mên. The main body of the Russians also entered the Chinese City by the Tung-pien mên, and General Liniévitch arrived at the Legations about 6 p.m. by the Sluice Gate. The troops with him moved east to the Ha-ta mên, and opened it for the entrance of their main body, who afterwards occupied the south-east quarter of the Tartar City.

Major-General Fukushima with a battalion of Japanese infantry also reached the Japanese Legation in the evening by the same route.

The Japanese, however, had not abandoned their attack on the eastern gates of the Tartar City, and about 9 p.m. the outer gate of the Tung-chih mên was blown in, and very shortly afterwards the inner gate was also destroyed. The infantry at once occupied the wall and guard-houses, and advanced towards the Chih-ho mên, while a detachment moved north towards the An-ting mên.

In the meanwhile the outer gate of the Chih-ho mên had also been assaulted and blown in about 9.40 p.m., and ten minutes later the inner gate was similarly entered, and the infantry stormed the wall and advanced along it north and south, two battalions eventually marching along the wall to the Legation Quarter.

These various assaults had entailed very heavy fighting, and the Japanese casualties throughout the day amounted to one officer and 33 men killed, and seven officers and 123 men wounded. The Russians lost fairly heavily in their unsuccessful attack on the Tung-pien mên, but the remainder of the Allies had veryfew casualties. The British casualties amounted to one man died, three wounded, one missing.

It was impossible to get any reliable information at this time about the disposition of the Chinese forces, but it was generally supposed that the Court and high officials had left Peking some time before, on receiving news of the advance of the relieving columns. As a matter of fact the Emperor and Empress Dowager were still in the Forbidden City, and did not leave till the morning of the 15th August, but this was not known till some days later. No doubt the defeat of the Chinese troops had been kept secret, and their majesties imagined themselves perfectly safe within the massive walls of the capital, which, had they been defended by resolute troops, might have set the small force of the Allies at defiance, unprovided as it was with heavy guns.

On the 15th the Allies were busily engaged in clearing the city of the Chinese troops, who still occupied many parts of it in considerable force. The British cleared the houses near the Legations, and also a large part of the Chinese city. The Engineers blew a hole in the wall of the Imperial City, to the north of the British Legation, just west of the Sluice Channel, and the south-east part of the Imperial City was cleared and occupied by the Royal Welsh Fusiliers. This hole was afterwards enlarged into a gateway to admit carts, and was known as "The Hole in the Wall"; and eventually General Gaselee established his headquarters in this part of the town.

The 42nd Regiment of Japanese Infantry advanced early in the morning west from the Chih-ho mên, and broke in the Tung-an mên, or eastern gate of the Imperial City, meeting with considerable opposition from a large body of Chinese troops. The 21st Regiment had also succeeded in capturing the Ti-an mên, or north gate of the Imperial City, and had inflicted heavy loss on the Chinese. They had further cleared the whole of the northeast part of the Tartar City, and before evening had seized the An-ting mên and Te-sheng mên, the two great gates in the north city wall. Their casualties during the day were 17 men killed and 88 wounded.

The Americans captured the great gates leading north from the Ch'ien mên to the Forbidden City. These had to be assaulted in succession, and as they were stubbornly defended, the attacking troops had several of their number killed and wounded.

The Russians cleared the south-east part of the Tartar City.

The French had bivouacked on the canal for the night, and did not enter Peking till the morning of the 15th, when they bombarded the Forbidden City from the wall near the Sluice Gate.

On the morning of the 15th, a conference of the general officers was held, and preliminary dispositions were arranged for the occupation of the city by the allied troops, and for the relief of the Pei-t'ang Cathedral, which was still being besieged by the Chinese.

On the morning of the 16th a column, under the command of Major-General Frey, commanding the French troops, started to

RELIEF OF THE LEGATIONS.
14th August 1900.

REFERENCES
- British
- Americans
- Russians
- Japanese

Scale 3 Inches to 1 Mile

Heliozincographed at the Ordnance Survey Office Southampton 1901.

I.D.W.O. N°.1634ᵈ

Tung-pien mên — Attacked by Russians early morning.

Sha-huo mên — British at 12·30 P.M.

Ha-ta mên — 2 Battalions at 10 P.M.

1 Battalion

7th Bengal Infantry

Party of Russians which opened Ha-ta mên for main body

Sluice Gate

At 7 P.M.

At 2·40 P.M.

LEGATIONS

At 6 P.M.

At 4·30 P.M.

1st Sikhs

2 guns R.T.A.

Chien mên — Occupied by Americans

Genl. Sir A. Gaselee, Staff and 70 men, 1st Sikhs & 7th B.I.

1st B.L. and 24th P.I.

TEMPLE OF HEAVEN

1st B.L.

24th P.I.

Detachment

Yung-ting-men

Main Body proceeding to Temple of Heaven

TARTAR CITY

CHINESE CITY

Magnetic

relieve the Pei-t'ang. It was composed of the French troops, reinforced by detachments, of about 400 men each, from the British and Russian contingents, while the Japanese co-operated from the north, moving round from that side of the Imperial City. Leaving the Ch'ien mên, the southern column marched west against the Shün-chih mên, or western gate, in the south wall of the Tartar City, which was still occupied by Chinese troops. The gate was bombarded by a 12-pr. of the Hongkong Artillery, posted on the Ch'ien mên, and by the French guns at close quarters, whereupon the garrison at once fled. The gate was then occupied by the French, and was afterwards held by a guard of British troops.

The column next turned north and marched up the main road from the Shün-chih mên till it arrived opposite the Hsi-an mên, or west gate of the Imperial City. This gate had already been forced by the Japanese, who were engaged with the enemy occupying two strong barricades constructed across the road facing the gate, and also the houses on each side of the road. After some sharp fighting the barricades were captured, and the enemy were driven out of the houses, many of which were set on fire. The relief of the Pei-t'ang, which lies inside the Imperial City to the north-east of and close to the Hsi-an mên, was thus effected.

The troops continued to fight their way east till they arrived at the marble bridge across the Imperial Lakes. Crossing this they occupied the Empress Dowager's temple at the east end, and then moved north and east to the Mei-shan or Coal-Hill. The Japanese seized the Hsi-hua mên, or western gate of the Forbidden City, of which they now guarded the north, east, and west gates, while the United States troops held the south gate, but it was decided that for the present no one was to be allowed to go inside.

After a short rest, a force of French and British troops cleared all the Chinese out of the houses to the east and north-east of the Pei-t'ang, and then returned to the Coal Hill, where the various detachments bivouacked for the night. The French occupied the Hall of Ancestors to the north of Coal Hill, and here General Frey established his headquarters. The Russians occupied the Winter Palace.

In the fighting the Japanese had had one man killed and seven wounded. The French had four men killed and two officers and three men wounded. The British had no casualties, as they had formed the reserve, and had taken no active part in the attack on the Hsi-an mên. The Chinese lost very heavily.

To return to the Pei-t'ang. The small garrison had, indeed, made a gallant defence. It originally consisted of thirty-five French marines, eleven Italian marines, the Roman Catholic priests, and a few native converts, for whom, however, very few rifles were available. Yet this small force had held a perimeter over half-a-mile in length, and had successfully repulsed all the attacks of the Chinese. It had withstood an even longer and fiercer siege than the Legations, had been subjected to a heavier shell fire, and had been responsible for the safety of about 2,500 nuns and native converts, most of the latter being women and children. Nearly all the brave defenders had been wounded, and several had been killed, and, with the necessity of sleeplessly defending so long a line, it was inconceivable that the place could have held out. Only the cowardice of the attackers, who could not screw up their courage to rush some point of the defence, had saved the garrison from certain destruction.

The chief danger was from mines, which the Chinese had used with great success, but luckily with little perseverance. They had exploded four of these with very heavy charges. Two had done but little damage, being outside the defended zone, but the other two had been most destructive. By the first about twenty-five persons, including five Italian marines of the guard, had been killed; while a much larger number, chiefly native children, had perished in the second. The large craters caused by the explosions, half full of débris from the fallen houses, were about forty feet in breadth, and fifteen feet deep. In the bombardment the two churches, more especially, had been much damaged by shell fire, but, as most of the projectiles had struck high up, the casualties had been comparatively few. It was said that most of the artillery fire had come from the east and north.

When relieved the inmates appeared to be fairly healthy and cheerful, though rather famished. Food was running very low, and consisted chiefly of meal, but the constant anxiety must have been far more trying than the mere scarcity of supplies.

With the operations of the 16th August the occupation of Peking had been practically completed. The Chinese troops had all melted away, and there was no further opposition inside the capital.

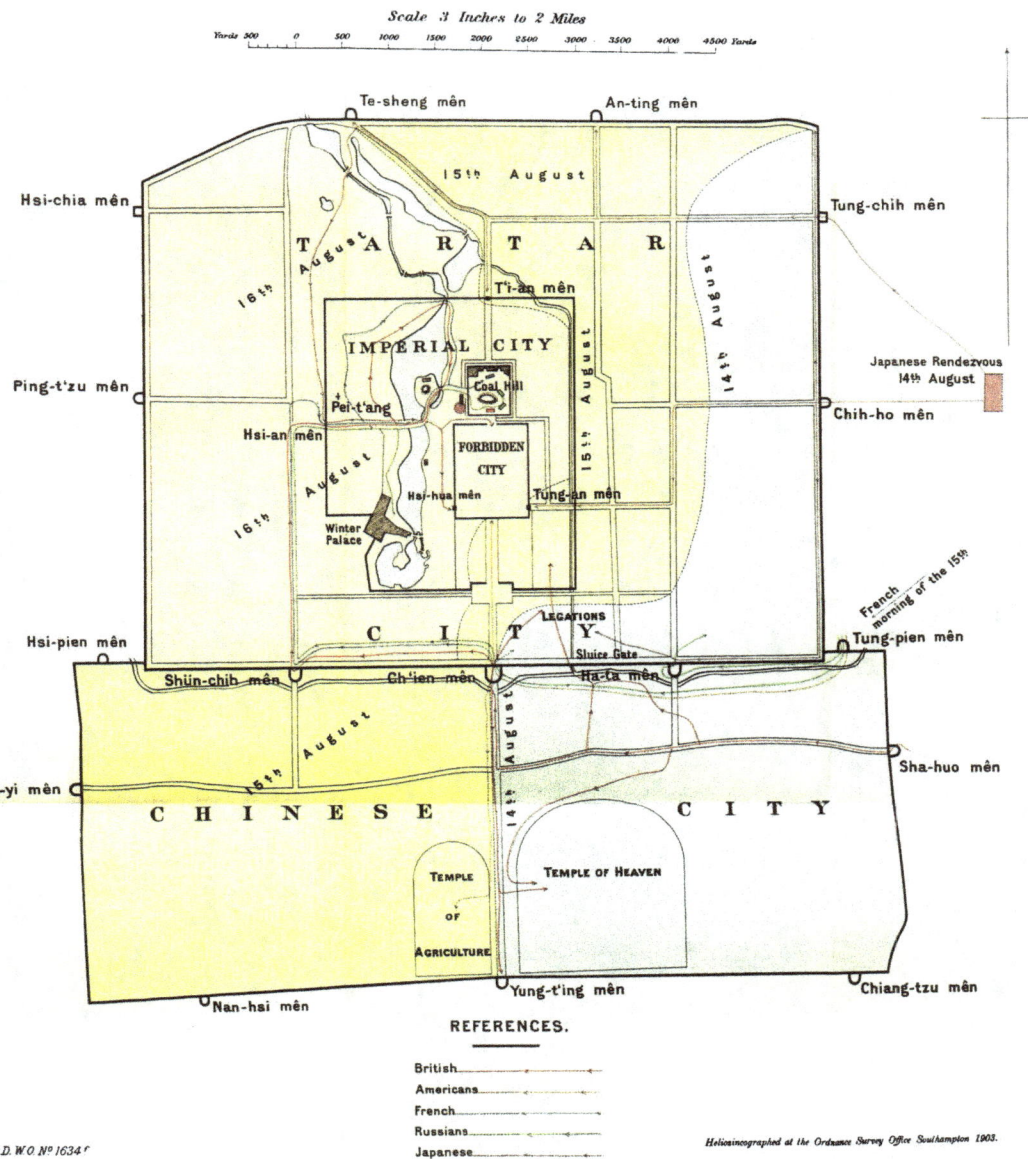

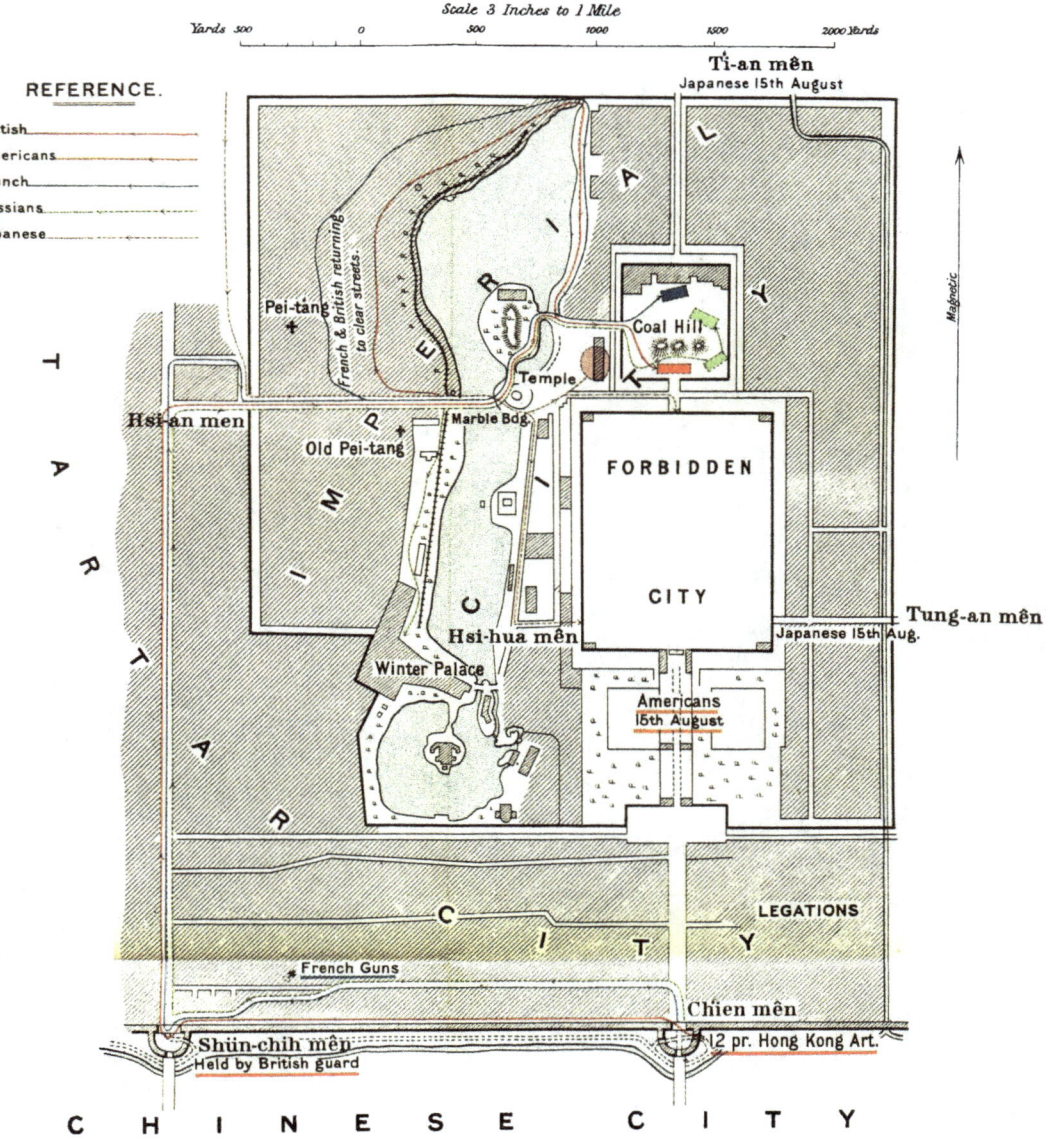

CHAPTER VIII.

SIEGE OF THE LEGATIONS.*

The Legation Quarter in Peking (*see* plan facing page 88) is divided into two parts by the canal, mentioned in the last chapter as carrying off the surplus water from the Imperial City through the sluice gate. This canal runs due south from the wall of the Imperial city to the Tartar City Wall, and in the Legation Quarter is about twenty yards broad and eight feet deep, the sides being perpendicular and faced with stone. Along each bank runs a road and it is spanned by three bridges, one at the foot of the Tartar City Wall, by which the road along the bottom of the wall crosses; the second about 130 yards north of the wall, by which Legation Street crosses ; and the third, usually called the North Bridge, about 600 yards further north, over which passes the road running east and west, north of the Han-lin and the Su-wang-fu.

On the west of the canal, between the Tartar City Wall and Legation Street, lies the United States Legation, to the west of which were situated the Russo-Chinese Bank and the Dutch Legation. Just north of the American Legation, across Legation Street, is the Russian Legation, and north-east of it, but separated from it by a strip of Chinese houses and shops, stands the British Legation. North of the Russian Legation and west of the southern end of the British Legation is an open space called the Mongol Market, surrounded by Chinese houses, and north of these and separated only by a high wall from the British Legation was the Imperial Carriage Park, a large open space of ten or twelve acres, containing four large yellow-tiled buildings, in which the royal carriages and chairs with their paraphernalia and trappings were kept.

Between the Carriage Park and the canal, just north of the British Legation, was the famous Han-lin academy, also surrounded by high walls ; and 100 yards still further north is the wall of the south-east corner of the Imperial City. This wall is nearly thirty feet high and six feet thick, being built of brick, and roofed with Imperial yellow tiles.

To the east of the canal, just opposite the British Legation and about sixty yards from it, lay the Su-wang-fu, or Palace of Prince Su, one of the hereditary Iron Princes, who was well disposed towards foreigners. His palace covered an area of about 200 yards from west to east and 300 yards from north to

---

* A full account of the siege by Sir Claude MacDonald is given on pages 240–300.

The defenders of the Legations numbered :—

| British | - 82 | Americans | - 58 | French | - 48 | Italians | - 29 |
| Russians | - 87 | Germans | - 51 | Austrians | - 35 | Japanese | - 25 |

south and was surrounded by a high wall. During the siege it was always referred to as the "Fu."

East of the "Fu" was a mass of houses, mostly Chinese, and including also those occupied by Sir Robert Hart and the Chinese Maritime Customs officials.

Still further to the east was the Austrian Legation and the Imperial Chinese Bank.

East of the canal, between the "Fu" and Legation Street, were the Spanish and Japanese Legations, the Hôtel de Pékin and the French Legation. Still further to the east was the Italian Legation, separated from the Austrian Legation to the north of it by a mass of houses occupied by Chinese.

Opposite the Hôtel de Pékin, between Legation Street and the Tartar City Wall, is the German Legation.

The Belgian Legation was at some distance from the others, to the north-east of the Austrian Legation, and no attempt was ever made to hold it.

In the beginning of June, when affairs first began to appear critical, and before the general attack on the Legations on the 20th, there was some idea of defending all the Legations, and the buildings in their vicinity occupied by Europeans, from attack by Boxers. Barricades were accordingly erected across the principal roads leading into the quarter. Thus a barricade between the Imperial Maritime Customs compound and the Austrian Legation commanded the road from the north. Others in front of the Italian Legation, and between the Russian and American Legations, commanded Legation Street, both east and west. The Germans had also erected one at the foot of the Tartar City Wall, facing east, and the Americans held the road at the back of their Legation, facing west.

The North Bridge was held by a picket of British Marines, and the roads beyond the barricades were watched by patrols.

These arrangements were fairly adequate as long as attacks by Boxers only were to be apprehended, as they were unprovided with fire-arms. When, however, the Imperial troops joined in, a very different complexion was placed on the state of affairs, and the defensive arrangements had to be greatly modified, in view of the probability of having to withstand a regular siege.

The British Legation was selected as the *réduit* of the position. It was surrounded by a strong, high wall, which with the substantially built houses, afforded excellent protection from rifle fire, and in some respects it was less liable to attack than any of the other Legations. Here nearly all the ladies and children were assembled, and also the Ministers of Russia, France, Belgium, Italy and Japan, besides many other Europeans and some 600 or 700 Chinese Christians. Here also was stored a large amount of provisions collected from the neighbouring shops, the daily distribution of which throughout the siege entailed much trouble and forethought.

From the very commencement the defences of the British Legation were constantly being improved and strengthened, under the direction of the Rev. F. D. Gamewell, of the American Methodist Mission, and they became by far the strongest and best planned in any part of the position. Walls and roofs which might be subjected to artillery fire were strengthened and strutted, floors were shored up, new barricades and breastworks were constructed wherever required, and were provided with loopholes and adequate head cover. Traverses and caponiers were built and also bomb-proof shelters, to protect the women and children when the Legation was subjected to shell-fire, and, in those parts where attack by mining might be resorted to, deep trenches and counter-mines were dug. Most of the work was carried out by Chinese christian refugees, who worked admirably, many of them being killed while employed on the defences.

It was at once recognised that the "Fu" must be included in the line of defence, as, if occupied by the enemy, it would render the British Legation almost untenable. Prince Su was informed of this decision, and, being powerless to oppose it, departed with his family, and the enclosure was garrisoned by the Japanese. Throughout the siege this was the weakest point in the defence, and the enemy's chief object of attack. The Japanese held it with the greatest gallantry, and their small force, which was quite inadequate for the area to be defended, had repeatedly to be reinforced with troops from elsewhere. Seven times were they compelled to fall back from their line of defence, and occupy one further to the rear, and, when the relieving troops arrived on the 14th August, about half the area of the "Fu" had been lost to the enemy. When the Italian guards were driven from their Legation they were sent to reinforce the Japanese in the "Fu," and remained there throughout the siege. Part of the Austrian guard was also quartered here, along with a considerable body of volunteers, and later, when the garrison was still further reduced by casualties from the enemy's fire, a party of British Marines was permanently detached from their own Legation for duty in the "Fu."

Another important part of the defence was the Tartar City Wall.

It was evident that if the enemy got possession of this, they would completely command the American and German Legations, which were just below it, and also, to a less degree, the other Legations. They would also hold the Sluice Gate, through which it was hoped that the relief column would eventually arrive. It was therefore imperative that this part of the wall should be included in the defence and held at all costs. The wall is about sixty feet high and forty feet broad at the top, the outer face is formed of square bastions at regular intervals, and access to the top is gained by double ramps on the interior face, the bastions opposite the head of these ramps being larger than the rest. The foot of one of these ramps is about one hundred yards to the west of the Sluice Canal, just in rear of the American Legation, and the foot of another about four hundred yards east of the canal beyond the German Legation.

On the 24th June, the Americans and Germans respectively constructed barricades at the top of these ramps and thus held about 600 yards of the wall, but on the 1st July, when the guards temporarily withdrew from the wall, the German barricade was lost to the Chinese and was never regained by the Allies. The American barricade was reoccupied and held throughout the siege, along with about two hundred and fifty yards of the top of the wall, the eastern barricade in the direction of the Hu-ta mên being just east of the Sluice Gate. The ramp leading up to the American barricades was protected from reverse fire by overlapping traverses of brick, and covered ways were also constructed, to facilitate movement on the top of the wall from one barricade to another.

Almost all the attacks by the Chinese on the top of the wall were made from the west, from the direction of the Ch'ien mên, by the troops of Tung Fu-hsiang's army. Except at the very commencement of the siege, there was very little fighting on the wall towards the Ha-ta mên, held by the troops of Jung-lu. Had these been as enterprising as the soldiers on the west, they could easily have advanced their barricades well beyond the German Legation, and so have taken its defence in reverse, but this they did not do.

With the exception of those made upon the "Fu," the heaviest attacks of the Chinese were directed against the French Legation. As in the case of the "Fu," its main weakness was due to the enemy being able to approach right up to the defences under cover of the Chinese houses outside, and also bring up Krupp guns, with which they battered the houses and barricades at point blank range. The French and German Legations, with the Hôtel de Pékin, were also subjected to heavy shell fire from the direction of the Ha-ta mên.

On the 13th July the Chinese succeeded in exploding two mines under the main buildings of the French Legation, and setting the latter on fire. This necessitated the withdrawal of the garrison to a third line of defence, and the abandonment of about two-thirds of the Legation enclosure.

The only other attempt at mining made by the Chinese was against the north-west corner of the British Legation, from the direction of the Carriage Park. The sound of digging having been detected, the British commenced a counter-mine, and the enemy, losing heart, deflected their mine away from the Legation, and the attempt failed.

After the burning of the Han-lin, the British defences were extended to the north so as to include one-third of the enclosure, and, as the British Legation buildings were now left exposed on that side, the enemy mounted some guns of old pattern on platforms, erected inside the Imperial City Wall. These platforms were most elaborate and of considerable size. They were constructed of large spars, and had broad timber ramps leading up to them. Overhead shelter was provided for the gun detachments, and the embrasures were closed by iron shutters, as a protection against rifle fire when the guns were not in action.

Towards the end of the siege the British line was also pushed forward on the west side of the south stables, up to the edge of the Mongol Market, so as to include a strip of ruined Chinese houses outside the Legation area. Though the attacks from the west were heavy and fierce, there was more open space in front of the defences, and the enemy never made much headway, the chief danger, which, indeed, at the commencement of hostilities was a very serious one, being from their attempts to set the Legation buildings on fire.

The defenders were also subjected to a heavy shell fire from the direction of the Ch'ien mên, but this was chiefly directed against the American and Russian Legations and the barricades on the Tartar City Wall.

The Russian Legation was successfully defended throughout the siege.

To the west of the American Legation was the Russo-Chinese Bank which at the commencement was occupied by detachments of Russians and American Marines, but on the 23rd June it was set on fire by the Chinese and partly burnt down, the ruins being afterwards occupied by the enemy, who were, however, later on, expelled from their position.

Communication between the west and east portions of the defence was provided by two barricades across the canal, between the British Legation and the "Fu," access to them being gained by deep trenches from the interior of the defences. Heavy rain on the 3rd July filled the canal with water and threatened to carry away the barricades, but fortunately no great damage resulted.

On the 30th July the enemy barricaded the North Bridge, and thus commanded the roads along the banks of the canal. To obviate the effect of this a large traverse was constructed across the road at the smaller gate of the Legation, and the Legation Street bridge was also barricaded.

With this description of the actual state of the defences of the Legation Quarter to explain what is narrated hereafter, we may now turn to the history of events as they occurred in Peking, after communication with Tien-tsin had been cut off by the destruction of the telegraph lines on the 10th June.

At an interview, on the 5th June, between Sir Claude MacDonald and Prince Ch'ing, it was acknowledged by the Chinese officials that the Boxer movement had got beyond their control. It was stated that the rising was aimed against the converts and their priests, and was generally approved by the bulk of the Chinese people, who sided with the Boxers; and that there were indications to show that the Imperial troops were all more or less in their favour. It was evident at the same time that the Tsung-li Yamen had lost all power, and that only direct intervention by the Throne could now avert the impending danger. On the 6th the Tsung-li Yamen assured the Ministers that General Nieh, with Imperial troops, had received most stringent orders to suppress the Boxers, and was actually in conflict with the rebels, and that railway communication with Tien-tsin would be restored on the 9th.

At this time the Court was residing at the Summer Palace, and it was impossible to ascertain its attitude towards the Boxer movement, but, from the Imperial decrees issued on the 29th and 30th May and 6th June, it was evident that the desire of the Throne was to treat these rebels with great leniency, and to put the blame on bad characters, who had taken advantage of the movement to create disturbances; and also upon the Roman Catholic priests, who were stated to have interfered in cases of litigation, in favour of their Chinese converts. The result of these decrees was to represent the Boxers as patriotic and loyal Chinese subjects, and to encourage them in spreading their propaganda and preaching war against the foreigners.

The immediate result of the publication of the last decree was a marked increase in anti-foreign feeling in Peking, and, on the 8th June, news arrived that the Boxers were destroying the railway bridge at Yang-tsun, and that General Nieh's troops had withdrawn to Lu-tai. On the same day a number of American Missionaries arrived from Tung-chou, 13 miles to the east of Peking, where they had handed over their premises to the care of the Chinese authorities. They reported a widespread massacre of converts at that place.

On the 9th June, the day on which the Tsung-li Yamên had promised that communication with Tien-tsin would be restored, the grand stand of the European racecourse was burnt by Boxers, and a party of students from the British Legation, who were riding in that direction, were attacked by bodies of Boxers, and had to use their revolvers to extricate themselves.

On the same day the Court returned to the city from the Summer Palace, but it was now generally admitted that the Empress-Dowager favoured the Boxers, and was determined to drive the foreigners out of China, an enterprise which Tung Fu-hsiang had persuaded her he was able to execute with his famous Kan-su troops. The British Minister accordingly telegraphed to Tien-tsin, informing the Senior Naval Commander that the position in Peking was most critical, and that more troops should at once be sent to the capital. The following morning he received news by telegram that 700 troops under the command of Admiral Seymour had started by train for Peking, after which telegraphic communication with Tien-tsin was finally cut off.

On the 10th June Prince Tuan, the father of the heir-apparent, who was generally supposed to be one of the strongest supporters of the Boxer movement, was appointed vice-president of the Tsung-li Yamên, and the same evening the British Summer Residency in the Western Hills, along with the London and Church of England Missions, was burnt down by the Boxers.

The following day the officials of the Tsung-li Yamên called on the British Minister, to impress upon him that it was unnecessary to increase the guards in Peking, but at the very time of their visit the Chancellor of the Japanese Legation, Mr. Sugiyama, was brutally murdered by Kan-su troops just outside the south gate of the Chinese City.

The 12th June was uneventful, but on the 13th the Boxer rising broke out in Peking. In the morning a Boxer in full uniform was arrested in Legation Street, and the same evening a large force of Boxers entered the Tartar City by the Ha-ta mên, and soon the whole of the houses occupied by the Customs' employés, along with the Missions and Churches in the East City, were in flames, and the massacre of large numbers of converts began. Père Garrigues, the aged priest of the Tung-t'ang, or Eastern Cathedral, refused to leave his charge, even when it was set on fire by the Boxers, and perished in the flames.

On the 14th the Nan-t'ang, or Southern Cathedral, situated just inside the Shün-chih mên, and a place of great historical interest, was seen to be on fire. Great numbers of Chinese christians, who lived in the houses all round the cathedral, were brutally butchered. The Imperial troops did nothing whatever to prevent the Boxers from carrying out this inhuman slaughter, and Duke Lan, the brother of Prince Tuan, with Chao Shu-ch'iao, a minister of the Tsung-li Yamen, were actually present to encourage them in their horrible work.

It was now evident that the Legations were in immediate danger of attack, and, as it was reported that orders had been issued by the Grand Council to the troops, to assist the Boxers in opposing the march of the relieving force on the capital, it was expected that they would certainly join them in attacking the Europeans in Peking. During the night there were several attacks on the Legation pickets, but these were easily repulsed.

On the 15th parties of Russians, Americans, and British Marines went out to the Nan-t'ang and brought in a large number of women and children, the survivors of a very large community of Chinese converts, who had been ruthlessly massacred by the Boxers. These refugees were quartered in Prince Su's palace. The Roman Catholic fathers and sisters had been gallantly rescued, and brought in to a place of safety the day before, by a small party from the French Legation, only just in time to escape the Boxer onset.

At this time, however, the excesses of the Boxers seemed to have rather alarmed the Court, as an Imperial Decree appeared, on the 15th June, ordering the Imperial troops to suppress the rioters and restore order. The Boxer ringleaders were to be arrested and executed, their altars destroyed, and their followers dispersed. This decree, however, did nothing whatever to improve the state of affairs.

On the 16th a rescue party went out into the Eastern City towards the Tung-t'ang, in the hope of finding survivors, who might have escaped the general massacre. They discovered a party of forty-four Boxers in a Taoist temple engaged in offering up christians, as human sacrifices to their gods. The christians were bound and horribly mutilated, and many were already dead, but revenge was swift, and not one of their murderers escaped.

The same afternoon the Boxers attacked the wealthiest part of Peking, the quarter in the Chinese City, just outside the Ch'ien mên, where the jewellers and booksellers, the dealers in curios, silks and furs, the goldsmiths and silversmiths had their stores. Many christians lived in this part of the town, and the first place attacked was a foreign drug store, which was recklessly set on fire. From here the flames spread over a very large area and created the most devastating conflagration ever known in Peking. Rushing northwards before the wind they set fire to the great outer tower of the Ch'ien mên itself, the gate below which is only opened for the passage of the Emperor on his way to worship at the Temples of Heaven and Agriculture. It is said that this ominous accident caused great consternation in the Palace, alarming even the Empress-Dowager and arousing her wrath against its originators, the Boxers.

On the 17th appeared an Imperial Edict forbidding attacks upon the Legations, and specially ordering Jung-lu to protect them with his soldiers.

The foreign Ministers were advised not to leave Peking in the present disturbed state of the country, but to remain quietly in the capital till matters settled down and the railway could be repaired.

On this day and the 18th affairs were comparatively quiet, but the first conflict between the Legation guards and the Chinese troops occurred, a German patrol having fired on some of Tung Fu-hsiang's troops, who had thrown stones at it.

On the 19th news reached the Legations that Admiral Seymour's column had had to retire on Tien-tsin, and that the Allies had captured the Taku Forts on the 17th, and in the afternoon a despatch arrived from the Tsung-li Yamên requesting that, as the foreign Powers had practically declared war on China, and there was now great danger on account of the popular excitement, the foreign Ministers would leave Peking within 24 hours. To this demand the Ministers at first agreed, but protested that the time allowed was too short to allow of the necessary preparations being made for the journey. Luckily subsequent events rendered their departure impossible, and, in avoiding certain death for themselves, the Europeans afforded protection to the numerous refugees, who would certainly have been murdered by the Boxers, had they been abandoned by their only protectors, the foreigners.

The question of withdrawal was once for all decided by the tragedy which took place on the morning of the 20th June.

No reply had been received to the demand of the foreign Ministers, made the day before, for an interview with the Ministers of the Tsung-li Yamen, and, such being the case, it was considered to be useless and dangerous to visit the Yamen, with little prospect of finding any responsible official there. The German Minister, Baron von Ketteler, was, however, of a different opinion, and determined to go alone to the Yamen and interview the Chinese authorities at all cost. He started accordingly, accompanied only by his Chinese secretary, Mr. Cordes, and two Chinese grooms. Both gentlemen travelled in chairs. All went well until more than half the distance to the Yamen had been covered, when suddenly Mr. Cordes, who was being carried in the second chair, saw a Manchu bannerman soldier, in full uniform, step forward close to the Minister's chair, level his rifle and fire, evidently with immediately fatal effect. Almost at the same moment Mr. Cordes was himself shot in the body, but, though badly wounded, was able to escape through back streets and reach the Legations.

There can be little doubt that the Chinese Government was directly responsible for this deliberately planned murder. No Minister was waiting at the Yamen to receive Baron von Ketteler, but no message requesting him not to come had been sent in answer to his demand for an interview. The man who fired the fatal shot was not a Boxer, but an Imperial soldier, acting, as it appeared afterwards at his trial, on orders received from his superiors, and the intention was to kill the German Minister himself and him only, as otherwise Mr. Cordes would not have escaped. None of the Chinese chair-bearers and attendants were attacked, but were allowed to return unharmed to the Legations.

Later, on the same day, a despatch from the Yamen was received, stating that, as it was considered unsafe for Europeans to travel to Tien-tsin, the Ministers should remain in Peking. No mention was made of the murder of the German Minister, though, at the time the despatch was written, the officials knew it had been committed. Although the ultimatum, requiring the Ministers to leave Peking before 4 p.m. on the 20th had thus been formally withdrawn, punctually at that hour the Chinese troops opened fire on the Legations, and the siege began.

The Austrians at once abandoned their Legation, and retired to that of France.

Everything was now done to strengthen the defences, all stores that could be obtained were collected, communications were constructed between the different parts of the defence, guards were posted, and the garrisons prepared to fight for their lives.

On the 21st June the American Mission, just inside the Ha-ta mên, which had been evacuated the previous day, was burnt down, as were also the Austrian Legation and the Chinese Bank.

On the 22nd the Chinese attacked on the east side of the Legation Quarter, and drove in the Italians, who fell back on the French Legation. The Chinese promptly set fire to the Italian Legation. The attack now seemed to be general, and at the first moment of alarm the Austrian, French, Italian, German and Japanese troops received the order to retire on the British Legation, whither they were shortly afterwards followed by the Russian troops. The mistake was quickly rectified, and they were sent back to their positions.

Luckily they were able to at once reoccupy these, as the Chinese had failed to notice the absence of the defenders and had lost the opportunity of penetrating the defences. After this date Sir Claude MacDonald, at the request of the other foreign Ministers, assumed the chief military charge of the defence.

At first the losses from rifle fire were not very serious, and the erection of fortifications went on rapidly, but the great danger which threatened the position was incendiarism, and the Chinese were quick to grasp the fact; flames broke out on the west of the British Legation, and it was only by great exertions that they were prevented from spreading to the main buildings. The same day the Dutch Legation was burnt down.

Next morning the Han-lin academy, which stood just north of the British Legation, was seen to be on fire. Efforts were at once made to extinguish the flames, when it was found that they were being kindled by the Imperial troops, in the hope of destroying the hated foreigners.

The Chinese were soon driven out, many of them being killed, but nothing could be done to save the buildings, and thus these famous libraries, with their priceless literary treasures, perished. At the same time all the houses between the American Legation and the Ch'ien mên, including the Russo-Chinese Bank, appeared to be on fire, and to the east the Customs buildings were blazing. From all sides the bullets were flying, and casualties were frequent, but the gallant defenders succeeded in keeping the flames from the Legation quarter, and, as they burnt themselves out, the danger from this source greatly decreased.

On the 24th, about 600 yards of the top of the City Wall were occupied by the Americans and Germans.

The attacks of the Chinese on the " Fu," which formed the north-east corner of the defence, were particularly determined. Here were quartered most of the Chinese Christians, and it was defended by the Japanese and Italians, supported by detachments of British and Austrian Marines, and volunteers. The enemy were repeatedly repulsed, often with heavy loss, but the defenders were gradually forced to give ground, and the main part of the Palace was burnt down. On the afternoon of the 27th the Chinese succeeded in making a breach in the north-east wall, through which they poured into the " Fu," but were then met with such a murderous fire from a loopholed position, which had been prepared in rear, that they fled in panic, leaving about 30 dead inside the enclosure.

On the evening of the 28th the enemy opened a heavy fire on the British Legation, from two Krupp guns in the Mongol Market. After nearly destroying the south stable quarters the fire suddenly ceased, and the Chinese gunners must have suffered heavily, as they were much exposed during the attack to the rifle fire of the defence. Heavy attacks were also made on the " Fu," the American Legation, and the Hôtel de Pékin, and the enemy occupied the ruins of the Russo-Chinese Bank.

On the morning of the 29th an attempt was made to capture the two Krupp guns, which had been used against the British Legation the previous day. The Chinese had, however, removed them during the night, and the party returned, after setting fire to some of the houses usually occupied by the enemy's sharpshooters.

On the side of the German and French defences the casualties up to this date had been severe, though, considering the intensity of the fire, it is to be wondered at that the loss of human life was not greater than it was. On the 29th the Chinese succeeded in setting fire to part of the French Legation, which had been battered by Krupp guns at very close range.

The defence of the barricade on the City Wall was also a matter of great difficulty, involving most serious losses in the small garrison, and on the 30th June the Germans had three men killed and two wounded, and two British marines were also wounded, one fatally, at the eastern barricade on the wall.

On the 1st July, in a moment of panic, the wall was abandoned by the guards. The American position was shortly afterwards reoccupied, but the German barricade was lost.

On the same day an unsuccessful attempt was made to capture a Krupp gun, which was firing into the "Fu," and the party had to retire after losing two men killed and nine wounded. Next day the line of defence in the "Fu" was still further driven in. In this quarter the fighting had been perhaps heavier than anywhere else, the Chinese being apparently imbued with a frantic desire to wreak vengeance on the converts inside.

The same day the defences of the British Legation, especially those on the eastern side, were greatly strengthened, in view of the possibility of the "Fu" falling into the hands of the Chinese, in which case the British Legation would certainly be subjected to a heavy artillery fire at close range.

Early on the morning of the 3rd a successful sortie was made from the American barricade on the top of the wall by 26 British, 16 Russians, and 15 Americans; the senior officer, Captain Myers of the United States army, being in command. The Chinese had gradually extended the right of their barricades across the bastion in front of the American breastworks, by pushing forward a wall of bricks, at the end of which they built a tower actually overlooking the American defences. It became necessary to drive them out of this position, and the plan of attack agreed upon was that the British and Americans should attack the tower and turn the right of the enemy's barricade, while the Russians simultaneously assaulted their left. This operation was successfully carried out, the Chinese were taken by surprise and fled along the wall, many of them being shot down, and the Allies occupied the enemy's breastwork, and held it for the remainder of the siege. Captain Myers was wounded in the knee, and was not again fit for duty; two American marines and one Russian soldier were killed, and three British marines and two Russians were wounded; but the capture of the barricade was of great importance to the defence, as it included possession of a ramp by which the Chinese gained access to the top of the wall.

The next attack came from the north, where, on the 5th July, the Chinese mounted some old cannon, on platforms inside the wall of the Imperial City, and, at a range of about 250 yards, hurled round shot into the British Legation, but luckily without causing any loss of life among the inmates. On the same day Mr. David Oliphant, of the British Legation, was killed.

Still the pressure on the Prince's Palace continued and the Japanese were gradually forced back. A second attempt, on the 6th, to capture the Krupp gun failed, and by the 8th the strength of the garrison in the "Fu" was so greatly reduced, that a British reinforcement of eleven men had to be permanently detached to its assistance, and a new line of entrenchments was taken up, with open ground in front. On the same day the gallant Austrian commander, Captain Thomann, was killed by a shell, and daily the little garrison was being reduced by frequent casualties.

The attacks on the eastern defences were particularly heavy and continuous, and on the 13th the Chinese exploded two mines under the French Legation, killing two French marines and rendering the main buildings of the Legation untenable, but the garrison promptly fell back a short distance to another line of defence, the abandoned buildings being at once set on fire by the Chinese. A very heavy attack was also made on the "Fu," where the garrison had to fall back to a new line of defence. This was the eighth line occupied by the defenders, but it was maintained, without further retreat, until the end of the siege.

An assault by the Chinese on the German Legation on the 13th was repulsed with heavy loss.

On the 14th July communication by letter with the Chinese authorities was reopened. It may be noted that this was the date of the capture of Tien-tsin city by the Allies. The missive purported to come from "Prince Ch'ing and others," and was sent by a Roman Catholic convert, who had left the Legation four days before with a letter to the relieving force, had been captured by the Chinese, and had received the message which he brought back in General Jung-lu's Yamen. The letter contained a request that the Ministers would take their families and staffs, "in detachments," for safety to the Tsung-li Yamen, and so "preserve friendly relations intact from beginning to end," but no armed guard was to accompany them, "in order to prevent doubt and fear on the part of the troops and people."

Though the writers declared this to be the only chance of safety for the Europeans, there was never any question of accepting the suggestion, but, as it was of great importance to gain time, a distinct refusal was not sent back, but further particulars were asked for. While these negotiations were proceeding, the attack on the Legations continued as fiercely as ever. On the 15th Mr. Warren, a British student, was killed, and the following morning the senior British officer, Captain Strouts, R.M.L.I., was mortally wounded and died shortly afterwards. Dr. Morrison of the *Times*, and Colonel Shiba, commanding the Japanese troops, were wounded when Captain Strouts was hit. They were all three walking together in an exposed part of the " Fu."

These were amongst the last casualties of the siege, as the same afternoon another message arrived from " Prince Ch'ing and others," to the effect that, as the Ministers were unwilling to proceed to the Tsung-li Yamen, the Chinese Government would take measures to protect the foreign Legations. The result of this was the suspension of hostilities for several days, which showed that the Government had complete control over the troops when they chose to exercise it. To the north and west were the Kan-su troops of Tung Fu-hsiang's force, who were still hostile and sullen ; but Jung-lu's men on the east were curious and even friendly, and small supplies of eggs and vegetables were smuggled through their lines, and even messengers with letters were able to enter the Legations. But though the truce continued, the Chinese occupied the time in strengthening their barricades, and the defenders followed their example, and took precautions against treachery by perfecting their defences and digging counter-mines.

Food was becoming very scarce and the Chinese Christians, in particular, were nearly reduced to starvation.

On the 17th July, Sir Claude MacDonald replied to the letter received on the previous day, and pointed out that the foreign troops had only acted on the defensive, and, while willing to refrain from further hostilities, they could not allow the movement of Chinese troops close to the Legations, and the construction of barricades and gun platforms. He further demanded that these hostile preparations should stop.

An answer was received the same day, from " Prince Ch'ing and others," putting the blame of the hostilities on the foreign troops, and requesting that they should be removed from the City Wall, the key of the defence. To this Sir Claude replied on the 18th, reiterating his demand that hostile preparations, amounting to acts of hostility, should cease during the truce, and pointing out that, as much of the fire from the Chinese guns had been directed on the Legations from the Wall, it was impossible to withdraw the troops from that part of the defence. The British Minister also wrote to Jung-lu, suggesting that some responsible person should be sent to the Legations to discuss the situation, and sending him a copy of regulations to be observed by the foreign troops, who would only fire upon armed Chinese moving near the Legations, or persons opening fire upon them, or constructing defences or performing other hostile acts. Unarmed messengers, not more than two in number at one time, would not be fired on.

In the afternoon a Yamen secretary, named Wen-hsien, arrived at the Legation with an introduction from Jung-lu, but had nothing of importance to communicate.

On the same day the Japanese Minister received a letter from Tien-tsin stating that a relief force was being organised, and thus the hard-pressed garrison learnt, for the first time, that their situation was known to the outside world, and that every effort was being made to rescue them.

On the 19th a letter was received from " Prince Ch'ing and others" stating that, although the Government of China had all along been doing their utmost to protect the Legations, the animosity of the people against the converts had been so universal that it had become uncontrollable, and the Legations were therefore still in great danger. The Throne was therefore desirous that the Europeans and Ministers should retire to Tien-tsin, and would furnish efficient escorts to enable them to do so; but, if they still insisted on remaining in Peking, it could not accept the responsibility of protecting them.

With this letter came a copy of telegrams, purporting to have been despatched on the 3rd July to the rulers of Great Britain, the United States, Germany, Russia and Japan. This was the day on which Captain Myers was wounded, two Americans and a Russian were killed, and three British and two Russian marines were wounded, in expelling Tung Fu-hsiang's troops from their barricade on the wall; and the Chinese were completing their preparations for bombarding the British Legation from the wall of the Imperial City. Further, on the previous day an Imperial edict was published, extolling the Boxers and ordering the extermination of the christians, and the expulsion of all missionaries from China.

The message to the Queen represented the Chinese Government as endeavouring to suppress " disorderly people " who had committed lawless acts, and appealed to the self-interest of England to assist China in restoring order.

Sir Claude MacDonald replied to the letter the following day, pointing out the inconsistency of the Chinese in guaranteeing a safe passage to Tien-tsin for the Europeans, while professing themselves unable to protect them in the capital; adding that it was impossible for them to free themselves of their responsibility for the safety of the Envoys to their Court.

The same day a note was received from the Tsung-li Yamen, with eight cartloads of vegetables and melons, for the use of the people in the Legations.

The armistice continued, though sniping from the Chinese outposts was of constant occurrence, and on the 24th a heavy fusillade was directed against the Legations for a short time from the north and west. Sir Claude MacDonald wrote the following day to Jung-lu protesting against this breach of the truce, and in reply received three letters, the most important of which was from " Prince Ch'ing and colleagues," and was an answer to the letter of the 20th. The Ministers stated that "from first to last " we have never neglected the protection of the Legations," and proceeded to explain that, if the foreign Envoys retired from Peking, they could guarantee their safety for the short space of time which would elapse before they reached Tien-tsin, whereas if they remained in the capital, where " the numbers of disorderly " characters were daily increasing," the difficulty of protecting them, for an indefinite period, against any unforeseen danger which might arise, would be greatly increased. The argument was specious but hardly convincing, and the letter ended with a request that the Ministers would fix an early date for their departure, and inform the Chinese authorities of their decision.

The other letters were naïve requests that the Ministers should telegraph *en clair* through the Tsung-li Yamen to their Governments assuring them of their safety and well-being.

To these letters the British Minister replied on the 27th that, unless the telegrams were sent in cypher, they would not be received by the Foreign Governments as genuine, and, with regard to the departure of the Europeans from Peking, asked for further details as to transport and escorts.

On the same day a further supply of vegetables and melons, with some rice and flour, was received from the Tsung-li Yamen, together with a letter from " Prince Ch'ing and others," suggesting that as the Legations must be very crowded, the native Christians should be sent out " to quietly pursue their avocations."

These were followed the next day by a reply to Sir Claude MacDonald's letter, from " Prince Ch'ing and colleagues," saying that the suggestion of the temporary withdrawal of the Ministers to Tien-tsin was only prompted by a desire for their safety, and not by any unfriendly feeling towards them; also that every arrangement for carts, chairs, boats, and provisions would be made, and the escort to accompany them would be ready, on notice being received of the intended date of their departure.

During the last few days there had been increased activity among the Chinese, which pointed to the early resumption of hostilities. Heavy firing had also been heard from the direction of the Pei-t'ang, and on the 29th a strong barricade was thrown up on the North Bridge, from which a steady fire was opened on the Legation defences. This was afterwards attributed to the arrival in the capital of the Li Ping-hêng, an anti-foreign ex-Governor of Shan-tung, who doubtless lent the weight of his influence to the hostile side of the Council. The occurrence furnished a good excuse for further discussion of the question of departure, and Sir Claude MacDonald wrote on the 30th, asking for an explanation of these hostile actions, at a time when the Government was professing its desire to protect the foreign Ministers from attack.

The answer arrived the next day, in which it was explained that the firing at the Pei-t'ang was due to the converts, who were looting provisions, and had opened fire when interfered with. With regard to the barricade on the North Bridge, it was explained that the Chinese troops were not building a barricade at all, but a road, and the Legations had fired on them under a misapprehension, and this had led to their fire being returned. Thus the foreign Envoys need have no anxiety in deciding a date for their early departure.

On the following day, the 1st August, another letter was received from " Prince Ch'ing and others," accusing the converts of firing on the Government troops the night before, and killing two men. It further suggested that the foreign Ministers were prevented from leaving the capital by the converts, who hoped thus " to secure perpetual protection for themselves," but begged that they would not be influenced thereby, but would notify an early date for withdrawal.

Sir Claude MacDonald replied on the following day, expressing surprise at the contents of the above letters, and pointing out that the Legations were not defended by converts but by foreign guards, brought there for that purpose with the consent of the Chinese Government. Further, that during the two previous days not a shot had been fired at the Chinese from the Legations, though a steady fusillade had been maintained from the Chinese barricades, evidently, from the statements in the letters, not by "disorderly persons," but by Government soldiers, who, the foreign Ministers had been informed, were being used for their protection. It was thus impossible for them to leave the shelter of the Legations, while there seemed to be no prospect of security from the Chinese troops.

During the last few days several letters had arrived from Tien-tsin, with the news that a force was preparing to advance to the relief of Peking, but the writers unfortunately had been unable to fix a date on which the troops would start.

On the 3rd August two letters arrived, one of which enclosed a cypher telegram from Lord Salisbury asking for news. It was intimated that "peaceful telegrams" from the Ministers would be transmitted by the Tsung-li Yamen to their Governments. The second letter was in answer to Sir Claude MacDonald's of the previous day, and without taking any notice of his remarks beyond observing that the firing at night was again the result of a misunderstanding, and was "really hardly worth a smile," announced that Jung-lu had been entrusted with the duty of arranging for an escort to conduct the Ministers in safety to Tien-tsin, and again pressed for the early notification of the date on which they would be prepared to depart.

In reply several of the foreign Envoys sent cypher messages to be telegraphed to their Governments, and these brought back an answer from the Tsung-li Yamen that they had been despatched for transmission to Chi-nan fu, the capital of Shantung province, by runner, as telegraphic communication from Peking was interrupted.

The Yamen also requested an early reply, as to the date on which the Ministers would leave for Tien-tsin, stating that the European Foreign Offices had been pressing for their withdrawal from Peking under safe escort.

This naturally drew from the Ministers the reply that they could not leave their posts without direct orders and instructions from their Governments, and ten telegrams intended to ascertain these views were enclosed for transmission.

The same night there was a heavy fusillade from all sides, which lasted for half-an-hour, and the following morning a letter was received from "Prince Ch'ing and others" expressing great surprise that the foreign soldiers had, without provocation, attacked the Chinese positions. To this the British Minister replied that the reports that had reached them were false, as the attack had been made by the Chinese, and only two shots had been fired from the Legation, at a man who advanced towards our barricades.

On the 5th, "Prince Ch'ing and others" sent a letter to the Italian Minister, announcing the death of His Majesty King Humbert, and conveying the condolences of the Chinese Government, which, it was stated, would be represented at the funeral.

On the 7th, the Tsung-li Yamen wrote to announce the sad news of the death of His Royal Highness the Duke of Saxe-Coburg and Gotha, and that the Chinese Minister in London had been directed to convey to the British Government the condolences of the Chinese Court. This, at the very time when the British Minister with the members of his Legation in Peking were fighting for their lives against the Imperial troops.

Sir Claude MacDonald replied to this on the following day, and pointed out that, as the Chinese Government apparently professed to be at peace with Great Britain, they should take steps to prevent their troops from firing on the British Legation, and should allow supplies to be brought in for the use of the residents.

In the meanwhile there had been a short lull in the firing on both sides, but from this date onwards the attacks on the Legations became incessant, and continued until the end of the siege, though communication by letter with the Chinese officials did not cease. From this it would appear that, while there was a strong faction bent on the destruction of the foreigners, there was also a more prudent party, who at least attempted to keep up a show of friendliness. It was noticed too that new uniforms and banners had appeared recently among the ranks of the enemy, and it was correctly surmised that these were fugitives from defeats, inflicted by the relieving force in its advance from Tien-tsin, and that they had come to wreak vengeance, if possible, on the small body of white men, who were still holding their own against the cowardly hordes of their countrymen.

At last, on the 10th of August, letters reached the garrison from Generals Gaselee and Fukushima, stating that the relief column had reached Tsai-tsun on the 8th, and expected to arrive at Peking on the 13th or 14th. Great was the joy at the prospect of an early deliverance, but it was felt that all cause for anxiety was not yet at an end, and that, before reinforcements could arrive, the Chinese would probably make a last desperate effort to overwhelm the small force, which had so long held them at bay. Still, thanks to the ability of the Rev. F. D. Gamewell and the untiring energy of the besieged, everything had been done to render the defences as strong as possible, and they now contained few points of weakness, so it was confidently expected that the troops would still be able to hold out for the prescribed period. They had not long to wait, as, on the evening of the 11th, the enemy commenced a furious bombardment from all points, which lasted without intermission during the next two days,

The attacks were varied by the receipt of more or less pacific letters from the Chinese officials. On the 11th they wrote placing the blame on the converts, whom they accused of continually attacking their outposts. Sir Claude MacDonald replied that this could not be the case, as the converts were unarmed. With regard to supplies, the Ministers said that there was no prohibition to their sale, but the people were afraid to bring them in. They proposed, however, that each afternoon a Yamen official should visit the Legations and receive a list of the provisions required, which he would then purchase outside. To this the British Minister agreed and sent a first list of articles with his reply. It is needless to say that these were never supplied.

On the 12th August "Prince Ch'ing and others" proposed that the members of the Tsung-li Yamen should visit the Legations, and discuss measures for the suspension of hostilities, and asked Sir Claude to fix an hour for their reception. To this an answer was sent appointing 11 a.m. on the following morning for the interview, but, unfortunately, all the Chinese officials had "important official engagements" elsewhere and could not attend.

Sir Claude wrote on the 13th, warning the Chinese Court that particulars as to the attacks on the Legations, and resulting loss of life, were now known to the foreign Governments, who also knew that these attacks had been made by Chinese Imperial troops directed by Government officials. Luckily, so far, no Envoy, woman, or child had been injured, but, if in subsequent attacks any were wounded, those holding official positions in the capital would certainly be held personally responsible. In reply "Prince Ch'ing and others" proposed that all firing should cease on both sides, but this had no effect upon the ceaseless fusillade which was being poured into the Legations, and which continued all night; till early in the morning of the 14th the sound of guns to the east and the bursting of shells over the Tartar City Wall warned the Chinese that the foreign troops were at their gates, and told the tired garrison that their labours were nearly ended.

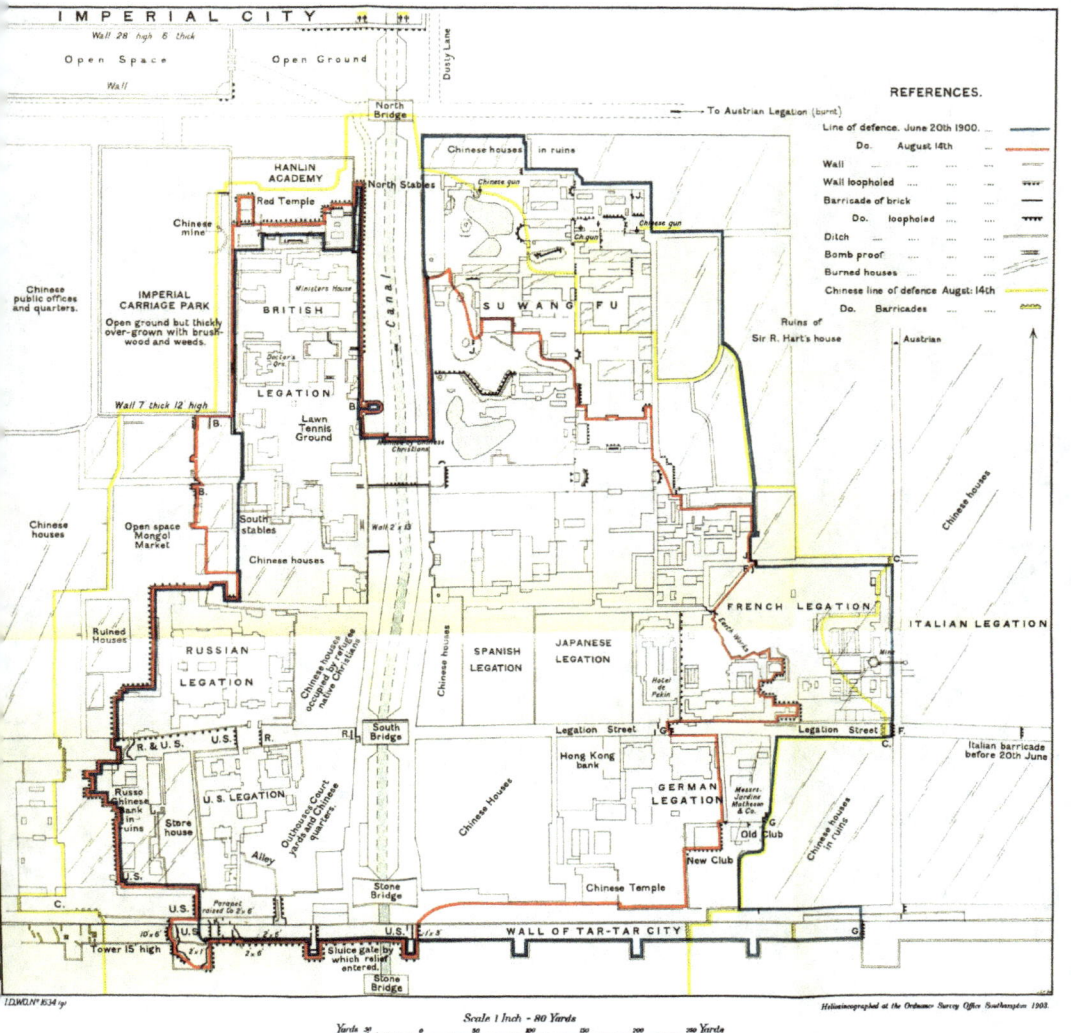

CHAPTER IX.

Progress of Events in and around Peking up to the end of September 1900.

The final expulsion of the Chinese troops and Boxers from Peking, as described in Chapter VII., completed the occupation of the capital, and the allied troops commenced to settle down in their new quarters and to make themselves comfortable.

On the morning of the 16th August a convoy was despatched to Tung-chou to bring up rations.

Looting was general throughout the city. General Gaselee had from the first given strict orders against the confiscation of property, but as almost all civilians, both European and Chinese, and also the troops of most of the Allied Powers, were busily engaged in appropriating large quantities of valuables of all sorts, it was only natural that our own men were greatly disappointed at being debarred from annexing a share.

It was evident that their not being allowed to participate would in no way enable the original owners to retain their property, as it would certainly be confiscated by others and merely go to swell their hoards. Most of the houses of the well-to-do in Peking were lying open, with their contents at the mercy of the first comer, their owners having fled, either during the disturbed times of the siege or on the arrival of the relieving troops. General Gaselee accordingly issued an order, which, while forbidding promiscuous looting by individuals, allowed the collection of booty by organised parties, from the houses of Chinese known to be hostile to foreigners or connected with the Boxers. These parties were to be under the charge of officers, and all confiscated property was to be deposited in a large building in the Imperial Carriage Park, under the charge of a military guard. The accumulated loot was afterwards sold by auction, the money realised forming a prize fund, for distribution among all the British troops who took part in the relief of the Legations.

Soon after the capture of Peking, the city was divided up into districts, which were allotted to the various nations for control and administration, and the troops of any one Power were debarred from going into the parts of the city told off to the charge of another nation, but certain main roads, leading to all parts of the city, were reserved for general use. Steps were also taken to reassure the peaceful Chinese inhabitants and to protect their property.

The rain, which had fortunately held off during the advance of the relieving force from Tien-tsin, had fallen in considerable quantities during the last few days, and rendered the forwarding of stores, from the junks at Tung-chou, a matter of considerable difficulty, on account of the state of the roads.

The telegraph line was brought into Peking on the 17th August. The entire line between Peking and Tien-tsin had been totally destroyed during the anti-foreign insurrection, and therefore a new line had to be constructed. Unfortunately only materials for repairs had been sent from India, and the personnel had been calculated on the same basis. An arrangement had therefore to be made with the American Signal Corps, which was also numerically weak, to erect a combined Anglo-American line, and in spite of deficiency of materials, an office was opened in the British Legation only three days after the relieving force marched in.

It had by this time been recognised by the military commanders that one of the first measures to be undertaken was the reconstruction of the railway from Tien-tsin to Peking, so as to ensure the troops being properly supplied with necessaries of all kinds, in the event of their having to remain in the capital during the winter. The Russians put forward a claim to the entire control of the railway, but this was opposed by General Gaselee, and the question remained in abeyance.

On the 19th a combined force of British, Americans, Austrians, and Japanese, about 1,000 strong, moved out of Tien-tsin, under command of Brigadier-General Dorward, and attacked a strong force of Boxers, who had occupied some villages about eight miles to the south-west of the settlements. The enemy were successfully dispersed with the loss of 300 killed and 60 prisoners. The Allies had 11 men wounded.

At Peking on the same day a reconnaissance, by the 1st Bengal Lancers, disclosed the presence of a large force of Chinese troops and Boxers in the Nan-hai-tse, or Southern Hunting Park, which lies about a mile and a half to the south of the city. Acting on this information a small British force, consisting of two guns 12th Battery R.F.A. two maxims, two squadrons 1st Bengal Lancers and 300 men of the 24th Punjab Infantry, marched out to the Hunting Park the following morning. It was hoped that a Japanese force would co-operate from the east with the British detachment, and the latter consequently waited for some time on the north side of the Park, expecting the Japanese to appear. From the position they occupied, a very extensive view was obtained to the south and west, and considerable bodies of Boxers and troops were visible, moving about in the distance. At one period a large body of Boxers collected in front of a village about two miles to the south-west, and the battery threw a few shells among them which dispersed them. A short time afterwards a body of Boxers attempted to attack our cavalry patrols, but were easily driven off by a few rounds of shrapnel, and disappeared to the south-west, followed by the Chinese troops in the vicinity. The British force shortly afterwards returned to quarters.

The 26th Bombay Infantry arrived at Peking on the 19th, and were followed the next day by No. 4 Company Bengal Sappers and Miners.

At this time there were undoubtedly considerable bodies of Chinese troops and Boxers in the immediate neighbourhood of Peking, to the north, west, and south, and on the 21st a combined movement was carried out by detachments of British, American, Japanese, and Russian troops, which reconnoitred the greater part of the Nan-hai-tse, without however encountering any of the enemy. In the afternoon the British and American troops returned to quarters, but the Japanese and Russians remained out for the night, which turned out very wet.

A large convoy, including most of the civilians, ladies and children, who had been present in the Legations during the siege, and who were now going away for change, was to have left Peking for Tung-chou on the morning of the 22nd, but had to put off its departure till the following day, on account of the state of the roads after the heavy rain of the night before.

On the morning of the 22nd, contrary to agreement, the Summer Palace was occupied by the Russians, to the exclusion of the other Allies, and they remained in possession for about two months. This Palace, called the Wan-shou-shan, had been built by the Empress-Dowager to replace the Yüan-ming-yüan, destroyed by the Allies in 1860. It was finished only a few years ago, and in it were collected most of the priceless treasures which Her Imperial Majesty had brought together from all parts of the Empire, during the preceding 40 years.

The same day the 5th Regiment of United States Infantry, with two batteries of American artillery, reached Tien-tsin, and the following day the 16th Bengal Lancers began to arrive.

While these events were happening the administration of the city was being organised, and there were constant reconnaissances, with occasional skirmishes, outside the walls.

For administrative purposes the city was divided as follows :—

The Japanese occupied the whole of the north and north-east part of the Tartar City, including the four great gates on the north and east sides. They also occupied the north-east part of the Imperial City, and guarded three of the four gates of the Forbidden City.

The Russians occupied the south-east part of the Tartar City, including the Ha-ta mên, also the Summer and Winter Palaces. When they withdrew their troops at a later date from Peking, the Germans took over their quarters in the city, and the Summer Palace was held by detachments of British and Italian troops.

The Germans had a long strip of the Chinese City, just outside the Tartar City wall, extending from the Ha-ta mên to the Hsi-pien mên, or north-west gate of the Chinese City, and south to the main street between the east and west gates of the Chinese City. They held only the Hsi-pien mên at first, but afterwards took over the Ha-ta mên from the Russians, and, later, the gates held by the Americans.

The Americans occupied the south-west part of the Chinese City, including the west and south-west gates and the Temple of Agriculture. They also held the Ch'ien mên and part of the Tartar City, lying south of the Imperial City, between the Ch'ien mên and the Shün-chih mên; and guarded the South Gate of the Forbidden City and the Hall of Ancestors. After their departure in the spring of 1901, their quarter was divided up between the British and Germans.

The British occupied the south-east part of the Chinese City, including the four gates, from the Tung-pien mên round to the Yung-ting mên, and the Temple of Heaven. They also occupied the south-west corner of the Tartar City and the Shün-chih mên. A new gate was also made in the west wall of the Tartar City, near the south-west corner, and was called the Ta-ying-kuo mên, or Great English Gate. This saved a long détour if the troops wanted to move out of the city to the west, and also admitted of supplies being brought direct into the English quarter from that side.

The British also occupied the south-east quarter of the Imperial City, and a strip of buildings to the west of the British Legation.

The French occupied the north-west and west part of the Imperial City, and that part of the Tartar City which lies west of the Imperial City, and includes the Ping-tsu mên, or west gate of the Tartar City.

The Italians occupied a portion of the Tartar City on the west side, lying between the French and Japanese, and held the Hsi-chia mên, or north-west gate of the Tartar City, conjointly with the latter. They also occupied another quarter of the Tartar City, on the east side of the Imperial City, between the Japanese and Russians.

The Austrian headquarters were in the north-east part of the Tartar City, in the Japanese quarter.

On the 25th August the Russians occupied Ma-chia-pu, the terminus of the Tien-tsin line, which lies about one and a-half miles to the south-west of the Yung-ting mén, and close to the north-west corner of the Hunting Park. The British had placed a small detachment there a week before, but it had been withdrawn, owing to a baseless rumour that a large Boxer force was advancing against the place from the south, and it had since remained unoccupied.

The same day a conference of the military commanders was held, and, after much discussion, it was decided that detachments of the allied troops should make a triumphal march through the Forbidden City on the 28th August, the order of march being

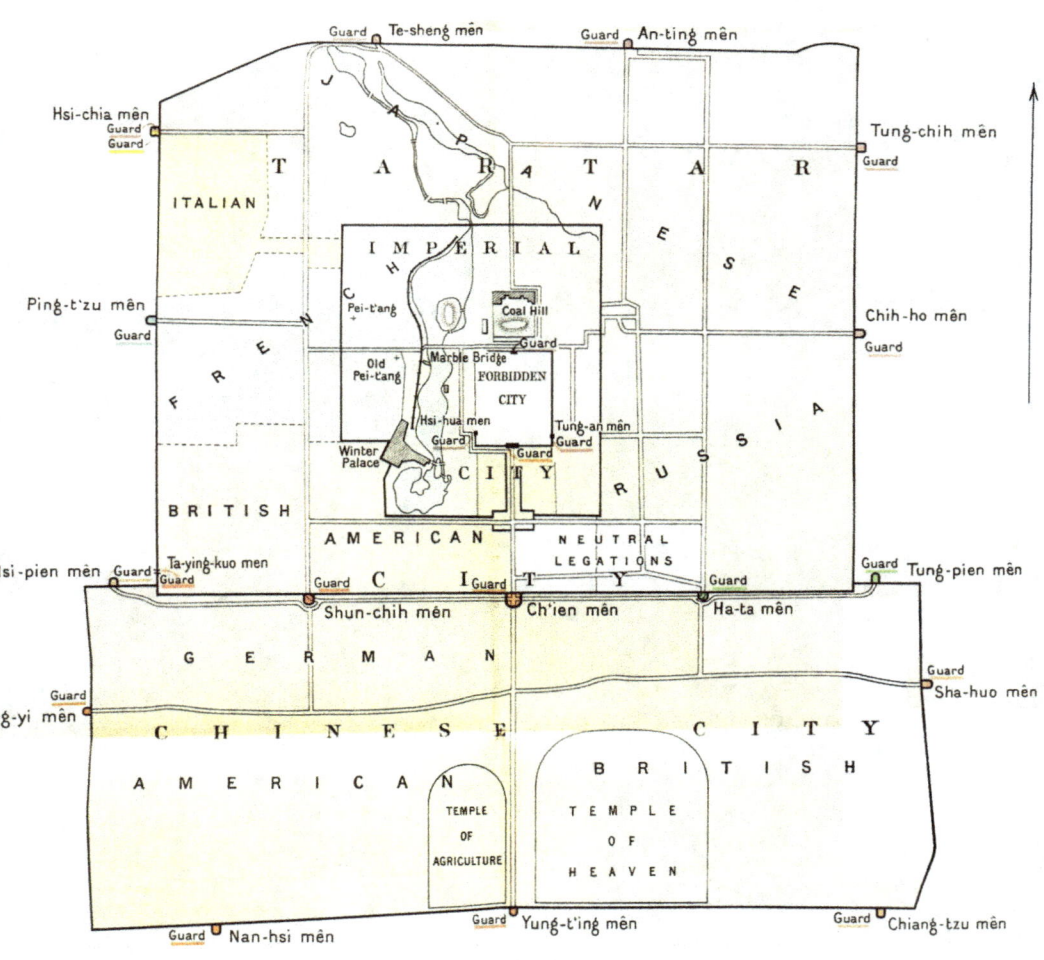

arranged, in accordance with the declared strength of the respective contingents. The Russians were to lead with 800 men, followed in order by the Japanese 800, British 400, Americans 400, French 400, Germans 200, Austrians and Italians.

On the evening of the 27th the great guard-house above the Ch'ien mên accidentally caught fire and was burnt down. It appeared that a beam near a place used for cooking had become ignited, and, as the building consisted almost entirely of perfectly dry and very inflammable timber, there was no chance of saving it. The outer guard-house had been accidentally burnt by the Boxers, soon after the commencement of the siege, and this completed the destruction of the great gate. The incident was looked upon as a most unlucky omen by the Chinese, as the Ch'ien mên is the principal gate of the Tartar City, and faces the Imperial Palaces in the Forbidden City.

The building was still burning when the contingents of the Allied forces paraded in front of the south gate of the Imperial City, for the march through the Forbidden City. Lieut.-General Liniévitch arrogated to himself the chief position in the ceremonial. Behind him and his staff came the Ministers of the various Powers, and then the detachments of Russian, Japanese, British, American, French, German, Austrian, and Italian troops, in the order named. As the head of the column started the 12th Battery Royal Field Artillery fired a general salute.

Crossing the next courtyard and passing through another large gate, the troops entered the great court, at the north end of which stands the southern and principal gate of the Forbidden City, through which no foreigner had ever previously passed. On marched the column with bands playing, through the gate, and over an artificial moat, spanned by five marble bridges, and across great courts, till it reached the foot of the high marble terrace, which forms the central and highest part of the Forbidden City. On the top of this terrace are two great halls, the first containing a carved wooden throne, stained to look like bronze.

Over the terrace and through succeeding halls swept the troops, till they reached the north gate, through which they passed, to be received outside by the remainder of the Russian troops, drawn up as a guard of honour, who cheered the various contingents as they arrived.

After the march through the Forbidden City the troops returned to quarters, and the Generals, Ministers, and their staffs, with many civilians, returned leisurely through the city, inspecting the various buildings.

The Imperial dwelling-houses are in the north-west part of the city, and there are also a great number of other buildings, usually occupied by the Court and by high officials. The city itself is disappointing, being grass-grown and neglected, but it must have presented a much finer appearance in the days of the Emperor Ch'ien-lung, when affairs in Peking were managed in a very different manner from that of the present day.

After the last of the visitors had left, the gates were closed, and the city was again handed over to the charge of the Americans and Japanese, such visitors only being admitted as were in possession of passes granted them by Major-General Chaffee, commanding the United States forces.

A curious part of the proceedings was the attitude of the Chinese officials, of whom there were a good number in the Palace. In order to save the Imperial " face ", they received the troops as guests, and conducted them through the city. Tea and refreshments were also provided, for those who chose to partake of them. No doubt they duly reported to the Court that the barbarians had desired to see the Palace, and had been admitted and treated as visitors. The following day some of the highest officials presented themselves at the British Legation, and thanked Sir Claude MacDonald for the orderly way in which the troops had behaved, during their march through.

On the 30th August, to nullify the effects of the Russian action at Ma-chia-pu, a British detachment occupied Feng-tai, the next station to Ma-chia-pu, and the junction of the Lu-han and Tien-tsin railways. The place had contained large railway workshops, all of which had been totally destroyed, along with a number of locomotives. The Russians from Ma-chia-pu were busy levelling the line and collecting sleepers and rails from the adjacent fields and villages, where they had been hidden, and the British were soon employed on the same work between Feng-tai and the next station, Huang-tsun.

On the 31st August the British occupied Kung-ch'i-ch'êng, an important strategical point, where the main road from Peking to the south crosses the Hun-ho by the massive stone bridge of Lu-kou-ch'iao. Some 300 yards higher up, the river is spanned by a fine iron-girder bridge, over which runs the Lu-han railway.

On the same day the Naval Brigade, and the Marines of the Legation Guard, who had fought so well during the siege, left Peking for Tung-chou, on their way to rejoin the fleet.

On the 1st September the 3rd Bombay Cavalry arrived at Tien-tsin, and two days later the 34th Pioneers reached the same place.

Everything was now quiet in the capital, and on the 3rd September Prince Ch'ing arrived in Peking, and took up his residence in the Japanese quarter. He was supposed to be accredited as a plenipotentiary from the Court, but had no powers to treat with the Allies.

On the 5th September " B " Battery, R.H.A., reached Tien-tsin, and the detachment of Mounted Bengal Sappers, attached to the Cavalry Brigade, arrived on the following day.

There were still a good many Boxers and disbanded soldiers scattered about the country, and skirmishes were of constant occurrence between them and the patrols of the Allies. On the night of the 6th the enemy attacked the Russian railway camp near Ma-chia-pu, and killed an officer and some men. In consequence the Russians made a raid to the south, along the west wall of the Nan-hai-tze, burnt some villages, and killed a number of Chinese, including some Boxers.

On the 8th September an expedition left Tien-tsin for Tu-liu, on the Grand Canal, which was reported to be occupied by Boxers. The town was entered without opposition, and, as the enemy had retired from the neighbourhood, the place was burnt, and the troops returned to Tien-tsin on the 14th September.

On the 11th September a German force of about 800 infantry and six guns attacked the walled town of Liang-hsiang-hsien, which stands on the main road to Pao-ting fu, about eighteen miles south-west of Peking. As they had no cavalry they were accompanied by forty-four sowars of the 1st Bengal Lancers. A Maxim gun, from the British detachment at Kang-ch'i-ch'êng, also joined the force. The German Krupp guns were each drawn by a team of six Chinese mules, and, as the road was very heavy after the late rains, their progress was very slow. To the east of Liang-hsiang-hsien, across the railway, is a very prominent pagoda, standing on a small, bare hill. As our cavalry approached the town they found it occupied by large numbers of Boxers, who rushed out to the attack, but, on the guns coming into action at long range, they retired, and began to rapidly disperse in all directions through the high crops. The principal body marched out in regular order by the southern road towards Pao-ting fu, and got away unharmed, but the cavalry killed about thirty armed Boxers moving off towards the west. After much delay the Germans finally blew in the east gate and entered the town, which they completely burnt, killing many of the inhabitants. The force returned the same evening to Kung-ch'i-ch'êng, and the following day to Peking.

On the 13th a detachment of British cavalry, with a force of Japanese, occupied Huang-tsun, near the south-west corner of the Nan-hai-tze, after driving out the Boxers, of whom about thirty were killed. The Japanese then commenced the repair of the railway, working north towards Feng-tai.

On the 14th September a very serious explosion occurred at Tung-chou, resulting in 29 deaths among the British troops, including Captain Hill of the Chinese Regiment. The men were employed, at the time of the accident, in removing and destroying Chinese powder from the temple near the junk landing-place, when from some cause, which has not been satisfactorily explained, a large quantity exploded with the above fatal results.

On the 16th the Australian Naval Brigade arrived at Tien-tsin, and on the same day a force, consisting of 800 British and 800 Americans, under command of Brigadier-General Wilson of the United States Army, accompanied by Major-General Barrow, the British Chief of the Staff, moved out by the paved road from the western gate of the Chinese City to Kung-ch'i-ch'êng, where it halted in the evening. It was intended that a converging attack should be made at daybreak the following morning on the temples of Pa-ta-ch'ü in the Western Hills, where a large body of Boxers were reported to have their headquarters. The British and Americans were to operate from the south and west, the Japanese from the north, and a party of Germans were to move out from Peking and attack the position from the east. The British and American column left Kung-ch'i-chêng at 1.30 a.m. on the 17th September, and reached Pei-hsing-an about 5 a.m. From there one body of troops moved by Mo-shih-k'ou on to the ridge west of Pa-ta-ch'ü, while the remainder moved along the foot of the hills. The Japanese were early in position to the north, but the Germans arrived after the affair was over. The Boxers had no warning of our approach, and were cooking their food when the first shots were fired. They rapidly dispersed, through the gap left by the non-arrival of the Germans, losing a few of their number in their flight. At the same time a party of British cavalry visited San-chia-tien on the Hun-ho, and destroyed the arsenal there.

A considerable number of cattle, mules, and ponies were collected and driven into Peking. Two of the pricipal temples, called Ling-kuang-ssu and Pi-mo-yüan, were found to contain Boxer insignia, documents, and arms, and from enquiries appeared to have been used by them as their headquarters. These two temples belonged to members of the Imperial family, who used them as country resorts during the heat of the summer months. As the European Missions and Residencies in the vicinity of these temples had been totally destroyed by the Boxers and priests, by whom also many of the Chinese christian converts, belonging to the Missions, had been brutally tortured and murdered, it was decided to destroy these two temples and the large white pagoda attached to them, as a punishment and a warning to the people of the neighbourhood. This destruction was effectually carried out by a party of Bengal Sappers and Miners.

A party of Americans had also been out on an expedition to the north-east, from which they returned on the 21st September. They found the country quite quiet, and the people busy with the harvest.

On the 18th September the 20th Punjab Infantry reached Sin-ho, and on the 20th and two following days the remainder of the 3rd Infantry Brigade reached Wei-hai-wei. This brigade had sailed from Calcutta between the 13th and 24th August, and had arrived at Hongkong in the first days of September, where they were detained till the 15th.

On the 20th September the Pei-t'ang forts to the north of Tang-ku were captured, and occupied by a combined force of Russians, Germans, and French. No intimation of the intention to carry out this operation was received by the British or Italian commanders at Tien-tsin, before noon on the 19th, and as transport by rail was not available, the British and Italian commanders arranged to transport their troops by boat, to a point on the Pei-ho near Chân-liang-chêng, and to march from there direct to Pei-t'ang. This force, which consisted of 1,100 British and 870 Italian troops, left Tien-tsin a little before midnight on the 19th, but owing to the darkness and the difficulty of landing, were much delayed, and did not reach Pei-t'ang till the following afternoon, by which time the forts were already in the hands of the allies who had used the railway. After halting for the night, the British troops returned to Tien-tsin on the 21st September. The Russians after the capture of the forts pushed along the railway to Lu-tai in the direction of Tong-shan.

All this time the British and Japanese were working on the railway between Feng-tai and Huang-tsun, collecting railway plant, and repairing the permanent way, but on the 20th September the Russian Commander issued a formal protest against the British and Japanese working on the line at all, the management of which he said had been handed over to the Russians by agreement of the Admirals. This was not the case, as that agreement had only referred to the line from Tang-ku to Tien-tsin, and General Gaselee informed General Liniévitch that he intended to go on with the reconstruction, on which his troops were engaged. It was of the greatest importance that the railway should be opened for traffic before the river was closed by ice, and the progress of the Russians was so slow that little hope of accomplishing this existed.

Mr. Kinder, who had originally built the railway, and who had managed it up to the outbreak of the war, undertook to repair the line from Tang-ku to Peking, and also that from Tang-ku to Shan-hai-kuan, within two months, provided the workshops and material at Tong-shan were found intact, which there was every reason to believe they were. This offer was strongly supported by General Gaselee, General Chaffee, and Sir Claude MacDonald, but pending the arrival of Count von Waldersee, nothing was done.

In the meantime the Russians were moving up the line towards Tong-shan and Shan-hai-kuan.

On the 23rd September Major-General Richardson and the staff of the Cavalry Brigade arrived at Peking with the 16th Bengal Lancers.

On the 25th General Gaselee proceeded on a visit to Tien-tsin. On the same day His Excellency Field Marshal Count von Waldersee arrived at Taku, and reached Tien-tsin on the 27th.

Meanwhile arrangements were actively proceeding in Peking and elsewhere for the housing and maintenance of the British troops remaining in garrison in North China for the winter.

In the middle of September General Gaselee gave it as his opinion, that a sufficient British garrison for North China, during the winter would consist of one infantry brigade, one cavalry regiment, one field battery, and one regiment of

Pioneers. He proposed to fix his own headquarters at Shanghai, as being the most central point from which to exercise command over his widely-scattered force. The reason for these recommendations were that—

1. Military operations in Chi-li were practically over, and, at any rate, the winter months are unsuitable for campaigning.
2. The climate of North China in winter is extremely rigorous, and the Indian troops might be expected to suffer greatly from the intense cold
3. Owing to the freezing-up of the mouth of the Pei-ho and the sea along the coast, the troops would be locked up in Chi-li for several months, and would not be available for service elsewhere if required.
4. With the railway unrepaired and means of communication very incomplete, the question of keeping a large force properly supplied might present great difficulties.

In view, however, of the large forces which the other Powers proposed to retain in North China, Her Majesty's Government decided on the following distribution of the British Contingent:—

In Chi-li.—1st and 4th Infantry Brigades, Cavalry Brigade, including the Horse Artillery Battery, 12th Field Battery, three companies of Sappers, Jodhpur Lancers, Maler Kotla Sappers, &c.

At Wei-hai-wei.—3rd Infantry Brigade, Hongkong Regiment, and heavy guns.

At Shanghai.—2nd Infantry Brigade.

This was practically the actual distribution during the winter, except that some troops, including the 1st Bengal Lancers, one company of Madras Sappers, &c., were sent to Hongkong and Shanghai, and the 3rd Infantry Brigade wintered at Shan-hai-kuan, while the Hongkong Regiment were at Tien-tsin instead of at Wei-hai-wei, which was garrisoned by the 28th Madras Infantry and the 1st Madras Pioneers.

The approximate strength of the Allies' Contingents which were present in China at the time of Field-Marshal Count von Waldersee's arrival at Taku, at the end of September, was as follows :—

American.

    4 battalions of Infantry.
    1½ regiments of Cavalry.
    1 Field Artillery battery (6 guns).
    1 company of Engineers.

British.

½ battalion of British Infantry.
½   „   of Australian Naval Brigade.
18 battalions of Native Infantry from India.
16 squadrons of Native Cavalry   „   „
1 Horse Artillery battery ⎫
1 Field Artillery battery ⎬ 14 field guns.
2 Naval 12-pr. guns ⎭
4 1-pr. Maxim-Nordenfelts.
21 Maxim guns.
12 siege   „
4 companies of Sappers.

French.

11 battalions of Infantry.
2 squadrons of Cavalry.
6 batteries of Artillery.
2 companies of Engineers.

German.

10 battalions of Infantry.
3 squadrons of Cavalry.
7 batteries of Artillery (40 guns).
3½ companies technical troops.

Italian.

2 battalions of Infantry.
4 Gardner guns.

Japanese.

13 battalions of Infantry.
3 squadrons of Cavalry.
9 batteries of Artillery (54 guns).
1 heavy battery (4 guns).
3 companies Pioneers.
½ Railway battalion.

Russian.

8 battalions of Infantry.
3 squadrons of Cavalry.
3 batteries of Artillery (22 guns).
4 technical companies.

CHAPTER X.

Course of Events in North China preceding Negotiations for Peace.

Before proceeding to describe "the further development of military operations it is necessary to refer more in detail to the contingents despatched to North China by the various Powers in consequence of the Boxer outbreak and the attack on the Peking Legations.

By the 12th June, 1900, it was known that the Legations were cut off from communication with their Governments, and there was reason to fear that the foreign envoys, with their families and the members of their staffs, and all other Europeans resident in the city had been made prisoners by the Chinese, and were probably in great danger of being murdered. It was therefore impossible to foresee the limits to which subsequent operations might not extend.

By the end of June the Japanese Government had ordered the mobilisation of 13,000 troops, including those already despatched to China, and they were directed to be in readiness for immediate embarkation should their services be required. By the middle of July the troops already sent from Japan, or under orders to proceed to Taku, numbered 22,000 men.

At the same time the Russian troops of the Amur Military District were ordered to be put on a war footing.

On the 16th June the Government of the United States issued orders to the commander of the American troops in the Philippines, to despatch an infantry regiment to Taku, and this was to be followed by large reinforcements from the garrisons of the Philippines and the United States, bringing up the strength of the contingent to a total of about 15,000 men. But, owing to the rapidity with which the Legations were relieved, and the armed resistance of the Chinese was crushed, only about one-third of this force ever reached Chi-li.

By the end of June France had decided to send two battalions of infantry and two batteries to Taku, from her troops in Tonkin, and a similar force from France, which, with some 600 troops already despatched, brought up the strength of her force in North China to about 4,000 men. These detachments were subsequently followed by a much stronger expeditionary force, under the command of Major General Voyron, which brought up the total strength of the French contingent to about 18,000 men.

Early in July the German Government decided to send a brigade, 7,000 strong, to North China, under command of Major-General von Höpfner, but this was subsequently increased, by the arrival of the main expeditionary force, to a total of about 20,000 men.

The Italian Government decided to send a force of about 2,000 men to China.

Great Britain, in addition to the garrisons of Hongkong and Wei-hai-wei, at first despatched from India a force of two infantry brigades, with line of communication and divisional troops. This was afterwards increased by two more infantry brigades, bringing the total strength of the British contingent in China up to about 21,000 men.

The total allied contingents, stated in round numbers, therefore amounted to about 100,000 fighting men.

At the end of June Lord Salisbury suggested to Japan that she should send an additional force of 20,000 men for the relief of the Peking Legations, as, owing to her geographical position, she alone was able to land a large force in Chi-li at short notice. Lord Salisbury at the same time informed the Governments of the various European Powers of the suggestion made by the British Government to Japan, and of the reason for making it. Germany replied that as no particulars of the proposed Japanese intervention were in their possession they were unable to judge whether the interests of third Powers would be affected by it, or whether the responsibility of supporting it could be undertaken by Germany. Russia welcomed the co-operation of Japan, but raised the objection that if Japan received a mandate from the other Powers for separate action in China, she might demand special conditions. It was explained that there was no suggestion of Her Majesty's Government that any mandate should be given to Japan, nor that she should be asked to undertake any operations beyond the relief of the Legations, nor was it intended that she should be entitled to any special privileges for her services.

On the 15th July, the Admirals at Taku unanimously agreed to ask the Japanese Admiral to telegraph to his Government, for the immediate despatch to Taku of the Japanese division of 13,000 men, mentioned above.

On the 9th July, the President of the United States received a telegram from the Emperor of China, appealing to him, through the long-continued friendship which had existed between the two countries, to bring about a concert of the Powers for the restoration of peace and order in China. This was very probably the real desire of Kuang-hsü, but he was quite unable to do anything to further it, and the telegram was only allowed to be sent, by the officials of the Empress Dowager's party, in order to throw dust in the eyes of the foreign Powers. On the next day the following Imperial decree was published : " It is written in the Confucian work ' Spring and Autumn ' that envoys shall not be killed. How can it then be supposed that the Throne's policy is to connive at allowing the troops and populace to vent their wrath upon the foreign Ministers ? For a month past, excepting the murder of the German Minister by the riotous people, which offence is being vigorously investigated, the other Ministers are being protected by the Throne with a ceaseless energy, and fortunately have suffered no harm."

This decree was of course carefully telegraphed to all the foreign Courts in Europe, though, on the very day on which it was issued, the Legations were being subjected to a particularly heavy bombardment by the Krupp guns of the Chinese Imperial Army. These communications were subsequently followed by several others of the same nature, all equally unsupported by any active measures, on the part of the Chinese Government, to enforce them.

While these events were happening in Chi-li the Russians occupied the treaty port of Niu-chuang, at the northern end of the Liao-tung peninsula.

Boxer agents had begun to spread their doctrines in the town and neighbourhood of Niu-chuang about the middle of June, and soon afterwards the missionaries from the interior, and the foreign employés on the Tien-tsin—Niu-chuang railway-line had begun to come into the port, to avoid attack by hostile Chinese. On the 30th June the Protestant Missions at Mukden were destroyed by a Chinese mob, and on the 2nd July the French Mission at the same place was attacked and burnt, and the bishop and his staff were murdered. All missionaries now retired from their stations. Those north of Mukden withdrew with the Russian railway people on Harbin and Vladivostock, and, though there was no further loss of life among the foreigners, their houses and property were all destroyed.

The women and children were sent away from Niu-chuang about the end of June, and the men guarded the foreign quarter, with the sailors from the Russian and Japanese gunboats.

South of Mukden the Russian railway employés had gradually fallen back before the Chinese to Ta-shih-ch'iao, the junction of the line from Niu-chuang and Port Arthur, which the Russians held with a strong detachment of troops.

On the 26th July the Russian Colonel Mischenkoff, with 400 or 500 Russian troops, attacked a stockade occupied by the tao-tai's troops, close to the mud wall of the town, and followed this action by moving a military force into the foreign settlement for its protection.

On the 28th the Russian Consul wrote to the tao-tai demanding the surrender of a Russian captive, reported to be in the city in the hands of the Chinese, on pain of the bombardment of the town. The threat of bombardment caused the greatest consternation and excitement among the Chinese, and finally led to an attack on the foreign quarter by the mob, mostly composed of Boxers, on the 4th August. This attack was easily repulsed, but the tao-tai fled, and the same afternoon the Russian gunboats opened fire on the city, which was then surrendered.

The same evening the Russians hoisted their flag on the Chinese Customs, under protest of all the Treaty Power Consuls.

On the 5th August Vice-Admiral Alexieff arrived from Port Arthur to confirm the Russian action.

On the 28th August the Russian Chargé d'Affaires in London explained to the Foreign Office that the occupation of Niu-chuang by the Russians had been forced upon them by the attack of the rebels on Russian troops; and that the despatch of Russian troops into Manchuria was solely due to the hostilities of the Chinese, including the unprovoked bombardment of Blagovieshchensk. M. Lessar also stated that these temporary measures had been solely dictated by the absolute necessity of repelling the aggression of the Chinese rebels, and not with any interested motives, which are absolutely foreign to the policy of the Imperial Government.

At this period there was much uncertainty as to the intentions of the foreign Governments with regard to China, and on the 2nd August the following statement of policy was made on behalf of the British Government in the House of Commons :—

"Great Britain will, in concert with other Powers, press forward by every means the relief of the Legations at Peking, and regards it as imperative to impress upon China the sanctity of Envoys, and the power of Europe to protect or avenge them.

"As regards the Yang-tse district and the adjacent region, assurances have been given to the Viceroys that the ships and forces of Great Britain will co-operate as far as possible with them in quieting unrest and securing order, and provision is being made for the due fulfilment of this assurance.

"Her Majesty's Government are opposed to any partition of China, and believe that they are in accord with other Powers in this declaration.

"Her Majesty's Government consider that the future government of China, whether directed from Peking or decentralised, must be a government by the Chinese, and they are not prepared to substitute for this an European administration.

"Similarly they hold that, in the common interest, much caution should be observed in any scheme which may be entertained for organising Chinese troops under foreign officers.

"Compensation must be made by China for the effects of the existing disturbances."

This declaration was followed on the 4th August by a statement that the British Government intended to give the Yang-tse Viceroys every support in maintaining peace and order in the Yang-tse basin, and in return the Viceroy Chang Chih-tung undertook to maintain the existing arrangements with Her Majesty's Government, in spite of any orders he might receive from Peking.

At this time the question of having a Commander-in-Chief in supreme command of all the allied forces began to be mooted. It was thought that more homogeneous results would be obtained, if the forces of all the Powers were under the direct control of one head. On the 7th August, Her Majesty's Minister at Berlin was informed, by Herr von Dermthall, that the Emperor of Russia had cordially agreed to place the Russian troops, operating in the Chi-li Province, under the supreme command of Field Marshal Count Waldersee, whose services had been offered to the Allied Powers by the German Emperor. The British Minister was at the same time requested to ascertain the views of Her Majesty's Government with regard to the appointment. On the 9th August Lord Salisbury, in reply, agreed to place the British troops in Chi-li under the supreme direction of Count Waldersee, provided that all the other Powers agreed to do the same, and the Governments of Austria, Italy, Japan, and the United States, whose views had also been asked for, replied in the same sense. A little later France notified to Germany that the officer in command of the French forces in North China would co-operate with the Field Marshal.

In the meantime the reactionary Court party in Peking were losing heart. The capture of the Legations appeared to be improbable, and the confident boast that they would sweep the country clear of the foreigner seemed unlikely to be realised. An apparent change of policy was thus brought about, and the party in favour of peace, having at last gained some ascendency, were making urgent proposals to the Powers to assist the Chinese Government in restoring order.

Their efforts had little effect, however, in stopping the continuous attacks on the Legations, and they invariably received the reply that no negotiations could be begun, until the Powers were placed in full and direct communication with their Ministers in Peking. It was daily becoming more evident that the cause of China was lost, that her resistance was falling to pieces, and that the day of reckoning, when she would have to sue for peace on any terms, was rapidly drawing near. At length, on the 7th August, the day after the defeat of the Chinese at Yang-tsun, an Imperial edict was issued appointing Li Hung-chang as Minister Plenipotentiary, to negotiate with the Powers for the suspension of hostilities, and to arrange satisfactory settlements for the approval of the Emperor. Shortly afterwards Prince Ch'ing was also appointed co-plenipotentiary with Li Hung-chang, and, by edicts dated the 31st August and 9th and 13th September, Liu K'un-yi, Chan Chih-tung, and Jung-lu were appointed Minister Plenipotentiaries to assist and co-operate with the two ministers already appointed.

Considerable anxiety was now felt, as to the effect the march of a relieving force on the capital might have on the fate of the Europeans shut up in the city. It was well known that they were hard pressed, and were possibly prisoners in the hands of the Chinese, who, if driven to extremities, might seek to avenge themselves by murdering them. Recognising this possibility the Japanese Government proposed to the other Powers, on the 11th August, that, as the advance of an allied army on Peking would

probably be the signal for the massacre of all the foreigners in the capital, and would cause the flight of the Emperor and Empress-Dowager into the interior, and a widespread outburst of anarchy, the Powers should agree to an armistice for a time, pending further negotiations, on condition :—
1. That the Chinese Government should order all their troops and the rebels to retire to a certain distance, to be determined by the commanders of the forces.
2. That a combined force should have free liberty to proceed to Peking, and escort the Ministers and foreigners back to Tien-tsin.

Long before these suggestions could be discussed or acted upon, the question had been settled by the entry of the relieving force into Peking, the rescue of the refugees in the Legations, and the final overthrow of the Chinese troops and Boxers, who were dispersing in all directions.

On the 19th August, immediately on receiving the news of the entry of the allied force into Peking, Li Hung-chang had the effrontery to telegraph to the Powers that, as they had all declared that the sole object for sending their forces to Peking was to rescue their Ministers, and, as this object had now been accomplished, and they had found their Ministers and others well and unharmed, hostilities should now cease and negotiations commence.

He requested that the Powers would each at once appoint a plenipotentiary to discuss the question of a settlement with himself at Peking, whither he was about to proceed.

On the 21st Li further telegraphed that the Court had left Peking, the Boxers were dispersed, and there was no further need for military operations. Therefore, he requested that all foreign troops should at once be withdrawn from the capital. In reply he was informed that, as the Chinese Government had done nothing to carry out the demands of the Powers to protect the foreign Legations in Peking, but the Powers had been compelled to rescue their Ministers by force of arms, unaided by the Chinese Government, the circumstances were entirely altered, and the question of a final settlement now rested on a different basis.

This question of future diplomatic action on the part of the foreign Powers with regard to China was, however, by no means an easy one to settle. The flight of the Emperor and the Court from Peking had left no responsible Government, with which the discussion of terms could take place, and, as yet, the Powers were not inclined to accept the plenipotentiaries appointed to conduct negotiations, as they had no guarantee that they were invested with full powers to represent the Emperor. The Chinese Government, moreover, did not appear to fully realise the very serious position in which they were placed, by their unprovoked assumption of hostilities against unprotected foreigners, living peacefully in their country under rights secured by treaty.

At first an idea prevailed in Europe that nothing could be done until the Court could be induced to return to Peking, and this view was strongly favoured by Russia, who was most anxious that all the Powers should at once issue orders to their Ministers and military commanders, to withdraw their Legations and troops from the capital to Tien-tsin, and to conduct negotiations from the latter place. She even issued orders to this effect to her own Minister and to the Russian General commanding her troops in Chi-li, and on the 29th August the Russian Government made the following declaration of her policy in China :—

"Having achieved the relief of the Legations, and aided the Chinese Government in suppressing rebellion, it is best now to withdraw the Legations and troops to Tien-tsin, so as to permit the Emperor and Empress-Dowager to return to Peking, after which negotiations can be entered upon.

"It has been necessary to occupy with Russian troops Niu-chuang and certain railways in North China, but the rights of foreign states and international companies in Niu-chuang, and in the railways repaired by Russian troops, remain inviolable.

"It is the intention of Russia to withdraw from Chinese territory as soon as pacification has been effected, provided such action does not meet with obstacles arising from the proceedings of the Powers.

"The Russian Government adheres to the principles announced by them from the first, viz. :—

1. The maintenance of the Agreement between the Powers;
2. The maintenance of the existing Government in China;
3. The prevention of the partition of the empire;
4. The establishment, by common effort, of a legitimate central power, capable in itself of assuring order and security to the country."

The remainder of the Powers nearly all agreed in principle to the declaration of policy made by Russia, except with regard to the withdrawal of their troops and Ministers from the capital. There appeared to be no cause to suppose that this withdrawal would accelerate negotiations for peace ; in fact, it was generally thought that it would have exactly the opposite effect, as the Chinese would most certainly view their retreat as a sign of weakness.

In the discussions which followed, Japan suggested that the Powers should bring pressure to bear on the Emperor and Empress-Dowager to induce them to return at once to Peking and form a responsible Government, in which case the troops would evacuate the city. The Court was known to be at or near Tai-yuan fu in the Shan-hsi province, but it was not clear how pressure could be brought to bear, so as to induce them to return to the capital; it was, however, decided that, before coming to any decision, the views of the Ministers at Peking should be ascertained.

In the beginning of September General Liniévitch officially announced that he had been instructed to retain 15,000 men in Peking during the winter; but the orders of his Government for withdrawal had not then reached him.

On the 4th September the Russian Minister announced that he was ordered to withdraw to Tien-tsin, and on the 10th of the month the French Government, in deference to the wishes of Russia, issued orders to her Minister at Peking to withdraw to Tien-tsin, with his Legation and all French troops. The other Powers had in the meanwhile decided that they would not withdraw from Peking, pending the settlement of negotiations with the Chinese Government, and, on the same date, the Marquis of Salisbury telegraphed to St. Petersburg that the British Government had decided to retain its Legation and troops at the capital.

Russia assured the other Powers that the withdrawal of her troops and Minister from Peking did not signify a separate course of policy towards China. Finally, at the end of September, the Russian Minister left Peking for Tien-tsin, and the Russian troops were withdrawn from the capital, leaving behind only one battalion, two Maxims, and half a company of sappers, or about 1,200 men in all.

CHAPTER XI.

Course of Events in other parts of China.

The widespread upheaval in the north had naturally caused great excitement throughout the empire, and the wildest reports, as to the doings of the Boxers, and their victories over the "foreign devils," were everywhere in circulation. In view of the universal distrust and hatred of foreigners throughout China, it was felt that the disturbances would almost certainly spread to the Yang-tse valley, and probably to Canton and the West River as well, the provinces of Kuang-hsi and Kuang-tung in the south being notoriously turbulent, and always ripe for rebellion. Hu-nan and Kiang-hsi to the south of the Yang-tse are also notably anti-foreign provinces, and might be expected to give trouble.

To protect British interests on the Yang-tse H.M.S. "Hermione" and "Linnet" were ordered, on the 15th June, to proceed to Nanking and Hankow respectively and to convey to Liu K'un-yi and Chang Chih-tung, the Viceroys at these places, assurances of the assistance of the British Government in maintaining peace in their jurisdictions.

On the 24th June the British consuls at Canton, Chung-king, and Ningpo all applied for gunboats, to protect British life and property at these treaty ports, but as no vessels were then available they were informed that gunboats could not be sent, but that in case of danger all Europeans must withdraw for safety to Hongkong or Shanghai. As a matter of fact, none of these places were ever seriously threatened.

In the meantime the Viceroys on the Yang-tse had a difficult part to play, as they remained perfectly loyal towards the Emperor and the Empress-Dowager, but, at the same time, being convinced of the hopelessness of China's success in a war against the united Powers of Europe, they determined to maintain peace, at all cost, in the central provinces, and to protect the lives and property of foreigners. They therefore decided to incur the great personal risk of refusing to obey the Imperial orders, sent from Peking, directing them to make war on all foreigners. In justification of their action, they declared that the decrees were sent out by Prince Tuan, whom they looked upon as a rebel to his country, and had not the sanction of the Emperor. One stipulation which they always insisted upon was a guarantee of the personal respect and safety of the Emperor and Empress-Dowager. They were supported by the Viceroy at Canton, Li Hung-chang, and by the governor of the Shan-tung province, Yuan Shih-k'ai, the latter of whom refused to obey the orders of the Court to march his army on Nanking, with the object of coercing the Viceroys.

The Viceroys also requested the British Government to hold a force in readiness to support them, in case of necessity, against a widespread Boxer rebellion. At the same time they requested that neither troops nor men-of-war should be sent up the Yang-tse River, unless their presence there became absolutely necessary. They pointed out that they were themselves able to keep order and to deal with any ordinary disturbances, but that the appearance of foreign soldiers or ships in the interior would most probably cause consternation and unrest among the people, and might precipitate a war.

All along the Yang-tse military preparations for defence were actively going on. Chinese troops were everywhere drilling, recruits were being enlisted in large numbers, and the armaments of the forts were being increased. It was noticed that the Wu-sung and Kiang-yin forts on the Yang-tse, and the Bogue forts at the mouth of the West River, were fully armed and garrisoned, but a good deal of this activity was no doubt due to orders issued by subordinate commanders, and not by the Viceroys themselves. Of course many of the Chinese officials were extremely hostile towards all foreigners, and sympathised with the anti-foreign party in the Court, and the Boxer movement in the north. One of the most important officials of this class was Li Ping-hêng, in chief command at the Kiang-yin forts. He had formerly been governor of the Shan-tung province, was strongly anti-foreign, and a staunch supporter of the Empress-Dowager. He several times telegraphed to Liu K'un-yi, the Viceroy at Nanking, for permission to open fire on any foreign men-of-war coming up the river, but to each application received a peremptory order not to commence hostilities. Finally, in disgust, he threw up his command and departed to Peking, where he impeached the Yang-tse Viceroys as traitors to the empire. His arrival at the capital, towards the end of the siege, was supposed to have been marked by a fresh outburst of energy on the part of the Chinese in their attacks upon the Legations, and he was said to be in high favour at Court, and to be received in almost daily audience by the Empress-Dowager herself. When news of the approach of the Allies was received in Peking, Li Ping-hêng was ordered to take command in the field and to oppose their advance, and he was reported to have died of a wound received in the neighbourhood of Tung-chou, about the 11th August, 1900.

At the end of June the unrest in the Yang-tse valley was very great. Large quantities of arms and ammunition were being sent up country from the arsenal at Shanghai to various destinations, and fresh guns were being mounted at the Wu-sung forts below the city. When this was brought to the notice of the Nanking Viceroy, he said it was being done without his knowledge and promised to issue orders to stop the work. At the same time it is undoubtedly the fact that large subsidies were continually being forwarded to the north, for the use of the Court. These chiefly went by way of the Grand Canal, and at first consisted of reinforcements of troops, while later on, after the Court had fled from Peking to Hsi-an fu, quantities of money, food, and supplies of all sorts were forwarded up the Han river to the capital of the Shen-hsi province.

It may be noticed that the levies sent north from the Yang-tse towards Chi-li consisted of raw recruits, untrained and badly armed. The prospect of fighting against the foreign troops was not viewed with enthusiasm by the Chinese soldiery, and the Viceroys were keeping all their own well-drilled and well-equipped troops to maintain order in their own provinces; but the question of paying these troops, and so keeping them contented, was causing them great anxiety.

Many of the soldiers were known to be secret-society men, and, though they had no particular sympathy with the "Boxers," they would probably cause trouble if their pay was withheld. Still, from loss of trade and revenue, due to the unsettled state of the country, the provincial treasuries were completely empty, and no money was available. Under these circumstances it became necessary to apply to Great Britain for a loan, and on the 10th August Lord Salisbury agreed to lend the Viceroy Chang Chih-tung, through the Hongkong and Shanghai Bank, the sum of 75,000$l.$ at $4\frac{1}{2}$ per cent., assured on the li-kin revenues of his provinces not already appropriated to the payment of interest on other loans.

In the month of June great excitement prevailed among the Chinese residents in Shanghai. There were several thousand regular Chinese troops quartered near the city, and at Wu-sung, all armed with modern rifles and provided with artillery. In times of trouble the presence of soldiers is always a cause of anxiety to the peaceful Chinese, and many of them began to remove their goods and families elsewhere. This action on their part alarmed the foreign residents, who demanded that guards of foreign troops should be sent to Shanghai for their protection. When the proposal was submitted to Liu K'un-yi he objected to it, as he said that the landing of foreign troops would probably precipitate the outbreak of hostilities, which it was designed to prevent; and further he represented that, although he had no great objection to the landing of a purely British force at Shanghai, he feared it would be at once followed by demands from other nations, to land contingents of their troops as well, and this would probably cause endless trouble; but it would obviously be very difficult to refuse the same concession to other Powers as that which had been granted to Great Britain.

Finally, on the 27th July, he agreed to the landing of a British force for the protection of Shanghai, the numbers being left to the discretion of the British Consul-General.

Admiral Sir E. Seymour had been informed that the British Government had no intention of sending a squadron up the Yang-tse River, or of attempting to garrison the valley with troops, but that everything was to be done to support the policy of the Viceroys in maintaining peace and allaying popular excitement. He was therefore at liberty to withdraw all his ships from the river, leaving only one powerful vessel at each of the four treaty ports of Chin-kiang, Nanking, Kiu-kiang, and Hankow, to render assistance to the European residents in case of emergency. At the same time the British Consul at Canton was informed that he could assure the Chinese officials of that city that there was no intention, on the part of the British, to commence hostilities in central or southern China, or to occupy Shanghai without the concurrence of the Viceroys.

The British Government again assured the Viceroys of their support in maintaining peace and order in the Yang-tse basin, and of their protection, should they find it necessary to disobey the orders of their own Government, and on the 2nd August Sir E. Seymour visited Liu K'un-yi at Nanking, and discussed the question of the defence of Shanghai and other treaty-ports with him. The Viceroy again agreed to the landing of a British force at Shanghai; but a week later he suddenly became alarmed and telegraphed to Lord Salisbury requesting him to countermand the disembarkation, and to trust the Viceroys to maintain peace themselves. Orders were in consequence sent to the British commanders that the troops were not to land at Shanghai, but were to proceed to Wei-hai-wei, but this action caused great consternation among the residents of the former place, who said that the cancelling of the order at the last moment, when the troops were on the point of landing, would appear to the Chinese to be such a sign of weakness, that it would probably encourage the badly disposed to break out into rebellion. The despatch of the troops to Wei-hai-wei was accordingly cancelled, and the whole of the Second Brigade of the China Expeditionary Force began to land at Shanghai on the 18th August. The French landed a force of 600 Marine infantry, a mountain battery, and a company of Annamite troops on the 30th August, and these were followed later by contingents from the Japanese and German forces.

While these events were taking place at Shanghai considerable anxiety was felt for the safety of foreigners in the interior.

In the provinces under Chang Chih-tung all the missionaries were withdrawn by the end of June, and their mission premises were handed over, for safe keeping, to the Chinese authorities. The Viceroy did all in his power to maintain order, and gave great assistance to other parties of missionaries who fled into his jurisdiction from the north, from the disaffected provinces of Shan-hsi, Shen-hsi, and Ho-nan. Thus many owed their lives to his protection. In the more remote districts there were a few cases of anti-foreign disturbances, due to the Imperial edict of the 24th June, which was published in a few places by local officials who were hostile towards foreigners.

In Hu-pei there were some cases of plundering of foreign property, and on the 3rd July the London Mission chapel at Heng-chou was burnt by a Chinese mob, and the following day the large Roman Catholic orphanage and mission at the same place were destroyed, and two priests were murdered. The Italian Roman Catholic bishop was also tortured to death about the same time.

The tao-tai, prefect, and magistrates then issued inflammatory proclamations, with the result that over 30 Protestant chapels were destroyed in the Heng-chou circuit, and a cruel persecution of the converts commenced. The anti-foreign Manchu governor of Hu-nan would do nothing to bring the guilty officials to punishment, but reported the execution of four of the rioters, though it was notorious that the men belonged to the *Ko-lao-hui*, (a secret society), and were beheaded on that account.

In the beginning of July there was considerable anti-foreign excitement in the Kiang-hsi province. The Imperial edict ordering the destruction of all foreigners, although ignored by the higher officials, had apparently reached the ears of the populace. On the 11th July the Roman Catholic premises at Jao-chou were burnt by the mob, and several native Christians were killed, but the priests and sisters had escaped to Kiu-kiang. In the beginning of August the feeling of unrest at this treaty-port had greatly subsided, owing to the action of the Chinese officials, and the removal of a troublesome band of 500 Hunanese soldiers, which had been quartered close to the foreign concession.

By the beginning of July all the treaty ports were protected by men-of-war, except Chung-king, and the British Consul, Mr. M. F. A. Fraser, was informed that, as it was impracticable to send a gunboat up there, he must retire, in case of necessity, to a place of safety further down the river. For this purpose the s.s. "Pioneer," capable of carrying all the Europeans at Chung-king, was retained at the port and placed at his disposal. He finally left Chung-king on the 3rd August, in consequence of alarmist rumours of native risings in the interior of Ssu-ch'uan. Many British and American missionaries had already left by native boat for the lower Yang-tse, and several of these were picked up by the "Pioneer" on her passage down stream, till she finally arrived at Ichang on the 5th August with 90 passengers on board. The French and Japanese consuls, with all the Roman Catholic priests under their bishop, and some other Europeans, preferred to remain at their posts, and tided over the crisis without molestation by the Chinese.

Towards the end of July the Consul-General at Shanghai had arranged for the withdrawal of all the women and children from the ports on the Yang-tse, but the danger of a general exodus was that it might be construed by the Chinese as a sign of impending hostilities, and the evacuation of Ku-ling, a summer station near Kiu-kiang, caused some excitement. The British and Americans left in some numbers, but the French, Belgians, and Italians mostly remained, and no actual outbreak against foreigners occurred.

While the Viceroys were doing their utmost to maintain order in the Yang-tse valley, a terrible outrage occurred at the town of Ch'ü-chou in the west of the Che-kiang province. The governor of Che-kiang, Liu Shu-t'ang, was a weak old man, who resided at Hang-chou. He was anxious to retire from public life, and he was surrounded by many anti-foreign officials, of whom the principal were the fen-tai or provincial treasurer, Yün Tsu-yi, and the nieh-tai, or provincial judge, Jung-ch'üan. The tao-tai, Ch'ing-lai, was well disposed towards foreigners.

It can thus be easily supposed that the maintenance of order and the suppression of anti-foreign risings were not very rigorously enforced in the province, and between the 21st and 23rd July eleven English and American members of the China Inland Mission were murdered at Ch'ü-chou by the local train-bands, which had been organised to defend the town against a rising of the secret society of *Vegetarians*.

There had been a rising of brigands, or secret society men, on the borders of Che-kiang, and they had sacked the town of Kiang-shan, about 90 *li* south-west of Ch'ü-chou; to protect the latter place, which was never attacked, the local officials and gentry raised a force of militia, or *t'uan-lien*. This force was then used by them to attack an unpopular magistrate of the name of Wu, who was butchered with over thirty of his retainers. Wu was friendly towards the missionaries, and so they were next attacked.

Mr. Thompson, his wife, and two children, and Miss Desmond were murdered in the tao-tai's yamen, in the city, on the 21st July, by the local militia and mob, practically in the presence of the Chinese officials and local gentry, who did nothing to save them, but in many cases encouraged their assailants. The same day two American missionary ladies, Miss Sherwood and Miss Manchester, were attacked in their house, but, though badly wounded, succeeded in escaping, and hid in the temple of the city god till the 23rd, when they were discovered, dragged out, and stabbed to death. While these things were happening at Ch'ü chou, Mrs. Ward, with her child, and Miss Thirgood had left Chang-shan, a town lying further to the west, by boat, as that place was on the point of being attacked by banditti. They arrived at Ch'ü-chou on the morning of the 22nd, and were there attacked and murdered by the militia. Mr. Ward, who was travelling by road, was also murdered at the village of San-shan-mo-chia, 15 *li* west of Ch'ü-chou.

The governor of Che-kiang, Liu Shu-t'ang, at once removed from office the chen-tai, tao-tai, and chih-fu of Ch'ü-chou, and expressed his sorrow at what had occurred, promising to punish the murderers. He was considered, however, to be responsible for what had happened, as the weakness of his policy had failed to prevent the outbreak, and in the beginning of December he was dismissed from his appointment.

Later on the Ministers at Peking demanded the banishment and degradation of the ex-governor, Liu Shu-t'ang, and of the ex-provincial judge Jung-ch'üan, and the confiscation of their property; the degradation and banishment of the Manchu brigadier, Yü Chun-ming, said to be out of his mind; the execution of the tao-tai, Pao Tsu-ling, and of the commander of the City Guard, Chou Chih-tê; the degradation and imprisonment of the prefect, Hung Szu-liang; and the degradation and banishment of the three gentry, Ch'êng Lien-shêng, Ch'êng Yung-hsi, and Lo Lao-su, and the confiscation of their property. To these punishments the Chinese Government eventually agreed.

About the beginning of August considerable uneasiness was felt, owing to reports of the activity of the "reform" party, who were said to be in league with the powerful secret society, the *Ko-lao-hui*, or "Society of the Elder brother."

A riot broke out at Ta-tung on the 9th August, owing to the refusal of a Chinese bank to honour a cheque, presented by the members of a secret society called the *Hsin-tang-hui*, who profess to be reformers and followers of K'ang Yu-wei. The tao-tai arrested nine members of the society, and the other members decided to attempt their rescue, and were helped by the crews of the numerous gunboats lying in the river, who supplied them with arms. The rioters then raided and looted the general and salt *li-kin* yamens and the Li-ho Bank, which had refused to cash their draft, and attempted to fire the town. Assistance was promptly sent from Nanking, and the rioters were dispersed by the troops with heavy loss. Numerous arrests were also made; 160 executions were reported to have taken place, and quiet was restored.

Several members of the *Hsin-tang-hui* and *Ko-lao-hui* also appeared at Wuhu about this time and attempted to raise a rebellion, but many of them were arrested by the officials and promptly executed, and the remainder took the hint and departed elsewhere.

The Chinese officials were very active, and many other arrests were made of suspected persons, at various places along the Yang-tse. It was also stated that the reformer K'ang Yu-wei was present in the valley, but all attempts to apprehend him failed.

The Ta-tung rebellion was said to have been part of a general rising, which was intended to take place at all the treaty-ports, but it broke out prematurely and so spoilt the whole scheme. The object of the reformers was supposed to be, to force the provincial authorities on the Yang-tse into war with the foreign Powers, and so to cause a general upheaval throughout the empire, in which the present Conservative Government would be destroyed and Kuang-hsü would be re-established on the throne, free from his anti-reform *entourage*.

The reformers were assisted by numbers of Japanese, and were well supplied with arms and ammunition, which had been imported from Japan. They even applied for assistance to the British authorities at Shanghai, but were warned that they could expect no sympathy from them, as the British were supporting the Viceroys in maintaining order. The Japanese Government was also asked to restrain its subjects from assisting in fomenting trouble in China, and promised to do so.

Another riot occurred at Kao-yo on the Grand Canal, said to have been got up by smugglers and *Ko-lao-hui* men, but it was suppressed without much difficulty.

About the middle of August "Boxer" placards appeared in Hankow and caused much alarm and excitement among the Chinese, but the Viceroy, Chang Chih-tung, at once had the city placarded with a strong anti-Boxer proclamation, which had an excellent effect in restoring confidence.

About a week later, however, a secret society plot was discovered, and a number of arrests were made in connexion with it, followed by several executions. Many important papers were also seized, along with flags, whistles, arms, ammunition, &c. The papers proved that the plot was connected with the Ta-tung rebellion, and several other risings planned to take place at different points. Most of the men arrested were natives of Canton and other places outside Hankow.

The proclamations issued by the "reformers" are curious, and are given below. From them it would appear that their intentions were not hostile towards foreigners, but, as they had enlisted large numbers of local blackguards and outlaws in their cause, it is very doubtful if they could have protected foreigners after the rebellion had begun.

PROCLAMATION ISSUED BY "REFORMERS" AT HANKOW, 24TH AUGUST 1900.

LADIES AND GENTLEMEN,
We, the members of the China Independent Association, in view of the Boxer movement, which has been clandestinely instigated and encouraged by Prince Tuan, Jung-lu, Kang-yi, and the whole pack of bigoted senile reactionists, have now risen in arms and do hereby inform you:

That we will no longer recognise the Manchu Government as a political organisation fit to rule over China.

It is our bounden duty to make a new China of the old: and to fill the land with happiness, instead of misery: and to make it a blessing to the Chinese Nation in particular, and to the world in general.

We resolve to reinstate H.M. Kuang-hsü as Emperor, and to construct a Constitutional Empire which in everything shall be made a model polity, worthy of the creation of the highest combined intelligence and enlightenment of the twentieth century. Its aim is to secure to the people civil freedom and constitutional liberty.

It is our firm conviction to agree with the Allied Powers, to put down the fanatical and insane movement, and to bring the anti-foreign and wicked usurpers of the Government to punishment.

All the foreign concessions in the Treaty Ports, churches of all kinds, and the life and property of foreigners and native Christians shall be protected from disturbance and injury.

We assure you, that you need not be afraid of our actions.

By the order of the Head of the Hankow Branch
of the China Independent Association.

Notice.

Notice is hereby given by the China Independent Association, that the intention of the Association to rise in arms is to save our beloved Emperor H.M. Kuang-hsü and to bring the anti-foreign and wicked usurpers of the Government to punishment.

Objects of the Association.

1. To maintain the independence of China.
2. To restore H.M. the Emperor Kuang-hsü to power.
3. To admit as a member any person anxious to preserve the integrity and independence of China.
4. To establish a firm union among the members, who must render mutual help to each other.
5. To treat with courtesy and humanity all harmless and good people who are not members of the Association.

Rules for action.

1. The life and property of all harmless people shall not be injured.
2. The life and property of foreigners shall be protected from disturbance or harm.
3. Churches shall be protected from being burnt, and native Christians from being disturbed or injured.
4. Lawlessness of all kinds, such as robbery, adultery, drunkenness, &c., shall be prohibited.
5. All foreign concessions in the Treaty Ports shall be protected from disturbance or injury.
6. Poisonous weapons, and cruel treatment towards the enemies shall be prohibited.
7. Captives shall be dealt with according to the Belligerent Laws of civilised nations, and shall by no means be murdered in a barbarous manner.
8. All tyrannical laws of the country shall be abolished in order to establish a civilised government.

By the order of the Head of the Hankow Branch
of the China Independent Association.

The events related above caused considerable panic in Hankow for a time, but, as nothing further occurred, confidence was soon restored.

Nothing of much importance happened at this period in the provinces to the south of the Yang-tse valley. The departure of the Viceroy, Li Hung-chang, from Canton, in the middle of July, caused some anxiety at Hongkong, as it was known that his strong rule had done much to restore quiet along the West River, and it was feared that on his departure the brigands and pirates would again cause trouble.

The Acting-Viceroy, however, continued to maintain excellent order, and no important outbreak took place. It was reported that the followers of the reformers, K'ang Yu-wei and Sun Yat-sen, were attempting to raise disturbances in the neighbourhood of Canton, and orders were issued by the British Government that no support was to be afforded them, and that any of their followers found in Hongkong were to be at once deported.

In July and August there was considerable persecution of Chinese Christians in the districts round Swatow, owing to the anti-foreign sympathies of the local tao-tai, but nothing very serious occurred, and, in consequence of orders issued by the Acting-Viceroy at Canton, tranquillity was soon restored.

In the interior of southern Che-kiang and Fu-kien provinces there was a certain amount of unrest, but the missionaries were not molested. Owing to reports of Boxer activity in the districts round about, Mr. P. E. O'Brien Butler, the British Consul at Wen-chou, removed to Shanghai, taking all the foreign residents at the port with him. No Boxer attack, however, took place, and the foreigners afterwards returned to find their property safe.

On the 25th August a Japanese temple was accidentally burnt in Amoy, and the Japanese naval commander landed a force of over three hundred men for the protection of foreigners. The feeling of the Chinese on the island was not hostile towards foreigners, and the fire was purely accidental, measures being at once taken to put it out. The action of the Japanese consequently caused a panic among the inhabitants, who began to leave in large numbers for the mainland, fearing that the Japanese intended annexation. The Chinese in the Fu-kien province look with great suspicion on the Japanese, whom they credit with designs on a protectorate over the province and the coast towns, on which Formosa is in a great measure dependent for her trade.

H.M.S. "Isis" landed 60 men at Amoy on the 30th August, for the protection of the British concession, and shortly afterwards, on representations having been made to the Japanese Government, all troops were withdrawn from the island and the state of affairs again became normal.

By the end of August the situation on the Yang-tse was quite peaceful. The action of the Viceroys and the presence of troops at Shanghai had restored confidence. The foreigners who had gone away at the commencement of the troubles gradually returned to the treaty ports, business began to revive, and there were no further outbreaks to cause anxiety.

On the 13th September the Viceroy Chang Chih-tung applied to the British Government for a further loan of 75,000*l*., and on the following day asked for another half-million *taels* in addition, undertaking to enter into no other loans without first consulting Her Majesty's Consul-General. As it was generally supposed that the money asked for was not for the payment of his troops, but for the use of the Imperial Court at Hsi-an, Her Majesty's Government declined to lend it, and informed the Viceroy that he was at liberty to raise it elsewhere if he felt so inclined.

There can be no doubt that to the Chinese officials alone, and especially to the Viceroys Liu K'un-yi and Chang Chih-tung, is due the credit of maintaining peace in the Yang-tse valley and the southern provinces. From the middle of June to the middle of August the political outlook was extremely critical, and the slightest encouragement, or even carelessness, on the part of the authorities, would have set the whole country in a blaze of rebellion. All anti-foreign demonstrations were, however, at once suppressed with a strong hand, before they could attain any serious proportions.

The success with which the Viceroys maintained the peace, during this period of dangerous unrest, affords a striking illustration of the fact that the officials, and not the people, are always responsible for anti-foreign risings in China, and that in cases where missionaries and other foreigners lose their lives at the hands of a Chinese mob, it is the punishment of the highest local authorities which should always be insisted upon, even more than that of the persons who actually commit the crime. Such crimes happen with the connivance, if not with the actual encouragement, of the local officials and gentry, and these men should always be held responsible, as they can invariably prevent the outbreaks if they wish to do so. Usually these responsible persons escape altogether, or with some slight nominal punishment, and the murderers are produced in the shape of criminals already condemned to death on some other charge, who are duly executed for the crime against the foreigner as well, with which they had nothing to do. The system is well understood, and the circumstances are carefully explained to the people, and so no real punishment for the crime is exacted. In the present instance the Viceroys chose to maintain peace; had they decided on war, the slightest hint from them would have been the signal for a general rising throughout central China, and for the massacre of every European in the Yang-tse basin.

Other illustrations of the influence of the local authorities are afforded by the outbreaks at Heng-chou and Ch'ü-chou. At the former place the attacks on the missions and the murders of the Roman Catholic priests were due to the direct encouragement of the officials, who afterwards atoned for the crime by the execution of some notorious criminals, who were unconnected with it.

The murders at Ch'ü-chou were, firstly, due to the want of firmness on the part of the governor of the province in enforcing the suppression of anti-foreign outbreaks ; and, secondly, to the connivance of the local officials and gentry at Ch'ü-chou itself, some of whom are reported to have actually incited the murderers to commit the crimes. The murders took place in one of the official yamens, actually in the presence of many of the local authorities, who made no attempt to protect the victims. That they could have done so is certain, as a Chinese mob is always perfectly under control of its officials, and thus, if the latter are not held personally responsible for crimes committed within their jurisdiction, the ends of justice are defeated and the guilty persons escape. In the case under consideration, when punishment and arrests began to be insisted on, the authorities took care to impress on the people that the punishments demanded were for the murder of the magistrate Wu, the case of the missionaries being passed over as a matter of no importance.

CHAPTER XII.

OCCUPATION OF SHAN-HAI-KUAN AND CHING-WANG-TAO AND ARRANGEMENTS FOR THE REPAIR AND WORKING OF THE RAILWAY FROM SHAN-HAI-KUAN TO PEKING.

Field-Marshal Count von Waldersee left Berlin for China on the 20th August, and embarked on the s.s. "Sachsen," after having paid a visit to the King of Italy at Rome.

Colonel J. M. Grierson, M.V.O., R.F.A., and Brevet Lieut.-Colonel C. H. Powell, Indian Staff Corps, were appointed British military representatives on the staff of the Field-Marshal. The French avoided appointing any officer, and the American army was also unrepresented; and it soon became apparent that the Russian officers considered their position ambiguous, as they asserted that the Field-Marshal was not now in command of the Russian troops at all, since that arrangement had only been made with the object of conducting operations for the relief of the Legations in Peking, and, as that had already been accomplished, the appointment no longer held good.

On his voyage out the Field-Marshal touched at various British ports, including Aden, Colombo, Penang, Singapore, and Hong-kong, and was everywhere received with marks of respect. At Hongkong he transferred his quarters to the German cruiser "Hertha," specially sent to meet him by order of the German Emperor.

Shanghai was reached on the 21st September, and here, on the following day, a complimentary parade was held in Count Waldersee's honour, as the troops forming the garrison were not under his orders. The troops on parade consisted of :—

British.—1 squadron 3rd Bombay Cavalry, and the 2nd Infantry Brigade (2nd Rajputs, 14th Sikhs, 30th Baluchis, and 1st Battalion 4th Gurkha Rifles).

French.—One battalion 8th Marine Infantry, and one battery of six mountain guns.

German.—1st and 2nd Companies 1st battalion 1st East Asian Regiment.

Shanghai Volunteers.—One mounted and seven dismounted companies.

The whole were under command of Major-General O'Moore Creagh, V.C.

On the 25th September the Field-Marshal arrived at Taku, and landed on the 27th, when he at once proceeded to Tien-tsin, where he was received by guards of honour of all nations.

The instructions sent to General Gaselee by the Secretary of State for India, regarding the appointment of Count Waldersee as Commander-in-Chief in North China, were as follows:—" Field-Marshal Count von Waldersee, of the " German Army, will shortly proceed to the north of China to " assume 'supreme direction' of the military operations to be " conducted in the Province of Chih-li. You will, as the " General Commanding the Forces of a loyal Ally, afford him " every support in carrying out the operations that he may " decide upon. You will foster, by every means in your power, " the most friendly relations and feelings of true comradeship " between all ranks under your command, and the soldiers of all " the foreign contingents employed in North China. The " command of the troops supplied by us will, however, rest " always with you, and the superior officers under your orders, " although their special sphere of action, or the part they are to " take in any particular operation, will be decided by Field-" Marshal Count von Waldersee, and all orders to the force " under your command should be given through you or your " Brigadiers. You will have complete control over your own " equipment, transport, commissariat, and medical arrange-" ments; and, whilst helping the troops of the Allies, when you " can afford to do so, without detriment to the interests of your " own troops, you must remember that the establishments sent " with your force are only calculated to supply its wants."

Immediately on his arrival at Taku the Field-Marshal requested Admiral Seymour to concert measures with Admiral Bendemann for the occupation of Shan-hai-kuan for the use of the allied contingents.

Admiral Seymour suggested that British troops should be landed to carry out the occupation. These troops could be conveniently drawn from the 3rd Brigade, which was quartered at Wei-hai-wei, and, on the arrival of General Gaselee from Peking on the 28th, he was directed by the Field-Marshal to make such arrangements as he considered suitable for the despatch of troops to Shan-hai-kuan.

He immediately ordered Major-General Reid to proceed from Wei-hai-wei, with the 4th Punjab Infantry and 6th Bengal Infantry, and to occupy Shan-hai-kuan; the 34th Pioneers from Tien-tsin, the Jodhpur Lancers from Shanghai and Hongkong, and the Maler Kotla Sappers from Hongkong were also ordered to the same place, while the 4th Brigade at Hongkong was ordered up to Tien-tsin for garrison duty there.

On the evening of the 29th September H.M.S. "Pigmy," with Sir Walter Hillier and Lieut.-Colonel Powell on board, left Taku, and arrived off Shan-hai-kuan the following morning under a flag of truce. The Chinese were summoned to hand over the forts to the Allies, and this they at once agreed to do. Sir Walter Hillier and Lieut.-Colonel Powell then landed a guard of 18 Blue-jackets and Marines, under Lieutenant Briggs, R.N., and the "Pigmy" returned to Taku to report. The guard took up its quarters in the railway station, and found that the line was in good order, and that trains were running daily both towards Tong-shan and Chin-chou.

On the morning of the 1st October the British flag was hoisted on all the forts, and also on the powder magazine, and guards were placed where possible. The Union Jack was also hoisted at Ching-wang-tao. The same evening a force of Russians landed at Shan-hai-kuan from Taku, and the following morning the rest of the Allies arrived. Later in the day a large force of Russians arrived from Tong-shan by train, and attempted to seize the railway station, but this was not allowed. They, however, laid claim to the whole line, and to the entire management of it.

On the 2nd the French landed at Ching-wang-tao, and marched on Tang-ho railway station, which they found occupied by Russian troops, but, mistaking them for Boxers, opened fire. The fire was returned, with the result that the French had one officer and two men killed and eight wounded, the Russians losing two men killed and three wounded.

Owing to a breakdown in telegraphic communication with Wei-hai-wei, the bulk of the British infantry did not reach Shan-hai-kuan till the evening of the 2nd October.

As regards the occupation of Shan-hai-kuan, the Field-Marshal issued orders that the fortifications and railway station should be occupied by the Allies in common.

Fort No. 1, nearest the sea, and the largest and most important, was to be held by guards from all the Powers, under a British officer as commandant.

Fort No. 2 was allotted to the Germans, Austrians, and Italians; Fort No. 3 to the French; Fort No. 4 to the British and Japanese; and Fort No. 5 to the Russians.

The railway stations of Shan-hai-kuan and Ching-wang-tao, with the rolling stock found in them, were to be under international control, and all nations had the right to post troops along the line from Shan-hai-kuan to Tang-ku and Peking.

General Zerpitsky, the senior Russian officer present, was appointed Commandant of Shan-hai-kuan city.

The restoration and working of the railway from Shan-hai-kuan to Tang-ku and Yang-tsun, was entrusted to the Russians, while that from Yang-tsun to Peking was to be taken over by the Headquarters Staff of the Commander-in-Chief.

The improvement and management of the harbours at Shan-hai-kuan and Ching-wang-tao were handed over to the British.

The British Admiral entrusted the harbour of Ching-wang-tao, and the railway thence to the main line, to a company, which had been working at it before the war broke out, and which undertook to finish the work in two months. At Shan-hai-kuan it was arranged that each nation that chose to do so could build a pier for itself, and that the British Pioneers would connect these piers with the main line by a light field railway.

By an army order of the 19th October the German, Austrian, Italian, and Japanese troops in the neighbourhood of Shan-hai-kuan, were placed under the orders of Major-General Reid, in addition to the British. This tended to bring about a better state of affairs, as much lawlessness had previously prevailed among the troops, and the surrounding country was being pillaged by Chinese banditti.

On the arrival of the Jodhpur Lancers at Shan-hai-kuan they were put into camp outside the Great Wall.

The work on the Ching-wang-tao pier was at once put in hand, and by the end of the year a length of about 1,100 feet was finished; nearly 300 feet remained to be built to reach the end of the bed of rocks on which it rested, and then a further 200 feet would give a depth of 14 feet at low water at the pier-head. By the middle of January the branch railway connecting the pier with the main line was completed, and by the end of the month 1,540 feet of the pier had been constructed. It was only a partial success, as it was not strong enough to carry an engine, and thus all goods had to be transported a distance of more than 600 yards from the lighters to the trains.

At Shan-hai-kuan the light railway between the beach and the railway station had been in full working order for some time, and the British and German piers were in course of construction. The British troops had supplies up to the middle of April 1901; they were well and comfortably housed, and their general health was excellent.

Closely related to this question of the occupation of Shan-hai-kuan is that of the railway from there to Peking. This railway is the property of a Chinese company and is built with money lent by the Hongkong-Shanghai Bank, the shareholders of the loan being nearly all British subjects.

The line has been built and very ably managed by British engineers, the chief of whom is Mr. Kinder, and it extends not only to Shan-hai-kuan but, on to the north-east, as far as the treaty port of Niu-chuang. At the time of the outbreak of the Boxer troubles the line was in working order as far as Chin-chou, and the remainder, up to Niu-chuang, was under construction.

From Shan-hai-kuan to Chin-chou, a distance of over 100 miles, the railway runs through a narrow defile, shut in on the west by the rugged spurs of the Mongolian mountains, and on the east by the sea. Through this defile lies the only really good line of advance for an army from the north into the capital province of Chi-li, and it cannot be easily turned. The hills on the west are steep and difficult, and the best of the landing-places on the coast, Shan-hai-kuan and Ching-wang-tao, are bad. Ning-yüan, in the middle of the defile, is historical, because for many years it held the Manchus at bay, when they attempted to invade China, and, though only garrisoned by Chinese troops, it was never taken, but was eventually treacherously surrendered to the invaders.

The question now arose as to how the line was to be administered. The Russians had, in the first instance, been given charge of the section between Tang-ku and Tien-tsin, by the conference of Admirals in July, and they had also reconstructed the 18 miles from Tien-tsin to Yang-tsun, but beyond that they had done very little towards repairing the line, and, on the arrival of Count Waldersee, they were informed that if they could not carry out the work, it would have to be taken over by other troops. It was then arranged privately between the Field-Marshal and the Russian Commander that the section between Yang-tsun and Peking should be taken over by the Headquarters Staff, and worked under the orders of the Commander-in-Chief, while the Russians were to retain the stretch from Yang-tsun to Shan-hai-kuan.

On the 1st October General Gaselee represented to the Field-Marshal that it was of the greatest importance to the allied contingents that the whole railway should be put into working order as soon as possible, and that the most effectual way of securing this would be to hand it over to the employés of the railway company, of whom the chief engineer, Mr. Kinder, was present on the spot with a trained staff, and with facilities for obtaining a large amount of trained coolie labour, and was ready to undertake the work.

This employment of civil labour was, however, entirely opposed to the rigid military system of the German headquarters, who insisted that the repairing of the line must be carried out by the troops, under military supervision, but this procedure was impracticable in the present instance, as there were not sufficient trained troops to do the work. The Germans themselves had neither men, tools, nor materials; no doubt they would all arrive in time, but in the meanwhile the repair of the railway was a matter of urgency. The other contingents had also only a certain number of technical troops, and they were too few to put the railway into proper working order before the arrival of winter. However, they did what they could, the Germans working from Yang-tsun towards Peking, while the British took charge of the 10 miles from Peking towards Huang-tsun and the stations at Peking and Feng-tai, and the Japanese worked from Huang-tsun towards Yang-tsun. The Russians undertook the section between Tang-ku and Shan-hai-kuan.

On the 13th October the proceedings of a railway convention, which had been summoned by the Field-Marshal to decide on railway matters, were signed. By it the railway station at Shan-hai-kuan was handed over to the Russians, with all the buildings, material, and working plant contained in it. At the same time it was stipulated that the railway and telegraph were to be available for the equal benefit of all the Allies, but that none of the material was to be used for the harbour works at Shan-hai-kuan and Ching-wang-tao, or for the lines leading from them to the main railway.

The British, American, and Japanese generals sent a joint telegram to Count Waldersee, protesting against the manner in which the railway was being managed, as giving no prospect of its early repair; the American general wired the same views to his Government, while the British commander addressed the Secretary of State for India on the same subject.

They strongly recommended that the whole railway from Peking to Shan-hai-kuan, together with all workshops, rolling stock, and material, should be handed over to the railway company, who alone were capable of obtaining the requisite labour and fully utilizing local resources.

Had the repair of the Tang-ku—Shan-hai-kuan line been taken in hand energetically from the time of its occupation in the beginning of October, there is no reason why it should not have been rapidly put in working order, throughout most of its length.

From Shan-hai-kuan the railway was intact to beyond Tong-shan, as far as a point four miles south-west of the station of Hsu-ko-chuang, but between this and Pei-t'ang it had been completely wrecked. All station buildings had been totally destroyed, and the sleepers, fish-plates, bolts, &c., removed from the line, though the rails were in most cases left lying on the track. An important girder bridge of eight spans between Lu-tai and Han-ku was completely destroyed, as was also the large girder bridge over the Pei-t'ang river, of which the girders were lying in the stream below.

A light line could have been easily constructed from Han-ku to Tang-fang, and the permanent way could have been put in working order for the rest of the distance, but the Russians did very little, and so a whole valuable month was lost.

The telegraph line was in working order, from Shan-hai-kuan to Tong-shan, up to the date on which the Russians occupied the latter place, but it was afterwards out of order.

The rolling stock and engines were neglected and in bad repair.

The workshops at Tong-shan were in fair order, but the machinery was being ruined by neglect and want of oiling, and by exposure to the weather.

The stores were, so far, intact, but the railway offices had been looted, and all papers, drawings, records, and valuable instruments had been taken away. Many of the houses belonging to foreigners had also been looted.

The Russians also occupied the coal mines, and refused to allow any of the Europeans connected with them or the railway to visit Tong-shan, and even objected to officers of the allied forces going there.

All work at the coal mines at Tong-shan and Lin-hsi was stopped, and this was a matter of great importance, as, from want of pumping, the head of water was rapidly gaining in the mines, and there was great danger of their being completely flooded. They had been working up to the time of the arrival of the Russians, and as this was the main supply for Tien-tsin and the neighbourhood the Allies were threatened with scarcity of fuel during the winter.

On the 2nd November General Gaselee informed the Field-Marshal that, from all he could hear, the line to Shan-hai-kuan was not being repaired, and in consequence Count Waldersee appointed a committee consisting of General Barrow, Lieut.-Colonel Gündell, and a Russian officer to be nominated by General Liniévitch, to report on the matter, and also to settle certain questions about the quartering of troops in the Shan-hai-kuan district.

It was now reported that the Russians were daily sending trains loaded with railway material from Shan-hai-kuan to Tong-shan, and so were, presumably, repairing the line. They had also handed over a certain amount of railway material to the British for the construction of the piers at Shan-hai-kuan.

On the 8th November General Liniévitch informed General Barrow that he had received orders to hand over the railway to Count Waldersee, and to withdraw all the Russian troops from Chi-li, except two companies at Tien-tsin and two at Tong-shan. The Field-Marshal, therefore, issued orders that no rolling stock was to be removed from the Peking—Shan-hai-kuan section of the line, east of the latter place. The Russians, however, put off giving any direct information of their withdrawal to the Field-Marshal, and, after being informed on the 13th November that the line from Tang-ku to Yang-tsun would be handed over to him immediately, General Gaselee was told that the Russians would retain it for the present, and that Russian troops would continue to protect the line.

On the 10th December it was notified by Count Waldersee that the Russians had finally agreed to hand over the whole line, from Shan-hai-kuan to Tien-tsin, to him on the 1st January (Russian style), and that he would thereafter hand over the whole line, from Peking to Shan-hai-kuan, to the British as soon as possible.

By the end of December the Russians had got the railway from Tang-ku to Shan-hai-kuan into some sort of working order, with the exception of the bridge at Han-ku. At this place the Pei-t'ang-ho was crossed by a raft, for the passage of which the ice was kept broken, and also by a road on the ice, the ends of which had to be bridged to the banks, as the ice, close to the edge, was broken by the rise and fall of the tide.

On the 26th December a railway convention was drawn up for the transfer of the railway from Shan-hai-kuan to Yang-tsun, by the Russians to the German Headquarters. By it the Russians retained the bridge works and part of the station buildings at Shan-hai-kuan for their own use, but General Gaselee refused to sign this agreement, without direct orders from his Government. The convention was finally signed on the 17th January, and the actual handing over took place between the 19th and 25th January, 1901.

While these events were happening in the east of the province, the work of repairing the line on the section between Tien-tsin and Peking had been steadily progressing, and on the 13th December the permanent way was in really good working order, and the first train had been run through to the capital.

The terminus had been brought into the Chinese City, where a railway station was in course of construction, opposite the Temple of Heaven. The Russians, however, had not handed over the necessary engines to the German Headquarters, but, within a few days, arrangements were made for a regular train service between Tang-ku and Peking, and this was afterwards effectively carried out without further interruption. It was further proposed to extend the railway into the Tartar City, in the neighbourhood of the Legations, but this suggestion remained in abeyance, though the earthwork was completed up to the Sluice Gate, under the Tartar City wall; the course to be taken by the railway being round the outside of the Temple of Heaven and to the east of it, inside the eastern wall of the Chinese City. Another scheme which was being carried forward was the extension of the line, through the north-east corner of the Chinese City, to the landing-place for junks on the Pei-ho, at Tung-chou.

The management of the railway from Yang-tsun to Peking had been handed over by the Field-Marshal to the British, and they had entrusted the charge of the traffic to the regular staff of the railway company, under their own military supervision.

After the Russians had handed over the Yang-tsun—Shan-hai-kuan section to the German head-quarters, towards the end of January, as already described, a further convention, transferring the Peking—Shan-hai-kuan Railway from the Germans to the British was signed on the 15th February, and the transfer of the line was completed on the 26th February 1901.

The whole of the permanent way was now inspected, and was found to require a great deal of repair. The line was not properly sleepered, and most of the bridges and culverts were in a dangerous condition. The civil railway staff, under Mr. Kinder, at once began the necessary work, and soon the trains were running much more regularly and smoothly. New engines were brought up from Shanghai, and by the 20th April six of these had been landed, put together, and got under steam, and two trains were running daily each way between Tien-tsin and Peking.

On the 8th May the Han-ku railway bridge, which had been constructed by the German railway troops, was opened for traffic, and thus through railway communication between the capital and Shan-hai-kuan was at last restored.

Trains were also running beyond Shan-hai-kuan to Niu-chuang, but the railway north of the Great Wall was still in the hands of the Russians.

CHAPTER XIII.

PUNITIVE EXPEDITION TO PAO-TING FU.

It is now necessary to turn to the course of military operations in Central Chi-li subsequent to the arrival of Count Waldersee, and his assumption of the duties of Commander-in-Chief.

After the dispersal of the Chinese forces in the neighbourhood of Peking, by far the greater part of them retired to the south-west, which was also the direction from which any reinforcements of fresh troops might be expected to arrive, and it was reported that a considerable force, said to be under the command of Tung Fu-hsiang, had its headquarters at Pao-ting fu, while every town and village south of the Hun-ho was occupied by bands of Boxers and Imperial soldiers. It was evident that before anything more could be done with regard to settling the country, all armed bodies within a wide radius of Peking must be broken up and dispersed, and the first step to be taken in this direction appeared to be the occupation of Pao-ting fu, the headquarters of the Chinese forces. There were other reasons why an early visit to this particular city appeared to be desirable. It is the provincial capital of the Chi-li province, and there, under the fostering care of its officials, the Boxer movement first declared itself in open attacks upon foreigners. As early as the month of May several British and American missionaries had been murdered by the populace just outside the walls of the city, and it was reported that three or four Europeans were still being held prisoners in the hands of the officials.

On the 28th September, 1900, General Gaselee called upon the Field-Marshal at Tien-tsin, and it was arranged that two columns should move out from Peking and Tien-tsin, with the object of making a combined attack on Pao-ting fu. At first it was intended that this force should consist of British, German, and Italian troops only.

The Americans, Japanese, and Russians did not wish to participate in the operations, and the French troops were not under Count Waldersee's orders.

The British were quite prepared to start at once, but the German arrangements were as yet incomplete. They were deficient of transport, and much of their clothing and supplies were still on board their ships. There seemed therefore to be every prospect of a long delay before a start could be made, when the news got about that the French were preparing to undertake a similar expedition, to the same place, with their own troops. This accelerated the German preparations, and it was arranged between the Field-Marshal and General Voyron, commanding the French forces, that the latter should combine with the two columns, which Count Waldersee proposed to despatch from Peking and Tien-tsin, in carrying out a general advance on Pao-ting fu. It was further arranged that the command of the Tien-tsin column should be given to Major-General Bailloud of the French army, while the column from Peking would be under General Gaselee, who would also assume supreme command of both columns, on their junction in the neighbourhood of Pao-ting fu.

Preparations now went rapidly forward, and the two columns started respectively from Peking and Tien-tsin on the 12th October.

The Peking column numbered about 3,500 men, and consisted of:—

    British.—Three squadrons of the 16th Bengal Lancers, four guns of the 12th battery. R.F.A., a half company of Madras Sappers and Miners, and 600 native infantry from the 1st Sikhs, 24th Punjab Infantry, and 26th Bombay Infantry; all under command of Major-General Richardson.

    French.—Two battalions of marine infantry.

    German and Italian.—Six guns, two battalions of German infantry, and one battalion of Italian infantry; all under command of Colonel von Normann.

The Tien-tsin column was numerically rather stronger, and consisted of:—

    British.—"B" Battery, R.H.A., two squadrons of the 3rd Bombay Cavalry, and one troop 1st Bengal Lancers; one company Victorian Naval Brigade, with two Maxims and one 12-pr. naval gun, six companies 20th Punjab Infantry, four companies Hongkong Regiment, two companies 1st Madras Pioneers, and half a company Bombay Sappers and Miners; all under command of Major-General Lorne-Campbell.

    French.—Two battalions of infantry, one squadron of cavalry, with some guns and engineers.

    German and Italian.—Four guns, one troop of cavalry, and two battalions of German infantry. One Italian battery, three companies of Bersaglieri, and a pioneer detachment; all under command of Major-General von Kettler.

The Peking column marched by the direct road to Pao-ting fu, the various contingents taking it in turn each day to lead the march. The Tien-tsin column marched by three roads, the French and German-Italian detachments to the north of the Pao-ting fu river, and the British contingent following a road to the south. The river was also utilised for the transport of supplies.

No opposition was encountered, as the Chinese took care to keep out of the way of the advancing columns. There are eight regular stages between Peking and Pao-ting fu, but as the march had to be accomplished in seven days, it entailed a slight alteration in the halting-places. However, there was nowhere any difficulty on this account, as the country passed through is a rich one, and the necessary supplies were everywhere obtainable, and water was also fairly plentiful.

It was reported that the Chinese regular troops had been employed everywhere in putting down the Boxers, and had killed a great many of them, and outside the gate of Cho-chou city several heads of reputed Boxers were suspended.

The road was unmetalled, but fairly good throughout, except where it crosses the great masonry bridges at Lu-kou-ch'iao, Liu-li-ho, and Cho-chou, the roadway of which was in a very bad state of repair, and calculated to smash any form of wheeled vehicle. Immediately after heavy rain the roads would undoubtedly become very bad, but they dry rapidly. Guides are essential, as branch roads constantly diverge to the right and left, and the road is also frequently double, and only a local guide knows which track at the particular moment is in the best state of repair. South of Liang-hsiang-hsien, a little " loess," is met with. This formation is said to be caused by wind-drifted dust, which, further to the west, in the Shan-hsi province, sometimes reaches a depth of two or three hundred feet. Constant traffic over this kind of soil quickly cuts a roadway, with perpendicular sides, many feet below the general surface of the surrounding country; as may be seen on the road to Pao-ting fu, where the bases of the old watch towers, built at intervals along the side of the road, are now many feet above the level of the road itself.

The advantages to the defence of a country, intersected by a network of defiles of this description, can be readily realised, but the march of the column was in no way interfered with.

The places at which halts were made were Li-pa-feng, Liu-li-ho, Sung-lin-tien, Ting-hsing, where the British encamped about two miles beyond the town on the bank of a small river called the Pei-ho, Ku-ching, and An-hsu, where a halt was made for a day to get in touch with the column from Tien-tsin, under General Bailloud. Pao-ting fu was reached on the 19th October. Throughout the march the British pitched their camp at each halting place, while the other troops were billeted in the villages and towns.

The column from Tien-tsin also arrived within a day's march of Pao-ting fu on the 17th, and halted for a day. The British contingent of this column was however delayed, as the route it had followed to the south of the river had proved much longer and more difficult than was expected, and, in consequence, it did not reach Pao-ting fu till the 21st October.

A small French column of about 1,000 men had preceded the main column from Tien-tsin, and had arrived at Pao-ting fu some days in advance of the rest of the allied force. They had occupied all the gates of the city, but were said to have been ordered by their General to remain outside, until the main columns arrived. They had also seized the railway, which was in working order from about six miles north of Pao-ting fu as far south as Ting-chou, and when the Peking column arrived they were already busy repairing it.

On nearing the city the column was met by the fen-tai, the chief magistrate, of Pao-ting fu and a number of other officials.

General Gaselee decided that the troops should remain outside for the night, and that the formal entry should be made next day, when the question of the occupation of the town and the portions of it to be allotted to each contingent would be decided.

Accordingly, on the morning of the 20th October, the General and his staff, accompanied by the other commanders with their staffs and mounted escorts, rode all through the city, which is divided into four quarters by main streets running north and south and east and west. It was a very wet, cold day, but the town appeared to be full of Chinese engaged in their usual occupations.

Immediately after visiting the town a conference of the commanders was held, when it was decided that the British should occupy and police the north-west quarter of the city, the French should take charge of the south-west quarter, the Germans of the north-east quarter and the Italians of the south-east quarter. Each Power also occupied one of the main gates, the British taking the North Gate, the French the West Gate, the Germans the East Gate, and the Italians the South Gate, while the flags of all the four Powers were hoisted over each gate.

The commanders of the other three nations decided to march their troops into the city, and quarter them in the houses, but the British Contingent remained outside, encamped to the north of the town. General Gaselee, however, removed his headquarters into the north-west section allotted to the British, and a strong force of police, under an officer, also took up their quarters in this district, while a strong British guard held the North Gate.

Cavalry reconnoitring parties were sent out into the hills to the west and north-west of Pao-ting fu, where Boxers were reported to be collected in considerable numbers, and these had one or two small skirmishes with the enemy.

Immediately after the arrival of the columns at Pao-ting fu grave suspicion fell upon the local officials of complicity with the Boxers in the murders of the British and American Missionaries, which had been committed at the outbreak of the recent troubles. To enquire into these charges General Gaselee appointed an international Commission, with General Bailloud as President. It appeared that the Boxer movement first assumed formidable proportions, in the neighbourhood of Pao-ting fu, during the month of May, and at the end of that month the Roman Catholic village of Chang-chuang to the south of the city was attacked. The Roman Catholics were however quite prepared for this onslaught and had fortified their village, and, being well supplied with arms by the priests, drove off the Boxers with heavy loss on several occasions.

Infuriated by this repulse, the Boxers next turned their attention to the Lu-han Railway, which they began to destroy. The foreign employés, most of whom were Belgians, seeing that serious trouble was impending, decided to withdraw to Tien-tsin and applied to the fen-tai, or provincial treasurer, of Pao-ting fu, for boats, and for protection on their journey. The fen-tai provided them with junks and a guard of fifty regular soldiers, and the whole party of nearly forty persons left for Tien-tsin in the beginning of June.

All went well until the morning of the third day, when a sudden attack was made on the small flotilla by a band of Boxers. The party had now to abandon their boats and all their possessions, and continue their journey on foot, as the guard of soldiers and the boat-men had all deserted. The last boat, in which were four Europeans, three of them men, and one woman, was cut off from the rest, and the occupants were undoubtedly murdered by the Boxers. The remainder, being well armed, succeeded in keeping the Chinese at bay and killing many of them, and at length, after suffering great privations, arrived at Tien-tsin.

After the departure of the railway employés from Pao-ting fu, an order reached the city from the Viceroy Yü-lu, at Tien-tsin, stating that the foreigners at that place had been overcome by the Chinese troops; and that now the soldiers and the Boxers were to unite together to destroy all foreigners and all Chinese christians. This message clearly indicated that the foreign missionaries at Pao-ting fu were to be put to death, but the fen-tai was timid about carrying it into effect, as he feared that the foreigners might again get the upper hand, and exact vengeance for any harm that had befallen their countrymen.

The nieh-tai, or provincial judge, was, however, entirely in favour of carrying out the order, and did all in his power to encourage the Boxers.

There were at this time three Christian missions at Pao-ting fu. Two of these were American, and the other English. The American Presbyterian Mission was outside the north gate of the city, while the American Board Mission and the British China Inland Mission were outside the city on the south side, and not far from the south gate.

At the end of June a large mob of Boxers and local Chinese made a sudden attack on the American Presbyterian Mission, and set fire to the buildings. The inhabitants, on trying to escape from the burning houses, were driven back again by the mob, and so perished in the flames. In this manner nine American subjects lost their lives, besides a large number of Chinese christians and servants, who were in the mission at the time of the attack. Far from rendering the foreigners any assistance, the local officials are reported to have praised and rewarded the Boxers.

Encouraged by this success, the latter now decided to attack the other missions, and the following day, accompanied, it is said, by many of the regular soldiers in garrison in the city, they marched against the American Board Mission, and there attacked and murdered Mr. Pitkin and a number of Chinese christians, while they made prisoners of two American ladies, Miss Morrell and Miss Gould.

They next attacked the British China Inland Mission, where they killed Mr. Bagnall, and seized his wife and two children and Mr. Cooper. They, together with the two American ladies, were carried off to a Boxer temple inside the city, where they were kept all day, and in the evening they were taken outside the town and beheaded near the south-east corner of the city wall. Thus, at Pao-ting fu, 17 British and American missionaries were murdered in cold blood.

About this time the reports got about that the fen-tai was lukewarm in the cause, and inclined to favour the foreigners. The Boxers therefore threatened to kill him, so he fled from the city; and the nieh-tai, who had been the warm supporter of the Boxers from the first, succeeded him in authority, and this was the official who came out to meet General Gaselee on his arrival at Pao-ting fu.

He, along with several other officials, was immediately taken into custody on suspicion, and their cases were all tried before the International Commission, with the result that T'ing-yung, the fen-tai; Kuei-hêng, the Tartar governor, commanding the Manchu garrison; and Wang-chan-kuei, a colonel commanding the provincial troops, to whom the missionaries had in vain applied for protection from the Boxers, were all three sentenced to be beheaded. These sentences were duly carried out on the 6th November, outside the south-east corner of the city wall, at the spot where the missionaries had been murdered three months earlier.

The astonishment and horror of the fen-tai, when he realised that he was to be executed for his guilt, were almost ludicrous. It was impossible, to his Chinese mind, that a magistrate of his rank could be in such a position, without hope of escape.

In addition to these executions, several Boxers implicated in the murders of the missionaries were also captured, tried, and shot; and, as a punishment to the town itself, the city temple, dedicated to the tutelary deities, and also the temple in which the Boxers practised their rites, and in which the missionaries had been confined while awaiting death, were blown up and totally destroyed by fire. The south-east corner of the city wall, outside which the missionaries had been murdered, was also razed to the ground, and a heavy fine was imposed on the town.

The punishment of Pao-ting fu having been effected, General Gaselee determined to withdraw his troops, as did the commander of the Italian contingent, but the Germans and French decided to retain garrisons at this point during the winter. The troops from Peking were to return, on a broad front, by three roads, different from that taken on the march south; and the British column from Tien-tsin was also to return by a slightly different road from the one it had used in its advance on Pao-ting fu, with the object of visiting certain Boxer villages that required to be punished.

The first column to start was a battalion of German infantry, which would march *viâ* Yi-chou and the foot of the western hills to Peking. With it were some of the 16th Bengal Lancers, the detachment of mounted Sappers, and three companies of Italian infantry, all under command of Colonel von Normann. They left Pao-ting fu on the 23rd October, and, after visiting the Imperial Tombs at Yi-chou, they moved west into the hills, and encountered a considerable force of Chinese troops near the Great Wall, which they dispersed with heavy loss. They afterwards continued their march on Peking, which was reached without further incident.

On the 27th October the British Column for Tien-tsin started, and reached the latter place on the 6th November, having visited and punished several Boxer villages, collected a large number of mules and cattle, and captured and destroyed a large amount of arms and ammunition, and a considerable quantity of gunpowder loaded upon junks.

On the following day the British Column took a road which was well to the east of the main road, and which led through Yung-ch'ing-hsien and Lang-fang. General Gaselee started the same day direct for Peking, where he arrived on the 1st November.

The Italian Column, consisting of a battery of artillery and three companies of Bersaglieri, together with a battalion of German infantry and a few German cavalry, all under the command of Colonel Garioni, started on the 29th October, by a road passing through Ku-an-hsien, and running at some distance to the east of the direct road to Peking.

The British Column, consisting of all the remainder of the British troops, commanded by Major-General Richardson, reached Yung-ch'ing-hsien on the 31st October, and here a halt was made for a day, to enquire into the murder of two British missionaries, Messrs. Norman and Robinson, in the beginning of June.

The two missionaries had been attacked by the Boxers, and Mr. Robinson had been at once cut down and killed, but Mr. Norman was taken prisoner and carried off to the village of Wu-chia-ying, where he was murdered the following day after having been horribly tortured.

General Richardson imposed a fine of 40,000 *taels* on the town, and, in addition, ordered the total destruction of the town temple, and also of another temple, commonly used by the Boxers; and of the north gate of the town, near which Mr. Robinson had been murdered. The village of Wu-chia-ying, and another village called Ta-cheh-hsiang, where a chapel had been destroyed and several Chinese christians murdered, were also completely burnt down.

Beyond Yung-ch'ing-hsien the Hun-ho had to be crossed. It is here a broad shallow stream, flowing in a wide sandy bed, which is full of quicksands. At the time referred to the water was about 120 yards in breadth, and 3 feet deep in the deepest part, with a rapid current, and the river is very liable to flood after heavy rain. The cavalry, artillery, and baggage animals, without loads, forded the river without difficulty, and the infantry, baggage, and carts were taken across in four junks which had been collected at this point. As the Hun-ho is not navigable, junks are not so easily procurable as on most of the other streams of the Chih-li plain. The crossing occupied about five hours, and the force camped for the night a short distance beyond the ford.

Near Lang-fang certain Boxer villages were also burnt, and the force continued its march to Peking, which was reached on the 6th November, on which day the German column from Yi-chou also arrived at the capital, the Italian column having come in the day before.

CHAPTER XIV.

MILITARY OPERATIONS UP TO THE END OF DECEMBER, 1900.

With the return of the allied troops from Pao-ting fu active military operations in North China may be said to have practically ceased. It had been conclusively proved that there was no Chinese force in the field, which had the least wish to oppose our troops, and the Boxer bands had all been dispersed and scattered, and were being hunted down by the Imperial soldiery. The Russian and Japanese Governments were even withdrawing their troops from Chi-li, and were preparing to considerably reduce their garrisons, before the intense cold of winter set in. The first of the Russian forces to retire from Peking was the 9th East Siberian Rifle Regiment, which reached Tien-tsin on its way to Manchuria on the 2nd October. It was followed by a steady stream of troops, until the Russian contingent was reduced to about one thousand men, who formed their Legation guard during the winter.

On the 10th October the Russians, who had occupied the Summer and Winter Palaces since the relief of Peking, evacuated these places and handed them over to the Chinese, without giving any warning of their intentions to their allies in Peking. The Summer Palace was at once reoccupied by detachments of British and Italian troops, while the Germans took possession of the Winter Palace.

On the following day His Excellency Li Hung-chang arrived at Peking, escorted by a Russian guard.

On the 14th October a British detachment occupied the railway terminus at Ma-chia-pu, the Russians having withdrawn their troops, and at once commenced the construction of a post.

On the same day the 4th British Infantry Brigade began to arrive at Tien-tsin.

The Field-Marshal had remained at Tien-tsin until the departure of the Pao-ting fu column from that place on the 12th October, and also pending the settlement of certain railway questions with the Russian authorities. He left Tien-tsin for Peking with his staff on the 13th October, and travelled as far as Yang-tsun by the railway, which had been repaired up to this point by the Russians. From Yang-tsun the journey was continued by route march through Ho-hsi-wu and Tung-chou, the various posts and garrisons being inspected *en route*. Contingents of Japanese and Russian troops, retiring from the capital towards the coast, were met with, and on the 17th October Count Waldersee reached Peking. Outside the city walls he was received by the commanders and staffs of the allied forces, and from the Ha-ta mên, by which he entered the Tartar city, to the Winter Palace, where he finally took up his headquarters, the streets, through which he passed, were lined by troops.

Detachments from the British Native Regiments were drawn up in Legation Street, and the Royal Welsh Fusiliers furnished a part of the guard of honour drawn up opposite the gate of the Winter Palace.

A few days after, on the 20th October, the new British minister, Sir Ernest Satow, who had been appointed to succeed Sir Claude MacDonald, arrived at Peking and took over charge from his predecessor. On the 25th Sir Claude MacDonald left for Tien-tsin *en route* to Tokio, where he was going to take up his new appointment as British Minister at the Japanese Court.

Certain withdrawals of British troops from North China were also ordered at this time; on the 20th October the Chinese Regiment left Tien-tsin for Wei-hai-wei, and on the following day the Royal Welsh Fusiliers left Peking for Hongkong, after having been relieved by a detachment of 230 men of the New South Wales naval contingent. On the 22nd the Hongkong Artillery, and on the 26th three squadrons 1st Bengal Lancers also left Peking for Hongkong, the fourth squadron of the 1st Bengal Lancers remaining behind, until the return of the 16th Bengal Lancers from Pao-ting fu.

This left the distribution of the British contingent of the China Expeditionary Force for the winter roughly as follows:—

- At and around Peking the 12th Battery, Royal Field Artillery, the New South Wales contingent, the 16th Bengal Lancers, the First Infantry Brigade, and No. 4 Company Bengal Sappers.
- At and around Tien-tsin, "B." Battery Royal Horse Artillery, two pompoms, the Victorian contingent, the 3rd Bombay Cavalry, the Fourth Infantry Brigade, less one battalion at Wei-hai-wei, the 20th Punjab Infantry, the 1st Madras Pioneers, the Hongkong Regiment, and No. 2 Company Bombay Sappers.
- At and around Shan-hai-kuan, two pompoms, the Third Infantry Brigade, less one battalion at Tien-tsin, the Jodhpore Lancers, and the Maler Kotla Sappers.
- At Wei-hai-wei, the 2nd Company, Southern Division, Royal Garrison Artillery, the 28th Madras Infantry, and the 1st Chinese Regiment.
- At Shanghai, one squadron, 3rd Bombay Cavalry, the Second Infantry Brigade, and No. 3 Company Madras Sappers. The last-mentioned did not leave Peking for Shanghai till the 8th November, after their return from Pao-ting fu.
- At Hongkong, the 1st Bengal Lancers.

On the 26th October the Field-Marshal published an army order directing the commanders of troops under his orders to despatch patrols and reconnoitring parties in all directions, to break up gangs of Boxers, who were to be treated with the utmost severity. All Chinese regular troops were also to be expelled from the zone of country occupied by the allied troops.

This led to great activity on the part of the German troops, who scoured the country in all directions, under the pretext of searching for Boxers.

The other contingents, who had been in Chi-li from the commencement of the campaign, refrained from carrying out any expeditions, knowing well that the Boxers, as a fighting force, had long since been scattered and dispersed.

On the 12th November an expedition started for Kalgan, under command of Colonel Count Yorck von Wartenberg, consisting of four companies of German infantry, one battery and three companies of Italian infantry, and a company of Austrian infantry. A British survey party with a small escort accompanied it, with the object of mapping the country passed through. The Russians were very averse to this expedition, as they declared that its presence near Kalgan might throw the whole of Mongolia into insurrection, and endanger the Russian provinces in Siberia.

As the Field-Marshal had made all his arrangements for the expedition, he refused to give it up, but promised that it would not go beyond the Great Wall. It accordingly left Peking on the 12th November, and, following the direct trade road, arrived at Kalgan without meeting with any opposition whatever. This road, as far as Hsuan-hua fu, had been used by the Emperor and the Empress-Dowager in their flight from Peking, in the middle of August.

Kalgan itself is an important place, as all tea going into Mongolia and Siberia *viâ* Urga and Kiachta passes through it, and caravans bringing skins, felt, sheep, ponies, camels, &c., come down by this route to Peking. Kalgan is thus a great emporium for trade, and considerable British, Russian, and German capital is represented there.

About thirty miles north-east of Kalgan is situated the Belgian Roman Catholic mission of Hsi-wan-tzu, which had been more or less in a state of siege from Chinese and Boxers for a period of about three months. Here a great number of Chinese christians, and some Belgian Roman Catholic missionaries, had taken refuge during the troubles, and had held out successfully against all attacks. Great was their relief at the news of the arrival of the German force at Kalgan. The German Commander, however, would not advance to Hsi-wan-tzu, as it was beyond the Great Wall, and his instructions forbade operations in that direction; but the British party accompanying the force visited the place, and were most cordially received by the inhabitants. These consisted of eighteen priests, eight sisters, and about 6,000 or 7,000 Chinese christians. A Belgian officer,

Commandant Witthamer, who had been travelling in this region at the time when the troubles began, was also in the mission, and had greatly assisted in its defence; another Belgian, M. Dansette, had also taken part in the siege. The garrison was very badly off for arms, having only about 75 firearms among them, but the Chinese never seriously attacked the place, though they assaulted a smaller village called Wu-hao, about twenty miles further to the north, which was defended by some 400 converts under a priest. Being driven off with some loss they did not venture on a second attack.

Another village, called Ho-tu-wa, still further to the north, was held by about 1,100 converts under two priests, but it was not attacked.

A large village, called Hsi-eng-tze, four days' march west of Hsi-wan-tzu, was held by about 3,000 converts under three priests, and was four times attacked by the Chinese, but succeeded in driving them back each time with considerable loss, while sustaining very few casualties themselves.

Two villages, Sin-hua-cheng and Trai-lou-hou, lying to the west of Kalgan, were defended by about 800 converts each, and were not attacked, but Chih-su-mou in the same direction, held by about 400 converts under two priests, successfully sustained three attacks.

At Kuei-hua-cheng, further to the west, near the Yellow River, it was reported that about thirty Europeans had been murdered, among the number being one Englishman, Captain Watts-Jones, of the Royal Engineers, who was travelling from Ssu-ch'uan to Peking. At Khon-bu, one day's march north-east of Kuei-hua-cheng, fourteen Swedish missionaries, including three priests, four ladies, and seven children, and three Roman Catholic priests were murdered, being burnt to death in the Roman Catholic Church along with about 500 native converts.

At Sio-chou-pain ten Roman Catholic priests were besieged for forty-nine days, during which time one priest was killed and one wounded, but the Chinese eventually withdrew.

Having completed its visit to Kalgan, and exacted fines amounting in all to about 80,000 dollars, the German column returned to Peking by the same route as it had used in its advance. The British survey party made a détour through the hills, for purposes of mapping in fresh country, and rejoined the main body at Ch'a-tao on the Inner Wall.

A most regrettable accident occurred at Huai-lai village, whereby the distinguished commander of the German column lost his life. Count Yorck had gone to sleep in a small room heated by a Chinese stove, and without any means of ventilation, and was asphyxiated by the charcoal fumes. He was a most prominent officer on the staff of the German Army, and was well known on account of his able writings on military subjects. His body was brought back to Peking, and his funeral took place on the 5th December. It was a most impressive ceremony, and was attended by the Generals, Ministers, and staffs of all the allied nations.

At this time very little in the way of military operations was going on, though patrols of mounted troops were constantly moving about the country.

The Field-Marshal had appointed a committee, presided over by a general officer, to conduct the administration of the city of Peking. To this committee each nation was invited to appoint a member, who could speak either French or English, and who would act as its representative, in expressing the views of its military commander, on any question which might call for discussion.

The principal duties of the committee were the allotment of funds for carrying out the policing of the various districts, and the consideration of suggested improvements of different kinds.

It was empowered to employ Chinese officials, to assist in discussing and carrying out its ideas.

Early in December the portion of the Chi-li province in the occupation of the allied troops was divided into districts, and assigned to the various nationalities for purposes of administration. The Germans administered the district to the north-west of Peking, the Japanese that to the north-east; the Italians had a small district to the east, next to the Japanese. The Americans had a strip just south of the Italians, also on the east of Peking; and the British took the district south of the capital, through which runs the railway from Tien-tsin. To the west of the British, and south of the Germans, the country was controlled by the French.

This arrangement worked satisfactorily and without friction, and on the retirement of the Americans from North China their district was added to that of the British.

From the direction of Shan-hai-kuan reports of Boxer gatherings were occasionally heard, but usually proved to be groundless. In the middle of October a mixed column was despatched from there to Lan-chou, to operate against Boxers, who were reported by the Russians to be threatening the railway, but no trace of them could be found. On the 5th November a column, composed of 180 British, 350 French, and 200 Russians, moved north-west from Tong-shan to engage a large gathering of Boxers, reported to be in the neighbourhood of Tsun-hua-chou, but failed to discover the enemy.

In fact, the winter was now setting in in earnest, and it was too cold for the movements of any but small bodies of troops. On the 10th November the Pei-ho was for the first time covered with a sheet of thin ice at Tung-chou, but it remained open for junk traffic till the beginning of December. The disembarkation of stores for the British force was completed at Shan-hai-kuan and Ching-wang-tao by the 17th November, but the sea remained clear of ice, and the weather, being calm and temperate, was particularly favourable for boat work.

The Americans were at this time withdrawing part of their troops, and on the 2nd December a British detachment relieved them of the garrison duties at Tang-ku.

On the 4th of the month a German expedition marched south from Tien-tsin to Ts'ang-chou on the Grand Canal, with the idea of dispersing a Chinese force, reported to be assembled at this point. Ts'ang-chou was outside the area designated by the Field-Marshal as being under the administration of the Allies, and it was also the birthplace of the viceroy Chang Chih-tung, who was doing his utmost in the interests of peace at Hankow, on the Yang-tse. The Chinese troops, moreover, were those of General Mei, who had all along been energetic in suppressing the Boxer movement and maintaining peace in this troublesome district. On the advance of the German column he withdrew his troops to the south, and so avoided hostilities, but the expedition tended to weaken the authority of General Mei, by causing him to "lose face" with the Chinese.

On the 7th December the Pei-ho was frozen over, and all communication by boat with Tien-tsin was finally put a stop to; but, on the same day, a train succeeded in getting through from Yang-tsun to the old Peking terminus at Ma-chia-pu, and afterwards returned safely to Yang-tsun. On the 9th the first train from Tien-tsin entered Peking, and from the 12th a regular train service with the coast was commenced. By the end of the month, railway communication on the whole line from Peking to Shan-hai-kuan was possible, except for the gap at Han-ku, formed by the broken bridge over the Pei-t'ang-ho. This necessitated the transportation of stores, &c., for a short distance, by road.

On the 22nd December the French dispersed a body of Chinese troops to the east of Cho-chou, inflicting considerable loss upon them, and capturing four guns and a quantity of stores and ammunition. The casualties on the French side were *nil*. The Chinese fled precipitately to the south, through Pa-chou and Ho-kien fu.

At the end of December a German detachment, operating in combination with an American force, inflicted punishment on a Boxer force in the San-ho district, to the east of Tung-chou, and also dispersed a Chinese force in the neighbourhood of Mi-yun.

CHAPTER XV.

MILITARY OPERATIONS FROM THE COMMENCEMENT OF 1901 UP TO THE CONCLUSION OF THE CAMPAIGN.

On the 1st January, 1901, the strength of the combatant troops of the allied forces in Chi-li was approximately as follows:—

In and around Peking.

British	-	- Cavalry	- 4 squadrons.
		Artillery	- 6 guns.
		Infantry	- 4 battalions and 2 companies.
		Engineers	- 1 company and details.
French	-	- Artillery	- 24 guns.
		Infantry	- 5 battalions.
Germans	-	- Cavalry	- 2 squadrons.
		Artillery	- 3 guns.
		Infantry	- 6 battalions and 3 companies.
Italians	-	- Artillery	- 6 guns.
		Infantry	- 1 battalion and 3 companies.
Japanese	-	- Cavalry	- 2 squadrons.
		Artillery	- 12 guns.
		Infantry	- 3 battalions
Russians	-	- Cavalry	- 1 squadron.
		Artillery	- 2 guns.
		Infantry	- 2 companies.
United States		- Cavalry	- 1 squadron.
		Artillery	- 6 guns.
		Infantry	- 2 battalions and 2 companies.

In and around Tien-tsin.

British	-	- Cavalry	- 4 squadrons.
		Artillery	- 6 guns and 2 pompoms.
		Infantry	- 6 battalions and 2 companies.
		Engineers	- 1 company.
French	-	- Cavalry	- 1 squadron.
		Artillery	- 12 guns.
		Infantry	- 4 battalions.
Germans	-	- Cavalry	1 squadron.
		Artillery	- 18 guns.
		Infantry	- 4 battalions.
Russians	-	- Infantry	- 3 companies.
United States		- Infantry	- 2 companies.

At Tang-ku.

Germans	-	- Artillery	- 8 guns.
Italians	-	- Infantry	- 1 company.

Japanese	-	- Cavalry	-	1 troop.
		Artillery	-	6 guns.
		Infantry	-	2 battalions.
Russians	-	- Infantry	-	3 companies.
United States		- Infantry	-	2 companies.

On Railway line to Shan-hai-kuan.

| Russians | - | - Infantry | - | 2 battalions. |

At and around Shan-hai-kuan.

British	-	- Cavalry	-	4 squadrons.
		Artillery	-	2 pompoms.
		Infantry	-	3 battalions.
		Engineers	-	1 company.
French	-	- Infantry	-	1 battalion.
Germans	-	- Infantry	-	2 companies.
Japanese	-	- Cavalry	-	1 troop.
		Infantry	-	1 battalion.
Russians	-	- Cavalry	-	2 squadrons.
		Artillery	-	8 guns.
		Infantry	-	1 battalion and 3 companies.

At Pao-ting fu.

French	-	- Cavalry	-	1 squadron.
		Artillery	-	18 guns.
		Infantry	-	3 battalions.
Germans	-	- Cavalry	-	1 squadron.
		Artillery	-	18 guns.
		Infantry	-	4 battalions.

The actual strength of the British contingent of the China Expeditionary Force on this date was :—

British -	-	-	-	2,129
Native -	-	-	-	16,100
		Total -	-	18,229 officers and men.

On the 1st January the usual parade took place, in celebration of the assumption of the Imperial title by Her Majesty the Queen. All the British troops in Peking were present, and Field-Marshal Count Waldersee took command, having been invited by General Gaselee to hold the parade, as the representative of Her Majesty's grandson, the German Emperor. He was accompanied by a numerous staff, and many officers belonging to the other allied contingents were present. The **parade was held in the great court just outside the south gate of** the Imperial City, and the troops presented a fine appearance. Similar parades were held at Tien-tsin, Shan-hai-kuan and Shanghai.

Everything was now very quiet in the Chi-li province, and General Gaselee was instructed to arrange for the return of the Australian naval contingent to Australia before the end of March. He represented that, when withdrawn as directed, their place should be taken by a British battalion, as white troops were most desirable for police duties and employment on the railway, as guards, ticket collectors, &c., where they would be dealing with the troops of foreign contingents. Orders were consequently issued, towards the end of February, for the despatch of half a battalion of the Royal Welsh Fusiliers from Hongkong to North China, to relieve the Australian contingent, and they arrived at Tien-tsin on the 23rd March and at Peking on the 25th; the Australians at the latter place leaving the following day for Tien-tsin, en route to Australia.

At the same time General Gaselee was authorised to agree to the Convention between Count Waldersee and the Russian authorities, regarding the transfer of the railway by the latter to the German headquarters, provided that it was stipulated that this Convention was of an entirely temporary nature, and without prejudice to existing political and financial rights, which were fully reserved on the part of Great Britain; and that the whole line from Peking to Niu-chuang, together with all material, rolling stock, &c., would, on the conclusion of military operations, be at once restored to the representatives of the bondholders.

On the 12th of January a grass-cutting party belonging to the Jodhpur Lancers was attacked by Chinese armed brigands, about five miles to the north-east of Shan-hai-kuan, when out cutting grass under a small escort. Two of the party were killed, but the escort succeeded in driving off the enemy, killing six of them. The same day a party of Japanese, who were attacked in the same neighbourhood, had four of their number killed. As a result a punitive expedition, consisting of British and Japanese, visited the district and burnt some villages, but, owing to the very difficult nature of the country, it failed to come up with the brigands, who were reported to be in the neighbourhood, but to have retired into the hills.

By the middle of January the Russian troops had been reduced to two battalions of the 5th Rifle Regiment, four squadrons 1st Chita Cossacks, and the 4th Light battery of the 2nd East Siberian Artillery Brigade. All the other troops had been withdrawn to Manchuria, and the protection of the railway had been handed over to the Germans; the above force being quartered in small detachments at Peking, Tien-tsin, Tang-ku, and Shan-hai-kuan where they were to remain during the occupation of Chih-li by the troops of other foreign nations.

On the 24th January the sad news reached Peking of the death of Her Majesty, Queen Victoria, and on the 2nd February memorial services were held, first at the chapel in the British Legation, and afterwards in the great court to the south of the Forbidden City. The whole of the British troops in Peking were present at the latter service, as were also the Field-Marshal and his staff, and detachments from all the foreign contingents. During the service a royal salute of 101 guns was fired. The day was intensely cold, with a strong wind from the north, but many civilians, including a number of ladies, from the different Legations were also present at the service.

At the end of the month the first train belonging to the Lu-han railway passed over the Lu-kou-ch'iao bridge, and arrived at Feng-tai, thus signalising the opening of railway communication between Peking and Pao-ting fu.

All this time negotiations for peace had been dragging slowly along, and there seemed to be no prospect of any definite result being reached. With a view to waking up the Chinese authorities, Count Waldersee determined to show them that, if it became necessary, he was prepared to resume active operations, and to compel the acceptance of the terms demanded by the allied Powers. He therefore issued an Army Order on the 15th February, in which he stated that, as the season of the year would shortly be favourable for the movement of troops and the resumption of hostilities, all commanders should take steps to render their contingents thoroughly ready for mobilisation at short notice, in case it might be found necessary to undertake fresh military operations. All troops were directed to be prepared to move by the end of the month, and to be provided with such transport as would be suitable for a campaign in mountainous country.

This clearly pointed to the possibility of an expedition being sent into the Shan-hsi province, and, as such, it was undoubtedly regarded by the Chinese plenipotentiaries, who immediately wired to the Court at Hsi-an fu, urging the acceptance of the demands of the foreign Ministers, with regard to the punishments of the high officials implicated in the Boxer troubles and in the attacks upon the Legations in Peking. The result was a reply from the Court, accepting the terms in full, and the publication of a satisfactory edict, specifying the penalties to be inflicted, on the persons whose names had been included in the list presented by the foreign plenipotentiaries.

In consequence of this action on the part of the Chinese, the expedition was, for the time being, postponed, and eventually abandoned.

The British force, warned to be in readiness to take part in this movement, consisted of a brigade of cavalry, a brigade of infantry, and some divisional troops, including additional guns, with some engineer and pioneer troops. They were to take eight days' rations, and to move on light scale without tents, reserve rations being carried in regimental charge.

On the 14th March Field-Marshal Count von Waldersee left Peking on a visit to Kiao-chou. He was received at all stations along the railway by British guards of honour, and embarked at Tang-ku.

The railway was now working well, and trains were running punctually.

As early as the 6th November, 1900, the Russian consul at Tien-tsin had informed the consular body there that the land along the left bank of the Pei-ho, between the railway station and a petroleum depôt, about 1½ miles further down the river, had become the property of Russia by an act of war, Russian troops having established themselves there by right of conquest. The British Consul-General replied, reserving all British rights, as this area included land belonging to the railways; and, on the 28th November, Sir E. Satow explained that some of the ground on which the Russians had hoisted their flag was the property of British subjects, and that the British consul had therefore rightly objected to this arbitrary annexation.

On the 6th January the Russian consul at Tien-tsin further intimated to the consular body that, by an agreement arranged through Li Hung-chang, the Russian Government had obtained from the Chinese Government a concession of land on the left bank of the Pei-ho, opposite the foreign concessions, extending from the railway station for a distance of about 2½ miles down the river.

On the 8th March the Russian consul at Tien-tsin claimed, on behalf of Russian subjects, proprietary rights over certain railway land, on which it was desired to construct a new military line, required to meet the increased traffic. General Gaselee gave orders for the work to be commenced, leaving the Russians to protest, and on the 15th March the Russian authorities objected to the construction of the new sidings.

These new sidings were urgently required for the unloading of stores belonging to the allied Powers; but when the British pioneers prepared to continue work on the morning of the 15th March, they found a force of Cossacks posted, with orders to prevent their working. The Russians had thrown a shelter trench across the line to be taken by the proposed siding, and the troops remained opposite each other all day, but no hostilities took place. The situation remained unchanged for some days, but on the 21st March the dispute about the railway was arranged at an interview between Generals Barrow and Wogack, and the following day the troops of both Powers withdrew from the disputed area. The incident was thus closed.

Towards the end of March the Field-Marshal suggested that the negotiations for peace should be pushed forward with all speed, to allow of the reduction of the allied forces in Chi-li. He pointed out that troops with nothing to do were apt to cause trouble, that the hot weather with its attendant ill-health was approaching, and that the monsoon season would add to the difficulties of transporting troops by sea.

The approximate strength of troops in the various allied contingents on the 1st April was as follows :—

Germans	21,295
British	18,181
French	15,670
Japanese	6,408
Russians	2,900
Italians	2,155
Americans	1,750
Austrians	300
Total	68,659

At a conference of general officers, held at Peking on the 6th April, the Field-Marshal's proposition was accepted that the following fortifications, which by their nature and position might interfere with free communication between Peking and the sea, should be razed :—

1. The Military Camp at south exit from Yang-tsun, if not required for the accommodation of the garrison to be left there.
2. The Military Magazine of Hsi-ku. ⎫
3. The Yellow Fort. ⎬ Tien-tsin.
4. The Black Fort (citadel). ⎪
5. The East Arsenal. ⎭
6. The two camps at Chün-liang-ch'eng.
7. The four camps at Sin-ho.
8. All the fortifications at Taku, viz.: on the right bank of the Pei-ho, the coast battery with the camp attached to it, and the South Fort of Taku with its camp; and on the left bank, the North-West and North Forts.
9. All the fortifications at Pei-t'ang, viz.: the South Fort, the Central and North Forts, the two earthworks to the north of these, and the camps between the line of forts and the railway.
10. All the camps at Lu-tai, within a distance of 2,000 metres from the railway embankment.
11. The camps between Tang-ho and Shan-hai-kuan within a distance of 2,000 metres of the railway.
12. All the forts at Shan-hai-kuan, except those required for the accommodation of the international garrison to be left at Shan-hai-kuan, which might be temporarily retained.

The West Arsenal at Tien-tsin, which is of no military importance, was not to be razed; and the high mud wall, which lies in the Russian concession, was to be placed at the disposal of the Russian authorities.

With regard to the garrison to be permanently left in Chi-li, for guarding the line of communication between Peking and the sea, its strength was fixed as follows, exclusive of the guards of the Legations in Peking.

Tien-tsin to be held by 2,000 men, with a further force of 1,500 men at Shan-hai-kuan and Ching-wang-tao, while the following nine posts along the railway were to be occupied by garrisons of about 250 or 300 men each:—Huang-tsun, Lang-fang, Yang-tsun, Chün-liang-ch'eng, Tang-ku, Lu-tai, Tong-shan, Lan-chou and Ch'ang-li; making a total of about 6,000 men.

It was further decided that these posts should be held as follows :—The Italians should furnish the guard at Huang-tsun, the Germans those at Lang-fang and Yang-tsun; the French those at Chün-liang-ch'eng and Tang-ku, the British those at Lu-tai and Tong-shan, and the Japanese those at Lan-chou and Ch'ang-li, while, as long as the railway remained under British military administration, that nation should maintain a small guard at each station for police purposes, and no other nation should interfere with the railway stations or their policing. All five nations were to furnish, approximately, equal proportions of the garrisons at Tien-tsin and Shan-hai-kuan; and, for the present, until the Chinese Government was fully re-established in power, an additional force of 4,000 men would be maintained at Tien-tsin, to be furnished in equal proportions by France, Germany, Great Britain, and Japan, with a smaller contingent of Italians.

The appointment of a Commander-in-Chief for the whole of the international guards was suggested, but considered impracticable.

The strength of the Legation guards was fixed at about 2,000 men, made up as follows:—

America	150 men.
Germany	300 ,,
France	300 ,,
Great Britain	250 ,,
Japan	300 ,,
Italy	200 ,,
Austria-Hungary	200 ,,
Russia	300 ,,

Early in April the Field-Marshal decided to send an expedition to attack a force of Chinese troops encamped in the hills near a place called Huai-lu, or Huo-lu, to the west of Cheng-ting fu. Huai-lu is on the main road to Tai-yuan fu, inside Chih-li province, near the inner Great Wall, which approximately follows the boundary line between that province and the adjoining one of Shan-hsi. These troops had been occupying Huai-lu for several months, and were under observation by the French at Cheng-ting fu, but showed no signs of any intention to commence hostilities. Count Waldersee, however, decided to drive them beyond the Great Wall, and invited the French to co-operate, which they agreed to do.

The first official intimation of the intended expedition was received by the British general on the 17th April, on which date the news was also communicated to the commanders of the Italian, Japanese, and United States forces.

The German troops from Peking, intended to take part in the expedition against Huai-lu, left the capital by train for Ting-chou, south-west of Pao-ting fu, on the 17th and 19th April. The total force was to consist of four battalions of infantry, one squadron of cavalry, and three batteries of artillery ; and the attack was to be made on the 22nd, unless the Chinese had withdrawn beyond the Great Wall before that date.

On receiving news of the approach of the Germans, the Chinese commander Liu had withdrawn most of his troops into Shan-hsi, between the 19th and 21st April, and the Germans met with very little opposition on their arrival at the Great Wall on the 23rd. What chance they might have had of inflicting punishment on the Chinese was lost by their pressing forward to the attack before the French were in position, on their left, to co-operate against the enemy's flank and rear. The losses of the Germans were reported as three men killed, and four officers and 28 men wounded.

On the 11th April orders were issued for the 4th Brigade of the British Contingent, China Expeditionary Force, to be broken up. The brigade staff and Ulwar and Bikanir regiments were to return to India as soon as transports could be provided, and the 28th and 31st Madras Infantry were ordered to be transferred to the lines of communication. Further, the 1st Bengal Lancers at Hongkong, the 14th Sikhs, and four sections of "pompoms," at Shanghai, were ordered up to Tien-tsin. On the following day orders were issued for the move of No. 3 Company Madras, Sappers and Miners, from Shanghai, and a wing of the 1st Madras Pioneers from Tien-tsin to Wei-hai-wei, for duty at that port.

A serious misfortune occurred on the night of the 17th–18th April, caused by an accidental outbreak of fire in the Winter Palace at Peking, occupied by the Field-Marshal and the German headquarters staff. In a short space of time the whole of the principal buildings were in flames, and nothing could be done to save them. General von Schwartzhoff, the chief of the German staff, lost his life in the conflagration. It is not known for certain how this occurred, but apparently he had returned to his room to secure important papers, and being overcome by the smoke or heat had fainted, and so perished in the fire. In the confusion and darkness his absence was not noticed until all question of rescue was impossible, and his body was not recovered till next morning, when the fire had burnt itself out. He was considered one of the most distinguished and able officers in the German army. Obtaining his commission after the battle of Sedan, he had risen rapidly and had held many important staff appointments, and at 30 years' service had reached the position of a major-general in the German army. His great ability and devotion to duty were recognised by all who came in contact with him, and his untimely end was deeply regretted by the entire allied force. His funeral, which took place on the 22nd April, was attended by the Generals of all the allied contingents, with their staffs, by the foreign Ministers and members of their Legations, and by large numbers of officers, and representative bodies of troops from the forces of the various Powers.

On the 20th April a party of the 4th Punjab Infantry, under Major Browning, when reconnoitring to the north of Fu-ning-hsien, came in contact with a force of Chinese brigands near the town of Tai-tou-ying. The enemy was strongly posted, under cover, in a village near the town, and Major Browning determined to attempt to dislodge them. This, however, he failed to do, and in the fighting that ensued he and one sepoy were killed, Lieutenant Stirling and six men were wounded, and the column had to retreat on Fu-ning. Reinforcements, consisting of the rest of the 4th Punjab Infantry, under Colonel Radford, 100 men of the 6th Jats, a squadron of the Jodhpur Lancers, and a detachment of 200 Japanese, were at once despatched to their assistance from Shan-hai-kuan. This force, which was subsequently joined by a company of French Zouaves, advanced on Tai-tou-ying on the 22nd, and captured it after some resistance, inflicting severe loss on the Chinese, who were driven beyond the Great Wall. Major Browning's body was recovered at the same time. The casualties in this second action were: 1 French, 2 Japanese, and 6 British soldiers wounded.

At the end of April the 2nd Squadron of the German Cavalry pushed out officer's patrols to the west and south-west of the line Ch'a-tao-Kalgan, which reconnoitred for a considerable distance into north Shan-hsi and Mongolia, and ascertained that the country was free from Chinese troops.

The question of the reduction of the whole allied force in North China was now assuming definite shape. On the 2nd May orders were issued for the return to India of No. 3 Company, Southern Division, Royal Garrison Artillery, the 1st Bengal Lancers, the 1st Madras Pioneers, the 28th Madras Infantry, and No. 3 Company, Madras Sappers and Miners. At the same time No. 15 Company, Western Division, Royal Garrison Artillery, and the 4th Balloon Section, Royal Engineers, were warned to be in readiness to embark for England.

On the 5th May the 6th United States' Cavalry, and F Battery, 5th United States' Artillery, left Peking, by route march for Tang-ku, *en route* to Manilla. They were followed, on the 22nd May, by Major-General Chaffee and his staff and by the 9th United States' Infantry, who travelled by train.

On leaving, they handed over to the British the district which had been policed by them, to the south-east of Peking, while in Peking itself the quarter occupied by the Americans was divided between the British and Germans, for administrative purposes, but the Americans retained their guards upon the south gate of the Forbidden City and the Temple of Agriculture.

The United States had been one of the first of the Powers to send troops to North China, as orders were sent, on the 16th June, 1900, to the General Officer commanding the United States forces in the Philippines, to despatch a regiment of infantry to Taku ; and on the 27th June the 9th Infantry, under command of Colonel Liscum, embarked at Manilla.

On the 1st July the 6th Cavalry sailed from San Francisco, and, later on, orders were issued for the despatch from the Philippines of the 14th Infantry and a light battery to Taku. These were to be followed by a considerably larger force of infantry, three cavalry regiments, two artillery regiments, and detachments of auxiliary services, collected from various garrisons in the United States.

The total expeditionary force thus set in motion was about 435 officers, 15,018 men, and 30 guns.

By arrangement with the Japanese Government, Nagasaki was to be used as a port of call by all American transports, coming from both America and the Philippines, where they would receive final orders as to their destination. Thirty-two large Government steamers were used for the conveyance of troops and stores, but no extra transports were hired.

On the 29th June Major-General Adna R. Chaffee was appointed to command the American forces in China. He arrived at Taku on the 20th July, where he found the 9th and 14th Infantry, one battery, and a battalion of marines already landed.

Two battalions of the 9th Infantry had landed as early as the 6th July, and had taken part in the attack and capture of Tien-tsin city on the 13th, being attached to the British force under Major-General Dorward. In this engagement they had suffered the loss of 18 killed, including their gallant leader, Colonel Liscum, and 77 wounded.

At the time of the advance of the allied relief force from Tien-tsin to Peking, on the 4th August, about 5,000 men of the United States' army had arrived in China, and of these about 2,500 formed part of the relief force, which entered Peking on the 14th August. Owing to bad weather, their cavalry had not arrived in time to take part in the advance.

Immediately on the receipt of the news that the Legations in Peking had been rescued, the American Government issued orders to General Chaffee that, as the object of the expedition had been accomplished, he was not to take part in any further aggressive action. The landing of additional troops was also countermanded, and they were diverted to Manilla ; orders were also issued for the return to the Philippines of a considerable portion of the American troops already in Chi-li, a force of about 3,000 men only being retained during the winter, and these, with the exception of the guards for the United States' Legation, were withdrawn, as above described, in May 1901.

During the entire campaign the American casualties amounted to 2 officers and 30 men killed, and 7 officers and 170 men wounded.

On the 10th May the French embarked one battalion of infantry, one field battery, and the balloon section at Tang-ku for France, and more troops were under orders for embarkation, but these movements were suddenly countermanded, probably on account of the fact that the Germans had received no orders as to the withdrawal of their troops from Chi-li.

Sanction to the Field-Marshal's proposals for withdrawing the German troops from North China was received by him on the 16th May.

On the 20th May General Gaselee received sanction, from the British Government, for the further reduction of the British force in Chi-li, by the return to India of the 1st Infantry Brigade, B Battery, Royal Horse Artillery, another cavalry regiment, the Jodhpur Lancers. These reductions were to be carried out *pari passu* with those of other contingents.

On the 25th May a further telegram was received, directing General Gaselee to take measures at once to reduce the British forces in China to the strength proposed for the transition period, and to forward suggestions for the reduction of the garrisons of Hongkong and Shanghai.

General Gaselee then suggested the following as the British garrison to be left behind in North China during the ensuing winter :—

Legation Guard—Peking.

2 companies, Royal Welsh Fusiliers.
Detachment No. 2 company, Southern Division, R.G.A.
2 Naval 12-pr. Q.F. guns.
2 siege trains, 6-inch howitzers from Hongkong, and Maxims.

Tien-tsin to Shan-hai-kuan.

3 sections of pompoms.
2 companies, Royal Welsh Fusiliers.
14th Sikhs.
1st Batt., 4th Gurkha Rifles.
31st Madras Infantry.
Hongkong Regiment.
Half a British Field Hospital.
2 Native Field Hospitals.

Shanghai.

Detachment of pompoms.
2nd Bengal Infantry.
30th Bombay Infantry.
1 section of a British Field Hospital.
2 sections of a Native Field Hospital.

The whole force to be commanded by Major-General Creagh, V.C., with his headquarters at Tien-tsin, and a full staff.

On the 1st June the Field-Marshal announced that he had received orders from the German Emperor, for the breaking up of the Army headquarters, and their return to Europe. In consequence, Count Waldersee, with most of his staff, left Peking on the morning of the 3rd June, spent the night at Tien-tsin, and left Taku on the 4th for Japan, on board the cruiser "Hertha."

A recrudescence of the Boxer movement, which took place towards the end of May, in the districts lying to the south of Pao-ting fu and east of Cheng-ting fu, was easily suppressed. A French column consisting of about 1,500 French troops, under General Bailloud, moved out from Pao-ting fu, and, in conjunction with a force of Chinese regulars under General Lu, attacked the Boxers and completely dispersed them. At the same time German columns, in the hills to the west of Pao-ting fu, encountered several bands of Boxers, probably fugitives from the fights with the French troops. These the Germans scattered, inflicting heavy loss.

Quiet having thus been completely restored, the outlying detachments of French and German troops were gradually withdrawn to Pao-ting fu and Peking.

On the 7th June the Japanese minister notified the other ministers that all Japanese troops in Chi-li would be recalled shortly to Japan, their place being taken by one fresh brigade. At the same time the French minister intimated that, of the two French brigades in North China, one would be withdrawn.

Everything was now very quiet in Chi-li except for the presence of large bands of armed banditti, in the mountains to the north-west of Shan-hai-kuan, who threatened to give trouble by invading the villages on the plains, but the Chinese Government was doing its best to make headway against these brigands with its Imperial troops, and, in the meanwhile, the withdrawal of the allied contingents from North China was proceeding rapidly.

The Home Government gave orders for the return of all the howitzers to England, as it considered them unnecessary for the defence of the Legations, as proposed by the general officer commanding. General Gaselee replied to this that, in the opinion of the International Committee of Defence, which had been entrusted with drawing up the scheme for the protection of the Legation quarter, the retention of the howitzers was necessary, as, in case of trouble they could drop large shells into any part of the city as required, and thus compensate to some extent for the comparative weakness of the defence.

The Home Government consequently agreed, but ordered two howitzers to be sent to Singapore. The artillery detachment at the Peking Legation was also increased to a strength of two officers and 50 men, making the total British garrison up to 270 men.

In the middle of July General Voyron informed the other allied commanders that he had received instructions to evacuate Pao-ting fu and the Lu-han railway as soon as possible, and that all French troops would, in consequence, be withdrawn from these places by the 5th August.

As the China Expeditionary Force might now be considered to have broken up, General Gaselee handed over command of the British troops in North China to Major-General Creagh, V.C., on the 21st July, and two days later left Chi-li for England, viâ Japan.

At the end of July the attitude of Li Hung-chang became so obstructive and insolent, that the British Minister requested General Creagh to again occupy the Summer Palace, with a view to bringing pressure to bear on Li, and the 12th Battery Royal Field Artillery, and two companies of the 7th Bengal Infantry were accordingly quartered there for a short time.

At this time the Home Government suggested that the garrison of Shanghai might be further reduced to one battalion of infantry, and enquired what the strength of the other foreign detachments at that place amounted to. In reply it was reported that the Germans had arranged to leave a garrison of one thousand men there for the winter, including a six-gun mountain battery with a personnel of 150 men, and 100 mounted infantry; while the French intended to send one battalion to Shanghai from Shan-hai-kuan, which would be made up to full strength from the troops already in garrison, after which the remainder would be withdrawn to Tonkin. The 2nd Bengal Infantry Regiment was accordingly sent to Hongkong from Shanghai in the beginning of September.

Towards the end of August the British Minister reported that he considered that the British troops in Chi-li were too few for the work they had to perform. At this time the strength of the other foreign contingents remaining in Chi-li were estimated as follows:—

Germans	3,690
French	3,860
Russians	1,900
Italians	1,170
Americans	300
Japanese	3,660

Against these the strength of the British force would be about 3,450 men, when the reduction was completed, but, from having to guard the long line of railway, very few troops were available for other duties, and the British garrisons at Tien-tsin and Shan-hai-kuan were unduly weak, especially in view of possible trouble with armed robbers in the neighbourhood of Shan-hai-kuan, and of the report that the Russians intended to place a considerably larger garrison in that place than they had at first stated. In consequence Sir Ernest Satow, after consulting General Creagh, strongly advised the retention in Chi-li of the 12th Battery

Royal Field Artillery, the 3rd Regiment of Bombay Cavalry, and the 4th Punjab Infantry, until the spring of 1902, in addition to the troops already arranged for. To this suggestion the Home Government agreed, but afterwards reconsidered its decision, and ordered the artillery and cavalry to be sent back to India, while the retention of the extra infantry battalion for the winter was sanctioned.

With the embarkation of the 3rd Bombay Cavalry and the 12th field battery, at the end of October and beginning of November, the reduction of the British contingent was finally completed.

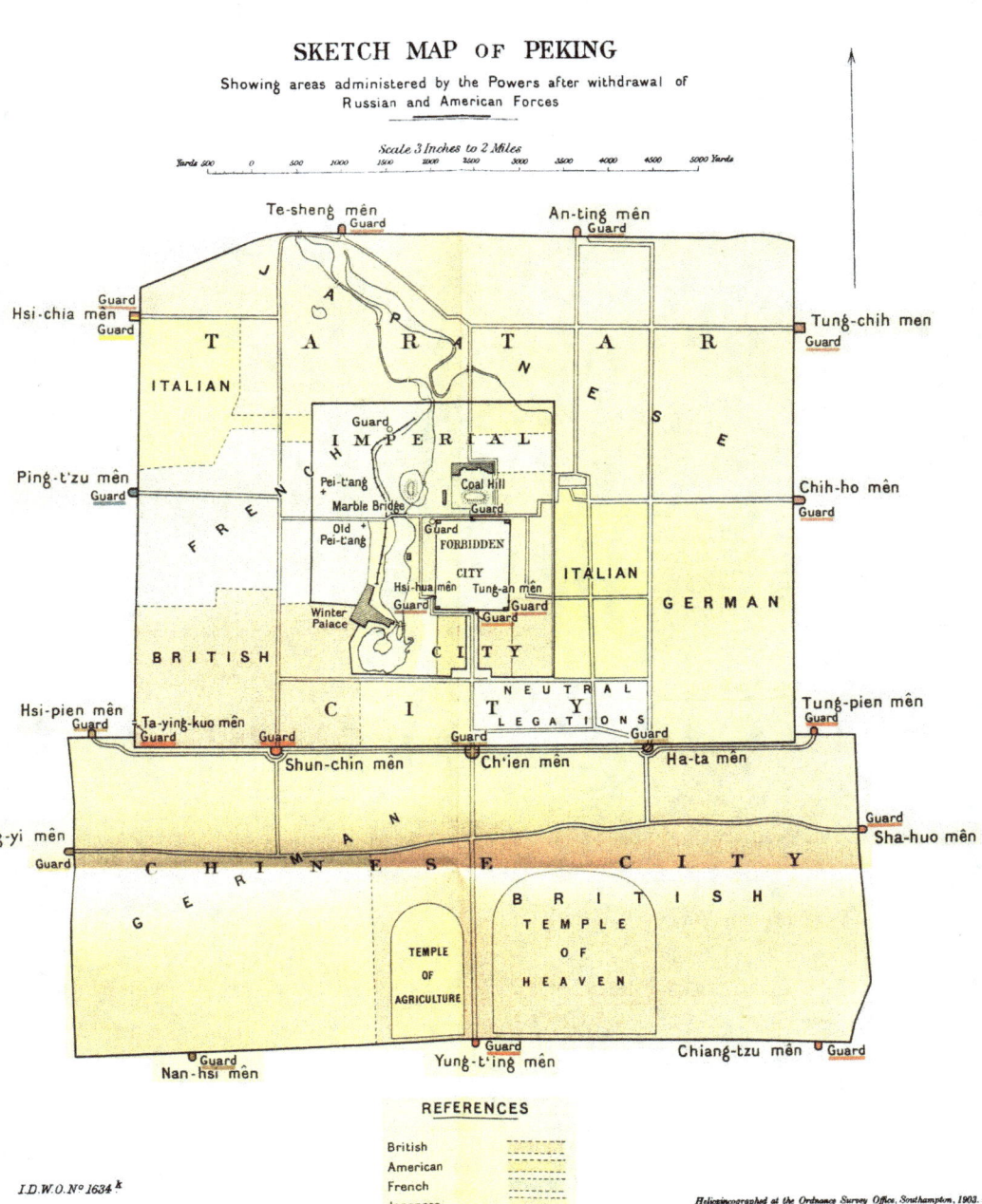

CHAPTER XVI.

NEGOTIATIONS FOR PEACE, RESULTING IN THE WITHDRAWAL FROM CHINA OF THE BULK OF THE FOREIGN CONTINGENTS, AND THE RETURN TO POWER OF THE CHINESE GOVERNMENT.

On the 11th September, 1900, the Powers were informed that Li Hung-chang and Prince Ch'ing had at last been invested with full powers to act as Plenipotentiaries, and to settle terms of peace on behalf of the Emperor.
It was therefore now possible to commence negotiations, and on the 15th September all the foreign Ministers in Peking, except the German Minister, sent separate letters to Prince Ch'ing, urging that the Court should return to the capital, and so demonstrate that the influence of its former advisers was now at an end. Prince Ch'ing replied that he had already urged the Emperor to return and thought that he might do so.
On the 18th September the German Government proposed to Lord Salisbury, through its Minister in London, and also to the other Powers, that, before entering upon diplomatic intercourse with the Chinese Government, they should insist upon the punishment of those persons, who were the primary and leading instigators of the crimes against international law, committed in Peking, as a preliminary condition to discussing terms of peace. It was suggested that the various Powers should instruct their representatives in Peking to indicate those leading Chinese, as to whose guilt in instigating and committing such crimes there was no room for doubt. To this the United States Government agreed, but considered that, instead of handing over the guilty persons to the Powers, their punishment should be carried out by the supreme Imperial Chinese authority itself, so as to vindicate its position before the world. Japan agreed to the idea, but saw great difficulty in enforcing the delivering up of the guilty persons. Russia considered that they should be punished by the Chinese Government. France, Italy, and Austria also agreed to the German proposal. Great Britain objected, as the strict enforcement of this demand would possibly necessitate the despatch of troops beyond Chi-li, the undertaking of extended operations in the interior, and the breaking off of all negotiations until the punishment of the offenders had been fully carried out.
After the appearance of an Imperial Edict, dated the 25th September, detailing certain punishments awarded to some of the leaders of the Boxer movement, the German Government

modified its proposal, and asked that the Powers would consult their ministers in Peking as to—
1. Whether the list of persons to be punished, as contained in the Imperial Edict, was sufficient and correct.
2. Whether the proposed punishments were suitable.
3. How far the Powers could control their being carried into effect.

To this the foreign Representatives in Peking replied that—
1. The list was correct as far as it went, but the names of Tung Fu-hsiang and Yü-hsien should be added to it.
2. The punishments were insufficient.
3. They should be carried out in Peking in the presence of representatives of the foreign Powers.

Japan agreed to these answers of the Ministers, and considered that all questions as to the terms of peace should be referred to them, for collective opinion. The edict of the 25th September was generally supposed to be merely intended to mislead the Powers as to the sincerity of the Court's regret, for the following day another edict appeared, in which Yü-hsien was removed from his governorship of Shan-hsi, and ordered to await *reappointment;* while by a decree of the 4th October, Huai-t'a-pu, the well-known anti-foreign Manchu, who had been cashiered by the Emperor in 1898 for his opposition to reform, was appointed to succeed Prince Tuan as chief of the Banner forces. Jung-lu and Tung Fu-hsiang, who in the opinion of the Chinese were quite as much to blame for the anti-foreign outbreak as any of the other officials, were not included in the list of the guilty at all, but they had strong forces of troops at their disposal, which was perhaps a sufficient reason for this. In the Yang-tse provinces various Manchus were also being promoted to high appointments, no doubt with the idea of counteracting the influence of the friendly Viceroys, and in October Yü-ch'ang, a violently anti-foreign Manchu, was appointed governor of Hu-pei, but on the representation of the foreign Ministers this appointment was cancelled.

Up to the end of September it was reported from Shanghai that, in the province of Shan-hsi alone, 140 foreigners had been murdered, of whom the greater part were British. For these murders the governor, Yü-hsien, was mainly responsible.

In the beginning of October the French Government formulated the following proposals, as preliminary terms to negotiations for peace with China:—
1. Punishment of the principal culprits, as designated by the Ministers at Peking.
2. Prohibition of the importation of arms into China.
3. Payments of equitable indemnities to States, societies, and individuals.
4. Establishment of permanent guards at the Legations in Peking.

5. Dismantlement of the Taku forts.
6. The military occupation of certain points, to be settled on by agreement between the Powers, to ensure free communication between the Legations and the sea.

These proposals were supported formally by the Russian Government.

The British Minister proposed the following additions :—

7. An edict to be posted for two years in every district, prohibiting membership of the Boxer Society, under penalty of death.
8. The abolition of the Tsung-li Yamen and the appointment of a Minister for Foreign Affairs.
9. The establishment of relations with the Court on a sensible basis.

The British Government agreed to the note generally, except as to the construction of forts between Peking and Taku, to be held by international troops, Lord Salisbury considering it preferable that any Power, who wished to do so, should have the right to construct a fort of its own, within easy reach of the sea, to which the members of its Legation might retreat in time of extreme danger. Japan also agreed generally, but said that the prohibition of importing arms might be given by China as a reason, or at least an excuse, if she failed to protect foreigners or to maintain order in the future. She also agreed to separate Legation guards, but considered an international guard impracticable.

While agreeing to the French note, the German Minister proposed the following addition to the bases of negotiation adopted by the Ministers, namely, the despatch of a mission to Berlin by the Emperor of China, to express regret for the assassination of the German Minister, and the erection of a monument to his memory by the Chinese Government.

A further proposal was that the Chinese Government should undertake to amend the Treaties dealing with commerce, inland navigation, and other commercial subjects, on lines agreeable to the Powers; and the Japanese Government also demanded the despatch of a Mission to Japan, to apologize for the murder, early in June, of Mr. Sugiyama, Chancellor of the Japanese Legation, by Imperial troops.

During the siege of the Legations in Peking the British cemetery outside the city was entirely destroyed and desecrated. All the tombstones and monuments were thrown down and broken, the 12-foot high brick wall round the cemetery was razed to the ground, and the caretaker's house was burnt down; all the trees, both inside and outside the cemetery, were cut down, and, lastly, thirteen graves were opened, the coffins broken up, and the bones removed from them and apparently burnt. The other foreign cemeteries were treated in a similar manner.

As some atonement for these barbarous outrages, the Chinese Government was called upon to erect expiatory monuments, in each of the foreign or international cemeteries, which had been thus desecrated.

All the foreign Ministers were agreed, in principle, as to the terms, and it was reported that the Chinese plenipotentiaries, finding that the Powers were firm, had decided to bow to the inevitable and accept them.

Considerable discussion ensued, however, as to the exact wording of certain clauses, and this involved telegraphic references to the home Governments. Owing, however, to mistakes in cipher messages, further misunderstandings took place, causing fresh delay.

In the meantime an Imperial decree was published on the 13th November,[*] which inflicted various punishments on the high Princes and officials responsible for the attacks on the Legations, and the encouragement of the Boxer rising. These consisted of imprisonment and banishment for the most guilty; and deprivation of rank or salary, or degradation, for the others.

At last the clauses of the amended note were finally agreed to by all the foreign Ministers, except the representative of the United States, and were signed by them on the 20th December. The American Minister signed on the 22nd, and the note was formally handed to Prince Ch'ing on the morning of the 24th December, by the doyen of the foreign Ministers, at the Spanish Legation; Li Hung-chang being prevented by illness from being present.

The text of the note now read as follows:—

Draft of Note embodying the Demands of the Allied Powers; to be presented to the Chinese Government.

(Translation.)

During the months of May, June, July, and August of the present year serious disorders broke out in the northern provinces of China, and crimes, unprecedented in human history, crimes against the law of nations, against the laws of humanity, and against civilisation were committed under peculiarly odious circumstances. Of these crimes the principal ones were the following:—

1. On 20th June his Excellency Baron Ketteler, German Minister, proceeding to the Tsung-li Yamên, was murdered, while in the exercise of his duties, by soldiers of the regular army, acting under the orders of their chiefs.

2. On the same day the foreign Legations were attacked and besieged. These attacks continued without intermission until 14th August, on which date the arrival of foreign troops put an

---

[*] *See* page 497.

end to them. The attacks were made by regular troops, who joined the Boxers, who obeyed the orders of the Court emanating from the Imperial Palace. At the same time the Chinese Government officially declared, by its Representatives abroad, that it guaranteed the safety of the Legations.

3. On 11th June Mr. Sugiyama, Chancellor of the Japanese Legation, in the discharge of an official mission, was killed by regulars at the gates of the city. At Peking and in several provinces foreigners were murdered, tortured, or attacked by Boxers and regular troops, and only owed their safety to their determined resistance. Their establishments were pillaged and destroyed.

4. Foreign cemeteries, notably at Peking, were desecrated, the graves opened, and the remains scattered abroad.

These events led the foreign Powers to send their troops to China in order to protect the lives of their Representatives and of their nationals, and to restore order. During their march to Peking the allied forces met with the resistance of the Chinese armies, and had to overcome it by force. China, having recognized her responsibility, expressed her regrets, and manifested the desire to see an end put to the situation created by the disturbances referred to, the Powers have decided to accede to her request on the irrevocable conditions enumerated below, which they deem indispensable to expiate the crimes committed and prevent their recurrence:—

Article 1.—(*a.*) Despatch to Berlin of an Extraordinary Mission, headed by an Imperial Prince, to express the regrets of His Majesty the Emperor of China and the Chinese Government for the murder of his Excellency the late Baron Ketteler, German Minister. (*Complied with by the Imperial Edict of the 9th June* 1901.)

(*b.*) Erection on the place where the murder was committed of a commemorative monument, suitable to the rank of the deceased, bearing an inscription in the Latin, German, and Chinese languages, expressing the regret of the Emperor of China for the murder. (*Complied with 25th June* 1901.)

Art. 2.—(*a.*) The severest punishment, in proportion to their crimes, for the persons named in the Imperial Decree of the 25th September 1900, and for those whom the Representatives of the Powers shall subsequently designate. (*Complied with by Imperial Edict of* 21*st February and subsequent Decrees.*)

(*b.*) Suspension of all official examinations for five years, in all the towns where foreigners have been massacred or have been subjected to cruel treatment. (*Complied with by the Imperial Edict of August* 19*th,* 1901.)

Art. 3. An honourable reparation shall be accorded by the Chinese Government to that of Japan for the murder of Mr. Sugiyama, Chancellor of the Japanese Legation. (*Complied with by the Imperial Edict of June* 18*th,* 1901.)

Art. 4. An expiatory monument shall be erected by the Chinese Government in each of the foreign or international cemeteries, which have been desecrated, and in which the graves have been destroyed. (*Agreed to.*)

Art. 5. Maintenance, under conditions to be settled between the Powers, of the prohibition of the importation of arms, as well as material serving exclusively for the manufacture of arms and ammunition. (*Complied with by the Imperial Edict of August 25th, 1901.*)

'Art. 6.—(*a.*) An equitable indemnity to Governments, societies, private individuals, as well as for Chinese who have suffered during the recent occurrences in' their persons or property, in consequence of their being in the service of foreigners.

(*b.*) China shall adopt financial measures acceptable to the Powers, for the purpose of guaranteeing the payment of the said indemnities and the service of the loans. (*Terms finally settled May 29th, 1901.*)

Art. 7. The right of maintaining, by each Power, a permanent guard for its Legation, and of placing the Legation quarter in a condition of defence. Chinese not to have the right of residing in that quarter. (*Agreed to.*)

Art. 8. The Taku and other forts, which might impede free communication between Peking and the coast, are to be razed. (*Agreed to.*)

Art. 9. Right of military occupation of certain points, to be determined by agreement between the Powers, in order to maintain communication between the capital and the sea. (*Agreed to.*)

Art. 10.—(*a.*) The Chinese Government shall cause to be posted up for two years in all the Sub-Prefectures an Imperial Decree embodying—

Perpetual prohibition, under pain of death, of being a member of an anti-foreign Society. (*Complied with by Imperial Edict of February 1st, 1901.*)

Enumeration of the penalties which shall have been inflicted on the guilty persons, including the suspension of all official examinations in the towns where foreigners were massacred or subjected to cruel treatment. (*Complied with by Imperial Edicts of February 21st, August 19th, 1901, and other decrees.*)

(*b.*) An Imperial Edict shall be issued and published everywhere in the empire, making all viceroys, governors, and provincial and local officials responsible for order within their jurisdictions; and whenever anti-foreign disturbances or any other treaty infractions occur therein, which are not forthwith suppressed, and in regard to which the guilty persons are not punished, these officials shall be immediately recalled, without the possibility of being given new posts or of receiving fresh honours. (*Complied with by the Imperial Edict of 24th December 1900.*)

Art. 11. The Chinese Government will undertake to negotiate regarding amendments to the treaties of commerce and navigation considered useful by the Powers, and also other subjects connected with commercial relations, with the object of facilitating them. (*Complied with.*)

Art. 12. The Chinese Government shall undertake to reform the office of foreign relations, and modify the Court ceremonial relative to the reception of foreign representatives in the manner which the Powers shall indicate. (*Complied with in the Imperial Edict of July 24th, 1901, and subsequent Decrees.*)

Until the Chinese Government have complied with the above conditions to the satisfaction of the Powers, the undersigned can hold out no expectation that the occupation of Peking and the province of Chi-li by the allied forces can be brought to a conclusion.

For Germany—
    (Signed)   A. VON MUMM.
For Austria-Hungary—
    (Signed)   M. CZIKANN.
For Belgium—
    (Signed)   JOOSTENS.
For Spain—
    (Signed)   B. J. DE COLOGAN
For the United States of America—
    (Signed)   E. H. CONGER.
For France—
    (Signed)   S. PICHON.
For Great Britain—
    (Signed)   ERNEST SATOW.
For Italy—
    (Signed)   SALVAGO RAGGI.
For Japan—
    (Signed)   T. NISSI.
For the Netherlands—
    (Signed)   F. M. KNOBEL.
For Russia—
    (Signed)   MICHEL DE GIERS.

Peking, December 22, 1900.

An Imperial Decree, dated the 27th December, accepted the principles laid down in the Joint Note in their entirety, and the Chinese plenipotentiaries thereupon requested that the Powers would now withdraw their troops from Chinese soil. The foreign Ministers, however, informed them that, before this request could be even considered, the Chinese Government would have to furnish clear proof of its determination to carry into effect the demands of the Powers, which the Emperor had accepted. At the same time they drew attention to the fact that Tung Fu-hsiang, one of the chief offenders, whose punishment they had demanded, was still in attendance on the Court, where his presence was most undesirable. Tung Fu-hsiang, however, had been deprived, by Imperial Decree, of his rank as commander-in-chief of the forces in Kan-su, and had been ordered to leave the Court and return immediately to his province.

To test the sincerity of the Chinese declaration of willingness to comply with the terms of the Joint Note, the foreign Ministers decided to demand, first of all, the carrying into effect of Article 2 of the Joint Note, which required the infliction of heavy punishments on the Princes and high officials, responsible for the troubles in Peking. It was considered that this would be the most difficult of all the clauses to enforce, and that if the Chinese Government could be induced to carry it into effect, the other clauses would also be complied with.

Much discussion now ensued as to the names of the high officials who were to be included in the list of those to be punished, and also as to the nature of the penalty to be awarded in each case. On the one hand, the Chinese plenipotentiaries did all in their power to mitigate the punishments required by the Powers, while, on the other, the Ministers continued to press for their demands to be carried out in full.

An attempt was even made to force the hands of the foreign Ministers by an Imperial Edict which appeared on the 13th February, 1901, and inflicted awards, which were much less severe than those proposed by the foreign plenipotentiaries. By it Prince Chuang was ordered to commit suicide; Prince Tuan and Duke Lan to be banished to Turkestan, and there perpetually imprisoned, no death penalty being recorded against them; Yü-hsien to be decapitated; Ying-nien and Chao Shu-ch'iao to be imprisoned, awaiting decapitation, implying the commutation of the death penalty; Tung Fu-hsiang to be degraded, but no mention was made of further severe punishment. The Court were evidently counting on disunion amongst the Powers, to help them to evade carrying out the demands in their entirety; but the Ministers, seeing the importance of not giving way over this first test clause, unanimously agreed to demand the execution of the full punishments by the Chinese Government. These punishments they had recorded in detail, in a despatch sent to the Chinese plenipotentiaries on the 6th February, but of which the Chinese Government had not acknowledged the receipt before the above Decree was published.

The penalties, the execution of which the foreign plenipotentiaries had finally agreed to insist upon, were as follows:—

Prince Chuang.—Official commander-in-chief of the Boxers, to be condemned to commit suicide.

Prince Tuan, chief patron of the Boxer movement and *Duke Lan*, his brother, one of the official chiefs of the Boxers, to be condemned to imprisonment pending their decapitation. If immediately after being condemned, the Emperor thinks fit to spare their lives, they shall be sent to Turkestan, there to be imprisoned for life, no commutation of the punishment being subsequently pronounced in their favour. (It was impossible to obtain the capital punishment in the case of these two men, owing to their close relationship to the Emperor.)

Ying-nien, one of the official chiefs of the Boxers, to be sentenced to capital punishment.

Kang-yi, one of the most active leaders of the Boxers, since dead. All the legal consequences of condemnation to capital punishment to be pronounced against him.

Chao Shu-ch'iao, a prominent leader of the movement against foreigners, to be sentenced to capital punishment.

Yü-hsien, original patron of the Boxers and responsible for the murder of missionaries in Shan-hsi province, to be beheaded.

Tung Fu-hsiang, chiefly instrumental in attacking the Legations, to be deprived of his command and suffer the severest punishment when such could be carried out.

Li Ping-hêng, and *Hsü T'ung,* prominent leaders of the Boxers, and markedly hostile towards foreigners, both dead. All the legal consequences of condemnation to capital punishment to be pronounced against them.

Hsü Ch'eng-yü, son of Hsü T'ung and equally guilty, and *Ch'i-hsiu,* a Mandarin notoriously hostile to foreigners, to be condemned to capital punishment.

It was further stated that the representatives of the Powers considered that the decrees announcing these resolutions should be immediately issued.

They should be carried out with the shortest possible delay; and the representatives of the Powers reserved to themselves the right to control their execution, by appointing delegates in Peking or the Provinces.

This list only included the names of Princes and officials responsible for crimes committed in Peking, and did not include those of Mandarins, who had been guilty of crimes against foreigners committed in the provinces, lists of whom were to be communicated later.

At the same time it was decided that the Emperor should be requested to publish Imperial Decrees rehabilitating the memories of the following five officials, who had bravely protested against the anti-foreign policy of the Court, and who had suffered death in consequence. This was complied with by an imperial decree of 13th February, 1901. Their names were Hsü Ching-ch'êng, Yüan Ch'ang, Hsü Yung-i, Lien-yüan and Lishan.

As already mentioned, in view of the obstructive tactics adopted by the Chinese, in order to put off complying with the terms demanded by the foreign Ministers, Count Waldersee issued an Army Order on the 15th February, in which he stated that all troops should be in readiness for the possible resumption of military operations at the end of the month. This strong hint that he might find it necessary to send a force into Shan-hsi produced the desired effect, and an imperial decree was published on the 21st February, accepting the penalties demanded by the foreign Ministers in full, with the exception that Ying-nien and Chao Shu-ch'iao were ordered to commit suicide instead of being put to death by strangulation, and this alteration was accepted by the Ministers.

It has been reported that Kang-yi had died about the middle of October 1900. Prince Chuang committed suicide on the 21st February 1901.

Yü-hsien was decapitated on the morning of the 22nd February at Lan-chou, the capital of Kan-su. The governor Li, charged with carrying out the sentence, committed suicide rather than obey the order, as he had formerly been a Mandarin of Tai-yuan fu under Yü-hsien. The nieh-tai then called on Yü-hsien to undergo the sentence pronounced on him, which was carried out by a military Mandarin, as the ex-governor's rank precluded his death at the hands of a common executioner. There seems to be no doubt that the sentence was carried out as above described.

Ying-nien and Chao Shu-ch'iao committed suicide on the 24th February.

Ch'i-hsiu and Hsü Ch'eng-yü were executed at Peking on the 26th February.

The question of punishments having thus been settled, the next clause which appeared likely to give trouble was that of the indemnities to be paid by China to the Governments of the foreign Powers. The first discussion on this subject took place on the 16th February, 1901, and it at once became apparent that the question was one of considerable difficulty, first, with regard to the classification of claims on which compensation could properly be demanded, and, secondly, with regard to the sources of revenue, which were available to the Chinese Government, for the payment of the sums total of the indemnities and the interest accumulating thereon. After some discussion it was decided to entrust the consideration of the sources from which China could furnish the indemnities, to a Committee, consisting of the British, French, German and Japanese ministers, who were empowered to call in the professional advice of bankers and others to their assistance.

The claims were furthermore divided into two classes, namely Government claims and private claims.

The Government claims consisted of:—

(*a*.) Destruction and damage of buildings of the Legations and Consulates, and of furniture.

The death or wounding of guards or civilians during the siege of the Legations.

Furniture, &c., belonging to the members of the Legations.

War expenses.

(*b*.) Buildings and other effects belonging to societies or individuals at Peking, Tien-tsin, or elsewhere.

Compensation for the death or wounds of civilians and missionaries.

Buildings and other effects, the property of missionary societies.

(c.) For the Chinese who have suffered in their goods or in their persons, owing to the fact of their being in foreign service.

Private claims by individuals, in addition to the above, were to be submitted to their Ministers, to be dealt with on their merits, and each nation was finally to submit the sum-total of its claims, to be included in the entire amount of the indemnity to be demanded from the Chinese Government.

After a great amount of discussion, the total amount of the indemnities, to be claimed by the Powers collectively from the Chinese Government, was fixed at four hundred and fifty million *taels*, to bear interest at four per cent. The annual payments were to commence in 1902, and the whole amount, including interest, was to be paid off by 1940.

These demands were agreed to by the Chinese Government.

In the meanwhile all the other clauses of the Joint Note had been gradually disposed of.

On the 28th February a long list of provincial officials, who merited punishment in connexion with the late troubles, was submitted to the foreign Ministers by a Commission appointed to inquire into the matter. It included ten names for whom the death penalty was demanded, and over ninety names for whom lesser punishments were considered sufficient. In the ensuing discussion the Russian Minister alone objected to the list, and stated that his Government had all along been opposed to the demand of the death penalty, and desired that a less severe form of punishment might be substituted. No Russian subjects had been killed in the interior of China.

The number of missionaries and other foreigners who were known to have been murdered by the Chinese in different provinces, up to the middle of March, was two hundred and forty persons. Consequently the British and French Ministers held that the list of death penalties was an extremely moderate one, and far below what might have been justly demanded. On the 13th March the list was finally approved by all the Ministers, except the Russian Minister, and was submitted to the Chinese plenipotentiaries, and was afterwards accepted by the Chinese Government with a few slight alterations.

The edicts dealing with these punishments, and also the suspensions of examinations in towns where foreigners had been murdered or cruelly treated, as demanded in clause 10 of the Joint Note, reached Pekin on the 5th September, and were considered to be satisfactory.

Article 1 of the Joint Note had been complied with by the departure of Prince Ch'un, a prince of the Imperial house, to Berlin, on the 12th July, on a mission to the Emperor of Germany ; and also by the commencement, on the 25th June 1901, of the foundations of a memorial arch, on the site of Baron von Ketteler's murder.

A special envoy had also been appointed, to convey the expression of regret of H.M. the Emperor of China to H.M. the

Emperor of Japan, for the assassination of Mr. Sugiyama, Chancellor of the Japanese Legation, as required by Article 3 of the Joint Note.

Article 4 had been agreed to, and Article 5 was complied with by an edict of the 25th August. Articles 7, 8, and 9 were being put into force by the allied Generals, and satisfactory Imperial edicts had been published by the end of August, dealing with all the clauses of Articles 10, 11, and 12. Thus, with the disposal of the question of the indemnities and of Article 6 in the beginning of September, the whole of the terms imposed by the Joint Note had been satisfactorily carried into effect.

This fact was placed on record in a final protocol, agreed to and signed by all the foreign Ministers, and by the Chinese plenipotentiaries, on the 7th September 1901, in which, after recapitulating the various points on which a settlement had been arrived at with the Chinese Government, the Powers agreed that hostilities were now finally at an end, and that, with the exception of the Legation guards, mentioned in Article 7 of the Joint Note, all the international troops should vacate Peking on the 17th September 1901, and, with the exception of the garrisons mentioned in Article 9 of the same note, should withdraw from the province of Chih-li on the 22nd September 1901.

Memorandum by Mr. C. W. Campbell, Chinese Secretary, British Legation, Peking, respecting Imperial Decrees on Reform.

In a Circular Decree of the 29th January, 1901, the high officers of the empire were all commanded to submit memorials on reform, and, on the 21st April, another Decree appointed a *Grand Council of Government Reform** to consider the shoal of documents forwarded to Hsi-an in response to the circular.

The members of this Council are leading men of State. They are :—

> Prince Ch'ing;
> Li Hung-chang;
> Liu K'un-yi :
> Chang Chih-tung;
> Jung-lu;
> K'un Kang;
> Wang Wên-shao;
> Lu Ch'uan-lin.

The members are directed to select " officials of probity and knowledge of the times " to assist them and act as secretaries of the Council, and much will, of course, depend on the experience and character of these men. The new Council is to report regularly " the results of their deliberations," and, the Decree

---

* The name " Chêng Wu Ch'u " is literally Place of Government Affairs, and might be translated Council of Government simply ; but up to the present it does not seem to supersede the existing Grand Council (" Chün-Chi Ch'u "), which continues to be the working Cabinet. I have added the word " Reform " to indicate its present functions.

says, the Emperor will submit them to "Her Imperial Majesty the Empress-Dowager for her decision." After the return of the Court to Peking, the "changes authorised shall be published throughout China."

However, the Court does not appear to consider it necessary to wait until the return to Peking to inaugurate some changes. It has always been notorious that the permanent clerks in the Central Government offices at Peking perpetuated a system of abuses which nothing but a root-and-branch reform could remove. The Presidents of Boards and higher officers have always been in the hands of their permanent staffs, who alone know how to thread the maze of precedents ruling the details of government—precedents which, as often as not, were ingenious subtleties devised to evade the plain law.

A Decree of the 28th May comments on these abuses in sweeping terms, and takes advantage of the fact that 50 or 60 per cent. of the archives of the principal Government offices at Peking were destroyed during last year's disturbances, to order the remainder to be burnt, "in order to make known our resolve to eradicate abuses." Establishments are to be cut down ruthlessly; responsible officials are warned to do their own work, and not delegate it to clerks, and, "precedents" having all been destroyed, the law is left to speak for itself.

A few days later, on the 1st June, these measures appear to have been found too drastic, and a Commission is ordered to ascertain what archives are useful for reference, draw up lists, and submit them to the new Council of Reform.

On the 3rd June the Emperor turned his wrath on the clerks in provincial Yamêns, who were declared to be "addicted to the same evil practices as their analogues in the Metropolitan Boards." The Provincial Governments were commanded to rigorously reduce their staffs of understrappers; employ the clerks at clerks' work only; make officers perform their legitimate duties and not delegate them to inferiors, and overhaul and simplify the archives. Here again the Council of Reform are to be consulted

On the same day (3rd June) a remarkable Decree of the Empress-Dowager—which marks the special importance of the subject—inaugurated a new special examination in political science. The Provincial Governments are commanded to submit the names of men "versed in home and foreign politics" as candidates, and the Council of Reform are directed to make regulations for the proposed examination. The number of possible candidates is, in any case, limited, and it is not at all likely that the names of the best qualified, who are men outside the leading official families, and, therefore, without influence, will be submitted. In this Decree it is declared that " mother and son are of one mind" on the subject of reform, and the Empress closes with a prayer that " the wealth of talent which characterised the zenith periods" of Chinese history may appear once more.

As an earnest of the Imperial desires to alter the existing type of education, there is another Decree of the 3rd June, dealing with the renowned " Han-lin Yüan " (Imperial Academy of Learning), admission to which is the great prize of successful scholars. In a scathing paragraph, the members are accused of frittering their time away on " verses and hard writing," on accomplishments rather than solid learning, and their Chancellor is told to set his house in order. A course of study is prescribed which may do a little to reduce the present ignorance of public law and international business. Once more the Council of Reform is called upon to consider rules to govern a new system of examinations of members of this ancient institution.

By way of convincing the world that there is no make-believe in all these Decrees, and that reform is seriously meant, both the Empress-Dowager and the Emperor, in another Decree of the 3rd June, command a " total and permanent discontinuance of the annual tributary offerings from the provinces," excepting tea, drugs, and eatables.

APPENDICES.

APPENDIX A.

DESPATCHES RELATING TO THE OPERATIONS IN CHINA.

LETTER No. 384, FROM COMMANDER-IN-CHIEF ON CHINA STATION, DATED 27TH JUNE, 1900.*
COMBINED NAVAL EXPEDITION TO ATTEMPT THE RELIEF OF LEGATIONS AT PEKING.

No. 384.

SIR, TIEN-TSIN, 27th June, 1900.

With reference to my submission No. 366 of the 30th May, forwarding copies of telegrams I had received from His Majesty's Minister on the above subject, I have the honour to report the course of events since that date.

On the 29th May I received a telegram from His Majesty's Consul at Tien-tsin reporting that Fengtai, the railway station next to Peking, had been burnt, also five stations on the Peking-Hankau Line, and on the following day (30th) His Majesty's Minister at Peking informed me that the situation there was "extremely grave, the soldiers mutinous and people very excited," and that European life and property was in danger.

Both the "Orlando" and "Algerine" were then at Taku, and thirteen ships of various other nationalities. The "Algerine" on her arrival on the 30th had immediately disembarked twenty-five marines who had been sent up as a guard for the Legation at Peking before it was known that affairs had assumed such a serious aspect. On the following day the "Orlando" landed fifty marines and sixty-seven seamen, and the "Algerine" ten seamen. The "Algerine's" men were subsequently sent back to their ship, from which they could not well be spared, and were replaced on the 4th June by a field gun's crew from "Centurion."

The men were disposed of as follows:—

Captain Bernard M. Strouts, R.M.L.I.,
  Commanding Tien-tsin Winter Guard
Captain Lewis S. T. Halliday, H.M.S.
  "Orlando" - - - -
Captain Edmund Wray, Wei-hai-wei
  Detachment - - - -
25 Marines, Tien-tsin Winter Guard -
26   „   H.M.S. "Orlando" -
25   „   Wei-hai-wei Detachment
} 79 Peking

Seamen and Marines - - - - 104 Tien-tsin

London Gazette, October 5, 1900.

The guards for Peking arrived there on the 31st May by train, the total number of all nationalities forwarded to Peking being 337.

After receiving the Minister's telegram before mentioned, I decided, in view of the gravity of the situation, to proceed off Taku myself, and left on the afternoon of the 31st with "Whiting" in company, leaving the Rear-Admiral (H.M.S. "Barfleur") at Wei-hai-wei, with orders to send on "Endymion," which was expected there the next day, and also the "Fame."

On arrival off Taku (13 miles distant from the anchorage) on 1st June, I telegraphed at once to His Majesty's Minister, and informed him I was prepared to land two hundred more seamen and marines, and awaited an intimation of his wishes. On the 2nd June a telegram from him was received (dated the previous day) stating that the guards had arrived at Peking without any opposition, and that affairs were quieter, at the same time asking if I was coming up. This I could not do, but on the 3rd June I landed at Tongku and went to Tien-tsin by train to see the arrangements made for our guards, and also to have some conversation with our Consul, and learn as far as I could the actual state of affairs at Tien-tsin and in the neighbourhood.

While there I heard that an attack had been made a day or two previously on an armed party of over thirty Belgians who were coming in with their families from Pao ting fu, on the Peking-Hankau railway line now under construction. It was supposed that some of the party had been killed, as nine were missing.

I was also informed of the murder of an English missionary, Mr. Robinson, and the abduction of another, Mr. Norman, at Yung-ching, some thirty miles from Tien-tsin. Bishop Scott asked me to send out a party to attempt to rescue Mr. Norman, but before any action could be taken it was ascertained that he too had been murdered.

The situation at the Palace was said to be strained, the Dowager Empress being credited with a wish to put down the Boxers, but not daring to do so on account of their numbers and support by some of the Princes. It was rumoured that she contemplated withdrawing from Peking to the ancient capital, Sian Fu, in Shensi Province. My object in going to Tien-tsin was also partly to return to Taku by river in order to know something about it in case we required to use it for a transport, &c. This I did, and returned to my flagship.

On the 4th June a gun's crew and gun were sent up from "Centurion" to Tientsin in response to a request from the Consul, and on the 5th a force of 100 men from "Centurion" was sent to H.M.S. "Algerine" in the river off Taku to be ready for immediate landing if required, as the distance at which the ships lie from Taku, about 13 miles, causes great delay in receiving messages; and sending in men such a long distance over a bar which can only be crossed even by a steamboat at near high water loses several hours. Matters remaining serious and the gravity of the situation in no way abated, but likely to increase, the Chinese Government being up to this time quite inactive, although the "Boxers" were near Tien-tsin in force and had committed outrages such as destroying property, and burning railway, in several places, I proposed to Rear-Admiral Courejolles (French), then the next senior naval officer present, on the 5th instant, that the senior naval officers should meet together to discuss the situation and arrange for mutual action. Rear-Admiral Courejolles agreed, and suggested that the meeting should be held on board "Centurion," in which I acquiesced, and at 4 p.m. the same day our first meeting took place, officers of seven nations besides our own being present. The proceedings were marked by great unanimity.

On the 5th June I received a requisition from His Majesty's Consul at Tientsin for a vessel to protect Pei-tai-ho (a watering place a few miles south of Shan-hai-kuan), as several British subjects and much British property were there. I informed him that I would send a ship there to protect lives of Europeans, and to embark them if necessary, but that I was unable to give protection to property, and that British subjects if in danger should embark and go to Chifu. The "Humber," then at Wei-hai-wei, was ordered to proceed there, taking twenty-five Marines in addition to her own crew. I sent her partly because she has accommodation for people.

The "Aurora," which had arrived at Wei-hai-wei on the 4th June, was ordered to Taku in case a larger landing force became necessary, and arrived on the 7th.

Having received a message from His Majesty's Consul requesting an increase of guard, fifty seamen of "Centurion" were sent to Tien-tsin on the 6th, and also seventy-five Marines. The latter were to be sent on to Peking if required by His Majesty's Minister, from whom I had received an inquiry whether that number could be spared, without stating whether they were actually required or whether he was only making an inquiry in case of further developments.

On the 5th June the Consul, in a telegram, advocated permission being given to guards "to take active measures of hostility"; but this I did not accede to, my view being that our mission here was solely for the protection of European lives, and property also, as far as might be, with which my colleagues concurred.

On the 6th a meeting of the Senior Naval Officers was again held, and it was generally agreed that, in case communication with Peking became cut off, it should be reopened, using whatever force was necessary with this object. The Austrian captain afterwards informed me that he would be glad if his. men at Tien-tsin might be placed under the orders of the Senior Naval Officer at Tien-tsin. I thanked him for the honour he paid me by making this request, and I instructed the officer in charge of our guards accordingly. Rumours were afloat that the Boxers intended to attack the Foreign Settlements at Tien-tsin on the 19th June—the anniversary of the massacres there in 1870. If this was to have been carried out the community should have been fully prepared to meet them.

On the 7th June I received intelligence that General Nieh, who had been ordered by the Chinese Government to march on the rebels then assembled in great force 20 miles from Tientsin, had an engagement, and had killed 500. It appeared from subsequent information that this number was greatly exaggerated.

On the morning of the 9th June another conference of the Foreign Senior Naval Officers took place. On the same day, at about 11.30 p.m., I received an urgent telegram from His Majesty's Minister informing me that unless those in Peking were relieved soon it would be too late. I immediately acquainted my colleagues with the tenor of the telegram, at the same time informing them that I was starting with all our available men at once, and expressing a hope they would co-operate.

The officers and men of the squadron were then sent on to Tongku in "Fame," "Whiting," and a tug, and about 6 a.m. were entrained and reached Tien-tsin about 7.30 a.m. After paying a visit to His Majesty's Consul, the train started about 9.30 a.m. for Peking. The numbers in the train were as follows :—

| 300 British, | 25 Austrian, |
| 112 United States, | 40 Italian. |

The train proceeded without any obstacle beyond Yungtsun, near which there was a camp of four thousand Chinese troops under General Nieh. About 3.30 p.m. the train had to be stopped for repair of damages to railway a few miles this side of Lofa, and remained for the night.

Two more trains joined here, bringing up the total force to

62 Officers ⎫	40 Italian,
640 Seamen ⎬ British,	100 French,
213 Marines ⎭	450 German,
	54 Japanese,
915 British,	112 Russian,
25 Austrian,	112 United States,

June 11th. Early next morning the trains proceeded to Lofa Station, where the engines were watered. A fourth train joined here with two hundred Russians and fifty-eight French, making a total force of over two thousand. The train proceeded at 11.30 a.m. A guard of one officer and thirty men (afterwards reinforced to sixty) was left at Lofa to protect the line.

About 6 p.m. when beyond some three miles short of Langfang station, some Boxers were seen approaching; they had previously endeavoured to cut off an advance party with railway repairing gear, but had failed, and now came to the attack of No. 1 train; they advanced in skirmishing order and were soon repulsed by our rifle fire, leaving about thirty-five killed.

June 12th. All trains proceeded to Langfang as soon as the line was repaired. It was found that the line beyond had been much cut up, the damage being apparently done recently by bodies of men as we approached, and evidently not far ahead. As some time would have to be spent at Langfang repairing bridges, &c., Lieutenant (G.) Smith, of "Aurora," commanding her men, was sent with a party of three officers and forty-four men to try to get, if possible, to Anting, thirteen miles on, to prevent more damage being done to the line, and to hold the railway station there. He occupied a village on the line the following morning, and early in the morning was attacked by Boxers three times in succession, who, however, retreated on a few volleys being fired, with a loss of 15 men. At 10.30 a final and more determined attack was made by about four hundred and fifty Boxers, who charged in line with great courage and enthusiasm, but were repulsed with heavy loss estimated (with those killed in previous attacks) to be about 150. The party being then short of ammunition, Lieutenant Smith wisely decided to return, and rejoined at 2.30 p.m.

June 13th. Major Johnstone was sent forward in the afternoon with 60 men towards Anting, to try to prevent the line being broken up ahead. He was attacked by the Boxers in a village adjoining the railway a few miles on the railway, which had been destroyed for about a mile and the sleepers, &c., carried away. The Boxers lost about 25 killed, and there were no casualties on our side. He returned on the evening of the 14th.

June 14th. Langfang. At about 10.15 a.m. the outposts were seen running in, and reported the Boxers close to in great numbers; they were closely followed by the Boxers, who made a most determined rush at the fore part of the train, which was then drawn up alongside a well, where many of our men were engaged in watering. They came on in great numbers in loose formation, and with the utmost courage under a withering fire, some of them even reaching the train before they were killed. They did not retreat until they had suffered a loss of about 100. I regret to say that we have to deplore the loss of five Italians, who formed the picket near a deserted village, which was used by the Boxers to conceal their approach. At 5.30 p.m. a messenger arrived on a trolly from Lofa Station to report that the guard there was being attacked by a large body of the enemy. No. 2 train then being ready, I took it down the line at once to assist the Lofa guard. On arrival it was found that the brunt of the attack was over, the Boxers then being on the retreat; they were harassed in their retreat by the reinforcements, and left about 100 killed behind. Two small cannon were taken from them. I regret to say that two seamen belonging to H.M.S. "Endymion" were here wounded, one seriously and the other dangerously, who has since died.

June 15th. The trains remained at Langfang while the line ahead was being repaired, a strong guard being detached with the construction train to protect the workers. A train which had been sent back to Lofa returned and reported that the line we had repaired had been much broken up again below that place. Later on the officer of the station guard at Lofa came up with an engine and reported that he thought an attack in force by Boxers might be expected, as he had seen three large bodies moving about in the distance. They eventually moved off without attacking, being probably only making for the line lower down to break it up towards Yungtsun.

June 16th. A train left at 4 a.m. to endeavour to get through to Tien-tsin, but came back at 3 p.m., having found the line too much destroyed to repair with their resources. It being evident that the line was much damaged between Yungtsun and Lofa, I decided to return and investigate, and left Langfang in No. 1 train at 4 p.m.; Nos. 2 and 3 remained at Langfang, and No. 4 at Lofa, to follow later on, if the development of affairs at those places seemed to render such a course desirable. It appeared to me probable that the attempt to relieve Peking might have to be made by river, for the following reasons:—

1. We were so much delayed that more provisions were required by many of the force, and would in a very few days run short; ammunition was also getting short.
2. That it seemed unlikely we could get nearer Peking than Anting, or a little beyond it; some transport would be needed, and we could not go without it.
3. That we were quite cut off from our base, and ignorant of what was happening there, having had no communication since 13th.
4. It was necessary to take some steps to protect the line in our rear, as trains had ceased to run.

June 17th. On the night of 16th–17th No. 1 train remained on the line between Lofa and Yangtsun, and in the morning, as soon as repairs were effected, reached the latter place, where the station was found to be entirely demolished, communication with Tientsin by rail impossible to re-establish with the resources at disposal, and consequently no possibility of obtaining any supplies or necessaries.

A few days previously I had endeavoured to send down orders to Tientsin for junks, provisions and ammunition to be sent to Yungtsun with a view to establishing a base there from which to start, if found desirable, by river to Tungchow, marching thence to Peking, as our alternative route. Not one of these couriers reached Tien-tsin, the surrounding country being at that time overrun with Boxers or hostile Chinese, but had they done so it would have been impossible to have complied with my requisition, owing to the state of affairs at Tien-tsin which was itself then in a state of siege and being bombarded by the Chinese. Of this I was in complete ignorance at the time, as no news whatever from outside reached me between 13th and 26th June. I had also tried to get messages to the General at Hong Kong to send immediately all available troops, having at the commencement of the march to Peking, when the hostility of the Chinese authorities and their active support of the Boxers was not known, only asked for the troops (650) then ready, whom it was intended to employ as guards at the railway stations selected to be held against attacks by Boxers and for guard at Peking, to enable men of the Fleet to return to their ships.

On 17th messages were sent back to Lofa and Langfang to recall Nos. 2, 3, and 4 trains, it being evident that the advance by rail was impossible, and the isolation and separate destruction of the trains a possibility.

June 18th. No 3 returned on the afternoon of June 18th, and in the evening Nos. 2 and 4 from Langfang. Captain von Usedom (H.I.G.M. Navy), the senior officer present with Nos. 2 and 4 trains, reported that they had had a severe engagement with the enemy, who unexpectedly attacked them at Langfang about 2.30 p.m. on that day, 18th, in great force, estimated to be fully 5,000 men (including cavalry), large numbers of whom were armed with magazine rifles of the latest pattern. The banners captured show them to have belonged to the army of General Tung Fu Hsiang, who commands the Chinese troops in the Hunting Park outside Peking, and it was thus definitely known for the first time that Imperial Chinese troops were being employed against us. The attack was made in front and on both flanks, the enemy pouring in a heavy fire on the allied forces coming out to engage them; they were driven off with much loss, but when they saw our forces retiring towards the trains, they rallied and made another attack; a halt was then made, and the men were once more beaten off with greater loss than before, and then finally retreated. In this action the Chinese lost over 400 killed, the Allied forces six killed and 48 wounded. While at Yangtsun we had endeavoured to open friendly relations with the headmen of the town (distant one mile), but their promises to furnish supplies were not fulfilled, probably owing to pressure from Boxers, who seemed to be in strength in the locality.

June 19th. At a conference of the officers commanding of various nationalities it was decided on the 19th to desert the trains and withdraw on Tien-tsin, marching by the left bank of the river and conveying the wounded and necessaries in junks, four of which had been taken by the Germans from some Boxers below Yangtsun on the previous day.

Preparations were rapidly made, and the wounded having been safely embarked and made as comfortable as possible under the circumstances, a start was made at 3 p.m. Soon afterwards some delay was caused by the junks grounding in a shallow reach of the river, but when this difficulty had been overcome, satisfactory progress was made, and we bivouacked for the night, 2½ miles down the river, without further incident. A 6-pr. Q.F. gun of the "Centurion" had to be thrown overboard to lighten one of the junks before she would float off.

June 20th. Early on 20th the march was resumed, progress being regulated by the speed of the junks with wounded, and none of our men being skilled in handling such craft and Chinese impossible to get, their movements retarded the advance of the forces on the river bank. At 9.15 the enemy opened fire on our approach to one of the villages; they were driven out after some resistance, falling back on the next in our line of advance. Several villages in succession had to be carried, either by rifle fire or, failing that, at the point of the bayonet. The charge with bayonets was always very effective, the cheers of the men as they advanced appearing to intimidate the Chinese, who without waiting to receive the charge would fall back immediately. In the afternoon a 1-pr. Q.F. gun was brought into action by the enemy for the first time, and although not much damage was actually done by it, the effect of its fire was harassing to those on the march, especially when an exposed space had to be crossed. Its position could not be accurately located, as the nature of the country and the use of smokeless powder enabled them to mask its position both on this and subsequent occasions. After fighting during the whole day, a suitable place for bivouac was selected at 6 p.m. The distance made good during the day was estimated to be about eight miles.

June 21st. March was resumed at 7.30 a.m. About an hour later a body of from 150 to 200 cavalry was observed in the distance on our left flank of advanced guard. At first it was hoped they might be Cossacks coming to our relief, but as they approached nearer to reconnoitre it was seen that they were Chinese troops. After satisfying themselves they withdrew, but hovered about the left flank for the remainder of the day, firing when favourable opportunities offered; several well-directed shrapnel from the nine-pounder did much to discourage them and to keep them at a distance.

A few minutes after the withdrawal of the cavalry referred to above the enemy opened fire with a field gun and 1-pr. Q.F. Their fire was returned by our 9-pr. and machine guns, and the position of their field gun being disclosed by its smoke, our fire was successful in checking it; although it was brought into action again during the day from time to time, but with the same result, as soon as its position was known.

Fighting was carried on continuously throughout a succession of villages and in the town of Peitsang, which is the chief place between Tien-tsin and Yangtsun, and at 6 p.m. the enemy being then in a very strong position, from which we were unable to dislodge them during the evening, a halt was made, and further movements considered. It was then decided that after supper and two or three hours' rest the forces should make a night march, starting after midnight as our best chance of getting through.

Our advance during the 21st was probably not more than six miles owing to the stubborn resistance of the enemy and their increased gun power.

The field and machine guns had been placed in a junk taken on the previous day, and at 1 a.m. the march commenced. As we passed along fires were seen at one or two places, a little distance off the river bank, evidently signalling our advance, but nothing occurred until about $1\frac{1}{2}$ mile had been covered, when heavy fire was opened on the advanced guard from a village about 200 yards off in the direct line of advance. The marines then fixed bayonets and carried the position without further opposition.

The lighter containing our guns filled and sank about this time, probably owing to the fire of a field piece from ahead of us, and so had to be abandoned, the Maxims only being saved.

At 4 a.m. we arrived opposite what proved to be the Imperial Chinese Armoury, near Hsiku (on right bank of river). Two unarmed soldiers were seen coming out of a house, 100 yards from the bank, evidently to communicate. A halt was made to hear what they had to say, which were some simple inquiries as to who we were and where we were going, &c. These advances seemed perfectly friendly, and the men walked leisurely back to the house, which they had no sooner reached than a heavy fire was opened on us from rifles and several guns. Fortunately good cover was close at hand in a village, and behind the river embankment, which was immediately taken advantage of. The rear columns had not come up, nor the junks with wounded, but the latter were carried down by the river before they could be brought up, and although placed in the best position possible under the circumstances, could not be entirely sheltered and were occasionally struck.

Rifle fire was directed to a 47-m.m. Hotchkiss gun at the north corner of the Armoury and two 10-c.m. guns on the river front. Some of the men at the guns were killed, and others driven from them. Major Johnstone, R.M.L.I., of "Centurion," was then sent higher up the river to cross over unobserved with a party of 100 Marines and seamen to rush the position at the north corner. There is a village about 150 yards from this, which enabled the attacking force to come up without being seen until they emerged from it, when they charged with a cheer, joined in by those on the other side of the river, and the Chinese in that part of the Armoury fled precipitately. At the same time lower down the river a German detachment crossed over and captured two guns (10-c.m. Krupp) in their front, and subsequently several others. The Marines also took two more guns (47-m.m. Krupp). The two detachments then cleared the whole Armoury grounds.

In the afternoon the Chinese made a most determined but unsuccessful attempt to retake the Armoury, trying to drive us from the place by shell fire and to carry it by assault. Their losses were heavy, but we also suffered severely, losing amongst others Commander Bucholtz, I.G.N., a valuable officer whose death was a blow not only to the Germans but to the whole force.

The main body of the forces and wounded crossed the river at 3 p.m., and occupied quarters in the Armoury. Conditions and prospects were now somewhat better than they had been, as the place could be defended by the captured guns, but as provisions for only three days at half allowances remained we were still in a somewhat precarious position.

The importance of communicating our position to our forces in Tien-tsin was urgent, as to proceed by water was impossible, and to carry our wounded would take nearly all our force and leave no one to protect them. I had sent various messengers without success, and therefore on the evening of the 22nd ordered Captains Richard O. M. Doig and Henry T. R. Lloyd, R.M.L.I., with 100 Marines to start after dark and try to make their way into the Foreign Settlement by a detour to the northward and along the railway. This was the route recommended by Mr. A. Currie, C.E., of the Imperial Chinese Railway, who accompanied our force for the repair of the line. Mr. Currie now gave his services as guide. The party reached the railway and at once encountered active resistance, the alarm bugles sounded in various places, and having lost four of their number they had no option but to return to us.

At daylight the Chinese made another unsuccessful attempt to retake the Armoury, which was continued until nearly 8 a.m. Captain Beyts, R.M.A. ("Centurion"), was killed while defending the east front, and there were several other casualties.

When everything was quiet and only a desultory shell fire kept up, a thorough search of the contents of the various buildings was made, about 15 tons of rice being found. In the Armoury we discovered immense supplies of guns, arms, ammunition, and war material of latest pattern. Their discovery gave us what we most needed—viz., food and ammunition, and enabled us if need be to hold out here for several days.

The necessity of carrying our wounded—now 230 in number—prevented our forcing our way down to Tien-tsin. Efforts were made to convey there information of our position and condition, but the couriers were at first killed or stopped.

Several guns were mounted on the various fronts, and in the afternoon we assumed the aggressive by bombarding a Boxer stronghold near the Armoury and a Chinese fort lower down the river. This seemed to have an excellent effect, as we were afterwards but little troubled by the enemy.

A native courier sent out this day managed to get through to Tien-tsin, and give an account of our condition. He had been captured by Boxers and tied to a tree, but having destroyed his message before being taken, nothing incriminating was found upon him, and he was eventually released; his life was for some time in danger, and after escaping from the Boxers he had some difficulty in getting safely inside the lines round Tien-tsin settlement. None of the couriers previously sent had got through, the surrounding country being so closely watched.

June 24th. A Chinese soldier wounded and captured while trying to enter the Armoury stated that General Nieh's army were much discouraged at their want of success, and that the attempts to retake the Armoury were made with 25 battalions (nominally of 500 men each, but probably of not more than 300 to 400 men). During the day the Chinese Fort was again bombarded.

June 25th. Early in the morning one of the guns in the Fort below the Armoury was observed to be firing towards Tien-tsin, and to create a diversion two of our guns were got into position and bombarded it. The gun then turned its fire towards the Armoury.

About 6 a.m. European troops were reported to be in sight, and at 7 a.m. a relief column under the Russian Colonel Shirinsky, composed of forces of the various nations, arrived outside the Armoury.

Preparations were then made—
I. For the evacuation of the Armoury. The wounded were transported across the river in the afternoon, the whole force following later, and bivouacking on the river bank for the night.
II. To set on fire and destroy this very important arsenal, said by some who should know to contain 3,000,000*l*. worth of warlike stores.

June 26th. At 3 a.m. on 26th the return march with the relieving column commenced, and the combined forces arrived at Tien-tsin about 9 a.m. without further incident. The wounded were immediately placed in the hospitals, and the various detachments joined their respective forces in Tien-tsin.

After the return march had commenced Lieutenant (G.) Edward G. Lowther-Crofton and Mr. Charles Davidge, acting gunner (T.), of H.M.S. "Centurion," remained behind to set fire to the ammunition and other store-houses in the Armoury. Fires were lit in five separate places, and judging by the great volume of smoke continually rising, with occasional explosions, the destruction must have been fairly complete. After doing their work, these officers crossed the river, mounted ponies which were waiting for them, and rejoined the main body.

During the expedition the hostile villages which afforded shelter to the enemy from which to attack the force had to be burnt and destroyed as a matter of military necessity.

The number of enemy engaged against us in the march from Yungtsim to the Armoury near Hsiku cannot be even estimated; the country alongside the river banks is quite flat, and consisted of a succession of villages of mud huts, those on the outskirts having enclosures made of dried reeds; outside, high reeds were generally growing in patches near the village, and although trees are very scarce away from the river, alongside it they are very numerous; these, with the graves, embankments for irrigation and against flood, afforded cover to the enemy, from which they seldom exposed themselves, withdrawing on our near approach. Had their fire not been generally high it would have been much more destructive than it was. The number of the enemy certainly increased gradually until the Armoury near Hsiku was reached, when General Nieh's troops and the Boxers both joined in the attack.

In the early part of the expedition the Boxers were mostly armed with swords and spears, and not with many firearms; at the engagement at Langfang on 18th, and afterwards, they were armed with rifles of late pattern ; this, together with banners captured and uniform worn, shows that they had either the active or covert support of the Chinese Government or some of its high officials.

The primary object of the expedition, viz., to reach Peking and succour the Foreign Legations, has failed—success was only possible on the assumption that the Imperial troops, with whose Government we were not at war, would at least be neutral; their turning their arms against us, and certainly conniving in the destruction of the railway (probably actually joined in it) made failure inevitable.

For the undertakings of the expedition, for its conduct, and its issue, I am responsible.

The destruction of the valuable "armoury" near Hsiku may be regarded as some object at least gained.

When the somewhat unusual character of the force, viz., the combination of eight different nationalities, is considered, it may, I think, be conceded that their harmonious action reflects credit on the various members of the expedition, and I venture to think it will tend to foster international sympathies.

I have with pleasure to acknowledge my gratitude to the various Commanding Officers for their hearty co-operation and accordance to my wishes, which is the more creditable to them as our position was often an anxious one.

Both officers and men have suffered a good deal of pecuniary loss of clothes, &c., as we had to leave behind in the trains nearly all that we could not personally carry ; yet no want of cheerfulness was observable. As regards our own service, I shall submit claims for compensation for the above to their Lordships.

I have written officially to the respective Admirals or Senior Naval Officers of the several foreign nationalities present to thank them for their cordial co-operation throughout our short campaign, and to express my sense of the service rendered by the officers and men in question.

I have especially referred to Captain von Usedom, of the Imperial German Navy, who was Senior Officer present after myself. I nominated this Officer to direct the expedition, should I fall ; and after I was deprived of the services of my Flag Captain by his wound at the battle of Peitsang, I requested Captain von Usedom to act as my Chief of the Staff, in which capacity he rendered very valuable service, and I beg to submit the same to their Lordships. Captain von Usedom was slightly wounded at Langfang.

I must also specially refer to Captain B. H. McCalla, of the United States Navy, who was of the greatest value to me and to all concerned. He was slightly wounded in three places and well merits recognition.

Before closing my despatch I have the very pleasing duty of reporting to their Lordships that the officers and men landed from His Majesty's ships and present with me acted throughout, as regards energy, courage, and cheerfulness, in a manner well worthy of the high traditions of His Majesty's Navy.

I might with truth mention favourably all names; it is hard justly to discriminate, and there are probably others who deserve special mention fully as much as those named below.

I feel it right specially to recommend for their Lordships' favourable consideration the following officers:—

Captain John R. Jellicoe, my Flag Captain, who was, as always, of most valuable help, both by his judgment and action, till disabled by a serious wound at the battle of Peitsang on 21st June.

Commander Charles D. Granville, of my flagship, who ably commanded the Naval Brigade with me after my Flag Captain was wounded.

Commander William O. Boothby of H.M.S. "Endymion," in command of the seamen from that ship, and, at times, of others also. He was in every engagement, and I specially noticed his energy and activity.

Lieutenant George M. K. Fair, of my flagship, employed on my Staff in Intelligence Department, &c., but diverted as required to other duties, such as the very important one of getting along the junks with the wounded.

Lieutenant Horatio W. Colomb, of H.M.S. "Endymion," was slightly wounded on different days. He had charge of Lofa Station Fort, defended it against various attacks, and showed good judgment while in separate command.

Lieutenant Edward G. Lowther-Crofton, of my flagship, most intelligent and active; with great risk to himself he remained behind in the Hsiku Armoury on 26th instant, when we left for Tien-tsin, to set fire to and destroy it, having made the preparations for so doing, which were carried out by him most satisfactorily. This important service reflects very great credit on him.

Lieutenant Arthur G. Smith, of H.M.S. "Aurora," led and commanded an advanced post above Langfang, on the line towards Peking, with zeal and good judgment.

Midshipman William B. C. Jones, of H.M.S. "Centurion," who took command of Lieutenant Wyndham L. Bamber's company in the operations on 21st June, after the latter officer was wounded.

Mr. Charles Davidge, Acting Gunner of "Centurion," who ably assisted Lieutenant Crofton in the destruction of Hsiku Armoury, and shared the risks with him, the two being alone.

Major James R. Johnstone, R.M.L.I., of "Centurion," has been most active throughout. He often commanded all the marines present. He kept pushing ahead of the trains on our advance, to clear and protect the line. He it was who led the storming party I sent round on 22nd June to carry the north angle of the armoury, near Hsiku, and he has rendered very good service.

Captain Richard O. M. Doig, R.M.L.I., H.M.S. "Endymion," has been very active throughout, and commanded the night expedition of 100 men, on 22nd June, sent from the armoury to try and communicate with Tien-tsin, which attempt he made with skill and credit.

Mr. Francis C. Alton, my secretary, has been near me throughout, and, as at all times, was of the greatest assistance and value by his grasp of matters and good judgment and sense.

Mr. Charles J. E. Rotter, Assistant Paymaster of my flagship, was in charge of the commissariat arrangements, a most difficult task under the circumstances, but performed by him with constant efforts and all possible success. To this, having regard to our foreign allies, Mr. Rotter's knowledge of German, and well-known tact and good temper, much contributed.

Fleet-Surgeon Thomas M. Sibbald, H.M.S. "Centurion," has had charge of the hospital arrangements throughout, and has also been much under fire. His activity, attention, and constant cheerfulness have gone far to mitigate the sufferings of the wounded, and have met with my entire approval.

Mr. George H. Cockey, Engineer, H.M.S. "Centurion," took over the duties of company officer of the "Centurion's" marine detachment after Captain H. W. H. Beyts, R.M.A., fell on 23rd June, until their arrival at Tien-tsin, 26th June, and was of the greatest assistance to Major Johnstone, R.M.L.I.

Mr. Arthur E. Cossey, Assistant Engineer, H.M.S. "Aurora," at much risk to himself, returned from our advanced post towards Anting Station to bring important news.

Mr. Clive Bigham, late Grenadier Guards, honorary attaché to His Majesty's Legation at Peking, has been attached to me as Intelligence Officer, and shown much zeal and ability as such; he has been of great value to me.

Mr. Archibald Currie, C.E., B.Sc., resident engineer in charge of railway line between Tien-tsin and Peking, came with us to take charge of the trains and their *personnel*, and to repair the line. In this he worked with a skill and energy not to be surpassed. He acted in opposition to the Chinese Director-in-Chief of the Railway, for our benefit and His Majesty's Service, and the Allies owe him a debt of gratitude which I submit must be acknowledged and repaid. He has lost his home and nearly all his wordly possessions out here, destroyed by the Chinese.

Mr. C. W. Campbell, His Majesty's Consul for Wuchow (on leave), accompanied us as interpreter, and was of the utmost value by his knowledge both of the language and customs of the

Chinese. He showed untiring zeal, and I would submit him for the decided acknowledgments of His Majesty's Government

When the fact of the Chinese having beheaded anyone they got is considered, the conduct of such officers or men as risked themselves to capture is to be praised far more than if against a civilized foe.

I have, &c.,

F. H. SEYMOUR, Vice-Admiral.

The Secretary,
Admiralty.

LIST of OFFICERS who accompanied EXPEDITION, and GUNS.

H.M.S "Centurion": Sir Edward H. Seymour, K.C.B., Vice-Admiral; Frederick A. Powlett, Flag Lieutenant; Francis C. Alton, Secretary; William G. Littlejohns, Secretary's Clerk; Hy. W. E. Manisty, Secretary's Clerk; John R. Jellicoe, Flag Captain, wounded 21st June, Peitsang; Charles D. Granville, Commander; George M. K. Fair, Lieutenant; Edward G. Lowther-Crofton, Lieutenant; John L. F. Luttrell, Lieutenant; James M. Faric, Lieutenant; Wyndham L. Bamber, Lieutenant, wounded 21st June, Peitsang; Claud H. Sinclair, Lieutenant; James R. Johnstone, Major, R.M.L.I.; Herbert W. H. Beyts, Captain, R.M.A., killed 23rd June, Hsiku; Rev. Ernest F. Harrison Smith, M.A., Chaplain and Naval Instructor; Thomas M. Sibbald, Fleet Surgeon; Morris E. Cochrane, Sub-Lieutenant; Edward B. Pickthorn, Surgeon; Charles J. E. Rotter, Assistant Paymaster; George H. Cockey, Engineer; George H. Starr, Assistant Engineer; Charles Davidge, Acting Gunner (T.); Frank Sammels, Acting Gunner (Q.D.D.); James Atrill, Carpenter; Hector Boyes, Midshipman; William B. C. Jones, Midshipman; Charles D. Burke, Midshipman, wounded 21st June, Peitsang; Sidney R. Bailey, Midshipman; St. Andrew St. John, Midshipman; Guy B. Alexander, Midshipman; Hardinge L. Shepard, Midshipman; Philip W. Douglas, Midshipman; Robert L. Jermain, Midshipman; Edward O. B. S. Osborne, Midshipman; Frank O'B. Wilson, Midshipman, wounded 21st June, Peitsang; John C. Davis, Midshipman; Augustus E. Tabuteau, Clerk, wounded 21st June, Peitsang.

H.M.S. "Aurora": Arthur G. Smith, Lieutenant; Hy. T. R. Lloyd, Captain, R.M.L.I.; Arthur E. Cossey, Assistant Engineer; Thomas R. Fforde, Midshipman; Charles B. Dickson, Midshipman; George M. Hill, Midshipman.

H.M.S. "Orlando": Francis E. M. Garforth, Lieutenant; Edward F. Murray, Assistant Paymaster; Patrick McGuire,

Gunner; Cloudesley V. Robinson, Midshipman; Herbert F. Littledale, Midshipman; Charles P. Dumaresq, Midshipman.

H.M.S. "Endymion": William O. Boothby, Commander; Horatio W. Colomb, Lieutenant, wounded 21st June, Peitsang, (wounded 27th June, Tien-tsin Arsenal); Frank Powell, Lieutenant; Richard O. M. Doig, Captain, R.M.L.I.; Rev. John C. Leishman, Chaplain; Lawrence W. Braithwaite, Sub-Lieutenant, wounded 22nd June, Hsiku; Eric D. Macnamara, B.A., Surgeon; Ethelbert S. Silk, Engineer; Henry J. S. Brownrigg, Midshipman; Guy D. Fanshawe, Midshipman; Eric G. Robinson, Midshipman; Edwin A. Homan, Midshipman; Norman M. C. Thurston, Midshipman; Fras. S. McGachen, Midshipman; Herbert R. McClure, Midshipman; Stuart E. Holder, Midshipman.

Numerical Strength of Expedition.

Austrian: 1 officer, 24 men, Lieutenant Prochasca in command. British: 62 officers, 640 seamen, 213 Marines, 1 6-pr. Hotch. Q.F., 3 9-pr. M.L., two ·45 Maxim, six ·45 Nord., Vice-Admiral Sir Edward H. Seymour, K.C.B., in command. French: 7 officers, 151 men, 1 field gun, Captain de Marolles in command. German: 23 officers, 427 men, 2 Maxims, Captain von Usedom in command. Italian: 2 officers, 38 men, 1 Maxim, Lieutenant Sirianni in command. Japanese: 2 officers, 52 men, Captain Mori in command. Russian: 7 officers, 305 men, 1 field gun, Commander Chagkin in command, United States: 6 officers, 106 men, 1 13-pr., 1 Colt automatic, Captain B. H. McCalla in command; making a total of 110 officers, 1,956 men, and 19 guns. (All the officers in command were naval officers.)

Casualty List.

British: "Centurion," officers, wounded, 5; seamen, &c., killed, 9; wounded, 36; Marines, killed, 1 officer and 6 men; wounded, 7. "Aurora," seamen &c., wounded, 2; Marines, killed, 3; wounded, 5. "Orlando," seamen, &c., killed 1; wounded, 13. "Endymion," officers, wounded, 3; seamen, &c., killed, 5; wounded, 15; Marines, killed, 5; wounded, 6. Weihai-wei detachment, Marines, wounded, 5; making a total of officers, wounded, 8; seamen, &c., killed, 15; wounded, 66; Marines, killed, 1 officer and 14 men; wounded, 23. Foreign: Austrian, seamen, &c., killed, 1; wounded, 1. French, seamen, &c., killed, 1; wounded, 10. German, officers, killed, 1; wounded, 6; seamen, &c., killed, 11; wounded, 56. Italian, seamen, &c., killed, 5; wounded, 3. Japanese, seamen, &c., killed, 2; wounded, 3. Russian, officers, wounded, 4; seamen, &c., killed, 10; wounded, 23. United States, officers, wounded, 2; seamen, &c., killed, 4; wounded, 25; making a total of officers, killed, 1;

wounded, 12; seamen, &c., killed, 34; wounded, 121; making a grand total of officers, killed, 1; wounded, 20; seamen, &c., killed, 49; wounded, 187; Marines, killed, 1 officer and 14 men; wounded, 23.

Summary.

Killed, 2 officers, 63 men, total 65; wounded, 20 officers, 210 men, total 230; making a grand total of 295 officers and men killed and wounded.

COPY of LETTER despatched to the Commander-in-Chief or Senior Officer of each Nationality on the Expedition's return to Tien-tsin.

YOUR EXCELLENCY (or SIR),— Tien-tsin, 27 June 1900.

The late allied Naval Expedition for the attempt to reach Peking and succour our respective Legations in that city having now terminated, I have the honour, as the Senior Naval Officer of the various National Forces engaged therein, to address your Excellency (or you) on that subject.

First, to officially thank your Excellency (or you) for sending the officers and men belonging to the (nation), in company with those of Her Majesty the Queen of England to act in concert with them.

Secondly, to express to your Excellency (or you) my highest sense of—

1. The valuable, cheerful, and constant co-operation and assistance I received from (Commanding Officer's name) and all others under his command.
2. The unfailing energy and zeal displayed, under somewhat trying circumstances, by (nation) officers and men, whose courage was worthy of their high traditions, and require no words of mine to describe.

Thirdly, to assure Your Excellency (or you) of my sincere belief and hope that the above Expedition, though both small and not of long duration, will help to cement between our respective nations that mutual good feeling and respect which happily now exists between our Sovereigns (or Government), and which, especially in China, is now so desirable in all the best interests of civilisation and advancement.

The following additions were made to the letters to respective nationalities:—

To His Excellency Vice-Admiral BENDEMANN, Commander-in-Chief H.I.G.M. Ships, China Station.

Though it may seem out of place for me to report on the conduct of an officer not placed under my command, yet I cannot close this letter without, Sir, expressing to your Excellency both my personal admiration of the ability and unfailing energy which Captain von Usedom, of H.I.G.M.S. "Hertha," displayed throughout the expedition, and also my high sense of the value of his services. The allied force at the battle of Langfang on 18th instant was under his command, I myself being some miles away at the time. In this determined attack on us, the first in which Chinese Imperial troops joined with the Boxers, Captain von Usedom was wounded. To his skilful conduct and arrangements for withdrawing the trains when it had become necessary the avoidance of a disaster then should be ascribed.

As second to myself in rank of all officers present, I often consulted him with much benefit, and I also officially nominated him to succeed me in the direction of the expedition, should I fall, and then felt our general interests would not suffer.

When my Flag Captain was disabled by a wound, I requested Captain von Usedom to do me the honour to act as chief of my staff which he acceded to, and was of the greatest value to me.

As regards the courage and high discipline shown by all His Imperial Majesty's officers and men accompanying us, I can only say they were well worthy of the high traditions of the great German Empire.

I have, &c.,
(Signed) E. H. SEYMOUR, Vice-Admiral.

To His Excellency Rear-Admiral COUREJOLLES, Commander-in-Chief, French Squadron, China Station.

Though it may seem out of place for me to report on the conduct of an officer not placed under my command, yet I cannot close this letter without, your Excellency, expressing my high sense of the valuable co-operation and support I received from Captain de Marolles, of the "D'Entrecasteaux," and all under his command; that in the various engagements they acted with us in a manner worthy of the high traditions of the great national French Navy was only what I felt sure I might expect, yet may be allowed with pleasure to dwell on.

When in the West Armoury, near Hsiku, Captain de Marolles took the honourable part of occupying and holding the Arsenal there, which, being most advanced towards Tien-tsin and also full of combustibles, with a fire of shell from the enemy's guns at times upon it, was a decided post of danger and of honour. Captain de Marolles also undertook, with his men only, a reconnaissance on the 25th instant towards the railway.

I would request your Excellency to express my thanks to Captain de Marolles for his cordial co-operation throughout our short campaign, which reminded me of our happy alliance with your great nation both in the Crimea and out here. May I add my hope that it may, though of small degree, help to draw together in friendship France and England, a thing certainly desirable for the civilisation of the world.

I beg, &c.,

(Signed)　　E. H. SEYMOUR, Vice-Admiral.

To Rear-Admiral KEMPFF, Second in Command, U.S. Squadron, China Station.

I cannot conclude my letter without expressing to you, Sir, the high admiration I have for Captain B. H. McCalla, who accompanied us in command of your officers and men. Their post was usually in the advanced guard, where their zeal and go was praised by all. I regret to state that Captain McCalla was wounded in three places, but considering the gallant way in which he exposed himself I am only equally surprised and thankful that he is alive.

Had he been thoroughly British he could not have more kindly and loyally stood by me in every way and carried out any wish I expressed. I may indeed say the same for all those under his command.

I hail this experience as a further proof of the real good feeling so happily existing between our nations, which is by no one more valued than by your brother sailors of our Navy.

I have, &c.,

(Signed)　　E. H. SEYMOUR, Vice-Admiral.

To Capitano di Frigato CASELLA, Senior Italian Naval Officer, Taku.

Permit me, Sir, to express the pleasure I have felt in co-operating with the officers and men belonging to His Majesty's Royal Navy, and allow me to add my tribute to the energy and readiness they have shown throughout to assist the expedition.

I have, &c.,

(Signed)　　E. H. SEYMOUR, Vice-Admiral

To Captain THOMAN VON MONTALMAR, S.M.S. "Zenta" (Austrian).

(No special addition.)

To His Excellency Vice-Admiral J. HILTEBRANDT, Commander-in-Chief, His Imperial Russian Majesty's Ships, China Station.

In conclusion pray let me express to your Excellency my high sense of the valuable service rendered to our joint expedition by Captain Chagkin of His Imperial Majesty's Navy, who was always ready, always to the front, and did me the honour to as exactly carry out any wish I expressed to him as if he had belonged to our own Navy.

I have, &c.,
(Signed)   E. H. SEYMOUR, Vice-Admiral.

To Captain SHIMAMURA, Senior Japanese Naval Officer, Tien-tsin.

Pray allow me, Sir, in conclusion, to express my satisfaction at this opportunity of sharing our efforts with officers and men belonging to His Imperial Majesty's Navy, who showed that energy and mobility which is well known to characterise the Japanese nation. I trust this may prove an instance of the friendly feeling now happily existing between our respective services, and the forerunner of long good fellowship between them.

I have, &c.,
(Signed)   E. H. SEYMOUR, Vice-Admiral.

YOUR EXCELLENCY,   Tien-tsin, 27th June 1900.

I cannot let the present occasion pass without doing myself the honour of addressing you to thank you from myself, and I feel sure I may add also for the other commanding officers of the various National Forces engaged in the late expedition towards Peking, for the very prompt and thoroughly efficacious way in which you, Sir, organised, and Colonel Shirinsky, in charge of the relieving force, carried out, on 25th and 26th instants, the arrangements for our return from the West Armoury near Hsiku to Tien-tsin, with the large number of wounded by whom we were encumbered.

It is not for me as a sailor to give any opinion on a military land movement, yet, as an officer of some experience, I may be permitted to express my admiration of the arrangements of Colonel Shirinsky, and I would request you, as you feel right, to express the same.

Such events are what help to draw nearer to each other civilised nations like our own, and this occasion is, I feel sure, as much a source of gratification to your Excellency as to myself.

I have, &c.,
(Signed)   E. H. SEYMOUR, Vice-Admiral.
To His Excellency Major-General STĖSSEL, Commanding Imperial Russian Troops, Tien-tsin.

LETTER No. 4 from the REAR-ADMIRAL on the CHINA STATION, dated 17th June, 1900.

No. 4.

"Barfleur," at Taku,
SIR,   17th June 1900.

I have the honour to report, for the information of the Lords Commissioners of the Admiralty, that on my arrival here on the 11th instant I found a large fleet, consisting of Russian, German, French, Austrian, Italian, Japanese, and British ships, and that in consequence of an urgent telegram from Her Majesty's Minister at Peking, Vice-Admiral Sir Edward H. Seymour, K.C.B., Commander-in-Chief, had started at 3 o'clock the previous morning (10th June), taking with him a force of 1,375 of all ranks, being reinforced by men from the Allied ships as they arrived, until he commanded not less than 2,000 men.

At a distance of some 20 to 30 miles from Tien-tsin—but it is very difficult to locate the place, as no authentic record has come in—he found the railway destroyed and sleepers burned, &c., and every impediment made by supposed Boxers to his advance.

Then his difficulties began, and it is supposed that the Boxers, probably assisted by Chinese troops, closed in on his rear, destroyed railway-lines, bridges, &c., and nothing since the 13th instant has passed from Commander-in-Chief and his relief force and Tien-tsin, nor *vice versâ*, up to this date; nor has any report whatever, to my knowledge, come in as to his movements, and the last we heard was that the British and German advanced party, probably about 500 men, had left the railway about 40 miles from Tien-tsin (Long Fa) for the purpose of making forced marches the rest of the distance (30 to 35 miles) to the relief of Peking.

During the night of the 14th instant news was received that all railway-carriages and other rolling stock had been ordered to be sent up the line for the purpose of bringing down a Chinese army to Tong-ku.

On receipt of this serious information a council of Admirals was summoned by Vice-Admiral Hiltebrandt, Commander-in-Chief of the Russian Squadron, and the German, French, United States Admirals, myself, and the Senior Officers of Italy, Austria, and Japan attended; and it was decided to send immediate orders to the captains of the Allied vessels in the Peiho River (three Russian, two German, one United States, one Japanese, one British—" Algerine ") to prevent any railway plant being taken away from Tong-ku, or the Chinese army reaching that place, which would cut off our communication with Tien-tsin; and in the event of either being attempted, they were to use force to prevent it, and to destroy the Taku Forts.

By the evening, and during the night of 15th instant, information arrived that the mouth of the Peiho River was being protected by electric mines.

On receipt of this, another council, composed of the same naval officers, was held in the forenoon of 16th June on board the " Rossia.' and in consequence of the gravity of the situation, and information having also arrived that the forts were being provisioned and reinforced, immediate notice was sent to the Viceroy of Chili at Tien-tsin and the commandant of the forts that, in consequence of the danger to our forces up the river, at Tien-tsin, and on the march to Peking by the action of the Chinese authorities, we proposed to temporarily occupy the Taku Forts, with or without their good will, at 2 a.m. on the 17th instant.

Necessary orders were given to the captains of the Allied ships in the river, acting under command of the Russian Post Captain of the " Bobr."

At 0.50 a.m. of Sunday, 17th June, the Taku Forts opened fire on the Allied ships in the Peiho River, which continued almost without intermission until 6.30 a.m., when all firing had practically ceased and the Taku Forts were stormed and in the hands of the Allied Powers, allowing of free communication with Tien-tsin by water, and rail when the latter is repaired.

In forwarding the reports of Commander Robert Hathorn Johnston Stewart, commanding H.M.S. " Algerine," and Commander Christopher George Francis Maurice Cradock, who commanded the Allied landing force, I wish to bring most strongly to the notice of their Lordships that the brilliant manner in which Commander Stewart handled his ship immensely contributed to the success achieved, which at one time was extremely doubtful, and his putting her so close under the forts that most of their shot went over him, accounts for his small loss. He and the captain of the German vessel " Iltis " were always contending for the post of danger, and the German officer is, I regret to say, severely wounded in several places.

The Japanese and British stormed the North-West Fort together, and the Japanese Commander was, I believe, the first man in, and then assisted Commander Cradock up, when I much regret to say that the Japanese Commander was killed.

Four destroyers of the Chinese Navy were boarded and captured by Lieutenant and Commander Roger John Brownlow Keyes, of the "Fame," and Lieutenant and Commander Colin MacKenzie, of the "Whiting," which was done by towing a boat astern with boarders under the command of Lieutenants John Alfred Moreton and Wilfred Tomkinson, of the "Whiting" and "Fame" respectively, who boarded and captured two destroyers each. I intend handing over three of the destroyers to the Admirals of our Allies—viz., the Russian, German, and French.

In the action slight damage was done to the "Algerine" by shell fire, principally to ventilators, &c., and a shell passed through the hull of the "Whiting," which necessitated her being sent to Nagasaki for repairs.

I regret to have to report that during the action William Theodore Bing, Ord. O.N. 188203, H.M.S. "Barfleur," was killed, and Mr. Herbert J. Hargraves, Assistant Paymaster in charge H.M.S. "Algerine," and 12 men were wounded; but, owing to the lack of any communication with the shore to-day (18th June), on account of the weather, I have not received any details.

I have, &c.,
JAMES BRUCE, Rear-Admiral.

The Secretary of the Admiralty.

THE ATTACK ON THE TA-KU FORTS.

Enclosure in Letter from Rear-Admiral, China Station.
(Dated 17th June, 1900. No. 4.)

SIR, Taku, 17th June, 1900.

I have the honour to report, that in conjunction with the Allied Forces on shore, the British Force, which I have the honour to command, stormed and assisted to take the North-West Fort of Taku, at 5 o'clock this morning, after which the outer North and South Forts were respectively occupied.

I regret to state that in the capture of the North-West Fort, W. T. Bing, O.S., of H.M.S. "Barfleur," was killed, and six other men of the British Force were wounded; the Foreign Forces on shore had also, I am sorry to say, some casualties, including amongst the killed the Japanese Commander.

The North-West Fort was first attacked. Half the British Force, the Russians on the left and the Italians on the right, composed the firing line, the other half were deployed to act as a close support.

The resistance at the North-West Fort was severe, other Forts were occupied with but slight opposition.

On the junction of the Allied Forces this morning, the German and Japanese Commanders were pleased to propose that I should take command of the proceedings of the combined forces, which I did.

At a meeting held by the Foreign Representatives after the operations, it was decided that the several nations should each occupy a fort; in consequence the British Force, under my command, take charge of the North-West Fort. The entire force has been landed as a result of fears expressed by the conference as to the descent of Boxers on Taku in large numbers at night, and I am endeavouring to place the Fort in such a state of defence that danger of its being rushed by weight of numbers will not be probable.

Machine guns are wanted, and also more rifle and pistol ammunition.

I have, &c.,
CHRISTOPHER CRADOCK, Commander,
Commanding the Allied Forces on shore at the
attack on Taku Forts.

To Rear-Admiral James Bruce.

Enclosure in Letter from Rear-Admiral, China Station.
(Dated 17th June, 1900. No. 4.)

SIR,   H.M.S. "Algerine," Taku, 17th June, 1900.

I have the honour to report that after receiving your orders of yesterday's date, I attended a conference of the Allied Squadron of Men-of-War inside the bar, when it was decided that we should take up our appointed positions by 4 a.m., and open fire on the Forts at that hour, should they not be surrendered before then.

I took up my position at once, shifting berth at 8 p.m., and prepared for action. At 1.30 a.m. I ordered the destroyers "Fame" and "Whiting" to seize the Chinese destroyers alongside the Government yard.

At 12.50 a.m. all the forts opened fire, and we engaged the enemy. At about 1.30 Commander Cradock and his landing party were landed on the north bank, and at about 5 o'clock the fire of the North-West Fort was, except for field and machine guns, practically silenced, and the Fort taken by the landing party.

At 6 o'clock the Allied Ships weighed and proceeded down the river. I anchored again, and it was not until 7.10 a.m. that the Chinamen finally abandoned their guns and the Forts were occupied.

No damage has been done to the hull of the ship, but there are several holes in the cowls, and one in the steam cutter.

A list of casualties will follow with a detailed report.

Reports from Lieutenants Keyes and MacKenzie as to their proceedings will be sent in with the detailed report, showing that the Chinese destroyers are all in our possession.

At a conference of Commanding Officers held this morning, it was decided that the British Forces should occupy the North-West Fort, the Japanese the North Fort, and the Russians and Germans the South Fort.

Our wounded have been landed and the Taku Hotel pretty well taken for them.

Captain Cradock will detail a guard for the hospital.

I have, &c.,
R. H. JOHNSTON STEWART, Commander.
To Rear-Admiral James Bruce,
H.M.S. "Barfleur."

Letter No. 385 from Commander-in-Chief on the China Station, dated 4th July.

SIR, Tien-tsin, 4th July, 1900.

I have received from Rear-Admiral Bruce, Second in Command, a copy of his letter of 17th June (No. 4), reporting to their Lordships the taking of the Taku Forts, and of the Chinese Dockyard with four destroyers there on that day.

It is my pleasing duty to inform their Lordships that these operations meet with my entire approval. In my opinion they were skilfully planned and executed in a most gallant manner, worthy of the highest traditions of our Service.

I concur in the Rear-Admiral's commendation of those concerned, and would specially mention Commander Johnston Stewart, of H.M.S. "Algerine," the Senior Naval Officer present at Taku (the Rear-Admiral being in his flagship outside the Bar, 12 miles off). Commander Stewart directed our part of the operations, and well and ably handled his ship under heavy fire from the forts in a most gallant and seamanlike way, and I desire to submit his name to their Lordships for their very favourable notice.

I have, &c.,
E. H. SEYMOUR, Vice-Admiral.
The Secretary of the Admiralty.

Affairs at Tien-tsin during Admiral Seymour's Absence.

Letter No. 388 from Commander-in-Chief on the China Station, dated 8th July 1900.

Affairs at Tien-tsin between 10th and 26th June 1900.

No. 388.

Sir, Tien-tsin, 8th July 1900.

I have the honour to report, for the information of the Lords Commissioners of the Admiralty, the following occurrences at Tien-tsin between 10th June, the date of the departure of the expedition to attempt the relief of Peking, until its return on 26th June.

Captain E. H. Bayly, of H.M.S. "Aurora," who was left in charge of the British forces at Tien-tsin, found immediately after my departure that the Chinese authorities were doing all they could to prevent trains being sent forward with reinforcements, and to keep up communication. Large and threatening mobs of Chinese came to the railway station to obstruct the work, but trains were with some difficulty sent through as required until 14th, when the tearing up of the line prevented further communication in advance.

On 10th June, Lieutenant C. D. Roper with 50 men was sent from Tien-tsin to Tongs-han to protect British railway employés there, at the earnest request of Mr. Kinder, the Engineer-in-Chief. They remained until 16th June, when, finding the position untenable, they withdrew with the European residents to Peitaho, and embarked on 21st in H.M.S. "Humber" for Taku.

On 11th June the Chinese began to leave the Settlement and shops to close. Reinforcements of 150 seamen and marines, under Commander Beatty, H.M.S. "Barfleur," arrived on that day, and on 13th some 1,600 to 1,800 Russians with cavalry and field guns.

A courier arrived from Peking on 14th, with news that the Summer Legation and all mission houses at the western hills had been destroyed.

June 15th. Some mission houses in the French Settlement and the cathedral in the Native City were burnt, and telegraphic communication with Taku interrupted. A search-light train patrolled the line between Tien-tsin and Tong-ku all night, and a guard of 200 Russians was left at Chun Liang Cheng, a station midway between.

June 16th. The first attack on the Settlement was made by some Boxers, who set fire to several stores and houses before they were driven out; they also attacked the railway station held by the Russians.

A train for repairing the up line was prepared with search-light and a 6·8 gun mounted; work had to be commenced within half a mile of the station. A train sent down to Tong-ku was fired at by the forts as it approached and returned to Tien-tsin next morning.

June 17th. Some Chinese were observed gathering together to destroy the line 1½ miles away; the repairing train was sent out with a small force under Mr. Henry C. Halahan, midshipman, to drive them off. Outside the station they came across a body of Chinese troops (80 to 90), who opened fire on the train; the fire was returned, and, after losing a few men, the Chinese made off.

The Russians afterwards went out with a force of 200 men and one of our 6-pr. with crew, under Lieutenant G. B. Powell, of "Aurora," and engaged the enemy.

The Military College on the river opposite the British Concession was taken by a party of the Allied Forces under Major Luke, R.M.L.I. ("Barfleur"); the guns found there were destroyed, and the building also. The British loss was one killed and four wounded.

The bombardment of the Settlement by guns in the Native City commenced.

June 18th. A train under Lieutenant Field ("Barfleur") started with a Russian force to bring back the 200 Russians from Chun Liang Cheng, but found the line badly damaged, and failed to reach that place. They were heavily engaged by the enemy, and returned in the afternoon in time to help, by a flank attack, to repulse the Chinese troops then attacking the railway station. During the engagement two British companies under Commander Beatty, with a 9-pr. field gun under Lieutenant P. Wright ("Orlando"), reinforced the Russians and did excellent service.

June 19th. Two Chinese field guns were placed near the railway embankment opposite the British Concession, and opened fire. Commander Beatty, with three companies of seamen, crossed the river and manœuvred to within 200 or 300 yards in the hope of capturing them with a rush; some Russians moved out at the same time to co-operate. While our men were waiting for the Russians to come up, a large force of Chinese appeared to the right behind a mud wall and poured in a heavy fire, wounding Commander Beatty, Lieutenants Powell ("Aurora") and Stirling ("Barfleur"), Mr. Donaldson, midshipman ("Barfleur") (the latter died on 3rd July of his wounds), and 11 men. The force then retired.

A 9-pr. gun was then brought up to the Bund outside the British Consulate, and succeeded in throwing shell close in front of the guns, upon which the Chinese brought up horses and withdrew them. During this action a piece of shell from one of the enemy's guns struck Lieutenant Wright, who was on the roof of the Consulate directing the fire of his gun, inflicting dangerous wounds on the head and arms.

Mr. J. Watts, of the Tien-tsin Volunteer Corps, undertook to ride to Taku with despatches, and left at 9.30 p.m. with a guard of only three Cossacks. Mr. Watts knows the country thoroughly well, and succeeded in getting through; his action was most gallant, and is well deserving of official recognition, as the whole country was swarming with Boxers and Imperial troops.

June 20th-21st. Only small attacks and skirmishes took place, but the Concession was still bombarded from the Native City.

June 22nd. Troops were seen in the far distance advancing from Tongku. A courier from Peking arrived with a message that all Europeans had been ordered to leave within 24 hours.

June 23rd. A column, composed of 250 seamen and marines, 300 Royal Welsh Fusiliers, 40 Royal Engineers, 150 United States marines, and 23 Italians (in all about 769), arrived from Tongku about noon. They left Tongku three days previously, under the command of Commander Cradock, of H.M.S. "Alacrity," and had not met with much opposition from the enemy until nearing Tien-tsin, when at the last bridge before coming to the Settlement they encountered a heavy fire. This was checked by a 3-pr. field gun, lent by the Americans, assisted by the artillery of a Russian force (about 1,200) also advancing to Tien-tsin, and the enemy driven off. During this last part of the advance the British force lost two killed, five wounded, from a galling flank fire.

The Russian force camped on the left bank of the river, opposite the Settlement, where it still remains. Major-General Stessel is in command.

June 24th. Detachments of the Chinese Regiment and 50 men from the "Terrible," with a 12-pr. arrived. In the afternoon the 12-pr., in conjunction with a 6-pr. on the wall, shelled the Western Arsenal and set it on fire. It contains a great quantity of small-arm ammunition, and some explosions took place.

Arrangements were made by Captain Bayly with the Russian general for the despatch of a force to relieve the Peking Expeditionary Force, then in the armoury near Hsiku, about five miles distant, from whom a messenger had arrived on the 24th asking for assistance. The Russian general provided 1,000 men with two guns, and 900 men were furnished by the remainder of the garrison at Tien-tsin (600 being British) with two Maxims, the whole force being under the command of Colonel Shirinsky, of the Russian Army. The various divisions met at a rendezvous on the left bank of the river at midnight, and after a night march arrived soon after daylight of the 25th outside the armoury. Next day (26th June) the combined force returned to Tien-tsin without incident.

On 25th June the "Terrible's" 12-pr. was placed in position on the river bank to shell the fort in the City, which had been bombarding the Settlement; the position of the gun (or guns) was not known, but by careful watching in the evening the flash was detected and the gun located. By directing the fire from the roof of some houses near, the direction and range was obtained, and after a few minutes the gun was silenced. This accounts for the return of the forces from Hsiku to Tient-sin on the following day having been unmolested.

Since the 14th June, Captain Bayly, as commandant of the British Settlement, has been ably assisted by Captain Burke, of H.M.S. "Orlando," whom I placed, and who still remains, in command of the Naval Brigade.

I am highly satisfied with the behaviour of all employed in these operations, which reflect very great credit on all concerned, but I desire to bring specially to their Lordships' favourable notice the conduct of the following officers and men:—

(1.) Captain Edward H. Bayly, of H.M.S. "Aurora," whose duties were most constant, harassing, and onerous. He displayed throughout great calmness, energy, and good judgment, and a tact and temper quite remarkable. He is now performing the same duties with equal efficiency, and also those of chief of my staff, which combination he has proved himself quite equal to.

(2.) Commander David Beatty, D.S.O., of H.M.S. "Barfleur," although suffering from two wounds only partially healed, one of which is likely to cause him considerable suffering and inconvenience for some time, begged to be allowed to accompany the expedition for the relief of the forces under my command. He is thoroughly deserving of any mark of appreciation of his services.

(3.) Lieutenant Philip N. Wright's (H.M.S. "Orlando") services have been of a most arduous nature and of the highest character. His coolness and gallantry on every occasion merit the highest praise. Lieutenant Wright's very dangerous wound caused a severe loss to the whole force, which was felt by everyone. I have recently ventured, by telegraph, to recommend this officer for special immediate promotion, and feel sure that if granted it will give pleasure and satisfaction to the whole force who served with him.

(4.) Lieutenant Herbert du C. Luard, of H.M.S. "Barfleur," who took on the duties of inspection of defences after Lieutenant Wright had been wounded, and the defence of the line—a very long and troublesome one, constantly "sniped" by night—has been most indefatigable.

(5.) Lieutenant Frederick L. Field, of H.M.S. "Barfleur," deserves mention for his very excellent and arduous services with the repairing and other armed trains, having been hard at work for almost 48 hours continuously on one occasion.

(6.) Major Edward V. Luke, R.M.L.I., of H.M.S. "Barfleur," whose excellent leading and handling of his men at the attack on the Military College contributed very largely to the success of the operation. After Commander Beatty had been wounded, Major Luke assumed the duties of that officer with regard to the military work of the British Defence Force.

(7.) Surgeon J. Falconer Hall, of H.M.S. "Barfleur," whose devoted care and attention to his patients (as well as his professional skill) during a most trying time, have been the admiration of all.

(8.) Mr. George Gipps, midshipman, of H.M.S. "Orlando," has been almost continuously in charge of a gun at an outlying and dangerous portion of the defences, and has displayed at all times great coolness and ability, calmly waiting the arrival of the enemy within effective range, when he has invariably dispersed them with a few well-directed shells.

(9.) William Christmas, P.O., 2 cl., of H.M.S. "Barfleur," for coolness and gallantry during the British attack on the Chinese field guns, on 19th June, when he carried Mr. Donaldson, midshipman, severely wounded, on his back out of the firing line while exposed to a heavy rifle fire.

(10.) Patrick Golden, A.B., of H.M.S. "Barfleur," on the same occasion assisted to carry Lieutenant A. J. B. Stirling, severely wounded, across an open ground swept by rifle fire, and was himself wounded in so doing.

(11.) William Parsonage, A.B., of H.M.S. "Aurora," on the same occasion assisted to carry Lieutenant G. B. Powell, wounded, to the rear over open ground swept by rifle fire, and was wounded in so doing.

Many of the civilian residents have been most helpful, working hard continuously and unselfishly for the benefit of the community. Their kindness and generosity to the regular forces have been great. Mercantile and private houses have been placed at the disposal of officers and men.

Our relations with the representatives and commanding officers of other nations have been most cordial.

I have, &c.,
E. H. SEYMOUR, Vice-Admiral.
The Secretary, Admiralty.

Enclosure to letter from COMMANDER-IN-CHIEF, China Station, dated 8th July 1900, No. 388.

Approximate numerical strength of forces in Tien-tsin on 24th June 1900 :—Austrian, original force present during siege, 50. British, original force present during siege, 393 ; relief force from Taku, 590—total, 983. French, original force present during siege, 50. German, original force present during siege, 110. Italian, original force present during siege, 40 ; relief force from Taku, 23 — total, 63. Japanese, original force present during siege, 50. Russian, original force present during siege, 1,800; relief force from Taku, 1,200 — total, 3,000. United States, original force present during siege, 43 ; relief force from Taku, 150 — total, 193, making a grand total of 4,499,

Enclosure to Letter from COMMANDER-IN-CHIEF, China Station, dated 8th July 1900, No. 388.

Abstract of casualties between 10th and 25th June at Tien-tsin :—" Barfleur," officers, killed, 1 ; wounded, 5 ; seamen, &c., killed, 1 ; wounded, 23 ; marines, wounded, 3. " Aurora," officers, wounded, 1 ; seamen, &c., wounded, 1. " Endymion," seamen, &c., wounded, 1. " Orlando," officers, wounded, 1 ; seamen, &c., killed, 3 ; wounded, 15 ; marines, killed, 1 ; wounded, 1 ; making a total of 6 killed and 51 wounded.

Enclosure to Letter from COMMANDER-IN-CHIEF, China Station, dated 8th July 1900, No. 388.

List of naval and marine officers present in Tien-tsin between 10th and 26th June 1900.

H.M.S. " Barfleur." — David Beatty, D.S.O., Commander, wounded 19th June ; Herbert du C. Luard, Lieutenant ; Frederick L. Field, Lieutenant ; Valentine E. B. Phillimore, Lieutenant ; Anselan J. B. Sterling, Lieutenant, wounded 19th June ; Edward V. Luke, Major, R.M.L.I. ; Harold G. B. Armstrong, Lieutenant, R.M.L.I. ; Edward C. Kennedy, Sub-Lieutenant ; John F. Hall, Surgeon ; Harry G. Wilson, Assistant-Paymaster ; Edgar C. Smith, Assistant Engineer ; Valentine F. Gibbs, Midshipman, wounded 21st June ; Archibald B. Donaldson, Midshipman, wounded 19th June, died 3rd July ; Ronald C. Mayne, Midshipman ; Charles C. Dix, Midshipman ; Harold L. Carmichael, Midshipman ; George C. Browne, Midshipman, wounded 18th June ; Francis N. A. Cromie, Midshipman ; Basil J. D. Guy, Midshipman ; James S. C. Salmond, Midshipman ; Richard B. England, Midshipman ; Gerald F. Longhurst, Midshipman ; Frank S. D. Esdaile, Midshipman, wounded 6th July, died 7th July ; Hamilton C. Allen, Midshipman ; Lionel H. Shore, Midshipman, wounded 25th June ; William E. Cornabé, Midshipman.

H.M.S. " Centurion."—Robert Kilpatrick, Assistant Engineer ; Edgar W. Riley, Assistant Engineer ; George H. Borrett, Lieutenant (T.) ; Colpoys C. Walcott, Sub-Lieutenant ; Cecil B. Prickett, Midshipman ; John W. Dustan, Captain, R.M.L.I. ; William A. Harris, Captain, R.M.L.I.

H.M.S. " Aurora."—Edward H. Bayly, Captain ; Thomas W. Kemp, Lieutenant ; George B. Powell, Lieutenant, wounded, 19th June ; Charles D. Roper, Lieutenant, detached to Tongshan ; Charles F. Ballard, Sub-Lieutenant ; Edward F. Power, Surgeon ; Augustus P. Hughes, Assistant Paymaster ; Francis C. Hanning-Lee, Midshipman ; Robert H. Clark-Hall, Midshipman, detached to Tongshan, 12th June ; Cecil R. Hemans, Midshipman, detached to Tongshan ; Henry C. Halahan, Midshipman ; Arthur F. Crutchley, Midshipman.

H.M.S. "Orlando."—James K. T. Burke, Captain. Arrived prior to 10th June, Philip N. Wright, Lieutenant, wounded 19th June; Herbert M. Perfect. Lieutenant; Frederick C. Fisher, Sub-Lieutenant; Edmund A. B. Stanley, Midshipman; George Gipps, Midshipman; John A. Collett, Midshipman; George W. Taylor, Midshipman; Dennis de C. A. Herbert. Midshipman. 14th June, John H. Young, Midshipman.

H.M.S. "Terrible."—John E. Drummond, Lieutenant (C.); Joseph Wright, Gunner (Acting); Alexander G. Andrews, Lieut.-Surgeon; George J. H. Mullins, Captain, R.M.L.I.; Frank B. A. Lawrie, Lieutenant, R.M.L.I.; Alwyne E. Sherrin, Midshipman; Henry T. Dorling, Midshipman.

H.M.S. "Alacrity."—Christopher G. F. M. Cradock, Commander; Eric Charrington, Lieutenant; Robley H. J. Browne, Surgeon; William S. May, Gunner, wounded 27th June.

TIEN-TSIN AFTER ADMIRAL SEYMOUR'S RETURN.

LETTER No. 402 from COMMANDER-IN-CHIEF on the CHINA STATION of 12th July 1900.

Affairs at Tien-tsin, 27th June to 11th July 1900.

No. 402. H.M.S. "Centurion," off Taku,
SIR, 12th July 1900.

I have the honour to report, for the information of the Lords Commissioners of the Admiralty, the following account of occurrences at Tien-tsin since my return of 26th June.

I found the Settlement presenting a very desolate appearance, the railway station wrecked, the mud huts or cottages of the labouring (but hostile) Chinese round the Settlement burnt to prevent the enemy taking cover there; many of the houses in the Settlement closed or unoccupied, the buildings generally more or less injured by shell fire, which had evidently been heavy, and some by incendiaries; the streets barricaded with bales of wool, rice, &c., and trade entirely suspended both in the Settlement and on the river.

Some of the residents had previously taken the precaution to send their families away, but many women and children still remained. Their number has since been much reduced by sending them, as opportunities offered, to Tongku to wait on board Her Majesty's or other ships until they could be sent away. Several of the ladies have cheerfully devoted themselves to nursing the wounded, and have well fulfilled their self-imposed task.

On the forenoon of 27th June the Russian forces began bombarding the large arsenal two miles east-north-east of the British Concession. Before doing so, the Russian General had asked me if I could send a British force to act as a reserve, and support the Russian attack, if necessary. This I consented to do, and sent out a force of seamen under Commander Cradock, and marines under Major Johnstone, R.M.L.I., about 600 strong, the whole under the command of Captain Burke. They were brought into action directly they arrived, and ordered to advance parallel to the left face of the arsenal, the Russians taking the centre and right face. When about 200 yards from the face a heavy rifle fire was opened on them, and they had to push forward on a flat plain for a considerable distance under a flanking fire, until they could turn and face the arsenal, when they advanced towards it subjected to a harassing shrapnel fire from a field gun at the left corner of the arsenal.

At about 250 yards from the arsenal our men fixed bayonets and charged, the enemy then quickly clearing out; the marines were left outside to fire at them while flying across the plain.

The Russians on their side had also succeeded in gaining entrance, and drove the enemy out from their end. As they then no longer required assistance, our force returned to Tien-tsin, and the arsenal was destroyed.

The British casualties were 7 killed and 21 wounded, the latter number including 2 officers. The bearing of our men under a heavy flanking fire was all that could be desired, and they worked splendidly.

On 28th June a courier arrived from Sir Robert Hart, and another on the following day, both with messages from Peking of the same date (8 a.m., 24th June), " Our case is desperate, come at once."

The Chinese on this day flooded a part of the country near the western quarter of the native city by opening the Grand Canal, whether for their own protection or with a view of injuring us is uncertain, but we have not suffered in consequence, as the floods are of small area, and near the native city.

On 4th July, at 5 a.m., the Chinese opened fire from several guns which had been mounted near the railway bridge over a canal. About noon large bodies of troops were seen moving towards the western arsenal, but on being shelled kept at a distance out of range. About 4 p.m. Chinese troops on the other side of the river attacked the railway station, but were repulsed.

On 4th July two additional 12-pr. guns were received from "Terrible" and two 9-pr. (about) Krupp guns from forts at Taku to oppose the enemy's guns, our guns up to this time being one 12-pr. Q.F., two 9-pr. M.L. field guns, and three 6-pr. Hotchkiss.

On the forenoon of 6th July an attempt was made to take a small gun (about 1-pr. Q.F.) which had been pushed up within short range of the settlement, and whose position had been discovered. The attempt would have been quite successful, the Chinese being taken by surprise, but it was found to be on the opposite side of the river, and the nearest bridge was too much exposed to risk crossing it.

About noon a bombardment of forts in the native city, and of the arsenal, took place, the two 12-pr. guns of "Terrible" being assisted by the French and Japanese field guns. The guns in the Chinese forts were silenced by our guns, the French guns set fire to the Viceroy's Yamen, and the Japanese guns shelled the arsenal, where two guns were mounted, and kept them from firing at the 12-prs. while they were engaged with the forts in the city.

In the afternoon Major Bruce, 1st Chinese Regiment, volunteered to make an attempt to silence the 1-pr. Q.F. gun above-mentioned by the fire of a 9-pr., which he said could be taken by a road he knew, sheltered from the enemy's fire, to within close range. The road was found to be too narrow for the gun, and it was then unfortunately decided to use the main road, which was swept by the enemy's fire. The gun and rifle fire was too heavy for the 9-pr. to be brought into action, and the force retired with the loss of two killed and five wounded, the latter including Major Bruce and Mr. F. Esdaile, midshipman, of H.M.S. "Barfleur," both severely.

On 7th July at noon another bombardment was made as on the previous day, partly to keep down the incessant Chinese shell fire on the European settlements. Our fire was returned by various guns, mostly very difficult to locate, the flash being amongst ruined houses. For half-an-hour the enemy's practice was very good.

Meanwhile a Japanese cavalry reconnaissance was made to the south-west towards the racecourse, which at once unmasked a heavy rifle fire from that position. The Chinese for the last day or two had evidently been trying to work round to the west and south from the native city, perhaps with a view to cutting our communications by river.

On 8th instant it was arranged that a combined movement of Japanese, British, Russian, and American forces should be made at daylight next morning (9th July) to clear the enemy out of their position near the racecourse. A force of nearly 1,000 British (400 naval), under the command of Brigadier-General Dorward, was sent as supports; the Americans sent 150 and the Russians 400, the latter being in reserve; the whole being under the command of the Japanese general (Brigadier-General Fukushima).

Before daylight on 9th July this force moved in a southerly direction and then wheeled to the right; the Japanese then brought their field guns and those of the Hong Kong Artillery into action against the Chinese, who occupied a village near the racecourse. The Japanese cavalry on the left came on a body of Boxers, whom they charged and dispersed, killing about 200; the infantry in the meantime advanced to some earthworks and captured four 3-pr. Krupp guns and about fifty rifles. The force then continued its advance in a northerly direction and occupied a village immediately south of the arsenal, and afterwards advanced towards the arsenal; a gun in the south-west corner of the city opened fire, but was silenced. At the same time a Japanese naval force and American marines advanced along Sankolin's Wall from the Settlement, and entered the western arsenal from that direction at the same time as the forces from the west. The arsenal was found to be evacuated, but two guns, about 9-pr. Krupp, were taken in it. The Japanese advanced beyond the arsenal towards the south wall of the city, but the Chinese troops were collected in force, and a heavy fusillade with gun fire and "sniping" rendered it inadvisable to continue, and after burning the arsenal—which was decided to be untenable by us, and rendering it so by the Chinese—the forces returned. It is estimated that the Chinese lost about 300 to 400 in killed. Our casualties (naval) were one killed and three wounded.

The Russians during the 10th constructed some pontoons, intending that night to convey them to the Lutai Canal (north-east from the city) to enable them to cross and attack the Chinese on their left flank on the other side, about a mile from the city, where they had made a strong position for themselves with several guns. The co-operation of the other Allies was asked, and parties told off from each nationality as supports and in reserve, but late that night it was discovered that the pontoons were not fit for the work intended. This is to be regretted, as a successful attack on the left bank following up that on the right two days previously would have had an excellent effect and done much to discourage the Chinese. I hope it is only postponed for a short time.

Early on the morning of the 11th July a most determined attempt was made by the Chinese, in force, to take the railway station, which has always been one of their main points of attack, either to destroy the rolling-stock or to acquire a near position from which to bombard the Settlement. The fight lasted for three hours and was stubbornly contested, when the Chinese were finally driven out; the losses of the Allies in killed and wounded were fully 150, principally between the French and Japanese. The Chinese loss must have been very heavy, but cannot be accurately given.

About midday the forts in the native city were bombarded for one hour by British and French guns. The "Terrible's" 12-prs. and one of the "Algerine's" 4-inch Q.F. did good work, and demolished the pagoda in the fort used as a look-out place. The enemy's reply was not so vigorous as usual.

The number of Chinese to the west of the native city have increased either by reinforcements or by withdrawal of troops formerly on the other side. With Boxers, their number cannot now be less than 20,000 men. The forces of the Allies are :—Austrian, 50; French, 2,160; Great Britain, 1,420; German, 400; Italian, 40; Japanese, 3,090; Russian, 4,450; United States, 560; total, 12,170.

The operations of the Allied Forces, owing to want of numbers and guns, have been limited to what is necessary for protection of the troops and defence of the Settlement.

The most difficult positions to defend have been the railway station and the French Settlement. The former was held by a mixed force of 100 seamen or marines in turn, 100 French, and 100 Japanese or more, as their General feels able to add to them, all these nations forming a reserve for their own men. At first the Russians held it, but declined to do so after the 4th instant. The French Concession is that part nearest to the Chinese city, hence its danger. It is mainly held by the French troops, but we and the Japanese offered protection also. The south-east part, so-called German Concession, has been quite quiet.

The river has been open throughout and traffic undisturbed; there has been no difficulty in forwarding supplies as far as lighter accommodation admitted. The railway is being repaired by the Russians, and should be open in a day or two.

With the foregoing exceptions the operations have not been of importance. Frequent small attacks on our defences have been made by the Chinese and repelled, and they have been continually "sniping" from cover near, and every day for some hours shelling the Settlement, occasional outbursts being followed by a corresponding lull.

Before closing my despatch I feel it right specially to recommend for their Lordships' favourable consideration the following officers:—

Lieutenant Thomas W. Kemp, H.M.S. "Aurora," has been brought favourably to my notice by Commander Cradock in the advance to Tien-tsin. I can also recommend him for zeal and usefulness, and his services as Russian interpreter have been of very great assistance.

Lieutenant John E. Drummond, of the "Terrible," in command of guns on or near south wall of defences, a very important and exposed position. He has, with all under his command, rendered most valuable service there, and merits their Lordships' recognition.

Lieutenant Frederick A. Powlett, my Flag Lieutenant, was with me throughout the expedition towards Peking, and since. He has been most useful at Tien-tsin, in addition to his other duties, in arranging the signals and communications with the tower and our batteries for firing on the Chinese guns, also in trying to surprise and capture Chinese signallers at night.

Sub-Lieutenant Edward C. Kennedy, H.M.S. "Barfleur," recommended by Major L. W. F. Waller, United States marines. Placed himself under Major Waller with a Maxim, and was most useful firing on the enemy or Chinese guns of the arsenal as they retreated.

Mr. George Ellis, signal boatswain of "Centurion." With me through all the operations hitherto, and has shown the zeal he always does; he was slightly wounded at Tien-tsin.

Mr. Joseph Wright, gunner (acting), "Terrible," with Lieutenant Drummond. I have noticed the great coolness, energy, and valuable service performed by this officer.

Mr. Edward O. B. S. Osborne, Midshipman of "Centurion," has been with me the whole time, and shown great zeal, coolness, and courage.

Mr. James Attrill, carpenter, of H.M.S. "Centurion," has been with the expedition towards Peking, and at Tien-tsin, and showed great zeal and energy, first working hard at repairs to railway ; secondly, in the mounting of guns. He has been very often under fire.

On the evening of 11th July, the Allies having received reinforcements of United States and Japanese troops, the officers and men of " Centurion " were sent back to their ship, and I then returned with my Staff to the flagship outside Taku bar.

I have, &c.
E. H. SEYMOUR, Vice-Admiral.
The Secretary, Admiralty.

STATEMENT of CASUALTIES, 26th June to 11th July 1900.

" Centurion ":—Officers : wounded, 2 ; seamen, &c. : killed, 5 ; wounded, 10 ; Marines : wounded, 2. " Barfleur " :—Officers : killed, 1 ; wounded, 1—seamen, &c. : killed, 1 ; wounded, 5— Marines : wounded, 2. " Terrible ":—Officer : wounded, 1— seamen, &c. : wounded, 4—Marines : killed, 1 ; wounded, 6. " Aurora ":—Seamen, &c. : killed, 1 ; wounded, 5—Marines : killed, 1 ; wounded, 1. " Orlando ":—Seamen, &c. : killed, 1 ; wounded, 5. "Endymion":—Officer : wounded, 1—seamen, &c : killed, 1 ; wounded, 4 — Marines : killed, 1. " Alacrity ":— Officer : wounded, 1—seamen, &c. : wounded, 1. Wei-hai-wei Detachment :—Marines : killed, 1 ; wounded, 2—making a total of officers : killed, 1 ; wounded, 6—seamen, &c. : killed, 9 ; wounded, 34—Marines : killed, 4 ; wounded, 13.

Summary.

Killed : 1 officer, 13 men ; total, 14. Wounded : 6 officers, 47 men ; total, 53—making a grand total of 67 officers and men, killed and wounded.

THE ATTACK ON TIEN-TSIN CITY, July 13 and 14.

LETTER No. 429 from the COMMANDER-IN-CHIEF on the CHINA STATION, dated 23rd July 1900.

Report of Occurrences in connexion with the Attack on the Native Walled City of Tientsin on the 13th and 14th July 1900.

The attached reports are submitted for information. The following officers and men have been brought to my notice on this occasion :—

Lieutenant Valentine E. B. Phillimore, H.M.S. " Barfleur," who commanded A. Company, went to the support of one half-battalion of American Marines who had so many wounded that they would have been unable to save themselves had it not been for the able and timely support which he gave them.

Mr. Basil J. D. Guy, Midshipman, H.M.S. "Barfleur," for the great coolness and bravery he displayed in stopping with and attending to a wounded man under an excessively hot fire, eventually assisting to carry him in across a fire-swept zone.

Ernest Whibbley, ordinary seaman, H.M.S. "Barfleur," for the great coolness and gallantry he displayed in assisting to carry in three men across a heavy fire-swept zone.

Thomas Gardner, sick berth steward, H.M.S. "Barfleur," for the great coolness and attention he displayed whilst attending to and caring for the wounded (including the Americans) under a very heavy fire.

James Drew, Petty Officer, 1st Class, H.M.S. "Barfleur," for his coolness and attention to the wounded under a very heavy fire.

To these names I should also have added that of Captain Henry T. R. Lloyd, R.M.L.I., had he lived. This officer was with me in the advance towards Peking, and was engaged in every action, showing on all occasions great courage and zeal.

E. H. SEYMOUR, Vice-Admiral.

Enclosure to Letter from the COMMANDER-IN-CHIEF on the CHINA STATION.

(No. 429, of 23rd July 1900.)

H.M. Naval Brigade, Tien-tsin,
SIR,   15th July 1900.

I have the honour to forward, for your information, the following details regarding the operations of the 13th and 14th instant, resulting in the complete capture of the native walled city and forts by the Allied Forces.

Early on the morning of the 13th a large force of Russians, accompanied by some Germans and French, attacked on the east and north-east, while the remainder of the forces from the Settlement marched out of the Taku Gate and proceeded to make a detour to the west, in preparation for an attack on the south gate of the city.

By request of General Dorward, I directed all the naval guns, including the 4-in. and 12-pr. guns mounted close to the Russian camp under the direction of Lieutenant Luard, of H.M.S. "Barfleur," and those in the Meadows Road, near the wool mill, and on the mud wall, to be in readiness to open fire at 4 a.m. The fire of these batteries I personally controlled by means of telephone from the signal tower on the Gordon Hall, some of them being unable to actually see the object aimed at from their positions.

Owing to the darkness and mist, fire was not opened until nearly 4.30 a.m.

The guns in the native city immediately replied by shelling the Settlement heavily for some time, one shell wrecking a portion of the hospital established in the Tien-tsin Club, from which, fortunately, nearly all the wounded had been removed on the previous day.

As the attacking columns advanced on their respective sides, the Russians soon came into conflict with the enemy, whom they steadily drove back towards the city.

At about 5 a.m. a tremendous explosion took place near the right flank of the Russians. This was caused by the blowing up of a magazine, said to be full of brown powder, close to the Lutai Canal, which had been set on fire by a shell from a French field gun.

A volume of black smoke was thrown up into the air for a height of at least 600 feet.

Much glass was broken in the settlement, and the signal tower rocked heavily for some seconds.

No deaths or severe casualties resulted from the explosion, but very many Russians who were nearest to it were thrown from their horses, and the general in command received a blow on the head and arm from some falling *débris*.

Soon after this the attack on the left was perceived by the Chinese, and a heavy fire opened from some of the guns in the city.

Both attacks were steadily pressed home until the Chinese were driven under the walls, after some very heavy fighting, as the casualty lists show.

During the time of the advance a heavy fire was kept up, by my direction, from all our guns, both on the east and west, on the forts and guns which seemed to be firing most heavily on the attacking columns.

After the Russian attack had closed in near the city, I ordered Lieutenant Luard's 4-in. and 12-pr. guns in the Russian camp to direct their fire on the fort in the city.

I may here state that the outlying guns were all captured by the Russians.

A most destructive fire was kept up by all the guns to the westward, under Lieutenant Drummond, of H.M.S. " Terrible," on the south wall of the city as the attacking force approached from the south-west, with the view of keeping down the enemy's fire, which was poured heavily from the wall on either side of the south gate when our troops had once passed the western arsenal.

Large portions of the wall were swept away, and the fire was considerably subdued, when a signal reached me from the general to request that all guns might cease fire on the wall, as the Japanese had entered the city. This subsequently proved not to have been the case, and was due to some misunderstanding of a report.

During the time the fire of the guns was taken off the south wall the Chinese re-manned the battlements and poured in a very heavy rifle fire, until the guns once more received permission to re-open on the wall, which they did with great effect.

The Chinese most gallantly stuck to their positions, keeping up a heavy rifle fire until literally swept away, wall and all.

It was then long past midday, and all our forces on the west were lying down under such shelter as was obtainable from houses and walls near the native city and the arsenal walls in the case of the supports.

Killed and wounded have been brought in in great numbers; the Americans lost very heavily in proportion to numbers engaged, but, naturally, the Japanese losses were actually very great, they having such a large number under fire.

In fact, search parties were employed yesterday evening in bringing them in, many of them having been shot in the long grass to the north-west of the canal.

The troops remained in position for the night, food and water being sent out to them.

At daylight next morning there was a little sniping from the walls, but nothing more.

The Japanese sappers blew in the first gate and climbed over and opened the next.

The enemy by this time had, it was found, practically quitted the city during the night, a large body being observed from the Gordon Tower to the north-west.

All the south side of the city was in possession of the Allied Forces by 6 a.m.

The large fort to the north-east had not then been captured, but was subsequently taken by the Japanese about midday, and the whole of the place was divided into four districts, to be held by the foreign troops as detailed, the British holding the north-west portion.

About 200 junks and a very useful stern-wheel steamer were captured in the canal to the north of the city, and will all be very useful later for water transport.

I have the honour to enclose despatches from Captain Burke and a letter from General Dorward, which will convey to you fuller details of the operations of the naval and marine brigade, about 300 strong.

The casualties in this force amounted to six killed and thirty-eight wounded, the former including, I deeply regret to say, Captain H. T. R. Lloyd, R.M.L.I., of H.M.S. "Aurora," who has been engaged in every action with the marines with the force under your command on its march to Peking, and in the vicinity of Tien-tsin since your return.

I have, &c.

EDW. H. BAYLY, Captain and Senior
Naval Officer, Tien-tsin.

Vice-Admiral Sir E. H. Seymour, K.C.B.
Commander-in-Chief.

Enclosure to Letter from the COMMANDER-IN-CHIEF on the CHINA STATION. No. 429 of 23rd July 1900.

REPORT OF OPERATIONS carried out by Naval Brigade against Tien-tsin (Walled) City on 13th and 14th July 1900.

SIR, Tien-tsin, 14th July 1900.

I have the honour to report that, at 3.30 a.m. on 13th instant, the Naval Brigade, numbering a little over 300 bluejackets and Royal Marines, marched out of the European settlement by the Taku Gate, and joined the left attacking column to support the Japanese in the attack on the southern gate of Tien-tsin (Walled) City.

After passing the end of a deserted village at 4 a.m. the head of the column turned to the right in the direction of the western arsenal. The British naval guns on the mud wall now opened fire on the arsenal and city. Soon after the Japanese had reached the plain they deployed, and immediately came in contact with a body of Imperial Chinese troops, whom they soon drove back, with apparently slight loss to themselves. The column then advanced until the bridge leading to the front gate of the western arsenal was reached. This was at about 5 a.m., when a halt was made to permit the Japanese to repair this bridge, which had previously been destroyed by fire on the 9th instant. The Naval Brigade was extended and ordered to lie down, and maintained this position for some time, when the Chinese small-arm men on the City Wall got the range very accurately and caused many casualities in our ranks, including the deaths of Captain Lloyd, R.M.L.I., H.M.S. "Aurora," and James Brown, A.B., H.M.S. "Barfleur." I then moved the brigade some distance to the right, and it was some little time before the enemy again obtained our range, when their fire was again very destructive.

At about 7.15 a.m. the Japanese having completed the repair of the bridge, the whole column advanced over it, the Japanese entering the arsenal, and the remainder taking cover under its mud wall. Here we remained without further casualty until noon, when the Japanese had cleared the arsenal and commenced the attack. Shortly after this the American marines joined in the attack, and were reinforced by our "A" Company of seamen.

About 1 p.m. our "B" Company and all our marines advanced under a heavy fire in support of the Japanese centre, and took cover as supports in a village, and remained there for the rest of the day. At 8 p.m. the remaining two companies of our seamen went out to occupy two large houses on our left to prevent this occupation by snipers, and an hour later were reinforced by 100 French Marines. All these men returned to the mud wall shortly after daybreak on the 14th instant. At 10 p.m. (13th) our "A" Company returned from the firing line, bringing in the American wounded, who were very numerous.

At 3.45 a.m. (14th) the Japanese succeeded in blowing in the Outer Southern Gate of the city, and opened the Inner Gate and entered, supported by our " A " Company and Marines. They then occupied this gate. The remaining three companies of our seamen advanced at 5 a.m., entered the city, and cleared the main road and side streets between the South and North Gates. Outside the latter were several junks in the canal, which were seized by us.

The behaviour of our officers and men was admirable under very trying circumstances, in which we lost very heavily.

An abstract of casualties is attached.

I have, &c.,

J. H. BURKE,
Captain Commanding Naval Brigade.

Captain Edward H. Bayly, R.N.,
Senior Naval Officer, Tien-tsin.

Enclosure to Letter from the COMMANDER-IN-CHIEF on the CHINA STATION, No. 429, of 23rd July 1900.

To Captain BURKE, R.N., Commanding Naval Brigade on 13th and 14th instant. Through the Senior Naval Officer, Tien-tsin.

From Brigadier-General DORWARD, Commanding British Forces, Tien-tsin.

SIR, Tien-tsin, 15th July 1900.

I wish to express my deep sense of the honour done to me by having under my command the officers and men of the Naval Brigade during the long and hard fighting of the 13th instant, which resulted in the capture of Tien-tsin city.

The success of the operations was largely due to the manner in which the naval guns were worked by Lieutenant Drummond, R.N., the accuracy of their fire alone rendering steady fire on the part of the troops possible against the strong Chinese position, and largely reducing the number of casualties.

The delicate operation of withdrawing troops from advanced positions at nightfall, to strengthen other parts of the line, and the bringing back of the wounded could not have been effected without the aid of the well-directed fire of the guns.

I desire to place on record my appreciation of the gallantry and fine spirit of the men, and to join in their regret for the heavy loss in killed and wounded, and particularly with the Royal Marines in regret for the death of Captain Lloyd.

The Naval Brigade had their full share in the fighting at the centre and right of the position, and had the honour of being among the first troops to enter Tien-tsin. The succour they brought under a heavy fire to the hard-pressed American troops on the right was highly appreciated by the 9th Regiment United States Infantry, who found themselves unexpectedly under the heaviest fire of the day, and were much heartened by the arrival of Lieutenant Phillimore, R.N., and his men. It will be my honour to bring their conduct to the notice of the Secretary of State for War.

I join with them in their admiration for the gallantry, soldierly spirit, and organization of our comrades of the Japanese Army.

I have the honour to thank you particularly for the ready and unquestioning assistance which you personally gave me at all times during the progress of the operations, and for the cheerful co-operation of your officers and men in instantly carrying out any duty assigned to them.

I have, &c.,
A. R. F. DORWARD,
Brigadier-General.

ABSTRACT OF CASUALTIES.

Killed. — "Barfleur," seamen, 4; "Aurora," officer, 1; total, 5. Died of wounds.—"Barfleur," seaman, 1. Wounded.— "Barfleur," officers, 2; seamen, 14; marine, 1. "Terrible," seaman, 1; marines, 8. "Aurora," seaman, 1; marines, 6.. "Orlando," seamen, 3; marine, 1. Wei-hai-wei guard, marine, 1; total, 38; making a grand total of 44.

J. H. BURKE,
Captain Commanding Naval Brigade.
Tien-tsin, 14th July 1900.

FURTHER ACCOUNTS OF THE ATTACK ON THE TAKU FORTS.

LETTER No. 24 from the REAR-ADMIRAL on the CHINA STATION, dated 27th June 1900.

H.M.S. "Barfleur" at Taku,
SIR,   27th June 1900.

In continuation of my letter of the 17th instant, No. 4, I have the honour to report the following for the information of their Lordships :—

Communication with the shore was cut off the whole of Monday the 18th on account of the weather, but heavy firing was heard in the direction of Tien-tsin during the night of the 17th, and on the 19th a letter was received from Captain Bayly, H.M.S. "Aurora," who is in command at Tien-tsin, stating that the Chinese troops had openly appeared on the 17th, and had fired on a party sent out to drive off rail wreckers, subsequently shelling the foreign settlement, and a series of skirmishes or small engagements took place during the whole day.

The Chinese Military College was taken and destroyed that afternoon; of our forces, 48 marines, under Major Luke and Lieutenant Armstrong of the "Barfleur," were engaged. Major Luke received a graze on the cheek from the bullet which killed Private Henry Robinson, R.M.L.I., of the "Orlando."

On the 20th a cipher message from the Consul at Tien-tsin, asking for reinforcements, was brought down by runner, and H.M.S. "Terrible," having arrived on the morning of the 21st with 350 officers and men of the Royal Welsh Fusiliers and Royal Engineers, they were landed as soon as possible, and sent on by train to join up with a party of seamen under Commander Cradock, which had started from the north-west fort at 5 that morning for the relief of Tien-tsin.

A strong party of Russian troops with a party of Americans had previously advanced, but fell into an ambush some few miles from Tien-tsin, and were repulsed with some loss; they eventually joined up with our men, who reached Tien-tsin on the 23rd, having engaged the enemy with the loss of one bluejacket killed and some wounded.

Commander Cradock reports that the British bluejackets were in Tien-tsin 20 minutes before any of the others arrived. The Consul at Tien-tsin, writing on the 25th, says that news had been received from Sir Robert Hart, dated 19th instant, saying that the foreign Ministers had been ordered to leave Peking within 24 hours; nothing has since been heard from them.

He further informs me that the Commander-in-Chief was a few miles to the north of Tien-tsin, very short of provisions, and that on the morning of the 23rd he had 40 killed and 70 wounded, but does not say what communication has been made with him.

A force of 2,000 men started to the relief of the Commander-in-Chief from Tien-tsin on the*, and at the time he wrote an action was taking place in that direction.

A large fort on the south bank of the Peiho, above Tong-ku, was reconnoitred yesterday, and being found to be deserted, Lieutenant and Commander Keyes, of H.M.S. "Fame," proceeded there this forenoon, and destroyed it by exploding the magazine.

This fort, which was armed with 6-inch guns, commanded the river, which is now believed to be open for communication with Tien-tsin.

In view of the probable number of wounded being too great for the medical staff of Her Majesty's ships to cope with, I have engaged two civilian doctors to serve where required; one I have sent to Wei-hai-wei in charge of the sick-quarters there, and the other is serving in the base hospital, which has been established at Tong-ku.

---

* Probably 24th June.

I have received a signal from the Russian Admiral this evening to the effect that the Commander-in-Chief was "disengaged," and I hope to be able to telegraph to-morrow that he has been relieved, but up to the present have had no confirmatory news from Tien-tsin.

I forward herewith printed copies of the protocols drawn up at meetings of the Allied Admirals held on the 17th, 20th, and 23rd instant.

I also enclose detailed reports from Commanders Stewart and Cradock of the attack on the Taku forts on the 17th instant, and the capture of the four torpedo boat destroyers of the Hai-Lung class on the same date.

As previously reported, I have turned over a destroyer to the Russian, German, and French Admirals; the one retained for H.M. service having been re-named the "Taku." Her boilers were found to be in need of cleaning and overhaul, but she will be ready for service in a few days.

A list of guns captured in the north-west fort at Taku is forwarded herewith.

I have, &c.,
JAMES BRUCE,
To the Secretary, the Admiralty.   Rear-Admiral.

Enclosure in Letter of REAR-ADMIRAL, CHINA STATION, dated 27th June 1900, No. 24.

Submitting Reports of Proceedings from His Majesty's Torpedo Destroyers "Fame" and "Whiting."

H.M.S. "Algerine," Taku,
June 19th, 1900.

SIR,
I have the honour to submit the reports of proceedings of His Majesty's ships "Fame" and "Whiting" during the operations for the reduction of the Taku Forts on the morning of 17th June.

I take this opportunity of bringing to your notice the very able and gallant manner in which Lieutenant and Commander Roger Keyes carried out my orders, and also the brilliant way in which both Lieutenant and Commander Keyes and Lieutenant and Commander Mackenzie handled their vessels under a heavy fire.

I have, &c.,
R. H. JOHNSTON STEWART,
Commander.

To Rear-Admiral James Bruce,
H.M.S. "Barfleur."

Enclosure in Letter of REAR-ADMIRAL, CHINA STATION,
dated 27th June 1900, No. 24.

SIR, H.M.S. "Fame," Taku, June 17th.

In compliance with your order of 16th instant to take H.M.S. "Whiting" under my command and capture the four Imperial Chinese destroyers lying between Taku and Tongku, so as to ensure the safe passage of the "Iltis," German, and "Lion," French gun vessels, at 3 a.m., I beg to report that, having visited the place during the evening with Lieutenant and Commander Mackenzie of H.M.S. "Whiting," and found them moored head and stern in single line off the south steep-to bank with wire hawsers laid out from each bow and quarter, I arranged as follows :—That the "Fame" should weigh at 2 a.m. followed by the "Whiting" at a distance of about $1\frac{1}{2}$ cables (the distance between the fourth and second destroyers). Each vessel to tow a whaler with a boarding party of 12 men under Lieutenants Tomlinson of H.M.S. "Fame," and Moreton of H.M.S. "Whiting." That we should pass well out in the stream to give them the idea we were proceeding up the river, and when the "Fame's" bow was abreast of No. 4 and the "Whiting's" abreast of No. 2, sheer in and board them over the bow, each whaler boarding the next astern, and each boarding party being covered by a rifle party and the guns.

When the forts commenced the heavy firing about 0.45, both ships being in a very exposed position and the necessity of clearing the river immediate, I directed the "Whiting" to weigh and proceed as arranged. This was effected most successfully. After a slight resistance and the exchange of a few shots, the crews were driven overboard or below hatches; there were a few killed and wounded; our casualties *nil*. No damage was done to the prizes, the "Fame's" bow was slightly bent when we closed to board, and the "Whiting" was struck by a projectile about 4 to 5 inches abreast a coal bunker. This was evidently fired from a mud battery on the bend between Taku and Tongku, which fired in all about 30 shots at us, none of the others striking, though several coming very close. I could not reply for fear of striking the Russian gun vessels lying behind it. There was a good deal of sniping from the dockyard, so I directed all cables of the prizes to be slipped, and proceeded to tow them up to Tongku. At this point, Mr. Macrae, the manager of the Tug and Lighter Company, came to my assistance; I cannot speak too highly of this gentleman's assistance, he took one destroyer off my hands, as did another of the same company's tugs for the "Whiting." In the former case Mr. Macrae had to use force, with the assistance of one of my men, on the Chinese crew, most of whom tried to jump overboard when we came under the fire of the mud battery. In the latter case, Mr. Mayne, midshipman of the "Barfleur," was in command of a guard of seamen with a Maxim, and also did very well. So soon as the destroyers were captured, the "Iltis" and "Lion" passed. The torpedoes were in the tubes, but war heads were not fitted. Ammunition for Q.F. guns in two destroyers was on deck.

By 5 a.m. they were securely berthed at Tongku. It was not a good position, owing to the exposure to shell passing over the bombarding ship, but the best I could find under the circumstances. Fortunately no damage was done.

Mr. Mayne, midshipman in charge of a tug with despatches and stores for Tien-tsin, informed me that his Chinese crew would not pass a fort 12 miles up the river at Lun Chang. So I proceeded in company with the " Whiting " to force a passage if necessary; finding no opposition I returned, as directed by you, to Taku.

Lieutenant Commander Mackenzie is forwarding a separate report. I can only say he did most excellently, as did Lieutenant Tomkinson in charge of the whaler boarding party, and Mr. Mascull, gunner, who took charge of the other destroyer. Mr. Knight, engineer, was of the greatest assistance in charge aft when I was left with a very small crew and no executive officer.

I have, &c.,
ROGER KEYES,
Lieutenant and Commander.
Commander R. H. Johnston Stewart, R.N.,
H.M.S. " Algerine."

Enclosure in Letter of REAR-ADMIRAL, CHINA STATION, dated 27th June 1900. No. 24.

H.M.S. " Whiting," Taku,
SIR,   June 17th, 1900.

I have the honour to report that, having received your order to attack and capture the four Chinese destroyers moored off the dockyard at Taku, acting in conjunction with H.M.S. " Fame " last night, I boarded and captured the two lying down stream at about 1.33 a.m., and as soon as prize crews were got on board and the four wire hawsers, with which each was secured, either cut, or the anchor attached to it weighed, I towed one to Tongku out of reach of the shell-fire of the forts, and was just returning to tow the other up (she had great difficulty in weighing her anchor) when she came in sight, in tow of the tug " Fa Wan."

The capture of the destroyers was effected without any casualties on our side and without much resistance.

In towing one of the prizes to Tongku, a mud fort, hitherto silent, opened a hot fire on us, and the " Whiting " received one 5-inch shot in the hull just forward of engine-room bulkhead, starboard side, passing through bunker (full), carrying away wing-door of boiler and damaging several tubes and putting No. 4 boiler out of action, otherwise not causing any more damage.

After placing the captured destroyers in a place of safety at Tongku with a skeleton crew in charge, I proceeded in company with the "Fame" to escort the tug "Fa Wan" past the fort at Sheng Shing, meeting with no opposition.

I beg to recommend to your notice Lieut. Moreton of this ship, who carried **out** the operation of boarding the first destroyer in a very able **manner**, and succeeded in raising steam and going to quarters for action in about two hours from the time of boarding.

I have, &c.,
C. MACKZENIE, Lieutenant and Commander.

Commander H. J. Stewart, R.N.,
H.M.S. "Algerine."

Enclosure in Letter of REAR-ADMIRAL, CHINA STATION, dated 27th June 1900. No. 24.

North-West Fort, Taku,
SIR, 20th June 1900.

I have the honour to lay before you a further despatch with inclusive details of the operations conducted by the Allied Forces on shore, when capturing the Taku Forts.

The British force detailed for the purpose embarked in a tug from the outer anchorage, and at 3 p.m. on 16th June each man, having been supplied with 100 rounds of ammunition and three days' provisions, proceeded to H.M.S. "Algerine" for the purpose of being berthed, prior to being landed.

Immediately on arrival at Taku on the same evening, a conference was held on board the Russian gunboat "Bobr," among the commanding officers of the several allies, and a plan of attack for the shore forces was prepared.

It was arranged that the British landing party was to land abreast of H.M.S. "Algerine" at a certain hour, and meet the other forces marching from Tongku at the rendezvous on the military road.

The Chinese opened fire on the ships rather earlier than was expected, but the proposed meeting was satisfactorily accomplished, and the men were put into the boats at the commencement of the bombardment to clear the "Algerine's" decks. Each man of the force received a ration of optional cocoa, handed down into the boats before shoving off, and this was consumed before the boats were allowed to leave.

Landing occupied half an hour, and was completed under heavy shell-fire by 2.30 a.m. without mishap.

Allied forces consisted of :—
British: 23 officers, 298 men, commanding officer, Commander C. Cradock, H.M.S. "Alacrity"; total, 321.
German: 3 officers, 130 men, commanding officer, Commander Pohl, H.I.M.S. "Hansa"; total, 133.

Japanese: 4 officers, 240 men, commanding officer, Commander Hattori, I.J.S. "Kasagi"; total, **244**.

Russian: 2 officers, 157 men, commanding officer, Lieutenant Stankewitch, 12th Regiment Tirailleurs, "D'Orient," Luberie; total, 159.

Italian: 1 officer, 24 men, commanding officer, Lieutenant J. Tanca, H.M.S. "Calabria"; total, 25.

Austrian: 2 officers, 20 men, commanding officer, Lieutenant Ernt. Tatniams Qenta; total, 22—making a total of 904 officers and men.

It was arranged that, after an effective bombardment, the north-west fort should be the first to be attacked, then the north fort (on same side of the river), and finally, the long string of south forts on the other bank; before the advance it was agreed that half the British should leave the firing line with the Italians on the left, Germans, Japanese, and that the other half of the British, the Russians, and Austrians should form the supports and reserves.

The German and Japanese commanders were pleased to propose that I should direct proceedings, which I had the great honour to do.

At 2.45 a.m., when some 250 yards from the north face of the fort, the advance commenced, deploying from the right, which flank rested on the river bank; the whole ground a thousand yards this side of the fort was hard mud, but unfortunately quite flat, without a vestige of cover.

The objective of the British was to force or scale the west gate, and this done, to endeavour to gain an entrance into the inner fort, by means of another gate, the whereabouts of which was not quite clear. To do this they were to advance in skirmishing order, to within 50 yards of the moat on the north face, then close on the right, and swinging round the corner of the fort along the military road, the right flank leading in loose formation, seeking what cover the right bank might afford, and charge on the west entrance.

The advance continued until within 1,000 yards of the fort, when I could plainly see that, owing to the darkness, it had suffered little from gun fire, and was practically intact, no guns being silenced. I therefore halted the men and returned myself to consult the other commanding officers as to continuing; it was at once unanimously agreed, that to take it in its present condition, all its guns being still in action, would entail a serious and unnecessary loss of life, and it was therefore decided to retire slightly for the cover afforded by a bend in the river, and wait until the fort was further reduced.

It was not until 4.30 a.m., half-an-hour after dawn, that the heavy ordnance was finally silenced by the ships, although two field guns which had been previously silenced now commenced to play on the attacking party.

The second formation of attack was different to the first; on the previous retirement the "Alacrity" and the "Endymion's" men had been ordered to remain 300 yards to the front, as an observation party. They were under cover of a small rising, and shortly before the advance were joined by the Russians on the left.

In the firing line were the "Alacrity's" and "Endymion's" on the right, Russians on the left, and Italians in loose formation immediately on the right flank, the military road slightly interfering with their getting into line. The "Barfleur's" closed in the rear of the fighting line, reinforcing while the charge was sounded. The foreign forces and the remainder of the British were in close support, the Russians inclining to the left to make their attack on the right rear.

When the charge was sounded the Japanese doubled up from the supports in column of route along the road, and raced with the British along the intervening 300 yards to the west gate, the two nations scaling the parapet together.

Part of the British force also gained an entrance through two gun ports, and over a low part of the ramparts to the right of the gates which were held by my officers through the instrumentality of Lieutenant Duncan of H.M.S. "Algerine," who from previous observation on shore had found these weak spots.

The inner and second gate was forced by rifle fire from the British and Japanese, and this done the fort was practically ours.

As mentioned in my previous despatch, the remaining forts were taken with slight resistance, and after the north fort was captured, the British and Germans were each able to turn and work one of the fort's guns on the still active artillery in the south fort across the river.

Enclosed is a despatch I have the honour to forward.

I have the honour to enclose a letter received from Lieutenant Jno. Tanca, I.M.S. "Calabria," whose force of 25 men had been linked with the British, which he had insisted I should forward, and I have, therefore, given him a letter couched in similar terms.

I cannot close this despatch without mentioning the capital behaviour of the men, more especially as there were amongst them many ordinary seamen and lately-joined stokers. I would especially remark on the fine example set by Lieutenant Eric Charrington, of H.M.S. "Alacrity," and Lieutenant R. Hulbert, of H.M.S. "Endymion," in the firing line, both being worthy of the highest praise. I would also respectfully bring before your notice the pluck and ability of my A.D.C.'s, Midshipman Dennis Herbert, H.M.S. "Orlando," and Midshipman Lionel Shore, H.M.S. "Barfleur," also the conduct of Midshipman C. Dix, H.M.S. "Barfleur," who undoubtedly saved his lieutenant's life.

Surgeon Robley Browne, I.M.S. "Alacrity," was quick in his aid and assiduous in his attention to the wounded.
I have, &c.,
CHRISTOPHER CRADOCK,
Officer Commanding British Land Force, Taku.
To Rear-Admiral J. Bruce, H.M.S. "Barfleur."

Enclosure in Letter of REAR-ADMIRAL, CHINA STATION, dated 27th June 1900, No. 24.

On board the "Algerine,"
17th June 1900.

I have the honour to report to you that in the fight of this morning round the Taku Forts no casualty happened among my 24 men. I have also the honour to thank you very much for your kindness, in the same time that I cannot find sufficient words to praise the conduct and direction of your troops, which I tried, though very poorly, to emulate. Hoping that in any other occasion may I have the honour to be put under your orders, and to fight side by side with the gallant British sailors.
I remain, &c.,
Lieutenant JOHN TANCA.
To Commander C. Cradock,
Commanding the Naval Brigade.

Enclosure in Letter of REAR-ADMIRAL, CHINA STATION, dated 27th June 1900, No. 24.

"Algerine," at Tongku,
SIR,   22nd June 1900.
I have the honour to submit a full report of the operations for the reduction of the Taku forts, which took place on the morning of the 17th June.

Having about 6 p.m. on the 16th instant received your instructions, and a landing party of 350 men under Commander Cradock, from the ships outside, together with 20 Italians from the "Elba," having arrived, Commander Cradock and I attended a conference on board the Russian ship "Bobr," when it was decided that if the forts were not surrendered by 2 a.m. on the 17th the allied squadron should bombard them. It was also arranged that the bombardment should commence at 4 a.m., and that the ships should by that hour be in the positions assigned to them. The "Algerine" was at the position, next above her the German "Iltis," then the Russian ships "Bobr," "Koreytz," and "Gilyak," the French gunboat "Lion," and the Japanese "Atago," the U.S.S. "Monocacy" remaining at Tongku to look after the railway and the various landing parties.

On my return from the conference at about 8 p.m., I shifted berth to my allotted position, and found there the "Bobr," "Koreytz," and "Gilyak," the forts taking no notice of my movements.

I instructed Lieutenant and Commander Keyes, of H.M.S. "Fame," to take the "Whiting" under his orders and seize the four Chinese torpedo-boat destroyers moored alongside the Government yard at 1.30 a.m., so that they should not interfere with the passage of the "Iltis" and "Lion" to their allotted positions.

At 12.50 a.m., when all the ships, except the "Iltis" and "Lion," were in position, and I had the landing party on my upper deck, the forts opened an almost simultaneous and heavy fire, which was replied to almost at once by the Allied ships. I directed my fire with 4-inch guns on the north-west fort, but finding that much ammunition was being expended, and that the shooting in the moonlight was not very accurate, I simply kept one 4-inch firing. I did not use my searchlight, as I judged that it would only draw the fire of the south fort on the ship.

At 1.30 a.m. the "Iltis" took up her position, followed shortly afterwards by the "Lion." As soon as possible the tug "Fa Wan," which was alongside, shoved off and proceeded up the river to Tien-tsin, and the landing party were got into the boats, and disembarked at about 2 o'clock at a previously selected point a short distance below the ship on the north bank of the river.

At about 2.45 a.m. I received a message from Commander Cradock that the landing party were about to assault the north-west fort, and requesting the ships not to fire on it, which message was passed on to the other Allied ships by boat, and the fire continued on the south and north forts. At about 3.45 another message was received from Commander Cradock to the effect that the north-west fort was practically untouched and too strong for them to assault. It was now daylight, and I opened fire on the fort with all my starboard 4-inch guns, together with the "Iltis," whose firing was very well directed. By about 4.30 the return fire had practically ceased, and shortly afterwards the fort was carried by assault.

At 5 o'clock I hoisted the pre-arranged signal, and when it had been repeated by the foreign ships I weighed at about 5.30, and, closely followed by the "Iltis" and the other ships, except the "Gilyak," which had a compartment full of water, and could not move, I led the squadron down the river, firing on the north fort with my forecastle guns, and engaging the south forts with the remainder of my starboard broadside. The north fort made no return, and had been deserted by the garrison, but the fire from the south fort was very heavy, and it was only by God's mercy that we were not hulled. It was at this period that all our casualties occurred.

At about 6.20 a.m. I anchored in position C, and the "Iltis," which had followed me closely, passed ahead and anchored about a ship's length from us, the remainder of the foreign ships being some way astern. At about 6.55 a magazine blew up, after which there was practically no return to our fire, and at 7.10 I ceased firing.

A list of casualties is attached, and I submit that H.M.'s ship under my command, though always in the thick of it, was extremely lucky in not suffering more damage, three or four shots through cowls, one through our steam cutter at the davits, and some standing and running rigging shot away being the extent of the damage.

The behaviour of officers and men was admirable, and where all did their duty it is difficult to particularise. Lieutenants Chambers and Duncan were indefatigable in the performance of their duties and in superintending the firing, while Lieutenant Robinson navigated the ship down the river as cooly as if nothing was going on.

Commander Cradock is sending in a separate report of the operations of the land forces.

The ships engaged were the Russian vessels "Bobr," "Koreytz," and "Gilyak," the German "Iltis," and the French "Lion."

The reports of Lieutenant and Commander Keyes of the "Fame," and Lieutenant and Commander Mackenzie of the "Whiting," have already been submitted, and I have nothing to add to my remarks already made thereon, except cordially to endorse Lieutenant and Commander Keyes' remarks as to the indefatigable manner in which Mr. A. J. Macrae, of the Taku Tug and Lighter Company, assisted us by every means in his power, both before and during the operations, and I respectfully submit that his services are deserving of some recognition.

The ship which suffered most was the Russian "Gilyak," which had 10 men killed, and two officers and 47 men wounded. She was disabled by a shot which severed one of her steam-pipes, and most of her casualties were caused by a shell which penetrated one of her smaller magazines, and exploded some charges in it. She also had one or two below the water-line.

The "Iltis" also lost her gunner and seven men killed, while the captain and about 30 men were wounded. The manner in which this ship was fought was the admiration of the whole squadron.

The "Lion" had one man wounded, since dead.

The "Koreytz" had two officers and several men killed and wounded.

The "Bobr" had no casualties.

I have, &c.
R. H. JOHNSTON STEWART,
Commander.

Rear-Admiral James A. F. Bruce,
 Commanding H.M.'s Ships
  and Vessels at Taku.

Enclosure in Letter of REAR-ADMIRAL, CHINA STATION, dated 27th June 1900, No. 24.

List of Guns captured in North-West Fort, Taku, 17th June.

Number.	Calibre, &c.	Description.
4	12-cm.	Krupp, B.L.
4	12-pr.	Smooth bore, M.L.
8	40-pr.	Rifled, M.L.
2	6-in.	Vavaseur, B.L.
4	8-cm.	Krupp field guns, B.L.
3	4-in.	Brass, rifled, M.L.
3	8-cm.	Krupp, iron carriages, B.L.
4	6-pr.	Smooth bore, wooden carriages, M.L.

Guns bearing on the river.

4	12-cm.	Krupp, B.L.
5	40-pr.	Smooth bore, M.L.
2	5-in.	Vavaseur, B.L.
2	8-cm.	Krupp, on field carriages.

Chinese killed at N.W. Fort.

Found dead, 450.
Estimated by prisoner to have been thrown into moat by Chinese, 50.

LETTER No. 26 from the REAR-ADMIRAL on the CHINA STATION, dated 11th July 1900. No. 26.

"Barfleur," at Taku,
SIR, 11th July 1900.
IN continuation of my general letter No. 24 of 27th June, I have the honour to report the following proceedings at this port.

The Council of Admirals sat on the 5th and 6th instant.

I forward a report from Lieutenant and Commander Keyes, H.M.S. "Fame," of the destruction of the Hsin Cheng Fort.

This fort commanded the river, and it is most important that it should have been destroyed.

It is with much pleasure I forward to your Lordships a letter received from the Russian Admiral, conveying the appreciation expressed by Captain Dobrovolsky, who commanded at Taku during the attack on the Taku Forts, for the services of the British on that occasion; my reply to Admiral Hiltebrandt is also enclosed.

H.M.S. "Whiting" returned from Nagasaki on the 9th July, her repairs having been expeditiously and efficiently executed by the Nagasaki Dock Company, and I have asked Her Majesty's Consul at that port to convey to the directors my thanks, they having put aside other work in order to hasten her.

A composite squadron was despatched to Shan-hai-kwan on the evening of the 8th instant. The decision to send this squadron was reached at the Council of the 5th July.

The squadron consisted of:—1 German ("Hansa," Senior Officer); 1 French; 1 Japanese; 1 Russian; 1 British ("Aurora").

This squadron returned to Taku to-day.

I have, &c.,

JAMES BRUCE, Rear-Admiral.

The Secretary, the Admiralty.

Enclosure to Letter from the REAR-ADMIRAL on the CHINA STATION, dated 11th July 1900, No. 26.

Reporting the Destruction of the Hsin Cheng Fort.

H.M.S. "Fame," at Taku,
SIR, 26th June 1900.

I have the honour to report that, in accordance with your order of the 25th instant, to reconnoitre, and if possible destroy all munitions of war in the Hsin Cheng Fort, I embarked Lieutenant Duncan and 12 men of H.M.S. "Algerine," at 6 a.m. this day, and proceeded up the river.

On arriving there I anchored the "Fame" in the most suitable position for covering the operations, and landed with 32 men, 24 being armed with rifles, the remainder with cutlasses and pistols. After posting sentries and taking every precaution against surprise, I entered the fort without opposition and blew up the magazine and disabled the guns.

The guns disabled were six in number, and were 15-cm. Krupp B.L. on recoil mountings; these guns command the river and Tien-tsin road, and if they were properly manned the passage of the river would be extremely difficult to force. They were in excellent order.

A 2¼-lb. charge of gun-cotton was placed under the trunnions of each gun, with the result that the carriage was shattered and bent and the gun rendered unserviceable, but, except in one case when a primer was also placed in the breech of the gun, the guns themselves were not permanently injured should they be required for Her Majesty's Service.

The magazine contained about 50 tons of powder pebble, prism, black, and small grain.

The explosion was very severe, and though I took every precaution to ensure the safety of my men and the villagers, I regret to have to report that two men were slightly injured by the falling *débris* at a distance of a quarter of a mile from the magazine.

It is possible that there is more ammunition in the fort, but the time at my disposal was limited and did not admit of a systematic search being made. The 6-in. B.L. shell-room was not discovered.

On the outside to the eastward of the fort, there is a large store of projectiles (round) for the numerous obsolete guns which evidently were mounted all round the ramparts and in the three cavaliers; also some hundreds of war rockets, and the carriages and limbers of 27 field pieces—the guns for these could not be found.

I would submit that further investigation be made, as munitions of war must presumably still remain there in large quantities.

Mr. Baldwin (the manager of the mining company), who accompanied me, acted as interpreter, and his services were invaluable.

Lieutenant Duncan was in charge of the gun-cotton party; he performed the work with celerity and great success.

I have, &c.,
ROGER KEYES,
Lieutenant and Commander.

To Captain George Warrender,
Commanding Naval Brigade at Tongku.

Enclosure to Letter from the REAR-ADMIRAL on the CHINA STATION, dated 11th July 1900, No. 26.

Imperial Russian Pacific Squadron.

No. 1,648.

SIR, Taku Roads, 9th July 1900.

Captain Dobrovolsky, who commanded the combined column of gunboats during the bombardment of the Taku Forts, expresses the highest praise of the gallant conduct of Commander Stewart, the officers, and crew of H.M.S. "Algerine," and Lieutenants and Commanders Keyes and Mackenzie of the torpedo-destroyers "Fame" and "Whiting," which took part in the action and did good business under fire of the forts.

I am glad to be able to state this to you, sir, and on behalf of the Russian Fleet to acknowledge that we are proud to co-operate with the British Navy.

I am, &c.,
J. HILTEBRANDT,
Vice-Admiral.

His Excellency
Rear-Admiral Bruce.

SIR, "Barfleur," at Taku, 10th July 1900.

I have much pleasure in acknowledging your kind letter in which you express the appreciation of Captain Dobrovolsky, who commanded the combined column of gunboats at the attack on the Taku Forts, of the gallant conduct of Commander Stewart, the officers, and crew of H.M.S. "Algerine," and Lieutenants and Commanders Keyes and

Mackenzie of the torpedo-boat destroyers "Fame" and "Whiting" on that occasion.

In thanking you, sir, for your letter of appreciation of the services of the officers and men of the British Fleet who assisted at the capture of the Taku Forts, I have the honour to inform you, sir, that the British Navy are proud to have co-operated with the Russian Navy, and been under the command of Captain Dobrovolsky.

         I have, &c.,
         JAMES BRUCE, Rear-Admiral.

To His Excellency Admiral Hiltebrandt,
  Commanding the Imperial Russian
  Squadron at Taku.

THE APPROVAL OF THE ADMIRALTY.

In connection with the operations referred to in the foregoing despatches the Lords Commissioners of the Admiralty have caused a letter, of which the following is a copy, to be sent to the Commander-in-Chief on the China Station:—

SIR,   Admiralty, 1st October 1900.

  My Lords Commissioners of the Admiralty having had before them your letter of the 27th June last, No. 384, reporting the proceedings of the Allied forces in the gallant attempt to relieve the Legations at Peking, desire me to convey an expression of their high appreciation of the tact and judgment displayed by you on that occasion, which contributed so greatly to the harmonious feeling that prevailed between the various sections under your orders.

Their Lordships consider that, having been suddenly called upon to assume command of a mixed force comprising representatives of almost every nation, great credit is due to you for the rapidity with which this force was organised, and for the manner in which the expedition was conducted, in view of the great difficulties necessarily attending it, and the overwhelming numbers of the opposing forces.

My Lords have read with pleasure your testimony to the courage shown, and the hardships cheerfully endured by Her Majesty's officers and men during the period in question, and they desire that you will express to Captain Jellicoe (your Flag Captain); Commander Granville, of H.M.S. "Centurion"; Major Johnstone, R.M.L.I., of H.M.S. "Centurion"; and to all concerned, their unqualified satisfaction at receiving this high commendation of their conduct.

The further reports contained in your letters of the 8th, 12th, and 23rd July, Nos. 388, 402, and 429, respecting the state of affairs at Tien-tsin during your absence and subsequent to your return, have also been laid before their Lordships, and they desire that you will inform Captain Bayly, of H.M.S. "Aurora," whose tact and untiring energy contributed materially to the successful defence of that place; Captain Burke, of H.M.S. "Orlando," who ably assisted him; Commander Beatty, of H.M.S. "Barfleur"; Lieutenant (now Commander) Wright, R.N., of H.M.S. "Orlando"; Major Luke, R.M.L.I., of H.M.S. "Barfleur," and the officers and men under their orders, how fully their Lordships recognise the valuable services rendered by them during a time of great peril and anxiety.

My Lords, having had before them a letter from the Rear-Admiral dated the 17th June, No. 4, containing reports on the storming and capture of the Taku Forts, desire that you will convey to Commander (now Captain) Stewart, of H.M.S. "Algerine," who most ably handled and fought his ship; to Commander Cradock, of H.M.S. "Alacrity," who skilfully led the allied landing force; to Lieutenants and Commanders Keyes and Colin Mackenzie, who did good service in the "Fame" and "Whiting" respectively, especially in their smart cutting out of four Chinese destroyers, and to the other officers and men engaged, an expression of their thorough approbation of the gallantry displayed by them during these successful operations, which their Lordships are pleased to find from your letter No. 385 of the 4th July, have met with your entire concurrence.

Further letters from the Rear-Admiral dated the 27th June and 11th July, Nos. 24 and 26, have also been received relating to other events which occurred whilst you were on shore, and their Lordships wish to take this opportunity of recording their appreciation of the manner in which Rear-Admiral Bruce conducted the important duties which devolved upon him during your enforced absence, and of the excellent relations which he maintained with his foreign colleagues throughout a period of exceptional gravity.

I am to inform you that the Secretary of State for Foreign Affairs entirely concurs in the expressions of approval which it has given their Lordships great pleasure to signify in this letter.

The despatches will be published in the "London Gazette" with the names of the officers and men of the Royal Navy and Royal Marines specially recommended.

My Lords cannot conclude without expressing their deep regret at the casualties which have occurred amongst the officers and men in the various engagements and operations, especially at the valuable lives which have been lost to Her Majesty's Service, notably that of Captain H. T. R. Lloyd, Royal Marine Light Infantry, mentioned favourably on several occasions; and I am to add that they have caused expressions of sympathy to be conveyed to the relatives of those who have fallen.

I am, &c.,
EVAN MACGREGOR.

Vice-Admiral Sir EDWARD H. SEYMOUR,
K.C.B., Commander-in-Chief of His
Majesty's Ships and Vessels, China
Station.

DESPATCHES RELATING TO THE FIGHTING AT TIEN-TSIN
AND THE RELIEF OF PEKING.

War Office, 6th November 1890.
The following despatches have been received by the Secretary of State for War :—

From the GENERAL OFFICER COMMANDING IN CHINA AND HONG KONG to the SECRETARY OF STATE FOR WAR.*

SIR, Hong Kong, 5th July 1900.
I have the honour to forward herewith a despatch received by me to-day from Major F. Morris, 2nd Battalion Royal Welsh Fusiliers, by which it would appear that his small force was fortunate enough to have been the means of at any rate assisting to open out the relief of Tien-tsin.

The reason this despatch was addressed direct me to was no doubt the fact that Major Morris had been detailed by me to command the force sent from Hong Kong, and it was only after he had left Hong Kong, and when all telegraphic communication with the North was interrupted, that I learnt that Colonel Dorward had been appointed to the command. Colonel Dorward had not joined at the time this despatch was written.

From what I learn, both H.M.S. "Terrible," in which Major Morris and this force went up, and the transport in which the remainder left, encountered such severe weather as to delay their arrival at Taku; H.M.S. "Terrible," though leaving Hong Kong a day later than the hired transport, arriving first at Taku. As troops were urgently needed, Major Morris started with his party, leaving the rest of the force sent by me to follow as soon as they landed. I learn, from unofficial sources, that these latter joined him later on, and the whole are now under the command of Brigadier-General Dorward.

It will, I think, be a source of satisfaction to you to know that the arrival of a British force enabled the relief to be successfully carried out.
I have, &c.,
W. J. GASCOIGNE, Major-General,
Commanding in China and Hong Kong.

From Major F. MORRIS, Royal Welsh Fusiliers, Commanding North China Field Force, to the GENERAL OFFICER COMMANDING, Hong Kong.

SIR, Tien-tsin, 24th June 1900.
I have the honour to make the following report with reference to the relief of Tien-tsin.

---

* *London Gazette*, November 6, 1900.

On 21st June I arrived in H.M.S. "Terrible" at Tonku at 5 a.m., with details as per margin,* and left by train a few hours later for the front. I was joined by Captain Cradock, R.N.,

Royal Welsh Fusiliers, officers 7, rank and file 328 ;
Royal Engineers, officers 1, rank and file 32 ;
Royal Army Medical Corps, officers 1, rank and file 9 ;
Army Service Corps, officers 1 ;
Army Pay Department, officers 1, rank and file 1,

with the Naval Brigade. We proceeded to Chun-lien-shang Station, our advance being greatly retarded owing to the two leading trucks being derailed and overturned at some points, and also through having to repair the line where the sleepers had been burned. At Chun-lien-shang we encamped for the night, and found a combined force of Russians and United States Marines,† who, on the previous day, had attempted to enter Tien-tsin, but had been repulsed with the loss of their gun. Major Waller, in command of the United States Marines, informed me that the position was too strong to take without guns, I, therefore, in consultation with Captain Cradock, R.N., agreed that it was advisable to delay a day till a Russian Field Battery should arrive. In the meantime my force was occupied in clearing the line of communications of Boxers and other rebels ; this was carried out completely, and a base for stores, &c., established at a place 10 miles west of Tientsin, where the line was so much destroyed that it was impossible for the train to advance further.

On the 23rd June a Russian force‡ joined the British force, the latter consisting of seven officers and 287 non-commissioned officers and men of the Royal Welsh Fusiliers, under myself, and the Naval Brigade under Captain Cradock, R.N., and advanced to the attack of Tien-tsin at 4 a.m. The whole advanced along the railway line, the Russians were on the right, and the British and Americans on the left.

At a distance of about 6 miles from Tien-tsin the attack was opened and a heavy fire returned by the enemy. From this point the Russians made the railway station their objective, and I was ordered by the Russian General in command to diverge, and in conjunction with the Naval Brigade and American Marines attack the Military School. For about 5 miles the force fought its way under a very heavy rifle fire ; many villages were rushed and taken at the point of the bayonet. The Military School was not strongly held, and was easily cleared of the enemy, who retreated out of it, leaving 25 killed and wounded. This school was the enemy's strongest position holding the European settlement, the relief of which was effected at 1 p.m., the inhabitants pouring out of their entrenchments to greet our soldiers and sailors as they crossed the river. I wish

---

* Military Force. Naval Force—about 150 strong.
† Russians about 300, United States Marines about 100.
‡ Infantry, Artillery, 4 guns, 1,500.

to testify to the great steadiness of my force under a very heavy fire and the heroic manner in which the various villages were assaulted, and the enemy driven out. I attribute my casualties being small to the fact that the men availed themselves of cover on every possible occasion.

The following are my casualties :—

Killed.

3752 Private F. Power.

Wounded.

4977 Private J. Jones, gunshot wound in knee.
4017 Private G. Martin, gunshot wound in thigh.
Self, slightly.

I wish to bring to your notice the names of the following officers for favourable consideration :—

 Captain J. H. Gwynne, Royal Welsh Fusiliers. This officer has done most excellent work, and was conspicuous in leading some of the principal attacks on the various villages.
 Lieutenant F. J. Walwyn, Royal Welsh Fusiliers. This officer managed, under great difficulties, to make local arrangements to bring up the reserve ammunition into the firing line and assisted in saving the killed and wounded from falling into the hands of the enemy.
 Lieutenant O. S. Flower, Royal Welsh Fusiliers, afforded me valuable assistance as Staff Officer.
 Major Watson, Royal Army Medical Corps, performed excellent work under great difficulties.

In forwarding this despatch, I should like to point out the difficulties under which I laboured.

The whole of my stores, reserve ammunition, stretchers and medical comforts were on board the chartered steamer "Hansing," which did not arrive till four days after me, so that I had to borrow ammunition and food in small quantities from the Royal Navy at different times.

There is no transport of any kind available, except a few odd mules and donkeys found in the country, but they have no saddlery or gear.

I am now organizing a company of Mounted Infantry, under Lieutenant Walwyn, 100 strong. The ponies and saddlery are provided by the civilians in Tien-tsin.

I find that the number of officers under my command is inadequate, and I request that you will send me four more for duty with the present detachment, and one more complete company of 100 men, to include as many men as possible who have been through a course of Mounted Infantry.

    I have, &c.,
     FRED. MORRIS, Major,
      Royal Welsh Fusiliers,
   Commanding North China Field Force.

From the GENERAL OFFICER COMMANDING NORTH CHINA BRITISH FIELD FORCE to the SECRETARY OF STATE FOR WAR.

SIR, Tientsin, July 11, 1900.

I have the honour to submit the following report on the action which took place near here on the 9th instant.

2. At 3 a.m. on 9th July a combined force of Japanese, Russian, American, and British troops moved out from the Taku Gate at the southern end of the Foreign Settlements with the object of clearing the Chinese Imperial troops and Boxers and their guns from the villages south of the Mud Parapet and also from the Western Arsenal.

3. The force consisted of 1,000 Japanese, including three troops of Cavalry, a battery of Mountain Artillery, and a party of Engineers, under General Fukushima, and of 950 British (2 companies 2nd Battalion Royal Welsh Fusiliers, 2 2·5in. guns, 2 Maxims of the Hong Kong Royal Artillery, ½ company Hong Kong Regiment, 2 companies 1st Chinese Regiment, 400 Marines and Blue-jackets), 400 Russians, and 200 American troops under my command.

4. The whole force, with the exception of the Americans, who advanced on the Arsenal along the Mud Parapet, proceeded south by the main road for one and a half miles to the village of Tung-lou; there the force turned to the west and half a mile further on deployed, when opposition from the enemy was met with, the Japanese being on the left and the British troops on the right. The Russians acted as reserve to the British column.

5. Four guns, that for several days had annoyed the Settlements by their fire from the village of Hei-niu-chuang, were quickly silenced and captured, and the Japanese cavalry were able to execute three successful charges among a considerable body of flying enemy, who had made but slight resistance to our attack.

6. The line then wheeled to the right and attacked the Western Arsenal.

7. The Japanese Engineers had to make a bridge across a small stream before the Artillery could advance. The bridge was made under cover of our combined artillery fire, slowly replied to by the enemy's guns left at the Arsenal.

8. At 7.30 a.m. the Artillery crossed the stream and took up positions on the further side; the remainder of the force followed, the left of the line resting on the road leading to the Arsenal and the City. The whole of the country to the west of the road had been flooded by the enemy and rendered impassable for troops.

9. The Arsenal was quickly captured by a rush of the Japanese and Americans, and was entered at 9 a.m. by the combined forces, which also spread along the Mud Parapet to the west. Artillery was brought up close to the Parapet

and a heavy fire opened on the city, which was answered with vigour by the enemy.

10. It had been intended to leave a force to prevent the reoccupation of the Arsenal by the enemy, but, owing to its gutted condition and exposed position, it was considered untenable. The houses surrounding it, which might give cover to guns or snipers, were burned, and the bridge leading to the city from the south destroyed.

11. The combined forces then returned along the Mud Parapet to the Settlements.

12. The success of the attack has relieved our batteries in the British Settlement from both direct and enfilade fire to which they had been exposed, and has also diminished the number of guns bombarding the Settlements.

13. The most arduous work of the day was done by the Chinese Regiment, who, as escort to the guns, worked indefatigably in getting them over broken and swampy country.

14. The casualties in the British Force were — 1 private Royal Welsh Fusiliers, 1 private Royal Marine Light Infantry, and 1 Chinese hospital attendant, killed; 3 privates Royal Welsh Fusiliers, 1 private Chinese Regiment, and 1 Chinese hospital attendant, wounded. The Americans and Russians had no casualties. The Japanese lost 50 killed and wounded.

15. The Chinese lost 350 killed, and the number of their wounded must have been considerable. As a result of the action, General Nieh, one of the best of the Chinese generals, is reported to have been killed or to have committed suicide.

I have, &c.,
A. R. F. DORWARD, Brigadier-General.

From the GENERAL OFFICER COMMANDING BRITISH FORCES, Tien-tsin, to the SECRETARY OF STATE FOR WAR.

SIR,   Tien-tsin, July 19, 1900.

On the afternoon of the 11th instant I arranged with General Fukushima, commanding the Japanese Forces, to carry out as soon as possible the capture of Tien-tsin City. Owing to our heavy losses during the daily bombardment of the Settlements we considered this movement necessary.

2. The Russian General was approached on the subject and said he would co-operate in the movement by an attack on the Chinese batteries and fort to the north-east of the city. He desired to get his pontoon train in readiness, and said that as soon as he had done so he would give me notice of his readiness to move. His Staff Officer gave me that notice at 5 p.m. on the 12th instant, and it was arranged that the Russian Forces, who had the longer march, should move in time to deliver their attack on the batteries about 10 a.m. on the following day and that the Japanese-British Force should deliver their attack on

the city as early as possible, in order to attract the bulk of the Chinese troops to their side and so facilitate the capture of the batteries by the Russians.

3. I then called on Colonel de Pelacot, commanding the French Forces, and Colonel Meade, commanding the American Forces, and together with them visited General Fukushima to discuss the plan of operations.

4. It was decided that the Allied Forces would parade at 3 a.m. and move in three columns—about 500 yards apart—on the Western Arsenal.

5. The French force 900 strong was to form the right column and, crossing the Mud Parapet in the British Extra Concession, was to move on the south side of it and under its cover direct on the Arsenal, timing its movement to agree with that of the other columns. Two companies were detailed to advance from the French Settlement and clear the houses between it and the city of troops. They were unable, however, in the face of a heavy fire to make much headway.

6. The Japanese column 1,500 strong under General Fukushima was to move out from the Settlement by the Race Course Gate at 3.30 a.m. and move parallel to the Mud Parapet about 500 yards from it.

7. The left column, consisting of 800 British troops (500 military and 300 naval), 900 Americans and 30 Austrians, moved out of the Taku Gate at 3.30 a.m. under my command and marched parallel to the Japanese column and about 500 yards from them. About 500 yards on the left of the left column was the Japanese cavalry 150 strong.

8. The left column was somewhat delayed in clearing villages of small parties of the enemy, and its head arrived at the road leading to the Arsenal and South Gate of the city about a quarter of a mile behind the head of the Japanese column.

9. The French column suffered a check at a bridge in the Mud Parapet about a quarter of a mile from the Arsenal, in crossing over which their troops were exposed to fire. The Arsenal was cleared of the enemy principally through the agency of the Japanese troops.

10. The advanced British troops, consisting of the detachment 2nd Battalion Royal Welsh Fusiliers, and the American Marines moved forward and lined the Mud Parapet west of the Arsenal, the 9th American Infantry being also brought forward under the parapet as support. The reserve, consisting of two companies Chinese Regiment and the Naval Brigade, were halted about 2,500 yards from the city and suffered some loss from long-range fire.

11. All the Artillery of the combined force, consisting of mountain guns with the exception of three 3·2-inch guns belonging to the Americans, formed up a short distance south of the Mud Parapet and bombarded the city (5.30 a.m.).

12. One 4-inch gun, three 12-pr. and a few 9-pr. and 6-pr., worked by the Navy from a position in the British Extra

Concession, did excellent service in keeping down the fire from the city walls.

13. After about an hour's bombardment it was decided to attack. The French were to be on the right, the Japanese in the centre, and the British on the left, the centre of the attack being the South Gate. Owing to the attack being pushed on somewhat too hurriedly in the centre, the Fusiliers and American Marines had to move forward rather too quickly under a heavy fire to get into their position on the Japanese left (7.15 a.m.).

14. General Fukushima had asked me to give some support to the left of his line during the attack, and the 9th American Infantry was directed by me to give this support and also to support the attack of the Fusiliers and Marines.

15. When the 9th Regiment had crossed the Mud Parapet, a body of men estimated at 1,500 strong, made up of cavalry and infantry, appeared about 2,500 yards away from our extreme left. I directed the detachment of the Hong Kong Regiment, who up to this time had been acting as escort to the guns, to take up a favourable position at a bend in the Mud Parapet about 1 mile from the Arsenal to meet any attack. They had no difficulty in repulsing this threatened attack with the aid of two Maxim guns sent to assist them as soon as possible.

16. The Japanese attack extended considerably more to the left than had been intended, so that the Fusiliers and Marines were pushed more to the left than had been contemplated and brought close to heavy enfilade fire from the suburbs south of the south-west corner of the city. They faced that fire in the steadiest way, taking up a position under fairly good cover, and during the whole day prevented a large body of the enemy from making any forward movement.

17. Meanwhile seven or eight guns of the enemy's artillery were replying to our artillery fire from a fort about $1\frac{1}{4}$ miles west of the West Gate of the city.

18. The reserves were ordered up to take cover under the Mud Parapet, and the whole of the artillery moved inside the parapet and took up the best positions obtainable to continue the bombardment.

19. Moving back from the Hong Kong Regiment position I could see nothing of the 9th American Infantry, but when I reached the Arsenal I saw that only a few Japanese troops were extended on the right of the road, and that the French troops were all in compact bodies in the villages on the road leading to the South Gate behind the Japanese, from which I judged that the fire on the right had been so heavy that the French attacking line could not be formed.

20. At the Arsenal I met the Acting Adjutant of the 9th Regiment, who said he had been sent back with news that his regiment was in a very exposed position, which from his description I made out to be near the French Settlement, and that they had lost heavily, their Colonel, amongst others, being mortally wounded. He said he had been ordered to ask for reinforce-

ments, and I directed 100 men of the Naval Brigade under Lieutenant Phillimore, R.N., to proceed to their assistance.

21. I signalled in to Lieut.-Colonel Bower, who was in command of the forces left in the Settlement, to send me out two more companies of the Chinese Regiment with all the stretchers he could collect, and on their arrival sent the stretchers forward, carried by the men of the regiment under Major Pereira. Major Pereira made two trips out to the American position and brought back many of their wounded under a very heavy fire, losing several men and being himself wounded. He told me on returning from his second trip that the Americans and the men of the Naval Brigade had got into a fairly safe position, so I decided to leave them there till nightfall. They detained a considerable body of the enemy in front of them, and prevented any attack being made on the right flank of the Japanese.

22. Major Pereira also informed me that the Americans were very badly off for ammunition, so I directed Captain Ollivant and a party of the Chinese Regiment to take a further supply to them. While performing this service I regret to say that Captain Ollivant was killed.

23. A Japanese Staff Officer afterwards told me that he had seen the 9th Regiment moving along the right rear of the Japanese attack in column of fours, and that he was afraid they must have suffered heavy loss.

24. The naval guns were all this time making splendid practice, keeping down the fire from the city walls, and we were anxiously waiting for the sound of the explosion which would tell that the Japanese sappers had reached the city gate and blown it in. Shortly after 1 p.m. I received the following note from the Japanese Chief Staff Officer:—

"MON GÉNÉRAL,

"Nos soldats sont déjà entrés dans la cité. Je vous prie donc de faire cesser le feu de vos canons immédiatement.

"AOKI, Lieutenant-Colonel."

25. Orders were accordingly given for the cessation of all artillery fire and the advance of our troops to support the assault on the city. The advancing troops were met with a very heavy fire from the walls, which continued to increase in intensity, and it soon became apparent that the Japanese troops had not entered the city. The troops were then forced to take cover close to the canal round the city. I shortly afterwards heard from the Japanese General that he had been misinformed and that his troops had not entered the city.

26. Orders were sent for all guns to open fire again, and owing to the beautiful practice of the naval guns very little loss was suffered by the troops in the advanced trenches.

27. Towards evening the 1,500 troops on the left flank again advanced and began preparing a long line of shelter-trenches. I received a request from General Fukushima asking me if I could undertake arrangements for the protection of his troops and the French, while in their advanced positions, from attack

from the left flank or rear, as his cavalry had informed him that bodies of the enemy were threatening us from those directions.

28. The naval guns were then requested to direct their whole fire on the enemy facing the extreme left of our position and, under cover of that fire and of volleys from the detachment, Hong Kong Regiment, directed on the various points from which the enemy were harassing the retirement, the Fusiliers and American Marines were withdrawn with very slight loss and formed up behind the Mud Parapet. The movement reflected great credit on Colonel Meade, commanding the Marines, and Captain Gwynne, commanding the Fusiliers.

29. The more delicate manœuvre of withdrawing the 9th American Infantry and the company of the Naval Brigade had then to be undertaken. The naval guns were directed to sweep the barriers constructed along the fringe of houses between the French Settlement and the city from which the fire on the American troops proceeded. The American troops themselves were only about 300 yards from this fringe, and there was great danger of the fire from the naval guns injuring them as well as the enemy. The dead and wounded, of which the Americans had still a considerable number with them, were brought back with the assistance of the company of the Naval Brigade, and shortly afterwards the 9th Regiment arrived at the Mud Parapet in safety. I would specially bring to notice the conduct of Major Jesse Lee during the retirement; in him the regiment possesses an officer of exceptional merit.

30. The whole force is under the greatest obligation to Captain Bayly and Lieutenant Drummond, Royal Navy, for their working of the naval guns.

31. After posting troops to secure our flank and rear from attack, the troops turned in for the night, during which there was some rain.

32. About 3 a.m. next day the Japanese sappers, crossing the canal by a bridge they had made during the night, blew in the South Gate, and in less than an hour, after some desultory street fighting, the city was in our possession.

33. The British force seized a large number of junks and one small steamer on the canal north of the city, which will be useful when we advance on Peking, and also the eight guns which had kept up a steady fire on our artillery throughout the previous day.

34. News was then received that the Russian attack on the other side of the city had been delayed by unforeseen causes, but when made had proved very successful, resulting in the complete rout of the Chinese and the capture of 11 guns; the Russian loss was about 120 killed and wounded.

35. The losses of the Allied Forces in the attack on the South Gate were as follows:—

Royal Marine Light Infantry.—Killed, Captain Lloyd; slightly wounded, Major Luke; wounded, 16 men.

Royal Navy.—Slightly wounded, Lieutenant Field; killed, 5 men; wounded, 19 men.

Royal Welsh Fusiliers.—Killed, 5 men; wounded, 12 men.

Hong Kong Regiment.—Wounded, 8 men, of whom 1 afterwards died.

Hong Kong Companies, Royal Artillery.—Killed, 2 men; wounded, 5 men.

Chinese Regiment. — Killed, Captain Ollivant; slightly wounded, Major Pereira and 1 European non-commissioned officer; killed, 3 men; wounded, 13 men, of whom 1 afterwards died.

American forces, 9th Infantry.—Colonel Liscum and 22 men killed, 3 officers and 70 men wounded. Marines, 5 killed and 27 wounded.

French forces.—110 killed and wounded.

Japanese forces.—400 killed and wounded.

Austrians.—Five wounded. The Austrians were my personal escort during the greater part of the day and were sent forward to enter the city with the advanced troops.

36. On returning to the settlement it was found that 7 men of the Royal Welsh Fusiliers had been wounded, and 1 American killed and 4 wounded by a shell at the railway station on the 13th instant.

37. Among many instances of personal bravery in the action, I would specially bring to notice the conduct of First Lieutenant Smedley D. Butler, United States Marine Corps, in bringing in a wounded man from the front under heavy and accurate fire. Lieutenant Butler was wounded while doing so, and was himself carried out of the firing line by the Adjutant, First Lieutenant Henry Leonard, who, I regret to say, was dangerously wounded in so doing.

38. Captain Lawton, Acting Adjutant of the 9th Regiment, brought me news of their condition under a heavy fire, and, when returning with the reinforcements to guide them to his regiment, was severely wounded.

39. The Royal Welsh Fusiliers were well handled throughout the day by Captain Gwynne; they were very careful of their ammunition and wasted less than any other body of troops on the ground.

40. No. 5653 Private Doodson, of the Royal Welsh Fusiliers, volunteered to carry back to medical assistance—across 300 yards of open and fire-swept space—Lance-sergeant Pearce, of the same regiment, who was severely wounded; this he successfully accomplished, and afterwards brought back a severely wounded Japanese soldier from the advanced trenches to medical assistance and safety.

41. No. 4617 Private Crew, of the Royal Welsh Fusiliers, attempted to carry back Private Bonner over the same ground;

Private Bonner was hit twice during the attempt, and Private Crew was shot dead.

42. I would also bring to notice the bravery and collected conduct of No. 4575 Sergeant C. W. Taylor, of the same regiment, throughout the day. He was prominent in bringing in the wounded men and was generally a splendid example to the half-company of which he was in charge.

43. Captain Watson, of the Chinese Regiment, led his men well, and the two companies with him were among the first troops to enter the city. He has specially brought to my notice the conduct of No. 94 Sergeant Gi-Dien-Kwee, who was in command of a half-company without any European.

44. The artillery under Major St. John were very well handled, and managed to make their ammunition last considerably longer than the artillery of the other nations did. As they were firing black powder, they were at a distinct disadvantage with the artillery of the enemy, which was using smokeless powder, thus rendering the exact location of their guns very difficult. Major St. John has specially brought to my notice the coolness and accuracy of fire of No. 353 Havildar Roshan Khan, who succeeded in putting out of action in four rounds an enemy's gun which had done us much damage.

45. The Naval Brigade under Captain Burke, R.N., had their full share of the fighting in the centre and right of the position, and had the honour of being among the first troops to enter the city. The companies were splendidly led by Commander Beatty and Lieutenant Phillimore, and nothing could have been finer than their spirit and conduct. I have already brought to notice the exceptionally fine work done by Captain Bayly and Lieutenant Drummond, R.N., and the naval guns. I received at all times the most ready and unquestioning assistance from Captain Burke.

46. The medical arrangements for the treatment, care and removal of the wounded reflected great credit on Major Watson, R.A.M.C., and his subordinates. Not only were those arrangements sufficient for the British wounded, but he was also able to take medical charge of American, French, and Japanese patients and to send them into hospital. Captain Prynne, R.A.M.C., and Assistant-Surgeon Pullen, S.M.D., were in the advanced fighting line all day dressing cases under fire. They are both valuable officers, always cool and collected.

I have, &c.,

A. R. F. DORWARD, Brigadier-General.

Report on the Siege of the Legations, Peking, by Sir Claude M. MacDonald.*

This account is compiled from two diaries, both kept during the siege in accordance with my instructions: one by Captain Poole, my Adjutant, and one by Mr. Meyrick Hewlett, who acted as my Private Secretary, from the reports of the various Commanders of detachments given me verbally or in writing, sometimes direct and sometimes through their various Ministers, and lastly, from my own personal observation.

Before the 20th June, barricades, but not of a very substantial nature, had been erected across the road which runs between the Imperial Maritime Customs compound and the Austrian Legation, in front of the Italian Legation in Legation Street, facing east. This was composed mainly of upturned Peking carts, and was to meet any attack from the east, whilst against an enemy advancing along the street from the west, one had been put up between the Russian and American entrance gates.

The British marines held the North Bridge over the canal with a picket; the other detachments also patrolled the roads in the vicinity of their Legations, and pickets were stationed at various points.

The German detachment had made a barricade in the street between their Legation and the Tartar city wall facing east, and the Americans one at the back of their Legation facing west.

Immediately the death of the German Minister became known, it was clear that we had a different foe to deal with, and preparations were made to defend the Legations in grave earnest.

A plan which had been sketched out previously by the commandants of the Legation guards was immediately put into execution; all barricades were hastily strengthened and outlying pickets withdrawn. All women and children were ordered into the British Legation. This order was pretty generally carried out, only a very few remaining at the Peking Hôtel, situated in Legation Street. More than 100 women and children came in during the afternoon, for all of whom accommodation had to be found. This does not include some 600 to 700 Chinese Christians, servants, converts, &c., of whom more than half were women and children.

The student interpreters gave up their quarters and slept in the "tingerhs," or open reception halls; most of the staff also gave up their houses. The Second Secretary's (Mr. Dering's) was handed over to the Russian Legation and bank. The Accountant's was handed over to the members of the French Legation and their wives and families. The ladies of the American Legation occupied the doctor's quarters, and one block of the students' rooms was given over to the Imperial Maritime Customs. Fifteen ladies were accommodated in the ball-room of the Minister's house, twelve others lived in the smoking-room, two families occupied the billiard-room, whilst many missionaries slept in the corridors. The Belgian, Japanese, and Italian Ministers and their families, together with the

---
* Parliamentary Paper, China No. 4 (1900).

widowed Baroness Ketteler, were also accommodated in the Minister's house. In all, 78 Europeans slept in this building, which usually accommodated a dozen; whilst nearly 900 lived within the four walls of the Legation during the eight weeks' siege, the normal number being about sixty.

The whole day was occupied in bringing in and storing provisions and making further arrangements for the defence. Punctually at 4 p.m. the Imperial troops opened fire from the north and east, mostly on the Austrian and Italian barricades, and then commenced the organised attack on the Peking Legations by the forces of the Chinese Government.

So far as the Boxers were concerned, the garrisons of the various Legations could have routed their entire force in Peking, for the *bonâ fide* Boxer believed implicitly in his supernatural powers, and disclaimed to use a fire-arm; but, with Mauser and Mannlicher bullets humming through the air, we knew that a different order of things had begun. Captain Strouts withdrew the picket from the North, or Yu Ho Bridge, to a barricade which we had erected at the main gate of the Legation; the enemy, from the roofs of houses, opened fire on this barricade, and the fire was at once returned. The removal of this picket was in accordance with the plan decided upon by the military authorities; it was in a very exposed position, useful against Boxers, but untenable against rifle fire. Across the canal, which runs from the Imperial city past the main gate of the Legation, is situated the Su Wang Fu, or Palace of Prince Su, a direct descendant of one of the Ironcapped Princes. This Prince had been friendly and helpful, allowing part of his Fu inclosure to be used as a shelter for the Christian refugees. I had, on this account, had some communication with him through a Mr. Huberty James, a professor at the Peking University, one of the refugees in the Legation. When the firing commenced, Mr. James informed me that Prince Su seemed very much distressed at hostilities having broken out, and asked him to convey a message to me, stating that he was convinced that if he could carry the Court an assurance that the foreign Powers had no intention of partitioning the Empire, orders would be given for a cessation of the attack. I authorised Mr. James to say that the mission of all the foreign Representatives in Peking was to maintain friendly relations with the Chinese Government and that Great Britain, and so far as I knew, none of the other Powers, had any designs whatsoever on the integrity of the Chinese Empire. Mr. James departed with my message and returned shortly afterwards saying that he had delivered it to the Prince, who had immediately mounted his horse and galloped off in the direction of the Palace. Mr. James returned to the Fu; suddenly, to the consternation of the small detachment holding our barricade at the main gate, he was seen to run out on the North Bridge, which at that time was swept by the enemy's fire and our own; instantly three Chinese cavalry soldiers charged the unfortunate man and with blows of their sabres drove him before them off the bridge; he was not actually seen to fall, but there is no doubt that he was then and there cut down. A hurried volley was fired at the cavalry, but owing to the failing light it was impossible to see with what result. Mr. James, who spoke Chinese well, had without doubt left the north gate of the Fu and proceeded on to the bridge to expostulate with the soldiery, but orders had evidently now been given to kill all foreigners at sight, orders which Tung-fu Hsiang's men were only too ready to obey.

The attack now became fairly general, and if pressed home must have been attended with disastrous results for, as I have stated, none of the Legations had at that time been put into a thorough state of defence. Desultory attacks took place during the night, all of which were repulsed. On the following day work was continued on the barricades and the provisioning of the British Legation was proceeded with.

June 21.—The Austrian Legation was vigorously attacked; a French marine was killed and an Austrian wounded behind the Austrian barricade; this led to the Austrians falling back on the French Legation, thereby exposing the entire east side of the large block of Customs buildings, which up to this had been held by volunteers belonging to the Maritime Customs. Before long, immense volumes of smoke arose, and the roar of flames and crash of falling timbers were heard, denoting that the Chinese had not been slow in taking advantage of this retirement. The incendiarism continued, and during the day the Austrian and Dutch Legations were burnt, as well as the greater part of the Customs quarter and the Chinese Bank. The enemy were particularly bold in their attacks, exposing themselves freely, and suffering in proportion; it was noticed that nothing fanned their failing courage so much as a conflagration. From the French and German Legations it was reported that some troops, presumably Prince Ching's, were seen to open a heavy fire on the Boxers in the neighbourhood of the Hata Gate. Meanwhile, Tung-fu Hsiang's troops, noticeable by their uniforms—red, with black velvet facings, the cavalry having on their breasts three characters denoting "the cavalry of Kansu"—were very busy in their attacks on us from the north and west. At 9 a.m. a determined onslaught was made on the Students' Mess, a two-storied building overlooking the Imperial Carriage Park; the upper storey of this building, which formed the library, had been barricaded, and was held by a garrison of marines and volunteers. The enemy were driven off, leaving six of their number, making picturesque dots of colour in the long grass. German marines reported that Prince Ching's troops had entered into conversation with them on the wall; these troops said that they had orders to prevent any Boxers coming on the wall of the city, and Prince Ching had issued the strictest injunctions to shoot any Boxers doing so; they added that foreign soldiers could come up there as much as they pleased.

All day the garrison not actually engaged in repelling the attacks of the enemy were busy in assisting the organization of the defence within the British Legation; a Committee of Public Comfort was appointed, the members consisting of representatives of the various Legations, the Maritime Customs, and the various missionary bodies. Various sub-committees were also appointed, one of the most important being the Fortification Committee, under the Rev. F. D. Gamewell, of the American Methodist Mission; this committee, under its intelligent and energetic head, subsequently rendered the most invaluable services; the Food Supply Committee, to look after and regulate the stores and supply of food; the Water Committee, in charge of the five wells in the Legation, to measure each day the depth of water and regulate its consumption; the Committee on Native Labour, a most important one, very ably presided over by the Rev. W. Hobart, an American missionary; by the proper management and organization of native refugees splendid results were obtained. There was, of course, some little confusion at first, but before many days everything worked smoothly, and by applying to the proper committee even watches could be mended and boots repaired free of charge.

June 22.—In the forenoon it was reported to me that, owing to a mistaken order, the garrisons of the various Legations were all falling back on the British Legation, and on going to the main gate I found this to be the case.

Fortunately, the Chinese were not aware of the critical state of affairs, or, at any rate, did not take advantage of it. Before it was too late the matter was rectified, and the various marine detachments marched back to their respective Legations, the Germans, however, losing two men in doing so.

While this was going on, a certain amount of confusion naturally prevailed, as a result of which the Russian, French, and Italian Ministers begged me, as having some previous military experience, to take general command of the defence of all the Legations, and I accepted the task. I subsequently saw the American and Japanese Ministers, who confirmed the above request. I will take this opportunity of stating that during the remainder of the siege I was throughout supported with the greatest loyalty and willingness by my colleagues, and also by the Commanders of the various detachments. I would also beg to acknowledge the splendid assistance given to the defence in general, and myself in particular, by the missionaries, especially the Americans, to whose powers of organization the comfort and comparative safety of the British Legation were mainly due.

The Italians, who, previous to their enforced retirement, had gallantly, by a bayonet charge, repulsed an attack of the enemy, found, on returning, that their Legation was in flames. Their Commander immediately reinforced the nearest post, which was the German, and together with their detachment held a barricade on the city wall above the German Legation, and also one in the street below. By my direction the Italians subsequently occupied, together with the Japanese, the Su Wang Fu. This Palace or Fu subsequently formed one of the principal parts of the defence; it consisted of an inclosure of some 12 to 14 acres, surrounded by walls 20 feet high. Inside were some thirty buildings of various sizes, beautiful gardens, houses, pavilions, rockeries, summer-houses, &c.

The garrison of the Fu now consisted of the Japanese detachment of one officer and twenty-three men, besides nineteen volunteers, most of whom had served in the army; the Italian detachment of one officer and twenty-eight men, the whole under the command of Lieutenant-Colonel Shiba, Japanese Military Attaché; also twelve British marines and the same number of volunteers, mostly from the Maritime Customs, a small garrison to hold so extensive a post. This was the weak point of the entire defence, the garrison being altogether too few in numbers for the area defended; it was, however, under the circumstances, unavoidable, as it would have been impossible to have surrendered any single point of the defence without seriously endangering the rest.

A general glance at the position held may here be useful.

The garrison were fighting practically with their "backs against a wall," in this instance the wall being that of the Tartar city, 50 or 60 feet high, and 30 feet wide at the top.

The German and American Legations were the two which abutted on to this wall, a narrow street only dividing them from it. The line of defence on the 21st June commenced on the east at the German Legation, and, crossing Legation Street, took in the French Legation, a compound of 5 or 6 acres, containing the Minister's residence and those of his staff.

The line then followed the wall of, and included, the Su Wang Fu; from there it crossed the canal, and took in the British Legation going south. It included the Russian and American Legations, finishing again at a point on the wall some 500 yards from where it commenced.

In the defence the French Legation formed a sort of salient, open to close attack from the north and east, and also from the city wall and houses to the south-east. By the burning of the Customs quarter the Su Wang Fu, generally called the "Fu," became open to attack from the east; its north wall faced the enemy, its west side was covered by the British Legation.

On the south of the Fu were situated the Spanish and Japanese Legations, which were included inside the lines of defence and never suffered from a direct attack. The British Legation was completely open to attack from the north and west; abutting the north face were the buildings, temples, examination halls, and library of the world-renowned Hanlin Yuan or Hanlin College, commonly called "The Hanlin." On the west was the Imperial Carriage Park, consisting of an enclosure 12 acres in extent, with handsome trees and capacious storehouses tiled with Imperial yellow, in which were stored the Imperial chairs and carriages.

This Carriage Park was held throughout the siege by the enemy; it was noticeable that the yellow-tiled roofs of the storehouses, though they commanded the British Legation at close range, were never utilized by the enemy; to the south of the Carriage Park, and abutting the west wall of the Legation, in some places actually built against this wall, were the houses which surrounded an open space some 2 acres in extent, which went by the name of the Mongol Market; as its name implied, this inclosure was used by the Mongols, who visit Peking in the winter, as a market-place for their wares.

The south of the Legation was defended from direct attack by the Russian Legation, but between these two, which are some 50 yards apart, was a large collection of Chinese and Mongol houses. These houses were a source of grave danger to both Legations, on account of the ease with which they could be set on fire. South of the British Legation was situated the Russian, the north-east half of which was protected from direct attack by the British, but the north-west formed part of the Mongol Market, and was under fire from the north and west; abutting the west of this Legation were Chinese houses, the whole of the south wall faced Legation Street, on the opposite side of which was the American Legation, which was separated from the Tartar city wall by a narrow street. It was commanded at close range from the wall. The position is clearly shown in the inclosed excellent map, compiled after the siege by Lieutenant Fergusson, of the United States Engineers.

At the commencement of the siege the west of the American Legation was protected by the Russian Bank, which for some few days was held by the Russian and American Marines and volunteers. It was evident from the commencement that to the general defence the most important points were the Tartar city wall and the Fu, the former because an enemy holding it commanded easily the entire circle of defence, and the Fu, because its loss would render the British Legation almost untenable, and here were assembled, by the decision of the Military Commandants, the women and children, spare ammunition and provisions, also; an enemy holding the Fu would menace the retreat of the German and French Legations. The wisdom of the abovementioned decision on the part of the Commandants was amply borne out by subsequent events.

Late in the afternoon the enemy developed their attack from the west, opening fire from the Mongol Market, the houses surrounding which had been loopholed. A private of the marines was shot dead on the west wall of the Legation whilst returning the enemy's fire. Two 9-pr. Krupps also opened fire from the Chien Gate of the city, doing damage to the Russian Bank and American Legation.

The buildings in the Hanlin College were, from a military point of view, a source of great danger to the British Legation, owing to the possibility of their being set on fire, and it was proposed to destroy them. As the buildings were, however, of a very substantial nature, it would have been difficult to do this without explosives, of which we had none; to set them on fire would have been the best course, but one attended with very great danger to ourselves. One could only hope, therefore, that the Chinese, a nation of *literati*, would hesitate to commit this act of vandalism and destroy their national library. By way of precaution, however, a hole was made through the wall which separated us from the Hanlin inclosure, and a search party sent out under Captain Poole, the various buildings were found unoccupied by the enemy, neither were any signs of preparation for setting them on fire visible.

June 23.—Communication with the Russian Legation was established through a hole in the South Wall, and the work of destroying the shops and small buildings situated between the two Legations was commenced; this was a most important necessity in order to establish safe communication between the two Legations, and to ward off all danger from incendiarism; the enemy kept up a heavy rifle fire on the working party, some of whom were wounded, including Mr. Peachy, a student interpreter, but considerable progress was made.

A brisk fire was now commenced and kept up by the enemy from some high roofs belonging to the recently established Electric Light Company, as also from the adjoining premises of the Chinese Colonial Office; these buildings lie some 300 yards to the north-east of the British Legation; the Italian quick-firing 1-inch gun was brought up and together with our sharpshooters from the north stable picket returned the fire with telling effect. This Italian quickfirer was by far the most useful of the machine-guns brought by the various detachments. The others were an Austrian Maxim, a British five-barrelled Nordenfelt, very old pattern, and an American Colt automatic. Unfortunately, there were only 150 rounds brought up with the Italian gun. In the course of the siege the entire gun detachment of this quickfirer, consisting of five men, were either killed or wounded.

At 11.15 A.M. a determined attack was made on the Hanlin inclosure. It was preceded by a sharp infantry fire from the Imperial Carriage Park; the greater part of the Hanlin was then set on fire by the enemy; the fire-bell rang and all hands were soon at work endeavouring to extinguish the flames; the Chinese had carefully selected their day and had evidently no qualms whatever as to the vandalism they were committing; a fresh north wind was blowing, and the flames were carried nearer and nearer to the Legation buildings; a stubborn fight was maintained until late in the afternoon, when the flames were got under, but not before more than three quarters of the temples, examination halls, and libraries, forming the Hanlin College, had been destroyed. There remained only one building entirely intact, the heavy wooden eaves of which overshadowed and almost touched the students' quarters in the Legation; had these caught fire, the Legation would most probably have been doomed, but owing to the splendid efforts of the garrison, men, women, and even children joining in the work of passing water to the engines, as well as to a providential change of the wind to another quarter, the danger was averted. Orders were given to save as many of the valuable books in the Hanlin as possible; the greater part had, however, been destroyed either by fire or water; a good many were taken away as mementoes by members of the garrison.

The enemy pursued these incendiary tactics at other parts of the defence, and at 3 p.m. a fire was reported from the Russian Legation, but M. de Giers reported that he thought he could cope with it with the resources at his command. Late in the afternoon the American detachment reported a determined attempt to set fire to their Legation buildings. I sent over immediately a reinforcement of twenty-five men and some members of the fire brigade. The Russo-Chinese Bank next to the American Legation was on fire, and partially burnt down, but the Legation escaped. For the next five days the enemy endeavoured to burn out the garrison, and a daily and hourly fight took place, resulting in a complete victory for the defenders.

The practice from the enemy's Krupp 9-pr. battery on the Chien Gate now became very accurate, and for a time they paid particular attention to the national standards flying over the entrance gates of the Russian and American Legations. The American flagstaff was shot away,* and a considerable hole made in the gateway. The Russian flag had also some narrow escapes, and they were both eventually removed to places where they could not be seen from the wall. This battery also shelled the barricade on the wall at the back of the American Legation, bursting two shells in the barricade itself, the range being about 800 yards. Unfortunately we had no artillery heavy enough to silence these guns, and our riflemen were so scattered it was all we could do to keep in check those of the enemy. The 9-pr. which was to have accompanied the Russian detachment had most unfortunately been left behind on the platform of the railway station at Tien-tsin, though the ammunition had been brought.

June 24.—Early on this morning an attack was made on the American and Russian Legations, resulting in some casualties on our side. A determined attack was also made on the Fu, the Chinese trying to breach the high wall on the north-east corner, but were driven off with loss. They also effected a lodgment on the Tartar city wall immediately behind the American Legation, where they displayed their banners, and seemed to be waiting for orders to fire. A brilliant charge along the top of the wall by a small force of Germans and Americans, led by the intrepid Lieutenant von Soden, put the enemy to flight, and the pursuit was kept up almost to the Chien Gate. Here the pursuing party had to retire, finding themselves face to face with a Chinese barricade. In this gallant affair the enemy lost from eight to ten killed and three banners. While this was

---

* N.B.—Sir C. MacDonald telegraphed on the 29th January, 1901, to the effect that this incident took place not on the 23rd June, but later, on the 6th July.

going on the British Legation was attacked in a determined manner from the Mongol Market, the attack being directed against the south stable quarters, the enemy working their way through the Chinese houses up to the wall of the Legation. They then set fire to part of the stables, and threw stones and other missiles into the stable-yard. A sortie was instantly decided upon, a hole was made in the wall, and a party of marines headed by Captain Halliday dashed into the burning buildings, and cleared them at the point of the bayonet. Unfortunately Captain Halliday was almost immediately wounded very severely by a rifle-shot through the shoulder and lung, and had to give up the command. Notwithstanding the severe nature of his wound, Captain Halliday shot three of his assailants, and, refusing all aid, walked to the hospital, a distance of some 200 yards. I regret to say, owing to the severity of the wound, the services of this excellent officer were lost to the defence for the rest of the siege. Captain Strouts now took command of the sortie, and inflicted considerable loss on the enemy, killing thirty-four in one house. One marine was mortally wounded, and others slightly in this affair, which had a most excellent effect, as it destroyed some 200 yards of cover which the enemy possessed, and drove them back to their barricades situated at the same distance from the Legation wall. During the morning an equally brilliant sortie was made by Colonel Shiba from the north-east corner of the Fu at the head of ten French, ten Italians, and ten Japanese marines, and some British and Japanese volunteers, driving the enemy out of and past the Customs buildings. In the meanwhile the American detachment under Captain Myers had effected a lodgment on the Tartar wall, and a barricade had been commenced, a special gang of coolies to work on it being told off under an American missionary. By the following morning this barricade was completed. Unfortunately it was constructed at the head of the east ramp leading up to a bastion, thus leaving the bastion and the west ramp to be taken possession of by the enemy should they be so minded. The ramp leading up to the barricade was under fire from the Hata Gate, and many casualties occurred in going up to it. I myself saw three "converts" shot on the ramp in the space of five minutes. The enemy maintained a smart fire on this position, as also on the barricades across the street below. The fire on the wall was so severe that any casualties which occurred could not be attended to until nightfall, and the dead had to remain where they fell. The French and German Legations had meanwhile been keeping up a stubborn defence. The Germans held a barricade facing the Hata Gate, on the wall, and also on the road between the Legation and the foot of the ramp, and the French a barricade across Legation Street looking east. As evening closed in a British marine was dangerously wounded whilst walking inside our Legation compound. At the time he was shot down several ladies and children were within a few yards. It is a noticeable fact that during the entire siege only three casualties took place in the actual grounds as distinguished from the defences of the Legation. A marine was shot dead coming out of the guard-room by a bullet which skimmed the roof of the constables' quarters; the third casualty was a lady seriously wounded on the tennis-lawn a few minutes after the relieving force entered the Legation.

June 25.—During the night and early morning the barricades on the wall and in the street at the back of the American Legation were badly damaged by shell fire from the Chien Gate; ten Germans and ten British marines were sent to reinforce, two British marines were almost immediately wounded by shell fire, one of whom subsequently died.

French reinforcements, together with Customs and Legation volunteers, under Captain Poole, were sent to the Fu, which was hard pressed; in this attack one French marine and two Japanese were killed and two Italians wounded.

Shortly after 4 p.m. great excitement was caused in the British Legation by the appearance of a small group of men carrying a board on the North Bridge, and word was passed to the northern defences and to the Fu to cease fire. By means of glasses from the north stable the board was made out to be an Imperial Decree stating that the Chinese troops were sent to protect the Legations and stop the firing, and adding that a despatch would be handed to the Legations on the North Bridge. One of the garrison, a Chinaman, volunteered to go out and receive the despatch; he was furnished with a notice board with black characters painted thereon, to the effect that the Imperial Decree had been understood, and that the despatch would be received; wearing an official hat the messenger sallied out watched by an expectant garrison; on arrival at the bridge he was received with cries of "Lai, la" ("He has come"), whereupon his courage seemed to fail him, and dropping the board he retreated hurriedly back to the Legation, arriving unhurt. Two Mandarins accompanied by soldiers appeared round the corner of the bridge and everybody hoped that communications with the enemy were about to be opened, but some dropping shots were heard and the Mandarins and soldiers quickly disappeared. It was thought at the time that some too zealous sentries in the Fu had been unable to resist the temptation of shooting a Mandarin, and had disobeyed orders; but I have subsequently ascertained that the shots were fired by Tung-fu Hsiang's soldiers at the party bearing the Imperial Decree, and that one of the bearers was actually shot dead, the rest taking to flight. The board with the Imperial Decree inscribed thereon remained for many days on the bridge a curious commentary on the thousands of bullets which swept over it and pattered on the roofs and defences of the Legations.

The immediate effect, however, of this notice was a sounding of horns in the Imperial city, which was taken up all round the defences and the firing immediately ceased, thus showing very clearly the complete command the *de facto* Government, whether Dowager-Empress, Prince Tuan, or both had over the troops.

The lull in the firing was the signal for increased activity in the British Legation on the part of Mr. Gamewell and his Fortification Committee, and soon some hundred of converts were busily at work strengthening weak places and adding to the defences. Our advanced posts in the Hanlin entered into conversation with the Chinese soldiers; from the latter it was gathered that Yung Lu had ordered the "cease fire," and that a communication was coming from him to us, but it never came.

Previous to the appearance of the board, the Germans and Americans had been hotly engaged, and the Italian gun had been sent to the wall barricade to endeavour to keep down the shell fire from the Chien Gate, but had itself been put out of action, both gunners having been seriously wounded and carried to the International Hospital. By 8 p.m. the firing had altogether ceased; shortly after a few shots were exchanged between the French in their Legation and the opposing barricades; a few desultory shots were also fired on the wall. On this day the Chinese took to building barricades of a more substantial nature and scientific design; up till now they had fired from barricades hastily constructed, from roofs of houses, and from behind ruined walls, and must have suffered severely.

About midnight, Prince Tuan and the war party having presumably again got the upper hand, a tremendous fusillade was opened from all sides, but principally from north and north-west. This was the heaviest fire to which we had yet been subjected, and the bullets struck and ricochetted off the roofs of the various buildings like hailstones; this fire was kept up all through the night, and very few of the garrison obtained any sleep. The Americans were badly pressed in the barricade below the wall and reinforcements were called for from the French Legation, but Captain d'Arcy was unable to send them, his own post being hotly attacked; 10 British marines were accordingly sent as soon as they could be spared.

June 26.—In the morning the enemy, exhausted evidently by their efforts of the previous night, kept fairly quiet, allowing the worn-out garrison to snatch a few hours sleep. At 9.30 desultory sniping took place all round the defences.

Mr. Cockburn, Chinese Secretary, and Mr. Ker, Assistant Chinese Secretary, remained with the picket in the north stables the whole day, in case any message should come from the Imperial city, but in vain; and it was now evident that the war party was in the ascendant, and that a policy of extermination of the Legations had been decided on. The enforced retreat of Admiral Seymour and the successful blockade and bombardment of Tien-tsin, of which we were, of course, unaware, would be sufficient to account for this decision.

To-day was organised the last reserve, and the following order was posted on the Bell Tower:—

"In case of heavy firing, all men with guns of any description who are not on special duty at the time are to assemble at once at the Bell Tower and there await the orders of Captain Strouts."

Subsequent instructions were given that the assembly should only take place at the ringing of the "general attack bell."

The French Legation was severely attacked towards evening, and heavy volleys were fired into it from the enemy's barricades.

June 27.—This promised to be a lively day. The firing became very heavy all round as early as 2 a.m. At 8 a.m. the firing slackened somewhat ; but a smart attack was made on the Fu, and Colonel Shiba sent for the Italian gun. Fresh gunners having been procured, the gun was sent to him.

At 2.30 the American Legation called for reinforcements, and a reserve of five British marines, which were now always kept ready at the main gate, were immediately despatched with a promise of 10 more, if necessary. Ten British marines were already in the American barricade ; this made 21 British marines, rather more than one-third of the available force, on duty outside the British Legation.

At 4 p.m. a heavy fusilade commenced on all sides, and the bugle sounded to general quarters. There was also heavy firing from the north-east corner of the Fu, and a Japanese orderly came hurriedly over with a note for me from Colonel Shiba. It ran thus :—

"Dear Sir,—They are nearing to break down the Fu's wall. I want to crush them when they come in. Will you please send some more reinforcements to me with the bearer."

Five marines and five volunteers were immediately sent. Shortly afterwards Colonel Shiba came over and reported that the enemy, having breached a hole in the north-east corner of the wall, had poured through into the Fu. He was, however, prepared for this incursion, and opened a murderous fire on them from surrounding loopholes. The enemy fled in panic, trampling each other down in their efforts to escape through the hole by which they had entered, and leaving over 20 of their dead in the inclosure.

To cover their retreat they set fire to a temple at the corner of the Fu, and for the rest of the afternoon occupied themselves in dragging their dead through the hole in the wall by means of long poles with hooks attached to the ends.

At 8 p.m. the American detachment reported that 200 Boxers, compelled by Chinese soldiers to advance, had attacked the street barricade, but had been forced to retire with a loss of 50 killed. This number is, I think, somewhat excessive.

At 10.30 the "general attack" bell was sounded. The reserves turned out smartly and in very creditable numbers. The firing ceased shortly after 11, and a fairly quiet night ensued.

June 28.—The enemy had evidently constructed gun platforms during the night for their two Krupp guns in the Fu, and with these they devoted themselves to bombarding the north wall at close range (about 10 yards) in order to breach the wall further. They also turned their attention to the "Hôtel de Pékin." The upper storey of this building was struck 26 times by shell, without, however, doing any harm to the occupants, who were in the lower storey. The ruins of the Russo-Chinese Bank were occupied this day by the enemy.

At 6.30 p.m. the "general attack" bell was again sounded. The enemy had manned their loophole in the Mongol Market, and opened a heavy musketry fire against the stable quarters. Suddenly a gate at the north-west corner of the market flew open, and two Krupp guns opened fire at the top storey of the stable quarters at a range of about 200 yards. Shell after shell crashed into the building, completely wrecking one window, shattering the barricades of the next, and driving the defenders out of the two upper rooms down below into the stable yard. Our men were not slow to return the fire, but having been driven out of the top storey of the building, we could only bring a few rifles to bear. These, however, delivered an effective fire into the gateway, where, through the smoke, we could see the gunners at work. These, however, stuck to their guns, and it was only when it seemed as if the upper storey of the house must come down that the fire suddenly ceased.

Experts say that two or three more rounds and the supporting walls would have given way, sending the heavy Chinese roof crashing into the storey below. The Chinese gunners must have suffered severely, for they were considerably exposed, and they never again attempted an artillery attack upon the Mongol Market.

The food supply suffered considerably during this bombardment, two mules and a pony having been killed by exploding shells. Several of the men had narrow escapes, but only two were wounded.

The wall behind the American Legation and the Legation itself were hotly attacked during the day. Mr. Conger, writing from his Legation, says :—

"Besides the attack of last evening our people on the wall and in the street below had two heavy attacks during the night. This morning they can be seen in largely increased numbers; they have occupied the inclined ramp opposite ours, and have planted a banner near the top, within 100 yards of our position, but we cannot touch them. If they attack, Captain Myers can repulse them, if not in great numbers. I have instructed him to hold on to the last minute, and am sure he will."

The enemy did not leave their barricade, but contented themselves with a continuous fusillade from their loopholes.

June 21.—Two sorties had been arranged for this morning: one under Captain Wray and one under Captain Poole. The former consisted of 26 British, 10 Russians, 5 French, and 5 Italians, and the latter, of 5 marines and 10 volunteers. Captain Wray's party attacked the Mongol Market with a view, if possible, of capturing the two Krupp guns which had done such damage the day before; the guns had, however, been removed, and the sortie retired, setting fire to some houses; there were no casualties.

This sortie would have effected more, but so many nationalities were represented on one spot that orders given were not understood, and some confusion resulted. Captain Poole's party penetrated into the Carriage Park, but were brought up by a high barricade; when near the same they came under a heavy cross-fire at close range, and had to retreat, fortunately without any casualties, though the fire was very hot, the bullets pattering like hail all round the hole in the wall through which the retreat had to be effected.

During the forenoon the enemy's artillery at the north-east corner of the Fu was particularly energetic; the gunnery, however, was erratic, several of the shells coming over the Legation, and finding a home in the Chinese city south of the Tartar wall. Reinforcements were sent into the Fu, 5 marines and 5 volunteers. Shortly after 10 the Chinese set fire to a large pavilion at the north-east corner of the Fu, and effected a lodgment in the grounds. They crept up under cover of ruins, &c., with long poles, at the end of which tow dipped in kerosene was tied. With these they set fire to the heavy overhanging wooden eaves of the Chinese buildings, which were very old, and burnt like tinder. It was only by being burnt out that the plucky defenders were forced to fall back.

Dr. Lippett, surgeon of the American detachment, was dangerously wounded whilst talking to his Minister. The wound was a very serious one, and he was still in hospital when the relieving troops entered.

Captain D'Arcy, the gallant defender of the French Legation, was severely attacked and sent for reinforcements: 5 British marines, 5 volunteers, and 10 Japanese were immediately sent and assisted in repelling this attack. The British detachment was cheered by their French comrades when leaving the Legation.

Lieutenant Herbert, second in command of the French detachment, was killed whilst directing the defence, and two French marines were brought in wounded to the International Hospital, which had been established in this Legation under Drs. Poole and Velde, surgeons of the British and German Legations respectively.

This had been a bad day for the defence: every single nationality had to deplore the loss of some of its members, and the French and Japanese, after hard fighting, had lost ground.

It had always been supposed that heavy rain would have the effect of driving the Chinese under shelter, and that a rainstorm while it lasted would result in quiet times for us. At 10 p.m. heavy rain commenced, and was the immediate signal for a most tremendous fusillade that quite surpassed anything that had ever taken place before. There was little or no artillery fire, but the roar, for it can be called by no other name, of musketry continued without intermission until daylight. There was no necessity to ring the alarm bell, for the entire garrison stood to arms during the whole night, thinking that this waste of ammunition must be the precursor of something more serious. Nothing, however, happened, and the damage done, except to trees and roofs, which were badly cut about, was practically nil. To maintain so continuous a fire I am of opinion that the Imperial regiments must have relieved each other in the firing line. The vast majority of the hail of bullets were going very high, and again the Chinese city must have suffered seriously. At a low computation 200,000 rounds must have been fired by the Chinese during the night.

June 30.—Up till 9 a.m. the enemy remained quiet, having without doubt passed a sleepless night, but shortly after 9 they showed in large numbers opposite the German posts, and, in reply to a communication from the German Chargé d'Affaires, a reinforcement of ten British marines was sent to assist in repelling the attack; two of this reinforcement were soon carried back severely wounded by splinters from shells; one has since died. Fighting had now become severe, and three German marines were killed and two wounded, but the enemy were repulsed, having suffered heavily; the French also, though attacked and hard pressed, drove off their assailants with loss.

At 11 p.m. the picket in the south stable reported what looked like a search-light far away on the southern horizon. I watched the light in question for some time; it certainly had the appearance of a search-light, or rather lighthouse, low down on the horizon; its resemblance to a search-light, however, was not sufficiently pronounced to warrant a notice being put up on the Bell Tower, where all events of interest were posted.

July 1.—This morning began quietly, but at 9 a.m. the enemy, notwithstanding their lessons of the previous day, showed in force towards the Hata Gate, and creeping up in the ramps surprised the German guard of ten men, under a non-commissioned officer, who retired down the reverse ramp, thereby exposing the rear of the American barricade some 450 yards distant; the latter coming under a reverse fire also left the wall, and the situation for a time was very critical; the Chinese, however, did not realise, or at any rate did not avail themselves of the advantage they had gained: Russian reinforcements were at once sent to the Americans, and shortly afterwards they reoccupied their barricades, but the German barricades on the wall remained in the hands of the enemy until the end of the siege. At 10.30 a further reinforcement, consisting of ten marines under Captain Wray, was sent to relieve Captain Myers on the wall; seven marines also went to the German Legation. Whilst this was going on a fierce attack was made on the French Legation; Mr. Wagner, one of the Customs volunteers, was shot dead, and the garrison momentarily fell back to their last line of defence, leaving the German Legation in a somewhat exposed and critical position. M. von Below,

German Chargé d'Affaires, sent word to me informing me of the state of affairs, and asking for reinforcements; though the Kansu troops were busy attacking our north and north-west defences, Captain Strouts was able to detach six men and a corporal to the relief; the French had in the meanwhile advanced and reoccupied their Legation. The enemy had during the night built formidable barricades in the north of the Carriage Park; to cope with this the Italian quickfirer was with some difficulty hauled up into the Students' Library, a large upper storey room, and opened with deadly effect on the said barricade, completely silencing its fire. At 2 p m. Captain Wray, who, it will be remembered, had been sent to Captain Myers' assistance on the wall, was brought in with a Mauser bullet through the shoulder. I had given this officer orders whilst on the wall to commence a barricade some 200 yards east of the American one in order to hold the enemy in check from the Hata Gate side and to cover the rear of the Russo-American position. On advancing towards the spot indicated he and his party were met by a severe cross-fire from both the Hata Gate and Chien Gate, the Mauser bullets from the latter just clearing the top of the American barricade in rear of the little party, and ricochetting along the wall, they nevertheless continued to construct the work. Captain Wray, whilst directing his men, was wounded soon after; one of his party was also shot down. The fire now became so hot that it was quite impossible to continue the work; Captain Wray, therefore, ordered a retreat, which was carried out with most exemplary coolness under a severe fire.

At 3.15, Lieutenant Paolini, the officer commanding the Italian detachment in the Fu, reported that the Krupp gun, which had been firing all day, had been moved nearer, and he thought, by making a sortie, he might be able to take it; he asked for assistance, and also for permission to make the attempt. Thinking the proposition rather risky, I consulted Colonel Shiba, in whose judgment of affairs in the Fu I had the fullest confidence.

Colonel Shiba replied that he thought the capture of the gun practicable, and that the sortie should be made. I accordingly gave orders that the desired reinforcements should be sent to Lieutenant Paolini, and that he might proceed. There was no time to discuss the details of the sortie, as the position taken up by this gun was evidently only temporary, but the general idea was for Lieutenant Paolini's party to attack from the west, while Colonel Shiba attacked from the east. The reinforcements detached by Captain Strouts consisted of seven British marines and five volunteers, the latter all student interpreters in the Consular service. I ordered all firing to cease from the north stable picket and main gate, and waited results. The attacking party sallied out of the gate of the Fu, and going along the wall, disappeared round the corner, up a lane which forms the north boundary of the Fu. A heavy fusillade was heard, and a marine was seen staggering back, waving his hand as if to attract attention; he had not gone very far when he fell. Three of the garrison instantly dashed out and brought him in. No man of the attacking party returned, and it was hoped that the attack had proved successful; this, however, proved subsequently not to be the case. Lieutenant Paolini was severely wounded, two Italian marines killed, and seven marines wounded, two of the latter being British. Mr. Townsend, one of the student interpreters, was also severely wounded. It appeared that when the party turned into the lane they were met by a severe fire from a barricade some 40 yards in front, as well as from the left wall of the lane, which was only some 18 to 20 feet broad. Lieutenant Paolini was shot almost immediately, whilst gallantly leading the party; two Italian marines also fell, one shot dead, the other mortally wounded (he died almost at once). The barricade in front, some 8 feet high, was a blaze of fire, as well as the side wall. The little party, finding themselves in a death-trap, sought to escape through a hole or breach in the wall of the Fu, which was, however, only large enough to allow of two passing through at a time; it was whilst getting through this breach that two other men were wounded. Mr. Russell, a young student interpreter, with great presence of mind, ordered his party of four volunteers to take cover behind a small heap of earth and bricks, and wait till the regulars had got through the hole. As soon as all had passed through, the students dashed across the lane one at a time; it was in doing this that Mr. Townsend was shot in the shoulder and thigh, and fell. He was, however, pulled through the hole, still retaining possession of his rifle. Mr. Bristow, another of the party, with great coolness and presence of mind, picked up and brought in the rifle belonging to the Italian marine whose dead body was lying in the lane. But for Mr. Russell's cool action, the confusion and consequent loss amongst the attacking party would most certainly have been greater. A fight now took place over the dead body of the marine, but the fire was so deadly in the lane it was found impossible to recover it; three of the enemy, tempted, doubtless, by the reward offered by the Chinese Government for the head of a foreigner, came out from behind their defences, but were instantly shot down by the north stable picket from an advanced post on the other side of the canal.

Lieutenant-Colonel Shiba came over to me at once and reported the ill-success of the sortie, for which he very generously took the entire blame.

It was impossible to reconnoitre the ground outside our defences, so that sorties were at all times very risky, and, with so small a garrison, only to be undertaken under very special circumstances. Colonel Shiba's party had also encountered an unexpected barricade, and been forced to retire. Had we been able to capture the enemy's gun and its ammunition, the loss we suffered would have been small in comparison to the addition to our strength in the shape of even one piece of artillery. Lieutenant Paolini's wound was found to be severe, and he was detained in hospital; his place was immediately taken by

M. Caetani, Secretary of the Italian Legation, an ex-officer of Italian cavalry.

The evening passed fairly quietly. At 10.30 the light I have alluded to was again reported. I went, together with the signalman of Her Majesty's ship "Orlando," to the upper storey of the First Secretary's house, and the light was plainly visible; the signalman said it was evidently a flash-light. As it might possibly belong to the force which was on its way (we hoped) to relieve us, and by way of cheering up the spirits of the garrison, the following Notice was posted up the next day on the Bell Tower :—

"Last night, between 10 p.m. and 2 a.m., an electric flash-light was seen on the south-eastern horizon; its approximate distance from Peking, 25 miles. The flashes were regular, and occurred at intervals of almost a second, with a pause of between five to ten seconds between 40 or 50 flashes."

July 2.—Gangs of coolies were at work all night on the American barricades on the Tartar city wall, and some excellent work was put in, the barricades being very considerably strengthened. Spies coming in to Colonel Shiba stated that troops were being withdrawn from Peking towards the south. These statements were received with caution.

Up to 10 o'clock, however, very little firing took place, and it seemed as if the enemy were either withdrawing part of their force or engaged in making fresh plans for attack. At 10.30 the Krupp guns opened fire on the Fu, and an occasional shot took effect on the defences; the majority, however, were going high. During the forenoon the enemy commenced to construct a large barricade in front of the main gate of the Hanlin, about 60 yards from our northern barricades. A few well-placed shell from the invaluable Italian quickfirer, which had again been hauled up to the Students' Library, demoralised their working party, and they did not continue.

Various important defences were commenced to-day in the British Legation. It was evident that the enemy were concentrating their attack on the Fu, either because they knew how important a point it was in the defence, or because they were aware from their spies that the buildings immediately to the south of it had been allocated to the converts, and it was against these latter that the Chinese seemed especially incensed. Should the Fu fall into the hands of the enemy, the British Legation would be completely commanded by its west wall, and the enemy would be able to bring up their Krupp guns to within 40 yards of the east wall of the British Legation and batter it down in the same way as they had done to the north wall of the Fu. By my orders the Fortification Committee, under Mr. Gamewell, commenced to strengthen the east defences; the wall itself was furnished with a double row of loopholes and thickened to a breadth of 10 feet, so as to render it proof against artillery, and traverses were erected to protect the western defences from reverse fire.

At 9 p.m. the American Minister and Mr. Squiers, his Secretary of Legation, both of whom had seen military service, and whose experience was invaluable to the defence, came over to report that the Chinese had advanced across the bastion in front of the Russo-American barricade on the wall under cover of a species of sap or stone wall, and had erected a tower at the end of the sap, from which they could actually throw stones at the defenders of our barricade, from which the tower was only distant some 25 feet. They pointed out that it was absolutely necessary to take this tower and the Chinese barricade by assault, to prevent the enemy rushing our position on the wall which was in imminent danger.

I immediately fell in with their views, and promised a reinforcement of 15 men, which, with the 10 marines already on duty, made up a total of 25; with them went Mr. Nigel Oliphant, who volunteered for the sortie. The attacking party, under Captain Myers, United States Army, collected behind the wall barricade at 1.30 a.m. on the 3rd July; the party consisted of Captain Myers and 14 American marines, a Russian officer, Captain Vroubleffsky, and 15 Russian marines, Mr. Nigel Oliphant and 25 British marines. No marine officer was available, two, Captains Halliday and Wray, being in hospital wounded, and Captain Strouts could not be spared from the British defences. Captain Myers addressed the men in a short speech, pointing out clearly the plan of attack: the Anglo-American detachment, under his immediate command, was to attack the tower, follow along the sap, and then assault the barricade on its left or southern side; the Russian detachment was to attack the Chinese barricade on the right or northern end, where it abutted on to the top of the ramp.

At the given signal the whole party swarmed over the American barricade; the night was very dark and threatening rain. The English and Americans, with Captain Myers at their head, entered the tower, which they found unoccupied. They followed along the sap. Here Captain Myers received a severe spear wound in the knee and was disabled. At the south end of their barricade the Chinese had left a small lane or opening to connect with the sap. Through this the Anglo-American party streamed and engaged the enemy hand to hand, Mr. Oliphant shooting two with his revolver. A small encampment of tents was found behind their barricade. The enemy was cleared out of these, and driven down the ramp, leaving 25 of their dead on the wall.

The Russians, gallantly led by Captain Vroubleffsky, had in the meanwhile climbed over the right of the barricade and joined in the combat.

The enemy's position, including the whole bastion, was now in our hands, and work was commenced to strengthen what we had taken. A tremendous musketry fire was opened on the working party from a second barricade some 60 yards further along the wall, severely wounding a non-commissioned officer of marines. Just before dawn heavy rain came on, which lasted several hours and caused great discomfort to the men. Our losses were two American marines killed and Captain Myers wounded; one Russian killed and two wounded, and three British marines wounded, all severely.

The above was one of the most successful operations of the siege, as it rendered our position on the wall, which had been precarious, comparatively strong. Work was continued day and night, and every opportunity taken to improve the advantage gained. At dawn the Krupp guns again began pounding away at the Fu defences, which were severely knocked about, and several casualties took place. The rain which had set in at dawn continued until sunset; the canal which separated the British, American, and Russian Legations from the remainder of the defence came down in flood, and threatened to carry away the covered way and barricade which had been constructed across it: as soon as the water subsided, which it fortunately did next morning, work was started on this, and a culvert to carry off the water was constructed. The heavy rain had an excellent effect from a sanitary point of view, as it helped to clear out the canal, which from the number of decaying bodies of horses, mules, and dogs, which had been killed in or near the same by the wild fire of the enemy, had become very offensive and insanitary; but it played havoc with the earthworks and defences generally, and the fortification gangs were hard at work repairing damages. The enemy's works were also much impaired, and they lost heavily when repairing them.

During the afternoon the halyard of the Union Jack flying over the British Legation gatehouse was cut by a bullet, and the flag came down with a run. Attempts were made to rehoist it by the signalman and armourer of Her Majesty's ship "Orlando," but the fire on the top of the gatehouse was too hot; the flagstaff was let down to the ground through the tower, the flag nailed to the staff, and then rehoisted into its old place. Amongst the small crowd of bystanders who helped with a will to hoist the heavy staff were the Representatives of three of the Great Powers.

At 9 p.m. heavy firing began against the Russian Legation, and our new position on the wall resulting in a few casualties. One of the enemy crept up in the dark to the Russian barricade, and thrust a spear through one of the loopholes, narrowly missing a Russian sailor. The owner of the spear was instantly fired at from the neighbouring loopholes, but owing to the darkness it was impossible to see with what result. The flash-light was again seen, but clearer and with more movement. It was particularly bright at 2 a.m.

At my request a return was furnished to me this day by the various officers commanding the detachments of the number of casualties which had taken place since the 20th June. They were as follows:—

British marines, 2 killed, 15 wounded, including 2 officers.
Bluejackets, Italian, 5 killed, 7 wounded, 1 officer.

Bluejackets, Russian, 3 killed, 11 wounded.
Bluejackets, Japanese, 5 killed, 11 wounded.
German marines, 8 killed, 7 wounded.
Bluejackets, French, 6 killed, including 1 officer, 5 wounded.
Bluejackets, Austrians, 3 killed, 3 wounded.
American marines, 6 killed, 6 wounded, 1 officer.

All the wounds were severe, and necessitated removal to hospital. Total, 38 killed and 55 wounded.

July 4.—This being the anniversary of American Independence the Anglo-Saxon community amongst the besieged had decided that the relieving force would appear to-day; knowing the difficulties of transport I did not share in their anticipations, though when appealed to I did my best to encourage their hopes. Several attempts had been made through the converts to communicate with the outside world, from whom we had received no news whatever since the commencement of the siege. Our messengers were at first let down over the Tartar city wall, or went through the canal sluice gate under the same. None had succeeded, so far as we knew, in piercing the strict cordon drawn round us; some had returned baffled in their efforts; and some we feared had been killed. To-day a Shantung lad of about 14, well known to the American missionaries, volunteered to go; he took a letter from me to the British Consul sewed up in a piece of oil-cloth; the package was flat, just an inch long and half-an-inch broad; instead of concealing it in the thick sole of his shoe or sewing it into his clothes, hiding places with which the enemy had become well acquainted, he concealed it in a bowl of rice which he carried with him, after the fashion of some Chinese mendicants. As this was the first of our messengers who got through, his adventures are worth recounting. He left the water gate at night, and after having narrowly escaped capture, reached the south gate of the Chinese city; watching his opportunity he slipped through with some mendicants and gained the open country, working his way with great caution from village to village. As he was not certain of the road to Tien-tsin, and fearing to excite suspicion by making inquiries, he used, on arrival at a village, to join the children at play, and from them ascertain by degrees the general lie of the country, the names of adjoining villages, and the direction of Tien-tsin. The country was overrun with Boxers, and the villages were full of wounded, the result of the fighting with Admiral Seymour. When within sight of Tien-tsin he was commandeered by the enemy and made to work for them for over a week; at last he managed to escape, and slipping through the allied sentries, which was undoubtedly the most risky part of the journey, he arrived at Tien-tsin on the 19th, five days after the taking of the Chinese city by the allies. He wandered about for a couple of days before he met any European who could talk Chinese, but at last he was fortunate enough to do so, and was at once taken to the British Consul, where he delivered his letter on the 21st instant, which, though dated the

4th, was the latest news received from Peking. He started back on the 22nd, and made the return journey in six days. The lad stated that when he arrived in the vicinity of Tien-tsin the enemy were in the greatest state of demoralisation, flying in every direction, and leaving their artillery in ditches and hidden in the millet fields. On the return journey he noticed that finding they were not pursued they had recovered most of their guns and were entrenching themselves at Peitsang and other places. All the above we ascertained on the 28th instant, when the lad returned.

The letter which was received on the 21st by the British Consul was the *facsimile* of several others I had sent on previous occasions, the number of casualties only being altered from day to day. On this day, the 4th July, we had 46 killed, including civilians, and about double that number severely wounded; of these 8 civilians had been killed and 11 wounded. The slightly wounded were not entered in the returns, and only went to hospital to have their wounds dressed, and then returned to duty. The letter gave the relieving force, for of course we always counted on a relieving force, all needful information with regard to the position we held, and also pointed out that the water or sluice gate through the Tartar city wall afforded the easiest means of entering the Legation quarter. It was by this way that the troops eventually entered.

July 5.—At a European shop within our lines were found some Japanese fireworks. The light-hearted Japanese garrison amused themselves at night by a pyrotechnic display, but one of their number discovered that a very effective missile might be constructed by opening these fireworks and filling them with nails, scrap iron, &c.; this was accordingly done, and used against the Chinese with considerable effect.

The upper storey of the "Hôtel de Pékin" was again severely knocked about by the enemy's shells from the Chien Gate; the Secretary's quarters in the German Legation were rendered untenable from the same cause. The enemy were during the morning very active in the Hanlin. A party under Captain Poole were out clearing the ruins, the fire became very severe, and a retreat was ordered. Mr. David Oliphant, of my Consular staff, was busy cutting down a tree in company with the signal-man of the "Orlando," and before he had time to obey the order, was shot through the body and fell; the signalman stayed behind him under a shower of bullets until a stretcher was brought. The wound was mortal, and the poor young fellow died and was buried the same afternoon; his loss was deeply felt by the whole British community, with whom he was an immense favourite; owing to his coolness under fire, and his knack of commanding men, I had appointed him in charge of the eastern defences of the Legation, and I felt his loss very keenly.

At midday the sentries in the upper storey of the Students' Library and quarters reported the enemy at work amongst the yellow tiles on the top of the Imperial city wall, which is distant some 200 yards from the north wall of the Legation. At first it seemed as if they were loopholing it for musketry, but by means of field-glasses through the foliage of the trees two guns could plainly be made out. How the enemy had succeeded in getting them up to their position it was difficult to ascertain, for the wall was over 20 feet high and only some 3 feet thick. Fire was instantly opened upon the battery by our riflemen. The position, owing to the foliage and the very small part of the wall disturbed, was not easy to locate with the naked eye, but with glasses the gunners could clearly be seen getting their guns into position.

We were not long left in doubt as to the enemy's intentions, for the first missile, a 7-lb. round shot, came crashing into the students' quarter, where a group of riflemen were endeavouring to pick off the gunners. The bricks were sent flying in every direction, but no harm was done. This was the introduction to several more, all of which took effect on the buildings in the Legation, the Minister's house and upper students' quarters being particularly favoured.

The round shot were of two sizes, one weighing 7 lbs. and the other 14 lbs. The bombardment continued with intervals day and night for the next 10 days, and over 150 rounds of shot were fired into the Legation and the Hanlin buildings alone. Curiously enough, the only casualty resulting from this fire was an old Chinese woman, whose leg was broken by a round shot, from the effects of which she died. Some people were hurt by falling bricks, displaced by the shot, but no one seriously.

There were, of course, some narrow escapes. The British Nordenfelt, which was temporarily in action on the balcony of the nursery in the Minister's house, was struck by a round shot, which came through the wall and broke the wheel; the seaman who was working the gun escaped uninjured. Another struck a chimney high up, fell down the same, and rolled out of the grate on to the floor occupied by three young ladies of the garrison. One crashed through the smoking-room of the Minister's house and fell amongst the occupants, all ladies, but without touching any of them. Another, after carrying away part of the coping of one of the bedrooms in the Minister's house, smashed its way through a thick wall in the escort quarters occupied by the Maritime Customs and fell between two ladies without touching either. And, lastly, one entered the big dining-room through the north wall, and passing behind a large picture of the Queen without in any way injuring it, pierced the south wall of the dining-room and fell into the little central garden, where children were playing at Boxers, and barricades, sorties, and mimic warfare generally.

Though the enemy's fire from these two batteries—for very shortly a second appeared some 30 yards to the right of the first, also furnished with two smooth-bores—was ineffective, the same cannot be said of our return fire, which seemed to annoy the enemy considerably. The invaluable Italian gun was got into position and the second shell exploded in the westernmost battery, completely silencing one gun for the rest of the siege; the others continued to fire at intervals. Our rifle fire was so searching, however, that the gunners were unable to take aim; on the other hand, at that short range they could not help hitting some part of the Legation. The rifle practice, nevertheless, prevented the enemy from concentrating their fire on any one part of our defences and thus making a breach. Very shortly, owing doubtless to their losses at the guns, each embrasure was provided with an iron door, which opened at intervals; the muzzle of the gun was hastily protruded and the gun fired. The opening of these doors was a signal for a volley from our people, who had the range to a nicety. These volleys must have rendered the firing of the gun a somewhat unhealthy occupation.

After the siege was over these batteries were found to consist of very elaborate gun platforms, 20 feet by 16 feet, made of scaffolding strong enough to hold guns of a much heavier calibre than those actually used. They could accommodate from thirty to forty men, and were made of timbers 9 inches in diameter, some 700 to 800 being employed to make each battery. The constructing of the platforms must have taken from a week to ten days, and occupied from thirty to forty workmen a piece. Ramps 12 feet broad led up to the platforms. A small gallery supported by scaffolding ran along to right and left of the batteries just below the yellow-tiled coping on top of the wall. This gallery was loopholed for musketry. The place where the guns stood was roofed over as a protection from sun and rain. The iron doors mentioned were found in the battery after the relieving force arrived. They consisted of folding doors on hinges of wrought-iron half-an-inch thick, but had been pierced over and over again by our rifle fire, and the left battery had a hole through its door as if made with a punch. This was the work of the Italian gun. Towards evening the sound of big guns was heard to the west of the city. This was not the bombardment of the Roman Catholic missionary establishment known as the Peitang. The sound came from further off, and was almost due west of the Legation.

July 6.—The morning commenced by a severe shell fire against the Fu. The Chinese, emboldened by the failure of our last sortie in this direction, moved one of their Krupp guns up to within a few yards of the wall of the Fu, through which they had made a breach. Colonel Shiba seized the opportunity to make a sortie to capture the gun. Previous to so doing he came to me for orders, and to explain the situation. The gun was located some 10 yards in a lane to the right of the breach above mentioned, and the idea was to dash through the breach and seize the gun and limber. Several Chinese converts provided with ropes for dragging the gun away were to follow the attacking party, which was composed entirely of Japanese marines and volunteers, headed by an ex-officer of the Japanese army serving as a volunteer. A feint attack was to be made from the west by the Italian detachment, reinforced by a corporal and 10 British marines. The Japanese detachment charged through the breach. Unfortunately, their leader was almost immediately shot through the throat and fell, but the men pressed on, and actually seized the gun, the Chinese gunners taking to flight. The converts were, however, panic-stricken and refused to advance. The enemy, taking advantage of their hesitation, rushed back to their loopholes, and a terrific fire was opened upon the attacking party, causing them to retire through the breach with three more of their number *hors de combat*. The gun and limber were now standing disconsolately in the lane, which formed a *cul de sac*. To venture into the lane was certain death, as every wall and building which commanded it was loop-holed, and at every loophole stood one of Tung-fu Hsiang's men with a magazine rifle. On the other hand, any of the enemy who attempted to pass the breach in the wall to get at the gun was shot down by the Japanese. This state of affairs lasted till dark, when the Chinese from their side of the wall threw bricks and stones in front of the breach, gradually filling it up, and during the night they withdrew the gun. The Russian and French Legations were severely shelled from the Chien Gate, the fire being mainly directed against the American flag, which could be seen from the enemy's battery. At the fourth or fifth shot the flagstaff was struck at the base by a shell, which exploded and shot away a large portion of the roof of the gate-house, bringing down the staff, flag and all. It was rehoisted in a neighbouring tree, the roof of the gate-house being too damaged to allow of it being rehoisted there. The Russian flag was also attracting the fire of this battery, the shooting from which was very true. The flag was therefore removed to another building. It is to be noted that the flags of such Legations as remained unburnt were kept displayed throughout the siege. These were the flags of America, Russia, Great Britain, France, Germany, Japan, and Spain, the Chinese gunners distributing their favours amongst them with absolute impartiality. A Russian Consular student, whose mind, it appeared, had been somewhat affected by the strain of the siege, suddenly left the French barricade in Legation Street, and, before he could be stopped, advanced alone and unarmed towards the Chinese barricade some 60 yards distant. The enemy allowed him to approach to within 10 yards, and then shot him down. Instantly several Chinese soldiers rushed forward to seize the dead body, but the French sharpshooters were on the alert, and man after man of the enemy dropped, until 11 had paid the penalty of their temerity with their lives. During the night his body was removed by the Chinese. Since the commencement of the siege this was the third and last European whose dead body fell into Chinese hands. The gallant garrison of the Fu were this day burnt out of some more of the buildings held by them. Since the fighting began they had lost by this means about one quarter of the Fu.

July 7.—A quiet morning, but matters became lively as the day advanced. At 9.15 a sharp attack was made against the Fu defences, but repulsed. At 9.30 the French Legation was bombarded by the guns north of the Fu, and also from the Hata Gate. Firing of heavy ordnance was heard to the south and south-west of the city in the direction of the railway terminus. This firing had been distinctly heard throughout the night, and had been reported to me by the officers commanding the French, Austrian, and German detachments, and a notice to this effect was posted on the Bell Tower, and greatly cheered the garrison. The enemy started a fresh barricade near the North Bridge at the end of the road known as "Dusty Lane," but one or two well-placed shells from the Italian gun, which had been brought to the main gate of the Legation, made them desist. The ammunition for this gun was unfortunately getting very low. The cannonading from the Imperial city wall became very brisk; a round shot came through the north corridor of the Minister's house, and fell on the roof of the cellar, which had been converted into a magazine; as this contained some 20,000 rounds of Lee-Metford and Mannlicher ammunition, as well as 90 rounds of shell, common and shrapnel, for the Russian field gun, it was considered advisable to have the cellar further protected by a roofing of sandbags.

There were now only 14 shells remaining for the Italian quickfirer, so this gun was only used when the case was urgent. The armourer of H.M.S. "Orlando," with considerable ingenuity devised a new cartridge for the same; taking one of the empty copper cases, most of which had been converted into playthings by the children, but which were now collected, he cast some conical solid shot made from pewter vessels, teapots, candlesticks, &c., which had been found in the neighbouring houses; the charge consisted of pebble powder taken from the Russian shells. The difficulty was the percussion cap; this was surmounted by removing the cap of a ·45-inch revolver cartridge, which exactly fitted the hole made in the copper case by the removal of the original percussion cap. One of these projectiles was used experimentally in the Italian gun, and answered admirably; the shot being solid pewter, and weighing more than the old shell, the shooting was not so accurate, neither was the effect [of the solid shot so good as the explosive shell, but as a makeshift it was excellent. As soon as the shells were finished, these projectiles were taken into use, and continued until the end of the siege; so far as I know, though upwards of 70 were utilized, not one missed fire.

Towards evening much shouting and firing could be heard in the Chinese city; it seemed as if the Boxers and Chinese troops, or different factions of the latter, had fallen out and were settling their differences. Our guards on the wall reported skirmishing between what seemed to be Boxers and Imperial troops, and several of the former were seen to fall.

July 8.—At 2 a.m. a very heavy fusillade took place, but lasted only 15 minutes: it was so severe that the "general attack" bell was rung, and the garrison stood to their arms; the smooth-bores on the Imperial city wall joined in the chorus, and the din was deafening.

The morning passed quietly until shortly after 10, when the raitle of musketry burst out all round the north-east of the Fu, accompanied by the fire of the two Krupp guns, which were so close that they made the windows of the British Legation rattle again. At 10.15 the following note was brought to me by a Japanese volunteer :—

"Pressed hard; please send a strong reinforcement.—
SHIBA."

Warned by the musketry fire, a reinforcement was in readiness; a non-commissioned officer and six marines, also six volunteers, were at once hurried over. I also wrote to the Russian Legation, and they sent ten sailors; the attack had, however, in the meanwhile been repulsed, and their services were not required. The French Legation, to whom Colonel Shiba had also applied, had not been able to help, as they were themselves hard pressed, being subjected to a severe shell and rifle fire from the Hata Gate. Captain Thoman, of the Austrian frigate "Zenta," who had come up to Peking as a visitor, and had been unable to return to his ship, was killed on this occasion in the French Legation by a fragment of shell; he was a courteous and gallant officer, and his loss was much felt by those who knew him.

On the previous day one of the gangs of Chinese converts at work under the supervision of Dr. Dudgeon, discovered at an old foundry within our lines what appeared to be an old piece of iron but proved on closer examination to be a small cannon. The trunnions had been knocked off, and it was one mass of rust and dirt; it was handed over to Mr. Mitchell, the master gunner of the American detachment, and after much hard work, scraping and cleaning, it presented quite a creditable appearance. It was at first lashed to a heavy spar; when this was found unsatisfactory, it was mounted on a spare set of wheels belonging to the Italian gun; the shell of the Russian gun, when removed from its projectile fitted, with some coaxing, the bore of this new gun, which was found on closer examination to be rifled and apparently either made of steel or fitted with a steel lining, and probably dated back to 1860, when the Anglo-French forces were in Peking. As the gun was found by Chinese converts in charge of a British subject, and was probably of either British or French manufacture, as it fired Russian ammunition, was mounted on an Italian carriage, and further was put together and fired by an American, it was with much truth christened the "International" gun, though our marines more often called it the "Dowager-Empress," or "Betsy." The performances of this piece of ordnance were erratic, but owing to the close quarters at which the fighting was carried on, eminently satisfactory. The first shot was aimed at the corner battery on the Imperial city wall, about 240 yards distant (as there were no sights, the aiming consisted of pointing the gun generally in the direction of the object aimed at), the projectile went screaming over the battery into the Imperial city; the result was received with great cheering by the onlookers in the Legation, who, truth to say, had not much confidence in their new acquisition, and by an astonished silence on the part of the enemy, who were apparently startled to find that after so many days we had at length opened fire with comparatively heavy ordnance. The second shot went woefully short, but the third landed in the battery. This woke the enemy up from their astonishment, and the Mauser bullets began to whistle all round in uncomfortably close proximity; the "International" was therefore temporarily withdrawn, and transported, not without considerable difficulty, over to the Fu, where it was twice fired under Colonel Shiba's orders with telling effect at a barricade some thirty yards distant. The first shot carried away one of the enemy's standards, and the second discharge, which consisted of old nails and bits of scrap iron, was fired into the barricade, and judging from the yells which followed did considerable damage. One drawback to this gun was that immediately the enemy located its whereabouts (which was not at all difficult to do, as the noise and smoke created by it were out of all proportion to its size), they opened a heavy rifle fire on the spot and the gun could not be used for more than three or four shots in succession from the same place. From this evening on, a corporal and five British marines, and five volunteers were permanently stationed in the Fu, as affairs were very critical there; the Japanese detachment having been reduced by casualties from one officer and twenty-five men to one officer and seven men, and the Italian detachment had suffered in like manner.

The British marines also supplied a permanent guard of ten men to the American and Russian barricades on the Tartar city wall; this had been the case since the 1st July and lasted till the 17th July; this guard was changed every twenty-four hours. During the afternoon the enemy had been very persistent in their attacks from the Mongol Market and Carriage Park side, they brought up a 1-inch quickfirer and shelled the British Legation; in the space of fifteen minutes three shells exploded inside the roof of the Chinese Secretary's house, the fragments coming through the ceiling in a very unpleasant manner; several of these shells exploded in the trees around the tennis-ground, some struck the hospital, which fortunately was well barricaded, and one exploded in front of the Second Secretary's house, then occupied by the Russian Minister's family; the fragments entered a room full of children and buried themselves in the wall and furniture, but happily touched no one. It was impossible to locate this gun, as it was skilfully concealed amongst the ruins of the Mongol Market houses and was using smokeless powder; fortunately it never returned to this particular position.

July 9.—The "International" gun again changed position. This time it was unlashed from its carriage and hauled up into the Students' Library and fired at a barricade which the enemy had erected in the Carriage Park. Considerable damage was done to the enemy, but nearly every pane of glass was smashed in the library although the windows were open, and the wall of the mess-room below was cracked. The whole of this day the firing all round was incessant, but nothing of particular interest in the fighting-line occurred. All our positions were maintained; constant work was kept up on the fortifications, repairing the old and making new.

A Christian convert volunteered to go into the city and, if possible, obtain news of what was going on. The American missionaries stated that the man in question was reliable. Towards the evening he returned, having had many narrow escapes. He said that the soldiers that surrounded us were Yung-lu's and Tung-fu Hsiang's men. In the north of the city business was proceeding as usual, the hucksters crying their goods in the streets. He had himself bought some small articles, which he brought back with him. The Emperor and Empress were both at the Palace, only a few hundred yards from us. The "Peking Gazette" was published as usual. The Chinese troops had lost heavily, and were afraid of the foreigners in the Legations. He could hear nothing of any foreign troops coming to our rescue.

July 10.—The forenoon was quiet after a night of incessant fusillade. It was evident that the Chinese troops indulged in a siesta between the hours of 11 and 1. During the night they never seemed to sleep; the above hours were, therefore, in future, reserved for demonstrations on our part.

Shortly after two a fierce fusillade commenced against the Fu, and the enemy seemed to be concentrating all their efforts on this part of the defence. Twenty marines under Captain Poole were sent over; also ten Russian marines. One of the Krupp guns suddenly turned its attention from the Fu to the Union Jack over the Legation gateway. Three shells in quick succession struck the gateway, and several exploded on the tennis-lawn, just missing the staff.

As the latter was apparently drawing the enemy's fire and thereby endangering the women and children's lives, the question of hauling the flag down, or at any rate moving it to another position, was mooted to me by the missionaries. Captain Strouts, whom I consulted, was of opinion that this would only encourage the enemy to further efforts, and would lead to great discontent on the part of the British marine guard.

Fortunately the enemy settled the difficulty by turning their attention to other parts of the defence, and never again made a deliberate target of the flag.

July 11.—A message carried by one of the Christian refugees was sent out through the water gate. He was received with a volley from a loopholed house opposite, and beat a hasty retreat. The enemy had evidently discovered this means of exit from our lines and were prepared.

During this afternoon Baron von Rahden reported to me that Chinese soldiers had been seen leaving their defences carrying away their bedding, and that heavy firing had been heard south of the Chinese city.

No satisfactory reason for this heavy cannonading to the south and west of the city has ever been given. Rumour said that Prince Ching's troops had fought with Tung-fu Hsiang's and had been defeated, but no corroboration of this came to hand.

Mr. Nigel Oliphant, who, as already mentioned, had been with the sortie on the Tartar city wall, was brought in from the Fu this afternoon shot through the leg. The day's casualties in the Fu alone amounted to 1 Japanese marine killed and 2 wounded, 2 British marines and 2 volunteers wounded.

The temperature to-day registered 102° in the shade; it had not fallen below 90° for some days. The heat and a perfect plague of flies, together with the stench from dead bodies of men and animals, was very trying, especially for the wounded. The poor living—pony and mule broth—was beginning to tell on the children.

July 12.—During the night, which was as noisy as usual, the Chinese built a new barricade in the Imperial Carriage Park inclosure, close to the high west wall of the Hanlin, and also established a sandbag battery on top of it. Behind this they placed a large black silk flag with the Chinese character for "artillery" inscribed thereon. This battery abutted on to our advanced post in the Hanlin. Mr. Mitchell, the American gunner, and Sergeant Preston, of the Marine Guard, in the Hanlin, made a dash for the flag, and jumping up seized it. Instantly a volley of rifle shots went whizzing in all directions: one struck a stone sending the fragments into Sergeant Preston's face; stunned by the blow he let go his hold and fell. Mitchell, however, retained his hold of the flag, and a species of see-saw ensued, with the wall as a fulcrum; several marines and volunteers dashed forward and seized hold of Mitchell. The added weight broke the staff, and the flag and part of the staff was triumphantly retained on our side of the wall. This plucky act was the signal for a tremendous outburst of firing from all the enemy's positions which commanded the Hanlin, but our men keeping well under cover no damage was done. The French garrison the same afternoon made a gallant sortie and captured a large silk flag with scarlet characters on a white ground, setting forth that the flag was presented by the Dowager-Empress to General Ma, commanding the left wing of Yung-lu's army. Dashing forward the French sailors deliberately lassoed the flag and hauled it over to their side of the barricade. A tremendous outburst of rifle fire was the result, by which, unfortunately, four marines were wounded.

July 13, and a Friday.—This was the most harassing day for the defence during the whole course of the siege. During the night Tung-fu Hsiang's men had been particularly active in the

Hanlin. Shortly after daylight the Fu was heavily shelled by four guns with shrapnel; the defenders could do nothing with such a hail of shot except keep close under cover. The attack became so severe that notwithstanding reinforcements and a most stubborn resistance on the part of the Japanese, Italian, and British, they were compelled to fall back to the last position but one.

Colonel Shiba had originally planned nine lines of defence, one behind the other. The seventh had been held since the 9th instant but had now to be abandoned, as most of its buildings were in flames, and the enemy's Krupp guns were riddling them with common shell and shrapnel shell at a range of 150 yards.

About 4 a tremendous fusillade broke out on all sides. The "general attack" bell sounded, and as many men as could be spared were fallen in ready to reinforce any part of the defences which were more than usually hard pressed. The firing in the Fu was heavier and more continuous than I have ever heard it before, and accompanied with yells of "Kill, kill," which could be distinctly heard in the Legation; the sound of the firing seemed as if the defenders were being gradually driven back, and I expected every minute to see our people coming out of the Fu gate, crossing the canal, and falling back on the Legation. I had sent over every man that could be spared, for on all sides we, too, were being attacked.

I wrote to the Russian Legation for reinforcements and very soon ten marines came over at the double. As soon as they had got their breath I sent them over in charge of M. Barbier, a Russian volunteer, who did good service throughout, and who knew the geography of the Fu well. They had hardly disappeared through the gate of the latter when a welcome messenger came from Colonel Shiba to say that he was holding his own and had driven off the enemy, and for the moment required no further men. I was about to recall the Russians when Herr von Bergen, Second Secretary of the German Legation, came running across the lawn with an urgent written message from the German Chargé d'Affaires, saying that he was very hard pressed and begging for immediate help. The ten Russian marines no longer required at the Fu were at once sent to his aid, and arrived in the nick of time. The enemy, after a smart fusillade, had left their defences and charged into the open with waving banners and loud shouts. They were met by a volley which accounted for six or seven of their number; the rest wavered. The Russians coming up at that moment, the united forces under Lieutenant von Soden charged with fixed bayonets and pursued the enemy, capturing one of their standards.

In the meanwhile the French Legation was being vigorously attacked, and shortly after 7 the Chinese exploded two mines underneath the Second Secretary's house and the east side of the Minister's; the explosion completely destroyed these buildings and set fire to those adjacent; two French sailors were killed and buried under the ruins. Captain D'Arcy, the Commandant, was also partially buried and badly cut about the head by falling stones ; his wounds were fortunately not serious. The enemy not having properly judged the force of the explosion, suffered severely, and the spy stated that carts next day carried away 30 of their dead from the vicinity of the crater formed by the explosion. The command of the French detachment for the moment devolved upon Captain Labrousse, an officer of Marine Infantry, a visitor to Peking. When he had satisfied himself that it was impossible to recover the bodies of the buried men, he ordered a retreat to the next line of defence. After the explosion the Chinese, notwithstanding their losses, seemed to be greatly elated at the success of their mining venture and opened a sharp fusillade, but did not leave their defences. The French and Austrians now occupied a trench which they had prepared, and also the Legation chapel, which was loopholed, and held the enemy at bay. In spite of their severe repulse by the Russian and German detachments, the Chinese attempted another attack along the road leading at the back of the German Legation under the city wall. The Americans were at this moment changing guard at this post; in the half light they detected the attempt, and the double guard opened a withering fire on the advancing enemy, who retired in confusion, leaving twenty dead on the road.

While all this fighting had been going on in the east and north-east, the enemy had also made demonstrations against the Hanlin, but had been kept in check by the fire from the loopholed defences and the upper windows of the students' quarters; just in front of the west corner of the Hanlin defences against the Carriage Park wall there had been a temple; this had been burnt by the enemy on the 23rd June, and only the four walls remained standing. Captain Strouts saw it was important to occupy this inclosure, as the enemy had pushed their attack to within a few yards of it; a hole was made through the wall, and a party under Captain Poole dashed in and occupied the place; a heavy fusillade was opened, but by keeping close to the west wall no one was hit; here two sentry posts were established, so close to the enemy's sandbag entrenchment on the Carriage Park wall, that amenities in the shape of bricks, stones, and water-melon rinds were freely exchanged between the besiegers and the besieged, and our sentries could hear the enemy quarrelling over their rice rations and discussing matters generally. The net result of this day was that the enemy had undoubtedly lost heavily and had been severely handled, and our defences had been pushed forward in the Hanlin, as shown above, but we had lost ground both in the French Legation and in the Fu; our losses amongst the fast-diminishing garrison were very serious, amounting to five killed and about double that number wounded.

That evening, together with Colonel Shiba, I inspected the new position in the Fu to which we had been driven back; the left of the line was pretty strong, consisting of two buildings defended by a high parapet with a species of small fort built against the wall; the ground in front of this was clear, but the enemy had crept up and made a high barricade, its right resting against the wall some 15 yards from the little fort: the parapet was now extended to the right, but unfortunately it was impossible, owing to the nature of the ground, to construct it parallel to the enemy's attack, but it fell back considerably, taking in a little artificial mound whereon a redoubt had been constructed. The fort and buildings above mentioned were held by an Italian guard under M. Caetani, Lieutenant Paolini being still incapacitated by his wound. The little hill redoubt was held by Austrians and Italians. The line then proceeded east some 30 yards, where a building half in ruins was arrived at; this was held by Japanese sailors and volunteers. Looking through the loopholes one could see the enemy's positions amongst the still smoking ruins some 50 yards off; the parapet was carried south-east again till it met a high wall which divided the Su Wang Fu into two portions, the official buildings being on the right and the private dwelling-houses on the left; the defence line followed this till it came to a hole made by the Japanese; here it went due east inclosing two buildings east and west of the big centre gateway to the Prince's official residence. In front of this entrance was a large courtyard with gates east and west; in this courtyard the Christian converts had originally taken refuge, but had been obliged to abandon it owing to shrapnel and rifle fire; this courtyard formed the right of the line of the Fu defences; it was 200 metres south of the fort held by the Italians, and 220 metres east. The two gates of the courtyard were held by the Japanese marines and British marines and volunteers, the advance sentries being posted by Colonel Shiba and myself at loopholes in the two buildings above mentioned. Looking through these loopholes manned by a British and Japanese sentry side by side, the flames from the burning buildings in front actually touched the muzzles of their rifles. Fortunately, what little wind there was came from the south, increasing in strength as the night advanced; it blew the fire back towards the enemy; but for this the buildings must have caught, the main gate would have followed, and the enemy entering here the whole position would have been taken in reverse. When this fire had burnt itself out our position was strengthened, for it had cleared a space in front of the advanced sentries.

During the night it rained heavily, and the enemy, in consequence, kept up a brisk fusillade; the forenoon was quiet. In the afternoon matters livened up somewhat, and an attack was made on the Russian Legation, the Minister's house being shelled, and his study riddled with shrapnel. The Italian gun was sent over, and assisted in repelling the attack. The "International" went to the French Legation, where, under the able direction of the American gunner, it did excellent work, bursting a shell in a Chinese barricade and scattering the enemy. On this day a Chinese convert, late gatekeeper at the Roman Catholic Cathedral, called the Nan Tang, who had volunteered to take a message to Tien-tsin, came with a letter addressed to me, signed "Prince Ching and others." A full account of the correspondence which ensued, and which lasted up to the last day of the siege, is given in a previous despatch. The messenger bore evidence of having been badly beaten, and he told a sad tale of his experiences. He had been caught attempting to leave the Chinese city, and compelled to give up his letter, which the enemy read. After beating him, they took him to Yung Lu, who ordered that his life should be spared, and handed him this letter. The Roman Catholic missionaries gave the man an indifferent character, so he was kept apart from the rest of the converts, and not allowed to roam about the defences. On the following day he quite willingly took back an answer to Yung Lu.

The enemy having been successful with their mining operations in the French Legation, were evidently bent on trying this means of attack at other points. Sounds of picking were distinctly heard by placing one's ear at the back of our foremost barricade in the Hanlin, close to the Carriage Park wall. Mr. Wintour, of the Imperial Maritime Customs, obtained leave and commenced a countermine just at the back of the barricade, and worked in the direction of the sound; three of the Chinese converts, who had proved themselves expert diggers, were told off and put under his orders.

July 15.—A quiet night. Chinese, judging by the sound, were very busy in the early morning in the Carriage Park with pick and shovel, though no signs of what they were at, or exactly where they were, could be detected. One of our marines was brought in dangerously wounded from the Fu. During the afternoon the Russians made a successful sortie, and pulled down some houses outside their defence, which had been giving cover to the enemy.

At 6.30 Mr. Warren, student interpreter, was brought in from the Fu mortally wounded by a splinter of a shell in the face; he died within a few hours without recovering consciousness; he had only been in Peking a few months, and was much liked by his fellow students.

Heavy firing in the direction of the Peitang, the celebrated Roman Catholic Mission presided over by Mgr. Favier. We were aware that several thousand refugees, as well as a number of foreign priests and sisters, were besieged within its walls. When the Legation guards had first come up, a French officer and 30 men, and an Italian officer and 11 men, had been sent to assist in the defence of this important Mission. Though several attempts were made, we never succeeded in establishing communication with this place, which lay only some 4 miles off, but through streets packed with the enemy.

Colonel Shiba reported to me that the men of his detachment, sailors and volunteers, were quite exhausted; they had all been up on duty night and day since the commencement of the siege, and had none of them even changed their clothes since the

20th June, nor had they had more than three or four hours of consecutive sleep during that time; he begged that, if possible, half might be taken off duty for a clear 24 hours, and replaced by British marines and volunteers, after which the second half might be relieved in a similar manner. I consulted with Captain Strouts, and it was arranged that, although our people were in the same plight, an effort should be made to carry out Colonel Shiba's wishes. The marines and volunteers responded with alacrity to this call made upon them, for they knew what splendid work the Japanese had done and were doing. It was decided that the Japanese sentries should be relieved by ours at 7 o'clock on the following morning.

July 16.—At 7 a.m. Captain Strouts took over the relief party; he was accompanied by Dr. Morrison, "Times" correspondent. After having posted the last sentry, they were returning, and had just left the Italian post, when a shower of bullets came over the barricade, and Captain Strouts fell mortally wounded by a bullet through the groin, which shattered the upper part of the thigh-bone. Dr. Morrison was shot almost at the same time by a bullet through the thigh, but which, fortunately, did not strike the bone. Colonel Shiba, who was coming towards them at the time, seeing Captain Strouts and Dr. Morrison fall, ran forward to help them; stretchers were procured, and both wounded men were brought into hospital; this was done under heavy fire, a bullet passing through Colonel Shiba's coat. From the first there was no hope for Captain Strouts, and he died within three hours of his entry into hospital. He was a first-rate officer, cool, calm, and fearless, and his death was a great blow to me and to the entire defence. He was buried at 6 p.m. in the same grave with young Warren, who had been killed the day before. The funeral was attended by all the foreign Representatives, the officers commanding detachments, and as many of the garrison as could be spared from their defence duties. While the mournful procession was proceeding through the Legation grounds to the little cemetery close by the First Secretary's house, the old Chinese messenger who had taken a letter to "Prince Ching and others," bearing a large white flag aloft in one hand, and holding in the other what proved afterwards to be a sufficiently friendly reply to our letter, was marching solemnly along the side of the canal from the North Bridge towards the Legation. The enemy—whether they had in the meantime relented of the friendly tone of the letter he carried, or whether they wished to accelerate their messenger's movements—deftly exploded a shell over his head, fortunately without doing him any harm; the next two shells followed in the same line, exploding in the trees just above the funeral party, but the fragments were carried into the ruins of some neighbouring houses, and did no damage.

The document from "Prince Ching and others," which was an answer to my letter of the previous day, practically initiated a species of armed truce, which lasted until 10 or 12 days before the entry of the relieving force.

For the first day or two the enemy were embarrassingly demonstrative in their endeavours to be friendly, and came out unarmed from behind their barricades in considerable numbers, and advanced towards ours. They had repeatedly to be warned back, for we were afraid of treachery; neither did we wish them to see how few were the defenders behind barricades which otherwise looked formidable to them.

As time wore on this friendliness became less and less apparent, and by the end of the month matters had become almost normal, and the attacks and counter-attacks were as brisk and determined as ever. The precious days of comparative peace which followed the 16th were utilised by us in working with increased energy at our defences. At no time, however, after the 20th of the month was it safe to show for one second outside the defences. The slightest exposure was a signal for a hail of bullets. The old Chinese messenger, besides the official despatch from Prince Ching, brought a cypher telegram for Mr. Conger from the State Department at Washington. This the messenger said he had received from the Tsung-li Yamên.

The arrival of this telegram created great excitement amongst the besieged, as it was the first news we had had from the outside world since the 18th June. There could be no question of the genuineness of the message, as it was in a cypher possessed only by Mr. Conger and the State Department. Mr. Conger replied in the same cypher. This message was duly forwarded by the Yamên, and duly arrived at Washington, but the public were unwilling to credit it, having apparently quite made up their mind that the Legations had been destroyed and the besieged massacred.

July 17.—At the east barricade in the Fu, the Chinese came from behind their defences in considerable numbers and advanced up to Colonel Shiba's post. Six of them were forthwith made prisoners, the rest beat a hasty retreat. Colonel Shiba reported the matter to me, and I ordered the men to be released with a message to their commander to the effect that if more than two left their barricades together they would be fired on.

The same afternoon I was on the Tartar City wall, inspecting the defences, together with Mr. Squiers, whom I had appointed Chief of the Staff. The Colonel commanding Tung-fu Hsiang's troops in the opposing barricade, some 60 yards off, had shouted a message across for permission to bury his dead which were lying at the foot of our barricade, the result of the sortie of the 3rd instant. This permission, as may be imagined, was readily granted.

The Chinese barricade was swarming with men, at least 250 being crowded on it and the adjacent walls; their arms were all out of sight. They were dressed in a variety of uniforms, scarlet and black of Tung-fu Hsiang's men predominating. Six of the

Chinese soldiery descended with spades and large pieces of matting, on which they proceeded to carry away the rotting corpses. Through Mr. Splingard, our interpreter, I requested the Colonel to come and have a talk with me. After some demur he consented. I offered him a cigar, which he gladly accepted, and we sat on the outside of our barricade and chatted until our cigars were finished. He told me that he belonged to the Kansu troops, but was at present under the immediate orders of Yung Lu, who was desirous of stopping the fighting. I remarked that the fighting was none of our doing, but we were quite prepared to defend ourselves whenever attacked. I said that, to prevent misunderstandings, it would be better if not more than two men left their barricades at a time. If more than that number did so I should be compelled to open fire. He said he thought it would be a good thing if some such understanding were arrived at, and suggested my writing a letter to Yung Lu to this effect. He assured me that any letter handed to him for Yung Lu would most certainly reach its destination. On my return from my interview, whilst standing on the top of our barricade, I could see the enemy's positions stretching away to the north until they disappeared in the direction of the Carriage Park.

There were barricades in the streets below the wall. A large temple was loopholed and put into a state of defence and full of men. More men were amongst the ruins west of the Russian Legation, and a species of mound which commanded this Legation and the Mongol Market was gay with the uniforms of hundreds of Imperial infantry. Following the line west of the Mongol Market the tops of the houses carried nests of these bright-coated soldiery. Altogether from my position I saw some 1,500 to 2,000 men, and many more must have been hidden behind the walls and ruined houses. From where I stood I noticed that the men in the opposing barricade could overlook certain portions of our position on the wall, and would probably remark the very small garrison we were able to maintain. I therefore requested the American and Russian Commandants to send up as many of their reserve men as could be spared, with orders to show themselves as much as possible on the barricades. This order was promptly and quietly carried out, and very shortly our position was occupied by a goodly number of Russian and American sailors, as well as by some 20 of our marines.

On my return to the Legation I wrote a despatch to Yung Lu, and stated that in view of the negotiations which had commenced with the Tsung-li Yamên the defenders of the Legation would not fire unless they were fired at, but to prevent misunderstandings it would be better if not more than two soldiers left their barricades, and these must be unarmed. Any armed soldier leaving his barricade would at once be fired at. I also added that if the enemy were seen making new barricades in advance of those already existing fire would be opened on the working parties, even if they were unarmed. This letter was delivered into the hands of my friend the Colonel, who promised to deliver it to Yung Lu.

The Commanders of all portions of the defence reported that the enemy had ceased firing, and showed a friendly disposition and a desire to enter into conversation with the besieged. This was much less the case in the north and west, where they were decidedly treacherous and unfriendly, though they had evidently received the same orders as their comrades. From information picked up by the Japanese at their barricade it was evident that the cause of this sudden change in the demeanour of our assailants was due to the news which the high authorities, whoever they may have been at that time, had received of the capture of the native city of Tien-tsin by the Allies, and the rout of the Chinese army. By some friendly soldiers we were warned against mines which were especially to be directed against the British Legation. In addition to the counter-mine begun by Mr. Wintour on the 14th, and which by now had been sunk to a depth of some 9 feet, and then for a short distance carried under the Carriage Park wall, a system of counter-mines had been organised in the north and west of the Legation, and carried out most efficiently under Mr. Gamewell's direction. They consisted of trenches some 11 or 12 feet deep close up against our advanced lines, and it would have been impossible for the enemy to pass these trenches without being immediately detected.

On the 18th July a messenger who had been sent out by Colonel Shiba returned from Tien-tsin with a letter from the Japanese head-quarters staff at that place. It contained the news that the native city had been taken by the Allies, and that a relief force was being organised consisting of 24,000 Japanese, 4,000 Russians, 2,000 British, 1,500 Americans, and 1,500 French, and would leave on or about the 20th July and advance on Peking. This notice was posted on the Bell Tower. It was the first news we had had from Tien-tsin, and was joyfully welcomed by the besieged, though many were disappointed that the force was not already well on its way. As a matter of fact the message was far less hopeful. It mentioned the heavy losses sustained by the Allies, and also spoke of the absolute absence of transport. To keep up the spirits of the besieged, however, the message as posted was made as cheerful as possible.

As an instance of the curious state of affairs which existed at this time between the besiegers and besieged, especially on the east side where the Japanese and French were in contact with the enemy, a young Frenchman, by name Pelliot, wandered over to the opposing barricade and entered into conversation with the Chinese soldiery; without thinking he stepped inside their barricade and was instantly made prisoner; he was not roughly treated but taken to a Yamên at some distance where he was brought before some high Mandarins who courteously asked him several questions regarding our strength, losses, &c., all of which he answered in an evasive manner; eventually he was conducted under an escort of Yung Lu's men through streets full of Boxers and soldiery, back to the barricade, and set at liberty.

The Japanese started a small market for eggs which the Chinese soldiers brought over hidden in their capacious sleeves and sold to our people; the eggs were mostly distributed by the Food Supply Committee to the hospital, and amongst the women and children. The weather was very hot and the latter began to feel the want of proper food; between now and the arrival of the relieving force six of the younger ones died in the Legation.

On the 20th it was reported to me that the Chinese were heard mining in close proximity to the Hanlin. I went down Mr. Wintour's countermine and heard them distinctly at work; they seemed quite close but somewhat above my level; a pick was handed down and at the first few blows the enemy stopped working. From that time a strict watch was kept at this countermine, but the enemy had either abandoned their mine or had changed the direction, for the sounds gradually died away and then stopped altogether. After the entry of the relieving force the mine was thoroughly examined by the Royal Engineers; it was found to commence in one of the large buildings in the Carriage Park inclosure and to proceed straight for our barricade in the Hanlin. It arrived within a few feet of Mr. Wintour's countermine and then suddenly changed direction to the south and followed parallel to the dividing wall for some 40 feet, till it arrived opposite the centre of the building, forming the students' library and mess-room when, instead of turning east under this building, it turned west, described a curve, and ended at a point some 30 yards due south of where it started. There is no doubt that Mr. Wintour's countermine checked the enemy's advance underground and headed them south, but why, when they got to a convenient striking point, they went away from their objective, it is impossible to say.

During this spell of comparative quiet the enemy were very busy working at their barricades, and besides the one I have mentioned, mines were started by them on the top of the Tartar city wall endeavouring to get under the Russo-American barricade, also in Legation Street working towards the Russian barricade; similar mines were commenced against the French and Japanese defences on the east, we, in the meanwhile, were equally busy working at our defences and countermines. After the arrival of the relieving force, amongst some documents seized by the German troops was found a letter addressed to the General Commanding at the Hata Men, on the subject of mines. The writer had been a teacher at the British Legation in the employ of Her Majesty's Government for four years and was well known to the student interpreters; together with all the other teachers he disappeared about the middle of June. The letter was dated the beginning of July and pointed out that the General's methods of attacking the Legation were faulty and were bound to lead to considerable loss in the future as they had done in the past. The proper method of attack, the writer said, was by mining; to assist the General in his attack he inclosed a correct plan of the British Legation, with which he was well acquainted, and marked on the plan the most suitable place for the mine to be driven. Eager inquiries have been made, since the siege was raised, for the writer of the letter, but as yet he has not been found.

On the 18th July one of Yung Lu's men advanced with a flag of truce along the city wall, and came down to the German defences with a letter for me from Yung Lu, accepting the arrangement suggested with regard to terms of a truce. This man was very intelligent and friendly; he had been specially selected to come, as he had had to do with foreigners, having been a policeman on the Peking-Tien-tsin Railway. He was recognised by one or two Europeans in the Legation. The same afternoon another soldier came in with his ear partially severed; he had been in the employ of Sir Robert Hart, and was bugler to the regiment at the Hata Gate. He came in, he said, to have his ear seen to, as he knew that foreign surgeons were good and humane men. His officer had wounded him with a blow of his sword for not being sufficiently proficient on his bugle. He informed us, further, that the men were very discontented, and were sick of fighting the foreigners. The same story was told by three soldiers who strolled along the wall from the direction of the Hata Gate to the American barricade.

It was very evident throughout the siege that the enemy on the east were much more friendly, and had not the same stomach for fighting as our friends in the north and west; from this direction not a single man ever came in, neither did any of our messengers ever succeed in getting out. My conversation with the Colonel on the city wall was the only instance of a friendly act on that side.

Even when the truce was at its height, from the 17th to the 20th, it was unsafe to show oneself for an instant at the barricades in the Hanlin. On the 19th some of the enemy held out a water-melon at the end of a pole on one of the Hanlin barricades; a volunteer of ours advanced to take it, and was instantly fired at, the bullet passing within an inch of his head. On the 20th and subsequent days several of our people, mostly Chinese converts, were hit whilst working at the defences; this was, of course, in accordance with the terms of truce, and we returned the compliment.

On the 24th the supply of eggs began to dwindle down, and the men who brought them reported to the Japanese that their officers had threatened to execute anybody found bringing in anything to the besieged. On the 23rd two men were beheaded for this reason within sight of the Japanese.

On the 28th July the boy messenger, who had been sent out on the 4th July, returned from Tien-tsin. His arrival caused great excitement; he brought, sewed in the collar of his coat, the British Consul's letter in answer to mine. The news ran like wildfire through the Legation, and eager crowds surrounded the Bell Tower, waiting to hear what was posted on the notice board. This was the message :—

"Yours of the 4th July. 24,000 troops have now landed, and 19,000 here. General Gaselee expected Taku to-morrow. Russians hold Pei Tsan. Tien-tsin city under foreign government, and Boxer power has exploded. Plenty of troops are on the way if you can hold out with food. Almost all ladies have left Tien-tsin."

This letter caused great disappointment amongst the garrison, as the general opinion was that ample time had elapsed between the 20th June and the 21st July to organise and start a relief expedition.

In justice to Mr. Carles, who has been blamed for not sending more information, it is right to state that, had he written the true state of affairs which then existed in Tien-tsin, the effect on the beleagured garrison would have been crushing; he consequently made the note as cheerful as he could under the circumstances. Had not the arrival of the messenger been witnessed by numbers of people, it is more than probable no notice of the contents of the letter would have been posted on the Bell Tower.

During the early days of the armistice from their barricades on the east of the Fu, the Chinese adopted a novel way of communicating with the Japenese defenders. One day a large dog trotted into the Japanese barricade with a note tied round its neck. This was from the Chinese General commanding in that quarter, pointing out the futility of further defence, and recommending unconditional surrender. A reply, declining the suggestion in somewhat forcible terms, was tied on the dog's neck, with which it trotted back.

This was repeated several times, the advisability of surrender being urged with greater insistence each time. The answers varied only in the strength of their language. Letters demanding and suggesting surrender were also tied to arrows and shot into the Japanese lines. A remarkable instance which took place at this time of filial obedience and good faith on the part of a Chinese soldier, was recounted to me by Colonel Shiba.

Amongst the men who brought eggs for sale was one who belonged to Yung Lu's force, who was distinguished from his fellows by the hard bargains which he drove for his wares. Noticing this, Colonel Shiba thought the man might be induced for a price to carry a letter to Tien-tsin and bring back an answer. He was accordingly approached on the subject, and after considerable discussion about the amount, he agreed to go for the sum of 250 dollars, the money to be paid over on his return with the answer. The man left on the 22nd and returned on the 1st August, bringing with him a reply from the Chief of Staff of the Japanese division. It ran as follows :—

"Your letter of 22nd received. Departure of troops from Tien-tsin delayed by difficulties of transport, but advance will be made in two or three days. Will write again as soon as estimated date of arrival at Peking is fixed."

The letter was dated the 26th July. The bearer refused to accept the 250 dollars, and no amount of persuasion could induce him to do so. Thinking that perhaps he was unwilling to be discovered in possession of so large a sum, he was offered a letter to the Consul at Tien-tsin in the form of a promissory note, but he declined everything. On being asked why he refused now, when he had been previously so keen to acquire the money, he told Colonel Shiba that on arrival at Tien-tsin, after delivery of the letter and receiving the answer, he went to his own home; his mother did all she could to prevent his returning to Peking, but he said he had promised the foreign officer to return, and return he must. "Then," said she, "you must accept no money, for what you are doing is for the good of your country." He, therefore, in obedience to his mother's wishes, steadfastly refused any money whatever. He offered to take a letter back to Tien-tsin if it was written at once, but he could not, he said, bring back an answer. Seeing that it was impossible to shake the man's resolution, Colonel Shiba wrote another letter which the messenger duly delivered at the Consulate at Tien-tsin, but again refused all offers of money.

On the afternoon of the 29th July the Chinese began to throw out heaps of bricks and stones at the corner of some ruined houses at the east end of the north bridge. This bridge was commanded by the north stable picket, and by a caponier which had been constructed in front of the main gate of the Legation, called by the marines "Fort Halliday.' The road across it is one of the main arteries of the city from east to west, and to avoid the bridge the Chinese had to make a considerable detour through the Imperial city. It had always been a source of surprise to us that no barricade had been constructed across the bridge, because in addition to allowing passage across, the fire from it, the barricade, would command the whole length of the canal with the roads on either side, and would sweep the south bridge, which was one of our means of communication (the only one for carts), between the east and west defences. During the night time the bridge was undoubtedly used by the enemy; but in the daylight the fire of our pickets was so deadly, that after losing several men, they gave up all attempts at crossing it.

It soon became evident that the heap of bricks and stones was the commencement of the long-expected barricade; immediately a lively fusillade was opened on the inoffensive-looking heap, and bricks and stones were sent flying, but so soon as they were shot away others appeared in their place. Very shortly wooden cases, evidently filled with bricks and stones, were pushed forward from behind the heap and the barricade stealthily crept forward.

The enemy's sharpshooters in the ruins on the other side of the canal were in the meanwhile very busy, and some very pretty shooting took place. They had the most modern rifle with smokeless powder, and the men in the north stable picket had some very narrow escapes, bullets pattering round their loop-holes, and in some instances coming through.

The "International" gun was at that time doing good service in the French Legation, so could not be used, but the Italian 1-pr. with its solid pewter bullet was hauled up on to a sandbag battery on the roof of the cow-house, which formed part of the north stable picket, and opened fire. The enemy were not slow to return the compliment, and the Mauser bullets soon began to knock the sandbags about at the close range of 60 yards, cutting them into shreds.

The Italian gunner behaved with great coolness. Unfortunately, as he was laying the gun for the third round his hand was smashed by a Mauser bullet, and he was taken to hospital. The serjeant commanding the marine detachment went up and fired the round, but the enemy's fire now became so hot, pieces of silk damask and sand being scattered in every direction by the hail of bullets. It was found impossible to continue the gun in action; it was also impossible to remove it. This was eventually done under cover of darkness.

On the following morning it was found that the enemy had succeeded in building a barricade 6 foot high the whole length of the north bridge, a distance of 30 to 40 yards.

In the correspondence which was at this time proceeding between the Diplomatic Body and the Chinese Government as represented by "Prince Ching and others," expostulations had been made respecting the strengthening of our defences. Attention was, therefore, drawn to the building of this formidable barricade by the Chinese Imperial troops. The reply received was that "we must not be alarmed as the troops of Tung-fu Hsiang were only engaged in mending the road!"

Fire was immediately opened from this barricade, and the road along the canal became very dangerous. To obviate this a large traverse was run across the road at the smaller gate of the Legation and a barricade constructed across the south bridge.

On the 2nd August the fortifications having been thoroughly strengthened on the north and east, it was determined to improve our western defences. Consequently, a small party of British marines and volunteers of various nationalities, mostly belonging to the Imperial Maritime Customs, under M. von Strauch, an ex-officer of the German army, were directed to cut a hole through the west wall of the stable quarters and occupy some buildings forming the east side of the Mongol Market. The hour chosen was that of the Chinese siesta, shortly before noon. The houses were successfully occupied without the enemy becoming aware of our intentions. They were found to be in a good state of preservation, and a party of Christian converts under Mr. Gamewell's orders were at once set to work to loophole the walls and make barricades where necessary. Three Chinese soldiers were found dead in the houses, where they had evidently dragged themselves to die.

In a few days this position, which was one of considerable importance, was greatly strengthened. Thus on the north and west the British Legation defences had been pushed forward in the direction of the enemy. The latter very soon discovered this new occupation, and the whole of the Mongol Market barricades blazed out on our working parties. These, however, kept well under cover, and only a few casualties took place.

For the remaining few days of the siege this position was the scene of constant attack. The enemy, whose barricades by the Carriage Park wall were within stone-throwing distance, kept up a constant fire, also hurling bricks and stones over the ruined walls. One of our marines was badly cut on the head by one of these missiles.

On this day a messenger arrived from Tien-tsin bearing many letters. The following were posted on the Bell Tower :—

" From the American Consul, Tien-tsin, to American Minister, dated the 28th July.

"Had lost all hope of seeing you again. Prospect now brighter. We had 30 days shelling here, nine days siege, thought that bad enough. Scarcely a house escaped damage. Excitement at home is intense; of course, our prayers and hopes are for your safety and speedy rescue. Advance of troops to-morrow probable."

Another from Lieut.-Colonel Mallory, United States Army, dated the 30th July :—

"A relief column of 10,000 is on the point of starting for Peking; more to follow. God grant they may be in time."

The one which contained the most news was written by Mr. Lowry, of the American Legation, who was in Tien-tsin when the railway was cut. The letter was to his wife, one of the besieged. It was as follows :—

"The bearer arrived last Friday with news from Peking. The 9th, 14th United States Regiments already at Tien-tsin. 6th Cavalry at Taku on its way up. An advance guard of several regiments has already started. There was fighting this morning at Pei Tsang. Everything is quiet here now. Word came to-day Boxers killing Christians at Tsun Hua and many other places. Tien-tsin full of foreign troops and more coming all the time. Railway open between here and Tangku. Many ladies and children went back to United States on transport 'Logan.' All property at Pei-tai Hoa destroyed."

This letter was dated the 30th July.

The news greatly cheered the spirits of the garrison.

On the 7th August "Prince Ching and others" sent condolences on the death of the Duke of Saxe-Coburg and Gotha and the firing was heavier than usual. The enemy seemed now to be concentrating their attention on the British Legation, the fire from the Mongol Market being particularly severe; the bullets were also coming lower. Mr. Gamewell reported that our fortifications in this quarter were being damaged by rifle fire to an extent which had not before occurred. We ascertained afterwards through spies that a new division of troops had come from Shansi under a Brigadier-General, who had sworn to take the Legation in five days. This division was stationed in the Mongol Market.

Orders were posted on the Bell Tower that women and children were not to walk about the grounds while firing was going on, several very narrow escapes having taken place. To meet the attacks from the west the Nordenfelt was mounted on a platform on the top of the wall at the back of the Chinese Secretary's house and did excellent work. A platform was also made in our new defences in the Mongol Market for the "International" gun, which was still in charge of the indefatigable American gunner, Mitchell.

On the 9th August the Fu, which had enjoyed a spell of comparative quiet, was again attacked, and fresh flags were planted behind the enemy's barricades. The attack was evidently now closing in. We had, however, worked so hard on the defences that our casualties were very few.

August 10.—At 3 in the afternoon a tremendous fusillade took place against the Fu and all our defences, Hanlin, Carriage Park, and Mongol Market. The big-gun fire had entirely ceased since the commencement of the armistice, but the rifle fire was very heavy, and cut our fortifications about considerably.

On this day a messenger, who had been sent out on the 6th to the advancing forces, returned with the following letter from General Gaselee, dated the 8th August, Tsai Tsung:—

"Strong force of Allies advancing. Twice defeated enemy. Keep up your spirits."

Colonel Shiba also received a letter from General Fukushima, dated Camp at Chong Chiang, 2 p.m., north of Nan Tsai Tsung, the 8th August:—

"Japanese and American troops defeated the enemy on the 5th instant near Pei-tsang and occupied Yang-tsun. The allied force, consisting of Americans, British, and Russians, left Yang-tsun this morning, and while marching north I received your letter at 8 p.m. at a village called Nan Tsai Tsung. It is very gratifying to know that the Foreign community at Peking are holding on, and, believe me, it is the earnest and unanimous desire of the Lieutenant-General and all of us to arrive at Peking as soon as possible, and relieve you from your perilous position. Unless some unforeseen event takes place the Allied force will be at Ho Si Wu on the 9th, Matou, 10th; Chang Chia-wan, 11th; Tung Chou, 12th, and arrive Peking 13th or 14th."

On the 6th Mr. Squiers, my Chief of the Staff, had drawn up a plan of the city, showing the sluice gate through the Tartar city wall, and our position on the wall, which was marked by three flags, a Russian on the western extremity, a British flag in the centre, and an American on the east. Directions were given in this letter in English and American cypher as to the best means of entrance. The letter was addressed to the American and English Generals, and was duly delivered to them on the 8th instant.

August 12.—From the various quarters of the defence reports came in that the enemy were very active, and it became evident that the relief force was nearing. From the Russo-American position on the Tartar city wall numerous bodies of troops were reported leaving the Cheng Meng. From the north stable picket bodies of cavalry were seen to advance up to the bridge, dismount, and lead their horses across under cover of the barricade; their movements were considerably accelerated by our riflemen from that post and the Main Gate caponier; the Krupp gun by the Hata Gate, which had been silent for several days, again opened fire. Nickel-plated bullets, fired at a range of 20 yards, pierced our defences in the Mongol Market and elsewhere. In their eagerness to press forward, the enemy overthrew one of their barricades. Instantly our sharpshooters opened a deadly fire, and the Nordenfelt was brought to bear. Before they could escape this hail of bullets 27, including their leader, fell in a riddled heap. The next day "Prince Ching and others" wrote an indignant protest, saying that the "converts" had again opened fire on the Imperial troops, killing an officer and 26 men. We subsequently heard that the officer was none other than the General of Division whose rash oath has been recorded.

When the evening closed in the enemy had made no advance in any direction and had lost severely. Our casualties were few, but they included Captain Labrousse, of the French Staff, an officer who had done excellent service both in the French Legation and on the Tartar city wall; in this capacity he came particularly under my notice, his reports being very lucid and of great service to the defence. In him the French army lost a smart and capable officer.

The morning of the 13th commenced with sharp firing in every direction, which lasted with scarcely an interval thoughout the day. Towards evening it was reported to me that the enemy were at work in the battery on the Imperial city wall. I immediately proceeded to the north stable picket, and in the failing light, through glasses, saw that work of some kind was being carried on. The sergeant of the picket reported that previous to my arrival he had seen what he thought was a modern piece of artillery owing to the light catching on brass mountings. As the enemy had not fired from this battey since the 16th July, I thought that it would be advisable to let sleeping dogs lie and not to draw the fire unnecessarily, especially as the relief force was so close; but, to be on the safe side, before the light died away altogether the Austrian Maxim was brought into the north stable and careful aim taken at the battery. The American gunner in charge of the automatic Colt, in the Main Gate caponier, was instructed also to lay his gun on the embrasure. Both had orders that immediately fire was opened from it the two machine-guns were to return the fire. The ranges were 200 and 350 yards. Shortly before 8 a tremendous rifle fire opened all round, and instantly the above-mentioned battery joined in. The sergeant had been right in his surmise, for, instead of our old friend the smooth-bore, it was a 2-inch quick-firing Krupp which opened on us with segment and common shell. Hardly had the crash of the first exploding shell taken place when the Austrian Maxim and the American Colt rattled out their reply. At the seventh round this gun was silenced, but not before it had done considerable damage; three shots struck Fort Halliday, stunning the inmates, though hurting nobody; one carried away a tall chimney in the Minister's house, another struck a brick pillar in the upstairs balcony of the north-east corner of said house (a post commonly known as Rosamond's Bower), completely demolishing the pillar and part of balcony, and one pierced the roof and exploded in my dressing-room, creating very considerable havoc; fortunately, not a single casualty resulted from all this cannonade. Four times between sunset and sunrise the "general attack" bell was sounded, when all reserves turned out and stood ready for emergencies. The enemy seemed particularly active in the Mongol Market; reinforcements were urgently requested from this quarter, and were promptly sent. The Chinese officers were heard inciting the men to charge, laying stress on the fact that they far outnumbered us and the distance was very short. The firing ceased, and an ominous silence followed, as if they were in reality gathering for the attack. It was then that our Commandant sent for reinforcements; before they arrived the enemy had evidently thought better of their intention to attack with the bayonet, and had recommenced firing and throwing bricks. The din of rifle fire, the rattle of bullets on the roofs, and the scream and crash of large ordnance was deafening.

At about 2 a.m. there was a pause, when very distinctly the delighted garrison heard the boom of heavier guns away to the east, and the sound of many Maxims evidently outside the city walls. The scene in the Legation was indescribable. Those who, tired out, had fallen asleep were wakened by these unwonted sounds, and there was much cheering and shaking of hands. The enemy, too, had heard it. For a moment there was silence; then the rifle fire broke out more angry and deafening than before, instantly responded to by the rattle of our sharpshooters and the grunt of the five-barrelled Nordenfelt, which, under the able management of the "Orlando's" armourer and Sergeant Murphy of the marines, refused to jam, but hailed volleys of bullets into the Mongol Market barricades. The "International" was also particularly active, and fired at point-blank range into the said barricade until the gallant gunner Mitchell had his arm badly broken by a Mauser bullet, and was taken to hospital. After the relieving force entered, the little garrison of the Mongol Market defences found that the "International" was loaded, but owing to the accident to the gunner had not been fired. As it was impossible to draw the charge, the muzzle was elevated, and the last shot fired from this unique gun descended amongst the yellow-tiled pavilions of the Pink or Forbidden City.

With daylight the firing died down, and there was a period of calm. A sharp look-out was kept from all the posts, especially the Tartar city wall, for any possible appearance of the relieving force. Mr. Squiers, my energetic Chief of the Staff, reported from the American Legation shortly after daybreak: "On the "wall there has been no sign of the approach of our troops "beyond the firing of the machine-guns. The direction of the "firing seemed to be the Chinese wall just to the right of the "part where it joins the Tartar city wall. There is no com- "motion in the Chinese city or at either of the gates. Your "flagstaff was shot away during the night, the flag falling over "the wall. Fortunately it was secured, and pulled back before "the Chinese had a chance to capture it. If you will send a "carpenter I will attend to repairs." The armourer and signal- man of the "Orlando" were sent, the staff was mended, and the flag rehoisted.

At 6 a.m. Mr. Squiers again reported: "The Chinese have "three guns mounted at the Hata Men, which they have been "firing in an easterly direction. All the musketry-fire seemed "to be on the wall between the Hata Men and the tower at the "corner. No excitement in the Chinese city. The Chien Men "is still open, but few passing in or out." Again, at 7 a.m.: "Heavy firing at the Chi-hua Men; also further machine-gun "fire beyond the Hata Men. No movement in the Chinese "city." This was the Japanese, Russian, and American attack developing along the east side of the Tartar city. As can be seen, Mr. Squiers is careful to report any movement in the Chinese city, for in accordance with the plan sent out it was in this direction the relief was expected. At 9.15 he reports: "For the past half-hour Chinese soldiers have been pouring "out of the Chien Men, going in the direction of the south "gate; cavalry, infantry, and two pieces of artillery. In the "direction of the Hata Men there is heavy cannon fire, and a "large shell has just exploded in the roof of the tower in the "south-east angle of the Tartar city."

At 11 the report came: "Large numbers of Chinese soldiers are passing through the Chien Men into the Imperial city." The defending troops were evidently being withdrawn from the Chinese city to meet the Japanese attack on the east gate of the Tartar city.

Shortly before 3 p.m. a breathless messenger from the Tartar city wall arrived to say that foreign troops were under the city wall opposite the water gate. I immediately followed him, and arrived in time to receive General Gaselee and his Staff as they came through the said gate and stood on the canal road. From there I led them through the Russian Legation to the British, where they were welcomed by the rest of the besieged garrison. The regiment which first entered the Legation quarter was the

7th Rajpoots under Major Vaughan. With them was Major Scott, of the 3rd Sikhs, attached to the 1st Sikhs, with a few men of this regiment. This officer with several men ran along the canal road from the south bridge to the gateway opposite the First Secretary's house, and were the first to enter the British Legation. This portion of the canal road was under the enemy's fire from the north bridge barricade, and three casualties occurred here later in the afternoon.

On arriving in the Legation, which was still being hotly attacked by the enemy from the Hanlin and Mongol Market, a small detachment of the 7th was sent into the Main Gate caponier to assist in repelling the attack. A man of this regiment was almost immediately seriously wounded; one of the ladies of the garrison was also wounded on the lawn. In the meanwhile, Mr. Squiers with a small party of Russian and American marines, under Captain Vroubleffsky and Captain Perry Smith, had proceeded along Legation Street to the Chien Gate, which they opened, allowing the 1st Sikhs, under Colonel Pollock and the Hong Kong Artillery to enter, the Chinese making a stand here and charging up to the Maxims of the artillery. The American troops under General Chaffey, and Russians under General Linievitch, had, with considerable loss, forced the north-east gate of the Chinese city, and proceeding underneath the wall, had entered, some by the water gate and some by the Chien Gate. Two guns of Major Johnson's Battery, Royal Artillery, had also been got through the water gate and up an improvised ramp on to the canal road. One of these guns was brought on to the south bridge, and effectively shelled the north bridge barricade, and the battery on the Imperial city wall. The besieged lost no time in taking the offensive. As has been seen, the American and Russian Legations were instrumental in opening the Chien Gate; Lieutenant von Soden with a detachment of his men attacked the enemy and drove them to the Hata Gate, capturing their guns and banners; the Italian and Japanese detachment in the Fu drove the enemy from their positions and reoccupied the entire Fu.

A detachment of British marines and volunteers under Captain Poole cut a hole through the Carriage Park wall and occupied the whole of this inclosure, killing three of the enemy.

Two days later a detachment of French, Russian, and English troops relieved our gallant fellow prisoners in the Peh-tang, whose sufferings had been worse than ours, and the siege of Peking came to an end.

During the siege the following number of cases passed through the International Hospital : 126 wounded, all severely, of whom 17 died; 40 cases of sickness, mostly enteric and dysentry, of whom 2 died. Of the 166 cases treated 142 were soldiers or sailors, the rest civilians; 165 were men; 1 woman was wounded. Of the above cases 21 were Germans; Americans,

17; English, 55; French, 17; Dutch, 1; Japanese, 14; Italians, 17; Austrians, 6; and Russians, 18.

The slightly wounded are not mentioned in this return; many of these were treated on the spot by the excellent French and Japanese military surgeons, who remained with their detachments in the French Legation and Fu.

The latter post has frequently been mentioned as the scene of severe fighting. The following return of the numbers killed and wounded therein will be of interest :—

	Killed.	Wounded.
English	2	11
French	1	2
Russians	—	2
Austrians	1	1
Italians	7	11
Japanese	9	21
Chinese	18	85
Total	38	133

The Chinese were mostly employed working in the defences, though Colonel Shiba had organised a force of some 20 Chinese armed with swords and spears who were very useful in keeping watch.

A return of the officers killed and wounded of the various marine detachments will be of interest :—

	Officers arrived.	Killed.	Wounded.
British	3	1	2
Italians	2	—	2
Russians	2	—	—
Japanese	2	1	1
German	1	—	—
French	3	2	1
Austrians	4	1	2
Americans	2	—	1
Total	19	5	9

The total number of foreigners killed during the siege from the 20th June to the 14th July inclusive, was 66.

I enclose two maps: one, of the defences of the Su Wang Fu, and the other, of the French Legation, both drawn to the same scale.

A careful examination of these maps will show that from the 20th June to the 13th July the garrisons of both these important posts were driven back step by step, disputing every inch of the ground, yielding only to superior numbers, and having to cope with shell fire, incendiarism, and in the case of the French Legation, subterranean mines, until, after twenty-three days' fighting, three-quarters of each of these two positions was in the hands of the enemy. Had the latter pressed on after the 13th July with the same persistence they showed up to that date, and also having an attenuated and worn-out garrison to deal with, they would have captured both positions by the 20th July at latest. Fortunately, on the 14th instant Tien-tsin was taken by the allies; this produced a marked effect on the besiegers, and the besieged received nearly 20 days' respite, which enabled them to materially strengthen their defences and recuperate generally, so that the final attacks of the enemy were repulsed with ease.

[Three plans annexed.*]

No. 4.

SIR C. MACDONALD TO THE MARQUESS OF SALISBURY.
(Received November 22.)

MY LORD, Peking, 20th September, 1900.

I have the honour to bring to your Lordship's notice the following facts :—

On the 24th June the enemy, consisting of Boxers and Imperial troops, made a fierce attack on the west wall of the British Legation, setting fire to the west gate of the south stable quarters, and taking cover in the building which adjoined the wall.

The fire, which spread to part of the stables, and through which and the smoke a galling fire was kept up by the Imperial troops, was with difficulty extinguished, and as the presence of the enemy in the adjoining buildings was a grave danger to the Legation, Captain Strouts, with my sanction, organised a sortie to drive them out.

A hole was made in the Legation wall, and Captain Halliday,† in command of 20 marines, led the way into the buildings and almost immediately engaged a party of the enemy. Before he could use his revolver, however, he was shot through the left shoulder at point blank range, the bullet fracturing the shoulder and carrying away part of the lung ; notwithstanding the extremely severe nature of the wound Captain Halliday killed three of his assailants, and, telling his men to " carry on and not mind him," walked back unaided to the hospital, refusing escort and aid so as not to diminish the number of men engaged in the sortie.

---

* Not printed. † Awarded the Victoria Cross.

For some days the surgeons feared the wound was mortal, but I am happy to say that, though still in the convalescent hospital, Captain Halliday is out of danger.

I attach the evidence of two men of the Royal Marine Light Infantry, who were present on the occasion; also a letter of Mr. R. E. Bredon, of the Imperial Maritime Customs, addressed to me in the name of a committee consisting of representatives of all nationalities amongst the besieged.

I have, &c.,
(Signed)   CLAUDE M. MACDONALD.

Inclosure 1 in No. 4.

STATEMENT of EVIDENCE *re* Captain HALLIDAY, Royal Marine Light Infantry.

1st Witness.—No. 8653 (Plymouth) Private J. Murray, Royal Marine Light Infantry, states:—

"On the 24th June, 1900, at about 3 p.m., I was with Captain Halliday when he went through the hole in the wall.

"The enemy immediately opened fire, and Captain Halliday was wounded.

"He then fired three shots from his revolver at the enemy, three of whom I saw fall.

"He then said 'I am wounded,' propped himself up against the wall and emptied his revolver at the enemy; after that he said 'Carry on, don't mind me,' and walked inside the wall, directing us to fire at three of the enemy who were visible."

2nd Witness.—No. 9008 (Portsmouth) Private J. Rumble, Royal Marine Light Infantry, states:—

"At about 3 p.m. on the 24th June, 1900, I followed Captain Halliday through the hole in the wall to make a sortie.

"He was wounded, and I saw him empty his revolver at the enemy.

"He then said 'Carry on and don't mind me,' and went back inside the wall."

This evidence was taken down by me on this 24th day of August, 1900, in the presence of the witnesses.

(Signed)   F. G. POOLE, Captain,
                East Yorkshire Regiment.

Her Britannic Majesty's Legation.

Inclosure 2 in No. 4.

MR. BREDON TO SIR C. MACDONALD.

YOUR EXCELLENCY, [Undated.]

I am requested by the members of the General Purposes Committee to put on record and bring specially to your notice its high appreciation of the bravery and energy displayed by Captain Halliday, Royal Marine Light Infantry, now unfortunately lying severely wounded.

On the occasion of the fire in the Hanlin Yuan, and also at the one near the south-west stables, Captain Halliday was always to the front, and at the stable fire led his men with conspicuous courage into a close quarter filled with armed enemies, several of whom he disposed of after he had been himself wounded.

The committee trust that you will bring Captain Halliday's gallant conduct to the notice of the proper authorities, and use your influence to secure him appropriate reward.

I am, &c.
(For the Committee),
(Signed) R. E. BREDON.

No. 5.

SIR C. MACDONALD TO THE MARQUESS OF SALISBURY.
(Received November 22.)

MY LORD, Peking, 20th September, 1900.

I have the honour to recommend the following officers and civilians, who rendered exceptionally good service during the siege and attack on the Legation quarter from the 20th June to the 14th August.

Of those not belonging to the Diplomatic and Consular staff I would beg to recommend Captain F. G. Poole, of the East Yorkshire Regiment, who was in entire charge of the volunteers and of the northern defences of the Legation, and also acted throughout the siege as my personal adjutant.

Captain Poole was not absent from duty for a single night or day of the fifty-five during which the siege was maintained, and this, although wounded in the face, and notwithstanding that he suffered on several occasions from malarial fever.

I cannot praise too highly the devotion and gallantry of this young officer, who set an excellent example to all the volunteers under his command.

Captain Strouts, Commandant of the Royal Marine detachment, was my right hand from the commencement of the siege until he fell, mortally wounded, on the 16th July. He was a most excellent officer; his readiness of resource and calmness under fire were the admiration of all the besieged.

The case of Captain Halliday, of the Royal Marines, has already been brought to your Lordship's notice in a separate despatch.

Of the British civilian volunteers under Captain Poole's command, I cannot speak too highly. They were enrolled from the Diplomatic and Consular staff, from the Imperial Maritime Customs, and from gentlemen who were in Peking either on pleasure or business when the siege began. The British volunteers consisted of thirty-five capable of bearing arms. Of these, two were killed and seven wounded.

The two killed were both in the Consular Service—Mr. David Oliphant and Mr. H. Warren. Mr. Oliphant had been in Peking since 1897, and I had the very highest opinion of his abilities and worth; he was exceedingly cool and collected under fire, and, although he had no military training, showed so much military aptitude that I specially selected him in sole charge of part of the defences. His death was a severe loss to me and to the Consular Service. Mr. Warren had only been in Peking as Student-Interpreter a few months. He had volunteered to assist the Japanese detachment in the park of Prince Su, and was mortally wounded whilst pluckily repelling the enemy's attacks. He succumbed to his wound in a few hours, and was buried in the same grave and at the same time as Captain Strouts.

Of the other British volunteers, without a single exception, all rendered excellent service. Mr. Dering, Second Secretary of the Legation, was in charge of an important part of the defences, and was always alert and at his post when the enemy attacked. He was also in charge of all ponies and mules, for six weeks our only meat supply, a service requiring considerable tact, owing to the somewhat natural desire of everybody to keep their ponies to the last. Mr. Cockburn, besides acting as a volunteer in the barricades of the West Wall, was in charge of the very important correspondence which took place between the enemy and myself, commencing on the 16th July. By means of this correspondence much valuable time was gained, which enabled our defences to be considerably strengthened, so that, when the final assaults were delivered, they were repulsed with heavy loss to the attackers. Mr. Cockburn's house was especially selected by the enemy for their attentions; several shells struck and burst on the roof, and rifle bullets pierced the mosquito curtains, besides other parts of the house.

Mr. Ker was a very able second to Mr. Cockburn; he came particularly under my notice as a conscientious hard worker.

Captain Percy Smith, a retired officer in the 38th Regiment, performed very good service, undertaking the most disagreeable and dangerous duties with ready and cheerful alacrity, and keeping up the spirits of the men under his command in exceedingly difficult and depressing circumstances. This was more particularly the case on our barricades on the South Wall during the earlier days of the siege, when the fire was so deadly that the bodies of those shot behind these barricades had to remain where they fell until night-time, when they were carried down to be buried, it being found impossible to do this during daylight, owing to the accuracy of the enemy's fire. Many dead bodies of the Chinese lay rotting in front of the barricades. This combined with the tropical heat of the sun, alternating with heavy rain, rendered the post a more than usually trying one.

Mr. Clarke-Thornhill, late of the Diplomatic Service, on a visit to Peking, was a most active and willing volunteer, always ready to undertake any duty, however dangerous, several times carrying messages for me to other parts of the defences under a very smart fire. He was also very useful as a prominent member of the very important Food Supply Committee.

The Rev. F. Norris, Chaplain to the Legation, rendered invaluable service, outside his own special duties, in working with pick and shovel in the trenches and on the barricades ; also in taking charge of and encouraging the Chinese converts in their work on the defences. He was always ready, willing, and cheerful ; though severely wounded by the explosion of a shell in the park of Prince Su he stuck to his work, and was at all times a splendid example to those around him.

Mr. Tours, of the Consular Staff, and Mr. Tweed, of the Hong Kong and Shanghae Bank, were indefatigable as Captains and organizers of the fire brigade, and were mainly instrumental in staving off the greatest danger to which the Legation was subjected. On the two occasions when the enemy set fire to the Hanlin buildings, which abutted on the north wall of the Legation, and the Mongol Market buildings, on the west, the Legation was in eminent danger of destruction, the fire brigade, under the personal orders of these two gentlemen, coped successfully with the danger. In addition to these duties Mr. Tours and Mr. Tweed served as volunteers at the barricades. Mr. Tours, owing to his intimate knowledge of the Chinese and their language, was also invaluable in looking after the large number of refugees and servants who lived within the walls of the Legation. Mr. Tweed, like Mr. Oliphant, showed special military aptitude, and I therefore appointed him one of my special orderly officers.

Mr. Tours' duties were so arduous, on watch practically day and night, and he carried them out with such conscientious zeal, that a few days after the arrival of the troops his health completely gave way, and he was struck down with a severe attack of brain fever and paralysis, and is still very dangerously ill.

Dr. Morrison, "Times" correspondent, acted as Lieutenant to Captain Strouts, and rendered most valuable services. Active, energetic, and cool, he volunteered for every service of danger, and was a pillar of strength when matters were going badly. He was severely wounded on the 16th July by the same volley which killed Captain Strouts, and his valuable services were lost to the defence for the rest of the siege.

Of the conduct of the Student-Interpreters I cannot speak too highly. They behaved with a pluck and dash, yet steadiness under fire, worthy of veteran troops. On the occasion of a sortie made from the park of Prince Su under the command of Lieutenant Paolini of the Italian navy, volunteers were called for, and Messrs. Russell, Townsend, Bristow, Hancock, and Flaherty immediately came forward. The party, which consisted of Italian and British marines as well as the student volunteers, came suddenly upon a barricade 8 feet high, which effectually barred all further advance, and from which a heavy fire was opened at a distance of a few yards. Lieutenant Paolini fell severely wounded, two Italian marines were shot dead; several of the marines, both British and Italian, were also wounded. The party was thrown into disorder, and crowded through a hole in the park wall. Mr. Russell, who was the senior student, with great coolness ordered the others to take cover behind a projecting piece of wall on the north side of the lane, from which they opened a smart fire on the barricade, and when the marines had all got through, several being wounded in doing so, he ordered the party to dash across the lane two at a time. They did this under a withering fire. All got across in safety except Mr. Townsend, who was shot through the shoulder and thigh, but was pulled through the hole, still retaining hold of his rifle. Fire-arms had been served out to the volunteers, but there were more of the latter than of the former, so the loss of a rifle was a very serious matter. Mr. Bristow in his dash across the lane with great coolness stopped and picked up the rifle of one of the killed and brought it in. I venture to think that, but for the presence of mind displayed by Mr. Russell, very few of the students would have escaped being killed or wounded. The above is only a specimen of the spirit which actuated my entire staff throughout the siege. Amongst the remaining students I also noticed Messrs. Kirke, Barr, and Hewlett, the latter acting as my Private Secretary and special orderly. The conduct of Mr. Townsend (above mentioned as wounded) and Mr. Russell was on several occasions brought to my notice by both Captain Strouts and Captain Poole. They were always foremost in volunteering for any service of danger, and they behaved when under fire with the greatest pluck and coolness. Mr. Townsend's wounds were of so severe a nature that he was incapacitated for the remainder of the siege. I specially selected Mr. Russell as one of my orderly officers. Mr. Rose, another of the Student-Interpreters, suffered from typhoid during the siege, and was only available for duty the last few days, on one of which he was wounded, though not seriously.

Of the volunteers belonging to the Imperial Maritime Customs, Messrs. Brazier and Brewitt-Taylor came under my eye as doing special good work. Captain Poole reports very highly respecting Messrs. Sandercock, Ferguson, Wintour, Richardson, Simpson, De Luca, and Dupree; the latter was specially promoted by the Inspector of Customs. Mr. Nigel

Oliphant, brother of Mr. David Oliphant, did excellent work. After Captain Myers, of the United States army, was wounded in the night attack on the Chinese barricades, Mr. Oliphant remained in command and conducted the operations most successfully. He was always to the front whenever volunteers were called for. On the 18th July he was severely wounded, and is still in hospital.

One of the most important departments in the system of defence was the international hospital. The two doctors doing duty were Dr. Poole, Legation surgeon, and Dr. Velde, of the German Legation. During the siege 166 cases passed through the hospital, 20 suffering from illness; the rest were all severely wounded. Owing to the devotion and skill of these two medical officers, 110 of the wounded were eventually discharged cured, and this, notwithstanding that towards the end of the siege, the resources of all the dispensaries having proved unequal to the strain, medical appliances, such as bandages and medicated wool, had to be replaced by makeshifts made from cast-off linen, the wool being replaced by sterilized sawdust. Dr. Poole was indefatigable at his work, always sympathetic and cheerful. The wounded of all nationalities spoke most warmly of his devotion and skill. At the conclusion of the siege he was struck down with fever of a very dangerous description, and had to be invalided. Dr. Poole speaks most highly of the sick-bay steward, Fuller, of H.M.S. "Orlando," and his commendation is fully endorsed by Dr. Velde and all the besieged. From personal observation, I can say that his care and gentle treatment of the wounded, and the willing and cheerful manner in which he carried out his duties, was beyond all praise.

I cannot conclude this despatch without saying a word of praise respecting the ladies of all nationalties who so ably and devotedly assisted the defence, notwithstanding the terrible shadow which at all times hung over the Legations—a shadow which the never-ceasing rattle of musketry and crash of round-shot and shell, and the diminishing number of defenders, rendered ever present. They behaved with infinite patience and cheerfulness, helping personally in the hospital, or in making sandbags and bandages, and in assisting in every possible way the work of defence. Especially to be commended are two young ladies —Miss Myers and Miss Daisy Brazier—who daily filtered the water for the hospital (a by no means easy task in the tropical heat with a hand-pump filter), and carried it there themselves, as often as not with the bullets whistling and the shells bursting in trees overhead. Miss Brazier, whilst on her errand of mercy, was struck by the fragment of a shell, but happily only slightly. Dr. Poole, in his report, will, I am sure, bear testimony to the devoted behaviour of the hospital nurses and the ladies who assisted them in their work.

I have, &c.
(Signed) CLAUDE M. MACDONALD.

No. 6.

SIR C. MACDONALD TO THE MARQUESS OF SALISBURY.
(Received November 22.)

(Extract.) Peking, 20th September, 1900.

I have the honour to request that your Lordship may be pleased to convey the thanks of Her Majesty's Government to the following officers, who commanded the detachments of foreign troops which took part in the defence of the Legation quarter :—

> Lieutenant Baron von Rahden, of the Imperial Russian Navy;
> Captain Myers, United States Marines, wounded;
> Lieutenant d'Arcy, French Navy, wounded;
> Lieutenant Baron von Soden, Imperial German Marines;
> Lieutenant Paolini, Italian Navy, wounded; and
> Lieutenant Hara, Japanese Navy.

On the 22nd June, owing to a misunderstanding caused by an order given by the Officer Commanding in one of the Legations (who was subsequently killed), the garrisons of all the Legations fell back on to the British, and great confusion resulted. The Ministers of Russia, France, Italy, and Japan begged me to take charge of the defence; this request was subsequently confirmed by the Ministers of the other Powers. I accepted the post, and, consequently, had a good deal to do with the above-mentioned officers: without a single exception they conducted themselves with the utmost gallantry and loyalty, and I never had the slightest difficulty in my dealings with them. To their loyal and cordial co-operation with myself our successful resistance to the enemy is, without doubt, due.

No. 7.

SIR C. MACDONALD TO THE MARQUESS OF SALISBURY.
(Received November 22.)

MY LORD, Peking, 20th September, 1900.

I have the honour to bring to your Lordship's notice the conduct of the following gentlemen, not being British subjects, who particularly distinguished themselves during the attacks on the Legation quarter by Imperial troops and Boxers, and who gave invaluable assistance to me in particular as well as to the defence in general.

At an early stage of the proceedings it was evident that the retention of the Su Wang-fu or Park of Prince Su in our hands was vital to the general scheme of defence, as it completely commanded the British Legation, and its loss would also have cut off the retreat of the garrisons of the French and German Legations.

Lieutenant-Colonel Shiba was appointed by me in command of the defences of this Park, which covers some 8 acres and contains many buildings of a substantial nature.

Lieutenant Shiba was fully alive to the importance of his post, and resisted the attacks of the enemy, which were fierce and persistent, with a skill, tenacity, and courage above all praise.

In the fighting which took place between the 20th June and the 16th July, his detachmennt of 25 men had been reduced to 8, and 115 per cent. had been killed or wounded, many of the latter having been wounded more than once, and one man five times in succession. An Italian detachment of one officer and 28 marines who were under his orders in the Park lost 8 killed and 13 wounded, including their officer.

Lieutenant-Colonel Shiba's dispositions were taken with the greatest skill, and he contested every inch of the ground, thereby giving time for the defences of the British Legation to be thoroughly put in order, and as a direct cause of this the lives of very many of the garrison were saved.

I beg respectfully that this officer's services be favourably brought to the notice of his Government.

On the 1st July Lieutenant Paolini, commanding the Italian detachment under Lieutenant-Colonel Shiba, was wounded, and I had to call for a volunteer to replace him.

Don Livio Caetani, Second Secretary of the Italian Legation, immediately volunteered, and at once took up his duties, which he continued to do with great devotion and ability until the end of the month, when he was relieved.

During the whole of this time he never once quitted his post, which was a barricade exposed to a very severe shell and rifle fire. M. Caetani entirely won the confidence of the detachment, consisting of Italians and Austrians, under his orders, and did most excellent work.

I beg that this gentleman's name be brought to the notice of the Italian Government as one who rendered special service to the defence.

I have also the honour to request that the names of the following two gentlemen be brought to the notice of the American Government, the Rev. F. D. Gamewell, of the American Methodist Mission, and Mr. Herbert Squiers, Secretary of the United States Legation.

The latter gentleman served as Chief of Staff after the death of Captain Strouts to the end of the siege.

His earlier services in the United States army were of great use to the defence; for the period I have mentioned Mr. Squiers was under my special orders, and I cannot speak too highly of his zeal and ability.

The barricades on the Tartar City Wall were initiated, designed, and carried out by him, and under my orders he drew the plan for the entry of the troops, which plan was conveyed to General Gaselee by a messenger who was let down from the wall; by this means the British troops entered the Legation quarter some two hours before any others.

The Rev. F. D. Gamewell carried out the entire defences of the British Legation.

These defences have excited the admiration of the officers of various nationalities who have since inspected them; a tribute to their excellence is the fact that, notwithstanding the constant rain of rifle fire, which was directed against the Legation during five weeks of the siege, not a single woman or child of the 217 who had sought shelter was touched. A deep debt of gratitude is owed to him by all the besieged.

M. von Strauch, a member of the Imperial Maritime Customs, formerly an officer of the Prussian army, was in command of the Customs Volunteers.

He was most useful in the defence of the British Legation, and also for some time assisted in the defence of Su Wang-fu. He was of the greatest assistance to me personally, and I was much struck by his zeal and loyalty, and also by his intrepidity under fire.

Dr. Velde assisted Dr. Poole, Legation surgeon, in the international hospital which was started in this Legation. All those who came under his treatment praised very highly his skill and untiring attention during the siege; 166 cases passed through the hands of the two surgeons in charge, and it is remarkable as an instance of the skill displayed and precautions taken, that not a single amputation was necessary.

I have the honour to request that the names of Dr. Velde and M. von Strauch be brought to the favourable notice of the German Government.

One of my personal orderlies was M. Fliche, an ex-officer of the French cavalry; for the first six weeks of the siege he was under my special orders and personal observation.

He carried messages and orders from me to the various parts of the general defence at all hours of the day and night, and nearly always under fire. Nothing could exceed the gallantry and smartness of this young officer. I beg that his name be specially brought to the notice of the French Government.

I have, &c.

(Signed) CLAUDE M. MACDONALD.

LIST OF MEMBERS OF THE IMPERIAL MARITIME CUSTOMS RECOMMENDED BY SIR C. MACDONALD.

Mr. Macoun was for some time in charge of the Customs contingent of volunteers, arranged their roster, and was himself unceasingly on duty in either the dangerous Prince Su's Park or West Hanlin. He was an indefatigable worker. He was wounded in the thigh by a bullet in Prince Su's Park on the 12th July, and, though lame from the effects, cheerfully resumed his duties after a week's rest. I understand that he is not even now fully recovered.

Mr. de Courcy was also conspicuous by his hard work, and cheerfully resumed his dangerous duty in the park and elsewhere before his health really rendered it advisable for him to do so. After the siege his health completely broke down, and he died at Tien-tsin on the 29th September. He was also slightly wounded in the Legation compound.

Mr. Smythe, too ill at the commencement for work, took his duty at the very earliest opportunity, and was always only too eager to supplement his own watches by relieving those who were worn out by the extreme length of the watches towards the end of the siege. His health suffered severely under the strain of his self-denying good nature, resulting in an attack of typhoid after the relief.

Mr. Bethell's extreme youth made the work done by him as a volunteer the more specially noticeable. The strain and hardship brought on a sickness which necessitated his going to hospital for a short time during the siege, yet, in spite of this, he resumed his duty at the earliest chance.

Mr. Russell's arduous, willing, and self-denying services in the commissariat, where he had charge of and dealt out daily the rations of the plainer foodstuff to foreigners and natives, excited general admiration, and they were always rendered with the greatest cheerfulness. The important and difficult work of milling the grain, in obtaining which he was also largely instrumental, was also intrusted to him.

No. 3.

THE MARQUESS OF LANSDOWNE TO SIR C. MACDONALD.

SIR, Foreign Office, 10th February, 1901.

I have received and laid before the King your despatch of the 24th December, inclosing a report, in continuation of those already received, with accompanying maps, on events at Peking from the 20th June to the 14th August regarded from the military aspect.

As the present report completes your account of the siege and relief of the Legations, I desire to take this opportunity of stating how highly His Majesty's Government value these admirable and exhaustive records of an episode of the deepest historic interest.

The gallantry with which the defence was maintained by all the foreign forces engaged, more especially after the failure of the first relief expedition, and the consequent disappointment to the besieged, coupled with the energy and courage with which the efforts of the regular forces were seconded by the Legation staffs and other civilians, has commanded the admiration of the whole civilised world.

His Majesty's Government desire also to place on record their appreciation of the important part borne by yourself throughout this crisis. On the 22nd June, at the request of your colleagues, you took charge of the defence, a position for which, from your military training, you possessed exceptional qualifications; and from that date you continued to direct the operations of the garrison until the relief took place on the 14th August.

Information has reached His Majesty's Government from various sources that the success of the defence was largely due to your personal efforts, and more particularly to the unity and cohesion which you found means of establishing and maintaining among the forces of so many different nationalities operating over an extended area. Competent eye-witnesses have expressed the opinion that if it can be said that the European community owe their lives to any one man more than to another, where so many distinguished themselves, it is to you they are indebted for their safety.

I cannot conclude this despatch without asking you to convey to Lady MacDonald the thanks of His Majesty's Government for her unceasing and devoted attention to the comfort and welfare of the sick and wounded. Her work, and that of the ladies who assisted her, have earned the lasting gratitude not only of those who benefited by her ministrations, but also of their relatives in Europe who were kept for so many weeks in a condition of the most painful anxiety and suspense.

I am, &c.

(Signed) LANSDOWNE.

Admiralty, December 10, 1900.*

ENCLOSURES in China Letters Nos. 573, 605, and 613 of 5th, 17th, and 18th September 1900, respectively.

H.B.M. Legation, Peking,
SIR, Saturday, August 18, 1900.

I have the honour to forward to you this my report of the guard of Royal Marine Light Infantry which did duty in this Legation and in the defence of the Legations Settlement in Peking during the late siege.

The guard was under the command of Captain B. M. Strouts, and left Tien-tsin the 31st May, arriving here the same night. Trouble began with the Boxers in the city the 13th June. An ultimatum to quit the city within 24 hours was received by the Ministers from the Chinese Government. It was decided to remain, and hostilities began the night of the 20th. The active siege continued until the 17th July, when there was a practical cessation of firing until the 5th August, during which period the Tsungli Yamen communicated several times with the Ministers. The siege was raised the afternoon of the 14th August by the allied army.

Captain Strouts having died of his wound the 16th July, and Captain Halliday still suffering from his wound, I have been in command since that date.

I have, &c.,
EDMUND WRAY, Captain, R.M.L.I.,
The Senior Naval Officer, Commanding Guard.
  Her Britannic Majesty's Fleet,
    North China.

H.B.M. Legation Guard, Peking,
SIR, August 26, 1900.

I have the honour to forward to you this my report of the part taken in the defence of Peking by the Royal Marine Legation Guard. I beg to state that no accurate record of all the details of duties performed by the detachment was kept, as parts of it were daily employed in reinforcing other portions of the concerted defence of the Legations, and no reports were received from the foreign officers commanding those sections of the defence.

The guard arrived in Peking on the night of the 31st May, and consisted of 3 officers, 75 non-commissioned officers and men, 1 bugler, 1 armourer, 1 signalman, and 1 sick-berth steward, the

---

* *London Gazette*, December 11, 1900.

late Captain B. M. Strouts being in command. Ordinary guard duties were performed until the 13th June, on which date some 300 Boxers entered the Tartar City near the Légation Settlement, and it was from this date that the detachment was continuously on the alert and at their posts in the defence. I beg to report the subsequent events in the form of a diary:—

June 13.—A picket of an officer and 12 men was placed and kept on the North Bridge, to prevent Boxers from attacking the Legation.

June 14.—At about 10.30 p.m. some 100 Boxers wishing to cross the North Bridge from east to west, rushed at and attacked the picket, and were repulsed, losing 4 killed and 2 wounded.

June 15.—Captain L. S. T. Halliday, with a combined force of British and German Marines, rescued several hundred Chinese Christians from the Nantung Roman Catholic Mission, who were being massacred by Boxers, some 30 of the latter being killed.

June 16.—I was sent with 20 British, 9 American, and 5 Japanese Marines to rescue a Christian family from the northeast city. A reputed Boxer temple, which I intended visiting on my return, was passed on the way. Hearing shrieks issuing from the temple, as of victims being tortured, and seeing signs of Boxers holding their rites, I approached the temple with some men. Bricks were hurled and spears thrust over the walls, so I decided to force my way in. I succeeded in doing so, and killed about 45 Boxers, none of them being able to escape. The mutilated bodies of two native Christians were found. My native guide having meantime run away, I returned to the Legation, and learnt that the Christian family had come in.

June 17.—Chinese Imperial troops fired on the picket on North Bridge.

June 19.—An ultimatum for all Ministers and foreigners to leave Peking within 24 hours was received by the Ministers that evening. It was decided to remain and defend the Legations.

June 20.—The German Minister was killed; the picket on North Bridge was withdrawn. It was decided that all women and children should be brought into the British Legation, which would be the last line of defence. Our sentries at the Front Gate opened fire for the first time on Imperial troops, who shot an unarmed European on North Bridge. A heavy fusillade was opened by the enemy all around the settlement during a thunderstorm that night. Captain F. G. Poole, East Yorkshire Regiment, who was in Peking studying Chinese, and who was attached to the Marine Guard in June, was given a section of the defence of the Legation to command. Captain C. Percy Smith, late of the South Staffordshire Regiment, also became attached, and commanded another section.

June 21.—At the request of all the Foreign Ministers, Sir Claude MacDonald, K.C.M.G., K.C.B., Her Britannic Majesty's Minister Plenipotentiary, took supreme command of the Legations

Settlement, the commanding officers of each guard being in command of their several Legations.

June 22.—An unsuccessful attempt was made to burn the Legations at the south-west corner. Captain Poole, with 15 marines, reconnoitred the Hanlin. Private Scadding was killed.

June 23.—The Hanlin was set on fire by the enemy with the object of burning the Legation from the north; the wind changing in time, our front was cleared. Captain Poole, with a force of British and American marines and volunteers, drove out the enemy and occupied the southern part.

June 24.—Captain Halliday, with 30 marines, was sent by Captain Strouts to drive the enemy from the houses behind First Chinese Secretary's house. He was dangerously wounded almost immediately after, killing four out of five of his assailants with his revolver, returned to the Legation, and has been disabled ever since. Captain Strouts, who was on the spot, then took charge and led the force. Driving the enemy back some 100 yards, he succeeded in taking several arms and much ammunition, besides burning several houses, thus clearing our front. Germans and Americans occupied South City wall. Privates Sawyer and Goddard wounded this day.

June 25.—Captain Strouts formed and took command of a company of 85 volunteers of all nationalities living in the British Legation.

June 26.—Lance-Corporal Allin wounded.

June 27.—Lance-Corporal Sparkes wounded.

June 28.—Enemy opened fire with a 2·7-inch Krupp gun and a "1-pr. field gun" against the south stable quarters, doing considerable damage to the building; this was silenced by rifle fire.

June 29.—I made an unsuccessful sortie at daylight to capture the Krupp gun with a mixed force of British, German, and Russian marines and volunteers. It was discovered that the gun had been withdrawn. Captain Poole, with a force of British marines and volunteers, at the same time made an unsuccessful sortie to destroy the enemy's barricade on the Imperial Carriage Park wall near the West Hanlin. On this occasion Corporal T. Johnson showed great bravery in covering the retreat carried out under a very heavy rifle fire. Private Philips killed on this day.

June 30.—Privates Tickner and Hornes wounded.

July 1.—The Germans having had to abandon their barricade on the South City wall near their Legation, I was sent with a party of 12 British, 3 American, and 2 Russians to try and build a barricade as near the canal as possible so as to cover the rear of the American barricade. After working for four hours, losing 2 men wounded and being wounded myself, I was ordered to give up the attempt, so retired the force to the American barricade. Corporal D. J. Gowney showed great coolness in carrying out the retirement, and Private T. A. Myers showed great tenacity and courage in building the barricade under a heavy and accurate front and rear fire, and in spite of damaged hands. Five British marines took part in an unsuccessful sortie made by the Japanese and Italians to capture a Krupp gun in the Suan Fu. This day Privates King, Harden, and Heap were wounded, also Privates Deane and Buckler very slightly. Volunteers took an important part in the sortie.

July 3.—Captain Myers, the officer commanding American Marine Guard, with a force of 15 Americans, 25 British marines under Sergeant Murphy, and 15 Russians, carried and occupied two Chinese barricades on the South City wall towards the Chun Min Gate. Sergeant T. Murphy showed great courage and coolness in leading the second assault after Captain Myers had been wounded. This action was carried out at night. Corporal Gregory wounded.

July 5.—Enemy mounted four smooth-bore M.L. guns firing round shot on the Imperial City wall. They opened fire on a working party, which, with its covering force of British marines in the Hanlin, was forced to retire into the Legation. It was during this time that Leading Signalman Swannell distinguished himself. Considerable damage was done to the buildings at north end of Legation with these guns.

July 8.—An old smooth-bore gun was found and mounted by an American gunner, assisted by Armourer Thomas, Royal Navy, who also manufactured the ammunition: the projectiles being the shells of a modern Russian field gun. In the evening the enemy opened fire at the roof of the First Chinese Secretary's house with a 1-pr. Corporal D. J. Gowney showed great coolness and pluck by firing at the flash of the gun from the fort on the top of the First Chinese Secretary's roof. The enemy's gun was only 100 yards off, and was silenced by Corporal Gowney at the ninth round.

July 11.—From this date eight British Marines were sent daily to reinforce the Japanese and Italian posts in the Suan Fu. (I beg to mention here that since about the 8th July the enemy seem to have given up trying to force their way into the British Legation, but to have made the Christian converts the object of their attacks, so that henceforth their worst attacks were against the Italians, Japanese, French, and Germans.)

July 12.—The Italian officer having been wounded, Captain Strouts allowed my services, which I had offered, to be accepted, and I took command of the Italians at their post, together with eight British Marines.

July 13.—It happened that during this day British Marines were used in reinforcing every post outside the British Legation. Lance-Sergeant T. E. Preston distinguished himself on this day. (His conduct will be mentioned later.) Private Westbrook wounded.

July 16.—Captain Strouts was mortally wounded, and died three hours later. He was returning from visiting my post in the Suan Fu. His loss was deeply felt by all. Captain Halliday was the next in seniority, but being still unfit for duty, I took command of the Royal Marines, and was relieved from the command of the Italians by Lieutenant Von Stranck, late of the Prussian Army, and now in the Chinese Imperial Maritime Customs. Sir Claude MacDonald now took command of the British Legation, and Captain Poole took command of the Volunteers. I have been in command of the British Marines ever since. A message was received from the Chinese Government saying they would protect us, and had given orders to stop all firing. Firing on the part of the enemy actually ceased about noon on the 17th.

From the 17th July until the 4th August, except for sniping on both sides, but chiefly on the part of the Chinese opposite our western defences, there was a cessation of hostilities. This sniping gradually increased on the part of the enemy, until on the 4th severe fusillades and attacks were made on the Legations Settlements; but, as before, the enemy never rushed in the open, but only approached behind brick barricades which they built, even under a heavy fire on our part.

August 2.—The houses east of Mongul Market were occupied by Marines and Customs Volunteers under Lieutenant Von Stranck.

August 4.—Sergeant Murphy did great execution with the five-barrelled Nordenfeldt, mounted at the south-east corner of Imperial Carriage Park, in covering the subsequent occupation of the "Ruins" behind the Chinese Secretary's house, and the holding of the Mongul Market by us. Severe fusillades at night.

August 8.—The "Ruins" were occupied and fortified. Heavy fusillades all round the settlement, especially at night. This happened every night, more or less frequently.

August 9.—In the afternoon the enemy made three heavy attacks on the "Ruins," and the Chinese officers in their barricades only 15 yards off were heard ordering their men to charge. But we were using our ammunition more freely than at any time during the siege, and firing volleys at their barricade, doing considerable damage to it. The last attack, and one at night, we were able to repulse by merely throwing bricks and stones.

August 13.—A note was received from the Chinese Government saying orders had been given for any Chinese soldiers firing on us to be court-martialled. During a total cessation of firing in the afternoon the enemy mounted two Krupp guns on their fort in the Imperial City wall over the canal, with which they opened fire on the Legation during a heavy combined attack on the whole settlement at 7.45 p.m. They were also heard again trying to urge an attack on the "Ruins" at 3 a.m. next morning, but never came, our men, with reinforcements of volunteers, remaining at their loopholes for over two hours.

August 14.—Very heavy cannonading was heard, and from the South City walls shells were seen bursting against the gates of the Tartar City. This increased during the morning, and it was realised that relief was at hand. At 3 p.m. the allied army sent to our relief reached us; the first to enter the settlement, and two hours in advance of any others, being British native troops, one company of 1st Sikhs, followed immediately by General Sir Alfred Gaselee and his Staff.

I have the honour to bring before your notice the conduct of, and to recommend for the Conspicuous Gallantry Medal, Lance-Sergeant T. E. Preston, of Her Majesty's ship "Orlando." On the 14th July, after the enemy had been driven down from their barricades on the Imperial Carriage Park wall, near the West Hanlin, by shell fire, this non-commissioned officer climbed on to the wall, some 12 feet high, with the intention of capturing a banner left on the barricade by the enemy. Finding that he could not reach it, he called for his rifle to be given to him, and pushing down part of the barricade he kept the enemy, some .50 in number, at bay, while an American gunner, named Michell, was enabled to lay hold of the flag. Sergeant Preston then jumped down and assisted Gunner Michell in drawing the flag over with difficulty, as the enemy had laid hold of the other end. He was struck on the head at the same time by a brick, which partly stunned him.

I have the honour to bring before your notice also the conduct of Leading Signalman H. Swannell, Her Majesty's ship "Orlando," and to request that you will be pleased to recommend him for that reward which you think his action deserves. I beg to enclose from Captain Poole his account of the deed, of which he was an eye-witness.

I have the honour to bring before your notice and to recommend for promotion the following :—

Lance-Sergeant T. E. Preston, Her Majesty's ship "Orlando."
Corporal W. Gregory, Wei-hai-wei Detachment.
Corporal D. J. Gowney, Wei-hai-wei Detachment.
Acting Lance-Corporal T. R. Allen, Wei-hai-wei Detachment.

Also the following Naval ratings :—
Armourer T. S. Thomas, Her Majesty's ship "Orlando." This man showed great ingenuity in constructing the charges, and in utilising the modern Russian projectiles for the muzzle-loading gun. Also in making projectiles for the Italian 1-pr. field gun, as well as bullets for the German and Russian modern rifles. His services were invaluable.

Sick Berth Steward, second class, R. G. Fuller.

In conclusion, I beg to report that the behaviour of the whole detachment during a very trying time, and under fatiguing circumstances, was exemplary and deserving of all praise. As a proof of their steadiness and coolness, I beg to state that out of

18,000 rounds of Lee-Metford ammunition brought from Tien-tsin some 9,000 remain.

      I have, &c.,
    EDMUND WRAY, Captain, R.ML.I.,
      Commanding British Marine Guard.

To the Senior Naval Officer,
 Northern Division,
Her Majesty's China Fleet, Taku.

       H.B.M. Legation, Peking,
SIR,   July 31, 1900.

 I have the honour to bring to your notice particularly the conduct of Leading Signalman H. Swannell, Her Majesty's ship "Orlando."

 On the 5th instant, being in command of the Hanlin outposts, at 10.30 a.m. I heard that Mr. Oliphant, Her Britannic Majesty's Consular Service, had just been wounded.

 I ran out to the spot and found Leading Signalman Swannell attending to Mr. Oliphant, who was mortally wounded, under the close and accurate fire of the enemy.

 He remained with Mr. Oliphant until he was brought into a place of safety.

      I have, &c.
      F. G. POOLE, Captain,
The Officer Commanding, East Yorkshire Regiment.
 Royal Marine Light Infantry
  Detachment, Peking.

       H.B.M. Legation, Peking,
SIR,   August 24, 1900.

 I have the honour to forward to you the enclosed letter from Dr. Wordsworth Poole, Physician to the Legation, and Medical attendant to the Royal Marine Guard, referring to the conduct of Sick Berth Steward, second class, R. G. Fuller, R.N.

 I beg to state that, from my own observations and experience, his behaviour and treatment of wounded and sick was beyond all description. The recommendation of Dr. Poole speaks for itself.

 I have the honour to request that you will be pleased to recommend Sick Berth Steward Fuller for what reward and distinction you may think he deserves, for his exemplary behaviour during a very trying time.

      I have, &c.,
       EDMUND WRAY, Captain, R.M.L.I.
         Commanding British Legation
The Senior Naval Officer,   Guard.
 Northern Division, China Fleet,
  Taku.

        H.B.M. Legation, Peking,
SIR,   August 24, 1900.

  I have the honour to bring before your notice the conduct of Richard G. Fuller, Sick Berth Steward of H.M.S. "Orlando," who worked under me in the International Hospital during the siege of Peking. The work was excessively arduous, and he proved himself an invaluable assistant. He was indefatigable at his work, of which he has an excellent knowledge. He managed the sick of eight different nationalities with great tact. Both myself and my colleague, Dr. Velde, formed a very high opinion of his capabilities. In fact, it would be impossible to overpraise his conduct.

      I have, &c.,
       WORDSWORTH POOLE,
        Physician to the Legation.
Captain E. Wray, Royal Marines,
 Commanding British Legation Guard,
  Peking.

        British Legation, Peking,
SIR,   September 7, 1900.

  I have the honour to bring to your notice the conduct of the detachment of Royal Marine Light Infantry commanded by the late Captain Strouts, which your Excellency was good enough to send as a guard in this Legation on the 31st May.

  I cannot speak in any other terms but those of the highest praise of the behaviour of the officers, non-commissioned officers, and men of this detachment. They were exposed, day and night, for two months to the most arduous, irksome, and responsible duties, which they fulfilled with a cheerful alacrity and with a courage and endurance which excited the admiration of everybody. Their bearing under fire was quite excellent, and could not have been surpassed by the best veteran soldiers. During the entire siege I did not observe the slightest sign of liquor in any of the men, neither was a case reported to me, and this though the facilities for obtaining drink were great. To sum up, the general good conduct, soldierly bearing, and steadiness under fire of the men of the detachment was worthy of the highest traditions of the British Army and of the corps to which they belong.

This high state of excellence was undoubtedly in a great measure due to the officers and non-commissioned officers. Captain Strouts was an excellent soldier and a gallant gentleman. He was killed in the defence of the Legation on the 16th July, and his loss was to me, and to the defence generally, irreparable. Had Captain Strouts lived, I should certainly have recommended him to the Lords of the Admiralty, through your Excellency, for promotion or for the Distinguished Service Order.

Captain Halliday was dangerously wounded whilst leading a sortie on the 24th June, and his valuable services were lost for the rest of the siege. Under another cover I am recommending this officer for the Victoria Cross.

Captain Wray, who was also wounded in taking part in the defence of the Tartar City Wall, one of the most dangerous posts in the defence, commanded the detachment very efficiently until the end of the siege. This latter officer has, I understand, recommended several non-commissioned officers. Those that came under my special notice were Sergeants Murphy, Saunders, and Preston, and Corporals Gregory and Gowney, who are all worthy of the highest praise.

I have, &c.,
CLAUDE M. MACDONALD,
British Minister.

Sir Edward Seymour, K.C.B.,
Commander-in-Chief,
H.B.M. Squadron in China and
Japan.

LETTER No. 605 from COMMANDER-IN-CHIEF, CHINA, 17th September 1900, to the Admiralty.

It is clear that the Marine Guard well and ably fulfilled the duties required of them under very trying circumstances, and worthily upheld the traditions of their corps. Captain Strouts, who was in command until his death on 16th July, earned the respect and admiration of all. After his death Captain Wray took command, and carried out the responsible duties successfully. Captain Halliday was severely wounded on the 24th June, soon after the siege commenced.

Captain Wray brings forward the names of several men whom he considers deserving of special recognition, and I submit them for their Lordships' favourable consideration.

E. H. SEYMOUR,
Vice-Admiral.

DESPATCHES FROM SIR A. GASELEE, GENERAL OFFICER COMMANDING CHINA EXPEDITIONARY FORCE.*

No. 36 S. Headquarters, China Expeditionary Force,
MY LORD, Peking, August 19, 1900.

Now that the first and paramount duty of relieving the Legations has been successfully performed, I am in a position to address to your Lordship a preliminary despatch, describing the operations of the British forces in Northern China from the 27th July, the date I arrived at Tien-tsin, to the 14th August, the date on which we entered Peking.

2. On my arrival at Tien-tsin I at once put myself into communication with the General Officers commanding the American and Japanese forces, and soon came to a satisfactory understanding with them. We decided to collectively impress upon the Allied Commanders the absolute necessity of pressing forward towards Peking at the earliest possible moment, and happily our views were eventually accepted.

At a conference held on the 3rd August it was arranged to commence the advance on the 4th, with approximately 20,000 men, viz. :—

    10,000 Japanese with 24 guns.
    4,000 Russians with 16 guns.
    3,000 British with 12 guns.
    2,000 Americans with 6 guns.
      800 French with 12 guns.
      200 Germans.
      100 Austrians and Italians.

    20,100 with 70 guns.

3. The Chinese were believed to occupy a strongly intrenched position near Pei-tsang, astride the Pei-ho. It was decided to force this position and push on to Yang-tsun, so as to secure the passage of the river at that important strategical point. The general idea was that the Japanese, British, and Americans should operate along the right bank of the river, the other allies along the left bank. It was then settled in direct communication with General Chaffee, United States Army, and General Yamagutchi, Japanese Army, that, as regards the left attack—i.e., that on the right bank of the river, the movement should be of a turning nature along the embankment marked A———B in the attached sketch, the Japanese leading, followed in succession by the British and Americans. The turning movement to commence at 2 a.m. on the 5th.

4. In pursuance of the above agreement, the British troops marginally noted† moved from Tien-tsin to Hsi-ku on the

---
* *London Gazette*, November 6, 1900.
† Naval Brigade, 4 guns; Royal Marine Light Infantry, 300; 12th Battery Royal Field Artillery, 6 guns; Hong Kong Artillery, 2 guns

x 2

afternoon of 4th and bivouacked in the area marked C. Annexure A. (Field Force Order No. 140) shows the arrangements for the march. The British were followed by the Americans and Japanese, who bivouacked at the points marked D and E.

5. As arranged, in the early hours of the 5th instant, the turning movement commenced. At daybreak the column came under a heavy fire from the right front and the action began with a vigorous forward movement of the Japanese against the entrenchments, supported on the right by the British. The brunt of the action fell on the Japanese, who attacked and stormed line after line in the most gallant manner. Our troops, in consequence of their position, scarcely fired a shot, and I readily accord to the Japanese the whole credit of the victory. Their loss was, I understand, about 300 killed and wounded, while ours was only 25 (*vide* Annexure B). The Chinese rout was complete, and before noon they had entirely disappeared, having fled to the left bank of the river. The other allied forces were scarcely engaged at all and practically had no loss.

6. After the victory at Pei-tsang we pushed on for a mile or two along the right bank, but, being stopped by inundations, were compelled to return to Pei-tsang, and cross over to the right (*sic*) bank, where we bivouacked for the night, covered by a strong outpost, two or three miles in advance.

7. On the 6th instant the whole of the Allied Forces marched on Yang-tsun, by the right bank, with the exception of about 6,000 Japanese, who continued to advance by the left bank. Owing to the direction taken by the several columns the British troops were leading along the direct road when we came in sight of Yang-tsun, the Americans being on our right flank. The enemy's main position was apparently along the railway embankment, with one flank resting on a village close to the Pei-ho railway bridge. It was at once arranged to attack this position with one Russian battalion on the left, the British troops in the centre, and the Americans on the right, while the 1st Bengal Lancers covered the extreme right flank. I thereupon directed the 1st Sikh Infantry to extend for attack, supported by the Royal Welsh Fusiliers, and the 24th Punjab Infantry, the advance to be covered by the fire of No. 12 Battery Royal Field Artillery. The remainder of our troops were too far in rear to be utilised at the moment. The advance to attack was made in beautiful order over about 5,000 yards of level plain, covered with high crops. At about half this distance the troops came under a hot shell and musketry fire; nevertheless, owing to the open order in which we worked, the

---

4 Maxims; detachment Royal Engineers,—; 1st Bengal Lancers, 400; Royal Welsh Fusiliers, 300; 7th Bengal Infantry, 500; 24th Punjab Infantry, 300; 1st Sikh Infantry, 500; Hong Kong Regiment, 100; Chinese Regiment, 100.

British loss was comparatively small. The further advance was a rapid one, and the embankment was carried by a rush of the 1st Sikh Infantry and 24th Punjab Infantry. The Welsh Fusiliers, owing to the conformation of the ground, were rather wedged out of the assaulting line. This practically ended the fight, as the Chinese fled precipitately in all directions. The enemy's guns were in a retired position and thus escaped capture. Our loss on this occasion was as shown in Annexure C.

8. On the 7th instant the Allies halted to bring up supplies, and on the 8th the movement was continued. On the 9th, at Ho-hsi-wu, a squadron of the 1st Bengal Lancers caught up some retreating Tartar cavalry, inflicting on them heavy loss, and on the 12th Tung-chao was occupied without opposition. At a conference held on that day it was decided to send forward strong reconnoitring forces on the 13th, to concentrate on a line about five miles from Peking on the 14th, and to attack on the 15th. The positions of the several forces were assigned, the British taking the extreme left. On the 14th, however, owing to the premature advance of a battalion of one of the Allied Forces, the intended concentration was abandoned, and the troops all hurried forward to assault the city of Peking.

9. I have above endeavoured to give a connected account of the military operations preceding the attack on Peking, and I will now try to briefly relate what occurred on the 14th, so far as Her Majesty's troops are concerned. Our forces on the night of the 13th were concentrated on the river south-east of Tung-chao, about 15 miles from Peking, with two guns, the 1st Bengal Lancers and the 7th Bengal Infantry, about nine miles in advance as an observation force. At 2.30 a.m. on the 14th, hearing heavy firing in the direction of Peking, I caused the rouse to be sounded and marched without delay towards the supposed scene of action. About 7 a.m. I reached the point held by my advanced force, and at once pushed on with the troops there available, directing the main body to follow after an hour's rest. About noon I got into touch with the Americans, who were on the south bank of the canal, and as they and the French were preparing to assault the Tung Tien Gate, I decided to push straight on and assault the south-east gate of the Chinese city, Sha-chia-men. Here I met with no opposition, and about 1 p.m. the British troops passed through the city wall. I then ordered the 1st Bengal Lancers and the 24th Punjab Infantry to march straight to the Temple of Heaven Park, which I wished to secure as a camping ground, and also as a protection to my left and rear, while with the rest of my available troops I pushed on through streets and alleys towards the Water Gate of the Tartar City, a point which I had learnt from a cypher message from Sir C. MacDonald would probably be the most vulnerable. Our troops were much exhausted by the long march and intense heat, and were much scattered in groups, but they struggled gamely on without attempting to reply to the desultory and ineffective fire of the enemy At a few minutes before 3 p.m., I, with a few officers

of my Staff and about 70 men of the 1st Sikhs and 7th Bengal Infantry, reached a point opposite the Water Gate. The British flag was still flying on that portion of the Tartar wall which we knew the Legations had occupied, but an ominous silence made us fear that the worst had occurred, and that the flag was only a ruse to lure us on; when suddenly, to our great relief, we saw a flag signal being made. "Come up Sluice Street by Water Gate." Our small party at once rushed across the almost dry canal, and entered into the Legation zone through the Water Gate under the Tartar wall. As we crossed a hail of ill-aimed fire was directed on us from the Hata-men Gate, but not a man was touched, and at 3 p.m. Her Majesty's troops had the supreme gratification of finding they were the first to relieve the sorely-pressed beleaguered garrison.

10. Our loss* during these operations was quite insignificant, which may be attributed to the fact that the enemy had never expected attack from this quarter, and had concentrated their defence on the eastern wall of the Tartar city, where the resistance was, I understand, of a most obstinate description.

11. The operations I have described have, happily, not been attended with the loss that might have been expected; nevertheless, the troops engaged have been subjected to a severe strain on account of the intense heat, the want of good water, the heavy mud or dust which characterises the roads in this country, and, above all, the want of sufficient rest. The patient endurance and ardour of the troops has, however, more than compensated for these difficulties, and I am proud of the manner in which Her Majesty's British and Indian troops have acquitted themselves.

12. In conclusion, I do not propose in this despatch to bring specially to your Lordship's notice the services rendered by many officers of this force, but I take the opportunity of mentioning the names of those few who had a special opportunity of distinguishing themselves at the action of Yang-tsun. They are:—

Major T. E. Scott, D.S.O., 1st Sikh Infantry (attached).
Lieutenant W. F. Bainbridge, 1st Sikh Infantry.
Captain J. H. Gwynne, Royal Welsh Fusiliers.

No. 4995, Private Jackson, Royal Welsh Fusiliers, whose commanding officer reports that "as some shells from one of the batteries engaged were taking our troops and the Americans in reverse, he volunteered to get up on the embankment and tried to communicate with the battery." While doing so, he was exposed to fire from both sides.

I would also like to mention the names of two American officers who gallantly supported our fighting line, viz.:—

Major William Quinton, 14th United States Infantry.
Captain J. R. M. Taylor, 14th United States Infantry.

---

* *Vide* Annexure D.

As regards other officers and men, I deem the conclusion of the campaign to be the most fitting moment to bring their services to your Lordship's notice.

I have, &c.

ALFRED GASELEE, Lieutenant-General,
Commanding China Expeditionary Force.

The Right Honourable the Secretary of State for India.

ANNEXURES.

Annexure A.

CHINA EXPEDITIONARY FORCE ORDERS.

Tien-tsin, 4th August, 1900.

140. Movements.—The enemy is in position in the direction of Pei-tsang on both banks of the Pei-ho. The position is believed to be intrenched with outposts thrown forward.

(ii.) The Russian, French, and German forces will operate on the left bank of the river Pei-ho, the British, Americans, and Japanese on the right bank.

(iii.) The British forces will march to Hsi-ku to-day, where they will bivouac for the night.

(iv.) The British forces will march in the order given below:—

Royal Welsh Fusiliers with advance guard of one company
Detachment Royal Engineers.
One Field Troop 1st Bengal Lancers.
Headquarters Staff of Division.
One half Company 1st Sikhs (General Officer Commanding's escort).
12th Battery Royal Field Artillery.
R. 7 Ammunition Column Unit.
Hong Kong Royal Artillery.
1st Brigade Staff.
7th Rajputs, less one Company.
1st Sikhs.
Chinese Regiment.
1st Bengal Lancers.
Divisional and Brigade Headquarters Transport.
Commissariat and Transport.
Field Hospitals.
Rear Guard one Company 7th Rajputs.

(v.) The route will be by the Temperance Hall on the Taku road, through the Chinese city, entering by the south gate and over the iron bridge to Hsi-ku. The road to be followed will be shown by the Deputy-Assistant Quartermaster-General for Intelligence, who will head the column.

(vi.) The troops will keep closed up as much as possible, water bottles are to be filled with boiled water or tea, and all mussacks filled with good water.

(vii.) The head of the column will leave the Temperance Hall at 2.30 p.m. Officers commanding units will hold their units in readiness to join the line of march in the order detailed above. No interval between units.

(viii.) Camp colour men of all units and one officer or non-commissioned officer per unit will accompany the advanced guard.

(ix.) No fires or cooking will be allowed in bivouac to-night.

(NOTE.—All units not mentioned in paragraph iv. had marched to Hsi-ku the previous evening.)

By order,
E. G. BARROW, Major-General,
Chief of the Staff, China Expeditionary Force.

All transport of units will march immediately in rear of their own units.

Annexure B.

Detail of casualties in the action at Pei-tsang.

British non-commissioned officers and men, slightly wounded, 4.

Native officers, slightly wounded, 3.

Native non-commissioned officers and men, killed, 1; dangerously wounded, 1; severely wounded, 9; slightly wounded, 7.

Total.—Killed, 1; dangerously wounded, 1; severely wounded, 9; slightly wounded, 14.

Annexure C.

Details of casualties in the action at Yang-tsun.

British officers, dangerously wounded, 1.

British non-commissioned officers and men, killed, 1; died of sunstroke, 1; dangerously wounded, 1; severely wounded, 3; slightly wounded, 4.

Native non-commissioned officers and men, killed, 5; dangerously wounded, 3; severely wounded, 6; slightly wounded, 20.

Total.—Killed, 6; died of sunstroke, 1; dangerously wounded, 5; severely wounded, 9; slightly wounded, 24.

Annexure D.

Casualties from 8th to 14th August.

8th August, native non-commissioned officers and men, died, 1, accidentally drowned.

At Ho-hsi-wu, 9th August, native non-commissioned officers and men, slightly wounded, 2.

At Peking, 14th August, British non-commissioned officers and men, died, 1, heart disease.

Native non-commissioned officers and men, severely wounded, 2; slightly wounded, 1; missing, 1.

Total, died, 2; severely wounded, 2; slightly wounded, 3; missing, 1.

No. 198 S.*

Headquarters, British Contingent,
China Field Force,
My Lord,   Peking, 17th January 1901.

As the conclusion of the year 1900 and the winter season together mark the cessation of active operations at least for the present, I deem the moment a fitting one for reviewing the events which have occurred since the 14th August, as well as for placing on record my appreciation of the good work done by both officers and troops during the last few months.

2. In my despatch No. 36 S., dated 19th August,† I made no reference to the part played in the attack on Peking by those portions of the British forces which were not with me at the moment of the relief of the Legations, as I had not, on the date of my despatch, received any reports on these operations. In paragraph 8 of that despatch I informed your Lordship that on entering the Chinese city I ordered the 1st Bengal Lancers and the 24th Punjab Infantry to occupy the Temple of Heaven enclosure, which I wished to secure as a camping ground, and also as a protection to my left and rear. This was effected about 2.30 p.m. without serious opposition, but the south gate of the Chinese city close to it was held by a strong body of Chinese till late in the afternoon, when the 12th Battery, Royal Field Artillery, and portions of the 24th Punjab Infantry and Hong Kong Regiment, under the command of Lieutenant-Colonel O'Sullivan, Assistant Adjutant-General, arrived to reinforce the Temple of Heaven. Fire was then opened on this gate, a company of the 24th Punjab Infantry being detached to cut off the retreat of the enemy along the wall to the east, with the result that the gate fell into our hands, the enemy losing heavily as they retired.

3. At the time that I, with a portion of the 7th Rajputs and 1st Sikhs, was moving towards the Water Gate, as already described in my previous despatch, another party (*vide* margin‡) under the command of Brigadier-General Sir Norman Stewart, pushed along the main street until they reached the great thoroughfare running north into the Tartar city through the Chien-men (gate), where they turned to the right. At this point some 40 or 50 of the enemy emerged from a side lane, but were easily dispersed. The advance of the party was then continued towards the Chien-men, where the force was met with

---

° *London Gazette*, May 14, 1901.
† *Vide* Sketch No. 1 (red line).
‡ Detachments.—12th Battery, Royal Field Artillery; 2nd Battalion Royal Welsh Fusiliers; 1st Bengal Lancers; Hong Kong and Singapore Artillery, Maxim Section; Hong Kong Regiment; 7th Rajputs; 1st Sikhs.

a sharp fire from the enemy on the wall of the Tartar city. The bridge leading to the gate was at once seized and held. Lieutenant Bainbridge was the first to occupy this bridge with a small party of the 1st Sikhs, and he there remained in an exposed position holding a Union Jack to attract the notice of the Legation defenders occupying a portion of the wall to the east, who, for a short time, failed to recognise our men, and were firing on them. The Royal Welsh Fusiliers meanwhile covered the left flank, occupying the roofs of the houses and firing on the enemy holding the wall to the west of the gate.

While arrangements were being made for forcing the Chien-men a sortie along the top of the wall from the Legation barricade, by Russian and American troops of the Legation garrison, carried the large building over the inner gateway. At the same time a gun of the 12th Battery was brought into action by hand against the enemy on the wall to the west of the gate, and a few well-placed rounds crushed all opposition from that direction. By this time it had been ascertained that the east gateway of the hornwork of the Chien-men was not closed; the troops accordingly entered by it, and a passage was then found through a small hole in the inner gate, by which a party of the 1st Sikhs, with one Maxim gun of the Hong Kong and Singapore Artillery, and about 20 dismounted men of the 1st Bengal Lancers penetrated the Tartar city.

As the second Maxim gun was being taken through the hole of the gateway about 50 of the enemy occupying some ruined houses in the vicinity made a determined effort to capture it, actually closing with our men at the gate, but were beaten off and nearly all killed. The Chinese thereupon retired hurriedly westward from the direction of the Legations across the main road leading to the Imperial city, under a heavy fire from our Maxims and the troops holding the Chien-men. The 1st Sikhs then moved down Legation Street, clearing away the enemy still remaining, and entered the British Legation. At the same time the rest of the force, consisting of the Royal Welsh Fusiliers, two guns 12th Field Battery, and detachments of various regiments, moved along the foot of the wall outside the Tartar city, and entered the Legation by the Sluice Gate about 5 p.m. At about 7 p.m. some 500 of the enemy advanced along the wall from the westward against the Chien-men, but were easily driven back by a few rounds from the Maxims at the gate, abandoning two guns in their retreat. The fact that British troops had already forced an entrance into the Legations through the Sluice Gate fully accounts for the feeble resistance made at the Chien-men.

4. I would take this opportunity of observing, with reference to paragraph 10 of my last despatch, that I have since learnt that the absence of all opposition at the Chinese city wall was due to the premature attack made by the Russians and Japanese, which had the effect of drawing all the defenders of the Chinese city wall northwards. When we appeared it was too late to recall the troops thus withdrawn, and so mortified was the

responsible Chinese General at his mistake that he committed suicide on the spot.

5. The next operation in which our troops took part was the relief of the Peh-tang, the head-quarters of the Roman Catholic Missions in Peking.* This duty was entrusted by the Allied Commanders to General Frey of the French Army, but in accordance with agreement we co-operated with a detachment of 350 men (details in margin†) under the command of Major E. V. Luke, Royal Marine Light Infantry.

The force concentrated at the Chien-men on the morning of the 17th August, and was first directed on the Shun-chih-men (gate). The Hong Kong and Singapore Artillery opened fire on this gate from the wall near the Chien-men with a 12-pr. Q.F. naval gun, and under this fire the enemy evacuated the gate, which was immediately occupied by the Allies. The main body then advanced along the Shun-chi-men Street and entered the Imperial City. The British troops assisted the French in clearing the streets of the Imperial City of Chinese troops, and at nightfall bivouacked on the southern slopes of Coal Hill.

On the 21st October this detachment again co-operated with the French troops under General Frey in clearing the Imperial City north of the Pehtang Cathedral. Our men were never seriously engaged, but Major Luke appears to have acted throughout with tact and discretion, and Major-General Frey expressed himself as much gratified at the assistance thus rendered.

6. On the 17th August I sent a detachment to occupy the ruins of the railway terminus at Machiapu, with a view to asserting our interest in the railway to Tient-sin. Owing, however, to a Russian report that the enemy were advancing in force from the Hunting Park, this detachment was withdrawn on the 18th August, and a day or two afterwards the post was occupied by the Russians without reference to us. In consequence of this action, at the request of the British Minister, I sent detachment to occupy the railway junction at Fengtai and the walled town of Liukachao, commanding the road and railway bridges across the Hun-ho. These posts have been maintained ever since, and have proved of the utmost value in facilitating the collection of supplies and of railway material as well as in restoring confidence.

On the withdrawal of the Russians in October from Machiapu, that post was handed over to the Germans, and subsequently, by Field-Marshal Count Von Waldersee's orders, transferred to the British, to whom the construction of the railway line from Peking to Huang-hsun was entrusted.

7. Apart from various reconnaissances, the only military operations of any importance in which our troops have been

---

* *Vide* Sketch No. 1 (dotted lines).
† 150 Royal Marine Light Infantry ; 100 7th Bengal Infantry ; 100 1st Sikh Infantry.

engaged since the occupation of Peking are those detailed below :—

(i.) *Reconnaissance South of Tien-tsin on 15th August.*

On the 15th August a small cavalry reconnaissance, consisting of 30 men 1st Bengal Lancers and about 50 American cavalry, was sent south of Tien-tsin, supported by a detachment of Madras Sappers and Miners. As the advance party of the cavalry patrol approached within 300 yards of the village of Yaudshia-tsun a large number of Chinese troops suddenly showed themselves, and from the whole line of villages, nearly a mile in length, a heavy but badly-aimed fire was opened on them. The cavalry wheeled about and retired rapidly. At this point the horse of one of the American troopers suddenly came down, throwing the rider heavily; the Chinese soldiers dashed out to secure him, when Lieut. Gaussen, 1st Bengal Lancers, seeing how matters stood, at once rode back in the face of a heavy fire, took the American trooper on his horse, and brought him back into safety. The force then returned to Tientsin.

Both Lieutenant-Colonel Wint, 6th U.S. Cavalry, and Major-General Chaffee, Commanding the United States Forces in Northern China; have brought Lieutenant Gaussen's services on this occasion to my special notice.

(ii.) *Action 19th August South of Tien-tsin.*

As it was evident that an increasing number of Imperial troops and Boxers were collecting in villages from seven to ten miles south of Tien-tsin, a combined force * under the orders of Brigadier-General A. R. F. Dorward, C.B., D.S.O., was despatched from Tien-tsin on the 19th August to disperse them.

The cavalry, under Lieutenant-Colonel Wint, 6th United States Cavalry, covered the advance and came into touch with the enemy near the village of Wang-Landi. The cavalry were dismounted and returned the enemy's fire; meanwhile, the infantry changed direction to the left, and, pushing steadily on, intercepted a large body of Chinese who were advancing against the flank of the cavalry, and drove them back upon their main position, which they had not time to properly occupy before it was rushed by our infantry. Only a slight stand was made here, and the enemy was soon in full flight, pursued by the cavalry. Sixty prisoners, a quantity of arms, and a large number of standards were captured, and 300 killed and wounded were left on the field. Our casualties were one officer slightly wounded and one soldier severely, while the Americans and Japanese had a few more.

---

* 398 6th United States Cavalry ; 30 1st Bengal Lancers ; 20 Austrian Infantry; 200 Japanese Infantry. Detachments :—Bombay Sappers and Miners, Hong Kong Regiment, Chinese Regiment, 7th Bengal Infantry, 24th Punjab Infantry, 1st Sikh Infantry, 1st Madras Pioneers, 26th Bombay Infantry, aggregating 350 men.

The expedition, which was ably conducted by General Dorward, had a most excellent effect on the districts, and freed the peaceful villagers from the terrors of the Boxer rule.

(iii.) *Tiu-Liu Expedition.*

In order to free the country lying between the Grand Canal and Tien-tsin of Boxers who were raiding villages and cutting off supplies, a force was sent to the town of Tiu-Liu, 22 miles distant from Tien-tsin.*

Three columns † under the command of Brigadier-General A. R. F. Dorward, C.B., D.S.O., were despatched to operate against them.

The Left column moved from Tien-tsin on 8th, and the Central and Canal columns on the 9th September. The several columns were ordered to be in position round Tiu-Liu on the morning of the 10th September. Heavy rain fell on the night of the 8th and all day on the 10th, causing much discomfort to the troops and adding to the difficulties of the march; nevertheless, on the 10th Tiu-Liu was occupied without opposition, the enemy having fled on the approach of the attacking force. The troops then returned to Tien-tsin.

Brigadier-General Dorward reports that each column succeeded in carrying out its orders exactly, and was in the prescribed position round Tiu-Liu at 9 a.m. on the 10th September. As a manœuvre, therefore, over partially unknown country the expedition was, he considers, a distinct success, reflecting credit on Brigadier-General Richardson and on Colonel Garioni, of the Italian Army, commanding the left and centre columns respectively, which view I cordially endorse, and at the same time wish to bring to your Lordship's notice the excellent arrangements made by Brigadier-General Dorward on this occasion.

(iv.) *Affair at Matao.*

On the 9th September a small American foraging party was attacked by Boxers near Matao. On hearing of this Captain Browne, Central India Horse, with 21 Lancers at once proceeded to clear the village in which the Boxers, some 300 in number,

---

* *Vide* Sketch No. II.

† Left Column :— Brigadier-General Richardson ; B Battery, Royal Horse Artillery ; 16th Bengal Lancers ; 3rd Bombay Cavalry ; Mounted detachment Bengal Sappers and Miners ; 250 Japanese Infantry, with four guns ; 350 Italian Infantry ; 200 Russian Infantry ; 50 1st Chinese Regiment ; detachment Bombay Sappers and Miners ; 100 7th Bengal Infantry ; 100 1st Sikh Infantry.

Centre Column :—Colonel Garioni ; 2 Japanese siege guns ; 500 Italian Infantry ; detachment Bombay Sappers and Miners ; 100 34th Punjab Pioneers.

Canal Column :—Detachment 1st Bengal Lancers ; 200 United States Infantry ; 150 Italian Infantry ; 100 24th Punjab Infantry ; 100 1st Madras Pioneers ; 100 26th Bombay Infantry.

had established themselves. The enemy were completely dispersed with a loss of about 40 men, our only casualty being one man wounded.

(v.) *Affair at Liong-Hsian.*

A German column under Major-General Von Hoepfner marched out on the 11th September to attack Liang-Hsian,* about 10 miles south of Liukochao; a half squadron 1st Bengal Lancers and two Maxim guns, Hong Kong and Singapore Artillery, co-operated under the command of Captain Griffin, 1st Bengal Lancers. The detachment behaved most creditably, and General Von Hoepfner in his report stated that "Captain Griffin attacked the Boxers, who made an energetic resistance in the maize fields, several times with great valour. His horse was shot under him in a hand-to-hand combat." General Von Hoepfner adds that he has submitted Captain Griffin's name for a decoration.

(vi.) *Punitive Expedition to Pa-ta-Ch'u.*

This place is a group of temples in the low hills 14 miles west of Peking,† which temples have for many years been used as a summer resort by the members of the Corps Diplomatique at Peking, and near which were several prosperous mission stations as well as the new summer retreat of the British Minister. Since the troubles began Pa-ta-Ch'u has been a head centre of the Boxer movement, and the neighbouring foreign buildings have all been ruthlessly levelled to the ground. As a punishment for these acts and with a view to striking a blow at the Boxer movement a combined allied operation was decided on, the command being entrusted to Brigadier-General Wilson, United States Army.

The British Forces (as per margin ‡) were under the immediate command of Lieutenant-Colonel Tulloch, 26th Bombay Infantry, while Major-General Barrow accompanied General Wilson on my behalf.

The Anglo-American column marched to Liukochao on the afternoon of the 16th September, bivouacked there, and then, by a well-devised and successful night march, succeeded in gaining the south-west or rear of the enemy's position, while German and Japanese columns approached it from the east and north-west.

The resistance made was short and ineffective, and all the temples were occupied by the Anglo-American troops without a single casualty. Two Gatling guns were captured, and the Boxers who held the place were all dispersed or killed.

---

* *Vide* Sketch No. III (green line).
† *Vide* Sketch No. III (red line).
‡ 100 1st Bengal Lancers; 2 guns Royal Field Artillery; 2 Maxim guns; 89 Royal Welsh Fusiliers; 105 7th Bengal Infantry; 85 24th Punjab Infantry; 150 1st Sikh Infantry; 200 26th Bombay Infantry.

In the afternoon a small British detachment of sappers, cavalry, and infantry was sent to destroy the new arsenal at San-Chia-Tien This was most effectually carried out by Lieutenant Pearson, Royal Engineers, and on the following morning the bulk of the troops returned to Peking, a small British detachment only remaining, with a view to destroying the principal buildings as a punishment, these having been designated as the Boxer Head-Quarters by Imperial Edict.

(vii.) *Paotingfu Expedition.**

A punitive expedition to Paotingfu† having been decided on a combined converging force was despatched thither by Field-Marshal Count von Waldersee, one column operating from Tien-tsin under the command of Major-General Bailloud, of the French Army, and the other from Peking, under my orders. I was directed to assume command of the whole international force on the arrival of the two columns within striking distance of Paotingfu

Major-General Lorn Campbell commanded the British portion of the Tien-tsin column, and Major-General G. Richardson, C.B., C.I.E., the British portion of the force despatched from Peking.

The force from Peking commenced its march on the 12th October. The country was quiet, the inhabitants were friendly, and the Chinese regular troops retired before us in the direction of Paotingfu.

On the 15th October the force advanced unopposed to the left bank of the Pei-ho River near Ting-hsing. I there heard that about 2,000 French troops had occupied Paotingfu two days previously.

On the 17th the Peking column reached An-hsu and halted there one day. Here I received visits from certain Chinese officials of Paotingfu, and was informed that all Chinese troops had withdrawn from the neighbourhood.

---

* Details.—Tien-tsin Column :—1. French detachment : Major-General Bailloud ; Cavalry ; Artillery ; Pioneers ; three battalions Infantry. 2. German-Italian detachment : Major-General von Kettler ; Colonel Garioni ; one section Cavalry ; two battalions Artillery ; one battalion Bersaglieri ; one Pioneer detachment ; two battalions Infantry. 3. British detachment :—Major-General Lorn Campbell ; one company Australian Naval Brigade, with one 12-pr. Q.F. gun, and two machine guns ; six guns Royal Horse Artillery ; five troops Cavalry ; two Vickers-Maxim guns ; half No. 2 Company Bombay Sappers and Miners ; four companies Hong Kong Regiment ; six companies 20th Punjab Infantry ; two companies Madras Pioneers ; 200 Alwar Imperial Sikh Infantry.

Peking Column.— 1. French detachment : Colonel Laluban ; two battalions Marine Infantry. 2. German detachment : Colonel von Normann ; section Cavalry ; six guns ; two battalions Infantry. 3. Italian detachment : Colonel de Salza ; one battalion Infantry. 4. British detachment : Major-General G. Richardson, C.B., C.I.E. ; 16th Bengal Cavalry ; four guns 12th Battery Royal Field Artillery ; detachment Mounted Sappers ; half No. 3 Company Mounted Sappers and Miners ; 200 24th Punjab Infantry ; 200 1st Sikh Infantry ; 200 26th Bombay Infantry.

† *Vide* Sketch No. IV.

On the 18th General Bailloud, commanding the French troops, arrived, and arrangements were made for cantoning the troops on their arrival at Paotingfu, to which town the force marched on the 19th.

On the 20th the Allied Generals rode through the town and allotted certain districts to the troops of each Power.

The Tien-tsin troops operated in two columns, one viâ Du-liu and Wen-an-hsien, the other by the river, escorting supplies and hospital boats.

The walled town of Wen-an-hsien was reached by the former column on the 14th, and a small party of Chinese Imperial Cavalry was there captured, while on the 17th October, at Maochao, 200 Chinese Imperial Infantry surrendered to our troops. Both columns reached Paotingfu on the 21st, after passing through the very heart of a Boxer district, the people of which were threatening and hostile in manner, though no actual hostilities were attempted.

A reconnoitring party which was sent out from Paotingfu on the 23rd October to Kushan, 32 miles west of Paotingfu, having met with some opposition, a small force under Colonel Phayre, 3rd Bombay Cavalry, marched on the 24th to punish the village. The place was easily taken, and about 100 of the enemy were killed.

The immediate object of the expedition, namely, the release of certain Europeans and the punishment of the officials principally implicated having been attained, the British portions of the force were ordered to return to Tien-tsin and Peking.

The Tien-tsin column left Paotingfu on the 27th October under Major-General Lorn Campbell. Several Boxer villages were occupied on the return journey, and large quantities of arms and ammunition were captured, while nine Chinese war junks, with one gun each and 600 good mules, were also seized during the operations, which, in my opinion, were conducted by Major-General Lorn Campbell with skill and judgment, while Lieutenant-Colonel Retallick commanded the river column in a satisfactory manner.

On the 23rd October, at the request of Major-General von Gayl, Quartermaster-General Allied Forces, I despatched a force, consisting of German troops, with a few British cavalry and mounted sappers, to I-chou, under Colonel von Normann, to occupy that place, and to reconnoitre westward to the Great Wall, returning thence along the foot of the hills to Peking. This column, with small loss to itself, took the gate in the wall near Tsu-king-kuan, and killed about 100 Chinese regular troops out of 1,200.

The remainder of the German and Italian troops of the Peking force, under Colonel Garioni, left Paotingfu on the 28th October for Peking, viâ Yungchen and Huang-tsun, while the bulk of the British troops of the Peking force, under the command of Major-General Richardson, returned to Peking viâ Yung-chen and Lang-fang. The first-named town, where two English missionaries were murdered in June 1900, was severely punished, and throughout the march various Boxer centres were demolished, the objects of the movement being successfully carried out by Major-General Richardson.

I myself left Paotingfu on the 28th October, after handing over the command to General Bailloud, and reached Peking on the 1st November.

The expedition was practically bloodless, but nevertheless has, I believe, had a salutary effect in convincing the Chinese of the power of the Allies to move where they like, and of the uselessness of armed resistance.

8. I must now refer to those other portions of my command which have not been under my immediate direction. The 2nd Brigade commenced to arrive at Hong Kong on the 29th July, and on the 10th August proceeded to Woosung under orders from your Lordship. The ships conveying them began to arrive at Woosung on the 14th, but on the 16th the Brigade was ordered to proceed to Wei-hai-wei. They had hardly started, however, before they were recalled, and on the 18th August the troops began to disembark at Shanghai, at which city they have since been quartered.

I have nothing further to relate regarding this Brigade, except that I understand the demeanour, discipline, and appearance of the troops have been unexceptionable, and that Major-General Creagh has established the most cordial relations with our Allies.

9. I now turn to the 3rd Brigade, under Major-General Reid, C.B.

The 3rd Brigade arrived at Wei-hai-wei between the 20th and 22nd September, and remained there till summoned by Field-Marshal Count von Waldersee to occupy Shan-hai-kwan, where the troops were landed on the 3rd October.

On the 5th October two companies of infantry were sent to Ching-Wangtao, with a view to protecting what is intended to be the winter port for the Allies.

On the 16th October a column, consisting of detachments of the Allies, was despatched through Lanchow to Nikkoo under the orders of Major-General Reid, in order to disperse Boxers who were reported to be threatening the railway line. The British portion of the force (as per margin*) left Shan-hai-kwan on the 16th October by rail for Lanchow, and marched to Nikkoo on the 17th, where they bivouacked for the night. No opposition was met with, and on the 20th the force returned to Shan-hai-kwan.

Major-General Reid brings to notice the loyal support he received from the commanders of the various nationalities, and particularly mentions Captain Oznobishine, of the Russian Army, who performed the duties of Chief of the Staff, and Colonel Génêt, German Contigent.

---

* Two squadrons Jodhpur Lancers; 200 6th Jats; detachment 4th Punjab Infantry with Maxim gun.

On the 5th November, 180 rifles, 4th Punjab Infantry, co-operated with a Russian and French column from Tongshan to Tsun-hwa, which place was occupied on the 7th November without opposition. The force returned to Tongshan on the 11th November and to Shan-hai-kwan on the 12th. Our detachment was under the orders of Colonel Tomasheffski, of the Russian Army, to whom much credit is due for the cordial relations that existed.

Since then the troops have been busily employed in hutting themselves and preparing for the severe winter of Shan-hai-kwan. General Reid has had many difficulties to contend with, and that he has surmounted them is due to his tact and discretion.

10. It will complete this general narrative of the British operations in North China if I here make a few brief remarks regarding the medical and commissariat arrangements for this force.

The Medical Department have, I rejoice to say, not been severely tested by this campaign, and ample provision for contingencies was made by Government. The number of sick and wounded on the march to Peking was comparatively small, and the river afforded an easy and rapid means of transferring the sick from the front to the base, while at Tien-tsin and Wei-hai-wei suitable hospitals had been prepared for their reception. Credit for the good arrangements on the march are chiefly due to Lieutenant-Colonel W. J. R. Rainsford, Royal Army Medical Corps, and Major C. C. Manifold, Indian Medical Service.

11. As regards the Commissariat-Transport Department, I may say at once that, considering the difficulties of the first advance, the results were eminently satisfactory. The only land transport at first available was that afforded by the obligatory mules of regiments, but the foresight and energy of General Dorward and the naval authorities secured for the force a sufficient supply of boats to supplement the transport; while, thanks largely to the exertions of Commander G. H. Borrett, Royal Navy, Captain R. P. Lee, Royal Engineers, and Captain H. O. Parr, 7th Rajputs, to whom the organization of river transport was first entrusted, and thanks also to the energy of Captain D. R. Adye, 6th Infantry, Hyderabad contingent, who commanded the land transport, the British contingent was, from first to last, well supplied with food and necessaries, while the anxious and responsible duties of supply during the march up were admirably performed by Major F. W. B. Koe, Army Service Corps. Since the relief of Peking both supply and transport arrangements have been perfected. We have now a well-organised cart train, formed chiefly from captured mules and ponies, and our stocks of food and clothing are ample and good. For these gratifying results I am chiefly indebted to the organizing faculty which distinguishes Lieutenant-Colonel W. J. H. Bond, Indian Staff Corps, and to the energetic assistance afforded him by Captains R. E.

Vaughan and F. E. Geoghegan, Indian Staff Corps, of the Indian Commissariat Department.

12. I take this opportunity of making a few general observations regarding regiments and other units of this force. In my despatch of the 19th August I commented on the arduous nature of the march, and it is gratifying to think of the spirit and endurance which all ranks displayed. The Naval Brigade and other British units* behaved admirably, and I only regret they had so little opportunity for displaying their fighting qualities. The 1st Bengal Lancers did good service throughout the march by covering the advance ; these duties were the more important as the Allies as a whole were somewhat deficient in cavalry. The 7th Rajputs afforded me the most lively satisfaction. In marching powers they were second to none, while their spirit, discipline, appearance, and steadiness has been a credit to the Indian Army. I particularly mentioned these two corps, because the experience of this campaign tends to show that good Bengal regiments may be thoroughly relied on. The 1st Sikhs and 24th Punjab Infantry maintained their previous high reputation, while the small detachment† of the Hong Kong Regiment, whom I detailed as escort for the Artillery throughout the operations, exhibited great endurance in always keeping touch with the guns.

13. In an over-sea expedition like this much of the success of the operations must always be due to the exertions of the Royal Navy and Royal Indian Marine, and in addition to the officer named in paragraph 11, I desire to place on record the great assistance I have received in sea and river transport business from—

Captain P. F. Tillard, Royal Navy.
Commander J. B. Eustace, Royal Navy.
Commander E. F. A. Gaunt, Royal Navy.
Lieutenant A. G. Alston, Royal Navy.
Assistant Paymaster E. F. Murray, Royal Navy.
Gunner A. E. R. Brock, Royal Navy.
Commander F. H. Elderton, Royal Indian Marine.
Lieutenant S. D. Vale, Royal Indian Marine.
Lieutenant A. Rowand, Royal Indian Marine.
Lieutenant A. E. Harold, Royal Indian Marine.
Lieutenant E. J. Headlam, Royal Indian Marine.

In this connection I would also wish to notice Mr. Tamplin, master of the steamship "Eldorado," who was largely responsible for unloading transports at Taku

14. It is now my pleasing duty to bring to your Lordship's special notice those officers whose duties have been performed in such a manner as to call for my recognition.

---

* 12th Battery, Royal Field Artillery. Detachments :—25th Company Royal Engineers ; 2nd Battalion Royal Welsh Fusiliers ; Royal Marine Light Infantry.
† 100 rifles.

General Officers and Headquarters Staff.

Major-General E. G. Barrow, C.B., as Chief of the Staff, has throughout given me most valuable support and assistance. His high reputation as a Staff Officer is already well established, but I venture to bring his services most particularly to your Lordship's notice.

Major-General L. R. D. H. Campbell has carried out the important duties of General, lines of communication, thoroughly and satisfactorily. He is a zealous officer with untiring energy, whose services are worthy of recognition.

Major-General A. R. F. Dorward, C.B., D.S.O., was for some time in command at Tien-tsin, where he displayed much tact and judgment in dealing with difficult situations and gave me invaluable help in pushing on supplies, while at the same time clearing the country of gatherings of the enemy who were then threatening to interrupt our communications. His services throughout have been of a high order.

Major-General Sir Norman Stewart, Bart., had the good fortune to command the 1st Infantry Brigade on the advance to Peking, and I am indebted to him for his ready help on all occasions.

Major-General O'Moore Creagh, V.C., commanding 2nd Brigade at Shanghai, although not actively employed in the field, has fully maintained his reputation as a thoroughly good officer, while the fact of his presence at Shanghai, in a necessarily detached command, has been a great relief to me.

Major-General A. J. F. Reid, C.B., since the beginning of October has been employed at Shanhaikwan, where he has had many difficulties to contend with. He has proved himself thoroughly reliable as a commander.

Major-General J. T. Cummins, D.S.O., is an officer with a good record, who has commanded his brigade satisfactorily.

Major-General G. Richardson, C.B., C.I.E., commanding Cavalry Brigade, has twice commanded troops in the field with credit and has proved himself a good officer.

Sir W. Hillier, K.C.M.G., who was attached to my Staff as Political Adviser, has rendered invaluable services to this force. It is chiefly owing to his tact and great knowledge and experience of the country that our relations with the Chinese round Shanhaikwan have been so satisfactory.

Lieutenant-Colonel G. H. W. O'Sullivan, Royal Engineers, Assistant-Adjutant and Quartermaster-General, is an officer of wide experience. During the march to Paotingfu he was my Senior Staff Officer, and in dealing with officers of the Allied Forces showed much tact and judgment. I recommend him to your Lordship's notice for advancement.

Captain I. Philipps, Indian Staff Corps, Deputy-Assistant-Adjutant and Quartermaster-General, has had very hard work throughout, which he has performed with zeal and ability. He is a Staff Officer of much promise whose advance would be in the interests of the public service.

Colonel J. B. Bookey, Principal Medical Officer during the first part of the operations, is an experienced officer of long service whose advice was valuable, and who performed his duties to my satisfaction until he was unfortunately invalided.

Major (local Lieutenant-Colonel) G. K. Scott-Moncrieff, Royal Engineers, was Commanding Royal Engineer during the first part of the operations until relieved in October by Colonel W. T. Shone, C.B., D.S.O., Royal Engineers. He performed his duties with great credit.

Lieutenant S. G. Loch, Royal Engineers, in charge of Telegraph Section, has had considerable difficulties to overcome in completing telegraphic communication. He has not spared himself, and I have much pleasure in commenting favourably on his work.

Major (local Lieutenant-Colonel) W. J. H. Bond, Chief Commissariat Officer, has carried out his arduous duties in a most satisfactory manner, and I consider the force is much indebted to him for his care and forethought. I desire to bring his services especially to your notice.

Captain E. W. M. Norie, Deputy-Assistant Quartermaster-General for Intelligence, has carried out his duties with judgment and zeal, and has shown much ability in utilizing all sources of information. He was much aided in the march to Peking by Captain A. W. S. Wingate, Indian Staff Corps, whose previous knowledge of North China was of great value.

Captains C. H. Selwyn and G. de S. Barrow, Indian Staff Corps, Special Service Officers, have been employed since the occupation of Peking as police officers in charge of the portions of the city under British control. They have performed their duties with tact and discretion and fully maintained the British reputation for justice and good government.

Captain M. E. Willoughby, 2nd Bengal Lancers, as Special Service Officer on the Yangtse has shown special aptitude for Intelligence duties.

I would wish to bring to notice Captain B. T. Pell, the "Queen's" Regiment, my Aide-de-Camp, whom I consider to be an officer of considerable capacity; he rendered most valuable assistance on the advance to Peking, and, on the day we entered the city, carried out alone a reconnaissance which proved of great value.

I also beg to mention Lieutenant Commander (now Commander) Roger Keyes, Royal Navy, whose services were most useful to me as Orderly Officer; and the following officers of the Headquarters Staff, who, according to their opportunities, have done good service and proved themselves to be efficient and deserving officers:—

Captain G. C. Rigby, Superintendent Army Signalling.

Captain R. B. Low, D.S.O., Indian Staff Corps, Provost-Marshal.

Veterinary-Captain E. H. Hazelton, Senior Veterinary Officer, who has had onerous duties.

Captain C. H. C. Ryder, Royal Engineers, Survey of India Department.

Lieutenant R. A. Steel, Indian Staff Corps, my Aide-de-Camp, and Captain Boyce Kup, Tien-tsin Volunteers, Interpreter, who were most active and useful on the march to Peking.

15. In so large a force, and under circumstances which have not called for prolonged active operations in the field, it is difficult to discriminate; but although I am convinced that generally speaking all have done their best, still there are many officers whom I would particularly wish to bring to notice.

Cavalry Brigade.—Staff.

Major F. W. P. Angelo, Deputy-Assistant Adjutant-General.
Captain V. B. Fane, Deputy-Assistant Quartermaster-General.
Captain F. W. Hawks, Commissariat Department.
Lieutenant A. S. H. Teed, Assistant Brigade Commissariat and Transport Officer.

Royal Horse Artillery.

Major C. F. Blane, B Battery.

16th Bengal Lancers.

Colonel A. de V. Alexander.
Ressaidar and Wordie-Major Chanda Singh.

3rd Bombay Cavalry.

Major (temporary Lieut.-Colonel) A. Phayre.
Risaldar Kudrat Khan.

Royal Engineers.

Lieutenant E. Tylden-Patterson, Commanding detachment of Mounted Sappers.

1st Infantry Brigade.—Staff.

Captain T. Jermyn, Indian Staff Corps, Deputy-Assistant Adjutant-General, was most active during the march to Peking and afterwards as Senior Staff Officer in the Brigade.

Captain H. T. Brooking, Indian Staff Corps, Deputy-Assistant Quartermaster-General, is a very efficient Staff Officer, who looks well after the comfort and welfare of the troops.

Captain R. E. Vaughan, Indian Staff Corps, Brigade Commissariat and Transport Officer, has been invaluable in stocking Peking with supplies. He adapts himself to the circumstances and is full of resource. His services will, I hope, meet with recognition.

Captain D. R. Adye, Indian Staff Corps, is a very hard-working officer, whose management of the transport on the march to Peking, and ever since, calls for special commendation.

7th Rajputs.

Major H. B. Vaughan deserves credit for the fine work done by his fine regiment, which on all occasions has rendered excellent service. He was well supported by—

Captain A. H. Bingley, an exceptionally able officer.
Captain E. F. Hood.
Subadar-Major Gurdat Sing (since deceased).

26th Bombay Infantry.

Major (temporary Lieut.-Colonel) J. W. G. Tullooh is an officer of good capacity, whose regiment, although unfortunately not able to take part in the march to Peking, has since done good work.

Captain (temporary Major) G. H. Turner.
Lieutenant A. W. Chitty; and Lieutenant J. Macpherson.

The last-named has been specially brought to my notice for gallant conduct.

1st Sikhs.

Lieutenant-Colonel J. A. H. Pollock is an officer of high merit; his regiment, under his leading, distinguished itself at Yang-tsun and at the taking of Peking.

Captain and Brevet Major W. C. Barratt, D.S.O.
Captain H. A. Cooper.
Lieutenant W. F. Bainbridge.
Subadar-Major Hira Singh.

24th Punjab Infantry.

Lieutenant-Colonel J. G. Ramsay has proved himself a thoroughly good commanding officer, and under his command his regiment has done very good service. I would also mention—

Captain and Brevet Major S. H. Climo, D.S.O.
Captain G. J. Soady.
Lieutenant S. Morton.
Subadar-Major Yasin Khan.

2nd Infantry Brigade.

In the 2nd Infantry Brigade I desire to call special attention to the services of Captain J. M. Stewart, Indian Staff Corps, an officer of considerable experience on field service, who, as Senior Staff Officer of the Brigade, has been of great assistance to Major-General Creagh in his dealing with officers of the Allied Forces; also

Captain F. C. Rampini, Deputy-Assistant Commissary-General, who has satisfactorily performed his duties as Commissariat Officer.

3rd Infantry Brigade.

Lieutenant-Colonel O. C. Radford, Commanding 4th Punjab Infantry.
Lieutenant-Colonel J. B. Woon, 20th Punjab Infantry.

Captain H. Hudson, Deputy-Assistant Quartermaster-General.

Captain A. J. Shaw, 34th Pioneers.

Captain J. F. Barry, Indian Staff Corps, Brigade Commissariat Officer; also

Colonel His Highness the Maharaj Dhiraj Sir Pertab Singh, G.C.S.I., C.B., Commanding Jodhpur Lancers, and

Lieutenant Asaf Ali Khan, Commanding Maler Kotla Sappers, attached to 3rd Brigade.

4th Infantry Brigade.

Major (temporary Lieutenant-Colonel) H. D'U. Keary, D.S.O., Commanding 31st Madras Infantry.

Major F. C. Colomb, Deputy-Assistant Adjutant-General.

Major His Highness Maharaja Raj Rajeshwar Siromani Sri Ganga Sing Bahadur of Bikanir.

Divisional Troops.—Naval Brigade.

I have already brought the good services of the Naval Brigade to Admiral Sir E. H. Seymour's notice, and though many of them have already been rewarded, this despatch would not be complete if I did not here mention the names of—

Captain G. A. Callaghan, C.B., Royal Navy.

Major (now Lieutenant-Colonel) Ev. V. Luke, Royal Marine Light Infantry.

Royal Artillery.

Major G. F. W. St. John, Hong Kong and Singapore Artillery, was the Senior Artillery Officer in the force during the march to Peking. I would also mention—

Captain W. St. C. W. Bland; and

Second Lieutenant T. M. Wakefield.

Major F. E. Johnson, Commanding 12th Battery, Royal Field Artillery, did good service with his battery at Yangtsun and Peking.

The Royal Welsh Fusiliers.

As the only British Infantry corps with the force this regiment was invaluable to me. I understand they did good service at Tien-tsin before my arrival, and I am certainly much indebted to them for their services on the march to Peking. I trust Lieutenant-Colonel the Honourable R. H. Bertie's services will be recognised.

1st Bengal Lancers.

The services of Lieutenant-Colonel R. F. Gartside-Tipping deserve special mention; his regiment bore the brunt of the advance cavalry work on the march to Peking, and did good service at Yangtsun and in an affair with Tartar cavalry near Hoshiwu, as well as at the final capture of Peking. I trust

Lieutenant-Colonel Gartside-Tipping's services may be considered worthy of recognition.
Major (now Lieutenant-Colonel) C. H. Hayes.
Captain C. P. G. Griffin.
Captain A. P. Browne.
Lieutenant J. R. Gaussen.
Risaldar-Major Abdul Ghafur Khan.

1st Madras Pioneers.

This regiment was unfortunately too late to join in the march to Peking, but has done very good service at Tien-tsin and Paotingfu. Major (temporary Lieutenant-Colonel) E. C. W. Mackenzie-Kennedy is a capable and efficient officer. He did good work as Assistant Adjutant-General with the Tien-tsin column of the Paotingfu Force.

Sappers and Miners.

No 3 Company Madras Sappers and Miners, under Captain J. A. S. Tulloch, Royal Engineers, took part in the march to Paotingfu, and throughout have fully maintained their reputation.

No 2 Company Bombay Sappers and Miners, under Lieutenant G. H. Boileau, Royal Engineers, have done useful work at Tien-tsin.

No. 4 Company Bengal Sappers and Miners, under Captain H. R. Stockley, Royal Engineers, have been mainly employed on railway work, which has been satisfactorily carried out.

Hong Kong Regiment.

Major (local Lieutenant-Colonel) J. M. A. Retallick, Indian Staff Corps, did useful work on the Paotingfu Expedition, and Captain E. C. Rowcroft, Indian Staff Corps, was in command of a detachment of the regiment on the march to Peking, when the detachment did well.

Subadar-Major Sardar Khan also deserves recognition.

1st Chinese Regiment.

A detachment of the regiment was present on the march to Peking, and afterwards did well on the lines of communication. The services of Captain A. A. S. Barnes call for recognition.

Australian Naval Brigade.

The New South Wales and Victorian Naval contingents have been a great support to this force since the departure of the Royal Welsh Fusiliers. Their conduct and bearing has been admirable, and I bring to your Lordship's notice—

Captain A. Gillespie, Royal Navy.
Commander E. R. Connor, New South Wales contingent.
Commander F. Tickell, Victorian contingent.

Line of Communications.

The following officers on the line of communications in their various capacities have rendered good service :—

Major (temporary Lieutenant-Colonel) J. C. Swann, Assistant Adjutant-General, an experienced officer of much common sense, tactful, self-reliant, and resourceful, one whom I can confidently recommend for advancement.

Major (local Lieutenant-Colonel) H. Bower, Commanding 1st Chinese Regiment, and Captain (local Major) G. H. G. Mockler, Indian Staff Corps, have done excellent service in the civil administration of Tien-tsin, the one as a member of the Provisional Government, the other as Chief of Police.

Captain and Brevet Major T. E. Scott, D.S.O., 1st Sikhs, as Post Commandant at Tungchao, the most important point on the line of communications, and as a Road Commandant, has proved himself a capable Staff Officer.

Lieutenant L. M. R. Deas, Deputy-Assistant Commissary-General, was in charge of the advance Commissariat Depôt at Tungchao, a most responsible and difficult post, in which he acquitted himself well.

Major J. V. Jeffreys, Royal Engineers.

Captain M. R. E. Ray, Deputy-Assistant Adjutant-General, line of communications.

Captain Ross, Shanghai Volunteers, who did good service as Staff Officer to General Dorward during the Tien-tsin operations.

Captain the Honourable H. D. Napier, Indian Service Corps, Post Commandant at Sinho.

Captain F. G. Batten, 1st Madras Pioneers, Post Commandant at Hoshiwu.

Lieutenant C. L. Peart, Indian Staff Corps, Transport Officer.

Lieutenant W. L. O. Twiss, Indian Staff Corps, Water Transport Officer, Tungchao.

Base.

Major (temporary Lieut.-Colonel) W. H. Lowry, 28th Madras Infantry.

Major C. Penrose, Royal Engineers.

Captain G. H. G. Colomb, 1st 4th Gurkhas, Deputy-Assistant Adjutant-General.

Captain (temporary Major) W. S. Delamain, Commandant, Native Military Base Depôt.

Ordnance Department.

Captain M. S. C. Campbell, Royal Artillery.

Commissariat Transport Department.

In addition to those already named, I desire to mention the following :—

Major H. D. MacIntire, 8th Madras Infantry.

Major S. G. Radcliff, 33rd Madras Infantry.

Captain A. W. Cripps, Deputy-Assistant Commissary General.
Captain J. A. Douglas, 2nd Bengal Lancers.
Captain G. A. H. Beatty, 9th Bengal Lancers.

Medical Department.

In addition to the officers named in paragraphs 10 and 14, I would mention for their good services the following:—

Major J. M. Reid, Royal Army Medical Corps.
Major H. E. Cree, Royal Army Medical Corps.
Lieut.-Colonel E. M. Damla, Indian Medical Service.
Lieut.-Colonel L. A. Waddell, Indian Medical Service, who has shown himself to be a particularly good organizer.
Lieut.-Colonel D. B. Spencer, Indian Medical Service.
Lieut.-Colonel G. E. Fooks, Indian Medical Service.
Major W. W. White, Indian Medical Service.
Major H. F. Whitchurch, V.C., Indian Medical Service.
Captain W. H. Kenrick, Indian Medical Service.

I would further wish to here record the great value to this force of the hospital ship "Gwalior," which was so loyally and generously placed at the disposal of Her Majesty's troops in China by Colonel His Highness the Maharaja Sindhia of Gwalior, G.C.S.I.

16. I trust it will not be deemed out of place in this despatch if I venture to draw attention to the invaluable service rendered to this force by the loyal and zealous co-operation of the military authorities at Hong Kong. They have had an arduous, responsible, and thankless task in striving to ensure the success of this expedition, and none know better than myself how much the State is indebted to their self-denying co-operation. I trust the services of Major-General Gascoigne, C.M.G., will meet with their due recognition.

I would also call attention to those of Colonel N. P. O'Gorman, Deputy-Assistant Adjutant-General;

Lieutenant-Colonel J. L. A. Wheeler, Chief Ordnance Officer; and

Major M. M. Morris, Royal Garrison Artillery, Deputy-Assistant Adjutant-General.

17. I wish to take this opportunity of paying a tribute to some of the foreign officers with whom British troops have been associated. By the force of circumstances this contingent has been more in touch with the American and Japanese forces than with those of the other Powers, and in consequence of their close co-operation with us on their march to Peking, I have good reason for particularising these forces among our Allies. General Chaffee and General Baron Yamaguchi, who respectively commanded the United States forces and Imperial Japanese contingent, have been most loyal in all their relations with me, and I may say the same of General Wilson, United States forces, and General Fukushima, Chief of the Staff of

the Japanese contingent, while among the many officers with whom we have been closely associated, I desire to mention the following :—

    Colonel Dickman,
    Major Mills,
    Captain Grote Hutchieson,
    Major Waller, of the United States Marine,
        on the Staff of the United States contingent;

Colonel Negata, Colonel Shiba, Lieutenant-Colonel Harada, Major Yui, on the Staff of the Japanese contingent; while Colonel Aoki has done good work in the Allied cause as the Japanese member of their Tien-tsin Government. I must also express my thanks to another of the members, Colonel De Wogack of the Russian service.

In the Russian and French contingents Generals Linevich and Frey shared with us the hardships and hazards of the march to Peking. Other officers whom I would bring to notice are—

    General Wasiliewski, Chief of the Staff, Russian contingent, and
    Colonel Tamasheffski,
    Colonel Comte, 18th Regiment (French), and
    Colonel Rondoney; also
    Captain De Mandat Grancey of the French Navy.

On several occasions since the relief of Peking, and especially during the Paotingfu Expedition, we have also co-operated with the German, French, and Italian contingents, and I desire to particularly mention—

    General Von Hoepfner, General Baron Von Gayl, General Von Kettler, Colonel Von Normann, German Army;
    General Bailloud, Colonel Lullubin, Colonel Drude, French Army;
    Colonel Garioni, Colonel Salsa, Italian Army; with all of whom my relations have been most cordial.

18. Finally, I should like to mention that several warrant and non-commissioned officers, as well as native soldiers of all ranks, have been brought specially to my notice, but, in my opinion, the operations have, as regards these ranks, not been such as to call for the distinction of a "mention in despatches." I shall, however, take steps to bring their services to notice in the proper quarters, with a view to obtaining for them regimental or departmental promotion, as the case may be.

    I have, &c.
        ALFRED GASELEE, Lieutenant-General,
            Commanding British Contingent,
                China Field Force.

The Right Honourable
    the Secretary of State for India.

No. 241 S.

Head-Quarters, British Contingent,
China Field Force,
My Lord,   Peking, 20th February 1901.

In continuation of my despatch No. 198 S., of the 17th January 1901, and with reference to paragraph 17, I would wish also to bring to notice the following foreign officers who have latterly been more or less connected with the British contingent, and who in their respective positions have facilitated our operations in Northern China :—

Austro-Hungary :—Captain Sambochi, Imperial Navy.

France :—Lieutenant-General Voyron, Commanding French Expeditionary Corps.

Germany :—Major-General Von Schwarzhoff, Chief of the Staff to the Field-Marshal.

Colonel Gundell, Chief of the Staff, German Expeditionary Force.

Major Bauer, Railway Battalion.

United States, America :— Colonel Heistand, Assistant Adjutant-General.

Lieutenant Stamford, United States Signal Corps (Telegraph Section).

I have, &c.
ALFRED GASELEE, Lieutenant-General,
Commanding British Contingent,
China Field Force.

The Right Honourable
the Secretary of State for India.

No. 380 S.*

Head-Quarters Staff Office,
British Contingent, China Field Force,
My Lord,   July 6, 1901.

Now that I have received the orders of His Majesty's Government for the gradual reduction of the China Field Force, I submit, for your Lordship's information, what I presume will be my final despatch as the General Officer Commanding the China Field Force.

2. In my despatch No. 190 S., of the 17th January, I reviewed the events of last year, and brought to your Lordship's notice a number of officers whom I considered worthy of commendation. In this, my final despatch, it will therefore only be necessary to allude to what has since occurred, and to submit to your Lordship a further list of officers who have done good service during the present year.

---

* *London Gazette*, September 13, 1901.

3. Military operations during this phase have, as far as the British troops are concerned, been confined to the repression of brigandage, the only operations of any importance being the affair near Funing, in which the late Major Browning lost his life, vide my despatch No. 4227 of the 5th May, in which I specially brought to notice the officer commanding the column, Lieutenant-Colonel O. C. Radford, 4th Punjab Infantry.

4. The only other feature of the occupation worthy of note has been the transfer of the Peking-Shanhaikwan Railway from the Russian military authorities to German headquarters, and thence to the railway administration under the control of the British military authorities. I have fully described the history of this transfer in my despatch No. 205 S., dated 23rd January 1901, and my despatch No. 337 S., dated 8th April 1901, in which I dealt with the so-called Tien-tsin incident.

5. The troops have been mainly employed on detached duties, guarding the 250 miles of railway, and have performed these duties in a thoroughly satisfactory manner which reflects credit on all ranks.

6. I have now the honour to bring to your Lordship's notice the following officers who have not been mentioned in my previous despatches:—

Brigadier-General W. T. Shone, C.B., D.S.O., occupied the important position of Chief Engineer from 31st August 1900 to 25th February 1901, and rendered me valuable assistance therein.

Brigadier-General H. Pipon, C.B., Commanding Royal Artillery, an officer thoroughly versed in artillery questions, has been a useful adviser to me in all such matters.

Colonel J. McB. Davis, M.D., C.B., D.S.O., Indian Medical Service, Principal Medical Officer, has performed his duties to my satisfaction.

Major F. T. Williams, 26th Madras Infantry, Deputy-Assistant Quartermaster-General, 4th Infantry Brigade.

Captain J. A. Houison Craufurd, 7th Bombay Infantry, Deputy-Assistant Quartermaster-General, 2nd Infantry Brigade.

Captain A. Nicholls, 2nd Punjab Infantry, Deputy-Assistant Adjutant-General, 3rd Infantry Brigade.

Captain P. W. Drake Brockman, 5th Bengal Infantry, Deputy-Assistant Quartermaster-General, Line of Communications.

Major T. F. B. Renny-Tailyour, Royal Engineers, Survey of India.

Major A. L. M. Turner, Royal Artillery, Principal Ordnance Officer, has controlled the Ordnance efficiently.

Lieutenant-Colonel H. E. Passy, Indian Staff Corps, Field Controller.

Major H. E. F. Goold Adams, Royal Artillery, has been invaluable in his dealings with the Chinese in the Shanhaikwan district.

Major C. M. Ducat, 4th Bombay Cavalry, has done good service in a similar capacity under the Tien-tsin Provisional Government.

Lieutenant-Colonel J. R. L. Macdonald, C.B., Royal Engineers, has been a tower of strength as Director of Railways. I cannot too highly commend his energy, tact, and good sense in a difficult post. He has been ably supported in railway business by—

Major C. A. R. Browne, Royal Engineers.
Captain P. G. Twining, Royal Engineers.
Lieutenant H. E. C. Cowie, Royal Engineers.
Lieutenant H. D. Pearson, Royal Engineers.
Major F. V. Whittall, 1st Infantry, Hyderabad contingent.
Captain L. C. Dunsterville, 20th Punjab Infantry.
Captain H. C. Holman, 16th Bengal Lancers.
Lieutenant E. F. Orton, 26th Bombay Infantry.
Lieutenant C. G. W. Hunter, Royal Engineers.

I would also bring to your Lordship's favourable notice Messrs. C. W. Kinder, C.M.G., J. E. Foley, A. G. Cox, and D. R. Ricketts, of the Civil Staff of the Chinese Imperial Railways, but for whom it would have been difficult to have collected the Chinese employés, or, indeed, to have worked the railway at all.

Major W. A. Watson, 2nd Central India Horse, and Captain G. W. Johnson, 3rd Punjab Cavalry, have done good service as Provost-Marshals at Shanghai and Tien-tsin respectively.

The following officers have rendered good service in duties connected with the communications :—

Major St. G. L. Steele, 4th Bengal Lancers.
Captain J. L. Rose, 2nd Battalion 1st Gurkha Rifles.
Captain E. H. Cole, 11th Bengal Lancers.

I may also mention Captain E. L. C. Berger, Hong Kong Regiment, who has been most energetic and successful in the repression of brigandage.

Lieutenant-Colonel O. C. Radford, 4th Punjab Infantry, has commanded a punitive column with credit, and in connection with the operations of this column near Funing I would specially bring to your notice—

Captain C. G. Prendergast, 4th Punjab Infantry.
Lieutenant J. D. Stirling, 4th Punjab Infantry.
Lieutenant H. A. Williams, Indian Medical Service.
Colonel Pares, French Army.
Captain Inoya, Japanese Army.

The services of the following officers also appear to me deserving of mention :—

Brigadier-General F. T. N. Spratt-Bowring, Commanding Royal Engineers.
Major L. H. Reid, Indian Staff Corps, Deputy-Judge Advocate-General.
Major T. McCulloch, M.B., Royal Army Medical Corps, Secretary to the Principal Medical Officer.

Lieutenant-Colonel M. C. Cooke-Collis, Commanding 34th Pioneers.

Lieutenant-Colonel J. W. Hogge, C.I.E., Commanding 14th Sikhs.

Lieutenant-Colonel C. H. Westmoreland, Commanding 6th Jats.

Major J. C. Turner, 2nd Bengal Lancers, on special duty, Jodhpur Lancers.

Captain G. S. F. Napier, Oxfordshire Light Infantry, Special Service Officer.

Major J. E. Dickie, Royal Engineers.

Major A. R. Reynolds, Royal Engineers, Brigade Major, Royal Engineers.

Major A. B. C. Williams, Indian Staff Corps, Assistant Commissary-General.

Assistant-Commissary and Honorary Lieutenant J. Craig, Commissariat-Transport Department.

Assistant Commissary and Honorary Lieutenant A. Watt, Public Works Department, Engineer Field Park.

Deputy Assistant-Commissary and Honorary Lieutenant S. Durrell, Ordnance Department.

Subadar Jan Muhammad, Hong Kong Regiment.

Ressaldar Sher Khan, 1st Bengal Lancers.

Subadar Jag Singh, No. 4 Company Bengal Sappers and Miners.

Subadar Devasahayam, No. 3 Company "Q.O." Sappers and Miners.

Subadar Krishnaji Gaekwar, No. 2 Company Bombay Sappers and Miners.

Subadar Major Man Singh, Sardar Bahadur 14th Sikhs.

Jemadar Asa Singh, 24th Punjab Infantry.

Subadar Lakka Singh, 4th Punjab Infantry.

Jemadar Puran Singh, Ulwar Imperial Service Infantry.

Commandant Jas Singh, Jodhpore Lancers.

Rao Bahadur Thakur Dip Sing, Bikanir Infantry.

Sirdar Bahadur Natha Sing, Alwar Infantry.

Jemadar Jahandad Khan, 40th Pathans, who has been my orderly officer throughout, and has given me valuable help.

7. Owing to the special circumstances of this expedition, a great amount of correspondence, often of an exceptional nature, has devolved upon the Head-Quarters Office, and I desire to acknowledge the services rendered by the clerks, and their help on all occasions:—

I specially mention—
    Conductor C. E. Donaldson, and
    Sub-Conductor H. Watts.

8. The Postal Department has had many difficulties of a somewhat novel nature to contend with. These difficulties have latterly been successfully overcome, and credit is due on account thereof to Mr. W. T. Van Someren, C.I.E., Superintendent Post Offices, and his assistants.

I may mention here that our postal service has been conducted throughout in complete harmony with the Chinese Imperial Post Office.

9. Finally, I beg permission to bring to notice the following foreign officers who have rendered effective assistance in connection with railway communications :—

Captain Yamakushi, Japanese Army, Deputy Director British Railway Administration.

Captain Hornle, German Army, Deputy Director British Railway Administration.

Lieutenant Prestorius, German Army, Railway Staff Officer.
Lieutenant E. Pruneau, French Army, Railway Staff Officer.
Captain Bellecocq, French Army, Railway Staff Officer.
Major Gerhard,
Captain Krenzlin,
Both of the German Army, who did good work in rebuilding the Hanku railway bridge.

10. In concluding this despatch, I venture, once more, to assure your Lordship of the excellent discipline maintained in the force throughout a long period of trying inaction, in the face of many demoralizing conditions and some provocation. The Indian Army in China has not had great opportunities of adding to its laurels, but by its discipline, its fine soldierly appearance, and its thorough efficiency, I feel sure that its reputation has been largely enhanced in the eyes of our allies, while, at the same time, the loyal spirit and just pride of all ranks in themselves has been appreciably stimulated by their employment on a service of Imperial importance outside Indian limits.

I have, &c.,
ALFRED GASELEE, Lieutenant-General,
Commanding British Contingent,
China Field Force.

The Right Honourable
the Secretary of State for India.

Head-Quarters Staff Office,
China Field Force,
No. 385 S.　　　　　　　　　　　　　　　July 13, 1901.

To the Right Honourable the Secretary of State for India,
India Office, London.

MY LORD,

In continuation of my No. 380 S., dated 1st July 1900, I have the honour to bring to your Lordship's notice the services of Captain J. L. Coxhead, D.S.O., Royal Artillery, Brigade Major Royal Artillery, of whom Brigadier-General H. Pipon, C.B., reports most highly.

I have, &c.,
ALFRED GASELEE, Lieutenant-General,
Commanding British Contingent,
China Field Force.

War Office, July 24, 1901.*

The King has been graciously pleased to give orders for the following promotions in, and appointments to, the Most Honourable Order of the Bath, and the Most Distinguished Order of Saint Michael and Saint George, and for the following appointments to the Distinguished Service Order and promotions in the Army, in recognition of the services of the undermentioned officers during the recent operations in China. Except where otherwise stated these rewards will bear date of 29th November 1900 :—

To be Ordinary Members of the Military Division of the Second Class, or Knights Commanders of the Most Honourable Order of the Bath :—

Colonel Sir Claude Maxwell MacDonald, G.C.M.G., K.C.B. (Civil), Reserve of Officers.
Colonel Alexander John Forsyth Reid, C.B., Indian Staff Corps.
Colonel Edmund George Barrow, C.B., Indian Staff Corps.
Colonel Arthur Robert Ford Dorward, C.B., D.S.O.

To be Honorary Member of the Military Division of the Second Class, or Knights Commanders of the said Most Honourable Order :—

Colonel His Highness the Maharaja Dhiraj Sir Pertab Singh, G.C.S.I., C.B.

To be Ordinary Members of the Military Division of the Third Class, or Companions of the said Most Honourable Order :—

Major-General Sir Norman Robert Stewart, Bart., Indian Staff Corps.
Colonel James Turner Cummins, D.S.O., Indian Staff Corps.
Colonel Lorn Robert Henry Dick Campbell, Indian Staff Corps.
Colonel John Thomas Brownrigg Bookey, Indian Medical Service.
Lieutenant-Colonel Robert Francis Gartside-Tipping, Indian Staff Corps.
Lieutenant-Colonel the Honourable Reginald Henry Bertie, the Royal Welsh Fusiliers.
Major Wensly James Hodson Bond, Indian Staff Corps.
Major (now Lieutenant-Colonel) John George Ramsay, Indian Staff Corps.

To be an Ordinary Member of the Second Class or Knights Commanders of the Most Distinguished Order of Saint Michael and Saint George:—

Major-General William Julius Gascoigne, C.M.G.

---

* *London Gazette*, July 25, 1901.

To be Ordinary Members of the Third Class, or Companions of the said Most Distinguished Order :—

Commander Edward Richard Connor, New South Wales Naval contingent.
Commander F. Tickell, Victorian Naval contingent.

To be Companions of the Distinguished Service Order :—

Commander Ferdinand H. Elderton, Royal Indian Marine.
Major Frank Ernest Johnson, Royal Artillery.
Major George Edward Pereira, Grenadier Guards.
Captain Ivor Philipps, Indian Staff Corps.
Captain Cecil Pender Griffiths Griffin, Indian Staff Corps.
Captain Beauchamp Tyndall Pell, the Queen's (Royal West Surrey Regiment).
Captain Ernest Cave Rowcroft, Indian Staff Corps.
Captain Francis Gorden Poole, the East Yorkshire Regiment.
Lieutenant James Robert Gaussen, Indian Staff Corps.
Lieutenant William Frank Bainbridge, Indian Staff Corps.
Lieutenant Fulke James Walwyn, the Royal Welsh Fusiliers.

To be Major-General (Supernumerary) for Distinguished Service in the Field. Dated 3rd July 1900 :—

Colonel Sir Alfred Gaselee, K.C.B., Indian Staff Corps, Aide-de-Camp to the King.

To be Honorary and Extra Aide-de-Camp to the King :—

Colonel His Highness the Maharaja Sindhia of Gwalior, G.C.S.I.

BREVET.

To be Colonels :—

Lieutenant-Colonel G. H. W. O'Sullivan, Royal Engineers.
Lieutenant-Colonel J. B. Woon, Indian Staff Corps.
Lieutenant-Colonel J. A. H. Pollock, Indian Staff Corps.

To be Lieutenant-Colonels :—

Major (now Lieutenant-Colonel) J. R. Johnstone, Royal Marine Light Infantry.
Major J. C. Swann, Indian Staff Corps.
Major F. W. B. Koe, Army Service Corps.
Major H. Bower, Indian Staff Corps.
Major E. V. Luke, Royal Marine Light Infantry.
Major G. F. W. St. John, Royal Artillery.
Major J. W. G. Tulloch, Indian Staff Corps.
Major E. C. W. Mackenzie-Kennedy, Indian Staff Corps.
Major H. B. Vaughan, Indian Staff Corps.

To be Majors :—

Captain E. W. M. Norie, the Duke of Cambridge's Own (Middlesex Regiment).
Captain T. Jermyn, Indian Staff Corps.
Captain J. H. Gwynne, the Royal Welsh Fusiliers.
Captain R. P. Lee, Royal Engineers.

Captain A. J. Shaw, Indian Staff Corps.
Captain H. T. Brooking, Indian Staff Corps.
Captain the Honourable H. D. Napier, Indian Staff Corps.
Captain A. H. Bingley, Indian Staff Corps.
Captain R. E. Vaughan, Indian Staff Corps.
Captain E. Wray, Royal Marine Light Infantry.

Army Veterinary Department.

To be Veterinary-Major:—
Veterinary-Captain E. H. Hazelton.

Reserve of Officers.

Major Sir C. M. MacDonald, G.C.M.G., K.C.B., to be Colonel.

The King has further been pleased to approve of the grant of the Medal for Distinguished Conduct in the Field to the undermentioned:—

Royal Marine Light Infantry.

Sergeant T. Murphy.
Lance-Sergeant T. E. Preston.
Corporal F. Johnson.
Corporal D. J. Gowney.
Private T. A. Myers.

Royal Welsh Fusiliers.

Sergeant C. W. Taylor.
Private W. Crew.
Private Doodson.
Private Jackson.

Hong Kong-Singapore Battalion Royal Artillery.

Havildar Roshan Khan.

Chinese Regiment of Infantry.

Sergeant Gi-Dien-Kwee.

India Office, July 24, 1902.*

The King has been graciously pleased to approve and ordain the following Special Statute of the Most Eminent Order of the Indian Empire:—

EDWARD THE SEVENTH, by the Grace of God of the United Kingdom of Great Britain and Ireland King, Defender of the Faith, Emperor of India, and Sovereign of the Most Eminent Order of the Indian Empire: To all to whom these presents shall come; Greeting!

---

* *London Gazette*, July 25, 1901.

Whereas, by virtue of the power in Us vested under certain Letters Patent under the Great Seal of the United Kingdom of Great Britian and Ireland, bearing date respectively the second day of August, one thousand eight hundred and eighty-six, and the tenth day of June, one thousand eight hundred and ninety-seven, and in the Statutes of the Order made for the Government of the Most Eminent Order of the Indian Empire, We deem it expedient, without permanently increasing the number of the Ordinary Members of the Order, to provide for the admission into the First, Second, and Third Classes of the Order of such persons as have rendered to us special and important Services : We, therefore, in pursuance and in exercise of the power so vested in Us, do make, ordain, and establish by these presents, sealed with the seal of the said Order, the following Statute and Ordinances namely :—

It is ordained that the persons whom We may think fit to admit into the First, Second, and Third Classes of the said Most Eminent Order of the Indian Empire in consideration of their services rendered during the recent military operations in South Africa and China, shall be Additional Members of the said Classes, and shall not, now or hereafter, be included within the number of the Ordinary Members allotted to such Classes.

It is ordained that the Additional Members so to be appointed shall have rank and precedence among the Ordinary Members of their respective Classes, according to the dates of their respective appointments, and that the Statutes of Our said Order shall in all matters and things apply in the same manner to the said Additional Members as to the Ordinary Members of Our said Most Eminent Order, any statute, decree, or usage to the contrary notwithstanding.

And it is Our will and pleasure that this statute, sealed with the Seal of Our said Order, shall be taken and received as part and parcel of the Statutes thereof.

Given at Our Court at Saint James's, this twenty-second day of July, one thousand nine hundred and one, in the first year of Our reign.

By His Majesty's Command,
GEORGE HAMILTON.

The King has been graciously pleased to make the following appointments under the above Statute to the Most Eminent Order of the Indian Empire :—

FOR SERVICES IN CHINA.

To be a Knight Grand Commander.

Colonel Sir Alfred Gaselee, K.C.B., A.D.C.

To be a Knight Commander.

Major His Highness Maharaja Raj Rajeshwar Siromani, Sri Gunga Singh, Bahadur of Bikanir.

To be Companions.

Lieutenant-Colonel William John Read Rainsford, Royal Army Medical Corps.

Lieutenant-Colonel Oswald Claude Radford, Indian Staff Corps.

Lieutenant-Colonel George Kenneth Scott-Moncrieff, Royal Engineers.

Major John James Carl Watson, Royal Army Medical Corps.

Captain and Brevet Major Thomas Edwin Scott, D.S.O., Indian Staff Corps.

Lieutenant-Colonel Lawrence Augustine Waddell, Indian Medical Service.

Lieutenant Asaf Ali Khan, Maler Kotla Sappers.

Subadar Major Sardar Khan, Hong Kong Regiment.

Subadar Major Yasin Khan, 24th Bengal Infantry.

India Office, July 24, 1901.

The King has been graciously pleased to appoint Colonel George Lloyd Reilly Richardson, C.B., C.I.E., to be a Companion of the Most Exalted Order of the Star of India.

War Office, December 10, 1901.*

The King has been graciously pleased to give orders for the following appointment to the Most Honourable Order of the Bath, and for the following appointments to the Distinguished Service Order and promotions in the Army, in recognition of the services of the undermentioned officers during the operations in China.

These rewards to bear the date of 29th November 1900.

To be an Ordinary Member of the Military Division of the Third Class, or Companions of the Most Honourable Order of the Bath:—

Major and Brevet Colonel James Moncrieff Grierson, M.V.O., Royal Artillery.

To be Companions of the Distinguished Service Order:—

Captain Herbert Campbell Holman, Indian Staff Corps.
Lieutenant Stewart Gordon Loch, Royal Engineers.
Lieutenant Henry Edward Colvin Cowie, Royal Engineers.

° *London Gazette*, December 10, 1901.

Lieutenant James David Stirling, Indian Staff Corps.
Lieutenant James Macpherson, Indian Staff Corps.
Lieutenant Herbert Armstrong Williams, Indian Medical Service.

Brevet.

To be Colonel.

Major and Brevet Lieutenant-Colonel J. R. L. Macdonald, C.I.E., Royal Engineers.

To be Lieutenant-Colonels.

Major A. L. M. Turner, Royal Artillery.
Major F. W. P. Angelo, Indian Staff Corps.
Major A. Phayre, Indian Staff Corps.
Major F. B. T. Renny-Tailyour, Royal Engineers.

To be Majors.

Captain W. M. Watson, the Duke of Wellington's (West Riding Regiment).
Captain (now Major) J. M. Stewart, Indian Staff Corps.
Captain (now Major) H. Hudson, Indian Staff Corps.
Captain R. B. Low, D.S.O., Indian Staff Corps.
Captain G. H. G. Mockler, Indian Staff Corps.
Captain D. R. Adye, Indian Staff Corps.

Indian Medical Service.

Major C. C. Manifold, Indian Medical Service, to be Lieutenant-Colonel.

Memorandum.

Services Worthy of Mention.

Captain W. H. Dent, the Durham Light Infantry.
Superintending Clerk G. J. Butler, Royal Engineers.

The King has also been graciously pleased to confer the decoration of the Royal Red Cross upon the undermentioned Nursing Sisters in recognition of their services to the sick and wounded during the operations in China :—

Miss Agnes Mary Waterhouse.
Miss Marian Jeannette Hislop.

The King has further been pleased to approve of the grant of the Medal for Distinguished Conduct in the Field to the undermentioned non-commissioned officers, in recognition of their gallant conduct during the operations in China:—

9269 Colour-Sergeant R. Ruxdon, Coldstream Guards.

396 Quartermaster-Sergeant E. Brooke, the Duke of Wellington's (West Riding Regiment).

Both attached to the Chinese Regiment of Infantry.

CHINA MEDAL, 1900.*

Admiralty, 1st January 1902.

His Majesty the King has been graciously pleased to confirm the authority given by Her late Majesty Queen Victoria to the Lords Commissioners of the Admiralty for the issue of a Medal to commemorate the Naval and Military operations in North China in 1900.

II. The Medal will be granted to all officers, warrant officers, petty and non-commissioned officers and men of the British, Indian, and Colonial Naval and Military Forces, who were employed in North China, and in the Yangtse Valley from 10th June 1900 to 31st December 1900, and to all who embarked in India for service in China in the expedition under the command of General Sir A. Gaselee.

III. The Medal will be similar in pattern to the silver medal granted for the China Wars of 1842 and 1860; except that the obverse of the Medal will bear the same effigy of Her late Majesty as appears on the South African Medal, with the legend "Victoria Regina et Imperatrix."

IV. His Majesty has further approved clasps being issued as follows :—

1. A clasp inscribed "*Taku Forts*" to all those who were engaged in the Peiho River, on 17th June 1900, in the operations which resulted in the capture of the Taku Forts.

2. A clasp inscribed "*Defence of Legations*" to all who took part in the defence of the Legations in Peking, between 10th June and 14th August 1900, both dates inclusive.

3. A clasp inscribed "*Relief of Peking*" to all those engaged in the operations on shore at or beyond Taku for the relief of Peking, between 10th June and 14th August 1900, both dates inclusive.

The Medal will be issued by the Accountant-General of the Navy to all officers and men of the Royal Navy, and Royal Marines, and Colonial Naval Forces who are entitled to it.

The cases of officers and men of the Imperial Military Forces will be dealt with by the War Office in concert with the Indian and Colonial Governments.

---

* *London Gazette*, January 3, 1902.

APPENDIX B.

Amalgamated Scheme for the Despatch of an Expeditionary Force to China, as Finally Approved by the Government of India.

PART I.—TROOPS.

1. At the request of the Imperial Government, a Force of all Arms, to be entitled "The China Expeditionary Force," as detailed below, will be mobilised at once and despatched to China :—

2. *Composition of the Force—*

Cavalry Brigade—
 "B" Battery, Royal Horse Artillery.
 R-2 Ammunition Column Unit.
 1st Bengal Lancers.
 3rd Bombay Cavalry.
 16th Bengal Lancers.
 Section A, No. 22 British Field Hospital.
 Section C, No. 62 Native Field Hospital.
 Sections A and B, No. 57 Native Field Hospital.
 No. 1 Brigade Supply Column.

1st Infantry Brigade—
 7th Bengal Infantry.
 26th Bombay Infantry.
 1st Sikh Infantry.
 24th Punjab Infantry.
 No. 39 Native Field Hospital.
 No. 43 Native Field Hospital.
 No. 2 Brigade Supply Column.

2nd Infantry Brigade—
 2nd Bengal Infantry.
 14th Sikhs.
 1-4th Gurkha Rifles.
 30th Bombay Infantry.
 No. 63 Native Field Hospital.
 No. 66 Native Field Hospital.
 No. 3 Brigade Supply Column.

3rd Infantry Brigade—
  6th Bengal Infantry.
  4th Punjab Infantry.
  20th Punjab Infantry.
  34th Pioneers.
  No. 51 Native Field Hospital.
  No. 61 Native Field Hospital.
  No. 5 Brigade Supply Column.

4th Infantry Brigade—
  28th Madras Infantry.
  31st Madras Infantry (6th Burma Battalion).
  Alwar Infantry (Imperial Service Troops).
  Bikaner Infantry (Imperial Service Troops).
  No. 53 Native Field Hospital.
  No. 58 Native Field Hospital.
  No. 6 Brigade Supply Column.

Divisional Troops—
  12th Battery, Royal Field Artillery.
  R-7 Ammunition Column Unit.
  1st Regiment of Sardar Ressala Jodhpur Lancers (Imperial Service Troops).
  1st Madras Pioneers.
  Mounted Detachment, Bengal Sappers and Miners.
  No. 4 Company, Bengal Sappers and Miners.
  No. 3 Company, Madras Sappers and Miners.
  No. 2 Company, Bombay Sappers and Miners.
  The Maler Kotla Sappers (Imperial Service Troops).
  1 Photo-Litho Section, Bombay Sappers and Miners.
  1 Photo-Litho Section, Madras Sappers and Miners.
  1 Printing Section, Bombay Sappers and Miners.
  1 Printing Section, Madras Sappers and Miners.
  10 Special Signalling Units (British Infantry).
  2 Special Signalling Units (Native Infantry).
  Section B, No. 22 British Field Hospital.
  Section D, No. 62 Native Field Hospital.
  No. 42 Native Field Hospital.
  No. 4 Brigade Supply Column.

Line of Communication Troops—
  22nd Bombay Infantry. ⎫
  3rd Madras Infantry. ⎬ Garrison troops at Hongkong.
  5th Infantry, Hyderabad Contingent. ⎭
  1 Telegraph Section, Madras Sappers and Miners.
  1 Telegraph Section, Bengal Sappers and Miners.
  1 Railway Section.
  1 Ordnance Field Park.
  2 Engineer Field Parks.
  Sections A and B, No. 15 British Field Hospital.
  Sections A and B, No. 16 British Field Hospital.

351

No. 47 Native Field Hospital.
Sections C and D, No. 69 Native Field Hospital.
Sections A and B, No. 38 Native Field Hospital. ⎫
No. 41 Native Field Hospital ⎬ For sick and wounded returning from the field.
Sections C and D, No. 57 Native Field Hospital. ⎭

Section B, No. 5 Field Veterinary Hospital.
Nos. 3 and 4 Field Medical Store Depôt.
1 Base Depôt of Medical Stores in Hongkong.
1 Base Veterinary Store Depôt.
1 British General Hospital in which Sections A and B, No. 25 British Field Hospital will be merged.
3 Native General Hospitals (500 beds each).
1 Native General Hospital (do.).
1 Native Military Base Depôt.
2 Base Supply Depôts.
1 Base Stationery Depôt.

3. (a.) *Staff of the Force*—

Commanding (with temporary rank of Major-General and local rank of Lieutenant-General.	Brigadier-General Sir A. Gaselee, A.D.C., K.C.B., I.S.C.
Aide-de-Camp - - -	Captain B. T. Pell, the Queen's (Royal West Surrey) Regiment.
Aide-de-Camp - - -	Lieutenant R. A. Steel, 17th Bengal Cavalry.
Deputy Adjutant-General (with the local rank of Major-General).	Brigadier-General E. G. Barrow, C.B., I.S.C.
Assistant Adjutant and Quarter-Master-General -	Lieut.-Colonel G. H. W. O'Sullivan, R.E.
Deputy Assistant Adjutant and Quarter - Master General.	Captain I. Philipps, 5th Gurkha Rifles.
Marine Transport Officer -	Commander F. H. Elderton, Royal Indian Marine.
Assistant Marine Transport Officers.	Lieutenant S. D. Vale, Royal Indian Marine. Lieutenant A. Rowand, Royal Indian Marine. Lieutenant A. A. Harold, Royal Indian Marine. Lieutenant E. Stocken, Royal Indian Marine. Lieutenant E. T. Headlam, Royal Indian Marine.

Deputy Assistant Quarter-Master-General for Intelligence.	Captain E. W. M. Norie, Middlesex Regiment.
Field Intelligence Officer	Captain MacC. R. E. Ray, 7th (D.C.O.) Bengal Infantry.
Colonel on the Staff, Royal Artillery.	Brigadier-General H. Pipon, C.B., R.A.
Brigade-Major, Royal Artillery.	Captain T. L. Coxhead, D.S.O., R.A.
Orderly Officer, Royal Artillery.	From officers sent with siege train bullocks. (*See* Part II., B.).
Colonel on the Staff, Royal Engineers.	Colonel W. T. Shone, C.B., D.S.O., R.E.
Brigade-Major, Royal Engineers.	Major J. G. Day, R.E.
Chief Ballooning Officer	Major and Brevet Lieut.-Colonel J. R. L. Macdonald, R.E.
Principal Medical Officer	Colonel J. T. B. Bookey, V.H.S., I.M.S.
Field Engineers	Major J. E. Dickie, R.E. Major F. V. Jeffreys, R.E. Captain A. R. Reynolds, R.E. Captain A. F. Cumberlege, R.E.
Assistant Field Engineers	Lieutenant H. E. C. Cowie, R.E. (for Railways). Lieutenant F. W. Brunner, R.E. (for Telegraphs). Lieutenant S. G. Loch, R.E. (for Telegraphs). Lieutenant A. Rolland, R.E.
Superintendent, Army Signalling.	Captain G. C. Rigby, 1st Battalion, Wiltshire Regiment.
Provost Marshal	Captain R. B. Low, D.S.O., 9th Bengal Lancers.
Principal Ordnance Officer	Major A. L. M. Turner, R.A.
Field Paymaster	Captain C. N. Baker, Military Accounts Department.
Staff Surgeon	To be detailed from the Force.
Chief Survey Officer	Major T. F. B. Renny-Tailyour, R.E.
Survey Officer	Captain C. H. D. Ryder, R.E.
Chief Commissariat and Transport Officer.	Major W. J. Bond, Assistant Commissary-General.
Assistant to ditto	Lieutenant H. N. Young, Deputy Assistant Commissary-General.

Divisional Transport Officer	Major F. C. W. Rideout, Assistant Commissary-General.
Assistant to ditto	Major H. D. McIntyre, 8th Madras Infantry.
Commissariat and Transport Officer for Divisional Troops.	Lieutenant L. M. R. Deas, Deputy Assistant Commissary-General.
Assistant to ditto	Lieutenant R. M. Hall, 13th Bengal Lancers.
Senior Veterinary Officer and Veterinary Inspector.	Veterinary Captain E. H. Hazelton, A.V.D.

(*b.*) *Cavalry Brigade Staff*—

Commanding with local rank of Major-General.	Colonel G. L. R. Richardson, C.B., C.I.E., I.S.C.
Orderly Officer	Captain S. B. Grimston, 18th Bengal Lancers.
Deputy Assistant Adjutant-General.	Major F. W. P. Angelo, 9th Bengal Lancers.
Deputy Assistant Quarter-Master-General.	Captain V. B. Fane, 1st Punjab Cavalry.
Brigade Signalling Officer	Lieutenant C. A. F. Hocken, 5th Bombay Cavalry.
Staff Surgeon	To be detailed from the Brigade.
Veterinary Officer	Veterinary Lieutenant H. J. Axe, A.V.D.
Brigade Commissariat and Transport Officer.	Lieutenant F. W. Hawks, Deputy Assistant Commissary-General.
Assistant to ditto	Lieutenant A. S. H. Teed, 14th Bengal Lancers.

(*c.*) 1*st Infantry Brigade Staff*—

General Officer Commanding with local rank of Major-General.	Brigadier-General Sir Norman R. Stewart, Bart., I.S.C.
Orderly Officer	Major A. W. Leonard, 5th Infantry, Hyderabad Contingent.
Deputy Assistant Adjutant-General.	Captain T. Jermyn, 2nd Sikh Infantry.
Deputy Assistant Quarter-Master-General.	Captain H. T. Brooking, 21st Madras Pioneers.
Brigade Signalling Officer	Lieutenant C. R. Scott-Elliot, 4th Madras Pioneers.

354

Brigade Commissariat and Transport Officer.	Captain R. E. Vaughan, Assistant Commissary General.
Assistant to ditto	Captain D. R. Adye, 6th Infantry, Hyderabad Contingent.

(d.) 2nd Infantry Brigade Staff—

General Officer Commanding with local rank of Major-General.	Brigadier-General O'M. Creagh, V.C., I.S.C.
Orderly Officer	Major W. A. Watson, 2nd Central India Horse.
Deputy Assistant Adjutant-General.	Captain J. M. Stewart, 2–5th Gurkhas.
Deputy Assistant Quarter-Master General.	Captain J. A. Houison-Craufurd 7th Bombay Infantry.
Brigade Signalling Officer	Captain J. Gaisford, 25th Punjab Infantry.
Brigade Commissariat and Transport Officer.	Captain F. C. Rampini, Deputy Assistant Commissary General.
Assistant to ditto	Lieutenant M. R. W. Nightingale, 2–5th Gurkhas.

(e.) 3rd Infantry Brigade Staff—

General Officer Commanding with local rank of Major-General.	Brigadier General A. J. F. Reid, C.B., I.S.C.
Orderly Officer	Captain J. S. Kemball, 29th Punjab Infantry.
Deputy Assistant Adjutant-General.	Captain A. Nicholls, 2nd Punjab Infantry.
Deputy Assistant Quarter-Master General.	Captain H. Hudson, 19th Bengal Lancers.
Brigade Signalling Officer	Captain H. W. Cruddas, 38th Dogras.
Brigade Commissariat and Transport Officer.	Captain J. F. Barry, Assistant Commissary General.
Assistant to ditto	Captain P. H. Cunningham, 1st Bombay Grenadiers.

(f.) 4th Infantry Brigade Staff—

General Officer Commanding with local rank of Major-General.	Brigadier-General J. T. Cummins, D.S.O., I.S.C.

Orderly Officer	Captain C.T. Swan, 4th Madras Pioneers.
Deputy Assistant Adjutant General.	Captain F. C. Colomb, 42nd Gurkha Rifles.
Deputy Assistant Quarter-Master General.	Captain F. T. Williams, 26th Madras Infantry.
Deputy Assistant Adjutant General for Imperial Service Troops.	Captain H. D. Watson, 2-2nd Gurkha Rifles
Brigade Signalling Officer -	Captain W. R. Walker, 15th Madras Infantry.
Brigade Commissariat and Transport Officer.	Captain F. W. Forteath, Deputy Assistant Commissary General.
Assistant to ditto - -	Lieutenant O. C. S. Watson, 2nd Battalion, Yorkshire Regiment.

(*g.*) *Line of Communications and Base Staff*—

Base Commandant and in charge of Line of Communications with local rank of Major-General.	Colonel L. R. H. D. Campbell, I.S.C.
Deputy Assistant Adjutant and Quarter Master-General, Base and Communications.	Lieutenant-Colonel J. C. Swann, 1st Bombay Grenadiers.
Commanding Royal Engineers with local rank of Lieutenant-Colonel.	Major G. K. Scott-Moncrieff, R.E.
Adjutant, Royal Enginners -	Captain R. E. Picton, R.E.
Principal Medical Officer, Line of Communications, with temporary rank of Colonel.	Lieutenant-Colonel H. F. P. F. Esmonde-White, I.M.S.
Principal Medical Officer, Shanghai.	Lieutenant - Colonel P. F. O'Connor, I.M.S.
Commandant, Native Military Base Depôt.	Major W. S. Delmain, 23rd Bombay Rifles.
Adjutant, Native Military Base Depôt.	Lieutenant E. C. Creagh, 4th Punjab Infantry.
Base Ordnance Officer - -	Captain M. S. C. Campbell, R.A.
In charge, Veterinary Store Depôt.	Veterinary Lieutenant W. R. Wright, A.V.D.

Base Commissariat and Transport Officers.	Captain A. W. Cripps, Assistant Commissary General. Captain A. B. C. Williams, Assistant Commissary General. Captain E. R. Howell, Deputy Assistant Commissary General.
Assistant to ditto -	Captain F. E. Geoghegan, Deputy Assistant Commissary General. Lieutenant W. St. G. Chamier, Deputy Assistant Commissary General. Lieutenant E. A. Swinhoe, Deputy Assistant Commissary General. Lieutenant H. M. Turton, Deputy Assistant Commissary General.
Field Controller -	Lieutenant Colonel H. E. Passy, I.S.C.
Assistant Field Controller -	Captain W. A. Bruce, I.S.C.
Senior Transport Officer for Chinese Transport.	Major S. G. Radcliff, 33rd Madras Infantry.
Transport Officers for Chinese Transport.	Captain J. A. Douglas, 2nd Bengal Lancers. Captain E. A. W. Stotherd, 4th Lancers, Hyderabad Contingent. Lieutenant W. L. O. Twiss, 25th Madras Infantry. Lieutenant C. L. Peart, 4th Sikh Infantry. Lieutenant G. H. Potts, Hong-kong Volunteer Corps.

(*h.*) *Special Service Officers*—

  (*i.*) Captain G. H. G. Mockler, 30th Madras Infantry.
  Captain the Honourable H. D. Napier, 1st Central India Horse.
  Captain G. de S. Barrow, 4th Bengal Cavalry.
  Major T. P. England, Royal Fusiliers.
  Captain J. W. Orchard, 15th Madras Infantry.
  Captain A. R. Dick, 2nd Punjab Cavalry.
  Captain H. Tweddell, 4th Bengal Infantry.

Brevet Lieutenant-Colonel E. F. H. McSwiney
Major H. E. F. Goold Adams, Royal Artillery
Captain W. D. McSwiney, 7th Dragoon Guards
Captain E. C. Pottinger, Royal Artillery
Captain W. A. Harrison, Royal Engineers
Captain C. M. Ducat, 4th Bombay Cavalry
Lieutenant C. G. W. Hunter, Royal Engineers.
} Detailed by the Imperial Government.

(*ii.*) For duty at Treaty Ports under the orders of the General Officer Commanding the Force, with the pay and status of Deputy Assistant Adjutant Generals:—

Major N. W. H. du Boulay, Royal Garrison Artillery.
Captain C. H. Selwyn, 12th Bengal Cavalry.
Captain G. S. F. Napier, 2nd Battalion, Oxfordshire Light Infantry.
Captain M. E. Willoughby, 2nd Bengal Lancers.
Captain F. Tweddell, 28th Punjab Infantry.
Captain H. R. Davies, 2nd Battalion, Oxfordshire Light Infantry.
Captain E. H. Cole, 11th Bengal Lancers.
Captain F. Rennick, 40th Pathans.

(*iii.*) For duty with Imperial Service Troops:—

Major J. G. Turner, 2nd Bengal Lancers
Major H. V. Cox, 21st Madras Infantry
} With pay and status as Deputy Assistant Adjutant Generals.

Captain E. M. Hughes, 14th Bengal Lancers.
Captain C. M. Crawford, 2-5th Gurkha Rifles.
Captain W. L. Conran, 25th Bombay Infantry.
Captain C. W. Tribe, 38th Dogras
Lieutenant W. A. Stokes, Royal Engineers.
} With status as staff Captains and staff pay at Rs. 300 per mensem.

(Those of the above-named officers who are now employed with Imperial Service Troops will, in addition to the rates given, draw any additional pay admissible under Article 70·(*e*), Army Regulations, India, Volume I., Part I., but no other allowances are admissible.)

4. *Strength, Establishments, Baggage, and Tentage.*—(*a.*) The units mentioned in paragraph 2 except Bikaner Infantry and Mounted Detachment of Bengal Sappers and Miners will

proceed at field service strength and scale of establishments, and field service scale of tentage. The Bikaner Infantry will proceed on a strength of 400, with establishment and tentage in proportion. Cavalry regiments will take their pay establishments with them.

For scales of baggage see Part III., General Regulations, paragraph 29.

(*b.*) The Native Cavalry Regiments will be provided with a complement of 11 British Combatant Officers and 1 Medical Officer; and a Native Infantry and Pioneer Battalions with 12 British Combatant Officers and 1 Medical Officer.

(This does not apply to Imperial Service Troops.)

(*c.*) The following will be the establishment of the Mounted Detachment, Royal Engineers:—

      1 Subaltern Officer, Royal Engineers.
      1 Sergeant, Royal Engineers.
      1 Hospital Assistant.
      1 Havildar ⎫
      1 Naick ⎬ Bengal Sappers and Miners.
      1 Lance-Naick ⎪
    20 Sappers ⎭
      1 Nalband (drawn from a Native Cavalry Regiment).
    12 Syces.
      1 Cook (for Sergeant, Royal Engineers).
      1 Langri.
      2 Bhistis.
      1 Sweeper.
      6 Dooly bearers.
    20 Riding horses.
      4 Pack horses.

The Sappers will include at least four good carpenters and two smiths.

The horses will be small walers or other steady horses and will be taken over, together with their saddlery and line-gear, from Native Cavalry, compensation being paid as in case of Native Cavalry horses sent to South Africa.

5. *Depôts.*—(*a.*) Depôts for units of the Regular Army will be formed as prescribed in the Field Service Equipment Tables. Native Infantry Depôts will be on Scale B.

(*b.*) Depôts for Imperial Service Troops will be arranged for by the Inspector General, Imperial Service Troops.

6. *Movements in relief.*—Relief movements will be carried out by river, road, and rail on relief scale, but without families, as soon as possible under the orders of the Lieutenant-Generals Commanding the Forces concerned. All units in possession of mobilisation equipment, except those specified, will take it with them to their new stations.

7. *Supply Batteries.*—" D " Battery, Royal Horse Artillery, Umballa, will be the supplying battery of " B " Battery, Royal Horse Artillery; and the 57th Battery, Royal Field Artillery, Meean Meer, will be the supplying battery of the 12th Battery, Royal Field Artillery.

8. *Equipment.*—(*a.*) All units will be equipped on the Field Service scale as laid down in the Field Service Regulations except as modified in paragraph 9.

(*b.*) Corps in possession of mobilisation equipment will take it with them. Other units will receive equipment as detailed hereafter.

(*c.*) The Imperial Service Troops will be equipped under the orders of the Inspector General, Imperial Service Troops.

(*d.*) The equipment for the Mounted Detachment, Royal Engineers, will be made up at Roorkee under the direction of the Commandant, Bengal Sappers and Miners, with a special view to rafting the saddlery and equipment and men of the Cavalry Brigade across streams.

Each mounted man (3 non-commissioned officers and 16 men) will carry light equipment of tools, &c., slung on his saddle.

Four pack horses, led by spare sappers under ordinary conditions of marching and by mounted men for **rapid** advances, will carry the bulk of the equipment.

Details of equipment will be left to the Commandant, Bengal Sappers and Miners, but will include—

    (*i.*) Felling axes, pickaxes and shovels with spare helves.
    (*ii.*) Hammers and spikes.
    (*iii.*) Guncotton, fuze primers, detonators.
    (*iv.*) Collapsible boat.
    (*v.*) Carpenters' and smiths' tools.
    (*vi.*) Steel wire, cable, and travellers.

(*e.*) " B " Battery Royal Horse Artillery, will exchange its 12-lbr. guns, carriages, limbers and wagons for 15-lbr. equipment, and will obtain a spare gun carriage of the same pattern, from some convenient station, under the orders of the Lieutenant-General Commanding the Forces, Bengal.

(*f.*) R-2 and R-7 ammunition column units will be equipped with pole and draught wagons and harness.

9. *Ordnance.*—(*a.*) All units not already in possession of them will be armed with ·303 rifles (or carbines) and be equipped with the necessary proportion of component parts, bayonets, bayonet frogs, appurtenances and ammunition.

(*b.*) Five additional spare vents per gun will be taken by the Ordnance Field Park for each battery of artillery.

(*c*.)—(1.) The following scale of small arm (·303) ammunition will be provided :—

	On Soldier.	1st Regimental Reserve.	2nd Regimental Reserve	Ordnance Reserve.	Total number of rounds per man.
Artillery, per carbine	20	—	—	—	20
Regiment of Native and Imperial Service Cavalry.	50	100	—	250	400
Battalion of Native and Imperial Service Infantry.	100	80	120	450	750
Battalion of Pioneers	60	120	120	450	750
Company of Regular and Imperial Service Sappers and Miners.	50	100	—	250	400
Mounted Detachment, Royal Engineers.	50	—	—	—	50

In addition to above scale, small-arm ammunition, at the rate of 50 rounds per rifle or carbine, will be furnished to all units for practice on voyage.

·303, Mark II, ammunition only will be taken.

(2.) 750 rounds of artillery ammunition per gun will be taken. This will include the usual proportion of case shot, or 4,500 rounds per battery in all, including ammunition in battery and ammunition column charge, and Ordnance reserve.

(*d*.) The Ordnance Field Park stores on the scale fixed for a division will be drawn from the Allahabad arsenal, supplemented as necessary from all four commands. The *personnel* will also be drawn from Madras and Bengal commands.

(*e*.) In addition to the signalling epuipment with corps units and with the special signalling units referred to in paragraph 13, 6 spare sets of signalling equipment complete, and 6 C. C. Lamps will be shipped by the Ordnance Department, who will also make over to the Superintendent, Army Signalling of the Force, 6 cavalry pattern heliographs.

(*f*.) The Enfield revolvers now in possession of Imperial Service Troops will be exchanged for revolvers of the Webley pattern at Calcutta.

(*g*.) The Director General of Ordnance will supply the following tents to the Bikaner Infantry at the port of embarkation :—

      30 G. S. tents, 160 lbs.
      3 G. S. tents, 80 lbs.

10. *Machine Guns.*—(*a*.) One ·303 Maxim gun on Infantry field carriage and 30,000 rounds of ammunition (of which 6,200 rounds will be in regimental charge and the balance in Ordnance reserve), will be issued to each Infantry battalion, except Imperial Service Troops and the units for the garrison of Hongkong.

(*b*.) One box of ammunition (1,100 rounds) per gun will be issued for practice on the voyage.

(c.) The 3rd Bombay Cavalry is permitted to take a private ·303 Maxim gun, for which 30,000 rounds of ammunition will be supplied free by the Ordnance Department.

11. *Reserve of horseshoes and nails.*—Staff and other mounted officers, and the mounted units (British and Native) will make their own arrangements for a reserve of horseshoes and nails. A reserve for the mounted detachment of the Bengal Sappers and Miners will be issued by the Director-General of Ordnance.

12. *Engineer Field Park.*—The Engineer Field Parks maintained at Fort William Arsenal and Roorkee will be mobilised and despatched with the Force; such modifications and additions being made as the Commanding Royal Engineer of the force may consider desirable.

13. *Signallers.*—(a.) The 10 special signalling units (British Infantry) and the two special signalling units (Native Infantry) for the force will be equipped as laid down in Field Service Equipment Tables, British Infantry, and Table V., Field Service Departmental Code, "Ordnance," and will be concentrated as soon as possible at Calcutta under the orders of the Lieutenant-Generals concerned in direct communication with the General Officer Commanding, Presidency District.

14. *Staff and Departmental Offices* (a.)—The Divisional Staff Office, 4th division, maintained at Ootacamund, is detailed as the divisional office of the force, and will be despatched to Calcutta in charge of a non-commissioned officer from the Madras command office. A Warrant Officer from the office of the Quarter-Master General in India will be detailed to take subordinate charge of the office in the Field.

(b.) Two military clerks will also be detailed from the Office of the Adjutant-General in India and one military clerk from the Office of the Quarter-Master General in India for duty with the Divisional Office.

(c.) A military clerk and one draughtsman will be attached to the Divisional Office from the Intelligence Branch, Quarter-Master General's Department, for duty with the Intelligence Staff.

(d.) A typewriter will be supplied to the Divisional Office at Calcutta under the orders of the Superintendent, Government Stationery.

(e.) A military clerk will be detailed from the Office of the Military Secretary to His Excellency the Commander-in-Chief to act as Confidential Clerk to the Lieutenant-General Commanding the Forces.

(f.) The Office of the Engineer-in-Chief, Army Staff, maintained at Simla, is detailed as the Office for the Colonel on the Staff Royal Engineers, mentioned in paragraph 3; and it will be despatched to Calcutta in charge of a Warrant Officer from Army Headquarters.

(*g.*) The Office of the Commanding Royal Artillery, Army Staff, maintained at Simla, is detailed as the office for the Colonel on the Staff, Royal Artillery, mentioned in paragraph 3; and it will be despatched to Calcutta in charge of a Warrant Officer from Army Headquarters.

(*h.*) The 4th Cavalry Brigade Office maintained at Mhow is detailed as the Cavalry Brigade of the force, and will be despatched to Calcutta in charge of a non-commissioned officer from the Mhow District Staff Office.

(*i.*) The Office of the 10th Infantry Brigade maintained at Jubbulpore is detailed as the Staff Office of the 1st Infantry Brigade of the force, and will be despatched to Calcutta in charge of a non-commissioned officer from the Nerbudda District Staff Office.

(*k.*) The Office of the 8th Infantry Brigade maintained at Lucknow is detailed as the Staff Office of the 2nd Infantry Brigade of the force, and will be despatched to Calcutta in charge of a non-commissioned officer from the Oudh District Staff Office.

(*l.*) The Office of the 11th Infantry Brigade maintained at Belgaum is detailed as the Staff Office of the 3rd Infantry Brigade, and will be despatched to Calcutta in charge of a non-commissioned officer from the Belgaum District Staff Office.

(*m.*) The Office of the 12th Infantry Brigade maintained at Secunderabad is detailed as the Staff Office of the 4th Infantry Brigade, and will be despatched to Madras in charge of a non-commissioned officer from the Secunderabad District Staff Office.

(*n.*) The Staff Office for Imperial Service Troops, 2nd Division, maintained at Umballa in charge of the Inspecting Officer, Punjab Imperial Service Infantry, is detailed as the Office of the Deputy Assistant Adjutant-General for Imperial Service Troops. It will accompany this officer to the port of embarkation.

(*o.*) The Section Commandant's Office maintained at Delhi is detailed as the Base and line of communications office of the force. It will be at once completed up to the scale prescribed in Table VIII., Section 1, Field Service Equipment Tables, for a line of communication office, and will be despatched to Calcutta in charge of a non-commissioned officer from the Station Staff Office, Delhi.

A military clerk will be detailed from the Office of the Deputy Adjutant-General, Bengal Command, to take subordinate charge of the Office in the field.

(*p.*) The Office of the Commanding Royal Engineer, 4th Division, maintained at Bangalore, is detailed as the Office of the Commanding Royal Engineer of the Line of Communication, and will be despatched to Calcutta in charge of a non-commissioned Officer from the Madras Sappers and Miners.

(*q.*) The Office of the Superintendent, Army Signalling, 3rd Division, maintained at Kasauli, is detailed as the Office of the Superintendent, Army Signalling of the Force, and will be despatched to Calcutta addressed to the officer for whom intended.

(*r.*) The books for Provost Marshal, 3rd Division, maintained at Naini Tal, are allotted to the Provost Marshal of the Force, and will be despatched to Calcutta addressed to the officer for whom intended.

(*s.*) The Staff Office of the Force will be supplied, under the orders of the Adjutant-General in India, with Army Lists (both English and Indian); and with G. G. O's, G. O.'s, G. O. C. C.'s, and Army Circulars from the date on which orders issue for mobilisation till its return to India. Two copies each of the Government Telegraph Code and Lane's Word Code for Foreign State Telegrams will also be supplied to the Staff Office of the Force, and the War Office requested to supply each Brigade Office with a copy of the Government Telegraph Code.

(*t.*) The Medical Staff Office for the field force will be furnished from the Bengal Command, and that for the Line of Communication from the Madras Command, and that for Shanghai from the Punjab Command.

(*u.*) The Veterinary Office will be furnished from the Bombay Command.

(*v.*) Departmental Offices will be formed, equipped, and concentrated at Calcutta under departmental arrangements.

15. *Base Stationery Depôt.*—A Base Stationery Depôt, equipped with a four months' supply of forms, stationery, &c., for all the Staff Offices and corps units detailed for the Force, will be organised by the Superintendent of Government Stationery and despatched with the Force. The establishment of the Depôt will consist of one assistant, one clerk, and three sorters.

16. *Native Military Base Depôt.*—Will be organised under the orders of the Lieutenant-General Commanding the Forces, Bombay, and despatched with the Forces. It will consist of one Native Officer as Jemadar Adjutant, two Colour-Havildars, two Pay Havildars, one clerk, two bhistis, and two sweepers.

PART II.—SPECIAL DETAILS.

17. By desire of the Imperial Government the following special details will be despatched to China for service as required :—

(A) Four coolie corps for transport duty.
(B) 1,304 siege-train bullocks for use with siege artillery.
(C) 54 horses for use with a Balloon Section.
(D) 198 Artillery horses for use with one-pounder Vickers-Maxim guns.
(E) The Establishment and Equipment of a remount depôt of 250 horses.
(F) A Survey Party.
(G) Two Telegraph Sections.
(H) A Railway Section.
(I) A Sanitary Establishment.
(K) Nine Dhanjibhoy's Tongas.
(L) Field Audit Office.
(M) Base Depôt of Medical Stores.
(N) Aërated Water Factory.
(O) Base Veterinary Store Depôt.

A.—PUNJAB COOLIE CORPS.

18. The four Punjab Coolie Corps will be raised at once under the orders of the Lieutenant-General Commanding the Forces, Punjab. The Corps will be composed of Punjabi Mahommedan coolies, recruited from men accustomed to carry loads and marching.

The following officers are detailed to command the several corps :—

First Corps—
    Commandant - Captain J. L. Rose, 2-1st Gurkhas.
    2nd in Command - Lieutenant C. H. Alexander, 6th Bombay Cavalry.

Second Corps—
    Commandant - Major St. G. L. Steele, 2nd Bengal Lancers.
    2nd in Command - Lieutenant H. S. Garratt, 3rd Bombay Infantry.

Third Corps—
    Commandant - Captain E. B. C. Boddam, 2-5th Gurkhas.
    2nd in Command - Lieutenant H. F. Goldthorp, 3rd Punjab Cavalry.

Fourth Corps—
    Commandant - Captain P. W. Drake-Brockman, 5th Bengal Infantry.
    2nd in Command - Lieutenant G. A. H. Beatty, 9th Bengal Lancers.

(*b.*) *Establishment.*—The establishment of each corps is as follows:—

    1 Commandant (Regimental Officer).
    1 Second in Command (Regimental Officer).
    2 British Non-Commissioned Officers (1 Departmental and 1 Regimental).
    20 Sirdars at 1 per 50 coolies.
    40 Mates ,, 1 ,, 25 ,,
    2 transport agents—2nd class.
    2 weighmen.
    2 peons.
    8 sweepers.
1,000 coolies.
    2 syces.
    1 Section, No. 54 Native Field Hospital.

Each officer will be allowed to take one charger, and each non-commissioned officer one pony.

(*c.*) *Equipment.*—British non-commissioned officers will proceed fully armed and equipped.

Four yards of coarse country cloth and a length of 12 to 15 feet of cotton rope should be provided to each coolie to secure the load on the back. Daos or kukries for arming the men should be arranged for by the Ordnance Department at the scale of one per sirdar, mate, and follower, and taken in bulk with the corps.

(*d.*) *Rations* with be issued free from date of arrival at port of embarkation. If concentrated near a port of embarkation, free rations will be issued from date of arrival there to date of embarkation on the following scale:—

Atta or rice	$1\frac{1}{2}$ lbs.
Dhal	3 oz.
Ghi	1 ,,
Salt	$\frac{2}{3}$,,
Fuel	$1\frac{1}{2}$ lbs.

From date of disembarkation the corps will receive rations at the scale authorised for followers.

(*e.*) *Tentage* at the rate of one G. S. 40-lb. tent per British non-commissioned officer and one N. C. 45-lb. tent to every seven men will be supplied.

(*f.*) *Rates of Pay.*—The following rates of pay will be allowed:—

	Rs.	
Commandants—Staff pay	300	per mensem.
Second in command—Staff pay	200	,, ,,
Non-commissioned officers—Departmental command allowance	20	,, ,,
Non-commissioned officer, Regimental. { Staff pay	20	,, ,,
{ Command allowance	20	,, ,,

Transport agents, 2nd class, Rs. 40 per mensem, *plus* 50 per cent. batta.

Weighmen } Rs. 6 each per mensem, *plus* 50 per cent. batta.
Peons

	Rs.	A.	P.	
Sirdar	18	0	0	(including batta) per mensem.
Mates	15	0	0	„ „ „ „
Coolies	12	0	0	„ „ „ „
Sweepers	9	0	0	„ „ „ „
Syces	10	8	0	„ „ „ „

The British officers of corps will draw the pay of their appointments from date of joining at the station to which ordered for the purpose of raising the corps.

(*g.*) Each corps will be furnished with one section of No. 54 Native Field Hospital, complete in every respect.

B.—Siege Train Bullocks.

19 (*a.*) The bullocks will be detailed under the orders of Lieutenant-Generals Commanding the Forces, Punjab and Bengal, as under:—

From Punjanb Command - - - 528 bullocks.
„ Bengal „ - - - 776 „
Total - 1,304 „

(*b.*) *Establishment of Train.*—The following will be the establishment of the train:—

Captain E. D. C. Cameron, No. 7 Company, Eastern Division, Royal Garrison Artillery, Commandant.
1 departmental warrant officer.
1 „ non-commissioned officer.
1 British regimental non-commissioned officer.
14 kote-duffadors.
27 naicks.
109 lance naicks.
608 drivers.
8 veterinary assistants.
10 shoeing-smiths.
5 blacksmiths.
5 hammermen.
5 bellowsmen.
8 carpenters.
3 clerks.
1 syce.
Sections A and B, No. 69 Native Field Hospital.

The kote-duffadors will be detailed under the orders of the Lieutenant-Generals Commanding the Forces, Punjab and Bengal (six from the Punjab and eight from the Bengal Command), and will proceed direct to Calcutta, where they will report themselves to the General Officer Commanding, Presidency District, and take over the bullocks as they arrive.

(*c.*) *Establishment for Supervision and Care of Bullocks on Voyage.*—The following establishment will be detailed for the supervision and care of the bullocks on the voyage to China, and will be placed at the disposal of the General Officer Commanding, Presidency District, who will arrange for their joining at Calcutta as ships are got ready :—

Captain J. S. Gooch, No. 24 Company, Southern Division Royal Garrison Artillery.
Captain W. A. W. Swettenham, No. 9 Company, Western Division, Royal Garrison Artillery.
Lieutenant J. A. Beasley, No. 7 Company, Western Division, Royal Garrison Artillery.
2nd-Lieutenant E. G. Hart, No. 7 Company, Western Division, Royal Garrison Artillery.

1 sergeant ⎫ From each of the Heavy Batteries
2 effective non-commissioned officers. ⎬ at Jhansi, Mooltan, Campbellpore, and Trimulgherry.

(*d.*) *Tentage and Cooking Utensils.*—At the Field Service scale will be arranged for under the orders of the Lieutenant-General Commanding the Forces, Bengal.

(*e.*) *Equipment.*—The departmental warrant and non-commissioned officer of the siege train establishment will take the arms and accoutrements authorised in Appendix 10, Field Service, Departmental Code, "Commissariat Transport." The British regimental non-commissioned officer of the siege train establishment will be provided with a sword and belt of the mountain battery pattern, also a revolver and 24 rounds of ammunition. The other non-commissioned officers (British and Native) will take their arms and equipment and 40 rounds of ammunition per rifle or carbine.

Each British officer will be allowed to take one charger, one native personal servant, and one syce. Regimental non-commissioned officers (British and Native) will not take horses and ponies, except the warrant and British non-commissioned officers of the siege train establishment, who will be provided with Government ponies.

The Ordnance Department will provide draught gear and I.P. poles; and the Commissariat Transport Department will arrange for 500 sets of bullock gear and for a reserve of repairing materials and shoes and nails for 1,500 bullocks.

(*f.*) The following rates of pay will be allowed for the establishment of the train :—

	Rs.	
Commandant, staff pay	300	per mensem.
Departmental warrant officer, command allowance	30	,,
Departmental non-commissioned officers, command allowance	20	,,

		Rs.	
Regimental non-commissioned officers.	{Staff pay	20	per mensem.
	Command allowance	20	,,

	Rs.	A.	P.			
Kote Duffadars (who held the appointment of Kote Duffadar previous to appointment) (2)	36	0	0*	(including batta)	,,	
Kote Duffadars (12)	28	8	0*	,,	,,	,,
Naicks	12	0	0	,,	,,	,,
Lance naicks	10	8	0	,,	,,	,,
Drivers	9	0	0	,,	,,	,,
Veterinary assistants	45	0	0	,,	,,	,,
Shoeing-smiths	22	8	0	,,	,,	,,
Blacksmiths	18	0	0	,,	,,	,,
Hammermen	10	8	0	,,	,,	,,
Bellowsmen	9	0	0	,,	,,	,,
Carpenters	15	0	0	,,	,,	,,
Clerks	60	0	0	,,	,,	,,
Syce	10	8	0	,,	,,	,,

Other British officers and non-commissioned officers will receive pay and allowances at Imperial rates from date of leaving India.

The Commandant, warrant, and non-commissioned officers, and all Indian establishments, and followers of the train may be granted three months' advance of pay; other British officers may be granted 60 days' advance of pay at British rates.

(*g.*) *Medical.*—The ambulance transport for the two sections of the Native Field Hospital will consist of 15 dandies and 99 bearers, with the usual scale of commissariat sergeants, ambulance agents and mates.

The obligatory mules required for the two sections of the Native Field Hospital will be provided from the spare mules belonging to the Force.

C.—Horses for Balloon Section.

20. (*a.*) The Lieutenant-General Commanding the Forces, Bengal, will, in communication with the General Officer Commanding Presidency District, arrange for the despatch of the following horses, with blankets, jhools, linegear, and saddlery complete for the Balloon Section :—

    10 riding horses,
    44 draught horses.

(*b.*) One syce will be sent with every two horses.

(*c.*) The horses should not be more than 12 years old, fit for service, and quiet.

---

* *Plus* any good conduct pay to which they may be entitled.

(*d.*) The horses will proceed with the Royal Engineer mounted detachment, the officer in charge of which will hand them over to the officer in charge of the Balloon Section on arrival at his destination.

D.—HORSES FOR VICKERS MAXIM GUNS.

21. (*a.*) *Establishment.*—Captain B. Vincent, Royal Field Artillery, will command the party.

The horses and *personnel* will be drawn from commands as under:—

Commands to supply.	Horses to be supplied from each Command.		Personnel to be supplied by each Command.								Remarks.
	Riding.	Draught.	British Non-Commissioned Officers.	Farrier Sergeants.	Shoeing-smiths.	Hospital Assistant.	Jemadar syces.	Syces.	Bhisties.	Sweepers.	
Punjab - -	10	43	1	—	—	—	1	31	1	1	
Bengal - -	40	17	1	—	—	—	1	34	1	1	
Madras - -	7	20	1	—	1	—	—	17	—	—	
Bombay - -	9	52	1	1	—	—	1	36	—	1	
Total -	66	132	4	1	1	1	3	118	2	3	

(*b.*) *Embarkation.*—The whole of the horses will be embarked in one ship.

(*c.*) The British officer will be allowed two chargers, two personal servants, and two syces.

(*d.*) *Equipment, Arms, and Ammunition.*—The necessary camp equipage for the *personnel* will be supplied by the Ordnance Department at the port of embarkation, and will be handed over, ready packed to the officer in charge of the detail.

The requisite cooking utensils for the British *personnel* will be supplied by the Commissariat Department at the port of embarkation, and will be similarly handed over.

The British *personnel* will proceed fully equipped, and will be armed with ·303 carbines and 50 rounds of ammunition per man; the necessary number of carbines, together with all equipment pertaining thereto, will be supplied by the Ordnance Department at Calcutta.

Each horse will be supplied regimentally with all articles of stable equipment and line-gear in thoroughly serviceable condition, including one set of spare shoes and nails and hay-net per animal.

The shoeing-smiths will take their tools with them.

(e.) *Medical.*—The equipment will consist of—
   1 field medical companion.
   1   „   „   haversack.

E.—REMOUNT DEPÔT.

22. (*a.*) *Establishment.*—The following will be the establishment of the depôt :—

Captain A. G. B. Turner, 13th Bengal Lancers.	Superintendent.
Lieutenant W. H. Norman, 11th Bengal Lancers.	Assistant superintendent.
1 sergeant, Royal Artillery 2 non-commissioned officers, Royal Artillery. 1 sergeant-farrier, Royal Artillery 1 shoeing-smith, Royal Artillery	For Artillery horses to be detailed by the Inspector-General of Artillery.
2 Native officers 4 Native non-commissioned officers 20 sowars 1 duffadar salutri 1 sowar-dresser 3 farriers	For cavalry horses to be detailed by the Lieutenant-General Commanding the Forces, Bengal.
1 farrier quartermaster-sergeant 150 syces (including 20 per cent. spare). 1 hospital assistant 5 bhisties 5 sweepers	For the whole depôt, to be supplied under the orders of the Lieutenant-General Commanding the Forces, Bengal.

Native officers, British and Native non-commissioned officers, salutri, and shoeing-smith will be seconded, and promotions made in their place.

If an additional officer is needed, one will be supplied under the orders of the General Officer Commanding, Hongkong, from the Hongkong garrison.

(*b.*) *Tentage, Equipment, &c.*—(1.) Tentage on the Field Service scale and cooking utensils for British details will be arranged for under the orders of the Lieutenant-General Commanding the Forces, Bengal. The non-commissioned officers (British and Native) and Sowars will be supplied at Calcutta with Lee-Metford carbines and equipment, and 50 rounds of ammunition per carbine.

Each British officer will be allowed to take two chargers, two Native personal servants, and two syces. Each Native officer will be allowed one charger, one personal servant, and one syce. Regimental non-commissioned officers (British and Native) will not take horses or ponies. The sergeant-farrier, farriers, and shoeing-smiths will take their shoeing implements.

(*c.*) *Depôt Equipment.*—The following equipment will be furnished by departments of supply and shipped with the above detail :—

(*i.*) For each 250 horses and 20 per cent. spare—

1 corn sack.	1 chagul.
1 nose-bag canvas.	1 head-stall.
1 watering bridle.	1 set of head and heel ropes.
1 horse brush.	1 set heel-pegs.
1 curry comb.	1 jhool.
1 eye-fringe.	1 blanket.
1 rubber.	1 set of shoes and nails.

(*ii.*) For the whole depôt—

68 water-buckets.
25 sponges.
50 hoof-pickers.
45 sets of saddlery, complete, of the smallest size.

(*d.*) *Horseshoes.*—A three months' supply of horseshoes, suitable for the descriptions of horses will be arranged for under the orders of the Director-General of Ordnance in India.

(*e.*) *Medical.*—The medical equipment will consist of one pair of field medical panniers, to be supplied from the Bengal Command.

(*f.*) *Veterinary.*—The following veterinary equipment will be supplied for the depôt :—

Two universal field veterinary chests.
One reserve field veterinary box.

F.—SURVEY PARTY.

23. (*a.*) The following party will be detailed for the force under the orders of the Surveyor-General of India :—

1 provincial assistant (European).
2 Native surveyors.
27 Khalassies.

(*b.*) The party will embark at Calcutta and will, previous to embarkation, be concentrated at some convenient station in the Bengal Command where, under the orders of the Lieutenant-General Commanding the Forces, Bengal, they will receive field service clothing and tentage.

(*c.*) In addition to the above survey party, four Native soldier surveyors, to be detailed by Army Headquarters, will accompany the force for duty with the Intelligence Staff. These men will also embark at Calcutta.

G.—TELEGRAPH SECTIONS.

24. (*a.*) One telegraph section from the Madras Sappers and Miners and one telegraph section from the Bengal Sappers and

Miners, each consisting of 2 British non-commissioned officers, 2 Havildars, 2 Naiks, and 12 Sappers, will accompany the force.

(*b.*) In addition to the above establishment, 60 military signallers (to be drawn from the four Commands) will be attached to the sections for duty.

(*c.*) Equipment for these sections will be issued by the telegraph department to the extent deemed necessary by the assistant field engineers (telegraphs) under the orders of Commanding Royal Engineer of the Force.

H.—RAILWAY SECTION.

25. (*a.*) A railway section consisting of two warrant or non-commissioned officers and 48 public followers will accompany the force.

(*b.*) Five miles of light railway plant and 100 trucks will be purchased and despatched with the force.

I.—SANITARY ESTABLISHMENT.

26. The Lieutenant-General commanding the Forces, Bengal, will, in communication with the General Officer Commanding the Presidency district, arrange for the despatch of the following sanitary establishmant for the force :—

Sweepers with brooms and baskets - -	210
Bildars or mahars with mamooties or belchas -	90
Bhisties with mussaks - - - -	60
Filth carts, with one bullock and one sweeper driver each - - - - - - -	90
Rubbish carts, with two bullocks and one sweeper driver each - - - - -	30

K.—DHANJIBHOY'S TONGAS.

27. (*a.*) The tonga train will consist of 9 tongas and 21 ponies, and will be attached to the cavalry brigade.

(*b.*) The following is the establishment and rate of pay :—

Per mensem.

	RS.
1 British non-commissioned officer - - -	40
1 jemadar - - - - - -	20
1 daffadar - - - - - - -	16
10 coachmen - - - - - -	12
12 syces - - - - - - -	7
1 carpenter - - - - -	20
1 mochee - - - - - - -	15
1 hammerman - - - - -	15
1 blacksmith - - - - - -	20
1 shoeing-smith - - - - -	20

(c.) The establishment will be equipped under the orders of the Commissary General-in-Chief.

(d.) Twelve months' supply of repairing material will be sent.

L.—FIELD AUDIT PAY OFFICE.

28. (a.) A special field audit office for the auditing of the accounts of the whole China force will be despatched. The establishment will be 45 clerks and the necessary menials.

(b.) The officer in charge will have the powers of a field controller and a consolidated salary of Rs. 2,000 per mensem.

(c.) The following special scale of baggage will be allowed to the port of debarkation :—

Clerks	80 lbs.
Menials	40 ,,

M.—BASE DEPÔT OF MEDICAL STORES.

A base depôt of medical stores will be mobilised at Calcutta under the orders of the Lieutenant-General Commanding the Forces, Bengal, for service in China, and will be despatched to Hongkong as soon as possible.

2. The establishment will consist of—

1 Indian medical service officer (field rank).
1 assistant surgeon, 1st class.
1 assistant surgeon, 2nd class.
2 writers
3 compounders
3 packers
2 cutlers   } Appointed by the Director-General,
2 tin-smiths   Indian Medical Service.
2 carpenters
1 water carrier } Provided by the Commissariat
1 sweeper   Department.

3. The equipment will consist of the following :—

(a.) Medicines, surgical materials, &c., laid down in Appendix No. 38, Regulations for Army Medical Services.

Medical companions	24
Surgical haversacks	48
Field medical panniers	pairs 12
Reserve field medical panniers	,, 6
Field surgical panniers	,, 12
Field fracture boxes	,, 12
Antiseptic cases	,, 14

This equipment has been ordered from England and will be despatched direct to Hongkong.

(b.) Commissariat, ordnance, and military works stores will be supplied from the Bengal Command.

(c.) 12 boxes reserve medicines, *vide* Appendix No. 20, Field Service Departmental Code, Medical.
(d.) 12 cases antiseptic dressings, War Office pattern.
(e.) 100 pounds sulphate of quinine.
} To be supplied by the medical storekeeper to Government, Bengal Command.

(f.) As many condemned, but thoroughly cleaned and disinfected hospital sheets as the Commissary General, Bengal, can obtain.

4. The embarkation of this unit from Calcutta will be arranged for by the Lieutenant-General Commanding the Forces, Bengal, in communication with the Director-General of Royal Indian Marine, Calcutta.

N.—Aërated Water Factory.

Three aërated water machines with bottles, accessories, and three months' supply of chemicals and necessaries for manufacture of aërated waters, for use of hospitals, will be sent to China from England; tubs for washing bottles will be sent from India.

2. The following establishment for working the machines will be sent from India:—

Per Mensem.

	Rs.
3 Supervisors	30
3 Bottlers	20
3 Mates	12
6 Coolies	7
3 Bhisties	8

This establishment will be equipped under the orders of the Commissary General-in-Chief.

O.—Base Veterinary Store Depôt.

A base veterinary store depôt, calculated for six months for 10,000 animals, will be mobilised at Meean Meer and despatched to China, under the orders of the Principal Veterinary Officer in India.

2. The establishment will consist of:—

British.

1 Veterinary officer.
1 Farrier quartermaster-sergeant.
1 Soldier clerk.

Native.

1 Veterinary assistant.

Followers.
1 Tent lascar.
1 Bhisti.
1 Sweeper.
1 Cook.

Private Followers.
1 Personal servant.
1 General servant.
2 Syces.
1 Grass-cutter.

Animals.
2 Chargers.
1 Pony (private).

PART III.—GENERAL REGULATIONS.

The following regulations apply to the whole of the units and details given in Parts I. and II. :—

29. *Baggage.*—Baggage will be taken on the Relief scale as far as the port of debarkation. From that point baggage on the Field Service scale only will be allowed. Officers will take all their uniform (except serge and mess dress), and troops will take serge or cloth clothing in addition to the Field Service kit.

30. *Concentration at the Port of Embarkation and Embarkation :—*
(*a.*) The following units will be embarked at Bombay :—
Staff, 2nd Infantry Brigade.
2nd Bengal Infantry.
14th Sikhs.
1-4th Gurkhas.
3rd Madras Infantry.
34th Pioneers.
No. 2 Company Bombay Sappers and Miners.
No. 54 Native Field Hospital. (For Punjab Coolie Corps.)
No. 63 Native Field Hospital.
No. 66 Native Field Hospital.
Sections C. and D., No. 69 Native Field Hospital.
The four Punjab Coolie Corps.
(*b.*) The following units will be embarked at Karachi :—
26th Bombay Infantry.
30th Bombay Infantry.
(*c.*) The following units will be embarked at Madras :—
5th Infantry, Hyderabad Contingent.
28th Madras Infantry.
Sections A. and B., No. 61 Native Field Hospital.
Sections A. and B., No. 58 Native Field Hospital.

(*d*.) The following units will be embarked at Rangoon :—
31st Madras Infantry.
Sections C. and D., No. 58 Native Field Hospital, will be embarked at Calcutta, and despatched thence to Rangoon.

(*e*.) The remainder of the force and details will be embarked at Calcutta.

(*f*.) The Director of the Royal Indian Marine will arrange as expeditiously as possible for the necessary sea transport for conveyance of the force and details to China, all vessels to call at Hongkong for orders. He will inform the General Officers Commanding at the ports of embarkation concerned of the vessels he proposes to charter These will then be surveyed in accordance with Army Regulations, India, Volume X., and reports made to Army Headquarters regarding the transports engaged, the date of sailing and the allotment proposed. As dates of sailings become known, the General Officers Commanding at the ports of embarkation will arrange by telegram, in direct communication with the General Officers Commanding the Districts concerned, for the movements of units and details to the port—copies of all such communications being sent to Army Headquarters and to the headquarters of the Command concerned.

The General Officer Commanding, Calcutta, will arrange for the movement of Imperial Service units to the port of embarkation as follows :—

(*i*.) For the Jodhpur Lancers with the Inspecting Officer, Rajputana Imperial Service Troops at Muttra ;
(*ii*.) For the Alwar and Bikanir Infantry with the Inspecting Officers, Rajputana Imperial Service Troops at Alwar and Bikanir ;
(*iii*.) For the Maler Kotla Sappers, with the Inspecting Officer Imperial Service Troops, Maler Kotla.

(*g*.) Slings at 25 per cent. of horses, siege-train bullocks, and transport animals on board, and at the rate of one for each mule embarking with No. 2 Company, Bombay Sappers and Miners, at Bombay, will be placed on board transports.

(*h*.) Until the embarkation of the force is completed, an additional Deputy Assistant Adjutant-General will be appointed to the staffs of the Presidency and Bombay Districts, with staff pay of Rs. 400 per mensem, in addition to Staff Corps pay and allowances of rank.

(*i*.) To facilitate the despatch of stores, the staff of the Commissariat-Transport Department of the Presidency and Bombay Districts will also be temporarily increased to such extent as may be considered necessary by the General Officers Commanding the Districts, who will at once communicate their requirements to the Lieutenant-Generals of the Command concerned.

(*k*.) The General Officers Commanding Presidency, Madras, Bombay, Sind, and Burma Districts will make immediate arrangements for the construction of such railway platforms as may be needed to facilitate the detrainment of troops, animals, and stores; for the hire of such storage accommodation as may be necessary; and also for the construction of additional railway sidings if absolutely required.

(*l.*) The General Officers Commanding at the ports of embarkation will be responsible for receiving transport and stores for the force, for their accommodation, and for their loading on the transports.

(*m.*) As far as possible, stores of one description will be loaded together; those which are likely to be first required being loaded last in each vessel.

(*n.*) Field hospitals will be embarked with units as under:—

With each battery of Artillery -	1 section, British Field Hospital.
With each regiment of Native Cavalry and Imperial Service Cavalry.	1 or 2 sections, Native Field Hospital.
With each battalion of Infantry and Imperial Service Infantry	2 sections, Native Field Hospital.
With each Coolie Corps - -	1 section, Native Field Hospital.

(*o.*) The arms, ammunition, and equipment of each unit will accompany the unit in the same vessel or vessels, so as to be available at once on disembarkation.

(*p.*) The Lieutenant-Generals Commanding the Forces concerned will make all necessary arrangements for rest-camps *en route*, and for the supply of ice for troops on the line of rail if considered necessary; and will sanction such reduction in the regulation number of troops allotted to each compartment as they may, for climatic reasons, consider desirable.

31. *Medical.*—(*a.*) The following British and Native General Hospitals will be equipped at Calcutta and despatched with the force under the orders of the Principal Medical Officer, Her Majesty's Forces in India :—

1 British General Hospital for 110 beds in China.
3 Native General Hospitals for 500 beds each in China.
1 Native General Hospital for 500 beds will be established in Calcutta to receive the sick and wounded from China.

(*b.*) The equipment of an additional Native General Hospital of 500 beds will be stored in readiness at Calcutta.

(*c.*) The s.s. "Carthage" will be taken up and equipped as a hospital ship by the Director, Royal Indian Marine, in direct communication with the Principal Medical Officer, Her Majesty's Forces in India.

(*d.*) Obligatory pack mule transport will accompany the field hospitals marked with an asterisk* in Appendix A. 1. Transport for the remainder will be embarked separately at Calcutta as a distinct transport corps. *See also* paragraph 38.

(*e.*) Mosquito nets will be provided for full number of beds in field and general hospitals under the orders of the Lieutenant-Generals Commanding the Forces, Bengal and Bombay.

(*f.*) 500 per cent. reserve of medical comforts will be taken, and a sufficient reserve of medicines.

(*g.*) Any further medical arrangements deemed necessary will be made under the orders of the Principal Medical Officer, Her Majesty's Forces in India.

(*h.*) Officers attached to Imperial Service units are to arrange that each State shall send some one in authority to be attached to the base, to help invalided men of the Imperial Service Troops to return to their States, and also to report all casualties, &c., to the Darbars concerned.

(*i.*) The following medical equipment will be supplied to the Mounted Datachment, Bengal Sappers and Miners :—

1 field medical companion.
1 „ surgical haversack.
1 „ dandy.

32. *Ambulance Transport.*—No pony ambulance or ambulance tongas will be taken. Each complete field hospital will be provided with 30 dandies, and each separate section with 8 dandies, with 6 bearers per dandie. A reserve of 10 per cent. bearers will be taken for all field and general hospitals. The usual scale of Commissariat sergeants, ambulance agents, sirdars, and mates will also be provided.

33. *Veterinary.*—(*a.*) The necessary veterinary arrangements for the force and for the voyage will be made under the orders of the Principal Veterinary Officer in India.

(*b.*) A base veterinary store depôt, with 6 months' supply for the whole force sent from India to China will be organised at Meean Meer under the orders of the Principal Veterinary Officer in India, and will be despatched from Calcutta for establishment at such place as may be determined by the General Officer Commanding the Imperial Forces in China.

34. *Commissariat Equipment.*—Field Service scale. Fifty chaff cutters and a reserve of 100 mussacks and 100 pairs of pakhals will be provided under the orders of the Lieutenant-General Commanding the Forces, Bengal. Linegear for 750 pack mules and repairing materials for 2,800 mules on the scale laid down in Appendix 59, Table I., Field Service Departmental Code, "Commissariat Transport," will be shipped by the Commissariat Department, also waterproof paulins, as may be necessary, will be arranged for under the orders of the Lieutenant-General Commanding the Forces, Bengal, and shipped from Calcutta.

34. *Clothing.*—(*a.*) All troops and followers will be supplied with clothing in accordance with Appendix A. 2.

(*b.*) The issue of summer clothing, Appendix A. 2., Table I., will be made to units before they leave their stations, if possible; otherwise the officer responsible for the equipment of the unit concerned will inform the General Officer Commanding at the port of embarkation, by telegram, of the articles required to complete, and these will be issued before embarkation.

(*c.*) The winter scale of clothing, Appendix A. 2., Table I., will be issued to units in bulk, and will be retained in bulk, and will only be distributed to individuals under the orders of General Officer Commanding the force. If sufficient coats, warm, British, to equip the force are not available, the deficiency will be made up as soon as possible and sent after the force to China, under arrangements which will be made by the Commissary General-in-Chief.

(*d.*) Further supplies of field service clothing will be sent, if required, on receipt of telegraphic demands.

(*e.*) Sea kit, as prescribed for the Cape route in Army Regulations, India, Volume V., Article 2,166 (but without mattresses), will be issued to all British troops before they embark.

(*f.*) Foreign service kit, as prescribed in Army Regulations, India, Volume V., Article 2,162, will be issued to all native troops and followers before they embark.

(*g.*) Imperial service units will make their own arrangements for the first issue and 20 per cent. reserve of the clothing in Appendix A. 2., Table I.

35. *Stretchers.*—Field and blanket stretchers will be taken by corps units on following scale:—

	Field.	Blanket.
Battery of artillery	2	4
Regiment of cavalry	8	16
Jodhpur cavalry	8	16
Company of sappers and miners and Maler Kotla Sappers	2	4
Battalion of infantry or pioneers and Alwar infantry	8	16
Bikanir infantry	4	8

36. *Fuel.*—Firewood sufficient for 10 days' supply on landing for the troops on board will be placed on board each transport. In addition 50 days' fuel for the whole force will be shipped by the Commissariat-Transport Department, if space is available on the transports.

37. *Supplies.*—(*a.*) Forty days' sea rations and a reserve of thirty days' land rations, included compressed fodder and grain

for horses and transport animals, will be placed on board each transport. The supply of tea, sugar (or goor) for tea, and rum (for non-abstainers) as "extras" will be sufficient to provide for a day's issue.

(*b.*) In addition two months' supplies, including grain for horses and transport animals, but exclusive of compressed fodder, will be taken from Calcutta for the whole force, making a total of three months' supplies in all.

A further two months' supply of compressed fodder will be prepared and despatched hereafter.

(*c.*) Supplies will be packed in waterproof bags where necessary.

38. *Transport.*—(*a.*) Obligatory pack mules and ponies, with the necessary establishment allotted to units in Appendix A. 1., will accompany the force. The transport of corps units marked with an asterisk* in Appendix A. 1, will be embarked on the same vessel or vessels as the corps units; the transport for the remainder will be embarked separately at Calcutta as a district transport corps. The transport for the 3rd Brigade (except 20th Pubjab Infantry) and for the 4th Brigade will be collected at ports of embarkation under orders of the Commissary-General-in-Chief. The Engineer Field Parks will be equipped from spare mules at the base. The transport for the two sections No. 58 Native Field Hospital, which proceed with the 31st Madras Infantry, will be provided in Burma and embarked at Rangoon.

(*b.*) The Imperial Service Troops will take their own obligatory transport, which will be embarked with each unit.

(*c.*) The obligatory mules, allotted to units, include mules for the carriage of reserve or emergency rations in the field as follows:—

Native infantry or pioneer battalion and Alwar infantry.	8 mules per battalion.
Bikanir infantry	4 mules.
Company of sappers and miners and Maler Kotla Sappers.	2 mules per company.
British Field Hospital	1 mule per section.
Native Field Hospital	2 mules per hospital.

(*d.*) One duffadar and five sowars to be drawn from Native cavalry regiments in the Bengal Command, and one duffadar and five sowars to be drawn from Native cavalry regiments of the Hyderabad Contingent, will accompany the force as transport assistants. They will proceed from stations without horses, saddlery, carbines, or lances, and will be equipped at Calcutta with ·303 carbines and 50 rounds of ammunition per man.

(e.) A reserve of 750 sets of transport pack saddlery, 200 Army Transport carts, and 400 sets of gear, as laid down in Army Regulations, India, Volume V., Appendix 46, Part I., clauses (a), (b), and (c), and Part II., clause (a), will be arranged for under the orders of the Lieutenant-General Commanding the Forces, Bengal.

39. *Post Office.*—Postal arrangements will be made under the orders of the Director-General of Post Offices.

40. *Maps.*—Maps and hand-books will be issued from Army Headquarters to all corps and units, for the use of all officers with the force, and also to all staff and departmental offices.

41. *Submission of Reports.*—(a.) The following periodical returns, laid down in Appendix F., Part XI., Field Service Manual, will be rendered by General Officer Commanding Force to Army Headquarters, India :—

(1.) Telegraphic health report, fortnightly.
(2.) Telegraphic report of general condition of wounded, weekly.
(3.) Telegraphic disposition return, weekly.
(4.) Telegraphic report of expenditure of ammunition and requirements when necessary.
(5.) Telegraphic report of all important events in cypher, with any additional information likely to elucidate the situation.

(b.) Corps units will forward on the 1st of each month to the Adjutant-General in India, and to the Deputy Adjutant-General of the Command from which they have been withdrawn a copy of the regimental monthly strength return.

The batteries of Royal Horse and Royal Field Artillery on A. F. B.-81.
Punjab and Bengal units on I. A. F. W.-744.
Bombay units on I. A. F. W.-732.
Madras units on I. A. F. W.-733.

(c.) Imperial Service units will forward a copy of their monthly regimental strengths to the Inspector-General, Imperial Service Troops, on the 1st of each month.

(d.) Casualties will be reported as directed in the Field Service Manual, Part XI., Appendix F., paragraphs 4, 5, and 6.

42. *Voyage Reports.*—Voyage reports in accordance with paragraph 412, Army Regulations, India, Volume X., will be furnished to Officers Commanding troops on board, with necessary instructions for their preparation under the orders of the General Officers Commanding at the ports of embarkation. On completion of the voyage two copies will be rendered, one to the Quartermaster-General in India, and one to the Director, Royal Indian Marine.

Voyage reports for Imperial Service Troops will be rendered through the Inspector-General, Imperial Service Troops.

43. *Special Returns.*—Reference Army Regulations, India, Volume III., paragraph 166, and Volume XI., Section 37, paragraph 3, each corps, hospital and details proceeding to China will prepare on boardship, in duplicate, a list of arms, accoutrements, tools, and stores on I. O. Form 273, clothing on M. A. form 595, and necessaries on M. A. Form 738. The actual number and condition of articles accompanying units out of India will be entered and the headings of the forms altered to suit circumstances. The returns will be posted at Hongkong to Controllers concerned. The General Officer commanding at the port of embarkation will obtain the requisite number of forms and issue them to each unit embarking.

44. *Officers' Messes.*—Scale discretional as far as the base of operations. On leaving base, as laid down in the Field Service Manual, Part XII., Section IV.

45. *Press Correspondents.*—Officers belonging to the force will on no account be allowed to act as Press Correspondents. Applications for permission to accompany the force as Press Correspondents will be made to the Adjutant-General in India. Not more than one correspondent will be allowed for each newspaper. Officers appointed Press Correspodents must not be employed in any military capacity.

46. *Pay, Concesions and Privileges.*—(*a.*) Staff Officers, Transport Officers, Special Service Officers and others will draw the pay of their appointments from date of taking up their duties. For British officers of coolie corps *see* paragraph 18.

(*b.*) British units will receive pay and allowances at Imperial rates from date of leaving India, but British officers on the Staff, including special service officers of the British Service, Indian pay and allowances.

(*c.*) Officers, including continuous service officers, warrant, and non-commissioned officers and men of Indian services and all Indian establishments and followers, may be granted three months' advance of pay; and British officers serving regimentally may be granted 60 days' advance of pay at British rates and 120 days' field allowance under paragraph 472, Allowance Regulations. Subsequent issues of field allowance will be made in China, at the end of the advance period, for such days as the officers are under canvas compensation will be allowed in addition to field allowance, up to the full value of new tent according to the rank of the officer on the understanding that the officer provides his own tent. Horse allowance, as laid down in paragraphs 477 to 481, Allowance Regulations, and servants allowance as authorised for Hongkong under paragraphs 510 and 520, Allowance Regulations, are also admissible.

(*d.*) The troops and followers of the force will be considered on Field Service for all concessions and privileges from the date of embarkation until they return to India. Batta is admissible to troops and followers from the date of their quitting their stations.

(*e.*) Free passages to their homes may be granted to the families of all Native followers.

(*f.*) Concessions which are admissible from or between certain dates will have effect from such dates.

(*g.*) The Hospital and Regimental (excluding Silladar) establishments will receive 50 per cent. batta. Commissariat-Transport establishments will receive universal rates of pay and 50 per cent. batta.

(*h.*) The sanctioned followers paid by the troops will receive from Government such extra pay as may be necessary to put them on a par with the public followers of a similar class.

(*i.*) Followers of corps and departments, including clerks, commissariat agents, and others will be allowed to make family allotments in accordance with Section V., Field Service Manual, 1887.

(*j.*) Officers of the Indian Army forming part of the China Expeditionary Force will be liable to income duty at the British rate, but they will not be required to pay more than they would pay if in India. The difference between the amounts payable under Imperial and those under Indian Regulations will be provided by the Imperial Government out of Army funds.

(*k.*) Substitutes for British non-commissioned officers, and for the Native officers, non-commissioned officers and men, temporarily detached from corps in India for duty in China will be paid by India. The Imperial Government will bear extra charges caused by substitutes afterwards becoming temporarily supernumerary; and generally such expenditure as would not have been incurred but for the expedition. But seconding not to be unnecessarily carried out, in cases of absence likely to be short.

47. *Accounts.*—The Accounts of British units serving in China, and the pay bills of officers not in receipt of Indian pay and allowances, should be submitted to the District Pay Master, Hongkong.

All native corps with the force will submit their accounts for audit to the Field Controller's office, with effect from the 1st of the month in which they left India.

The accounts of Imperial Service troops will be audited by the Native States concerned.

Charges incurred in India will after audit be debited through the Controller of Military Accounts, Bengal Command, against the Imperial Government.

48. *Debit Note Telegrams.*—(*a.*) The Staff and Departmental Officers of the force will be permitted to send telegrams on the "debit note" system from telegraph offices in Calcutta and Bombay.

(*b.*) The Lieutenant-Generals Commanding the forces in the four Commands will authorise the despatch of telegrams on the "debit note" system from such offices as may be concerned with the equipment of the force or its maintenance in the field. They should communicate to the Director-General of telegraphs the official designations of the officers they may empower to use the "debit note" system; their headquarters; and, as far as possible, the names of any other stations from which "debit note" telegrams are likely to be sent. (*Note.*—"Debit note" telegrams cannot be sent from Railway Telegraph Offices.)

49. *Expenditure.*—All horses, transport animals, supplies, stores, equipment, arms and clothing sent with the force other than the horses, arms, stores, equipment and clothing forming the ordinary peace equipment of the corps units, Field and General Hospitals and Medical Store Depôt detailed are to be replaced as soon as possible. All expenditure in connection with the force incurred up to the date of sailing which would not have been incurred if the despatch of the troops had not been ordered, and subsequently all charges, will be borne by the Imperial Government, all telegrams, indents, &c., should be endorsed "China Expeditionary force, 1900. Debit cost to Controller of Military Accounts, Bengal Command."

(*a.*) In the case of Imperial Service Troops proceeding with the force all expenditure under the heading specified in paragraph 405, Field Service Departmental Code, Military Accounts, and also expenditure referred to in paragraph 306 *ibid.*, which would not have been incurred had the troops remained at their stations and not proceeded on field service, should be debited to the Imperial Government.

(*b.*) All expenditure both ordinary and extraordinary (except for ordinary peace equipment) on account of depôts in India of regiments of the Native army (including the Hyderabad Contingent) sent to China should be debited to the Imperial Government.

(*c.*) Charges directly due to special recruiting of corps actually proceeded to China will be debited to the Imperial Government.

(*d.*) Cost of replacement of issues from stock for China will be treated as ordinary expenditure chargeable against the Indian Government.

50. *Seconding of Native Officers and men.*—Native Officers, non-commissioned officers and men detailed for duty with the force from corps remaining in India, who are likely to be detained in China for any length of time, may be seconded in their corps.

51. *Plague precautions.*—All troops and followers and coolie corps arriving at ports of embarkation must be railed direct to the docks, or where this is not possible must be marched direct from the railway station to the docks and embarked. None are to be encamped at ports of embarkation, but, if necessary, may be detained at suitable rest-camps outside ports of embarkation. All newly-entertained followers must be thoroughly disinfected with their clothes and bedding. All natives belonging to coolie corps must be thoroughly disinfected with clothes and bedding at places of concentration and railed thence to ports of embarkation.

APPENDIX B. 1.

Detail of the China

Units.	British.			Native.		Followers.		Horses.		
	Officers.	Warrant and Non-Commissioned Officers and Men.	Officers and Hospital Assistants.	Non-Commissioned Officers and Men.	Public (exclusive of Transport Followers).	Private.	Chargers.	Public or Troop.	Silladar.
Divisional Staff	*36	15	1	2	3	188	75	—	—
Total Divisional Staff	36	15	1	2	3	188	75	—	—
CAVALRY BRIGADE.									
Staff	8	1	—	—	—	44	22	—	—
"B" Battery, Royal Horse Artillery	5	164	—	13	103	22	11	198	—
R.-2 Ammunition Column Unit	1	3	—	21	25	3	2	43	—
1st Bengal Lancers	12	—	18	483	263	60	25	—	495
*16th Bengal Lancers	12	—	18	483	263	60	25	—	495
*3rd Bombay Light Cavalry	12	—	18	483	263	60	25	—	495
Section A, No. 22 British Field Hospital.	1	6	—	2	72	9	1	—	—
Section A, No. 42 Native Field Hospital.	1	1	2	5	61	9	1	—	—
Sections A and B, No. 57 Native Field Hospital.	2	1	4	8	111	15	2	—	—
No. 1 Brigade Supply Column	—	1	—	4	22	2	—	—	—
Total Cavalry Brigade	54	177	60	1,502	1,183	284	114	241	1,485
1ST INFANTRY BRIGADE.									
*Staff	7	1	—	—	—	35	16	—	—
*7th Bengal Infantry	13	—	17	721	59	35	13	—	—
*24th Punjab Infantry	13	—	17	721	59	35	13	—	—
*1st Sikh Infantry	13	—	17	721	59	35	13	—	—
26th Bombay Infantry	13	—	17	721	59	35	13	—	—
*No. 39 Native Field Hospital	4	1	8	15	224	28	4	—	—
*No. 45 Native Field Hospital	4	1	8	15	224	28	4	—	—
No. 2 Brigade Supply Column	—	1	—	4	22	2	—	—	—
Total 1st Infantry Brigade	67	4	84	2,918	706	233	76	—	—

* One from siege train.

APPENDIX B. 1.

EXPEDITIONARY FORCE.

	Ponies.			Engineer Equipment Mules.	Transports and Establishments.														Guns.	
Private.	Public.	Silladar.	Ambulance.		Pack Mules.	Warrant Officers.	Non-Commissioned Officers.	Veterinary Assistants.	Clerks.	Jemadars.	Duffadars.	Drivers.	Shoeing-smiths.	Saddlers.	Carpenters.	Blacksmiths.	Hammermen.	Bellows Boys.	Syces.	B.L., 15-pr.	Maxims, Machine, ·303.
37	—	—	—	—	48	—	—	—	—	1	2	16	—	—	—	—	—	—	—	—	—
37	—	—	—	—	48	—	—	—	—	1	2	16	—	—	—	—	—	—	—	—	—
8	—	—	—	—	36	—	—	—	—	—	1	12	—	—	—	—	—	—	—	—	—
7	—	—	—	—	12	—	—	—	—	—	1	4	—	—	—	—	—	—	—	6	—
1	—	—	—	—	12	—	—	—	—	—	—	4	—	—	—	—	—	—	—	—	—
14	—	207	—	—	87	—	—	—	—	1	2	59	—	—	—	—	—	—	—	—	—
14	—	207	—	—	87	—	—	—	—	1	2	59	—	—	—	—	—	—	—	—	—
14	—	207	—	—	87	—	—	—	—	1	2	59	—	—	—	—	—	—	—	—	—
6	—	—	—	—	12	—	—	—	—	—	—	1	4	—	—	—	—	—	—	—	—
8	—	—	—	—	12	—	—	—	—	—	—	4	—	—	—	—	—	—	—	—	—
9	—	—	—	—	12	—	—	—	—	—	—	4	—	—	—	—	—	—	—	—	—
1	—	—	—	—	—	—	—	—	—	—	—	—	—	—	—	—	—	—	—	—	—
82	—	621	—	—	357	—	—	—	—	3	9	209	—	—	—	—	—	—	—	6	—
7	—	—	—	—	36	—	—	—	—	—	1	12	—	—	—	—	—	—	—	—	—
8	—	—	—	—	96	—	—	—	—	2	4	35	—	—	—	—	—	—	—	—	1
8	—	—	—	—	108	—	—	—	—	2	4	36	—	—	—	—	—	—	—	—	1
8	—	—	—	—	108	—	—	—	—	2	4	36	—	—	—	—	—	—	—	—	1
8	—	—	—	—	108	—	—	—	—	2	4	36	—	—	—	—	—	—	—	—	1
16	—	—	—	—	12	—	—	—	—	—	1	4	—	—	—	—	—	—	—	—	—
16	—	—	—	—	12	—	—	—	—	—	—	4	—	—	—	—	—	—	—	—	—
1	—	—	—	—	—	—	—	—	—	—	—	—	—	—	—	—	—	—	—	—	—
72	—	—	—	—	480	—	—	—	—	8	18	163	—	—	—	—	—	—	—	—	4

DETAIL OF THE CHINA

Units.	British.		Native.		Followers.		Horses.		
	Officers.	Warrant and Non-Commissioned Officers and Men.	Officers and Hospital Assistants.	Non-Commissioned Officers and Men.	Public (exclusive of Transport Followers).	Private.	Chargers.	Public or Troop.	Silladar.
2ND INFANTRY BRIGADE.									
Staff	7	1	—	—	—	35	16	—	—
2nd Bengal Infantry	13	—	17	721	59	35	13	—	—
14th Sikhs	13	—	17	721	59	35	13	—	—
1-4th Gurkhas	13	—	17	721	59	35	13	—	—
30th Bombay Infantry	13	—	17	721	59	35	13	—	—
No. 63 Native Field Hospital	4	1	8	15	224	28	4	—	—
No. 66 Native Field Hospital	4	1	8	15	224	28	4	—	—
No. 3 Brigade Supply Column	—	1	—	4	22	2	—	—	—
Total 2nd Infantry Brigade	67	4	84	2,918	706	233	76	—	—
3RD INFANTRY BRIGADE.									
Staff	7	1	—	—	—	44	16	—	—
6th Bengal Infantry	13	—	17	721	59	35	13	—	—
4th Punjab Infantry	13	—	17	721	59	35	13	—	—
20th Punjab Infantry	13	—	17	721	59	35	13	—	—
34th Pioneers	13	—	17	721	59	35	13	—	—
No. 51 Native Field Hospital	4	1	8	15	224	28	4	—	—
No. 61 Native Field Hospital	4	1	8	15	224	28	4	—	—
No. 5 Brigade Supply Column	—	1	—	4	22	2	—	—	—
Total 3rd Infantry Brigade	67	4	84	2,918	706	242	76	—	—
4TH INFANTRY BRIGADE.									
Staff	8	2	—	—	—	50	18	—	—
28th Madras Infantry	13	—	17	721	59	35	13	—	—
31st Madras Infantry	13	—	17	721	59	35	13	—	—
Alwar Infantry (Imperial Service Troops).	2	—	20	689	95		5	—	—
Bikanir Infantry (Imperial Service Troops).	2	—	15	382	53		5	—	—
No. 53 Native Field Hospital	4	1	8	15	224	28	4	—	—
No. 58 Native Field Hospital	4	1	8	15	224	28	4	—	—
No. 6 Brigade Supply Column	—	1	—	4	22	2	—	—	—
Total 4th Infantry Brigade	46	5	85	2,547	914		62	—	—

389

EXPEDITIONARY FORCE—*continued.*

	Ponies.			Engineer Equipment Mules.	Transports and Establishments.														Guns.	
Private.	Public.	Silladar.	Ambulance.		Pack Mules.	Warrant Officers.	Non-Commissioned Officers.	Veterinary Assistants.	Clerks.	Jemadars.	Duffadars.	Drivers.	Shoeing-smiths.	Saddlers.	Carpenters.	Blacksmiths.	Hammermen.	Bellows Boys.	Syces.	B.L., 15-pr.	Maxim, Machine, ·303.
7	—	—	—	—	36	—	—	—	—	—	1	12	—	—	—	—	—	—	—	—	—
8	—	—	—	—	108	—	—	—	—	2	4	36	—	—	—	—	—	—	—	—	1
8	—	—	—	—	108	—	—	—	—	2	4	36	—	—	—	—	—	—	—	—	1
8	—	—	—	—	108	—	—	—	—	2	4	36	—	—	—	—	—	—	—	—	1
8	—	—	—	—	108	—	—	—	—	2	4	36	—	—	—	—	—	—	—	—	1
16	—	—	—	—	12	—	—	—	—	—	1	4	—	—	—	—	—	—	—	—	—
16	—	—	—	—	12	—	—	—	—	—	—	4	—	—	—	—	—	—	—	—	—
1	—	—	—	—	—	—	—	—	—	—	—	—	—	—	—	—	—	—	—	—	—
72	—	—	—	—	492	—	—	—	—	8	18	164	—	—	—	—	—	—	—	—	4
9	—	—	—	—	36	—	—	—	—	—	1	12	—	—	—	—	—	—	—	—	—
8	—	—	—	—	108	—	—	—	—	2	4	36	—	—	—	—	—	—	—	—	1
8	—	—	—	—	108	—	—	—	—	2	4	36	—	—	—	—	—	—	—	—	1
8	—	—	—	—	108	—	—	—	—	2	4	36	—	—	—	—	—	—	—	—	1
8	—	—	—	—	168	—	—	—	—	3	7	56	—	—	—	—	—	—	—	—	1
16	—	—	—	—	12	—	—	—	—	—	1	4	—	—	—	—	—	—	—	—	—
16	—	—	—	—	12	—	—	—	—	—	—	4	—	—	—	—	—	—	—	—	—
1	—	—	—	—	—	—	—	—	—	—	—	—	—	—	—	—	—	—	—	—	—
74	—	—	—	—	552	—	—	—	—	9	21	184	—	—	—	—	—	—	—	—	4
10	—	—	—	—	36	—	—	—	—	—	1	12	—	—	—	—	—	—	—	—	—
8	—	—	—	—	108	—	—	—	—	2	4	36	—	—	—	—	—	—	—	—	1
8	—	—	—	—	108	—	—	—	…	2	4	36	—	—	—	—	—	—	…	—	1
7	—	—	—	—	111	—	—	—	…	—	—	58	—	—	—	—	—	…	…	…	—
6	—	—	—	—	60	—	—	—	—	—	—	31	—	—	—	—	—	…	…	…	—
16	—	—	—	—	12	—	—	—	—	—	1	4	—	—	—	—	—	…	…	—	—
16	—	—	—	—	24	—	—	—	—	—	1	8	—	—	—	—	—	…	…	—	—
1	—	—	—	—	—	—	—	—	—	—	—	—	—	—	—	—	—	…	…	—	—
72	—	—	—	—	459	—	—	—	—	4	11	185	—	—	—	—	—	—	—	—	2

DETAIL OF THE CHINA

Units.	British.			Native.		Followers.		Horses.		
	Officers.	Warrant and Non-Commissioned Officers and Men.	Clerks.	Officers and Hospital assistants.	Non-Commissioned Officers and Men.	Public (exclusive of Transport Followers).	Private.	Chargers.	Public or Troop.	Silladar.
DIVISIONAL TROOPS.										
*12th Battery, Royal Field Artillery	5	164	—	—	11	72	21	10	143	—
*R.-7 Ammunition Column Unit	1	3	—	—	21	25	3	2	43	—
1st Regiment, Jodhpur Lancers	2	—	—	26	483	345	25	4	—	506
*1st Madras Pioneers	13	—	—	17	721	59	35	13	—	—
Mounted Detachment, Bengal Sappers and Miners.	1	1	—	1	23	24	—	—	24	—
No. 4 Company, Bengal Sappers and Miners.	4	2	—	4	189	19	18	8	—	—
*No. 3 Company, Madras Sappers and Miners.	4	2	—	4	189	18	18	8	—	—
No. 2 Company, Bombay Sappers and Miners.	4	2	—	4	189	18	18	8	—	—
Maler Kotla Sappers	1	—	—	6	132	63		3	—	—
*1 Photo-Litho. Section, Madras Sappers and Miners.	—	2	—	—	4	2	—	—	—	—
*1 Printing Section, Madras Sappers and Miners.	—	1	—	—	4	2	—	—	—	—
Printing Section, Bombay Sappers and Miners.	—	1	—	—	4	2	—	—	—	—
Photo-Litho Section, Bombay Sappers and Miners.	—	2	—	—	4	2	—	—	—	—
10 Signalling Units, British Infantry	—	60	—	—	—	—	—	—	—	—
2 ,, ,, Native ,,	—	—	—	—	12	—	—	—	—	—
Survey Party	1	—	—	—	6	27	—	—	—	—
*Section B, No. 22 British Field Hospital.	1	6	—	—	2	72	9	1	—	—
Sections B, C. and D, No. 42 Native Field Hospital.	3	1	—	6	12	180	22	3	—	—
Sections C and D, No. 62 Native Field Hospital.	2	1	—	4	8	111	15	2	—	—
Sections A and B, No. 38 Native Field Hospital.	2	1	—	4	8	111	15	2	—	—
No. 4 Brigade Supply Column	—	1	—	—	4	22	2	—	—	—
Total	44	250	—	76	2,026	1,375		64	210	506

EXPEDITIONARY FORCE—*continued*.

	Ponies.				Transport and Establishments.													Guns.	
Private.	Public.	Silladar.	Ambulance.	Engineer Equipment Mules.	Pack Mules.	Warrant Officers.	Non-Commissioned Officers.	Veterinary Assistants.	Clerks.	Jemadars.	Duffadars.	Drivers.	Shoeing-smiths.	Saddlers.	Carpenters.	Blacksmiths.	Hammermen.	Bellows Boys.	Syces.	B. L., 15-pr.	Maxim, Machine · 303.
7	—	—	—	—	12	—	—	—	—	1	4	—	—	—	—	—	—	—	6	—
1	—	—	—	—	12	—	—	—	—	—	4	—	—	—	—	—	—	—	—	—
—	—	305	—	—	—	—	—	—	—	—	—	—	—	—	—	—	—	—	—	—
8	—	—	—	—	168	—	—	—	4	7	56	—	—	—	—	—	—	—	—	1
—	—	—	—	—	—	—	—	—	—	—	—	—	—	—	—	—	—	—	—	—
5	—	—	—	18	72	—	—	—	1	3	24	—	—	—	—	—	—	—	—	—
5	—	—	—	18	72	—	—	—	1	3	24	—	—	—	—	—	—	—	—	—
5	—	—	—	18	72	—	—	—	1	3	24	—	—	—	—	—	—	—	—	—
—	—	—	—	—	105	—	—	—	—	—	23	—	—	—	—	—	—	—	—	—
—	—	—	—	—	} 12	—	—	—	—	—	4	—	—	—	—	—	—	—	—	—
—	—	—	—	—	24	—	—	—	—	1	8	—	—	—	—	—	—	—	—	—
—	—	—	—	—	6	—	—	—	—	—	2	—	—	—	—	—	—	—	—	—
6	—	—	—	—	12	—	—	—	—	1	4	—	—	—	—	—	—	—	—	—
13	—	—	—	—	—	—	—	—	—	—	—	—	—	—	—	—	—	—	—	—
9	—	—	—	—	6	—	—	—	—	—	2	—	—	—	—	—	—	—	—	—
9	—	—	—	—	6	—	—	—	—	—	2	—	—	—	—	—	—	—	—	—
1	—	—	—	—	—	—	—	—	—	—	—	—	—	—	—	—	—	—	—	—
69	—	305	—	54	579	—	—	—	7	19	181	—	—	—	—	—	—	—	6	1

U 21071.   D D

DETAIL OF THE CHINA

Units.	British.			Native.		Followers.		Horses.		
	Officers.	Warrant and Non-Commissioned Officers and Men.	Clerks.	Officers and Hospital Assistants.	Non-Commissioned Officers and Men.	Public (exclusive of Transport followers).	Private.	Chargers.	Public or Troop.	Silladar.
Line of Communication Troops.										
Staff	19	2	—	—	—	—	86	38	—	—
*22nd Bombay Infantry	13	—	—	17	721	59	35	13	—	—
3rd Madras Infantry	13	—	—	17	721	59	35	13	—	—
5th Infantry, Hyderabad Contingent	13	—	—	17	721	59	35	13	—	—
*2 Telegraph Sections	—	64	—	—	32	—	—	—	—	—
1 Railway Section	—	2	—	—	—	48	4	—	—	—
Post Offices	3	10	—	42	—	57	31	4	—	—
*Ordnance Field Park	(a)6	24	7	—	—	158	16	2	—	—
*Engineer Field Park (Fort William)	1	3	—	—	2	35	4	2	—	—
Engineer Field Park (Roorkee)	1	3	—	—	2	35	4	2	—	—
Sections A and B, No. 15 British Field Hospital.	2	12	—	—	2	42	18	2	—	—
Sections A and B, No. 25 British Field Hospital.	2	12	—	—	2	42	18	2	—	—
*No. 47 Native Field Hospital	4	1	—	8	15	224	28	4	—	—
Sections C and D, No. 69, Native Field Hospital.	2	1	—	4	8	111	15	2	—	—
No. 41 Native Field Hospital	4	1	—	8	15	224	28	4	—	—
Sections C and D, No. 57, Native Field Hospital.	2	1	—	4	8	111	15	2	—	—
Section B, No. 5 Field Veterinary Hospital.	1	4	—	—	1	9	5	2	1	—
No. 3 Field Medical Store Depôt	1	—	—	—	—	5	4	1	—	—
No. 4 Field Medical Store Depôt	1	—	—	—	—	5	4	1	—	—
3 Native General Hospitals (500 beds)	30	6	—	60	75	540	213	30	—	—
1 Native Military Base Depôt	—	—	—	1	5	4	1	—	—	—
2 Base Supply Depôts	—	28	—	—	28	76	42	—	—	—
Base Depôt of Medical Stores	1	2	2	—	—	14	6	2	—	—
1 Base Veterinary Depôt	1	2	—	—	2	4	5	2	—	—
1 Base Stationery Depôt	—	—	—	2	3	—	—	—	—	—
Transport assistants (to be drawn from Native Cavalry Regiments).	—	—	—	—	12	—	—	—	—	—
Transport Establishment, including spare drivers and spare mules.	—	—	—	—	—	—	8	—	—	—
Carried forward										

(a) Including 3 Departmental

EXPEDITIONARY FORCE—*continued*.

	Ponies.									Transport and Establishments.																Guns.	
	Private.	Public.	Silladar.	Ambulance.	Engineer Equipment Mules.	Bullocks.	Filth Carts.	Rubbish Carts.	Pack Mules.	Warrant Officers.	Non-Commissioned Officers.	Veterinary Assistants.	Clerks.	Jemadars.	Duffadars.	Drivers.	Shoeing-smiths.	Saddlers.	Carpenters.	Moclis.	Blacksmiths.	Hammermen.	Bellows Boys.	Coachmen.	Syces.	B.E, 15-pr.	Maxim, machine ·303.
	19	—	—	—	—	—	—	—	36	—	—	—	—	—	1	12	—	—	—	—	—	—	—	—	—	—	—
	8	—	—	—	—	—	—	—	108	—	—	—	—	2	4	36	—	—	—	—	—	—	—	—	—	—	—
	8	—	—	—	—	—	—	—	108	—	—	—	—	2	4	36	—	—	—	—	—	—	—	—	—	—	—
	8	—	—	—	—	—	—	—	108	—	—	—	—	2	4	36	—	—	—	—	—	—	—	—	—	—	—
	—	—	—	—	—	—	—	—	24	—	—	—	—	—	—	8	—	—	—	—	—	—	—	—	—	—	—
	2	—	—	—	—	—	—	—	—	—	—	—	—	—	—	—	—	—	—	—	—	—	—	—	—	—	—
	1	—	—	—	—	—	—	—	—	—	—	—	—	—	—	—	—	—	—	—	—	—	—	—	—	—	—
	16	—	—	—	—	—	—	—	12	—	—	—	—	—	1	4	—	—	—	—	—	—	—	—	—	—	—
	1	—	—	—	—	—	—	—	12	—	—	—	—	—	—	4	—	—	—	—	—	—	—	—	—	—	—
	1	—	—	—	—	—	—	—	12	—	—	—	—	—	—	4	—	—	—	—	—	—	—	—	—	—	—
	12	—	—	—	—	—	—	—	9	—	—	—	—	—	—	3	—	—	—	—	—	—	—	—	—	—	—
	12	—	—	—	—	—	—	—	12	—	—	—	—	—	—	4	—	—	—	—	—	—	—	—	—	—	—
	16	—	—	—	—	—	—	—	12	—	—	—	—	—	1	4	—	—	—	—	—	—	—	—	—	—	—
	9	—	—	—	—	—	—	—	12	—	—	—	—	—	—	4	—	—	—	—	—	—	—	—	—	—	—
	16	—	—	—	—	—	—	—	12	—	—	—	—	—	—	4	—	—	—	—	—	—	—	—	—	—	—
	9	—	—	—	—	—	—	—	12	—	—	—	—	—	—	4	—	—	—	—	—	—	—	—	—	—	—
	1	1	—	—	—	—	—	—	12	—	—	—	—	—	—	4	—	—	—	—	—	—	—	—	—	—	—
	1	—	—	—	—	—	—	—	—	—	—	—	—	—	—	—	—	—	—	—	—	—	—	—	—	—	—
	1	—	—	—	—	—	—	—	—	—	—	—	—	—	—	—	—	—	—	—	—	—	—	—	—	—	—
	96	—	—	—	—	—	—	—	—	—	—	—	—	—	—	—	—	—	—	—	—	—	—	—	—	—	—
	28	—	—	—	—	—	—	—	—	—	—	—	—	—	—	—	—	—	—	—	—	—	—	—	—	—	—
	—	—	—	—	—	—	—	—	—	—	—	—	—	—	—	—	—	—	—	—	—	—	—	—	—	—	—
	1	—	—	—	—	—	—	—	—	—	—	—	—	—	—	—	—	—	—	—	—	—	—	—	—	—	—
	—	—	—	—	—	—	—	—	—	—	—	—	—	—	—	T	—	—	—	—	—	—	—	—	—	—	—
	—	—	—	—	—	—	—	—	—	—	—	—	—	—	—	—	—	—	—	—	—	—	—	—	—	—	—
	—	8	—	—	—	—	—	—	108	2	6	10	2	13	11	120	5	26	3	—	8	8	8	—	6	—	—

officers with honorary rank,

394

DETAIL OF THE CHINA

Units.	British.			Native.		Followers.		Horses.		
	Officers.	Warrant and Non-Commissioned Officers and Men.	Clerks.	Officers and Hospital Assistants.	Non-Commissioned Officers and Men.	Public (exclusive of Transport followers).	Private.	Chargers.	Public or Troop.	Silladar.
Brought forward -										
4 coolie corps -	8	8	—	—	8	4,228	48	16	—	—
No. 54 Native Field Hospital for Coolie Corps.	4	1	8	—	15	224	28	4	—	—
Total Line of Communication Troops	132	187	9	188	2,398	6,433	736	161	1	—
Special Details.										
Siege Train Bullocks -	5	15	—	—	—	—	10	5	—	—
Sections A and B, No. 69 Native Field Hospital.	2	1	—	4	8	111	15	2	—	—
Baloon Section -	—	—	—	—	—	27	—	—	54	—
Vickers-Maxim Guns -	1	6	—	1	—	126	4	2	—	—
Remount Depôt -	2	6	—	3	29	160	12	6	—	—
Sanitary Establishment -	—	—	—	—	—	480	—	—	—	—
Dhanjibhoy's Tongas -	—	1	—	—	—	—	—	—	—	—
Special Service Officers -	29	—	—	—	—	—	145	58	—	—
Field Audit Office -	2	—	45	—	—	8	32	4	—	—
Aërated Water Factory -	—	—	—	—	—	18	—	—	—	—
Total -	41	29	45	8	37	930	218	77	54	—
Summary.										
Divisional Staff -	36	15	—	1	2	3	188	75	—	—
Cavalry Brigade -	54	177	—	60	1,502	1,183	284	114	241	1,485
1st Infantry Brigade -	67	4	—	84	2,918	706	233	76	—	—
2nd ,, ,, -	67	4	—	84	2,918	706	233	76	—	—
3rd ,, ,, -	67	4	—	84	2,918	706	242	76	—	—
4th ,, ,, -	46	5	—	85	2,547	914		62	—	—
Divisional Troops -	44	250	—	76	2,026	1,375		64	210	506
Line of communications troops -	132	187	9	188	2,398	6,433	736	161	1	—
Special details -	41	29	45	8	37	930	218	77	54	—
GRAND TOTAL -	554	675	54	670	17,266	13,090		781	506	1,991

(a) Includes 276 mules belonging

395

EXPEDITIONARY FORCE—*continued*.

Ponies.								Transport and Establishments.															Guns.	
Private.	Public.	Silladar.	Ambulance.	Engineer Equipment Mules.	Bullocks.	Filth Carts.	Rubbish Carts.	Pack Mules.	Warrant Officers.	Non-Commissioned Officers.	Veterinary Assistants.	Clerks.	Jemadars.	Duffadars.	Drivers.	Shoeing-Smiths.	Saddlers.	Carpenters.	Mochis.	Blacksmiths.	Hammermen.	Bellows Boys.	Coachmen.	Syces.	B. L., 15-pr.	Maxim, Machine ·303.
8	8	—	—	—	—	—	—	—	—	—	—	—	—	—	—	—	—	—	—	—	—	—	—	8	—	—
16	—	—	—	—	—	—	—	12	—	—	—	—	—	—	4	—	—	—	—	—	—	—	—	—	—	—
300	17	—	—	—	—	—	—	621	2	6	10	2	19	26	291	5	26	3	—	8	8	8	—	14	—	—
—	3	—	—	1,304	—	—	—	—	—	—	8	3	—	14	744	10	—	8	—	5	5	5	—	1	—	—
9	—	—	—	—	—	—	—	12	—	—	—	—	—	—	4	—	—	—	—	—	—	—	—	—	—	—
—	—	—	—	—	—	—	—	—	—	—	—	—	—	—	—	—	—	—	—	—	—	—	—	—	—	—
—	—	—	—	—	150	90	30	—	—	—	—	—	—	—	—	—	—	—	—	—	—	—	—	—	—	—
—	21	—	—	—	—	—	—	—	—	—	—	—	1	1	—	1	—	1	1	1	1	—	10	12	—	—
2	—	—	—	—	—	—	—	—	—	—	—	—	—	—	—	—	—	—	—	—	—	—	—	—	—	—
11	24	—	—	—	—	90	30	12	—	—	8	3	1	15	748	11	—	9	1	6	6	5	10	13	—	—
37	—	—	—	—	—	—	—	48	—	—	—	1	2	16	—	—	—	—	—	—	—	—	—	—	—	—
82	—	621	—	—	—	—	—	357	—	—	—	3	9	209	—	—	—	—	—	—	—	—	—	—	6	—
72	—	—	—	—	—	—	—	480	—	—	—	8	18	163	—	—	—	—	—	—	—	—	—	—	—	4
72	—	—	—	—	—	—	—	432	—	—	—	8	18	164	—	—	—	—	—	—	—	—	—	—	—	4
74	—	—	—	—	—	—	—	552	—	—	—	9	21	184	—	—	—	—	—	—	—	—	—	—	—	4
72	—	—	—	—	—	—	—	459	—	—	—	4	11	185	—	—	—	—	—	—	—	—	—	—	—	2
69	—	305	—	54	—	—	—	579	—	—	—	7	19	181	—	—	—	—	—	—	—	—	—	—	6	1
300	17	—	—	—	—	—	—	621	2	6	10	2	19	26	291	5	26	3	—	8	8	8	—	14	—	—
11	24	—	—	1,454	—	90	30	12	—	—	8	3	1	15	748	11	—	9	1	6	6	5	10	13	—	—
789	41	926	—	54	1,454	90	30	3,600 (a)	2	6	18	5	60	119	2,141	16	26	12	1	14	14	13	10	27	12	15

to the Imperial Troops.

APPENDIX B. 2.

Troops and followers of the China Expeditionary Force will be supplied with field service clothing as follows:—

TABLE I.—FIELD SERVICE CLOTHING (Summer and Winter) according to usual Scales.

	Summer.	Winter
BRITISH TROOPS.		
Blanket, barrack	1	1
Waterproof sheet	1	—
Putties (Royal Horse and Field Artillery and mounted men of heavy batteries), pair	1	—
Boots, ankle (cavalry only) pair	1	—
Coat, warm	—	1
Mittens, pair	—	1
Cap, Balaclava	—	1
NATIVE TROOPS.		
Waterproof sheet	1	—
Blanket, country	1	1
Boots or shoes, pairs	✺	—
Coat, warm	—	1†
Mittens, pair	—	1
Cap, Balaclava	—	1
Socks, worsted, pairs	2	—
Jersey (cardigan jackets, until present stock is exhausted).	—	1
Pyjamas, warm, pair	—	1
FOLLOWERS.		
Waterproof sheet	1	—
Putties, pair	1	—
Blanket, country	1	1
Boots, hobnailed and toeplated, pair	1‡	—
Haversack	1	—
Water-bottle, tin	1	—
Blouse, khâki	1‡	—
Pugri	1‡	—
Belt, leather	1‡	—
Coat, warm	—	1
Jersey (cardigan jacket, until present stock is exhausted).	—	1
Pyjamas, warm	—	1
Socks, pair	1§	—

✺ An allowance of Rs. 2-8-0 per pair.
† Specially sanctioned in place of the ordinary scale of 32 per troop or company.
‡ Not issued to permanent transport followers who have these articles in possession.
§ Specially sanctioned.

A 20 per cent. reserve of all the above, including boots for troops and followers with hobnails and toeplates affixed thereto, will be provided under the orders of the Lieutenant-General Commanding the Forces, Bengal. It will accompany the force and be stored at the base, or as may be ordered.

Table II.—Special Warm Clothing.

Item No.	Articles.	British Troops.	Native Troops.	Followers.	Remarks.
1	Fur cap	1	—	—	Good, but a lighter and smarter cap could be obtained.
2	Lambswool drawers, pairs	2	—	—	Excellent, and very suitable.
3	Blankets, barrack	2	—	—	
4	Postin, or blanket-lined canvas coat, or Canadian warm coat.	1	1	1	Not suitable. A loose sheep-skin coat would be much more serviceable for North China.
5	Puttoo gloves, pair	1	1	1	A poor glove. A fur lined glove is required.
6	Comforter, woollen	1	1	1	Very good.
7	Norwegian socks, pair	1	1	1	Not obtained. Long stockings were issued instead which were good and suitable.
8	Ankle boots (one size larger than usual), pair.	1	1	1	
9	Blankets, country	—	2	2	
10	Short, thick-flannel drawers (for wear under pyjamas), pairs.	—	1	1	Too short and too thin, and shrink so as to become unwearable.
11	Cap, Balaclava	—	—	1	Good.
12	Khaki serge coat	1	—	—	
13	Khaki serge trousers, pair	1	—	—	
14	Bedford cord pantaloons, mounted men, pair.	1	—	—	
15	Khaki serge blouse	—	1	—	
16	Khaki serge pyjamas (dismounted men), pair.	—	1	—	
17	Khaki cord pantaloons (mounted men), pair.	—	1	—	

(1) A 10 per cent. reserve of items 4 and 8 and a 20 per cent. of other items will be provided.

Lambswool vests for British troops were purchased at Shanghai and Hongkong by the Commissariat Department and were excellent and very suitable.

Leather mocassins were sent to North China from Canada, but were quite unsuitable having too thin soles. A long Kashmir boot would be far preferable.

Table III.—Scale of Clothing proposed as suitable for Troops and Followers in North China by the Lieutenant-General Commanding the China Expeditionary Force.

British Troops.

Names of Article.	Summer and Winter Scale.	Special extra Scale as recommended by Lieutenant-General Commanding.	Remarks.
Blankets, barrack	2	2	
Putties, pairs	1	—	
Waterproof sheets	1	—	
Boots, ammunition, pairs	1	—	*Of a large size to be worn over thick socks.

British Troops—continued.

Names of Articles.	Summer and Winter Scale.	Special Extra Scale as recommended by Lieutenant-General Commanding.	Remarks.
Socks, worsted, pairs	2*	—	*With a reserve of two extra pairs per man in commissariat charge to be issued as replacements during winter.
Stockings, long, pairs	—	1	
Coats, warm	1	—	
Coats, sheepskin, long (Chinese)	—	1	} For sentries only.
Gloves, sheepskin, pairs (Chinese)	—	1	
Jerseys	1	—	
Mittens, warm, pairs	1†	—	†With a reserve of one extra pair per man in commissariat charge to be issued as replacements during winter.
Caps, Balaclava	1	—	
Caps, fur	—	1	
Drawers, lambswool, pairs	—	2	
Vests, lambswool	—	2	
Comforters, woollen	—	1	

Native Troops.

Names of Articles.	Summer and Winter Scale.	Special Extra Scale as recommended by Lieutenant-General Commanding.	Remarks.
Blankets, country	2	2	
Boots or shoes, pairs	1	1*	*Boots of a large size to be worn over thick socks.
Boots, sheepskin, or felt, pairs (Chinese)	—	1	
Coats, sheepskin, long (Chinese)	—	1	For sentries only.
Gloves, sheepskin, pairs (Chinese)	—	1	
Socks, worsted, pairs	2†	—	†With a reserve of two extra pairs per man in commissariat charge to be issued as renewals during winter.
Stockings, long, pairs	—	1	
Waterproof sheets	1	—	
Putties, pairs	1	—	
Jerseys	1	—	
Mittens, warm, pairs	1‡	—	‡Renewals admissible as above.
Caps, Balaclava	1§	—	§Unsuitable for Sikhs, perhaps a Bashalik might take its place.
Pyjamas, warm, pairs	1	—	
Coats, warm, British	1	—	
Drawers, warm, pairs	—	—	
Vests, warm	—	2	
Comforters, woollen	—	1	

Followers.

Names of Articles.	Summer and Winter Scale.	Special extra Scale as recommended by Lieutenant-General Commanding.	Remarks.
Blankets, country	2	2	
Putties, pairs	1	1	
Haversack	1	—	
Water bottle, tin	1	—	
Blouse, khaki	1	—	
Boot, pairs	1	—	
Shoes, Chinese, pairs	—	1*	*In lieu of large sized boots.
Socks, Chinese, pairs	—	1†	†Also one pair as renewals about 1st January.
Pugris	1	—	
Belts, leather	1	—	
Coats, warm	1	—	
Coats, great‡	—	1	‡Chinese sheepskin.
Jerseys	1	—	
Pyjamas, warm, pairs	1	1	
Drawers, warm, pairs	—		
Vests, warm	—	2	
Gloves, sheepskin, pairs (Chinese)	—	1	
Comforters, woollen	—		

N.B.—It should be understood that all clothing is to last for the winter and not to be renewed at the expense of the State, except under special circumstances.

APPENDIX C.

Return of Stores Provided from England and Canada for the China Expedition.

Description of Articles.	Remarks.
Coal for transports - Tons 20,000	Deposited at Hongkong.
Guns, automatic, 1-pdr., with necessary ammunition - No. 20	Shipped to Wei-hai-wei. One gun, harness and saddlery for six guns, and 111,280 rounds ammunition, shipped to Shanghai for transhipment to Wei-hai-wei per S.S. "Canton," 15th September. Four guns, with 10,000 rounds ammunition, shipped from South Africa per S.S. "Antillian" (23rd July) Five more shipped in October, and the remaining ten in November.
Guns, Maxim, with pack transport mountings - - No. 10	10 Maxims with tripods and pack saddlery (complete, except boxes belt ammunition) shipped per S.S. "Alcinous," 21st July, consigned to Ordnance Officer, Wei-hai-wei, transhipping at Shanghai. The boxes, belt, were shipped per S.S. "Patroclus," 2nd August.

Forage :—
 Reserve to be maintained :—
   Hay - - - Tons 4,000
   Oats - - -   „ 4,000
   Bran - - -   „ 400
 	
 Requirements about 2,200 tons per month.
	See below.

RETURN OF STORES, &C.—continued.

Name of Vessel.	Approximate date of sailing from Melbourne.	Destination.	Cargo.	
S.S. "Claverden"	– July 1900	Wei-hai-wei, or any safe port in the Gulf of Pechili.	Hay - Oats - Bran -	Tons. - 849 - 948 - 179
S.S. "Kirklee"	31 July 1900	Do.	Hay - Oats - Bran -	- 939 - 1,064 - 180
S.S. "Venetia" (Shut out of S.S. "Ness.")	13 Aug. 1900	Wei-hai-wei	Hay - Oats -	- 1,190 - 1,140
S.S. "Guthrie" and S.S. "Australian."	28 July 1900	Wei-hai-wei, or any safe port in the Gulf of Pechili.	Hay - Oats -	- 307¼ - 700 (Approximate).
S.S. "Isleworth"	– Aug. 1900	Do.	Hay - Oats -	- 700 - 300
S.S. "Ras Dara"	5 Sept. 1900	Do.	Hay - Oats -	- 1,000 - 1,000

N.B.—The quantities shown by the last two vessels are only approximate; those by the first five are the actual quantities taken.

Shipping documents, consisting of Bill of Lading, Insurance Policy and Certificates as to the quality, weight, and condition of goods shipped, sent by the shippers to the military officer commanding at the port of discharge.

To enable payment to be made in England, it is requested that, as soon as practicable after receipt of the forage, a telegram may be sent to the India Office stating the number of packages of hay, oats and bran respectively, delivered in good condition by each vessel.

Description of Articles.	Remarks.
Tobacco for officers - - lbs. 720 " " men - - " 780	1,584 lbs. shipped per S.S. "Bombay," 11th August, to Wei-hai-wei. In accordance with War Office recommendation the tobacco supplied is of one quality only.
Comforters - - - No. 42,200 Lambswool drawers - Prs. 2,640	
Fur caps - - - No. 1,320	1,200 to Wei-hai-wei, 100 to Shanghai, 20 to Hongkong sent from Vancouver.
Coats, warm, Canadian - No. 31,800 Mocassins, leather - - Prs. 29,000 Stockings, long - - " 29,000 " thick Canadian " 14,300	Sent to China from Vancouver.
Tripod mountings for ·303-inch Maxim guns - - No. 9	Shipped to Wei-hai-wei per S.S. "Bombay," 11th August.

RETURN OF STORES, &c.—continued.

Description of Articles.	Remarks.
X-Ray apparatus, with latest improvements - - - No. 1	Shipped to Wei-hai-wei for Chefoo per S.S. "Socotra," 28th August.
Blankets for extra issues and exchanges for Indian brigade landing at Hongkong, 90 in. by 60 in. - - - No. 6,000	Shipped per S.S. "Bombay," 11th August, to Hongkong.
Balloon equipment - - - -	Shipped per S.S. "Bombay" to Wei-hai-wei.
Condensed milk, unsweetened— Tins 13,376	Shipped to Wei-hai-wei per S.S. "Bombay," 11th August.
Horses, Artillery, harness-trained - - - - 100 Cobs, saddle-trained - - 500	Shipped per S.S. "Perthshire" and S.S. "Cleverdale," from Sydney end of September or beginning of October. These vessels call at Tungsha Lightship for orders as to port of landing.
Ammunition, Mark II., ·303-inch. Rounds 2,000,000	1,001,000 shipped to Wei-hai-wei per S.S. "Bombay," 11th August. 1,001,000 shipped to Shanghai for Wei-hai-wei per S.S. "Socotra," 28th August.
Components for five Native Infantry Regiments, each armed with 705 Mark I.° M.L.M. Rifles— 1 year's supply.	Shipped to Shanghai for Wei-hai-wei per S.S. "Socotra," 28th August.
Components for— 2,635 M.L.M. Rifles Mark I.° 1 year's 446 M.L.M. Carbines - supply.	Shipped to Shanghai for Wei-hai-wei by S.S. "Mazagon," 22nd September.
Medicines, medical stores, and appliances, as specified in Appendix 38, regulations, army medical services, and medical and surgical equipment, as specified in Appendix 37 A, regulations, army medical services (except surgical saddle bags).	Shipped per S.S. "Socotra," 28th August, to Shanghai for Wei-hai-wei.
X-Ray apparatus - - - Set 1	Shipped by S.S. "Mazagon," 22nd September to Shanghai for Wei-hai-wei.

Nao food, No. 3 - - Tins 100
   „ for Hospitals—
     Thick soup - „ 100
     Albuminoid paste „ 100
     No. 7 Nao cup - „ 100
   „ for emergency rations—
     No. 1 - - Tins 2,500
     No. 2 A-5 - „ 2,500
	Shipped per S.S. "Socotra," 28th August, to Shanghai for Wei-hai-wei.

Aërated water machines with accessories, &c. - - No. 3	Shipped per S.S. "Socotra," 28th August, to Shanghai for Chefoo.

Return of Stores, &c.—continued.

Description of Articles.	Remarks.
Mechanic for above - - - No. 1	The demand for three supervisors was cancelled by telegram from Viceroy, but one had already been engaged and has been sent with the plant.
To be supplied to Base for Troops.	
Jams, tinned, assorted, in 1-lb. tins - - - Lbs. 10,000	10,464 lbs. shipped per S.S."Socotra" to Shanghai for Wei-hai-wei, 28th August.
To maintain reserves of Medical Comforts for Hospitals and Hospital Ships.	
Two months' supply, as under:—	Stores shipped per S.S. "Socotra" were landed at Shanghai for transhipment to Chefoo; stores per S.S. "Mazagon" were consigned to Shanghai, for transhipment to Chefoo.
Soup, concentrated:—	
Haricot - - - Lbs. 40	⎫
Household - - „ 40	⎬ Shipped per S.S. "Socotra," 28th August, to Shanghai for Chefoo.
Julienne - - „ 40	⎪
Pea - - - „ 40	⎭
Milk, condensed, unsweetened - - „ 40,000	38,532 lbs. per S.S. "Socotra," as above.
Cornflour - - - „ 2,800	Shipped by S.S. "Mazagon," 22nd September, to Shanghai for Chefoo.
Essence of mutton - „ 2,400	1,200 ⎫
Extract of beef - - „ 324	324 ⎬ Per S.S. "Socotra," as above.
Barley, English - • „ 126	126 ⎪
Oatmeal - - - „ 2,002	2,002 ⎭
Brandy - - - Doz. 560	Shipped by S.S. "Mazagon," 22nd September, as above.
Port wine - - - „ 672	
Whisky - - - „ 32	32 per S.S. "Socotra," as above.
Champagne, in half-bottles - - - „ 120	Shipped by S.S. "Mazagon," 22nd September as above.
In addition to the above, a *monthly* supply of half these quantities will follow until further notice from General Officer Commanding Line of Communications.	A part of this supply (oatmeal, barley soup, and whisky) will be shipped per S.S. "Sobraon" 4th October, *via* Shanghai.
Forage:—	
Additional supply as reserve for the first three months of 1901— Tons 8,000	

Return of Stores, &c.—continued.

Name of Vessel.	Approximate date of sailing.	Ports of loading and destination.	Cargo.
			Tons. (Approximate).
S.S. "Hyson"	5 Sept. 1900	Melbourne to Wei-hai-wei or other port between there and Taku, calling at Woosung for orders.	Oaten Hay - 400 Oats - 400
S.S. "Perthshire"	28 Sept. 1900	Do.	Oaten Hay - 1,600 Oats - 1,600 Maize - 250
S.S. "Claverdale"	28 Sept. 1900	Do.	Hay - 1,100 Oats - 1,100

Description of Articles.	Remarks.
For Base Medical Store Depôt.	
Dressing cases, antiseptic, War Office pattern - No. 52	Shipped to Shanghai for Wei-hai-wei, by S.S. "Sobraon," 4th October.
Supplied gratis, for trial, by Messrs. Burroughs and Wellcome.	
Wallets, containing antiseptics and drugs for medical officers - No. 6	Shipped per S.S. "Socotra," 28th August.
Thresh's Disinfectors:—	
For advanced base hospital, Taku 1	Shipped per S.S. "Sobraon" (4th October) *viâ* Shanghai.
„ British troops, general hospital, Chefoo - 1	
„ Wei-hai-wei - 1	Shipped later.
Berkefeld filters, field service pattern as supplied for use in South Africa:—	
For Taku - No. 147	67 per S.S. "Sobraon" (4th October) *viâ* Shanghai.
„ Hongkong - „ 22	22 to Hongkong per S.S. "Sobraon" (4th October).
„ Shanghai - „ 30	30 per S.S. "Sobraon" (4th October) to Shanghai.
X-Ray apparatus, 12″ spark with Grove's battery, spare condenser, and extra supply of acids - Set 1	Shipped to Hongkong by S.S. "Mazagon."
Compressed vegetables - lbs. 2,514 Preserved potatoes - „ 5,040	Consigned to Shanghai for tranship-ment to Sin-ho.

RETURN OF STORES, &c.—*continued.*

Description of Articles.	Remarks.
Tobacco - - - - lbs. 4,796 For Sin-ho ,, - - - - ,, 308 For Shanghai	Shipped per S.S. "Sobraon" (4th October) to Shanghai for transhipment.
Coffee shop stores. For issue on repayment :—	Consigned to Shanghai for Sin-ho.
Pickles, assorted, in bottles doz. 150 Butter, 1-lb. tins - - ,, 200 Bacon, 4 ,, ,, - - tins 200 Cornflour, 1-lb. tins - - doz. 50 Sardines, 18-oz. ,, - ,, 200 Herrings in tins - - - ,, 200 Kippered herrings in tins - ,, 200 Cheese in tins, in pieces of 2 to 4 lbs. - - - - lbs. 200 Milk, condensed, sweetened - - - doz. tins 100 Milk, condensed, unsweetened - - - - ,, 100 Sausages - - - - ,, 100 Soups, assorted - - - ,, 100 Worcester sauce, ½-pint bottles - - - doz. 50 Jams, assorted, 1-lb. tins - ,, 200 Marmalade, 1-lb. tins- ,, 200 Biscuits, assorted, 1-lb. tins - ,, 100 Ginger nuts, 1 lb. tins - ,, 100 Candles, 8 to the lb., 1-lb. packets - - - - ,, 100 Tobacco, Pioneer, cut in ¼-lb. tins - - - - ,, 100 Coffee, ground, in 1-lb. tins - ,, 100 Cocoa, ½-lb. tins - - - ,, 100	Shipped per S.S. "Sobraon" (4th October).

APPENDIX D.

Details of Troops, Animals,

Vessel in which Despatched.	Port of Embarkation.	Date of Sailing.	Troops conveyed.	British.		Native.		Followers.	
				Officers.	Warrant and Commissioned Officers and Men.	Officers and Hospital Assistants.	Non-Commissioned Officers and Men.	Public (exclusive of Transport Followers).	Private.
		1900.							
Nerbudda	Calcutta	25th June	Left wing, 7th Bengal Infantry.	5	—	8	360	10	14
			"A" Section, No. 43 Native Field Hospital.	1	1	2	4	48	2
Palamcotta	,,	29th ,,	Staff	4	—	—	—	—	7
			Headquarters Wing, 7th Bengal Infantry.	8	—	9	338	31	28
			"B" Section, No. 43 Native Field Hospital.	1	—	2	3	65	2
			Marine Department	1	—	—	6	—	1
Itinda	,,	2nd July	Staff	1	—	—	—	—	2
			12th Battery, Royal Field Artillery.	5	160	—	10	73	19
			R-7 Ammunition Column	1	6	—	20	22	2
			"B" Section, No. 22 British Field Hospital.	1	2	—	12	62	2
Zebenghla	,,	3rd ,,	General Officer Commanding Force and Staff (*).	15	6	—	—	—	40
			Section "A," No. 42 Native Field Hospital.	1	—	2	4	59	3
			Engineer Field Park	1	3	—	2	32	3
			No. 2 Brigade Supply Column.	1	1	7	—	22	3
			Special Signalling Units	2	36	—	—	2	2
			24th Punjab Infantry	—	—	—	2	—	—
			Telegraph Section	1	20	—	—	—	4
			Railway Section	1	1	—	2	50	—
			Base Supply Depôt	2	14	—	—	92	29
			Native Military Base Depôt.	1	—	1	5	4	2
			Pay Office	1	—	—	—	3	2
			Field Post Office	2	—	—	—	56	7
			Transport Assistants	—	—	—	12	—	—
			Divisional Commissariat-Transport.	1	—	—	—	11	6
Nairung	,,	3rd ,,	Wing, 24th Punjab Infantry.	6	—	9	369	39	21
			Section "C." No. 43 Native Field Hospital.	1	—	2	3	59	1

* These numbers do not include Staff Officers shown

APPENDIX D.

Guns, &c., Embarked.

Clerks, &c., not included in Column 6.	Coolies.	Chargers.	Horses. Public or Troop.	Horses. Siladar.	Ponies. Private.	Ponies. Public.	Transport. Drivers.	Transport. Pack Mules.	Transport. Bullocks.	Dhanjibhoy's Tonga Train. Ponies.	Dhanjibhoy's Tonga Train. Tongas.	Guns. Field.	Guns. Maxim, Machine ·303.	Ammunition. Boxes.	Date arrived Hongkong.
															1900.
—	—	4	—	—	—	—	21	49	—	—	—	—	—	80	} 9th July.
—	—	1	—	—	—	—	—	—	—	—	—	—	—	—	
—	—	3	—	—	—	—	—	—	—	—	—	—	—	—	
—	—	9	—	—	—	—	21	49	—	—	—	—	1	114	} 11th „
—	—	1	—	—	—	—	—	—	—	—	—	—	—	—	
—	—	—	—	—	—	—	—	—	—	—	—	—	—	—	
—	—	1	—	—	—	—	—	—	—	—	—	—	—	—	
—	—	9	142	—	—	—	5	15	—	—	—	6	—	—	} 14th „
—	—	1	43	—	—	—	4	12	—	—	—	—	—	—	
—	—	1	—	—	—	—	4	12	—	—	—	—	—	—	
2	—	22	—	—	—	—	—	36	—	—	—	—	—	—	
—	—	2	—	—	—	—	—	3	—	—	—	—	—	—	
—	—	—	—	—	—	—	4	12	—	—	—	—	—	—	
—	—	1	—	—	—	—	—	—	—	—	—	—	—	—	
—	—	—	—	—	—	—	7	24	—	—	—	—	—	—	
—	—	—	—	—	—	—	—	—	—	—	—	—	—	—	
—	—	3	—	—	—	—	—	—	—	—	—	—	—	—	} 15th „
—	—	1	—	—	—	—	—	—	—	—	—	—	—	—	
—	—	2	—	—	—	—	—	—	—	—	—	—	—	—	
—	—	1	—	—	—	—	—	—	—	—	—	—	—	—	
3	—	—	—	—	—	—	—	—	—	—	—	—	—	—	
46	—	1	—	—	—	—	—	—	—	—	—	—	—	—	
—	—	—	—	—	—	—	—	—	—	—	—	—	—	—	
—	—	2	—	—	—	—	—	—	—	—	—	—	—	—	
—	—	6	—	—	—	—	36	109	—	—	—	—	1	114	} 15th „
—	—	—	—	—	—	—	4	12	—	—	—	—	—	—	

against specific units, *e.g.*, Signalling, Telegraph, &c.

408

DETAIL OF TROOPS, ANIMALS,

Vessel in which Despatched.	Port of Embarkation.	Date of Sailing.	Troops conveyed.	British.		Native.		Followers.	
				Officers.	Warrant and Commissioned Officers and Men.	Hospital Assistants.	Non-Commissioned Officers and Men.	Public (exclusive of Transport Followers).	Private.
		1900.							
			Staff, 1st Infantry Brigade	6	1	—	2	—	17
Nuddea	Calcutta	3rd June	Wing, 24th Punjab Infantry.	5	—	9	354	27	22
			Section "D," No. 43 Native Field Hospital.	1	—	2	3	61	2
Nawab	,,	6th ,,	Wing, 1st Sikh Infantry	4	—	8	352	30	15
			Section "D," No. 42 Native Field Hospital.	1	—	2	3	54	6
Uganda	,,	6th ,,	1st Bengal Lancers -	3	—	6	154	87	12
			Section "B," No. 42 Native Field Hospital.	1	—	2	3	61	6
Umta	,,	6th ,,	1st Bengal Lancers -	3	—	6	155	88	14
			Section "C," No. 42 Native Field Hospital.	1	1	2	5	58	6
Itaura	,,	7th ,,	1st Bengal Lancers -	5	—	6	166	88	19
			Section "A," No. 47 Native Field Hospital.	1	1	2	3	58	1
			Surveyors -	—	—	—	4	—	1
			Staff -	5	1	—	—	—	15
			Headquarters Wing, 1st Sikh Infantry.	6	—	9	369	29	22
Warora	,,	7th ,,	Section "A," No. 25 British Field Hospital.	1	5	—	—	18	3
			7th Bengal Infantry -	—	—	—	23	—	—
			Telegraph Section -	—	—	—	—	25	2
			Post Office -	1	—	—	—	—	—
Virawa	Bombay	7th ,,	"A" and "B" Sections, No. 63 Native Field Hospital.	2	1	4	7	117	6
	Karachi	11th ,,	26th Bombay Infantry -	11	—	17	706	63	34
Duke of Portland	Bombay	7th ,,	"C" and "D" Sections, No. 63 Native Field Hospital.	2	—	4	7	112	6
	Karachi	11th ,,	30th Bombay Infantry -	13	—	17	694	67	34
Ballaarat	Bombay	8th ,,	3rd Madras Infantry -	11	—	17	720	59	26
			"C" and "D" Sections, No. 66 Native Field Hospital.	2	1	4	6	116	3
Wardha	Calcutta	9th ,,	Wing, 22nd Bombay Infantry.	5	—	9	355	29	15
			Section "C," No. 47 Native Field Hospital.	1	—	2	3	58	3
			Miscellaneous -	1	3	—	—	24	5

The number of mules shown against

GUNS, &c., EMBARKED—continued.

Clerks, &c., not included in Column 6.	Coolies.	Horses.			Ponies.		Transport.			Dhanjibhoy's Tonga Train.		Guns.	Ammunition.	Date arrived Hongkong.
		Chargers.	Public or Troop.	Silladar.	Private.	Public.	Drivers.	Pack Mules.	Bullocks.	Ponies.	Tongas.	Field.	Maxim, Machine, .303.	Boxes.	
															1900.
—	—	7	—	—	2	—	—	—	—	—	—	—	—	—	}16th July.
—	—	5	—	—	1	—	—	—	—	—	—	—	—	100	
—	—	1	—	—	—	—	—	—	—	—	—	—	—	—	
—	—	4	—	—	—	—	22	50	—	—	—	—	—	100	}19th „
—	—	1	—	—	3	—	1	3	—	—	—	—	—	—	
—	—	6	—	169	2	—	18	96	—	—	—	—	—	33	}18th „
—	—	1	—	—	2	—	—	1	—	—	—	—	—	—	
—	—	6	—	164	—	—	17	98	—	—	—	—	—	31	}18th „
—	—	1	—	—	2	—	—	3	—	—	—	—	—	—	
—	—	12	—	174	—	—	27	115	—	—	—	—	—	20	
—	—	—	—	—	—	—	1	3	—	—	—	—	—	—	}21st „
—	—	—	2	—	—	—	—	—	—	—	—	—	—	—	
—	—	7	—	—	—	—	—	—	—	—	—	—	—	—	
—	—	5	—	—	—	—	25	61	—	—	—	—	1	107	
—	—	1	—	—	—	—	—	—	—	—	—	—	—	—	
—	—	—	—	—	—	—	—	—	—	—	—	—	—	—	}21st „
—	—	—	—	—	—	—	—	—	—	—	—	—	—	—	
—	—	—	—	—	—	—	—	—	—	—	—	—	—	—	
—	—	2	—	—	2	—	—	—	—	—	—	—	—	3	}29th „
—	—	13	—	—	7	—	—	—	—	—	—	—	1	148	
—	—	2	—	—	—	—	—	—	—	—	—	—	—	2	}29th „
—	—	13	—	—	2	—	—	—	—	—	—	—	1	232	
—	—	11	—	—	—	—	—	—	—	—	—	—	—	225	}22nd „
—	—	—	—	—	—	—	—	—	—	—	—	—	—	—	
—	—	5	—	—	—	—	24	54	—	—	—	—	—	106	
—	—	1	—	—	1	—	1	3	—	—	—	—	—	—	}23rd „
—	—	—	—	—	—	—	4	12	—	—	—	—	—	—	

1st Bengal Lancers includes Silladar ponies.

410

DETAIL OF TROOPS, ANIMALS,

Vessel in which Despatched.	Port of Embarkation.	Date of Sailing.	Troops conveyed.	British.		Native.		Followers.	
				Officers.	Warrant and Non-Commissioned Officers and Men.	Officers and Hospital Assistants.	Non-Commissioned Officers and Men.	Public (exclusive of Transport Followers).	Private.
		1900.							
Patiala	Calcutta	9th June	Headquarters Wing, 22nd Bombay Infantry.	8	—	8	361	30	18
			Section "B," No. 47 Native Field Hospital.	1	—	2	3	59	3
			Miscellaneous	1	15	—	161	—	—
Vadala	"	10th "	Headquarters Wing, 1st Madras Pioneers.	7	—	9	377	26	24
			Section "D," No. 47 Native Field Hospital.	1	—	2	3	54	2
			Miscellaneous	1	—	—	—	—	2
Nevassa	"	12th "	No. 4 Company, Bengal Sappers and Miners.	4	2	4	189	8	18
			Native General Hospital	8	2	20	45	110	35
			Miscellaneous	—	—	—	—	—	1
Sirsa	"	13th "	No. 3 Company, Madras Sappers and Miners.	4	2	4	189	23	19
			Photo-Litho Section, Madras Sappers and Miners. Printing Section, Madras Sappers and Miners.	—	3	—	8	—	—
			Section "A," No. 39 Native Field Hospital.	1	1	2	4	62	3
			Miscellaneous	2	—	—	1	—	5
Islanda	Bombay	14th "	No. 1 Punjab Coolie Corps.	2	2	2	2	12	7
			"A" Section, No. 54 Native Field Hospital.	1	1	2	3	64	2
Canning	"	15th "	Headquarters Wing, 1-4th Gurkhas.	6	—	9	364	29	20
			"A" Section, No. 66 Native Field Hospital.	1	—	2	3	59	3
			No. 3 Brigade Supply Column.	—	1	—	—	29	—
Nowshera	"	15th "	No. 2 Company, Bombay Sappers and Miners.	4	2	4	189	18	13
			Wing, 1-4th Gurkhas	6	—	8	357	30	15
			"B" Section, No. 66 Native Field Hospital.	1	—	2	3	56	2
Urlana	Calcutta	17th "	"B" Section No. 39 Native Field Hospital.	1	—	2	3	62	2
			No. 4 Brigade Supply Column.	2	1	—	—	22	6
			Miscellaneous	1	—	—	—	6	5
			Transport Mule Corps	—	3	—	—	40	3
Pentakotah	"	17th "	Wing, 1st Madras Pioneers.	4	—	7	342	18	21
			Section "C," No. 39 Native Field Hospital.	1	—	2	4	51	4
			No. 4 Field Medical Store Depôt.	1	—	—	—	5	—
			Miscellaneous	3	—	—	—	—	7

GUNS, &c., EMBARKED—*continued.*

Clerks, &c., not included in Column 6.	Coolies.	Chargers.	Public or Troop.	Siladar.	Private.	Public.	Drivers.	Pack Mules.	Bullocks.	Ponies.	Tongas.	Field.	Maxim, Machine, .303.	Boxes.	Date arrived Hongkong.
			Horses.		Ponies.		Transport.			Dhanlibhoy's Tonga Train.		Guns.		Ammunition.	
—	—	7	—	—	—	—	23	54	—	—	—	—	—	106	1900.
—	—	—	—	—	—	•	—	—	—	—	—	—	—	—	24th July.
—	—	—	—	—	—	—	—	—	—	—	—	—	—	—	
—	—	7	—	—	—	—	35	84	—	—	—	—	1	118	
—	—	1	—	—	—	—	1	3	—	—	—	—	—	—	25th „
5	—	1	—	—	—	—	—	—	—	—	—	—	—	—	
—	—	6	—	—	2	—	11	18	—	—	—	—	—	33	
—	—	7	—	—	—	—	—	—	—	—	—	—	—	—	26th „
—	—	1	—	—	—	—	11	20	5	—	—	—	—	—	
—	—	6	—	—	—	—	33	90	—	—	—	—	—	34	
—	—	—	—	—	—	—	4	12	—	—	—	1	—	—	29th „
—	—	1	—	—	—	—	1	3	—	—	—	—	—	—	
—	—	3	—	—	—	—	—	—	—	—	—	—	—	—	
—	1,057	3	—	—	—	2	1	—	—	—	—	—	—	—	30th „
—	—	1	—	—	—	—	—	—	—	—	—	—	—	1	
—	—	6	—	—	1	—	—	—	—	—	—	—	1	256	1st Aug.
—	—	1	—	—	—	—	—	—	—	—	—	—	—	—	
—	—	—	—	—	—	—	—	—	—	—	—	—	—	—	
—	—	8	—	—	—	—	—	—	18	—	—	—	—	104	1st „
—	—	6	—	—	—	—	—	—	—	—	—	—	—	—	
—	—	1	—	—	—	—	—	—	—	—	—	—	—	—	
—	—	1	—	—	—	—	1	3	—	—	—	—	—	—	
7	—	2	—	—	—	—	—	—	—	—	—	—	—	—	1st „
—	—	4	—	—	—	—	—	—	—	—	—	—	—	—	
1	—	—	—	—	—	3	177	405	—	—	—	—	—	•	
—	—	4	—	—	—	—	37	84	—	—	—	—	—	110	
—	—	—	—	—	—	—	1	3	—	—	—	—	—	—	
—	—	—	—	—	—	—	—	—	—	—	—	—	—	—	1st „
—	—	4	—	—	—	—	—	—	—	—	—	—	—	—	

412

DETAIL OF TROOPS, ANIMALS,

Vessel in which Despatched.	Port of Embarkation.	Date of Sailing.	Troops conveyed.	British.			Native.		Followers.	
				Officers.	Warrant and Non-Commissioned Officers and Men.	Non-Commissioned Officers and Hospital Assistants.	Officers and Hospital Assistants.	Non-Commissioned Officers and Men.	Public (exclusive of Transport Followers).	Private.
		1900.								
MailSteamer P. & O. Chusan.	Bombay	17th June	2nd Infantry Brigade Staff.	7	—	—	—	—	20
Matiana	Calcutta	20th July	Ordnance Field Park	4	14	—	5	92	12
			Transport Mule Corps	1	2	—	—	20	3
			Section "D," No. 39 Native Field Hospital.	1	—	2	3	53	2
			Miscellaneous	2	—	1	—	—	5
			Base Stationary Depôt	—	—	—	—	—	—
Nankin	Bombay	21st "	No. 3 Coolie Corps	2	2	—	2	—	6
			"C" Section, No. 54 Native Field Hospital.	1	1	2	2	62	3
Zamania	"	26th "	2nd Bengal Infantry	12	—	17	721	59	35
			Sections "A" and "B," No. 41 Native Field Hospital.	2	—	4	8	112	4
			30th Bombay Infantry	—	—	—	27	1	—
			Royal Indian Marine	2	—	—	—	—	—
Nizam	Calcutta	28th "	Transport Mule Corps	—	1	—	—	6	1
			Miscellaneous	3	—	2	—	37	6
Muttra	Bombay	1st Aug.	No. 2 Coolie Corps	2	2	—	2	—	7
			"B" Section, No. 54 Native Field Hospital.	1	1	2	5	61	5
Nurani	Calcutta	2nd "	Squadron, 16th Bengal Lancers.	2	—	5	132	82	15
			Section "B," No. 57 Native Field Hospital.	1	—	2	3	55	2
Rewa	"	2nd "	Squadron, 16th Bengal Lancers.	3	—	4	120	67	15
			No. 1 Brigade Supply Column.	—	1	3	4	23	9
			Medical	—	—	2	2	3	1
			Survey Party	1	—	4	—	29	4
Clive	Bombay	3rd "	Five Companies, 34th Pioneers.	8	—	11	454	36	27
			Section "C," No. 41 Native Field Hospital.	1	1	2	4	59	2
			British Section Hospital Ship.	1	6	—	—	7	—
			Medical	1	—	—	—	—	1

413

GUNS, &c., EMBARKED—*continued.*

Clerks, &c., not included in Column 6.	Coolies.	Horses.			Ponies.		Transport.			Dhanji-bhoy's Tonga Train.		Guns.		Ammunition.	Date arrived Hongkong.
		Chargers.	Public or Troop.	Siladar.	Private.	Public.	Drivers.	Pack Mules.	Bullocks.	Ponies.	Tongas.	Field.	Maxim, Machine, .303.	Boxes.	
															1900.
—	—	—	—	—	—	—	—	—	—	—	—	—	—	—	19th Aug.
4	—	1	—	—	1	—	4	12	—	—	—	2	—	6,342	
1	—	1	—	—	—	2	138	317	—	—	—	—	—	—	
—	—	1	—	—	—	—	1	3	—	—	—	—	—	—	2nd „
—	—	2	—	—	—	—	—	—	—	—	—	—	—	—	
5	—	—	—	—	—	—	—	—	—	—	—	—	—	—	
—	1,069	2	—	—	—	2	1	—	—	—	—	—	—	—	6th „
—	—	1	—	—	—	—	—	—	—	—	—	—	—	—	
—	—	12	—	—	—	—	—	—	—	—	—	—	1	179	9th „
—	—	2	—	—	—	—	—	—	—	—	—	—	—	—	
—	—	—	—	—	—	1	140	325	—	—	—	—	—	—	11th „
—	—	2	—	—	—	—	—	—	—	—	—	—	—	—	
—	994	4	—	—	—	2	2	—	—	—	—	—	—	—	19th
—	—	1	—	—	—	—	—	—	—	—	—	—	—	—	
—	—	4	—	137	2	—	—	75	—	—	—	—	—	20	15th „
—	—	1	—	—	1	—	—	—	—	—	—	—	—	—	
—	—	6	—	126	3	—	21	70	—	—	—	—	—	14	16th „
—	—	—	—	—	—	—	—	—	—	—	—	—	—	—	
—	—	—	—	—	—	—	—	—	—	—	—	—	—	—	
—	—	1	—	—	—	—	—	—	—	—	—	—	—	—	
—	—	13	—	—	2	—	—	—	—	—	—	—	1	197	19th „
—	—	1	—	—	—	—	—	—	—	—	—	—	—	—	
—	—	—	—	—	—	—	—	—	—	—	—	—	—	—	
—	—	—	—	—	—	—	—	—	—	—	—	—	—	—	

414

DETAIL OF TROOPS, ANIMALS,

Vessel in which Despatched.	Port of Embarkation.	Date of Sailing.	Troops conveyed.	British.			Native.		Followers.	
				Officers.	Warrant and Non-Commissioned Officers and Men.		Officers and Hospital Assistants.	Non-Commissioned Officers and Men.	Public (exclusive of Transport Followers).	Private.
		1900.								
Sunda	Calcutta	4th Aug.	Cavalry Brigade Staff	7	1		—	—	—	30
			Squadron, 16th Bengal Lancers.	3	—		5	112	61	14
			Section "A," No. 57 Native Field Hospital.	1	—		4	3	59	2
Fultala	„	4th „	Squadron, 16th Bengal Lancers.	2	—		4	120	72	15
			Medical Department	1	—		—	—	—	—
			Section "B," No. 5 Field Veterinary Hospital.	1	4		—	1	10	3
			Cavalry Brigade Transport.	—	—		—	—	1	—
Upada	„	5th „	One Squadron, 3rd Bombay Cavalry.	2	—		4	119	63	10
			Section "C," No. 57 Native Field Hospital.	1	—		2	3	57	2
			Cavalry Brigade Transport.	—	1		—	—	—	—
Ula	„	5th „	One Squadron, 3rd Bombay Cavalry.	5	—		6	121	66	26
			Section "D," No. 57 Native Field Hospital.	1	—		1	2	54	2
City of Cambridge.	Bombay	7th „	No. 4 Coolie Corps	2	2		—	2	—	4
			No. 2 Coolie Corps	—	—		—	—	—	—
			Section "D," No. 54 Native Field Hospital.	1	1		2	5	61	3
Fazilka	Calcutta	9th „	One Squadron, 3rd Bombay Cavalry.	2	—		4	121	64	10
			Dhanjibhoy's Tonga Train.	—	1		—	—	—	20
			Section "B," No. 25 British Field Hospital.	1	6		—	—	82	2
Lawada	„	9th „	One Squadron, 3rd Bombay Cavalry.	2	—		5	121	64	14
			Medical Department	1	—		—	—	—	—
Hospital ship "Carthage."	Bombay	9th „	Establishment and guard	4	1		6	40	25	4
Palamcotta	Calcutta	12th „	1st Bengal Lancers	1	—		—	—	—	—
			Mounted Sapper Detachment.	1	1		—	24	23	3
			Balloon Section	—	—		—	—	26	4
			Sanitary Establishment	—	—		—	—	240	—
			Medical Department	—	1		—	—	4	—

Five miles of light railway were shipped in the "Fultala."

GUNS, &c., EMBARKED—continued.

Clerks, &c., not included in Column 6.	Coolies.	Horses.			Ponies.		Transport.			Dhanjibhoy's Tonga Train.		Guns.	Ammunition.	Date arrived Hongkong.
		Chargers.	Public or Troop.	Siladar.	Private.	Public.	Drivers.	Pack Mules.	Bullocks.	Ponies.	Tongas.	Field.	Maxim, Machine, -303.	Boxes.	
															1900.
—	—	17	—	—	3	—	—	2	—	—	—	—	—	—	
—	—	7	—	118	3	—	15	φ70	—	—	—	—	—	18	} 18th Aug.
*2	—	1	—	—	—	—	—	—	—	—	—	—	—	—	
—	—	6	—	123	3	—	16	φ72	—	—	—	—	—	28	
1	—	—	—	—	—	—	—	—	—	—	—	—	—	—	
—	—	2	1	—	1	3	—	—	—	—	—	—	—	—	} 18th „
—	—	—	—	—	—	—	9	27	—	—	—	—	—	—	
—	—	4	—	123	2	—	10	φ61	—	—	—	—	—	21	
—	—	1	—	—	—	—	—	—	—	—	—	—	—	—	} 20th „
—	—	—	—	—	—	—	38	81	—	—	—	—	—	—	
—	—	11	—	125	6	—	30	φ106	—	—	—	—	—	22	} 19th „
—	—	1	—	—	—	—	—	—	—	—	—	—	—	—	
—	1,066	2	—	—	2	—	2	—	—	—	—	—	—	—	
—	78	—	—	—	—	—	—	—	—	—	—	—	—	—	} 22nd „
—	—	1	—	—	—	—	—	—	—	—	—	—	—	—	
—	—	4	—	124	2	—	9	φ62	—	—	—	—	—	21	
—	—	—	—	—	—	—	—	—	—	20	9	—	—	—	} 22nd „
—	—	1	—	—	—	—	—	—	†1	—	—	—	—	—	
—	—	6	—	124	3	—	5	φ65	—	—	—	—	—	21	} 22nd „
—	—	—	—	—	—	—	—	—	—	—	—	—	—	—	
—	—	—	—	—	—	—	—	—	—	—	—	—	—	6	23rd „
—	—	—	—	—	—	—	—	—	—	—	—	—	—	—	
—	—	2	24	—	—	—	—	—	—	—	—	—	—	—	
—	—	2	54	—	—	—	—	—	—	—	—	—	—	—	} 25th „
—	—	—	—	—	—	—	—	—	75	—	—	—	—	—	
—	—	—	—	—	—	—	—	—	—	—	—	—	—	—	

* Commissariat Department.   † Also one conservancy cart.
φ Silladar ponies of 16th Bengal Lancers and 3rd Bombay Cavalry are included in number of pack mules.

DETAIL OF TROOPS, ANIMALS,

Vessel in which Despatched.	Port of Embarkation.	Date of Sailing.	Troops conveyed.	British.			Native.		Followers.	
				Officers.	Warrant and Non-Commissioned Officers and Men.	Officers and Hospital Assistants.	Non-Commissioned Officers and Men.	Public (exclusive of Transport Followers).	Private.	
		1900.								
Formosa	Bombay	12th Aug.	14th Sikhs	12	—	17	721	58	42	
			Sections "C" and "D," No. 69 Native Field Hospital.	2	1	4	9	111	6	
			Three Companies, 34th Pioneers.	5	—	6	267	23	13	
			Section "D," No. 41 Native Field Hospital.	1	—	2	3	55	3	
			3rd Bombay Cavalry	1	—	—	—	—	1	
Ujina	Calcutta	13th „	"B" Battery Royal Horse Artillery.	5	164	—	13	103	22	
			R-2 Ammunition Column Unit.	1	3	1	21	26	3	
			Section "A," No. 22 British Field Hospital.	1	5	—	2	67	4	
			Veterinary.	1	—	—	—	—	4	
			Transport Department	—	1	—	—	—	—	
Patia	„	13th „	Headquarters Wing, 20th Punjab Infantry.	7	—	8	377	29	20	
			Section "A," No. 69 Native Field Hospital.	1	1	2	3	59	5	
Nairung	„	15th „	Wing, 20th Punjab Infantry.	5	—	7	344	49	13	
			Section "B," No. 69 Native Field Hospital.	1	—	2	4	52	3	
			No. 5 Brigade Supply Column.	—	1	—	4	20	1	
			Transport, 3rd Brigade	—	1	—	—	7	1	
Dalhousie	Madras	18th „	Headquarters Wing, 5th Infantry, Hyderabad Contingent.	*4	—	8	401	36	4	
			3rd Brigade Staff	5	1	—	—	—	13	
Sumatra	Calcutta	19th „	Headquarters Wing, 6th Bengal Infantry.	7	—	10	383	32	23	
			Field Audit Office	3	—	—	—	8	30	
			Section "B," No. 51 Native Field Hospital.	1	—	1	3	45	3	
			Part of No. 2 Native General Hospital.	4	1	17	43	112	9	
Nerbudda	„	20th „	Staff and Miscellaneous	3	1	—	1	1	10	
			Wing, 6th Bengal Infantry.	5	—	7	333	29	14	
			Section "A," No. 51 Native Field Hospital.	1	1	2	3	49	2	
			Part of No. 2 Native General Hospital.	3	1	—	—	—	2	
Mombassa	„	21st „	Siege Train Bullocks	1	3	—	30	6	3	
			Section "B," No. 38 Native Field Hospital.	1	—	2	3	49	4	
			Postal	1	—	—	—	12	4	

* Includes Medical Officer.

GUNS, &c., EMBARKED—*continued.*

Clerks, &c., not included in Column 6.	Coolies.	Horses.			Ponies.		Transport.			Dhanjibhoy's Tonga Train.		Guns.		Ammunition.	Date arrived Hongkong.
		Chargers.	Public or Troop.	Siladar.	Private.	Public.	Drivers.	Pack Mules.	Bullocks.	Ponies.	Tongas.	Field.	Maxim, Machine, .303.	Boxes.	
															1900.
—	—	12	—		2	—	—	—	—	—	—	—	1	—	
—	—	2	—		—	—	—	—	—	—	—	—	—	—	
—	—	—	—		—	—	—	—	—	—	—	—	—	212	29th Aug.
—	—	1	—		—	—	—	—	—	—	—	—	—	—	
—	—	—	—		—	—	—	—	—	—	—	—	—	—	
—	—	11	197	—	5	—	—	—	—	—	—	6	—	—	
—	—	1	44	—	—	—	—	—	—	—	—	—	—	—	
—	—	1	—	—	2	—	—	—	—	—	—	—	—	—	27th „
1	—	2	—	—	—	—	—	—	—	—	—	—	—	—	
—	—	—	—	—	—	1	4	10	—	—	—	—	—	—	
—	—	7	—	—	2	—	23	58	—	—	—	—	1	109	26th „
—	—	1	—	—	—	—	1	3	—	—	—	—	—	—	
—	—	5	—	—	—	—	21	50	—	—	—	—	—	97	
—	—	1	—	—	—	—	1	3	—	—	—	—	—	—	28th „
3	—	—	—	—	—	—	—	—	—	—	—	—	—	—	
—	—	—	—	—	—	1	20	48	—	—	—	—	—	—	
—	—	—	—	—	—	—	—	—	—	—	—	—	1	134	1st Sept.
—	—	8	—	—	—	—	—	—	—	—	—	—	—	—	
—	—	8	—	—	1	—	25	60	—	—	—	—	1	—	
46	—	2	—	—	—	—	—	—	—	—	—	—	—	—	31st Aug.
—	—	1	—	—	—	—	—	—	—	—	—	—	—	—	
—	—	2	—	—	1	—	—	—	5	—	—	—	—	—	
—	—	5	—	—	—	1	—	—	—	—	—	—	—	—	
—	—	5	—	—	1	—	19	48	—	—	—	—	—	105	1st Sept.
—	—	1	—	—	—	—	4	12	—	—	—	—	—	—	
—	—	1	—	—	—	—	—	—	—	—	—	—	—	—	
—	—	2	—	—	—	—	119	—	259	—	—	—	—	—	2nd „
—	—	1	—	—	—	—	1	3	—	—	—	—	—	—	
15	—	—	—	—	—	—	—	—	—	—	—	—	—	—	

DETAIL OF TROOPS, ANIMALS,

Vessel in which Despatched.	Port of Embarkation.	Date of Sailing.	Troops conveyed.	British. Officers.	British. Warrant and Commissioned Officers and Men.	Native. Officers and Hospital Assistants.	Native. Non-Commissioned Officers and Men.	Followers. Public (exclusive of Transport Followers).	Followers. Private.
		1900.							
India	Madras	22nd Aug.	Wing, 5th Infantry, Hyderabad Contingent.	9	—	9	319	27	23
			"A" and "B" Sections, No. 61 Native Field Hospital.	2	1	4	7	113	7
			Non-Commissioned Officers for Intelligence work.	—	—	—	3	—	—
Pundua	Calcutta	22nd „	Headquarters Wing, 4th Punjab Infantry.	6	—	8	367	27	12
			Section "C," No. 51 Native Field Hospital.	1	—	2	3	68	2
			Special Signalling Units	1	6	—	6	1	2
Lalpura	„	25th „	Wing, 4th Punjab Infantry.	5	—	9	354	26	22
			Section D, No. 51 Native Field Hospital.	1	—	4	3	60	2
			Staff	1	—	—	—	—	4
Mohawk	„	25th „	Headquarters Squadron, Jodhpur Lancers.	1	—	15	119	99	36
			Section "A," No. 61 Native Field Hospital.	1	—	2	4	59	2
		(Vessel detained at Diamond Harbour for two days.)							
St. Andrew	„	26th Aug.	Section "A," No. 38 Native Field Hospital.	1	1	4	2	64	3
			Siege Train Bullocks	2	4	—	62	20	6
			Details, No. 2 Native General Hospital.	3	—	2	2	73	5
			Field Audit Office	—	—	—	—	—	1
Nuddea	Rangoon.	31st „	Wing, 31st Madras Infantry.	5	—	8	311	29	23
			Section D, No. 58, Native Field Hospital.	1	—	3	3	51	4
Warora	„	31st „	Wing, 31st Madras Infantry.	7	—	9	410	30	28
			Section C, No. 58 Native Field Hospital.	1	—	2	3	59	4
Wardha	Calcutta	1st Sept.	Staff, 4th Brigade	7	1	1	—	—	29
			Photo-Litho Section	—	3	—	8	—	—
			Printing Section						
			Bickanir Imperial Service Infantry.	2	—	17	388	57	7
			Section "B," No. 15 British Field Hospital.	1	6	2	—	69	5
			No. 6 Brigade Supply Column.	—	1	—	4	24	—
			Special Signalling Units	—	6	—	6	—	—
			Base Supply Depôt (portion).	2	2	—	—	4	4

419

Guns, &c., Embarked—continued.

Clerks, &c., not included in Column 6.	Coolies.	Horses.				Ponies.		Transport.			Dhanjibhoy's Tonga Train.		Guns.		Ammunition.	Date arrived Hongkong.
		Chargers.	Public or Troop.	Siladar.	Private.	Public.	Drivers.	Pack Mules.	Bullocks.	Ponies.	Tongas.	Field.	Maxim, Machine, ·303.	Boxes.		
—	—	13	—	—	—	—	46	108	—	—	—	—	—	98	1900.
—	—	2	—	—	—	—	5	12	—	—	—	—	—	—	3rd Sept.
—	—	—	—	—	—	—	—	—	—	—	—	—	—	—	
1	—	6	—	—	—	—	21	50	—	—	—	—	—	100	
—	—	1	—	—	—	—	—	—	—	—	—	—	—	—	3rd „
—	—	1	—	—	—	—	—	—	—	—	—	—	—	—	
—	—	6	—	—	1	—	26	58	—	—	—	—	—	—	
—	—	1	—	—	—	—	—	—	—	—	—	—	—	—	7th „
—	—	3	—	—	—	—	—	—	—	—	—	—	—	—	
—	—	25	—	120	11	—	10	79	—	—	—	—	—	—	9th „
—	—	—	—	—	—	—	—	—	—	—	—	—	—	—	
—	—	1	—	—	—	—	1	3	—	—	—	—	—	—	
2	—	2	—	—	1	—	242	—	519	—	—	—	—	—	9th „
—	—	2	—	—	—	—	—	—	—	—	—	—	—	—	
—	—	—	—	—	—	—	—	—	—	—	—	—	—	—	
—	—	4	—	—	—	—	27	56	—	—	—	—	—	—	12th
—	—	1	—	—	1	—			—	—	—	—	—	—	
—	—	8	—	—	2	—	30	65	—	—	—	—	—	—	12th „
—	—	1	—	—	—	—			—	—	—	—	—	—	
—	—	15	—	—	1	—	—	13	—	—	—	—	—	—	
—	—	—	—	—	—	—	4	12	—	—	—	—	—	—	
—	—	11	—	—	—	—	31	60	—	—	—	—	··	—	14th „
—	—	1	—	—	—	—	1	3	—	—	—	—	—	∴	
—	—	—	—	—	1	—	—	—	—	—	—	—	—	—	
—	—	—	—	—	—	—	2	6	—	—	—	—	—	—	
2	—	1	—	—	—	—	—	—	—	—	—	—	—	—	

DETAIL OF TROOPS. ANIMALS,

Vessel in which Despatched.	Port of Embarkation.	Date of Sailing.	Troops conveyed.	British.			Native.		Followers.	
				Officers.	Warrant and Non-Commissioned Officers and Men.	Officers and Hospital Assistants.	Non-Commissioned Officers and Men.	Public (exclusive of Transport Followers).	Private.
		1900.								
Ashruff	Calcutta	1st Sept.	Horses and Establishment for Vickers-Maxim guns.	1	6	—	—	125	3
			Section "A," No. 15 British Field Hospital.	1	6	2	—	22	5
			Siege Train Bullocks	—	1	—	—	1	—
			Miscellaneous	2	—	—	1	2	4
Nawa	Madras	1st „	Wing, 28th Madras Infantry.	6	—	8	351	25	13
			Section "B," No. 58 Native Field Hospital.	1	—	2	3	51	4
Itaura	Calcutta	5th „	Additional Headquarters Staff.	4	2	—	—	10	17
			"D" Squadron, Jodhpur Lancers.	—	—	4	118	66	3
			Mules for 34th Pioneers	—	—	—	—	8	—
			Section "D," No. 61 Native Field Hospital.	1	—	4	2	56	2
Rajah	„	7th „	Siege Train Bullocks	1	2	*1	6	4	2
	Madras	13th „	Wing, 28th Madras Infantry.	6	—	9	370	34	12
			Section "A." No. 58 Native Field Hospital.	1	1	2	3	62	6
			3rd Madras Infantry	—	—	—	1	—	—
Umta	Calcutta	9th „	Staff and Miscellaneous	3	—	—	—	—	15
			"B" Squadron, Jodhpur Lancers.	1	—	5	119	75	8
			Mules for 34th Pioneers	—	—	—	—	—	—
			Section "A" No. 53 Native Field Hospital.	1	1	4	3	59	2
Nevassa	„	10th „	Supplementary Ordnance Field Park.	2	11	—	—	75	5
			Staff, 4th Brigade	—	—	—	—	—	—
			Section "C," No. 62 Native Field Hospital.	1	1	2	4	62	3
			Medical Base Depôt	1	2	—	—	14	4
			Base Supply Depôt (portion).	3	10	—	—	37	23
			No. 3 Field Medical Store Depôt.	1	—	—	—	5	1
			British General Hospital	1	—	†2	—	‡31	2
Vadala	„	11th „	Maler Kotla Sappers	1	—	—	155	59	7
			Engineer Field Park	2	2	—	2	35	4
			Section "D." No. 53 Native Field Hospital.	1	—	2	3	53	2
			Orderlies from Imperial Service Troops.	—	—	—	6	—	—

* One Hospital Assistant belonging to No. 3 Native General Hospital.
† Two Hospital Assistants belonging to "A" and "B" Sections, No. 51 Native Field Hospital.
‡ Includes one public follower of A, No. 15 British Field General Hospital.

421

Guns, &c., Embarked—continued.

Clerks, &c., not included in Column 6.	Coolies.	Horses.			Ponies.		Transport.			Dhanjibhoy's Tonga Train.		Guns.		Ammunition.	Date arrived Hongkong.
		Chargers.	Public or Troop.	Siladar.	Private.	Public.	Drivers.	Pack Mules.	Bullocks.	Ponies.	Tongas.	Field.	Maxim, Machine, .303.	Boxes.	
															1900.
2	—	1	198	—	1	—	—	—	—	—	—	—	—	—	
—	—	1	—	—	—	—	2	6	—	—	—	—	—	—	13th Sept.
—	—	—	—	—	—	—	17	—	30	—	—	—	—	—	
—	—	1	—	—	—	—	—	—	—	—	—	—	—	—	
—	—	6	—	—	1	—	24	54	—	—	—	—	1	108	14th „
—	—	1	—	—	—	—	2	6	—	—	—	—	—	—	
—	—	7	—	—	4	—	—	—	—	—	—	—	—	—	
—	—	6	—	118	—	—	9	75	—	—	—	—	—	—	29th „
—	—	—	—	—	—	—	44	103	—	—	—	—	—	—	
—	—	1	—	—	—	—	1	—	—	—	—	—	—	—	
—	—	1	—	—	—	—	75	—	130	—	—	—	—	—	
—	—	6	—	—	1	—	24	53	—	—	—	—	—	91	24th „
—	—	1	—	—	—	—	2	6	—	—	—	—	—	—	
—	—	—	—	—	—	—	—	—	—	—	—	—	—	—	
—	—	8	—	—	2	—	—	—	—	—	—	—	—	—	
—	—	7	—	120	1	—	—	75	—	—	—	—	—	—	23rd „
—	—	—	—	—	—	—	28	65	—	—	—	—	—	—	
—	—	—	—	—	—	—	1	3	—	—	—	—	—	—	
3	—	1	—	—	—	—	—	—	—	—	—	—	—	—	
—	—	—	—	—	—	—	4	12	—	—	—	—	—	—	
—	—	1	—	—	—	—	1	3	—	—	—	—	—	—	
2	—	1	—	—	—	—	—	—	—	—	—	—	—	—	23rd „
12	—	—	—	—	3	—	—	—	—	—	—	—	—	—	
—	—	—	—	—	—	—	—	—	—	—	—	—	—	—	
—	—	1	—	—	—	—	—	—	—	—	—	—	—	—	
—	—	2	—	—	1	—	—	105	—	—	—	—	—	—	
—	—	2	—	—	—	—	—	—	—	—	—	—	—	—	27th „
—	—	1	—	—	—	—	1	3	—	—	—	—	—	—	
—	—	—	—	—	—	—	—	—	—	—	—	—	—	—	

Detail of Troops, Animals,

Vessel in which Despatched.	Port of Embarkation.	Date of Sailing.	Troops conveyed.	British.		Native.		Followers.	
				Officers.	Warrant and Non-Commissioned Officers and Men.	Officers and Hospital Assistants.	Non-Commissioned Officers and Men.	Public (exclusive of Transport Followers).	Private.
		1900.							
Uganda	Calcutta	13th Sept.	Staff	3	—	—	*1	—	4
			"C" Squadron, Jodhpur Lancers.	—	—	7	119	67	4
			Section "B," No. 53 Native Field Hospital.	1	—	2	3	52	2
			Orderlies from Imperial Service Troops.	—	—	—	3	2	—
Ludhiana	"	14th "	Right Wing, Alwar Imperial Service Infantry.	1	—	10	348	—	3
			Postal	—	—	—	—	12	—
			Section "C," No. 53 Native Field Hospital.	1	—	‡4	3	58	1
Landura	"	14th "	Headquarters Wing, Alwar Imperial Service Infantry.	1	—	13	353	46	8
			No. 3 Native General Hospital.	10	2	24	45	181	31
			Miscellaneous	—	—	—	1	—	—
Urlana	"	17th "	Sanitary Establishment	—	—	—	—	238	—
			Remount Depôt	2	6	3	29	159	11
			Veterinary Base Depôt	1	2	—	1	4	3
			Military Telegraphists	—	20	—	—	8	—
			Section "D," No. 62 Native Field Hospital.	1	—	2	4	51	4
			Spare Transport	—	—	—	—	—	—
			Miscellaneous	2	—	—	—	—	3
Pentakotah	"	22nd "	Siege Train Bullocks	1	2	—	2	7	5
			Orderlies from Imperial Service Troops.	—	—	§1	2	—	1
Nowshera	"	24th "	Seige Train Bullocks	—	3	—	2	28	2
			Miscellaneous	—	2	§1	—	1	—
Chusan	Bombay	26th "	Sections "A" and "B," No. 17 British Field Hospital.	2	13	—	—	133	4
			Pay Establishment, 3rd Bombay Cavalry.	—	—	—	3	—	1
Duke of Portland.	Calcutta	4th Oct.	Details	9	—	8	392	25	16
			Staff	1	—	—	—	—	2
			Medical Department	1	—	1	1	—	1
			Commissariat Department.	—	—	—	—	18	5
			Postal Department	—	—	—	—	1	—

* Belongs Hongkong Regiment.
‡ Includes one Hospital Assistant of No. 2 Native General Hospital.

Guns, &c., Embarked—continued.

Clerks, &c., not included in Column 6.	Coolies.	Horses.			Ponies.		Transport.			Dhanjibhoy's Tonga Train.		Guns.		Ammunition.	Date arrived Hongkong.
		Chargers.	Public or Troop.	Siladar.	Private.	Public.	Drivers.	Pack Mules.	Bullocks.	Ponies.	Tongas.	Field.	Maxim, Machine, ·303.	Boxes.	
															1900.
—	—	2	—	—	—	—	5	†15	—	—	—	—	—	—	} 26th Sept.
—	—	6	—	120	2	—	9	74	—	—	—	—	—	—	
—	—	1	—	—	—	—	2	3	—	—	—	—	—	—	
—	—	—	—	4	—	—	—	2	—	—	—	—	—	—	
—	—	2	—	—	—	—	60	45	—	—	—	—	—	—	} 29th ,,
9	—	—	—	—	—	—	—	—	—	—	—	—	—	—	
—	—	1	—	—	1	—	1	3	—	—	—	—	—	—	
—	—	3	—	—	—	—	32	59	—	—	—	—	—	—	} 1st Oct.
—	—	5	—	—	1	—	5	—	5	—	—	—	—	—	
—	—	—	—	—	—	—	5	12	—	—	—	—	—	—	
—	—	—	—	—	—	—	—	—	75	—	—	—	—	—	} 5th ,,
—	—	6	—	—	—	—	—	—	—	—	—	—	—	—	
—	—	2	—	—	—	—	—	—	—	—	—	—	—	—	
—	—	—	—	—	—	—	—	—	—	—	—	—	—	—	
—	—	1	—	—	—	—	1	3	—	—	—	—	—	—	
—	—	—	—	—	—	—	2	6	—	—	—	—	—	—	
—	—	1	—	—	1	—	—	—	—	—	—	—	—	—	
—	—	2	—	—	1	—	103	—	184	—	—	—	—	—	} 6th ,,
—	—	—	—	2	—	—	—	1	—	—	—	—	—	—	
—	—	—	—	—	—	1	84	—	182	—	—	—	—	—	} 10th ,,
—	—	2	—	—	—	—	2	6	—	—	—	—	—	—	} 14th ,,
1	—	—	—	—	—	—	—	—	—	—	—	—	—	—	
—	—	8	—	—	1	—	—	—	—	—	—	—	—	—	} 14th§ ,,
—	—	1	—	—	—	—	—	—	—	—	—	—	—	—	
—	—	—	—	—	—	—	—	—	—	—	—	—	—	—	
5	—	—	—	—	—	—	—	—	—	—	—	—	—	—	
—	—	—	—	—	—	—	—	—	—	—	—	—	—	—	

§ Hospital Assistant.
† Three mules belong to "A" Section No. 15 British Field Hospital.

Detail of Troops, Animals,

Vessel in which Despatched.	Port of Embarkation.	Date of Sailing.	Troops conveyed.	British.			Native.		Followers.	
				Officers.	Warrant and Commissioned Officers and Men.	Non-Commissioned Officers and Men.	Officers and Hospital Assistants.	Non-Commissioned Officers and Men.	Public (exclusive of Transport Followers).	Private.
City of Cambridge.	Calcutta	1900. 12th Oct.	Staff	1	—	—	—	—	—	1
			Medical Department	3	—	—	2	—	—	9
			Commissariat Department.	2	19	—	15	—	62	14
			Miscellaneous	—	—	—	—	13	6	—
Rewa	„	2nd Nov.	Details	2	—	—	—	8	1	6
			Telegraph Section	1	22	—	—	16	16	3
			Medical Department	—	1	—	—	—	—	1
			Miscellaneous	—	3	—	—	4	—	2
			Total	555	706		710	17,852	8,983	1,877

Mobilisation Section, Army Headquarters;
Simla, the 26th November 1900.

Guns, &c., Embarked—continued.

| Clerks, &c., not included in Column 6. | Coolies. | Horses. | | Ponies. | | Transport. | | | Dhanjibhoy's Tonga Train. | | Guns. | | Ammunition. | Date arrived Hongkong. |
		Chargers.	Public or Troop.	Siladar.	Private.	Public.	Drivers.	Pack Mules.	Bullocks.	Ponies.	Tongas.	Field.	Maxim, Machine, .303.	Boxes.	
															1900.
—	—	1	—	—	—	—	—	—	—	—	—	—	—	—	
—	—	3	—	—	—	—	—	—	—	—	—	—	—	—	} 21st Oct.
—	—	—	—	—	—	—	—	—	—	—	—	—	—	—	
—	—	—	12	—	—	5	—	—	—	—	—	—	—	—	
—	—	5	—	1	—	1	—	—	—	—	—	—	—	—	
—	—	2	—	—	—	12	—	—	—	—	—	—	—	—	} 26th ,,
—	—	—	—	—	—	—	—	—	—	—	—	—	—	—	
—	—	2	—	—	—	—	—	—	—	—	—	—	—	—	
181	4,264	686	717	2,092	112	39	2,253	4,595	1,470	20	9	14	14	10,122	

APPENDIX E.

TRANSPORT BY SEA OF THE BRITISH CONTINGENT, CHINA EXPEDITIONARY FORCE, FROM INDIA TO CHINA, 1900, FROM A REPORT BY CAPTAIN W. S. GOODRIDGE, R.N., C.I.E., DIRECTOR, ROYAL INDIAN MARINE.

1. Definite orders were received from the Government of India in the latter part of June 1900 for the despatch of an expeditionary force to China, consisting of one cavalry brigade, two infantry brigades, divisional troops, line of communication troops, and coolie corps. This force was subsequently augmented by two infantry brigades, horses for a Vickers-Maxim battery, a detachment of mounted sappers, and some 1,350 siege-train bullocks.

2. Owing to the south-west monsoon having broken and the track route to China being about four days less from Calcutta than from Bombay, the Government of India decided that the greater part of the force should be embarked at the former port, and that such units only as could not be concentrated at Calcutta without great delay and difficulty, should be embarked at Bombay or Karachi. All transport animals going from Calcutta.

3. A limited choice only of tonnage was available at either Calcutta or Bombay at the time it was required, but on this occasion, as previously, the local representatives of the British India, Peninsular and Oriental and Asiatic Companies took steps to place vessels of their fleets at our disposal with all possible despatch, but even then it was necessary to requisition four Imperial transports from South Africa. The vessel specially ordered up from the Cape, the "St. Andrew," was a type unobtainable in Indian waters, and, although not of a great deal more tonnage than the largest vessels available here, was capable of carrying almost double the number of animals; she carried to China 525 siege-train bullocks in exceptionally large stalls.

4. The first vessel left Calcutta on the 26th June, and, from that time until the whole of the force was despatched, vessels were leaving in quick succession within a few days of their being placed at the disposal of the Government by their owners for arranging, fitting, coaling, and embarkation.

5. The first vessels left Bombay on the 7th July; they proceeded to Karachi, where they embarked the 29th and 30th Regiments, Native infantry; these were followed, as quickly as the units could be brought down, by seven others and the R.I.M.S. "Clive" and "Canning," while the R.M.I.S. "Dalhousie" and the transport "India" were despatched to Madras to embark units there.

6. In order to secure the necessary tonnage, and with the view of assisting Calcutta, five vessels were taken up at Bombay and fitted for cavalry, previous to despatching them to Calcutta, to embark the units allotted to them, and about 800 horse stalls and 1,000 mule stalls were despatched from Bombay by rail at Calcutta at the commencement of operations. Messrs. Burn & Co., Calcutta, also furnished fittings.

7. Considerable difficulties were experienced at Calcutta in fitting the vessels, as the exceptional heat that prevailed at the commencement of the operations quite disorganised all labour arrangements ; then followed labour troubles, which are not uncommon in Calcutta. These difficulties were succeeded toward the end of the operations by heavy rains and floods, which very much retarded the work of fitting and loading vessels.

8. No troubles as described above occurred in Bombay, and were it not for the great difference in the price of coal at the two places, Calcutta and Bombay, the few miles saved in the length of a voyage, such as in the present expedition, at any time of the year would scarcely give Calcutta an advantage over Bombay as a port of embarkation for an expedition of any urgency or magnitude, as much of what is gained by the saving in mileage is lost by the delays due to berthing and negotiating the navigation of the Hooghly.

9. The P. & O. SS. " Carthage " was taken in hand at Bombay and transformed into a hospital ship, and has given great satisfaction under all circumstances.

10. The second hospital ship, the " Zayathla," since re-named the " Gwalior," was similarly fitted by private arrangement at Calcutta, at the expense of His Highness the Maharajah of Gwalior.

11. Arrangements were made with the Peninsular and Oriental Steam Navigation Company for the conveyance to Hongkong in their ordinary mail steamers of the 2nd Infantry Brigade Staff ; A. and B. sections, No. 16 British Field Hospital, and details ; 3rd Bombay Cavalry.

12. The total numbers carried were —
    55 officers.
    7 ladies, nurses.
    706 European warrant and non-commissioned officers and men.
    181 clerks, &c.
    710 Native officers and hospital assistants.
    17,852 Native non-commissioned officers and men.
    17,377 followers, coolies and drivers.
    3,495 horses.
    171 ponies.
    4,595 mules.
    1,470 bullocks.
    18 guns.

13. The British India Steam Navigation Company supplied the largest number of ships. The total number of steamers employed was—exclusive of the hospital ship—53. Of these—

    36 belonged to the British India Steam Navigation Company, Limited.
    5 to the Asiatic Steam Navigation Company.
    4 to the Peninsular and Oriental Steam Navigation Company.
    4 Admiralty transports.
    1 Hajee Cassum.
    3 Royal Indian Marine.
    ──
    53
    ──

Of these, 19 made two voyages, bringing the total of ships fitted to 72. Gross tonnage 283,225; average tonnage of each vessel 3,933.

14. The terms of hire were Rs. 15 per gross ton per month, *plus* the costs of fittings, which is borne by Government; period of hire, three months certain.

15. The first ship to be paid off was the "Islanda," which returned from China on the 8th September 1900; the last, he "Ujina," on the 6th January 1901.

16. The choice of vessels selected has given general satisfaction. It was noticed that certain vessels taken up rolled excessively, and this was brought to the notice of the British India Steam Navigation Company, to which they belong, and the owners took steps to have them fitted with bilge keels, which are not usual in the mercantile marine.

17. Suggestions with regard to alteration of the existing pattern of horse fittings have been received, and a local committee met in Bombay Dockyard to consider any alteration suitable, and increase in length of stalls was attended to.

18. Certain complaints have also been made regarding insufficient cooking space for Native troops, due allowance should be made for the altered condition of affairs on board ship, to which Sepoys are unaccustomed, and which is unavoidable under the circumstances, but the matter has been noted for future guidance.

REPORT by COMMANDER F. H. ELDERTON, R.I.M., Senior Marine Transport Officer, British Contingent, C.E.F., on DETAILS of ARRANGEMENTS for DISEMBARKATION and FORMATION of BASES at the VARIOUS SEAPORTS in CHINA.

Hongkong.—The arrangements for the disembarkation of small bodies of men and animals, and small quantities of stores, were worked under the military authorities with the launches and craft belonging to the Army Service Corps, but, when necessary, ships of any size can be berthed alongside the wharves at Kowloon and West Point, and the orders laid down in the Queen's Regulations and Admiralty Instructions regarding the division of naval and military responsibility can be adhered to.

The port was made the coaling depôt of transports during the expedition, each ship going north taking a sufficient quantity to bring her back to Hongkong, and then again taking enough to enable her to reach India.

The facilities of the port are very good. Coal and water in any quantity are obtainable with proper arrangements, and there is also good docking accommodation.

Shanghai.—The arrangements can be carried out as in Hongkong, but to reach this port (where the wharves are situated) the draft of ships should not exceed 20 feet, otherwise they have to lay in the stream below Wusung Bar, and must be cleared by lighters.

Shanghai also has good docks, and fair facilities for coaling and watering.

Wei-hai-wei.—Had no local facilities for disembarkation of troops; lighters were sent from Taku when required, but the landing-place is on the main land, whilst the transport's anchorage is off the island, which is inconvenient; there is also insufficient water at the landing-place.

The craft employed were under the orders of the Naval or Indian Marine authorities, except in a few cases when the military provided lighterage.

No coal or water available, no docks, and scarcely any labour.

Chih-fu.—The harbour is sheltered from some winds. Coal and water is obtainable in small quantities, but the despatch is very slow; no repairs are possible. This port has only been used by transports for the dropping and picking up of mails.

Taku.—Arrangements here were entirely under the naval and marine authorities, the labour alone in part being military, but under the direction of the Senior Marine Transport Officer.

At this port the disembarkation of men and animals was done in small steamers chartered by Government for the most part. Stores were conveyed in lighters in tow of tugs to Sin-ho and Tien-tsin as required by the authorities. Most of the tugs and lighters were the property of T. T. and L. Company and chartered by Government for this duty, but as there was not sufficient lighterage two tugs and eight lighters were purchased at Shanghai and are now the property of Government. Sin-ho was chiefly used for the landing of men and animals, and the stores were taken straight to Tien-tsin in lighters. Sin-ho is 22 miles from the transport's anchorage and Tien-tsin about 70; latterly, however, a large quantity of the stores were also landed at the former place, and were afterwards conveyed in lighters or junks to Tien-tsin, these being towed by small tugs. There is a good standing wharf at Sin-ho capable of accommodating two small steamers, and two temporary ones were made by the military authorities for lighters and junks to unload. The depth of water on the Taku Bar limits the draft of steamers on most occasions to 10 feet 6 inches, and the sharp turns in the river do not allow of a longer ship than 260 feet.

At Tien-tsin there is good wharf accommodation for landing stores, but the river is very narrow, and the Russian and German boat bridges below the British concession caused a great deal of inconvenience and delay. The depth of the river from Sin-ho to Tien-tsin limits the draft of steamers on most occasions to 7 feet 6 inches.

The facilities for transport work at Taku are bad, as there is no fresh water to be obtained; coal (even in small quantities) only with great difficulty, and no repairs of any magnitude can be undertaken on a ship that draws more than 11 feet of water; the weather is very uncertain, and being an open roadstead, the least breeze raises a sea that makes it impracticable and unsafe for steamers and lighters to work alongside transports.

Shan-hai-kuan. — The craft for disembarking troops and animals or stores must be obtained from other ports, there being no facilities whatever at this place. It is an open roadstead in which the transports must anchor from 1½ to 2 miles from the beach on which the landing has to be carried out, and which has shelter only from north-west by west to southerly winds. With the wind in any other direction the surf prevents the possibility of work, in addition to the difficulties of transhipment in an open seaway.

No coal or fresh water is obtainable nor is it possible to get any repairs done to ships; labour is very scarce.

The Gulf of Chih-li is notably a part of the world in which the weather is bad and uncertain, and the dates on which the last British transports left the ports of Taku and Shan-hai-kuan were not any too early (*i.e.*, the 30th and 24th November, respectively) as the Pei-ho river was frozen solid on the 6th December and floating ice obstructed the passage across the bar of the tug and lighters with weakly men on board from Sin-ho on the morning of the 30th November.

The division of responsibility between the naval and military authorities is clearly laid down in paragraph 1294 of the Queen's Regulations and Admiralty Instructions (extract attached), and this has been adhered to by me as far as possible in the transport operations of the China Expeditionary Force.

APPENDIX F.

Standing Orders, China Expeditionary Force, by Lieut.-General Sir Alfred Gaselee, K.C.B., Commanding the China Expeditionary Force.

1. *Discipline.*—The strictest discipline will be maintained in the force, and men are warned that any looting or ill-treatment of the inhabitants will be severely punished.

The great danger of straying outside the lines or cantonments and of straggling on the line of march when in China must be impressed on all ranks, as kidnapping is a favourite practice of the Chinese. Men should be warned that stragglers thus kidnapped will probably be tortured by the enemy and never seen again.

Ill-treatment of transport coolies will be severely punished. Officers and soldiers must bear in mind that as they treat the transport coolies, well or ill, so will they find them useful or the reverse.

2. *Tactics.*—It is not considered desirable at this stage to lay down any specific rules for the guidance of the force, but the General Officer Commanding wishes to point out that the conditions of warfare with the Chinese are very dissimilar to those ruling in the Transvaal or on the North-West Frontier of India.

The Chinese, however well armed they may be, are very indifferently trained, and are little accustomed to their weapons, consequently we have no cause to fear the enemy's musketry fire, and can, as a rule, adopt formations that would be quite inexcusable when operating against Boers or Afghans.

Again, the Chinese will probably operate in masses offering suitable targets, and consequently volley firing will, as a rule, prove more efficacious than independent fire, especially as regards its moral effect, and this is a point which should constantly be borne in mind by Brigadiers and Commanding Officers.

As regards the general attitude of the troops in action, it is hardly necessary to remind officers of the Indian Army that with Orientals, especially Mongolians, a prompt offensive is usually the most efficacious method of dealing with the enemy, and that there is nothing to which the Oriental is more susceptible than a threatened flank or rear.

The Chinese are not given to night attacks, but should such be delivered, there must be no firing except volleys.

3. *Scouting and Reconnaissance.*—Great attention must be paid to scouting and reconnaissance if the mistakes so frequently committed in recent campaigns are not to be repeated. As duties of this nature will always be best performed by selected men, a small body of selected scouts should be formed in every company and squadron, say 8 or 10 men under a non-commissioned officer, who, without being permanently detached from their companies or squadrons, should always be ready to take up the duties of scouting and reconnoitring for the column with which they march. An officer in each battalion should be specially detailed to train and lead these scouts, and it should be his particular duty and pride that no column covered by his scouts is ever surprised.

It must be borne in mind that scouts so employed are in no sense a substitute for skirmishers, but are supplementary thereto.

Skirmishing is not to be neglected because scouts are in advance. On the contrary, when scouts are used skirmishers are the more necessary, in order to support them.

As skirmishing in its proper sense has been very little practised of late years, Commanding Officers will take every opportunity of training their men therein, more especially in movements to a flank when in extended order.

4. *Lee-Metford Rifles.*—The magazine of the rifles should never be kept fully charged, as this weakens the spring of the magazines.

Mark I. rifles should never have more than six cartridges in the magazine, and Mark II. rifles never more than eight cartridges.

Regiments are to be practised in charging and uncharging magazines with ball ammunition. When practising this the "cut-off" must never be pulled out after the magazine is charged.

When examining arms, if the magazine is charged the "cut-off" must never be pulled out for examination.

5. *Revolvers and Pistols.*—Officers and others carrying revolvers or pistols will give the strictest orders to their orderlies and servants that they are on no account to remove these weapons from their holsters. Officers and others, when giving their revolvers or pistols to their orderlies or servants to clean, will themselves remove them from the holsters, and will invariably unload them before handing them over to be cleaned.

Care must be taken that orderlies and servants do not obtain access to ammunition.

6. *Dogs.*—No dogs are to accompany the force.

7. *Water.*—The necessity for boiling drinking water must be impressed on all ranks, and must be enforced by Commanding Officers and Heads of Departments, as the matter is of vital importance to the health of the force. Commanding Officers will take steps to ensure that all water bottles are filled with **tea or**

boiled water before starting on a march. With a view to facilitate this, a daily issue of ¼ oz. of tea and ½ oz. of sugar is sanctioned for all fighting men, and followers (British and Native) of the force, in addition to the field scale of rations.

This order may be held in abeyance when, in the opinion of the Medical Officer, the drinking-water supply is uncontaminated, as when springs and rivers are the sources of supply.

8. *Reserve (or Emergency) Rations.*—Each unit will have with it in the field at all times a reserve or emergency ration. These rations will be carried on obligatory mules, and will accompany the unit on the march and always remain with it.

These rations are only to be issued to the troops when, from any cause, there appears no probability of the ordinary field ration being issued, and then only under the orders of the Senior Officer present.

Officers Commanding Units will draw from the Commissariat Department such stores as they may consider most suitable as an emergency ration for their men, and on their being expended will replace them as early as possible.

Arrangements must be made for the turnover of these rations to prevent deterioration.

The weight of reserve rations for each unit will be limited as follows:—

	Maunds.		Mules.
Battery Field Artillery	4	=	2
Native Infantry or Pioneer Battalion	16	=	8
Company of Sappers and Miners	4	=	2
British Field Hospital	4	=	2
Native Field Hospital	4	=	2

These rations will be carried on obligatory mules, the number of which, as contained in the Field Service Equipment Tables, will be added to accordingly.

It is not intended that the above should contain a complete field ration for every man in the unit, but a sufficient ration for an emergency.

The Native Cavalry Regiment will make its own arrangements for the carriage of its emergency ration, which will be approximately equivalent to 8 maunds or 4 mules.

9. *Chargers.*—All officers should register their chargers in the Divisional or Brigade Staff Offices, the information required being—

    (*a*) Description.
    (*b*) Date of purchase.
    (*c*) Age when purchased.
    (*d*) Price paid.

10. *Officers Messes.*—Officers' messes will be provided, whenever possible, with transport for the following :—

Staff messes (of 5 or more officers)	4 maunds.
Battalion Native Infantry	6 ,,
Native Cavalry Regiment	6 ,,
Battery Field Artilery	4 ,,
Company Sappers and Miners	2 ,,
Field Hospital (4 sections)	2 ,,

11. *Newspaper Correspondents.*—Officers and men belonging to the force will, on no account be allowed to act as press correspondents, either directly or indirectly.

Applications for permission to accompany the force as press correspondents will be made to the Adjutant-General in India.

Not more than one correspondent will be allowed for each newspaper.

Officers appointed press correspondents must not be employed in any military capacity.

All telegraphic messages and all written communications, drawings, and photographs must bear the counter signature of the press censor.

All communications for the press must be confined to events that have occurred. On no account is information to be sent of future movements or intentions, if known, without express permission; nor are unofficial speculations as to what is likely to occur admissible.

The press censor will have full discretionary power to suppress the whole, or any portion, of a press message, article, drawing, or photograph, the publication of which he may deem detrimental to the interests of the force, or the operations in hand.

Intimation will be given from time to time as to the limits to be imposed on the length of telegraphic messages for the press in order to avoid the line being blocked.

12. *Baggage.*—All baggage and equipment in excess of Field Service Scale will be stored at the Base, under the orders of the Officer Commanding Base and Communications.

The battery will detail two men, the cavalry one non-commissioned officer and four men, and each battalion of infantry and pioneers one non-commissioned officer and eight men to take charge of the baggage of their corps.

The men detailed for this duty should be selected from those whose who are weakly and the least fit to undergo prolonged exposure and exertion.

Special arrangements will be made by the Officer Commanding Base and Communications for the care of the baggage of field hospitals, staff officers, and details.

Mess stores and extra camp equipment should be stacked separately from the heavy kit.

None of the heavy baggage or equipment is on any account to be sent forward without the special orders of the General Officer Commanding the Force.

The greatest care must be taken to ensure that baggage left behind is carefully and securely packed, and that each package is clearly marked with the name and regiment of the owner.

Should it be necessary at any time to send forward the force, or any portion of it, on a scale lighter than the field service scale, the baggage and equipment in excess of the light scale will be stored at the Base or elsewhere as may be ordered.

Arrangements similar to those described above for marking, storing, and protecting the heavy baggage will be made for the excess baggage.

13. *Light Scale of Baggage.*—Should it be necessary at any time owing to the scarcity of transport to move on a lighter scale of baggage and equipment than that laid down in the Field Service Equipment Tables, one or other of the following light scales will be adopted.

14. *Light Scale without Tents :—*

(i.) BAGGAGE.

(*a.*) General Officers, Commanding Officers of batteries, companies of sappers and miners, regiments of cavalry and battalions of Infantry and Pioneers, and all staff officers who are entitled to more than one charger. For each officer including servants, syces, and grass-cutters' baggage and horse kit - - 160 lbs.
(*b.*) All other officers ditto ditto - 80 „
(*c.*) British Warrant Officers and unattached Staff Sergeants (3 to the maund) - - - 27 „
(*d.*) All other British soldiers (5 to the maund) - 16 „
(*e.*) Native officers and hospital assistants (3 to the maund) - - - - - 27 „
(*f.*) Native soldiers (6 to the maund) - - - 13½ „
(*g.*) Followers (8 to the maund) - - - 10 „

(ii.) TENTAGE.

(*a.*) Field Hospital - - - Modified scale.
(*b.*) Offices - - - - Half normal scale.
(*c.*) Other Units and details. } No tents.
(*d.*) Officers.

15. *Light Scale with Tents :—*

(i.) BAGGAGE.

As in " light scale without tents " above.

(ii.) TENTAGE.

As per field service equipment tables.

When orders are issued directing the light scale of baggage to be adopted, General Officers commanding Brigades will issue such orders as will prevent the precribed loads per coolie or pack animal from being exceeded or spare men or animals from being used. The mobility of the force will depend on the prescribed scale being adhered to.

16. *Intelligence* :—

(*a.*) Intelligence Officers will be detailed, as required, to accompany bodies of troops moving through the country which may furnish opportunities for acquiring information. They will not be appointed to Brigades or Units but will be at the disposal of the D.A.Q.M.G. for intelligence under the orders of the General Officer commanding the China Expeditionary force.

(*b.*) It is the duty of all officers to assist in the collection of information and any person should, when time can be saved thereby, communicate direct to the D.A.Q.M.G. for intelligence or Field Intelligence Officer, information of an important nature which has come to his personal notice; such report should, however, also be made to his Commanding Officer.

(*c.*) When an Intelligence Officer accompanies a reconnaissance he will furnish a sketch and report. When no Intelligence Officer is present, a sketch and report will be prepared by or under the orders of the officer commanding the party.

(*d.*) Sketches and reports and all information obtained will be sent to the D.A.Q.M.G. for intelligence through the officer commanding the advanced brigade or force, unless the General Officer commanding the force is with the advanced force, in which case it will be sent direct to the D.A.Q.M.G. for Intelligence.

(*e.*) Scale for road and route sketches—2 inches to the mile. Scale for positions, camps, &c.,—6 inches to the mile.

(*f.*) The submission of an important report must on no account be delayed for the elaboration of the sketch. A sketch clearly finished in pencil is all that is required. If time permits, however, there is no objection to the sketch being finished in pen and ink or even in colours if preferred.

(*g.*) Points to be kept in view in a reconnaissance :—

 (i.) Information regarding the enemy.

 (ii.) State of road or track: whether fit for troops, pack mules or carts: amount of work to make it practicable.

 (iii.) Suitable camping grounds, capacity, whether liable to be flooded or not, suitability for defence, drinking water, quantity and quality.

(iv.) Rivers, canals, their width and depth, whether passable by fords or bridges, material available for bridging; whether navigable; if so, for what sized boat, number of boats obtainable.

(v.) Towns, villages, situation, defences, if any, line of approach.

(vi.) Details of transport or supplies procurable.

17. *Signalling.*—(*a.*) The British Signallers attached to the force will be distributed, as follows:—

Headquarters and lines of communication -	4 Units.
1st Brigade - - - -	2 ,,
2nd Brigade - - - - -	2 ,,

Regimental signallers will, as a rule, be left with corps, but the divisional and brigade signalling staff are authorised to call on regiments for the services of their signallers if required.

(*b.*) Divisional and brigade signalling officers will, under the orders of their respective general officers commanding, be responsible for the maintenance of communication between the several portions of the commands to which they belong, and commanding officers for the communication between the several portions of their corps.

(*c.*) Column commanders are responsible that suitable guards are told off daily to accompany signalling parties.

(*d.*) Signallers are not to leave their stations to carry messages. Orderlies will be provided from corps on the requisition of signalling officers.

(*e.*) The division and brigade signalling officers should be informed as early as possible of intended movements so that signalling details may be arranged. Brigade signallers will report themselves morning and evening to their brigade commanders for that purpose.

(*f*) No messages will be taken by signal stations unless they are in writing and signed and all erasures initialled by the originator.

(*g.*) The addressors are responsible that their messages are condensed, numbers being expressed in words when possible, time (in the text of the message) spelt out, and important words and addresses written in block letters. The writing should be as distinct as possible.

(*h.*) No private messages will be accepted unless countersigned by a staff officer.

(*i.*) No press messages will be accepted without the signature of the press censor.

(*j.*) In "Clear Line" messages the words "Clear Line" must be written at the commencement of the text of the message.

(*k.*) Unauthorised persons whether officers or others are prohibited from remaining near signal stations and the immediate vicinity of all signal stations is to be kept clear of all persons unconnected with the working of the line.

(*l.*) The position of the camp signal station will be indicated by a white flag with horizontal blue stripe (signalling flag, large white).

18. *Field Telegraphs.*—(*a.*) The field telegraphs should not be made use of when the ordinary post affords a sufficiently rapid means of communication or when the heliograph will answer the purpose.

(*b.*) State telegraphs in every case have precedence over all private telegrams, including press messages. If there is no likelihood of a private telegram being sent during the day, on which it is presented for despatch, the military signaller in charge of the telegraph office will inform the sender of the fact.

(*c.*) No press message is to exceed 256 words. If the wire is so blocked with State traffic that long messages cannot be sent every endeavour will be made to despatch a daily message not exceeding 64 words from each press correspondent.

(*d.*) All private telegrams must be countersigned by a staff officer and press telegrams by the press censor.

(*e.*) The text of every message (telegraph or heliograph) must commence with place and date, and, if the message is for more than one addressee, the address of each must be entered in the place for "name and address to," and the fact must be stated at the end of the message and the number of addresses filled in in the official instructions; thus—

To G.O.C. 1st Brigade.   Official   {   Three
    G.O.C. 2nd Brigade.   Instructions { addresses.
    Base Commandant.

100 A Peking Third November, * * * * * *
* * * * * * * * * * * * * * * * *
* * * * Addressed G.O.C. 1st Brigade repeated G.O.C. 2nd Brigade and Base Commandant.

(*f.*) The under-mentioned officers are authorised to send "Clear Line" telegrams and heliograms:—

    Chief of staff;
    Officers commanding base and communications;
    Officers commanding detached columns;

And in cases of great emergency, officers commanding posts on the line of communications.

(*g.*) Officers commanding detachments passing up and down the line of communications will look at the telegraph line and report the nature and extent of any damage to the line there may be.

19. *Time.*—Telegraph time (hours 0 to 24) will be kept by the China Expeditionary Force.

20. *Reports and Returns.*—(*a.*) *Monthly Returns.* Corps units will forward on the 1st of each month to the Adjutant-General in India and to the Deputy Adjutant-General of the command to which they belong a copy of the regimental monthly strength return :—

Artillery Units	- - -	Army Form B. 81.
Punjab ,,	-	⎫ India Army Form W. 744.
Bengal ,,	- -	⎭
Bombay ,,	-	India Army Form W. 732.
Madras ,,	- -	India Army Form W. 733.

(*b.*) *Field Service Form No. 1.* Strength and disposition return of the force.
(*c.*) *Field Service Form No. 2.* Nominal roll of Staff officers.
(*d.*) *Field Service Form No. 3.* Description, quantity, and disposition of ammunition.
(*e.*) *Field Service Form No. 4.*

To be submitted to the Chief of the Staff on the 1st of every month or as early as possible after by officers commanding brigades, base, and communications and any detached force working independently.

(*f.*) *Fortnightly Disposition Return of Force.*—To be submitted in the following form to the Chief of the Staff on the 1st and 15th of each month punctually without fail by Officers Commanding Brigades, Base, and Communications, and any detached force working independently.

This return will not be required from the troops at Hongkong.

Camp or Post.	Corps, Unit, Detachment, or Detail.	Officers.	British N.-C. Officers and men.	Native Officers, N.-C. Officers and men.
Hsiang-ho	2nd Bde. Staff	5	3	6
	24th P. 1.	3	—	170
	No. 42 N.F. Hospital	1	—	3
	Railway Section	1	1	—
Tai-tzu	1-4 Gurkha Rifles	4	—	380

(*g.*) *Weekly Diary.*—A weekly diary made up to Saturdays will be submitted by Officers Commanding Brigades, Base, and Communications, and detached forces. These diaries should contain full information regarding movements, casualties, intelligence received, characteristics of country traversed and of its inhabitants, roads, resources, weather, rainfall, and all matters of military interest.

These diaries form the basis of the historical record of the campaign, and should therefore be as complete as possible. Sketches illustrating operations should be attached if available.

The diaries of subordinate officers will not be forwarded, but all information of interest contained in them should be incorporated in the diaries submitted by Officers Commanding Brigades, &c. The submission of these diaries should not be delayed owing to the non-receipt of a subordinate's diary, the contents of which can be incorporated in a future week's diary if necessary.

(*h*). *Daily Strength Return.*—Officers Commanding Corps, Units, Detachments, and Details and Departments will forward to the medical officer of the hospital in which their sick are treated on each Friday, a return, in the form given below, of their actual strength for each day of the previous week. The returns for the British officers and men of British corps and British non-commissioned officers of Native corps and departments, will be sent to the British Field Hospital, those for British officers, of Native corps, Native troops, and followers of all corps and departments to Native Field Hospitals :—

Corps or Department_____

Station and date_____

Day of Week.	British Officers.	British Warrant and N.-C. Officers and men.	Native Officers, N.-C. Officers and men.	Followers.
Saturday				
Sunday				
Monday				
Tuesday				
Wednesday				
Thursday				
Friday				

(*i.*) *Followers.*—Whenever a Native follower, public or private, is sent to a field hospital, a memorandum giving his name and the corps or department to which he belongs, his place of entertainment, and the articles in his possession (with date up to and for which he has been paid), is to be sent with him.

21. *Military Accounts.*—(*a.*) Officers commanding corps and detachments and heads of departments will submit monthly to the Field Paymaster, on the 15th of each month, rough estimates of cash required for the ensuing month; *e.g.*, estimates for the month of September will be submitted on August 15th.

(*b.*) Any large unforeseen expenditure likely to come forward after the estimates have been submitted should be at once notified to the Field Paymaster.

(*c.*) To insure against losses of cheques and remittance transfer receipts in transit through the post staff and departmental officers are recommended to make their pay bills payable to a well-known banker or recognised agent in India. Application for permission to do so should be made on application in the prescribed form (which will be supplied by the Field Paymaster) to the Controller of Military Accounts, Bengal Command, who will issue the necessary instructions to the banker or agent concerned informing the officer through the Field Paymaster of the action taken in the matter.

This system of payment of salary bills of officers in the field, which was adopted during the late Tirah Expedition, worked satisfactorily.

This will not prevent officers from drawing advances in the field, but they must credit these sums to Government by deduction in their pay bills when forwarding them to their agents.

22. *Postal.*—Officers Commanding units will send in at once, to the Base Post Office, a nominal roll of all officers, with their units, officers' initials being given. Officers in charge of field hospitals, Engineer companies, and sections, &c., should also include in the roll the names of Warrant and Non-commissioned officers. The Post Office should be kept informed of any changes. Departmental and extra-regimentally employed officers should keep the nearest Field Post Office and the Base Post Office informed of their movements.

The earliest possible intimation of any movements of troops should be given to the postal officers with the division and brigades, to enable them to make the necessary postal arrangements.

Mail bags must not be opened in transit under any circumstances.

The arrival of the mail in camp will be intimated by a bugle call of four "Gs," to be sounded by the bugler of the guard nearest the Field Post Office, and to be repeated by the other buglers on duty in camp.

Orderlies will be sent to the Field Post Office on arrival of mails to take over letters and parcels.

The probable hour of arrival of the mail and the latest hour for posting letters will be given in a notice affixed to the Field Post Office tent. These should be notified periodically in brigade and post orders.

By order,
E. G. BARROW, Major-General,
Chief of the Staff, China Expeditionary Force.

Hongkong, 17th July 1900.

APPENDIX G.

REPORT ON THE WORKING OF THE COMMISSARIAT DEPARTMENT OF THE CHINA EXPEDITIONARY FORCE, BY LIEUT. COLONEL W. J. H. BOND, C.C.O.

Original Reserve.—Land supplies for three months, in addition to sea rations, and obligatory transport on a fixed scale were ordered to be sent with each corps unit. The arrangement was a most fortunate one, as, without it, considerable difficulty would have arisen in maintaining supplies at places so far distant as Peking with an inadequate reserve of supplies in hand. As it was, there was always a sufficient stock to work on, notwithstanding considerable losses of stores owing to rains, and difficulties in transit, until the market for local supplies opened. On the augmentation of the original force by two infantry brigades and one cavalry brigade, a three months' supply of land rations was shipped in each transport, but owing to the monsoon, it was not considered expedient to send the obligatory mules with the troops, and two transport corps of pack mules were despatched as a body, and were afterwards allotted to units, as contemplated in the scheme.

Commissariat Base. — The commissariat base was fixed at Tien-tsin, which is undoubtedly the most suitable base for operations in the Chih-li Province. In some respects it would possibly have been more convenient to have had the commissariat base at Sin-ho, the port of debarkation, but the accommodation for a large commissariat godown was wanting, and it would have entailed the breaking of bulk of stores at Tien-tsin, which is the terminus of the river steamer traffic.

Tien-tsin is admirably suited for a commissariat base. The wharfage is extensive and conveniently situated in immediate proximity to the large godowns which were taken up for the shelter of stores. The "bund" gives ample room for sorting and handling stores, and it was always possible to keep incoming stores separate and distinct from despatches. Labour, as required, is also available at a fairly cheap rate.

Landing Stores.—The landing of stores from transports, and their despatch onwards was at first in the hands of the senior marine transport officer, and was subsequently taken over by the Navy, a principal transport officer being appointed from England. On first arrival at Taku there was a great deficiency of lighters, and, in consequence, much time was unavoidably wasted in steaming to and from the transports which had to lie about 13 miles from the mouth of the river. Eventually a large number of light draught steamers, tugs, and lighters were engaged from various sources, and the general working arrangement was that all troops and animals and such stores as could be discharged from transports into the light-draught steamers, were landed at Sin-ho, to be sent on thence to Tien-tsin by river or rail, as might be most convenient ; and the lighters were tugged up to Tien-tsin, where they discharged their cargoes. Subsequently, towards the end of the working season, this arrangement was modified, with the view of expediting the discharge of the transports at the bar, and large quantities of fodder, grain, and fuel, which were not required for immediate use, were landed and stocked at Sin-ho, which thus became a subsiduary base to Tien-tsin.

Necessity for Legislation.—The question of landing stores in over-sea expeditions is one which needs consideration and special legislation on the part of the military and marine authorities. No mention is made of this subject in the Indian military regulations for field service, with the result that when the work has to be undertaken, an improvised system has to be devised with inadequate material. The Government of India insists on an account of receipts and issues of all stores, despatched for the use of a force in the field, being kept, and, from a commissariat point of view, this procedure is absolutely essential, as its omission renders it impossible to arrive at correct information as to the state of supplies.

A good deal of difficulty was experienced in complying with the rules of the Military Accounts Department owing to the numerous bases which have been formed at Hongkong, Wei-hai-wei, Chih-fu, &c., and the invoicing of stores intended for the contingent direct to these places ; and also to the postal communication with the outer world being very defective.

River Transport.—The transport of stores to Peking was in the early days of the expedition an important matter. The obligatory transport, with which regiments were equipped, was sufficient only for the carriage of the barest necessaries ; cart, or any kind of local transport, was not obtainable, and all stores had to be sent by river. A large number of junks had been collected at the taking of Tien-tsin city, and it was only by making every use of them that the transport of the relief column was arranged. But many of these junks were old and worn out, some were hardly found in gear and equipment, and the Chinese coolies, who were impressed to man them, were not of the boatman class. The first convoy—a very large one of 80 boats—was despatched on the 4th August to keep in touch with the Peking relief column on its land march, and this was succeeded at intervals of a few days by other smaller convoys.

Escorts.—The Hongkong Regiment was detailed to supply escorts on the boats as required, the water transport officer requisitioning on the officer commanding that regiment for the numbers he wanted. In the early part of the work two rifles per boat were supplied, but latterly one rifle was considered sufficient. Escorts always carried 15 days' rations

Numbering of Boats.—All boats were numbered.

Papers.— The difficulty of knowing one Chinaman from another was got over by giving each headman of a boat a printed slip with his boat number on it, and a last pay and ration certificate, and without these he could not be paid.

Payments.—For all payments the headman of a boat made his mark, or, in case of contractors' boats, the contractor signed, and the British transport officer witnessed it.

Length of Voyage.—The ordinary voyage to Tung-chou took 13 days.

Expeditions.—Besides the ordinary work done between Tientsin and Tung-chou and the other posts on the river three flotillas were supplied for three expeditions, viz., to Tu-liu, to Pei-t'ang, and to Pao-ting fu.

Number of Trips made.—The number of trips made was 977 in all.

Carpenters.—Repairs to boats were carried out by one lance naick from the Bombay Sappers and Miners, who had under him one Chinese head boat-builder and nine assistant carpenters. Two men from the Bombay Sappers and Miners worked as painters, and put all the numbers on the boats.

Replenishment of Supplies.— Owing to the delay, which was to be anticipated in obtaining supplies from India, steps had to be taken early to replenish the three months' land rations which accompanied the force in the first instance. It was ultimately arranged that three months' full supply for the force in Chih-li province should be landed in the early part of October, and a further six months' reserve of special articles, which were not obtainable locally, viz., ghi, preserved provisions, rum, limejuice, &c., should be despatched so as to reach Taku by the beginning of November. If large bulks of stores have to be obtained from India, it would be better to arrange for their delivery not later than the 15th October, as the delay in landing, owing to bad weather and great cold in October and November, is considerable.

Local Supplies.— Owing to the disturbed state of the province on our first arrival, and the desertion of practically all its inhabitants, it was impossible to rely on local supplies. It soon became evident, however, that the country was a very rich one, and as affairs became settled and the inhabitants began to return, a beginning was made to exploit its resources. The Chinaman is a keen trader, and quite alive to the advantages of cash payment, and consequently this system of supply has developed in the most surprising manner. It is now quite possible to feed our force, both men and animals, from the province, only obtaining from India the special articles noted in the previous paragraph. Tien-tsin is a large trading centre with business connections in all parts of the world, and all imported articles, including medical comforts, are to be obtained there at moderate rates. Coal is available from local mines. Firewood is to be had in large quantities, and need not be imported. Fodder is available in large quantities. Grain for transport animals is readily procurable, but as both fodder and grain are of somewhat inferior quality, it was found advantageous to import a reserve of oats and hay for Australian horses.

During September, October, and November a better country for fodder and grain could hardly be found. In September and part of October crops of kao-liang (jowari) and pao-ku (Indiancorn) stand green all over the country and afford excellent grain and fodder combined, on which horses thrive very well. When the crops are down kao-liang stocks were stacked in every village, and every house is full of grain.

The country is very much cultivated, but there is sufficient grass procurable for a large number of animals. Even if sufficient grass is not available, kao-liang stocks are plentiful. The following are some of the different descriptions of grain met with :—

(1.) Kao-liang, both red and white. This is not a first-class grain.
(2.) Lu-ton, a small pea, very nutritious, but heating for horses not doing very hard work. Horses seem to like this better than any other grain, but in an uncrushed or unboiled state it is liable to give colic. It requires a great deal of boiling.
(3.) Hai-ton, a small black bean.
(4.) Huang-ton, yellow bean.
(5.) Ta-mai, barley.
(6.) Bran of various grains also procurable.
Nos. 3, 4, and 5 should be boiled, and are first-class grains for putting on condition. Horses fed on them have also continued to do daily hard work.

Extra Rations.—The anticipation of a rigorous winter necessitated special provision being made to supplement the ordinary ration of British troops with the articles of diet to which they are accustomed, and the Commissariat Department laid in a stock of the articles usually procurable in coffee-shops, which were available for the troops on payment at rates notified in field force orders. The existing regulations for payments for extra rations and renewal of clothing were found not to be satisfactory and require revision.

Medical Comforts. — The supply of medical comforts was abundant. A 500 per cent. reserve accompanied each hospital from India, and consignments of 100 per cent. on the normal scale were subsequently despatched from India and England every fortnight. A reserve calculated as sufficient for nine months for the general and field hospitals and hospital ships was despatched from India with the last consignment of stores.

Lighting Barracks.—About 2,000 lamps of various kinds for kerosine oil were obtained from Shanghai and Horgkong for the lighting of the various barracks constructed for the accommodation of the troops.

Clothing.—Clothing on special scales was authorised for this expedition.

Transport.—The expedition was the first occasion on which the corps organisation of transport, which has recently been sanctioned by the Indian Government, as a tentative measure, had been tried on field service. The system was put to a severe test, inasmuch as the transport corps were broken up to provide obligatory transport for corps, but it achieved better results than anticipated. But the transport corps was not worked as a body of transport in departmental charge, and there was little or no difference from the old regimental transport system. If the transport corps system is to be a success on service, corps must be officered by commissioned officers. Warrant officers have not the position which allows them to take the responsibility which is inseparable from transport work in the field.

A great deal of extra work was thrown on the transport branch owing to the large numbers of animals which have been purchased or captured to augment our transport, and their subsequent organisation into cart corps. The China mule is better adapted to draught than to pack work, and it is altogether advantageous to use draught transport in this flat country. But in the event of more extended operations in hilly districts having to be undertaken, pack transport would be necessary, and, consequently, a scheme was devised by which cart corps, readily convertible into pack transport corps, were formed. Thus, in addition to the obligatory pack transport with cart corps unit in the division, one army transport cart corps of 500 carts, fully equipped, and two Chinese cart corps, totalling 528 carts, were available, which would have been sufficient carriage to allow of a division undertaking any military operations which might have become necessary. The numerous waterways throughout the country would generally afford the means of transporting heavy bulks of stores to advance depôts.

APPENDIX H.

Report on Transport Operations of the China Expeditionary Force, by Major H. D. MacIntyre, Divisional Transport Officer.

The transport taken from India to China for the original force consisted of :—

(1.) 2,600 obligatory pack mules.
(2.) 4 Punjab cooly corps.
(3.) 500 army transport carts.

Of the 2,600 obligatory pack mules, only those allotted to regiments and corps which embarked at Calcutta accompanied them. The remainder, about 1,000, allotted to regiments and units which embarked at Bombay, came separately and in three batches. These were all brought on to Tien-tsin. A number of the Bombay regiments were detained at Hongkong or Shanghai and their obligatory transport formed a useful depôt at Peking.

Great difficulty was experienced in enlisting Chinese coolies for transport purposes with the force, and eventually none were obtained. 200 carts, 400 ponies and 2,000 Chinese wheelbarrows were ordered from Shanghai, and 1,000 hand carts from Kobe.

Advance on Peking.—When the advance on Peking commenced on 4th August, none of the cooly corps, army transport carts, or spare mules referred to above had arrived. Only the obligatory mule transport of regiments and units which had then arrived at Tien-tsin, a few locally purchased or captured animals and carts and a few Japanese coolies were available. The numbers actually taken were :—

511 Indian pack mules.
36 Japanese ponies.
79 Chinese mules and ponies.
37 Country carts.

The Japanese coolies proved very lazy and disobedient, and were sent back from Peking as soon as possible and dismissed.

By the 10th August, the 1st Cooly Corps, and 700 spare Indian mules had arrived at Tien-tsin. The coolies were furnished with Japanese hand-carts —3 to a cart—load 3 maunds each.

On 13th August a column with 400 spare Indian mules, and 200 Japanese hand-carts with coolies and some 15 country-carts left Tien-tsin for Peking. The fodder obtained on the way was rich and plentiful, though it tended to keep the animals soft and liable to galls, and careful supervision had to be constantly taken to prevent these. The Punjabi coolies took willingly to their hand-carts and worked very well, though in places the road was stiff. These arrived at Peking on 19th August.

The above 400 spare Indian mules, shortly increased to 700 by fresh animals from Tien-tsin, together with the coolies, and all locally-purchased or captured transport, was formed into a depôt at the Temple of Heaven, Peking. The remainder of the 1st cooly corps, and the 2nd cooly corps arrived a little later on. The coolies were used for local work, such as bringing in firewood, fodder, &c., and the other transport for column work or convoy duty to Tung-chou.

The Peking cart was the chief means of transport and every endeavour had to be made to increase the locally-raised transport and to keep it in as efficient a state as possible to cope with the hard, continuous work. Their numbers soon increased, and as Pekinese drivers were tried and found quite unreliable, it was found necessary to indent on the cooly corps for transport attendants. The stage convoy system with 400 Indian mules from Tung-chou, meeting 400 from Peking, was introduced and found very successful. They had, however, soon to be withdrawn for column operations. On 18th September, 132 army transport carts arrived and were most valuable. Their numbers were later increasd to 198.

The locally-raised transport, consisting of Peking carts, Chinese mules and ponies, was organised as it was raised into troops, according to the Indian organization, with petty officers in charge and drivers told off to particular animals and carts. The animals were branded, and the carts numbered, and some system and chain of responsibility was established. The amount of supplies of all sorts brought from Tung-chou to Peking in three months on Government transport, was about 40,000 maunds. By the end of October there were about 400 Peking carts, and about 1,000 captured or purchased animals working. Glanders made its appearance among the Chinese animals, but with proper precautions only a very few cases occurred.

The column from Peking to Pao-ting fu started on 12th October with transport consisting of 1,000 Indian pack mules, 150 army transport carts, and 30 Peking carts. The carts did very well.

Punjabi cooly corps proved valuable in many ways, and at Peking, with their sirdars and mates, proved useful as muleteers. At Tien-tsin, Sin-ho and on the fleet they have also done very good work, loading and unloading stores, &c. A number were distributed among regiments and units as stretcher-bearers and out of the four corps, (4,000 coolies) only some 500 spare were sent back to India, including all those invalided.

2. *Indian mules.*—The Indian mules were good as usual. They stood the voyage to China well, and did hard work. The corps system, on which they are now organized, was greatly interfered with by their being told off to different regiments and units. This, however, was necessary, and even with this I think the corps system an excellent one. With their permanent warrant officers, &c., there was no trouble in Calcutta in distributing them to the various regiments there and in embarking them.

3. *Chinese mules.*—Very good animals, especially in draught. Up to any amount of work and never sick or sorry if looked after. The animals obtained generally aged 10 years or upwards, the Chinese having apparently removed all the young ones.

4. *Chinese ponies.*—Sturdy little animals, but nothing like so good as the mules. With hard work, they are apt to break down, and have not much heart.

5. *India army transport carts.*—These require no description. They stand almost any amount of knocking about and are the best kind of transport seen in China, and can quite well carry 10 maunds.

6. *Peking carts.*—Very well made and with the Chinese mules made good transport. When closed, they only hold about 6 maunds, but when open or cut down, they can easily carry 8 or even 10 maunds. They are easily convertible to double draught by fixing on a cross bar. Their weak points are the wooden pegs holding the axle to the body. With rough usage, these pegs are liable to break, with the result that the cart is for the time being useless. This weak point was remedied by either screwing on an iron band to the body over the pegs and axle or by supporting the pegs by triangular blocks of wood fixed to the body of the cart. The wheels and axles are of special wood and are very well constructed. The harness for these carts was the great difficulty and every expedient had to be resorted to.

7. *Japanese hand-carts.*—These were issued to the Punjabi coolies and were very useful. They are light and handy, but break down with hard usage. The tyres of the wheels want riveting to the felloes without which they are liable to come off.

8. *Shanghai carts.*—Far too heavy and unwieldy for transport purposes. With a couple of bullocks they might be useful for municipal conservancy work. The ends of the axle are liable to break off. None of these arrived at Peking, though a few started.

9. *Shanghai single wheelbarrows.*—Difficult to manipulate as the balance is very easily upset. With Chinese, who are accustomed to them, they are very useful and carry a heavy weight such as three or four maunds.

APPENDIX I.

MEDICAL ARRANGEMENTS FOR THE CHINA EXPEDITIONARY FORCE, BY SURG.-GENERAL W. TAYLOR, C.B., A.M.S., P.M.O. OF H.M.'s FORCES IN INDIA.

ADMINISTRATION.

3. Colonel J. T. B. Bookey, V.H.S., Indian Medical Service, was appointed principal medical officer to the force, and Colonel H. F. P. F. Esmonde-White, Indian Medical Service, principal medical officer of the line of communication. Their office establishments were provided from the Bengal and Madras commands, respectively.

4. Stationery was provided from the Stationery Department, Calcutta, the office tents from the arsenal at Fort William, and furniture from the military works services at Fort William.

CORPS UNITS.

5. Each unit was equipped as laid down in Appendix No. 1, Field Service Departmental Code, Medical, and first field dressing packets were issued to every officer and soldier.

6. Collateral medical charges were formed by the principal medical officer of the force for the Royal Artillery batteries and the several companies of Sappers and Miners, respectively.

7. A strict medical examination of officers, troops, and followers was made as laid down in paragraph 49, Field Service Departmental Code, Medical.

8. A staff surgeon as a collateral charge was authorised, both for the division and the cavalry brigade. The appointments being made by the general officer commanding on the recommendation of the principal medical officer of the force.

9. Command principal medical officers arranged for inoculating against plague all officers, soldiers, and followers who were warned for service in China. It was distinctly understood that the operation was purely optional, and that no one was to be inoculated who did not voluntarily desire to undergo the operation, but the advantages of plague inoculation were explained to the men, and inoculation was carried out before the units left their respective stations.

Field Hospitals.

10. Field hospitals were mobilised at the following stations :—

No. 15, British (Sections A and B), at Meeau Meer.
„ 22, British (Section A), at Peshawar.
„ 22, British (Section B), at Calcutta.
„ 25, British (Sections A and B) at Madras.
„ 38, Native (Sections A and B), at Meean Meer.
„ 39, Native, at Jubbulpore.
„ 41, Native, at Secunderabad.
„ 42, Native, at Umballa.
„ 43, Native, at Lucknow.
„ 47, Native, at Mhow.
„ 51, Native, at Kampti.
„ 53, Native, at Belgaum.
„ 54, Native, at Meean Meer.
„ 57, Native, at Calcutta.
„ 58, Native, at Allahabad.
„ 61, Native, at Wellington.
„ 62, Native (Sections C and D), at Poona.
„ 63, Native, at Poona.
„ 66, Native, at Bangalore.
„ 69, Native, at Meean Meer.

11. Field hospitals were, as far as practicable, embarked with units as follows :—

With the field battery, 1 section British.
With each Native cavalry regiment, 1 or 2 sections Native.
With each battalion of infantry, 2 sections Native.
With each cooly corps, 1 section Native.

12. The Commissariat Transport Department were directed to send 500 per cent. reserve of medical comforts to China, and take steps, by means of periodical shipments from England or India, to ensure that any withdrawal from the reserve stock was immediately made good so that it should always be maintained as nearly as possible at 500 per cent. in China.

13. Each field hospital was provided with a box of reserve medicines and a box of antiseptic dressings.

14. The ambulance transport consisted of 30 dandies with 180 bearers per field hospital (sections in proportion), with the usual quota of commissariat sergeants, ambulance agents, sirdars, and mates.

15. A reserve of 10 per cent. of bearers accompanied all field and general hospitals.

16. Mosquito netting bags, field hospital pattern, were provided for the full number of beds in both field and general hospitals.

17. With a view to reduce transport, such field hospital packages as were not required at the front were, stored, under the orders of the principal medical officer of the force, at the advanced base.

Field Medical Store Depôts.

18. Nos. 3 and 4 Field Medical Store Depôts were mobilized at Calcutta, and in addition to the authorised equipment, were each provided with six cases of antiseptic dressing, 500 first field dressing packets, and a reserve supply of 50 lbs. sulphate of quinine.

19. Field medical store officers indented on the base medical store depôt at Hongkong for supplies, care being taken to frame requisitions so as to anticipate the requirements of the force.

Base Depôt of Medical Stores.

20. A base depôt of medical stores was established at Hongkong, the establishment and equipment for which is shown in Appendix No. H. 1.

21. The base depôt of medical stores indented on the Calcutta medical store depôt for supplies, care being taken to frame requisitions so as to anticipate the requirements of the force.

Line of Communication.

22. The following field hospitals were employed on the lines of communication for the purpose of bringing the sick and wounded back from the front:—

No. 38 Native (Sections A. and B).
„ 41 „
„ 57 „ (Sections C. and D).

Hospital Ships.

23. The following ships were employed:—

1. His Highness the Maharaja of Gwalior's ship "Gwalior," equipped for 150 beds, and stationed at Taku, as an advanced base hospital for native sick.
2. The American ship "Maine," equipped for 175 beds, employed for bringing British sick from Taku to Chih-fu, and from Chih-fu to India.

3 The Indian Government hospital ship "Carthage," equipped for 165 beds, employed for bringing native sick from Taku to Chih-fu, and from Chih-fu to India.

GENERAL HOSPITALS.

24. A British general hospital for 10 officers and 100 soldiers, was established at Wei-hai-wei. Sections A. and B., No. 25 British field hospital, were stationed at Peking, and was fully equipped with bedding, clothing, diet, requisites, &c.

25. Section A., No. 15 British field hospital, fully equipped with bedding, clothing, &c., was ordered to be stationed at Tien-tsin as an advanced base hospital.

26. The following native general hospitals were ordered to be established :—

No. 1 for 500 beds in China. ⎫ Disposition left to the
„ 2 „ „ „ „ ⎬ General Officer Com-
„ 3 „ „ „ „ ⎭ manding the Force.
„ 4 „ „ „ at Calcutta.

The equipment of an additional native general hospital was held in readiness at Calcutta for despatch to China if required.

27. Each native general hospital in China was equipped with 500 heavy woollen jackets and drawers, and the one in Calcutta with 250 warm and 250 light woollen jackets and drawers.

28. The scale of furniture for general hospitals is given in Appendix No. H. 2, and the equipment for lady nurses in Appendix No. H. 3.

29. All serious cases and such as were not likely to be fit to return to duty within a reasonable period were treated in general hospitals. Patients requiring a change to India and those considered unfit for further service in China, were invalided to Calcutta, and from thence transferred to their respective depôts. The British sick from China were treated in the Calcutta station hospital, which was augmented to the extent deemed necessary for the purpose.

30. A Röntgen X-Rays apparatus was ordered to be provided for each native general hospital in China.

31. Arrangements were made for the supply of ice for the sick, and three soda-water machines were sent to China for the purpose of manufacturing aërated waters for the sick, *vide* Appendix No. H. 4.

32. Any article deemed necessary for the sick and wounded, which had not been provided from India and which was locally procurable, was authorised to be supplied under the authority of the general officer commanding the force.

33. Conservancy carts with cattle and drivers were sent from India for both British and native general hospitals.

34. Disinfecting apparatus was sent to China direct from England.

Returns.

35. Field service returns were commenced from date of embarkation for China.

Establishment and Equipment for a Base Depot of Medical Stores.

I.— *Establishment.*

1 Indian medical service officer (*field rank*).
1 assistant surgeon, 1st class.
1 assistant surgeon, 2nd class.

2 writers	⎫
3 compounders	⎪
3 packers	⎬ Appointed by the Director-General, Indian Medical Service.
2 cutlers	⎪
2 tinsmiths	⎭
2 carpenters	⎫
1 water-carrier	⎬ Provided by the Commissariat Department.
1 sweeper	⎭

II.—*Equipment.*

(a.) Medicines, surgical materials, &c., laid down in Appendix No. 38, Regulations for Army Medical Service.

Medical companions	24
Surgical haversacks	48
Field medical panniers	prs. 12
Reserve field medical panniers	„ 6
Field surgical panniers	„ 12
Field fracture boxes	12
Antiseptic cases	14

This equipment was ordered from England to be despatched direct to Hongkong.

(b.) 12 boxes reserve medicines, *vide* Appendix No. 20, Field Service Departmental Code, Medical

(c.) 12 cases antiseptic dressings, War Office pattern

(d.) 100 pounds sulphate of quinine

Supplied by the medical storekeeper to Government, Bengal Command.

(e.) As many condemned, but thoroughly cleaned and disinfected, hospital sheets as the Commissary-General, Bengal, could obtain.

(f.) COMMISSARIAT STORES—

Sundries.

Corkscrews - - - - - -	No.	6

Books.

Army Regulations, India, Volume V. (Commissariat) - - - -	,,	1

Necessaries.

Candles, stearine, carriage size - - -	lbs.	100

Miscellaneous.

Lanterns, kerosine, storm-proof, Ditmar's -	No.	6
Lanterns, red glass - - - - -	,,	1

Tools, Tinsmiths'.

One set as follows:—

Awl, scoring - - - - - -	No.	1
Bellows, country, single - - -	,,	1
Blocks, wooden, 18-in. × 3-in. × 4-in. -	,,	1
Chisels, blunt, with handles - -	,,	1
,, cold, tinsmith, 1-in. and ¾ in. -	Sets	2
Compass, common, 9-in. - - -	No.	1
Hammer, creasing - - - -	,,	1
,, hollowing - - - -	,,	1
,, riveting - - -	,,	1
Irons, creasing, tinsmiths' - - -	,,	1
Mallet, wooden - - - - -	,,	1
Mandrel, wooden, tapering, 3-ft. long, 2-in. diameter - - - -	,,	1
Mandrel, iron - - - - -	,,	1
Pincers - - - - - -	,,	1
Punches, of sizes - - - -	Sets	3
Shears, stock, tinsmiths' - - - -	No.	1
,, hand, spring, tinsmiths' - -	,,	1
Spike, square, for inside work - -	,,	1
,, round ,, - -	,,	1
,, grooving ,, - -	,,	1
Square metal - - - - -	,,	1
Tool, soldering, iron, with handle - -	,,	1
,, ,, copper, handle - -	,,	1
Karai - - - - - -	,,	1
Chest for tools with lock and key - -	,,	1

Carpenters' Tools.

One set as follows:—

Adze, carpenters'	No.	1
Augurs of sizes	Sets	3
Bits of sizes	"	3
Brace	No.	1
Chisels, mortice, of sizes	Sets	2
" joiners, $1\frac{1}{2}$," 1, $\frac{1}{2}$	"	3
Compass, iron	No.	1
Files, half round	Sets	3
" triangular, for sharpening saw	"	2
Gauge, marking	No.	1
Glue pot, iron, small	"	1
Hammer, claw	"	1
Jack plane, single iron	"	1
Nail puller (Victor)	"	1
Oil stone	"	1
Pincers	"	1
Rule, 2-foot folding	"	1
Saw, 18-in. blade	"	1
Screw-driver, 12-in.	"	1
Square, steel blade, 9-in.	"	1
Box, wooden, with two locks and keys	"	1

(*g.*) ORDNANCE STORES—

Camp Equipment.

Buckets, water, G. S. leather, I P.	No.	5
" " I. P., with lid	"	11
Lantern, I. P.	"	16
Tents, I. P., complete—		
G. S. $\begin{cases} 160 \text{ lbs.} \\ 80 \text{ " } \end{cases}$	"	2
	"	3
Privates	"	9
Staff-sergeants	"	2
Tents, I. P. Privates, Walls	"	2

Tools, &c. for Intrenching.

Axes, pick—		
Heads, $6\frac{1}{2}$ lbs.	No.	6
Helves, $31\frac{1}{2}$ inches	"	6
Mamooties—		
G. S.	"	6
Helves	"	6
Spades—N. P. (or O. P.)	"	6

Field Hospital Equipment.

Flags, distinguishing, I. P.—
    Hospital, Mark I. - - - - No. 1
    Poles   „ II. - - - „ 1
(*h.*) MILITARY WORKS STORES—
    Office chairs - - - - - „ 4
    Dispensing tables - - - - „ 2
    Office tables - - - - - „ 2

SCALE OF FURNITURE FOR GENERAL HOSPITALS.

Articles.	British 110 beds.	Each Native 500 beds.	Remarks.
Apparatus, hot-water - -	2	5	
Baths, foot, galvanised iron -	2	—	
„ hip - - - -	2	—	
Bedsteads, iron, with wire-woven mattress.	110	100*	*For serious cases.
Boards, diet-scale - - -	4	—	
„ hospital orders - -	4	10	
„ inventory - -	4	10	
Boxes, ice - - - -	1	2	
Carts, conservancy - -	2	5	
Chairs, portable - -	20	20	
„ folding, canvas reclining	20	—	In lieu of easy chairs.
Commodes, portable - -	12	—	With enamelware pans.
Cots, trestle - - -	—	500	
Frames, diet sheet - -	110	500	
„ for mosquito curtains -	110	500	
Head-rests, double incline -	4	10	
Receptacles, filth, small -	6	12	
„ kitchen, small -	6	12	
„ urinary „ -	6	12	
Screens, moveable - - -	4	10	
Stools, folding - - -	50	—	In lieu of " forms."
Tables, portable - - -	20	20	
Trays, dressing - - -	4	20	
Trestles, bedding - - -	8	10	
Tubs, galvanised iron, oblong, for bathing.	12	5	
Tubs, galvanised iron, for storing water.	2	5	
Wash hand stands, portable, with enamel ware fittings.	8	5	
Urinals, iron, complete -	6	—	

Scale of Equipment for Lady Nurses.

Articles.	Per Lady Nurse.	Per Hospital.	Remarks.
Basins, washing, enamelled iron	1	—	
Bedsteads, portable, with mosquito curtain and frames for ditto.	1	—	
Bottles, water, glass	—	2	
Candlestick, enamelled iron	1	—	
Cans, water, galvanised iron.	—	2	
Chairs, easy, folding, canvas seat	1	—	
Commode, portable, with enamel-ware pan.	—	3	
Cups, egg, enamelled iron	1	—	
Cups and saucers, enamelled iron	1	—	
Forks, dinner, electro-plate	2	—	
Glasses, wine	1	—	
,, looking, folding	1	—	
Jugs, enamelled iron, 12 quarts	—	2	
,, ,, ,, 1 quart	—	2	
Knives, dinner, white handle	2	—	
Lanterns, Orr's, complete, in case.	1 per 2 ladies.	—	
Mugs, drinking, enamelled iron	1	—	
Napkins, table	3	—	
Plates, dinner, enamelled iron	2	—	
,, soup ,, ,,	1	—	
,, pudding ,, ,,	1	—	
Pots, tea	—	2	
,, chamber, with cover, enamelled iron	1	—	
Salt cellars	1	—	
Spoons, electro-plate, dessert	2	—	
,, ,, eggs	1	—	
,, ,, tea	1	—	
,, ,, table	1	—	
Stools, camp	1	—	
Stoves, Rippingille's, complete	—	1	
Table, camp, dining	1 per 2 ladies.	—	
,, ,, toilet, small	1	—	
Tubs, ablution	—	2	
Table-cloths, white	1	—	
Kitchen Utensils.			
Kettles, 2 quarts	—	2	
,, oval, camp, with covers	—	2	
Knives, kitchen	—	1	
Saucepans, with covers, block tin, 2 quarts, 1½ quarts, and 1 quart	—	1 each.	
Shapes, pudding, block tin	—	4	
Spoons, kitchen	—	1	

STATEMENT SHOWING THE ESTABLISHMENT AND STORES SUPPLIED WITH EACH AËRATED WATER MACHINE.

Establishment.

Supervisor	1
Bottler	1
Mate	1
Coolies	2
Bhistie	1

Chemicals for three months.

Sugar	mds.	20
Essence of Lemon	lbs.	20
Tartaric Acid	,,	20
Soda Bicarb	mds.	30
Sulphuric Acid, pure	,,	20

Accessories.

Bottles	dozens	100
Spare set of tubes for godeometer		1
Indiarubber rings for bottles	gross	100
Spare set leather washers		6
Reservoir for water		1
Boiler for boiling water		1
Tubs for washing bottles		3

STATEMENT SHOWING TOTAL MEDICAL PERSONNEL WITH THE FORCE.

Detail.	R.A.M.C. Officers.	I.M.S. Officers.	Assistant Surgeons.	Hospital Assistants.
Principal medical officer of force	—	1	—	—
,, ,, ,, of line of communication	—	1	—	—
2 batteries, Royal Artillery	—	—	2	—
2 ammunition columns	—	—	—	2
regiments, native cavalry	—	3	—	3
18 battalions, native infantry	—	18	—	18
3 companies, sappers and miners	—	—	—	3
Mounted sappers detachment	—	—	—	1
Vickers-Maxim guns detachment	—	—	—	1
Ordnance field park	—	—	1	—

STATEMENT SHOWING TOTAL MEDICAL PERSONNEL WITH THE FORCE—*continued.*

Detail.	R.A.M.C. Officers.	I.M.S. Officers.	Assistant Surgeons.	Hospital Assistants.
Remount depôt	—	—	—	1
Imperial service troops	—	—	2	4
1 British field hospital	4	—	8	—
15 native field hospitals	—	60	—	120
1 British general hospital	4	—	4	--
3 native general hospitals	—	30	3	60
2 field medical store depôts	—	—	2	—
1 base ,, ,, ,,	—	1	2	—
Hospital ship "Maine"	5	—	—	—
Hospital ship "Carthage"	--.	4	1	6
Hospital ship (Maharajah Gwalior's) "Gwalior."	1	3	--	6
Total	14	121	25	225

APPENDIX J.

MEDICAL HISTORY OF THE CAMPAIGN, COMPILED UNDER THE ORDERS OF COLONEL G. MαB. DAVIS, C.B., D.S.O., P.M.O. WITH THE C. E. FORCE.

PRINCIPAL DISEASES, WITH THEIR CAUSES, SEPARATELY FOR BRITISH AND NATIVE TROOPS AND FOLLOWERS.

That North China is a healthy country for troops to serve in, is the conclusion arrived at as the outcome of the past twelve months' experience.

Notwithstanding climatic variability, and the difference between the rigorous cold of the winter and the heat of the summer, and further, although the force was largely composed of natives of India, with regard to most of whom exposure to rigorous cold was an experience being tried for the first time, the health of both British and native troops, and of the followers belonging to the force, was good throughout; better indeed than was hoped for. This good result was no doubt largely contributed to by the care bestowed in providing for the comfort of the men, and the attention paid to sanitation. Never before perhaps has the feeding, clothing, and housing of troops suitably been so carefully thought out. At the same time it has to be remembered that at the very onset of the winter last year the men were weeded out, and all who were considered unfit to withstand the rigorous cold of the winter in China were sent back to India.

Speaking of the force generally, the diseases which prevailed most were chest affections and venereal. There was a good deal of dysentery in the earlier phases of the campaign; but for an Indian force there was a remarkable absence of any widespread prevalence of malarial fevers. The winter was very trying to men who had a tendency to lung disease, and a considerable number of cases of tubercle of the lung showed themselves in consequence, particularly among the followers. Contrary to the usual experience on field service, there was comparatively little enteric fever, although the German troops suffered considerably from this disease both at Tien-tsin and Peking.

Of infectious disease—the most troublesome was mumps which occurred amongst the native troops and followers only, and which prevailed at Shanghai, Tien-tsin, and Peking, as well as at many of the smaller posts; measles was prevalent at Shanghai; and there were five cases of small-pox (Peking 3, Tien-tsin 2).

Small-pox is very rife in North China among the native population, and it is of interest to observe that the Chinese practise vaccination and freely avail themselves of its protection. On the occurrence of cases among the troops, a calf vaccine depôt was started at No. 3 Native General Hospital at Peking, to supply lymph for the vaccination of unprotected men; and here also a number of Chinese children were vaccinated.

British Troops.

Small-pox.—Three cases occurred in Peking; a fourth case was admitted at Tien-tsin. One of the cases had never been successfully vaccinated. All made good recoveries.

Enteric fever.—There were 26 admissions with 10 deaths. One of the fatal cases was a man who belonged to the Royal Marine Light Infantry. Of the 25 remaining cases, 15 with 7 deaths occurred at Peking, 9 with 2 deaths at Wei-hai-wei, and 1 case at Shanghai.

At Peking the majority of the cases occurred in the first few weeks of the occupation, but the immediate source of the disease could not be traced.

At Wei-hai-wei the disease appeared among the troops in September. It had been prevalent at the naval end of the station, and there were enteric cases in the naval hospital for some time before it appeared among the troops. Diarrhœa and dysentery were also prevalent at this time.

Dysentery.—The disease was most prevalent during the early part of the campaign, and was chiefly of a mild type. Some of the cases resembled inflammatory diarrhœa more than tropical dysentery. The two cases that proved fatal at Wei-hai-wei were men who had been transferred from the front. With the arrival of the cold weather the disease practically ceased.

Malarial fevers.—The cases returned under the headings of ague and remittent fever occurred mostly in men who had contracted the disease in India or Hongkong.

Two or three cases of Chinese remittent fever were admitted at Wei-hai-wei. It appears to be a most persistent fever, which continues week after week, reducing and emaciating the patient to an extreme degree. Quinine by the mouth appears to have small effect, but subcutaneous injections of quinine were found to control the disease.

Venereal diseases.—Latterly, admissions for venereal diseases have been increasing in proportion, probably because at first opportunities of contracting these complaints were fewer than is the case now. With regard to the type of the disease there is nothing that calls for special note.

Diseases of the respiratory system.—Bronchitis was fairly common, and there were a few cases of pneumonia and pleurisy, all of whom recovered.

Abscess of the liver.—Two cases of abscess of the liver were admitted at Wei-hai-wei. In neither was there dysenteric history. One was a case of multiple abscess; this case died.

The other diseases which occurred call for no special comment.

Native Troops.

Small-pox.—There was one case contracted locally. The necessary precautions were taken and the disease did not spread.

Mumps.—This was very prevalent, particularly at Tien-tsin and Shanghai. It was very difficult to check its spread, and as a matter of fact it gradually wore itself out.

Measles.—A small epidemic of measles occurred at Shanghai, chiefly affecting the 1-4th Gurkhas.

Dysentery.—This disease was fairly common among the native troops, but was usually mild in character. It was variously attributed to impure drinking water, exposure to chills and damp, errors of diet making up old standing dysenteric lesions. As among the British troops it was most common in the early months of service in China. It gradually and steadily subsided as the winter advanced.

Malarial fevers.—Although much of the country in North China is marshy in character, and mosquitoes are common from June to September, few of the cases of fever admitted to hospital can be attributed to a Chinese origin. Most of the cases admitted were probably recrudescence of disease contracted in India, brought out by exposure to the sun, or chill, or other cause. In June this year, ague was reported to be prevalent and of a severe type at Sin-ho. The severity of type was synchronous, with a fairly sudden onset of moist heat, produced by a strong sun on the surrounding country, which was at the time flooded by heavy rainfall and high tides.

Several specimens of anophiles cinensis were obtained last summer in one of the camps at Shanghai.

Venereal diseases.—These diseases have been much more prevalent among the native troops on service in China than is the case when the regiments are serving in cantonments in India. Its prevalence began to increase towards the end of the winter. The type of disease is reported to be generally mild.

Diseases of the respiratory system.—Respiratory affections were very prevalent all through the winter, due to a large extent to chills and exposure to cold. Catarrhs appeared often to take on an epidemic character, and without a doubt, their spread was to some extent assisted by the vitiated atmosphere of the living rooms brought about by the men often closing up all ventilating openings during the very cold weather. Bronchitis was very common and in many cases very persistent in character. There was a large number of cases of pneumonia, many of which were of a very severe type, and often with a fatal termination. None of these cases were associated with preventable causes, as ventilation usually, and warming always, were carefully looked after, and clothing and bedding had been issued to the troops on an unusually liberal scale.

Sunstroke.—There were 38 cases of sunstroke and one case of heatstroke. One of the cases of sunstroke had a fatal termination. Nearly all the cases occurred among the troops engaged in the advance on Peking.

Frostbite.—The cases of frostbite were all traced to want of common sense, or want of knowledge on the part of the patients, and never to insufficiency of clothing.

Followers.

The incidence of disease among the followers was much the same as that for the native troops.

WATER SUPPLY: ITS SOURCE, QUALITY, AND QUANTITY.

For the purpose of discussing the question of water supply, it will be convenient to divide the time reviewed into two periods —(1) while active operations were going on, and (2) while the troops were in winter quarters.

I.—During the period of active operations.

Advance on Peking.

During the advance for the relief of the Legations at Peking, the water for all purposes was obtained either from the River Pei-ho or from village wells.

The river at the time was a very undesirable source, as it contained many human corpses, and the water was very muddy. The water from the wells was less muddy, but the surroundings of the wells were filthy in the extreme. Purification of the drinking water was carried out by treating it with alum and permanganate of potash, and by boiling as much of it as possible. A number of small one-candle Berkefeld filters were also taken, but it was found that, with very muddy water, they soon choked, and as a matter of fact they were not much used, except for filtering drinking water for the sick. The measures adopted were evidently effectual, as no untoward results occurred, and the quantity of the supply was certainly abundant.

Pao-ting fu Expedition.

The water was obtained from wells in the neighbourhood of the various camping grounds.

These wells were the ordinary Chinese wells, bricked-faced, with a very contracted mouth, which only just permits of a bucket being lowered. They were usually situated on small patches of cultivated land close to the villages. There never was any attempt at well covering, and as the mouth of the well was nearly always flush with the ground, there was nothing to prevent filth washing or dropping in. At Paoting-fu, where the troops encamped for several days, a guard was placed over the wells used for the supply of drinking water. There never was any scarcity of supply, and there was a standing order which enjoined that only boiled water or tea was to be used for drinking purposes, whether in camp or on the march.

II.—While the troops were in winter quarters.

The water supply, generally, at all stations occupied by the troops in North China has been satisfactory and abundant.

Except that Chinese in this part of the country build their wells with contracted mouths, they take little care to prevent the pollution of the supply.

The wells in use were specially cared for; their surroundings were cleaned, and the wells, in some instances, enclosed and covered in. The necessity for boiling the drinking water was impressed on all ranks, and commanding officers were ordered to take steps to ensure that all water-bottles were filled with tea or boiled water before starting on a march. With a view to encourage the drinking of boiled water only, a daily issue of ¼ oz. of tea and ½ oz. of sugar was sanctioned from the outset of the campaign for all fighting men and followers (British and Native) in addition to the field scale of rations. Berkefeld filters were in general use, and were specially issued to all outpost stations.

Peking.

The water supply was entirely from wells.

The water was hard, and in a few instances somewhat brackish in taste; but, speaking generally, the quality was very satisfactory, and the quantity abundant.

Tien-tsin.

The water is obtained from the River Pei-ho. As this passes through alluvial soil and a flat country, it is full of sediment, and as it passes through the Native city of Tien-tsin before reaching the off-take of the waterworks it is by no means pure. Careful arrangements for filtration are therefore necessary.

2. *Settling Tanks.*—The water is pumped by the waterworks company to settling tanks, where it remains quiescent from 14 to 18 hours. In this time much of the suspended matter subsides.

3. *Filtration.*—It is then passed through filtering beds of sand 3 feet 6 inches deep. The depth of water over the sand varies with the condition of the filter, being never less than 1 foot 6 inches, nor more that 2 feet 9 inches. The speed of filtration never exceeds 3 inches an hour, and is generally 2 inches an hour. This is very effective, as the effluent is clean and good.

The filter beds are 32 feet by 40 feet, and are arranged in pairs.

The top layer of sand is periodically removed and washed.

4. *Service Reservoir.*—The water is then pumped up to a service tank, the bottom of which is above ground. The tank itself is 12 feet high, so the average head is about 70 feet. It then passes by gravitation through cast-iron mains to various parts of the British concession.

5. *Special Arrangements made for Troops.—Boiled Water.*— So far the work is done by the municipality for the benefit of all residents in the British concessions. The works are under European management, and embody in their construction the latest scientific ideas on waterworks engineering. For the troops, however, some further arrangements were made as an additional precaution against pollution. At a point on the Taku road a large tank, holding about 40,000 gallons, was erected, connected by steam pipes with a factory adjacent. The temperature of the water was raised by a steam jet to boiling point, and was subsequently drawn off from taps and hose by the British troops, Italians and Americans also being allowed to obtain their supplies there. The arrangements for the boiling and for distribution were under the supervision of men of the Australian Naval Contingent.

6. *Cold Water for Troops.*—A hydrant was erected at the end of the Pao-shun road for troops to draw cold water. This had, of course, been filtered, but not boiled previous to issue. To keep the hydrant from freezing, a small house warmed by a stove was built round it.

7. *Village Settlement.*—To supply the village settlement, a pipe line was laid about 4,000 feet long, with service tanks to hold about 20,000 gallons. Arrangements for boiling the water were made also. The object of this pipe line was two-fold—(1) to enable the troops to get water during the winter without having to go 1½ miles for it ; (2) to ensure a pure supply being readily obtained after the thaw came. The villages were surrounded by ponds of very questionable quality, and it was most desirable to remove all possible temptation to the drawing of water from these undesirable sources by giving a good supply of pure water in a central place. This was the more necessary as the village settlement was, in other respects, most suitable for Indian troops.

8. *Minor Distribution.*—The minor distribution of water from the various hydrants, &c., was done in barrels, buckets, and " mussaks " under regimental arrangements.

Shan-hai-kuan.

The drinking water was obtained entirely from wells. Stone huts were built over the wells, and sentries were posted over them. The supply was ample and of good quality. Washing water was drawn from ponds and rivulets, and was sufficient.

Wei-hai-Wei.

Troops were quartered on both the island and the mainland.

On the island (Liu-kun-tao), the only drinking water used was condensed water, the condenser being in the naval dockyard and belonging to the naval authorities. The quantity allowed per head was 1½ to 2 gallons a day for both cooking and drinking purposes.

There were some old Chinese wells, and recently a few new wells had been dug, but neither the new nor the old wells were taken into use for the troops. Most of the wells are close to the seashore, and the water is, in consequence, very hard and contains abundant chlorides. In some the water would probably be drinkable if the well was protected from surface fouling.

There are also some large reservoirs for water, made by damming up the nullahs, but during the past twelve months the supply of water in both reservoirs and wells has been very scarce. This scarcity was stated to be unusual.

The condenser tanks were cleaned out and flushed with permanganate of potash solution at regular intervals.

The water-supply on the mainland (Ma-to) was obtained from wells, both old and new. The water from one or two of the wells near the sea was a little brackish in taste, but, on the whole, the supply was stated to be of good quality and abundant in quantity. Berkefeld filters were in use.

Shanghai.

Water was supplied by the Shanghai Waterworks Company, and with the exception of Jessfield it was distributed to the various camps through pipes.

The pipes ended about a mile from Jessfield, and from there to the camp the water was conveyed by carts, and at the camp stored in iron tanks.

The quantity was abundant, and the quality very good.

Outpost Stations.

At the posts on the lines of communication, water was obtained from surface wells. These were very numerous in all the villages in this part of China; they were in most cases protected by brick steining and at the ground line the mouth of the well was raised, so as to prevent entrance, of surface water. The water in the hottest weather was cold and good.

FEEDING OF THE TROOPS.

The rations issued to the troops were uniformly of good quality. Supplies were abundant. Extra issues were made to both troops and followers on an exceptionally liberal scale in view of the severity of the cold during the winter months in North China. These were continued to the 14th April after which date the ordinary field service scales for both British and Native troops was reverted to.

For the greater part of the winter a varied and abundant supply of vegetables was available.

To this supply and the extra issues of fresh meat, may be largely attributed the comparative freedom from scorbutic complaints among the troops and followers. While the liberal scale of rations largely contributed to the excellent health of the force during the trying winter.

Rum was issued at various times during the winter to troops and followers after extra or severe work, long marches, or on account of unusual exposure on wet or very cold days.

A half dram of rum was issued to the troops at Shan-hai-kuan twice a week during the winter months owing to the severity of the cold there.

The medical comforts sent out to China comprised concentrated soups, essence of mutton, extract of beef, condensed milk, cornflour, barley, oatmeal, brandy, whisky, port wine and champagne. These were of good quality, and were supplied in most liberal quantities, a 500 per cent. reserve being maintained. After five-monthly shipments had been received, further shipments were stopped, because of the abundance of the supplies in hand.

Maggi's consomme, Nao soup and Nao cup were also tried, and were very favourably reported on.

A good and abundant supply of fowls, eggs, and various fruits was locally procurable.

On account of the great difficulty of obtaining fresh cow's milk in China, unsweetened condensed milk or evaporated cream was largely used, and it was found that the brands supplied made a very palatable and excellent substitute for fresh milk.

Medical Establishments.

The provision of hospital accommodation, and medical and surgical supplies was on an exceedingly ample and liberal scale.

Of the three Native General Hospitals sent out, No. 1 formed the base hospital for native troops at Wei-hai-wei. No. 2 was kept in reserve at Hongkong for some time, but it remained unopened, and was finally sent back to India. No. 3 was brought up to the front, one half being stationed at Tien-tsin, and the other half at Peking, to take the overflow from the field hospitals.

The general hospital for British troops was established at Wei-hai-wei.

The field hospitals had to be much separated up, as the sections had to be widely distributed in making suitable medical arrangements for troops at Peking, Tien-tsin and Shan-hai-kuan, and, for the long chain of outposts between Peking and Tien-tsin and between Tien-tsin and Shan-hai-kuan.

In the field and on the march the mobility of our field hospitals compared very favourably with that of the field hospitals of the allied forces.

The hospitals, both general and field, were housed for the severe winter months.

At Peking 250 beds of No. 3 Native general hospital, two sections of a British field hospital, and No. 43 Native field hospital were all housed in the Chih-yei-fu, a magnificent range of buildings, the spacious rooms of which were readily convertible into excellent hospital wards. Three miles distant from the Chih-yei-fu another section of a Native field hospital was housed in buildings within the Temple of Heaven enclosure; and in another direction, also about three miles distant from the Chih-yei-fu, two sections more of a Native field hospital were located in buildings in the Legation quarter.

At Tien-tsin the remaining 250 beds of No. 3 Native general hospital, and the field hospitals, British and Native, were accommodated in roomy godowns, the Temperance Hall, and in buildings belonging to the London and American missions.

At Shan-hai-kuan and at the various outposts, Chinese houses were utilised in the majority of instances.

At Wei-hai-wei the British general hospital was located for the winter in a number of converted Chinese buildings. No. 1 Native general hospital was accommodated in the hotel buildings at Ma-to on the mainland; but in the middle of April it was moved from the hotel to the flagstaff camp.

At Shanghai the hospitals were for the most part hutted, the huts being provided with wooden floors.

Beds and a certain amount of extra furniture were provided for all hospitals. The wards were well warmed. The accommodation generally was comfortable, and well suited to the climatic conditions under which the troops were serving.

When the troops were advancing to the relief of the Legations at Peking, the heavy equipment of the sections of the field hospitals accompanying the force was sent up the river in junks. It was found that the junks carrying the hospital equipment could not keep up with the troops, and as this was causing considerable inconvenience additional mule transport was asked for and obtained. A certain number of mules were also placed at the disposal of the senior medical officer to carry exhausted men.

The sun was very hot, and as the men had frequently to pass through very tall crops, with not a breath of air stirring, cases of sunstroke were not uncommon during some of the marches to Peking, and there were also many cases of heat exhaustion. On account of the number of men that fell out, it was decided to try marching in the afternoons, and this course was attended by good results.

After the occupation of Peking, sick convoys proceeding to the base were sent in junks from Tung-chou to Tien-tsin, *en route* to the hospital ships.

The railway was re-opened for traffic towards the middle of December 1900, and from that time it was used in the transport of the sick, a railway carriage being fitted for the purpose.

The sick transport arrangements worked smoothly and well throughout.

The hospital ships have done much good and satisfactory work. This is the first time that hospital ships have been specially provided in connexion with an expeditionary force from India.

APPENDIX K.

NOTES ON THE ACCOMMODATION OF THE TROOPS OF THE CHINA FIELD FORCE DURING THE WINTER OF 1900–1901, BY LIEUTENANT-COLONEL G. K. SCOTT-MONCRIEFF, C.R.E. LINES OF COMMUNICATION.

Accommodation how provided.—Accommodation at all stations and posts was provided, as far as possible, by adapting existing buildings, which sometimes required considerable alterations in order to provide better warming and ventilating arrangements. The numbers to be provided for were approximately 18,000 troops, 14,000 followers, and 10,000 horses and transport animals.

Floors.—At Peking, Tien-tsin, and Shan-hai-kwan it was found that in the dry climate of Northern China, after the summer rains had ceased, the original stone floors of the Chinese houses and godowns were suitable. At Shanghai, where the climate is much damper, it was necessary to provide boarded floors for living rooms.

Alterations required to Chinese buildings.—The principal alterations were repairs to "Kangs" (a kang is the Chinese bed consisting of a raised brick platform with internal flues, having a fire-place below or outside which serves for cooking and at the same time heats the flues), repairs to roofs, ceilings, glass and paper for windows, the addition of a very large number of fire-places, and stoves with flues. The number of stoves found necessary to heat the buildings for troops in the province of Chi-li was 1,950, the length of flue piping erected amounted to about $7\frac{1}{4}$ miles.

New buildings.—New buildings were constructed mainly for transport animals, for some of the artillery and cavalry horses, and in nearly all cases for subsidiary buildings, such as cook-houses, latrines, and ablution room, but the expense on these was kept as low as possible by utilising existing walls and ruins.

Types adopted for new buildings.—The usual type of building constructed has brick walls 1 to $1\frac{1}{2}$ bricks thick, ordinary rough Chinese doors and windows, lean-to roofs, covered by 2 inches of lime and mud mixed, on 2 inches of mud resting in turn on 4 inches of fascines or mats made of kao-liang (coarse millet) and supported by wooden rafters spaced according to the size of the timber procurable. In some cases bamboo matting was used under the fascines. Walls of timber framing filled in with kao-liang stalks, held upright by battens of wood on each side, the ends of the battens being nailed to the uprights of the framing, and the whole plastered over with mud or mud and lime, are very quickly constructed by the Chinese workman and were found quite sufficiently durable for temporary subsidiary buildings or stables. The Chinese carpenter is good, the mason, on the other hand, decidedly bad, and it is necessary to superintend his work constantly, or he invariably adopts his usual methods of building walls with two skins, filled in with rubbish.

Hired buildings, and cost compared with new buildings.—Buildings have been hired at Tien-tsin, Wei-hai-wei, and Shanghai, where it was impossible to provide other accommodation except by erecting new buildings. The saving in cost due to hiring temporary accommodation instead of building shows that for any period shorter than 15 months it is more economical to hire than to build huts of the cheapest sort, such as would be used in England for wagons, even allowing for the fact that such huts cost in China about half what they would in England.

General remarks on huts.—Tents with mat shelters have been used at Shanghai. Three-inch mats formed of millet straw, or mattresses filled with the same material, formed good beds and kept the men off the stone floors. The minimum wall space allowed per man was about 4 feet and per follower 3 feet, per horse 5 to 6 feet, per mule or bullock 3 feet. At Tien-tsin blocks of huts with rooms 10 feet by 10 feet for five followers each were built, as this facilitated heating arrangements. The stables at Shan-hai-kwan were sunk $3\frac{1}{2}$ feet below ground level.

An allowance of 44 dollars per mensem was sanctioned for all officers quartered at Shanghai and Hongkong on account of the extra cost involved by living in those places. A free issue of fuel and light was also sanctioned for officers in North China, and free quarters where such had been provided, or lodging allowance in the case where this had not been done, and quarters had had to be hired.

APPENDIX L.

VETERINARY NOTES ON FITTINGS OF TRANSPORTS AND MANAGEMENT OF HORSES ON BOARD SHIP, BY VETERINARY-LIEUTENANT H. J. AXE, A.V.D.

Method of Embarkation.—The horses were not slung on board, but walked on the decks by ramps. The sides of the ramps should be well covered, and not open. They were inclined to be too steep, and those leading from the upper to the lower decks were badly devised. They made a sharp ascent over the combings of the hatch, and then a sharp descent below on to the deck. There was only one stage, and it terminated so close to the fittings on the opposite side of the lower deck that there was hardly enough room for the horses to get out and turn round. They should be made with a more gradual descent, or in two stages, and should be constructed so that they can be put up and taken down during the voyage, for the removal of sick horses on to the upper deck.

The screen boards were nailed directly to the stanchions, to which the rear bar was attached. The result was that, meeting with a gale after the third or fourth day, all the horses on the upper deck had the whole of skin and hair removed from the croup and tail, the wounds being six and eight inches long and three inches wide. These screen boards were badly devised. They should have sloped back to the bulwarks, as horses, when swaying backwards and forwards in rough weather must catch their croups and tails against screen boards which are nailed direct to the stanchions.

The present 6-ft. 9-in. stalls are too short in rough weather, and require to be at least 8 feet; otherwise the horses rub their tails, croups, and breasts.

A number of horses got rubbed on the sides from the canvas pads. If necessary at all, they should be covered with softer material, such as sheepskin.

The canvas head pads are a great improvement on the old leather ones, but they are constantly slipping round, and are never in the proper position, consequently many horses get their heads injured. They should be made so as to keep a more or less fixed position.

To prevent horses biting each other, a blinker board, 18 inches by 9 inches, should be attached to the stanchions against the horses' heads in front. This is a very important matter, as many horses are rendered unfit to wear a collar for some time afterwards, owing to the nature of the injuries.

Front bars should be made so that they can be taken out above and below, either way, and can be lowered 6 inches to suit any sized horse or pony.

The rear bars were immoveable and made of long sections, and nailed on to stanchions, the width of five or six stalls. To show that this is incorrect, horses sometimes get their hind legs over, and before they can be extricated the rear board has to be sawn through. They should be made moveable above and below, the same as the front board, and in smaller sections.

The platforms were much better than the old ones. The inch spaces between each bar are sanitary, allowing urine to escape, but they get blocked up at the back owing to horses treading in their manure. Long iron pickers are necessary to clean out these grooves.

The arrangement of the battens was better, particularly the first and second. The small longitudinal battens on the end of the surface of the platform and between it and the deck are also an improvement, allowing of the urine getting away. Transverse battens should be spaced.

The wooden hoes used for cleaning out the stalls are absolutely useless. They were too fragile, and were constantly breaking. Something strong should be substituted for them.

Loose boxes for sick horses are absolutely necessary, and two or three should be allowed on each side, upper and lower decks, fore and aft.

Enough room on board ship should be provided to allow of giving all the horses daily exercise during calm weather.

Some method of driving air with fans by machinery should be introduced on horse transports for ventilating lower decks, the present system not being quite satisfactory.

A better system of drainage should be adapted on horse transports. In some parts of the lower decks urine collected in the two-foot way behind the horses, and had to be baled out through the port holes.

Horses do not take to linseed cake at first. If it is broken up and scalded with boiling water and made up into porridge, and and then mixed with the feeds, they will generally eat it.

Rock salt and carrots should be provided on all transports, for sick horses.

Great care should be taken on board ship of horses' feet. Owing to want of exercise, they are liable to congestion of the feet and sub-acute laminitis. Frogs are occasionally found fly-blown and under-run with maggots. The Commissariat issue of 6 lbs. of hoof ointment, and five gallons of Stockholm tar for the feet, is extremely useful, as the feet can be thus dressed daily.

Carbolic disinfecting powder is most useful.

A liberal supply of liquid carbolic acid is also most useful for flushing the platforms, and for cleaning the under surface and deck, also the two footways behind the horses and scuppers.

Permanganate of potash should be shipped in case the others run out, owing to its small bulk. Chloride of lime might be used on upper decks.

The simple web head collar answers admirably, but they should be made stronger at the joints and sufficiently large.

The veterinary dispensary consisted of two small cupboards, which were useless, and were never used. Through the kindness of the Officer Commanding I obtained a barricaded fodder store about 12 feet square, in which all the voyage medicine boxes, disinfectants, &c. were placed. This made an excellent surgery, and should be noted for future guidance. The cupboards should be put inside here in future.

It is not certain what the regulation allowance of coir matting is on board ship. Besides a number of small pieces, which could be adapted to separate standings, the rolls should not be more than 20 feet long. When longer than this, after getting wet they become very heavy and troublesome to carry about.

The brooms provided were useless, not being strong enough.

At Taku the horses were transhipped into two steam lighters, they walking on to the smaller boats on ramps. There were no casualties. Long ropes were tied along the centre of the boats, and the horses simply attached to them. There were some 170 in one boat, and over 90 in the other. Cinders were put down to prevent the horses slipping. The whole of the transhipment as regards the horses was done in two hours.

The ramps at the landing-place at Sin-ho were much too steep, and the horses were with difficulty got off the lighters, and a considerable amount of time was in consequence wasted.

APPENDIX M.

Report on the Working of the Army Veterinary Department with the China Expeditionary Force, 1900–1901, by Veterinary-Captain E. H. Hazelton, I.V.O.

In disembarking at Taku the 12th Battery Royal Field Artillery were slung from the transports into river steamers, which took them to Sin-ho on the Pei-ho river. From Sin-ho they were trained to Tien-tsin. There were no platforms of any kind available at Sin-ho, and the horses had to be taken up inclined "ramps" of boards into the high railway trucks, which were large open wagons accommodating 17 to 21 horses each. There were few doors to these wagons, so boards were nailed over the opening as the best possible substitute, and luckily the horses after their voyage were very quiet, and only a few accidents occurred.

Transport animals came with the units, and on the 4th August 1900 the force started on its march to Peking.

At Tien-tsin a quantity of medicines were purchased and made into a mule load, with two boxes for the use of transport and officers' horses, as few veterinary chests for use of the transport had arrived from the base camp. A site for a base veterinary hospital was arranged as a temporary measure at Tien-tsin until the arrival of a section of a field veterinary hospital from India.

On the march to Peking the weather was very hot, and the horses after a few days did not get much grain ration, as the junks on the Pei-ho, which were carrying most of our supplies, were not always handy; the whole country was under high crops of millet and Indian corn in the ear, and there was no lack of green forage. The cavalry horses worked night and day, the roads were sandy and heavy and the artillery horses pulled themselves to pieces; none of the horses or transport animals were hard and fit at starting, having just come off a sea voyage, and the consequences were that at the end of the advance there was an enormous number of sore backs, and all the animals were in low condition.

On the march from Ho-hsi-wu to Ma-tou, the horses of the force were very exhausted, and seven artillery and three cavalry horses dropped dead from exhaustion and the effects of the great heat.

On the 14th August 1900, the day of the capture of Peking, the horses were under saddle and in harness from 2 a.m. until late at night, and three horses died in the streets of Peking from exhaustion, and the majority of the horses of the force could not have gone on without a rest.

At the end of August a bad outbreak of rinderpest occurred among the slaughter cattle at the Temple of Heaven, and in September cases of glanders appeared among the captured Chinese ponies and mules.

With the exception of small outbreaks of skin affections and occasional cases of glanders at Peking and Tien-tsin, all in transport animals, the health of animals was good. The climate being very dry, but few cases of affections of the respiratory tract occurred. The horses and transport animals were provided with extra warm clothing, which was found very useful. Good stabling for the winter was provided for all the horses and transport animals, and they stood the cold, which was very great at times, well.

The base veterinary store depôt arrived at Hongkong on 4th October 1900, and was there disembarked; as the Port of Taku was shortly to become ice bound, instructions were issued to send half the medicines and necessaries to the officer in charge of the section of the Field Military Hospital, Tien-tsin, in order that they should be available if required for the portion of the force north of Taku; this was carried out without delay, and the stores arrived before the ice closed the river. It was not found necessary to draw to any great extent on this depôt.

Section "B," No. 5 Veterinary Hospital, arrived at Tien-tsin in charge of Veterinary-Lieutenant Pallin on 30th August 1900 and was opened there at once.

A field veterinary hospital should be always equipped with a field forge, which has not hitherto been deemed necessary. It would be then possible to arrange for the shoeing of chargers of staff and infantry officers without applying to batteries or regiments for such services, for it is often found that they have enough to do to carry out their own shoeing without being called upon for a large increase in their work; further, in the case of lamenesses it is almost an indispenable adjunct to a veterinary hospital.

Units were directed to make their own arrangements regarding shoeing, and did so; but as time went on and their stocks of shoes were exhausted, iron was purchased locally for their requirements. Shoes with cognails for ice-bound roads are unnecessary, as the climate is dry, and there is always a lot of dust. The horses of the 12th Battery were "roughed" for about a month.

Charcoal and coal of good quality are available in any quantity in North China.

The Chinese pony is a sturdy beast, ranging from 12 hands to 13-3, seldom higher, with a coarse head, thick jowl, ewe neck, ragged hips, good barrel, short legs with good bone, colour generally grey or white, of a quiet disposition with Chinamen, but rather nasty tempered with those he is not used to, difficult to handle and shoe, and quiet to ride when mounted. Geldings were mostly met with in the ponies found in and around Peking, very few stallions and mares; these ponies are used largely by the Chinese in their Pekin carts, and also by the farmers in their heavy carts for the carriage of grain, &c.; it is no uncommon sight to see a pony, a mule and a donkey harnessed tandem-wise to a loaded cart, and I have seen a pony, a donkey, and a bullock drawing a plough.* The pony is also used for pack work, and carries heavy loads on the wooden Chinese pack saddle; they are very strong, enduring ponies, and carry heavy weights long distances without distress; they are very sure-footed. The mares are largely used to breed mules. These ponies, if carefully selected, would be very useful for Mounted Infantry purposes.

The Chinese mule is certainly one of the best types of mule, the larger riding mules and those used by the wealthier Chinese for their Pekin carts being beautiful animals; they run up to 15 hands and over, and are very well proportioned and full of power and quality.

The smaller mules compare very favourably with any breed in India, and the Chinese pony mare must be a wonderfully good mare to breed mules from, for the Chinaman does not carefully select his donkey sires for getting mules. The Chinese are very careful to feed and look after their mules and ponies well; a big mule in hard work will get 10 or 12 lbs. of grain daily, and after their work they are allowed to roll in the sand and dust, and are walked slowly about until dry.

They are led by a chain looped around the lower jaw, and are frequently driven with a rope twitch applied under the upper lip and around the upper jaw.

The donkeys are not very remarkable for size, but are sturdy, small animals, and are used largely for draught, pack and riding purposes.

The cattle I have seen are thick-set animals on short legs, with slightly drooping quarters and a rather rising wither, with medium horns; red and black are the prevailing colors; they rather remind me of a poor class of Highland cattle.

The sheep are light silky fleeced, good-sized animals, with large fatty tails, and are of very good quality.

Much of the compressed grass sent from India was spoiled by the voyage to China, but it was dirty when shipped, each bundle containing a quantity of earth, which has to be dusted out before issue.

A quantity of the grain was also spoiled by damp during the voyage; it would keep better if it were uncrushed.

The oats supplied to the force were very fair, but some complaints were made that they were dirty and had a musty smell.

The oat hay, Australian, issued to the horses is good, but about 50 per cent. of the bales contain a large proportion of wheat in the ear, but no ill-effects have been noticed from its consumption.

The grains available in China are maize, the millets (locally " kao-liang "), black and green beans. Both maize and millet are largely used by the force, the former crushed when possible.

Good bran is also obtainable in large quantities. The millet stalks are used as a substitute for hay, and it was also chaffed and fed to the horses and transport animals. Hay of indifferent quality has been collected in large quantities at Peking and Tien-tsin. The grass was cut late, and was therefore very dry and wanting in flower and aroma.

Cases of glanders occurred among the Chinese transport animals, but by careful precautions being taken, the disease did not spread to the animals from India; the large majority of cases have been found in old, worn-out animals.

The disease presents the same appearances as in Europe and India, and sometimes runs a very rapid course, some cases being on the point of death from glanders within 48 hours of their having come under observation, but suspicious cases were generally destroyed before all the diagnostic symptoms developed.

Scabies mange appeared among transport animals at Wei-hai-Wei, Tien-tsin and Peking, during the winter. The animals all had long coats and were clothed, so that cases were difficult to find in the very early stages of the disorder. When they were clipped, it was comparatively easy to deal with them. The number of cases was greatest at Tien-tsin, principally among Chinese animals. The severe cases in old animals were destroyed. The outbreak at Peking was a mild one and soon yielded to treatment.

Rinderpest has occurred in Peking, Tien-tsin, Wai-hai-wei (possibly), and on the Lines of Communication, notably at Sin-ho. At this latter place it was introduced by cattle obtained from the neighbourhood of Chih-fu or Shanghai.

At Peking it was introduced by cattle which had marched up from Tien-tsin, and Tien-tsin was infected by cattle brought for the troops of all nations from the surrounding country and the ports south of Taku. From enquiries it appears to be common in North China.

An outbreak of sheep-pox occurred in a flock of 60 sheep at Peking. The sheep belonging to the force at Peking have not suffered from contagious disease; they were segregated in the Temple of Heaven during the outbreak of rinderpest among the cattle, and did not become affected; it was thought to be very inadvisable to keep a large flock, so arrangements were made to purchase them for slaughter as required.

APPENDIX N.

Report on Signalling, China Expeditionary Force, 1900–01, by Captain G. C. Rigby, Superintendent Army Signalling, C.F.F.

Eight special signalling units (six men per unit) were detailed to accompany the force.

On the 3rd and 4th Brigades being despatched from India, four additional units were sent.

Six units embarked on S.S. "Zebenghla" with the headquarters' staff. In Hongkong harbour a party was kept on duty to communicate with the flagship and the shore. On the voyage from Hongkong to Wei-hai-wei the "Zebenghla" was stopped during the night by a British cruiser. Signalling communication was opened by lamp and messages received and sent.

At Wei-hai-wei the signallers proved especially useful in keeping up communication with the shore and between transports.

At Tien-tsin a signal station was established on the top of the Gordon Hall tower, in communication with the junks on the river, near Sin-ho, the native city, and the picquets around the concession. These stations were worked by the Royal Welsh Fusilier signallers, and the marines and naval signalmen.

Little use could be made of signalling during the advance to Peking, owing to the nature of the country which was throughout level and covered with high crops.

On arrival at Peking on August 14th, the first communication with the Legations was received from a marine signaller of the Legation Guard, who sent a message directing the troops to the Water-gate.

After entering the Legations, endeavours were made to open communication from the Tartar city wall with the troops at the Temple of Heaven, but failed owing to intervening trees. Early the following morning communication was obtained through the Ch'ien mên gate tower. From this point communication was successively opened with the South gate Chinese city, the Naval Brigade at the East gate, Chinese city, the detachment at Coal Hill, and the south-west corner of the Tartar city.

The headquarters' station was established on the roof of the chief secretary's house in the British Legation.

The Ch'ien mên gate tower formed the most important intermediate station for all points until the 23rd August, when by cutting away a portion of the parapet on the Tartar city wall and building a platform on the roof of a bell tower at the Temple of Heaven, direct communication was obtained to the headquarters' station.

From the Bell Tower communication was maintained also with the south and south-east gates, Chinese city.

Communication from the south gate was successfully opened with Ma-chia-pu, and later on, with Lu-kou-ch'iao, Feng-tai, and the Summer Palace, as soon as these posts were occupied.

On the 16th September, two British units accompanied the expedition to Pa-ta-ch'ü. After the capture of the temples, communication was successfully opened with the South gate, Chinese city, and maintained daily whilst the force remained out.

In October and November telegraphic communication gradually superseded the visual signalling.

On 12th October two British units accompanied the expedition to Pao-ting fu. The nature of the country again prevented any use being made of signallers on the march. On arrival at Pao-ting fu, communication was opened between the British headquarters in the town and the camps of the Peking and Tien-tsin columns and the escort to the junks on the river.

By the commencement of the winter all parts of the force in and near Peking were connected by telegraph or telephone lines. The British signallers were put through courses of telegraphy. They quickly picked up telegraph work, and were for the most part distributed to different telegraph stations in and around Peking and the railway.

APPENDIX O.

The Police Administration of the British Quarter of the Chinese City, Peking, by Captain G. de S. Barrow, British Police Commissioner.

Introductory.—The administration of Peking was one of the first questions to occupy the attention of the allied commanders after the relief of the Legations.

The Tartar and Chinese cities were divided, for purposes of control and order, into sections which more or less approximated to the positions held by the various allied forces after the taking of Peking. The boundaries of these sections were at first only roughly indicated.

International Police Committee.—Early in September an International Committee was appointed by the generals commanding at Peking to consider how far the police arrangements could be unified. The committee laid down the exact boundaries of each section, as shown in the administration map, and these boundaries were practically adhered to till the withdrawal of the foreign troops commenced.

The system of administration varied considerably in detail in the different sections, which was only to be expected when the idiosyncrasies of the various nationalities concerned is taken into consideration.

International Police Commission for the Administration of Peking.—Some time after the arrival of F. M. Count von Waldersee, an International Police Commission was formed by his orders. The Commission was composed of a German general as president, and an officer from each of the contingents as members. It met at regular intervals, and promulgated from time to time such directions as it thought necessary for the guidance of the Police Commissioners. Police Commissioners submitted monthly to the Commission statements of the funds required by them to carry on the administration of their respective districts, the money being paid through the Commission by the Chinese representatives.

British Sections.—Two sections were allotted to the British. One of these sections was in the Tartar City, under Captain Selwyn, 12th Bengal Lancers, as Police Commissioner; the other was in the Chinese City, under Captain Barrow, 4th Bengal Lancers.

On the 19th August 1900, five days after the relief of the Legations, the sections were handed over to the Police Commissioners.

Of the two sections, that in the Chinese City was by far the largest, both in extent and population. It was also unique in the fact that it was the only one in Peking not actually garrisoned by foreign troops. The administration of this section will therefore be briefly described as being typical, more or less, of the others, and at the same time illustrative of how it was possible to control a very large Chinese population with a very small display of force.

It will be convenient to consider the various steps adopted for the proper administration of the section under the following headings :—

1. First measures taken to restore order and confidence.
2. The formation of a regular municipality.
3. Courts of justice; penal code; punishments; Chinese Police, &c.
4. Dealings with foreigners and foreign troops.
5. Population and trade.
6. Finance and taxes.
7. Hospital and school.
8. General feeling between Chinese and British.
9. Gradual handing over of the sections to the Chinese.
10. The Indian Military Police.

1. *First Measures taken to restore Order and Confidence.*—At the time when the Police Commissioners took over control of their respective sections, the City of Peking presented an extraordinary appearance. The streets were empty, the shops were rifled; the houses pillaged. In the main street alone was any sign of life to be seen—coolies proceeding to work at the Legations, or an occasional Chinaman, who disappeared completely at the approach of a foreigner. All women and children had disappeared. Every shop was open, and in most cases the wares, which had not been carried away, were strewn about in hopeless confusion. Houses were in a like state. The courtyards and rooms were heaped with clothing, books, and articles, in many cases of considerable value, and of every description. Everything that was breakable had, in the majority of cases, been broken—everywhere confusion, desolation, and ruin.

The police force at the disposal of the Police Commissioner was—

British soldiers—non-commissioned officers and men	8
Native soldiers:—	
7th Bengal Infantry—1 Native officer, and non-commissioned officers and men	60
24th Punjab Infantry—non-commissioned officers and men	40
Total non-commissioned officers and men	108

A headquarter post was established at one of the most central of the former Chinese police yamens.

The first thing to do was to restore order, and to restore order it was necessary to restore confidence. It was essential to at once put an end to all looting. The streets were patrolled, and all foreigners who could not give a proper account of themselves, and soldiers not on duty, were put outside the limits of the section. Those found with loot on them were made to give it up, and, when possible, it was restored to the owners. Within 24 hours the Chinese understood that the intention was to assist them by putting an end to disorder. They came from all directions, asking for aid and protection, which was readily granted to them. A proclamation was posted all over the section, calling on the inhabitants to open their shops and to return to their business, and that they would be sure of protectors. Grain and flour merchants were also called on to come forward and sell their grain for the British troops. Several merchants at once presented themselves, and entered into contracts with the British Commissariat officers, and with regiments, for the supply of grain, flour, sheep, &c.

Signs of life began to show in the streets, gangs of coolies were employed in clearing the main thoroughfares of *débris*, dead bodies, and filth; shops were opened; gradually the city assumed a more normal aspect.

2. *The Formation of a Municipality.*—At the time of the entry of the Allies into Peking a great number of the inhabitants had fled the city; those that remained had hidden themselves. When it became known that the desire of the allied commanders was to protect them from pillage and to restore order, and when they found that every endeavour was being made to do so, they began to return to their homes, shops, and business. The return was gradual, but soon the population had increased so much that it was necessary and expedient to conduct affairs, to a certain extent, through the medium of the Chinese themselves. A municipal council was formed. The section was divided into three districts. The inhabitants of each district were asked to elect three representative men, and this being done the committee was asked to elect its own chairman. From the time of the formation of the committee, all work was carried out as far as possible through its agency. It was consulted on all points. Whether the committee agreed with the Police Commissioner or not, every measure for the benefit of the section was carried out with its countenance. This pleased the Chinese, and made them all the more ready to trust us, and to assist us in our endeavours to restore and maintain order. Two members of the committee sat daily on the Police Commissioners' Court. The assistance of the committee was invaluable in giving advice on matters in which Chinese customs and law were concerned.

3. *Courts of Justice; Punishments; Chinese Police.*—At first the only court was that held by the Police Commissioner, which sat daily for as long as required. On this court, in addition to the Police Commissioner, were also a European interpreter and assessor, and two members of the Municipal Committee. A Chinese interpreter, a writer, and the Chief of the Chinese

Police were also in attendance. All cases were tried before this court, offences of Chinese against Chinese and against order. Offences of foreign or British soldiers arrested in the section were investigated, and subsequently the men arrested, together with a statement of the evidence, and in some cases the witnesses also were sent, in the case of British soldiers, to their corps, in the case of foreign soldiers, to the Police headquarters of the contingent to which they belonged.

It was surprising how soon the Chinese took advantage of this court. They brought all their complaints, both civil and criminal, and even their family squabbles, before it. The question of appointing Chinese magistrates was several times considered but negatived, partly on account of the difficulty of finding suitable men and partly for fear that in the existing state of partial disorder, such magistrates might make improper use of their powers.

About the end of January 1901, when conditions were almost normal, and the work became too heavy for one court to deal with, courts presided over by Chinese magistrates were instituted.

These Courts had limited powers granted them at first, which were gradually extended up to the time when the section was handed over to Chinese control. In consultation with the Chinese, a penal code was drawn up, and punishments administered as far as possible in accordance with Chinese law. No punishments were administered which did not accord with Western ideas of humanity. A prison was built and run on sanitary lines, and when later it was necessary to confine some of the prisoners in Chinese prisons for want of accommodation, these were constantly inspected and their cleanliness carefully attended to.

Shortly after the occupation of the section a small force of Chinese police, 30 in all, was raised. A portion of this force was used to deal with offences of Chinese against Chinese, the remainder being employed as detectives: the work done by them was most excellent. In October an additional force of 140 police and 100 night watchmen was formed, as the work, owing to the rapidly-increasing number of inhabitants, became too heavy for the military police to cope with. Moreover, the difference of language and ignorance of the manners and customs of the Chinese on the part of the military police made it absolutely essential to employ Chinese for these duties during a prolonged occupation. The Chinese police and night watchmen were all regularly drilled and uniformed. They eventually became indispensable.

4. *Dealings with Foreigners and Foreign Troops.*—As soon as the various sections of Peking were taken over by the different contingents, it was ruled that no soldier of one nationality should be permitted inside the section belonging to another without a pass. This plan worked very well. It was laid down that any man arrested for being in a district other than his own without a pass, should be sent to the nearest police station in his own section, with a view to his being punished. In order to avoid

undue friction this rule was carried out with a good deal of discretion. After order was once thoroughly re-established, but little trouble was given by the foreign soldiery in the British Section, though isolated cases of theft and violence occurred up to the time of the evacuation.

5. *Population and Trade.*—Six weeks subsequent to the relief of the Legations a census was taken which showed approximately 30,000 Chinese living in the British Section. By the end of May 1901 the population had gradually increased till it reached normal, and was calculated by the Chinese officials at 150,000. When the Americans left Peking a part of their district was taken over by the British and the population of the British Section, Chinese City, numbered from that time on not less than 200,000 (according to Chinese, American, and our own computation).

Trade.—As soon as the Chinese realised that looting was put an end to, trade began to revive. Shops and markets were opened, and the main thoroughfares were fitted with booths, restaurants and open air entertainments. Wine shops and opium dens began to flourish, but these latter were almost entirely suppressed within a very short time. Brothels were not allowed to open in the British Section, for they attracted foreigners, and increased the chances of collision between our troops and those of the Allies.

6. *Finance and Taxes.*—When the sections were first taken over, funds were required for carrying on the necessary municipal business, such as maintenance of the police stations, yamen establishments, cleaning of the streets, &c. The first expenses were met by a small house tax. Subsequently the commission for the administration of Peking paid over the money required as already described. In proportion to the area and population the British sections were administered more cheaply than those of any other nationality. The average monthly expenditure in the British Chinese Section for lighting, watering, allowances of military police, pay of Chinese police and night watchmen, sanitation carts, police posts, yamen expenses, prison expenses, &c. was 1,800 dollars.

7. *Hospital and School.*—A hospital was started in the Chinese City for the benefit of the Chinese. Major Manifold, I.M.S., kindly undertook the management of this hospital, and was ably assisted by Captain Walton, I.M.S. The services of a Chinese who had studied medicine in England were also procured. The hospital was very successful. In $3\frac{1}{2}$ months the total number of attendances amounted to over 4,000, treated free of charge. The Chinese of all ranks and sexes came for treatment. It was a proof of the confidence which the Chinese placed in us that the women submitted themselves freely to be operated on by our doctors. The hospital was left free of debt, stocked with medicines, &c. and 1,000 dollars to its credit, and arrangements were made for its continuance under the patronage of the British Minister and Sir Robert Hart after the evacuation of Peking by the foreign troops.

A school for teaching English, history and geography was opened at the headquarters of the Police Commissioner, one of the European interpreters kindly took charge of this school. It was well attended and was growing rapidly at the time of our leaving Peking.

8. *General Feeling of Chinese towards British.*—The general feeling of the Chinese towards the British after order was restored was one of great confidence. Chinese of all sorts and conditions brought their grievances to the police authorities. Great cordiality existed between the Chinese gentry and the Police Commissioner, who was a constant recipient of their hospitality. The poorest brought their family quarrels to be adjusted at the Police Yamen.

The success of the British administration may be in great part attributed to the employment of European interpreters. These were for the most part missionaries, who had spent many years amongst the people and could speak the language fluently. Their assistance was invaluable.

9. *Handing over to the Chinese.*—When the withdrawal of the foreign troops from Peking became imminent, arrangements were made for the gradual handing over of the section to the Chinese, so that at the last there might be no disorder. This was done with the assistance of Prince Ch'ing, who nominated the magistrates and officials who would eventually take over charge. In the majority of cases the magistrates detailed by Prince Ch'ing were the same as those already employed under the Police Commissioner, which greatly facilitated the work of transference.

Gradually the powers given to the Chinese were increased, the strength of the military police being reduced by degrees. Eventually the section which had been administered by the British for 11 months was delivered over to the Chinese without any friction whatsoever, and in a better state as regards sanitation and law and order than had existed previously under Chinese rule.

10. *Indian Military Police.*—It would be difficult to praise too highly the reliableness of the Indian troops—Rajputs, Sikhs, and Afridis—as military police. It must be remembered that there were only 100 men to control a population rising from 30,000 to 200,000, a condition of things which existed in none of the other sections, in all of which troops were quartered.

In dealing with the foreign soldiers they never flinched from performing their duty, often in the face of superior numbers. They quickly gained the confidence of the Chinese, and the most friendly relations existed between them and the inhabitants, while the respect with which they inspired the latter was never relaxed. They were often placed in trying positions, and they never failed to come out with credit to themselves and the Indian army.

APPENDIX P.

ULTIMATUM OF THE FOREIGN ADMIRALS TO THE VICEROY OF CHIH-LI PROVINCE DEMANDING THE SURRENDER OF THE TAKU 'FORTS.

PROTOCOL of a MEETING held under the Presidency of His Excellency ADMIRAL HILDEBRAND, the Senior Naval Officer here.

The allied Powers, since the beginning of the troubles, have landed detachments without opposition for the protection of their nationals and Diplomatic Body against the rebels, who are known by the name of Boxers.

At first the representatives of the Imperial authority seemed to understand their duty, and made apparent efforts to re-establish order, but now they clearly show their sympathy for the enemies of the foreigners by placing troops on the railway lines, and by placing torpedoes in the entrance to the Pei-ho. These acts prove that the Government forgets its solemn engagements towards foreigners, and as the commanding officers of the allied forces are bound to remain in constant communication with the detachments on land, they have decided to occupy provisionally, by consent, or by force, the Taku forts.

The limit of time for their surrender to the allied forces is 2 o'clock in the morning of the 17th June (2 a.m.).

This will be communicated to the Viceroy of Pechi-li at Tien-tsin and to the officers commanding the forts.

(Signed) ADMIRAL HILDEBRAND,
Senior Naval Officer.

[The signatures of admirals and captains of ships of Allied Forces here follow.]

On board of the Russian Imperial cruiser,
16th June 1900, 11 a.m.

APPENDIX Q.

IMPERIAL EDICTS, &C., RELATING TO THE BOXER MOVEMENT.

The famous ANTI-FOREIGN EDICT of the 5th Month, 28th Day (24th June 1900).

We have received from Yü-lu a memorial reporting that the foreigners had started trouble and suddenly seized a pretext for acts of war, but that in successive battles, lasting for several days, victories had been obtained.

The reading of this memorial greatly rejoiced and comforted us. China had lived in peace and harmony with all countries for years, but, after all, affairs have come to an open rupture owing to the hatred between the people and the converts to Christianity.

Relying on their strong ironclads and powerful armies, they (the foreigners) attacked the forts of our port of Taku, and issued from Tzŭ-chŭ-lin (*i.e.*, the foreign quarter of Tien-tsin) in all directions to fight. But Yü-lu was everywhere at once offering resistance; and also our Boxer troops aided him with all their heart and strength, opposing the rampart of their bodies to the assailing cannon and bayonets.

On the 25th, 26th, and 27th (21st, 22nd, and 23rd June) our forces destroyed two war-vessels and killed many of the enemy. The people's resolution had become like walls to protect their country, and the firmness of their minds raised the martial spirit of the troops.

The Boxers who helped the troops so much in these actions are men of the people; with them the State need not use a soldier nor spend a dollar. Even the little children wielded arms in defence of their altars and fields. In all their dangers the spirits of their ancestors, of the gods and sages, protected them. The myriads of the people are actuated by one ideal.

We hasten to promulgate this edict in praise of the patriotic Boxers, and to assure them that those of them who are in distress will be cared for.

When these troubles are over we intend to bestow on them special marks of our favour. Let these people's soldiers only still continue, with united hearts and utmost efforts, to repel aggression and prove their loyalty, without failing, till the end. This is our earnest desire.

Reverence this.

The EMPRESS-DOWAGER OF CHINA to the VICEROY OF SSU-CH'UAN PROVINCE.

IMPERIAL EDICT.
Dated 5th month, 29th day (25th June 1900).

At present war has broken out between China and foreign countries. At Tien-tsin, in Chih-li, our generals have gained victories with the patriotic Boxers helping the Government troops, and an edict has already been issued to praise and congratulate these. Such patriotic people are to be found in all parts of the empire; and if the viceroys and governors of all the provinces are able to unite and organise forces, we can put an end to foreign insults, and shall accomplish great results. Report immediately what steps are being taken. The provinces bordering on the river or the sea should particularly act quickly. Bring this 600 *li* a-day urgent edict to public notice.

Respect this.

DECREE dated June 26, 1900.

I, TING-CHIEH, have the honour to forward this reverent copy of a Decree received by me on the 27th June, having been handed out by the Grand Council on the 26th June, and forwarded at 600 *li* (200 miles a day) by the Board of War:—

"We yesterday announced to Li Hung-chang, Li Ping-hêng, Liu K'un-yi, and Chang Chih-tung the facts that it was equally difficult to repress or to soothe the feud of the Society men against the converts, and that hostilities were first resorted to by the Powers.

The reluctance of you Viceroys and Governors, after considering the position and estimating your strength, to provoke foreign enmity lightly may well be the policy of tried Ministers consulting the interests of their State.

But, unfortunately, in the present case the Boxer bands have spread over the whole capital, and their numbers are not less than several hundred thousand. From soldiers and people up to princely and ducal palaces, from all alike, comes one cry of hatred of the foreign religion: the two cannot exist together. Repression meant intestine trouble and the utter ruin of the people. The only course, therefore, was to turn the movement to account, while slowly devising reformation. The warning in your memorial not to endanger the State by believing their heretical talk leaves out of account the helpless position in which the Court is placed.

Did ye Viceroys and Governors realise how great is the crisis in the capital ye would surely be unable to eat and sleep in peace, and so anxious to do your duty that ye could never think of making one-sided representations.

The present state of things is one in which the incitement and pressure of providential opportunity and human affairs have combined to render war inevitable. Do not any of ye Viceroys and Governors longer hesitate and look on, but with all speed provide troops and supplies, and vigorously protect the territories, for any remissness it is ye that shall be called to account.

"Let this be enjoined by telegram on—

"Li Hung-chang, Governor-General of Liang Kwang.
" Li Ping Hêng, Admiral of the Yang-tsze.
" Yü-lu, Governor-General of Chihli.
" Liu K'un-yi, Viceroy of Liang Chiang.
" Chang Chih-tung, Viceroy of Hukwang.
" Hsu Yang-k'uei, Governor-General of Chekiang and Fukien.
" Kuei-chün, Governor-General of Szechuan.
" Tseng-ch'i, Military Governor of Mukden.
" Ch'ang Shun of Kirin, and Shou-shan, of Helu Chiang.
" Wei Kuang T'ao, Governor of Shansi.
" Ting Chen-to, Governor of Yünnan.
" Yuan Shih K'ai, Governor of Shantung.
" Yü-ch'ang, Governor of Honan.
" Lu Chu'an-liu, Governor of Kiangsu.
" Wang Chih-ch'un, Governor of Anhui.
" Sung-shou, Governor of Chiang-si.
" Yü Ying-liu, Governor of Hupei.
" Yü Lien San, Governor of Hunan.
" Tuan-ts'ai.
" Liu Shu T'ang, Governor of Chêkiang.
" Yao Ying-ch'i, Governor of Ili.
" Tê-shou.
" Huang Tung-sen, Governor of Kwang-si.
" Shao Chi-ch'êng, Governor of Kwei-chow."

Copy is being telegraphed to the others.

(Received June 29, 1900.)

Inclosure 1 in No. 16.

PROCLAMATION issued by the following PRINCE and MINISTERS appointed by Imperial Decree to superintend the Affairs of the I-ho T'uan (Boxer Association):—

PRINCE CHUANG,
KANG YI,
YING NIEN, and
TSAI LAN.

(Translation.)

WHEREAS, the members of the I-ho T'uan, having assembled in large numbers at the capital, we have called for subscription of money and rice to form this righteous organization and use it for destroying [foreigners]; and whereas we now learn that certain nameless characters, expect to derive pecuniary advantages therefrom, to the detriment of the interests of the I-ho T'uan; now, therefore we issue this Proclamation for the information of officials, scholars, merchants, and the people generally. Let all who are willing to subscribe in aid of the T'uan send their subscriptions to the office of the T'uan affairs at the residence of Prince Chuang. This will obviate fraud and give a guarantee of good faith. When subscriptions are paid in, the office will at once issue a receipt and carefully enter the names and amounts in a register. From time to time a list based on the entries in the register will be published for the information of the public. All sending subscriptions by messengers must instruct the latter to demand receipts.

We will continue to make secret inquiry, and should we discover any person fraudulently raising subscriptions, or should any such case be reported to us, those concerned will be most severely punished. All who arrest such bad characters, or who give information leading to their apprehension, will be suitably rewarded.

Kuang Hsü, 26th year, 6th moon, 2nd day,
(June 28, 1900).

Inclosure 2 in No. 16.

PROCLAMATION issued by the GENERAL COMMANDANT OF THE GENDARMERIE.

(Translation.)

WHEREAS, the religious chapels in Peking having been burnt and destroyed, and having no place wherein to conceal themselves, the foreigners must have scattered and fled into hiding, now therefore the scholars, people, soldiers, braves, and Boxers, are hereby informed that all who surreptitiously afford shelter to foreigners of a certainty render themselves liable to the legal penalty of death. If they are able to capture foreigners alive the following rewards will be paid : A male, 50 taels ; a female, 40 taels ; a child, 30 taels. They must, however, be actually alive, and after examination the full reward will immediately be paid.

Let all take note and carefully obey these orders.

Kuang Hsü, 26th year, 6th moon, 2nd day,
(June 28, 1900).

Note.—The Office of the Gendarmerie was at that time presided over by Prince Chuang; Ying Nien, Vice-President of Board of Punishments; Duke Lan, younger brother of Prince Tuan.

POSITION taken by the YANG-TSE VICEROYS towards the BOXER MOVEMENT.

PROCLAMATION by CHANG, Viceroy of Hu Kuang Provinces, and Yü, Governor of Hupei, issued in obedience to an Imperial Rescript to safeguard their Territory.

WHEREAS in the north the disturbances of ruffians having led to a rupture with the Powers, men's minds are agitated and the political situation involved :

And whereas we had the honour to receive, on the 25th and 26th June, transmitted Decrees to the effect that at present in the capital every effort continued to be made to protect the Legations of the Powers, and that the Viceroys and Governors of the provinces must take such measures as in their judgment the crisis necessitated to preserve their territories :

And whereas it is, of course, our duty to devise means to carry out reverently these Imperial orders, we have, with his Excellency Liu, Viceroy of the Liang Chiang Provinces, carefully devised a joint scheme to preserve the integrity of the south-eastern provinces :

That is to say, we have agreed with the Consuls of the Powers that, provided only the naval squadrons of the fleets of the Powers do not enter the Yang-tse, the local authorities shall do their utmost to protect the lives and property of all foreigners in our provinces. And we have reported to the Throne, by telegraph, the successful negotiation of this scheme. This is a perfect plan to safeguard the lives of individuals and families of the people of these parts. But, as it is quite possible that, until the present scheme, as reported to the Throne, is understood among the populace, local ruffians and wicked folk may find pretexts to stir up trouble to the detriment of the public interests. We, therefore, hasten to issue this notice for the information of all classes—civilians and military alike :

Know ye that the present hostilities in the north were not intended or expected by the Court, and that the present Imperial orders that in the capital the Legations continue to be protected, and in the provinces at present the Concessions and chapels are still to be protected, in accordance with the Treaty provisions promulgated year after year, are both designed to maintain the public interest intact. Now that the Powers are willing to leave protection to us, and to keep the naval squadrons of the fleets out of the Yang-tse, the inhabitants and trade may both remain as undisturbed as usual, and local ruffians will not have a chance to make disturbance. Very many are the blessings secured by thus safeguarding the lives of individuals and families of the people in the Yang-tse and inland provinces, and utterly wrong would it be lightly to give cause for strife. Thus may we humbly embody the desire of the Court to see to the integrity of the State.

Gentry and Elders are especially bound earnestly to impress on others that thus may the peace of the unimpaired territory of the Empire be secured, and thus may the perfection of the heavenly sympathy of our divine dynasty be the more displayed.

From the date of this notification, should any concoct lying tales, and delude men's minds, or assemble crowds and disturb the Concessions and chapels, they shall be straightly sought out and dealt with as local bandits and secret society ruffians.

At every point strong forces have been posted promptly to extirpate utterly such evil scoundrels as seek pretexts to stir up disturbances with the design of starting riots.

Should soldiers or police make trouble, or be guilty of violence, they will at once be punished under martial law.

Our aim is, by keeping the people and traders undisturbed, and maintaining the peace of the country, to second humbly the meaning of the Imperial commands to preserve our territories by such measures as in our judgment the crisis necessitates.

Let all obey in fear and trembling this special urgent Proclamation.

Dated K.S. XXVI, vi (July 1900).

WANING of the BOXER CAUSE.

IMPERIAL DECREE of 2 August, 1900.

WHEREAS on account of the recent troubles in the capital between the populace and missionaries and their converts, war has broken out between China and the foreign Powers:

And whereas all the Ministers of foreign countries resident in Peking should be protected; the Prince and Ministers of the Tsung-li Yamen have frequently addressed to them letters of encouragement and inquiry, pointing out that in view of the disorder prevailing in Peking full measures of protection were difficult to carry out, and the Tsung-li Yamen therefore suggested that they should proceed under escort to Tien-tsin, where they could retire for the time being, and avoid all cause for alarm.

We accordingly command the Grand Secretary, Jung-lu, to select reliable military and civil officers of high rank to escort the Ministers to Tien-tsin with an armed guard. When the Ministers have fixed a date for leaving Peking they shall be escorted with every care *en route*, and any attack upon them by banditti shall be rigorously punished, while no pains shall be spared to render their journey safe.

Before leaving Peking, each Minister shall, if he desires, communicate with his Government *en clair*, and the message shall be transmitted by the Tsung-li Yamen without any delay.

The good feeling of the Throne towards the strangers from afar will thus be apparent.

IMPERIAL DECREE of August 2, 1900.

DURING the present outbreak of hostilities between China and the Powers, the foreign merchants, missions, &c. throughout the Empire must be considered as outside the sphere of hostilities. All Viceroys and Governors have, therefore, already been commanded to protect them as usual, and now that our troops are massing round Peking, all general officers marching with their forces towards the capital shall also respect this command, and make arrangements for the protection of all foreign merchants and missionaries, in order to assist the Throne in demonstrating its kindly feeling towards the strangers from afar.

With regard to native converts, these are also children of our State, and of the same origin as ourselves; but since the troubles began between the " Ch'üan ". (Boxers) and the Christians, the converts in many places have taken up defensive positions in their villages, intrenching themselves and throwing up earthworks to resist the Imperial troops. Such people as these are acting as rebels, and must absolutely be exterminated. However, if they repent, in fear of the punishment due to them, and adopt a new line of conduct, the net of destruction may be opened, and they may be allowed to escape.

Recently the General Sung Ch'ing reported that the converts at Ta-po-tien, in the Pao-ch'i district,* when exhorted by him, all expressed their willingness to cast aside their weapons and destroy their fortifications. They then scattered and returned to their villages. It is, therefore, evident that these converts are not all of their own free will banditti and robbers. In all cases where converts express their willingness to surrender in the above manner, we hereby command all military and local authorities to act in the same way towards them, and not to put them to death indiscriminately. But all cases of 'robbers and banditti pretending to be patriots, and wreaking their vengeance on the converts must be investigated and dealt with according to their circumstances, in order that disorder may be put a stop to.

Obey this.

IMPERIAL EDICT, dated 13 November 1900.

To Prince Ch'ing and the Grand Secretary Li,

An Imperial Edict of to-day's date has been received from the Grand Council by telegraph, together with a telegram addressed jointly by Prince Ch'ing and Li, and a telegram addressed to Li, which it is requested may be sent forward with the least possible delay.

(The context shows that this telegram was sent by Sheng Taotai.)

---

* About 60 miles east of Peking.

On the 13th November the Grand Council received the following Imperial Edict :—

The present troubles are to be attributed to the leniency shown towards, and the protection afforded to, the Boxer rebels by various high officers of State. These troubles have caused us to become embroiled with friendly Powers, and have proved a source of grief to the spirits of our ancestors.

We have already published edicts on this subject, decreeing punishments for the guilty; but we are extremely vexed and annoyed to find that in the districts round about the capital the Boxer rebels have not yet been completely exterminated, with the result that the country has been completely devastated and the populace plunged into a state of abject misery.

Unless, therefore, some severe and additional punishments are meted out, we cannot conciliate popular feeling nor appease the resentment of the friendly Powers.

We accordingly ordain as follows :—

Tsai I, Prince Tuan, is deprived of his rank and offices, and is together with Tsai-hsün, Prince Chuang, who has already been degraded, to be temporarily handed over to the Imperial Clan Court for incarceration. When hostilities shall have ceased they are to be sent to Mukden, and there imprisoned for life. Pu Ching, Prince of I, already degraded, Tsai Ying, a Prince of the Fourth Order, likewise already degraded, are also to be handed over to the Imperial Clan Court for incarceration.

Tsai Lien, a Prince of the Fourth Order, who has been deprived of his rank and offices, is directed to shut his door and reflect on his misdeeds (confinement in his own house).

Tsai Lan, an Imperial Duke of the Second Degree, is deprived of his entire salary, degraded one step in rank, and transferred to a lower office.

Ying-nien, President of the Censorate, is degraded two steps in rank, and transferred to a lower office.

Kang-yi, former Assistant Grand Secretary and President of the Board of Civil Office, when sent on a mission to discover how to deal with the Boxer rebels, returned to Peking and submitted a report largely screening and extenuating their offences. He ought, properly speaking, to have been most severely punished, but as he has since died a natural death, he is left out of account.

Chao Shu-ch'iao, President of the Board of Punishments, was guilty of negligence, in that when sent out to inquire into circumstances attending the Boxer rising, he returned the next day. As his report did not, however, gloss over facts, he is deprived of his rank, while remaining in office.

Yü-hsien, while officiating as Governor of Shan-hsi, in that he protected and encouraged the Boxer rebels and killed missionaries and Christian converts, was guilty of having acted in a most arbitrary and reckless manner. The circumstances of the case are peculiarly grave, and he is accordingly sentenced for life to hard labour on the remotest parts of the frontier.

We alone are cognisant of full facts. Take, for instance, Pu Ching, Prince of I, the inferior Princes Tsai Lien and Tsai Ying. Although the high officials in the capital and in the provinces have sent in accusatory memorials, none have been directed against these Princes, nor have our envoys in foreign countries ever alluded to them in their telegrams to the Throne.

That we should thus, in accordance with the real facts of the case, mete out punishment to all alike affords evidence that we, in a spirit of true justice, and without the slightest impartiality, chastise the guilty in proportion to their crimes, and this action on our part should be taken into consideration by the world at large.

APPENDIX R.

Imperial Decrees giving Effect to the Terms of the Joint Note presented to the Chinese Plenipotentiaries by the Foreign Ministers, on 22 December 1900.

Imperial Decree of 24th December 1900, fixing the responsibility of all anti-foreign troubles and infractions of Treaties on the provincial and local officials.

It has been stipulated in treaties made between China and the foreign Powers that the nationals of these Powers shall have the right to penetrate into the interior.

The Court, in order to assure and to maintain relations with other countries, has already issued decrees ordaining that the most sincere efforts be made in the provinces to insure protection. Nevertheless, the local authorities having relaxed little by little (in the exercise of their functions), disturbances have been caused by ill-doers, and attacks have been directed against foreigners. Similar incidents have been several times repeated.

We understand that our qualities have been too feeble to bring the ignorant people to reform themselves, and this has caused us to commit immense faults. Not a single local Mandarin has been able, in ordinary times, to make European affairs understood, and not one has comprehended the importance of foreign relations. A conflagration has thus spread everywhere threatening the Empire, and if they question themselves they will not feel easy in their minds.

From this time forth each one of you must set to work to drive away his resentment and to get rid of his prejudices. You ought to know that, at all times, the maintenance of friendly relations with foreign countries has been a fundamental rule. People who arrive in China, coming from afar, either as merchants to exchange their products there, or as travellers to increase their scientific knowledge, or again as missionaries to preach religion, for the purpose of exhorting people to do good, have crossed the mountains and the seas at a cost of the greatest fatigue.

Since China is considered to be a civilized country, she ought to practise the duties of a host towards her guests. Besides, the Chinese who, in these last years, have gone abroad, number at the least several hundreds of thousands. Their persons and their goods depend on the guarantee assured them by the Powers who have extended to them their protection. How could we continue to treat their nationals differently ?

We command, once again, all high responsible civil and military authorities of all provinces to instruct their subordinates to protect, in the most effective manner, the agents and nationals of foreign Powers who come within their districts. Should any audacious ill-doers go so far as to ill-treat and massacre foreigners order must be immediately re-established, and the guilty must be arrested and punished. There must be no delay. If, owing to indifference, or even voluntary tolerance, great calamities should occur, or if infringements of treaties should take place, and should not be immediately repressed and punished, the governors-general, governors, and provincial or local authorities responsible will be recalled without the power of being appointed to new posts in other provinces, or the hope of being reinstated, or of receiving fresh honours.

This decree is to be printed and published in order to warn the Mandarins and the people to put an end to all these unworthy habits.

Respect this !

IMPERIAL DECREE of 27th December 1900, accepting the terms of the Joint Note presented by the Foreign Ministers on the 24th December.

We have made ourselves acquainted with the contents of the telegraphic memorial submitted by the Prince of Ch'ing and Li Hung-chang, and also with the text of the accompanying articles. How can we adequately convey an idea of the extent to which these weigh upon our heart ?

Considering, however, the dangers and difficulties of the present situation, we have no alternative but, in an indirect manner, to seek some satisfactory means of saving the same. We must, therefore, accord our sanction to the whole of the general principles laid down in the twelve Articles. As regards the detailed points which yet remain, the utmost endeavours to secure attenuation and reduction must continue to be made.

It is of essential importance that the Prince and others concerned put forth their best efforts and strain every nerve to wrestle with their hard task, in the hope that the interests at stake may be conserved.

This document is interesting in that it shows the extent to which the Chinese language can be used to convey double meanings, and thus satisfy parties with conflicting views according to the way in which it is read.

The phrases throughout are selected with the greatest care, and the draughtsman, who is understood to be Wang Wen-shao, is considered to have achieved a masterpiece in this particular style.

The words "weigh upon the heart" may mean regret for what has happened; they may, on the other hand, conceal a feeling of resentment with regard to the terms proposed.

"To save the situation in an indirect manner" may indicate a desire to do what is possible to make reparation; it may also signify an intention to evade as best one can the conditions imposed.

The characters used to "accord sanction" may be construed in the sense of assent; their generally accepted interpretation is, however, "vouchsafe permission." The Chinese Plenipotentiaries recognising this, had altered them to others expressing direct assent.

The decree winds up with a flattering appeal to the Chinese Plenipotentiaries to do their utmost, but holds out little hope of their being actively supported.

IMPERIAL EDICT of 1st February 1901, making Membership of Anti-Foreign Societies illegal and punishable with Death.

In all the provinces bandits have summoned adherents and founded anti-foreign societies. Various edicts have formally forbidden this. We have repeated it many times, yet, in these last years, there have still been, in all the districts of Shantung, sects of the name of Ta-tao-hui (Society of the Great Knives) and Y-Ho-Kien (Boxers), which have been propagated everywhere for the avowed purpose of killing and stealing. They have gradually gained the territory of Chih-li and suddenly penetrated into the capital, where foreign establishments have been burned and the Legations attacked. Crimes have thus been committed against neighbouring countries and mistakes made against the general interest. For not having insured protection we have incurred considerable responsibilities.

You, people, who in ordinary times are nourished by and live on the products of this land, on all of whom the benefits of the empire have been showered, you have nevertheless dared to incite these bandits to wish to fight, to teach methods of casting spells, and to devote themselves to false practices. You have had the temerity to resist your mandarins, you have massacred them, you have murdered foreigners, and have finally been the cause of those unheard-of calamities which, over and above all else, have overwhelmed with grief your sovereign and your fathers.

We cannot think of what has been done without feeling a still more profound resentment. We have already expressly ordered the commanders-in-chief of all regions to make the most sincere efforts to destroy these societies. It is necessary to suppress the evil in its very root; the princes and ministers, therefore, who have lent the Boxers their support, will undergo the most severe punishments in keeping with their crimes, and, in order to inspire dread, all civil and military examinations will be suspended for five years in all towns where foreigners have been massacred or have undergone cruel treatment.

Fearing lest the ignorant populations of the country may not have knowlege of these punishments, new and severe interdictions will be specially issued, in order to prevent the execution of people who had not been warned.

You, soldiers and people, ought to know that it is expressly forbidden by law to form secret societies or to belong to them. Our ancestors have never shown the least indulgence in the suppression of societies of malefactors.

Besides, the foreign Powers are all friendly countries, the Christians are children of our blood, whom the Court regards with the same favour, and it could not admit that it entertained different sentiments towards them. All Chinese, Christians or not, who are ill-treated should complain to the authorities, and await the pronouncement of a just and equitable judgment. How can you lightly believe all the rumours which are spread? How can you fail to consider the penal laws?

Afterwards, when all is lost, the clever ones flee to a distance, and the simple-minded are put to death. The law is slow to pardon, and all this is truly very sad. From the date of the publication of this edict each one should amend his ways, and repent of the teaching which he has received.

If hardened and incorrigible ill-doers again form clandestinely anti-foreign societies, they will be punished with death, as also whoever joins these societies. It would be impossible to show them any indulgence.

The Tartar marshals, the governors-general, governors, and high provincial authorities whose duty it is to direct the populations, must give very precise instructions to their subordinates to publish severe proclamations, and to have this decree printed on yellow paper, which shall be placarded everywhere. It is necessary that all families should be warned, that all should be exhorted to do right, and that none should be ignorant that the will of the Court is that all should know well that people will be punished in order to avoid inflicting other punishments.

Let this edict be made known to all throughout the Empire.

Respect this!

IMPERIAL EDICT of 13th February 1901. Rehabilitation of the Five Officials who were executed for protesting against the Boxer Movement and the Attacks upon the Foreign Legations in Peking.

The disturbances caused by the Boxers in the course of the 5th moon (May–June) having increased from day to day, the Court had two difficult courses open to it, either to adopt coercive measures or to calm them. In the hope that a way might be indicated to us, the Ministers were several times summoned to an audience.

We frequently questioned Hsü Yung-i, President of the War Office, Li-shan, President at the Ministry of Finance, Hsü Ching-ch'êng, Director of the Left of the Ministry of the Interior, Lien-yüan, Vice-Chancellor of the Chief Secretary's Office, Yüan Ch'ang, Director of the Board of Sacrifices.

In their speeches and in their thoughts all admitted that both methods were possible. Several Ministers, promoters of disorder, profiting directly by this circumstance, accused them unjustly, and handed in memoranda, in which they denounced them. They were therefore severely punished in their persons.

But, seeing that Hsü Yung-i and others have given evidence of great zeal for many years, and that they have always made a study of international questions, that they may have been faithful, and that they have shown themselves to be hardworking, it is our duty to confer on them a favour.

We command that Hsü Yung-i, Li-shan, Hsü Ching-ch'êng, Lien-yüan, and Yüan-Ch'ang be reinstated in their former rank.

Let the office concerned in the matter be informed.

Respect this !

IMPERIAL EDICT of 21st February 1901, ordering the punishment of the Princes and Officials concerned in the Boxer rising.

Edict issued and transmitted by telegraph on the 3rd day of the 1st moon (21st February 1901), and received on the 4th by the Grand Chancery.

By a former Edict we had already severely punished, according to their cases, all the high functionaries who were the chief authors of the present ills. But we received, a short time since, a telegraphic report from I-Kwang and Li Hung-chang, informing us that, according to an official note from the Ministers Plenipotentiary of the various Powers a fresh increase of punishments was necessary, and begging us to make a decision.

Besides Tsai-Hsun (Prince Chuang), who has been commanded to commit suicide, and Yü-hsien, on whom the penalty of immediate decapitation has been pronounced, and with regard to whom delegates will be charged to go and verify (the execution of the sentences), we have decided that the punishment applicable to Tsai-Yi (Prince Tuan) and to Tsai-Lan (Duke Lan) is postponed decapitation; however, in consideration of the ties of relationship which bind them to us, we grant them the very special favour of sending them to the borders of the Empire, to Turkestan, where they will be imprisoned for life. A delegate charged to conduct them under escort will be appointed and will start at the earliest opportunity.

As regards Kang-yi, whose crimes were more serious, the punishment to be inflicted would have been decapitation without delay, but as he has already died of disease, he will be granted the favour of a fresh examination of his case.

As regards Ying-nien and Chao-Shu-ch'iao, whose punishment, according to our previous decisions, was to be postponed decapitation. We command that they be invited to commit suicide, and we charge Ts'en-Ch'uan-huian, Governor of Shan-hsi, to go and verify their deaths.

As regards Ch'i-hsiu and Hsü Ch'eng-yü, whom the Powers designate as the determined protectors of the Boxer bandits, and as having especially done harm to foreigners, we had previously decreed their destitution; we command to-day I-Kwang and Li Hung-chang to request the Powers, by telegram, to hand them over to them, and to have them immediately executed. One of the Presidents of the Ministry of Justice will be charged to verify their execution.

As regards Hsu T'ung, who has compromised the general great interests by lightly placing confidence in the Boxers, and Li Ping-hêng, whose habits of boasting have deliberately engendered these misfortunes, the penalty to be inflicted on them would have been postponed decapitation; but, taking into consideration the fact that they have committed suicide on seeing the approach of the disaster, that they have already been degraded, and that the posthumous honours which had been accorded to them have been annulled and withdrawn, no further notice need be taken of their case.

The nature of the crimes committed by all the principal authors of the evil has been exposed, in a clear and detailed manner, in the preceding Decrees.

Respect this!

IMPERIAL EDICT of the 9th June 1901. Appointment of Prince Chün as Special Envoy to convey the message of Regret of the Emperor of China to the Emperor of Germany for the murder of His Excellency Baron von Ketteler, German Minister.

We confer upon Tsai-fêng, Prince of the first rank, Chün, the title of Ambassador Extraordinary, and we charge him to proceed to Germany in order to acquit himself respectfully of the Mission which we intrust to him.

Chang Yi, Reader at the Grand Chancery, and Yin Chang, Military Lieutenant-Governor, will accompany him as Secretaries.

Respect this!

(Prince Chün left Peking on the 12th July 1901 to carry out this mission.)

IMPERIAL EDICT of 18th June 1901. Despatch of a Mission to Japan to express the regret of his Majesty the Emperor of China for the murder of Mr. Sugiyama, Chancellor of the Japanese Legation.

Edict received by telegraph from Hsi-an fu on the 3rd day of the 5th moon (June 18, 1901).

We confer on M. Na-t'ong, Second Vice-President of the Treasury, the button of a Mandarin of the first rank, and we appoint him special Envoy to proceed to Japan and there acquit himself respectfully of the Mission with which we intrust him.

Respect this !

IMPERIAL EDICT of 24th July 1901, Transforming the Tsung-li Yamen into a Ministry of Foreign Affairs (Wai-wu-pu).

On the 9th day of the 6th moon the Grand Chancery received the following Edict :—

The appointment of functionaries and the settlement of their duties have hitherto been regulated according to the necessities of the moment. At this time, when a new Treaty of Peace has been concluded, international relations have assumed the first place amongst important affairs, and it is more than ever necessary to have recourse to capable men to undertake all that concerns the establishment of friendship in relations and of confidence in language.

The Board of Foreign Affairs, formerly created to deal with international questions, has indeed existed for many years, but considering that the Princes and Ministers who composed it discharged their functions, for the most part only, as an accessory to others, they were unable to devote themselves to them exclusively. It is necessary, therefore, to create special functions in order that each may have his own duty.

We consequently command that the Board of Foreign Affairs (Tsung-li ko kuo Che-wu Yamen) be converted into a Ministry of Foreign Affairs (Wai-wu-pu), and rank before the six Ministries, and we appoint I-Kwang, Prince of the first rank, Ching, President of the Ministry of Foreign Affairs.

Wang Wên-shao, Grand Secretary of State of the Ti-jen Ko, is appointed Assistant-President of the Ministry of Foreign Affairs; K'in Hong-ki, President of the Ministry of Public Works, is transferred, with the same title, to the Ministry of Foreign Affairs, of which he is appointed Assistant President; Hsü Shou-p'êng, Director of the Stud Establishment, and Lien-fang, Metropolitan Expectant Sub-Director of the third or fourth rank, are appointed First and Second Directors (Under-Secretaries).

As regards the arrangement of the staff, the regulations which are to govern its selection, the emoluments of the ministers, directors, and other agents, we direct the Government counsellors to consult with the Ministry of the Staff, and to promptly report to us their conclusions.

Respect this!

IMPERIAL EDICT of 19th August 1901, Suspension of Examinations for Five Years.

Edict received by the Grand Chancery the 6th day of the 7th month of the 27th year Kwang-Su (19th August 1901).

Whereas, in the report of to-day, I-Kwang and Li Hung-chang inform us that the foreign Powers have decided on the suspension for five years of the civil and military examinations in the localities which have been the scene of disturbances;

And whereas it is declared that this suspension shall remain applicable to the local degree examinations of Choun-T'ien and T'ai-Yuan;

And whereas the list comprises the localities of—

In Shan-hsi: T'ai-yüan Fu, Hsin Chow, T'ai-ku Hsien, Ta-t'ung Fu, Fên-chou Fu, Hsiao-yi Hsien, Ch'ü-wu Hsien, Ta-ning Hsien, Ho-ching Hsien, Yüch-yang Hsien, Lo-p'ing Fu, Wên-shui Hsien, Shou-yang Hsien, P'ing-yang Fu, Chang-tsŭ Hsien, Kao-p'ing Hsien, Tsé-chou Fu, Hsi-chou, P'u-hsien, Chiang-chou, Kuei-hua-ch'êng, Sui-yüan ch'êng.

In Ho-nan: Nan-yang Fu, Kuang-chou.

In Che Kiang: Ch'ü-chou Fu.

In Chih-li: Peking, Chun-tien Fu, Pao-ting Fu, Yung-ch'ing Hsien, Tien-tsin Fu, Shun-tê Fu, Wang-tu Hsien, Huai-lu Hsien, Hsin-an Hsien, T'ung-chou, Wu-yi Hsien, Ching-chou, Lan-p'ing Hsien.

In the three provinces of Manchuria: Shêng-ching (Mukden), Chia-tzŭ-ch'ang, Lien-shan, Yü-ch'ing-chieh, Pei-lin-tzŭ, Hu-lan-ch'êng.

In Shen-hsi: Ning-chiang Chou.

In Hu-nan: Hêng-chou Fu.

We command that in all these localities the civil and military examinations be suspended for a period of five years, and we order all governors-general, governors, and examiners of the provinces concerned to act accordingly, and to have proclamations published.

Respect this!

IMPERIAL EDICT of 25th August 1901, Prohibition of the Import of Arms for Two Years.

We command all Tartar marshals, governors-general and governors of provinces, and likewise the taotais of the Customs, to prohibit, at first for a period of two years, the importation of engines of war, as well as of materials which are exclusively employed in their manufacture, of foreign origin. Instruct the office concerned.

Respect this!

MEMORANDUM on the CEREMONIAL to be observed at SOLEMN AUDIENCES, and the Reception of Foreign Representatives by H.M. the Emperor of China.

1. Solemn audiences given by His Majesty the Emperor of China to the Diplomatic Body, or to the Representatives of the Powers separately, will take place in the hall of the Palace, called "K'ien-ts'ing Kong."

2. On going to these solemn audiences, or in returning, the Representatives of the Powers will be carried in their chairs as far as the exterior of the gate King-Yun. At the gate King-Yun they will alight from the chair in which they have come, and will be borne in a small chair ("i chiao") as far as the foot of the steps of the gate K'ien-ts'ing.

On arriving at the gate K'ien-ts'ing the Representatives of the Powers will alight from their chair and advance on foot into the presence of His Majesty in the hall K'ien-ts'ing Kong.

On leaving the Representatives of the Powers will return to their residence in the same manner in which they have come.

3. When a Representative of the Powers has to present to His Majesty his credentials or a communication from the Chief of the State by whom he is accredited, the Emperor will have sent to the residence of the said Representative, to bear him to the Palace, a sedan-chair with yellow upholstery and tassels, such as are used by Princes of the Imperial family. The said Representative will be conducted back to his house in the same manner. An escort of troops will also be sent to the residence of the said Representative to accompany him on his departure and on his return.

4. When presenting his credentials or a communication from the head of the State by whom he is accredited, the Diplomatic Agent, whilst bearing the said credentials or communications, will pass through the central openings of the gates of the Palace until he arrives in the presence of His Majesty. On returning from these audiences he will conform, as far as concerns the gates through which he has to pass, to the usages already established at the Court of Peking for audiences granted to foreign Representatives.

5. The Emperor will receive directly into his hands the credentials and communications above mentioned, which the foreign Representatives may have to present to him.

6. Should His Majesty decide to invite the Representatives of the Powers to a banquet, it is well understood that this banquet should take place in one of the halls of the Imperial Palace, and that His Majesty should be present at it in person.

7. In a word, the ceremonial adopted by China with regard to foreign Representatives can in no case differ from that which results from a perfect equality between the countries concerned and China, without any loss of prestige on the one side or on the other.

APPENDIX S.

RETURN OF THE TROOPS FROM CHINA ON THE REDUCTION OF THE CHINA FIELD FORCE.

Date of Departure.	Name of Corps.	From	To.	Date of Arrival.
1901.				
15th May	2 Squadrons, 1st Bengal Lancers	Hongkong	India	27th May and 7th June.
19th „	1 „ 1st „ „	Taku	„	10th „
28th „	Headquarters 4th Brigade, Bikanir Regiment.	„	„	21st „
31st „	Alwar Regiment	„	„	27th „
1st June	Balloon Section, R.E.	„	„	
3rd „	28th Madras Infantry	„	„	29th „
21st „	1st „ „	Wei-hai-wei	„	9th July.
29th „	26th Bombay „	„	„	17th „
3rd July	6th Bengal „	Taku	„	23rd „
4th „	Headquarters 1st Brigade and 24th Punjab Infantry.	„	„	23rd „
5th „	½ Jodhpore Lancers	„	„	26th „
7th „	34th Bengal Pioneers and 1 Company, 1st Sikhs.	„	„	28th „
9th „	½ Jodhpore Lancers	„	„	30th „
11th „	½ „ „	„	„	2nd Aug.
15th „	Details Head-Quarter Staff and ½ 16th Bengal Lancers.	„	„	2nd „
16th „	1st Sikhs	Wei-hai-wei	„	4th „
19th „	Headquarters 3rd Brigade, 20th B.I., and Maler Kotla Sappers.	Taku	„	8th „
6th Aug.	Pompoms and 1 Company, R.G.A.	„	„	26th „
20th „	7th Bengal Infantry	„	„	9th Sept.
24th „	No. 4 Co. B. S. and M., No. 2 Co. Bo. S. and M., and R.E. Field Park.	„	„	15th „
27th „	½ 16th Bengal Lancers and Mounted Sappers.	„	„	15th „
29th „	½ 16th Bengal Lancers	„	„	20th „
2nd Sept.	2nd Bengal Infantry	Shanghai	Hongkong	
17th „	No. 2 Company, S. Division, R.G.A.	Wei-hai-wei	„	
21st Oct.	"B" Battery, R.H.A.	Taku	India	11th Nov.
28th „	½ 3rd Bombay Cavalry	Shanghai	„	12th „
29th „	½ 3rd „ „	Taku	„	18th „ 19th „
3rd Nov.	12th Field Battery, R.A., and R.-7 Ammunition Column.	„	„	22nd „

INDEX.

A.

	PAGES
Administration, of Peking	89, 91, 141, 151
,, of Tien-tsin	41
Aërated water factory	374
"Alacrity," H.M.S.	12, 14
Alexieff, Russian Vice-Admiral	32, 40, 103
'Algerine," H.M.S.	9, 10, 12, 13, 14, 15

Allies—
    Strength of, in China - - - 22, 32, 55, 98, 143, 148, 155
    Reduction of forces of - - - - - 151
Ambulance tongas - - - - - 47
Americans in China - 11, 17, 20, 32, 35, 37, 38, 39, 40, 55, 56, 61, 100
    9th Infantry - - - - - 38, 39, 152
    6th Marines - - - - - - 39
    6th Cavalry - - - - - 152
    14th Infantry - - - - - 152
Ammunition—
    Ammunition columns - - - - 45, 47, 49
    Scale of, for Maxim guns - - - - 46
Amoy—
    Japanese force landed at - - - - 117
    British force landed at - - - - 117
Anchorage, at Taku - - - - - 10
An-hsu - - - - - - 131
An-ting - - - - - - 23
Aoki, Japanese colonel - - - - 41
Artillery—
    At Tien-tsin - - - - - 35
    C Battery, R.H.A. - - - - 47, 49
    B Battery, R.H.A. - - - - 49, 94, 138
    12th "Battery," R.F.A - - - 41, 43, 45, 55, 138
"Aurora," H.M.S. - - - - - 10, 11
Australia, supplies fodder - - - - 46
Australian Contingent - - - - 50, 138, 145
Austrians in China - - - - 11, 14, 17

B.

Baggage, Scale of	375
Bagnell, Mr., Mrs., and child	133
Bailloud, French Major-General	130
Balloon section	47
,, ,, Horses for	368
Bank, Imperial Chinese	72
Bar, at Taku	10
"Barfleur," H.M.S.	12, 34, 51
Barrow, Colonel E. G.	43, 44, 47, 95
Base Depôt Medical stores	374
,, ,, Native Military	373
,, ,, Stationery	363
,, ,, Veterinary stores	363
Base, Wei-hai-wei selected as	45

	PAGES
Bayly, Captain E. H., R.N.	11, 17, 21, 38
Beatty, Commander, R.N.	18
Beyts, Captain, R.M.A.	28
Blake, Sir Henry	46
"Bobr," Russian gunboat	13, 15
Bogue forts	109
Bombardment of Taku forts	13
"Bonaventure," H.M.S.	47
Bower, Lieut.-Colonel H.	9, 20, 21, 41
Boxerism, seat of	4
Boxers—	
Meaning and origin of name	1
Outrages committed by	3, 4, 5, 6, 11, 17, 78, 133
Railway destroyed by	6, 9
Brigades of China Expeditionary Force—	
1st	44
2nd	45, 47
3rd	49
4th	49
Briggs, Lieutenant, R.N.	122
"Brisk," H.M.S.	9
British—	
Contingent for China, strength in September 1900	99, 101
„ „ „ strength on 1st January 1901	144
„ „ „ reduction of	149, 151, 153, 155
Policy in China	103
Brooks, Mr.	4
Browning, Major, 4th P.I.	151
Bruce, Rear-Admiral	12, 16, 20, 22
„ Major, Chinese Regiment	34
Bucholtz, Commander, German Navy	27
Bullocks for siege train	366
Butler, Mr., P.E.O.	117

C.

Cable, submarine, between Shanghai and Taku	50
Canada, supply of warm clothing from	46, 401
"Carthage," hospital ship	48
Casualties—	
Of Allies at capture of Taku forts	15
British, at relief of Tien-tsin	20
„ during fighting at Tien-tsin	18
„ of naval force up to 10th June 1900	21
„ at Lofa on 14th June 1900	24
Of Admiral Seymour's column	30
British, at Tien-tsin on 27th June 1900	31, 34, 40
Of Allies	35, 36, 40
At Peitsang	59
At Yangtsun	60
At capture of Peking	67, 68
In American contingent	152
Cavalry brigade	47, 49
"Centurion," H.M.S.	10, 26, 34, 36
Chaffee, Major-General, U.S.A.	52, 151, 152
Chang Chih-tung, Viceroy at Hankow	33, 103, 104, 108, 110, 118, 168
Chang-chia-wan, action at	63
Chao-shu-ch'iao, and punishment of	77, 164
Che-kiang province	33
Ch'i-hsiu, punishment of	165
Chi-li, garrison of for winter 1900	98

	PAGES
China Expeditionary Force, despatch of, from India	42 et seq.
„ „ details of	349
China Independent Association	116
Chinese Court, anti-foreign Manchu faction	5
Chinese Imperial Troops—	
Attack allies	25
Strength of	33
Chinese Regiment	8, 9, 20, 21, 34, 38, 55, 138
Ching, Prince	75, 84, 104, 157, 168
Ching-wang-tao—	
Occupation of	122
Light railway at	123
Cho-chou, town	131
Cholera	48, 49
Chuang, Prince, punishment of	164
Chun, Prince	167
Chün-liang-ch'eng	17, 18, 20
Climate	56
Coal—	
Japanese	46
Mines at Tong-shan	126
Coolie corps	43, 364
Cooper, Mr.	134
Cordes, Mr	79
Cossacks	59
Council of Reform	170
Cradock, Commander, R.N.	12, 13, 14, 20
Creagh, Brigadier-General O'M.	45, 120, 154
Cummins, Brigadier-General J. T.	49
Currie, Mr. A.	27
Curzon, Lord	42, 43

D.

Dansette, Mr.	140
Davidge, Mr., R.N.	29
Decrees, Imperial	101, 160, 168, 170
Depôts	358
Desmond, Miss	113
Despatches—	
Vice-Admiral Sir E. H. Seymour's	171–228
Major-General W. J. Gascoigne's	229–231
Brigadier-General A. R. F. Dorward's	232–239
Sir Claude M. MacDonald's	240–310
Lieut.-General Sir A. Gaselee's	311–341
Dhanjibhoy, Khan Bahadur, supplies ambulance tongas	47
Distribution of British troops during winter, 1900-1	98
Doig, Capt. R. O'M., R.M.L.I.	27
Donaldson, Midshipman	18
Dorward, Colonel and Brigadier-General	20, 21, 35, 38, 39, 90, 152
Drummond, Lieut. J., R.N.	21, 38

E.

Eastern Arsenal, Tien-tsin	40
Edicts, Imperial	32, 146, 158, 160, 161, 164
"Endymion," H.M.S.	10, 14
Engineer Field Park	361
Esdaile, Midshipman F., R.N.	34

	PAGES
Europeans, total number murdered	167
Explosion	95

F.

"Falamas," s.s.	50
"Fame," H.M.S.	10, 11, 13, 15, 16, 21
Favier, Père, R.C. Bishop of Peking	5
Feng-tai, railway station—	
Burnt by Boxers	6, 9
Occupied by British	94
Field audit pay office	
Field batteries	45, 47, 50
Field hospitals	45, 49, 50
Fodder, from Australia	46
Fortifications, Chinese, razed	148
Fraser, Mr. M. F. A.	112
French in China	11, 17, 19, 33, 36, 37, 38, 59, 61
,, contingent for China	100, 101
,, reduction of	153, 154
,, strength of troops in September 1900	99
Frey, Major-General, commanding French troops	68
Fukushima, Japanese Major-General	35, 37, 67

G.

Gamewell, Rev. F. D.	72, 87
Garioni, Italian colonel	135
Garrigues, Père	77
Garrisons in North China	97, 138, 143, 149
Gascoigne, Major-General	46, 48
Gaselee, Lieut.-General Sir A.	41, 43, 44, 46, 48, 51, 52, 54, 66, 68, 89, 97, 121, 139, 155
Germans in China	11, 14, 17, 26, 31, 36, 37
,, contingent for China	100
,, strength of, in September 1900	101
"Gilyak," Russian gunboat	13, 15
Gould, Miss	133
Grand Canal	36
Grand Council of Government Reform	168
Grierson, Colonel J. M.	120
Gündell, Lieut.-Colonel, German army	126
"Gwalior," hospital ship	48
Gwynne, Captain, R.W.F.	39

H.

Hall of Ancestors	92
Halliday, Captain L. S. T., R.M.L.I.	9
Hang-chou, Viceroy of	33
Hanku, railway bridge	125
Hanlin, academy and library burnt	80
Hart, Sir Robert	31, 72
Hattori, Commander, Japanese navy	14
Hei-niu-chuang, village	35
"Hermione," H.M.S.	9, 108
Hill, Captain, Chinese regiment	95

	PAGES
Hillier, Sir Walter	121
Honan, headquarters of Ta-tao-hui, or Big Knife Society	1
Hongkong—	
British force embarks from for North China	19
Troops sent from	42
Garrison of	45
Hongkong artillery	21, 55, 138
Hongkong regiment	21, 35, 38, 48, 55, 138
Ho-hsi-wu	62
Höpfner, Major-General von	100
Horse shoes and nails, reserve of	361
Hospital ships	45
Presented by Maharajah Scindia of Gwalior	48
"Maine"	48
"Carthage"	48
Howitzers	47, 154
Hsi-an-fu, city	110
Hsi-ku armoury	21, 27
Captured by Admiral Seymour	27
Occupied by Russians	40, 53
Hsin-cheng, Chinese fort	16, 22
Hsi-wan-tzu, mission station	139
Hsu-tung, punishment of	165
Hsü-cheng-yü, punishment of	165
Hsü-ching-cheng, punishment of	165
Hsü-yung-i, punishment of	165
Huai-ho, or Grand Canal	36
Huai-ta-pu, anti-foreign Manchu	158
Huang-tsun	94, 95
"Humber," H.M.S.	10
Hunho River	56, 136
Hunting Park	92

I.

"Iltis," German gunboat	13, 14, 15
Imperial Chinese Bank	72
Imperial decrees	101, 160, 168, 170
Imperial edicts	32, 104, 112, 146, 158, 160, 161, 164
Indemnity, basis of claims for	166
India—	
Offers to send troops to China	19
First troops sent	41
Part taken by in sending troops	42 et seq.
Indian troops—	
1st Sikh Infantry	42, 44, 55, 62
1st Bengal Lancers	43, 45, 49, 53, 55, 138, 150
1st Jodhpur Lancers	50, 121, 138, 145, 151
1st Madras Pioneers	43, 45, 138
2nd Bengal Infantry	44, 45, 155
3rd Bombay Light Cavalry	47, 49, 138
3rd Madras Infantry	44, 45
4th Gurkha Rifles, 1st Battalion	44, 45
4th Punjab Infantry	49, 121, 151
5th Infantry, Hyderabad Contingent	49
6th Bengal Infantry	47, 49, 121, 151
7th Bengal Infantry	41, 42, 44, 55
14th Sikhs	44, 45, 48, 150
16th Bengal Lancers	47, 49, 91, 138
20th Punjab Infantry	47, 49, 96, 138
22nd Bombay Infantry	45
24th Punjab Infantry	41, 43, 44

	PAGES
26th Bombay Infantry	44
28th Madras Infantry	49, 138, 150
30th Bombay Infantry	44, 45
31st Madras Infantry	49, 150
34th Punjab Pioneers	47, 48, 49, 121
Bengal Sappers and Miners	45, 138
" " " Mounted Detachment	94
Bikanir Camel Corps	49, 150
Bombay Sappers and Miners	45, 138
Maler Kotla Sappers	50, 121, 138
Q.O. Madras Sappers and Miners	45, 138, 150
Ulwar Infantry	49, 150
Indian troops, raising of new regiments to replace those sent to China	48
"Isis," H.M.S.	117
Italians in China	11, 14, 17, 20, 24
Strength of, in September 1900	99
Contingent for China	101

J.

Japanese coolies	43
Japanese in China	14, 17, 33, 34, 35, 36, 37, 39, 40, 52, 54, 55, 56, 57, 58, 61, 63
Strength of, in September 1900	99
Mobilisation and strength of first contingent	100
Reduction of force	154
Jellicoe, Captain J. R., R.N.	26
Johnstone, Major, R.M.L.I.	10, 24, 27
Jung-Lu	78, 83, 104, 115, 158, 168
Junks—	
for carriage of wounded	26
" " " guns	26

K.

Kalgan, expedition to	139
Kang-yi, pro-Boxer	6, 115, 165
Kao-chia-chuang, action at	63
Ketteler, Baron Von, murdered	79
Keys, R., Lt., R.N.	13, 15, 21
Kiang-yin forts	109
Kinder, Mr.	97, 127
Ko-lao-hui, or "Society of the Elder Brother"	1, 114
"Koreytz," Russian gunboat	13, 15
Ku-ching	131
Kang-chi-chêng	94
Kun-kang	168

L.

Lan, Duke	77
"Landaura," s.s.	50
Langfang	11, 23, 25
Action at	24
Lee, Major Jesse, U.S.A.	39
Legations, Peking—	
Communication with outside world cut off	6
Attack on commenced	7

		PAGES
Guards		9
Attempted relief of, by Admiral Seymour		11
Defence of		71
and Sir Claude MacDonald's report, Appendix A.		240
Preparation of, for defence		73
Strength of guards left in China		149
„ „ British guard		154
Liang-hsiang-hsien		131
Attacked by Allies		95
Lien-yüan		165
Li Hung Chang		46, 104, 109, 117, 137, 157, 168
Linievitch, Russian Lieut.-General		52, 64, 67, 93, 107
Lines of communication between Peking and the sea, arrangements for guarding		149
"Linnet," H.M.S.		108
"Lion," French gunboat		13, 15
Li-pa-feng		131
Li Ping-hêng		85, 109, 165
Liscum, Colonel, U.S.A.		38
Lin Kun-yi, Viceroy of Nanking		33, 104, 108, 110, 118, 168
Liu-li-ho, town		131
Lloyd, Captain H. T. R., R.M.L.I.		27
Loans by Great Britain to Chang Chih-tung		110, 118
Lofa, fighting at		11, 23, 24, 25
Looting		89
Lorne Campbell, Colonel		45, 130
Lowther-Crofton, Lieut. E. G., R.N.		29
Luhan Railway		94
Luke, Major, R.M.L.I.		18
Lu-kou-chiao		94, 131
Lutai Canal		36

M.

Ma, Chinese General		40
MacDonald, Sir Claude		10, 41, 75, 83, 84, 85, 138
Ma-chia-pu, terminus of railway		92, 95
Machine guns		360
Macrae, Mr.		16
"Maine," s.s., American hospital ship		48
Manchester, Miss		113
Manchuria, Boxer outrages in		102
Marseilles, French troops leave for China		19
Matou		63
Maxim guns—		
Issue of to troops proceeding to China		46
Lent from England		46
Scale of ammunition for		46
Medal for operations in China		348
Medical stores, base depôt		373
Mei, Chinese General		142
Military College, Chinese, at Tientsin		18
Mischenkoff, Russian Colonel		102
Missionaries—		
Protected in South China		111
Murdered		112, 113, 133, 135, 140, 158, 167
"Monocacy," U.S. gunboat		13
Morrell, Miss		133
Morris, Major, R.W.F.		19, 20
Morrison Dr.		83
Mukden		41
Missions destroyed at		102

N.

	PAGES
Nanking, Viceroy of	33
Naval Brigade	38, 55
Negotiations for peace	105, 107
"Nerbudda," s.s.	45
New South Wales contingent	50, 138
Nieh, Chinese General	6, 11, 28, 75
Nieh-tai, of Pao-ting fu	134
Ning-yüan	124
Niu-chuang, occupied by Russians	102
Norman, Mr.	6, 135

O.

Offices, Staff and Departmental, of China Expeditionary Force	361
Officials responsible for outrages	118
Oliphant, Mr. David	82
Ollivant, Captain, Chinese Regiment	38
Operations—	
After relief of Legations	90
Up to end of December, 1900	137
Against Boxers	141, 142, 154
Against regular Chinese troops	142, 149
From 1st January 1901 to end of campaign	143
Against brigands	145, 151
Ordnance	359
Ordnance field park	46
"Orlando," H.M.S.	9
Outrages, committed by Boxers	3, 4, 5, 6, 11, 17, 78, 133
,, ,, ,, Chinese troops	7

P.

"Palamcotta," s.s.	45
Pao-ting fu—	
European railway employés attacked at	6
Murder of Christians at	5
Punitive expedition to	129
Fen-tai of	131, 133
Return of columns from	135
Evacuation of by French	155
Pa-ta-chü, attacked by Allies	96
Pay office, Field Audit	373
Peace negotiations	105, 146, 157, 158, 160
Pei-ho River	21, 26, 36, 56
Pei-tai-ho, destroyed	10
Peitang cathedral	6, 68, 69, 70
Peitang forts	96, 148
Peitsang, actions at	26, 54, 58
Peking, attack on by Allies	64–67
Occupation of	68, 69
Administration of	89, 91, 141, 151
Defence of Legations at	71, 240
Pelacot, French Colonel	37
Penrose, Major, R.E.	9
Pereira, Capt.	9
,, Major	38
Perrott, Col., R.A.	47

	PAGES
Phillimore, Lieut., R.N.	38
Pier at Ching-wang-tao	123
"Pigmy," H.M.S.	121
"Pioneer," s.s.	112
Pitkin, Mr.	133
Political situation in China	108
Pompoms from England and South Africa	46
Powell, Lieut., R.N.	18
,, Bt. Lt.-Col. C. H.	120, 121
Prize Fund	89
"Protector," South Australian cruiser	50
Punishments inflicted on Chinese	114, 157
,, of guilty persons demanded by Powers	164, 167
,, demands for, complied with	168

R.

Radford, Colonel	151
Railway—	
Destroyed by Boxers	6, 9
Handed over to Russians	41
Manchurian, destroyed by Chinese	41
Reconstruction of	90, 97
At Shan-hai-kuan	122
Light, to Ching-wang-tao	123
Repairs and administration of	124, 126, 128, 142, 146
Convention	125, 127, 145
Railway Section—	372
Workshops	97, 125
Rainy season	52
Reform Party	114, 115
Regulations, general, for China Expeditionary Force	375
Reid, Major-General	121, 328
Relief of Legations, Peking, attempted by Admiral Seymour	11, 12
,, ,, ,, by Allies	66
Remount Depôt	50, 370
Robinson, Mr.	6, 135
Roper, Lieut. C. D., R.N.	10
Royal Engineers in China	20
Royal Inniskilling Fusiliers	47
Royal Marine Light Infantry	55
Royal Welsh Fusiliers	19, 39, 41, 55, 138, 145
Russians in China	13, 14, 17, 20, 21, 31, 33, 35, 36, 37, 40, 59, 61
Strength of in September 1900	99
Withdrawal of from Peking	107
Russian policy in China	106

S.

San-chia-tien Arsenal destroyed	96
Sanitary establishment	372
Sappers, mounted detachment	48
Satow, Sir Ernest	138
Scheme for despatch of British Expeditionary Force to China—	349
Aërated Water Factory	374
Base Depôt, Medical stores	373
,, ,, Native Military	363
,, ,, Stationery	363
,, ,, Veterinary stores	374
Composition of the Force	349

	PAGES
Depôts	358
Dhanjibhoy's Tongas	372
Engineer Field Park	361
Equipment	359
Field Audit Pay Office	373
General regulations	375
Horses for balloon section	368
Horses for Vickers-Maxim guns	369
Machine guns	360
Ordnance	359
Punjab Coolie Corps	364
Railway Section	372
Remount Depôt	370
Reserve of horse shoes and nails	361
Sanitary establishment	372
Siege train bullocks	364
Signallers	361
Staff of the Force	351
Staff and Departmental offices	361
Strengths, establishments, baggage, and tentage	357
Survey party	371
Telegraph Section	371
Schwarzhoff, German General Von	150
Scottish Rifles	47
Scott, Major T. E.	66
Secretary of State for India	42
Secret Societies	1
Seymour, Admiral Sir E. H.	10, 17, 24, 25, 36, 41, 42, 111
Seymour's, Admiral Sir E. H., Column for relief of Peking	17, 21, 23 et seq.
Shanghai, garrison of	47, 98, 155
Excitement at	110
Troops landed at	111
Shan-hai-kuan—	
Occupied by Allies	121
Forts at destroyed	148
Shan-hsi Province, scarcity in	3
Shan-tung, seat of Boxerism	2, 4
Sherwood, Miss	113
Shiba, Japanese Colonel	83
Shirinsky, Russian Colonel	21, 29
Shropshire Light Infantry	47
Siege train bullocks	366
Signalling units	45, 50, 361
Sinho	51
Smith, Lieut. A. G., R.N.	23, 24
Special Service Officers	45
Staff of the China Expeditionary Force	351
Stessel, Russian Major-General	20, 52
Stewart, Commodore R. H. J., R.N.	13
Stewart, Brigadier-General Sir Norman	44
Stirling, Lieut., R.N.	18
Stirling, Lieut., 4th P.I.	151
Strengths of British units	358
Strouts, Captain B. M., R.M.L.I	9, 82
Su, Prince	71
Sugiyama, Mr	7, 77, 159
Summer Palace	91, 137, 155
Sung, Chinese General	40
Sung-ling-tien	131
Supply Column	44, 45, 49
Survey party	48, 139, 371
Swatow, persecution of Chinese Christians at	117

U 21071. M M

T.

	PAGES
Tai-yuan-fu	106
Taku—	
Anchorage and bar	10
Forts attacked by Allies	13
Forts destroyed	148
Arrival of first British transport at	45
"Taku," Chinese torpedo boat, destroyed	16
Tang-ku	13, 51
Tartar City, Peking	92
Ta-tao-hui, or Big Knife Society	1
Ta-tung rebellion	114
Telegraphs	50, 75, 90, 107
Telegraph Section	371
Tentage, Scale of	358
Temple of Agriculture	92
Temple of Heaven	92
"Terrible," H.M.S.	19, 20, 21, 34
Thirgood, Miss	113
Thomann, Austrian Captain	82
Thompson, Mr.	113
Tien-tsin—	
Allied Artillery at	34, 38
Attack on and capture of native city	37 *et seq.*
Administrative division of, among Allies	41
Defence of Settlement at	31 *et seq.*
Garrison of	21, 36
Tien-tsin—	
Governorship of	41
Reinforcements sent to	9, 10, 11, 12, 20, 21
Strength of Chinese forces employed against	33
Tien-tsin Tug and Lighter Co.	16
Ting-hsing	131
Tong-shan—	
Abandoned	10
Railway workshops at	97, 126
Torpedo boat destroyers, Chinese, captured by British	15
Torpedo boat destroyers, Chinese, disposal of	16
Tsung-li Yamen, abolition of	159
Transport—	
Taken up for shipping force to China	42
Chinese	45
Transports—	
Fitting up of at Calcutta	45
Troops, Chinese, outrages committed by	7
Tuan, Prince	33, 76, 108, 115, 164
Tu-liu, Expedition against	95
Tung-chou	63
Tung Fu-hsiang	6, 25, 158, 163, 164

V.

Veterinary Stores, Base Depôt	374
Vickers-Maxim guns, horses for	369
Victorian Contingent	138
Voyron, French Major-General	100

W.

Waldersee, Count Von	97, 104, 120, 121, 138, 153
Waller, Major, U.S A.	39

	PAGES
Wang-wên-shao	168
Ward, Mr. and Mrs.	113
Warren, Mr.	82
Watson, Captain, Chinese Regiment	9
Watts, Mr. J.	18
Watts Jones, Captain, R.E.	140
Wei-hai-wei	8, 9, 45, 98
Western Arsenal, Tien-tsin	21, 33, 35, 37
"Whiting," H.M.S.	10, 11, 13, 15, 16
Wilson, Brigadier-General, U.S.A.	95
Winter Palace	137
Withdrawal of troops from N. China	137, 168
Witthames, Belgian Commandant	140
Wogack, Russian Colonel	41, 147
Wray, Captain E., R.M.L.I.	9
Wright, Lieut., R.N.	18
Wu-chang, Viceroy of	33
Wu-sung Forts	109

Y.

Yamaguchi, Japanese Lieut.-General	52, 54
Yangtse Valley, situation in	117
Yangtsun, battle of	59
Railway station destroyed at	24
Yi-chou	134
Ying-Nien, punishment of	164
Yorck, Count Colonel Von Wartenberg	139
Yüan-chang	165
Yüan Shi-kai	4, 109
Yü-chang	158
Yü-hsien	2, 4, 158, 164
Yü-lu	8, 40, 61, 133

Z.

"Zayathla," hospital ship, renamed "Gwalior"	48
"Zebengla," s.s.	46, 47
Zerpitsky, Russian General	122

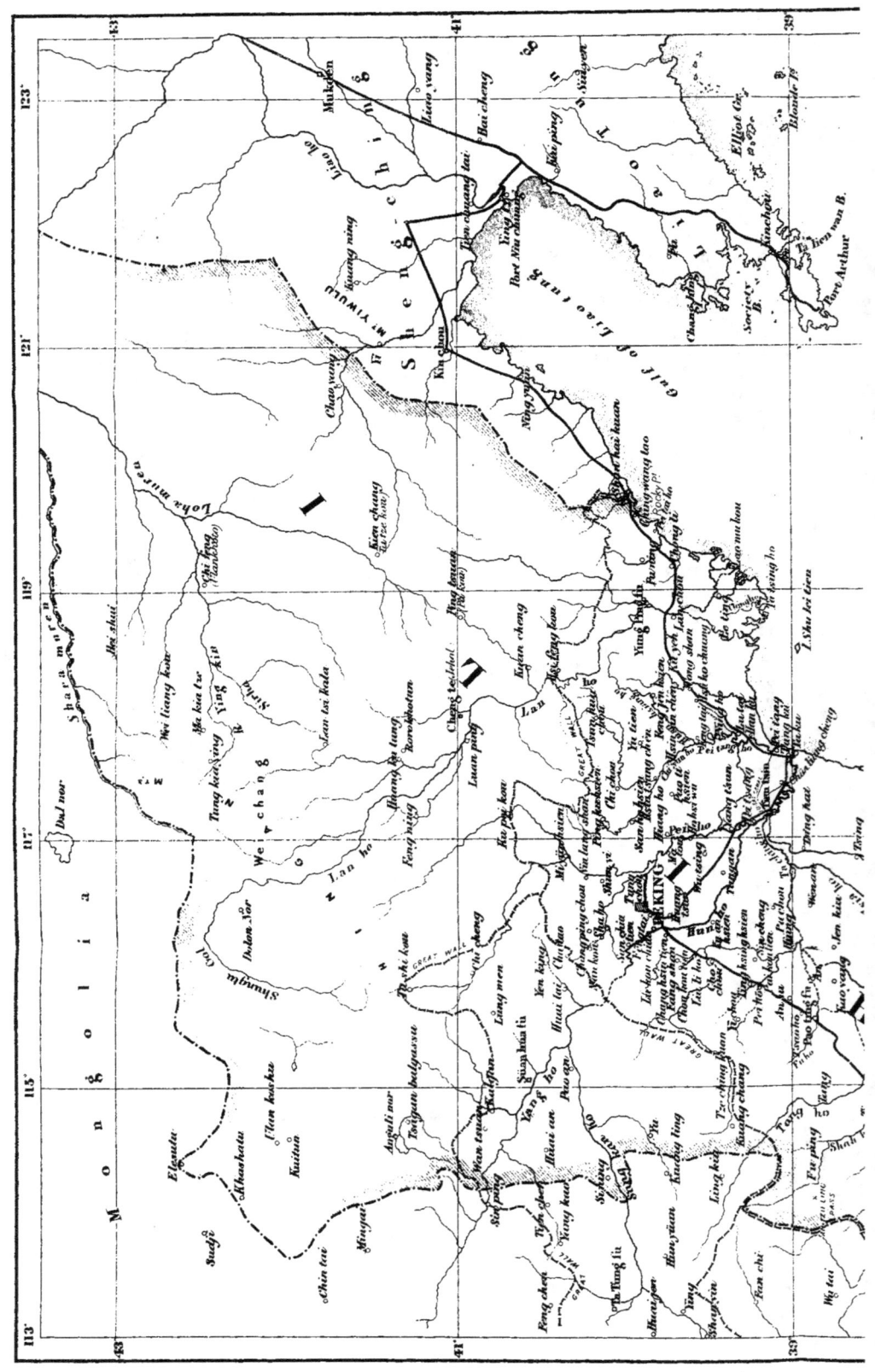

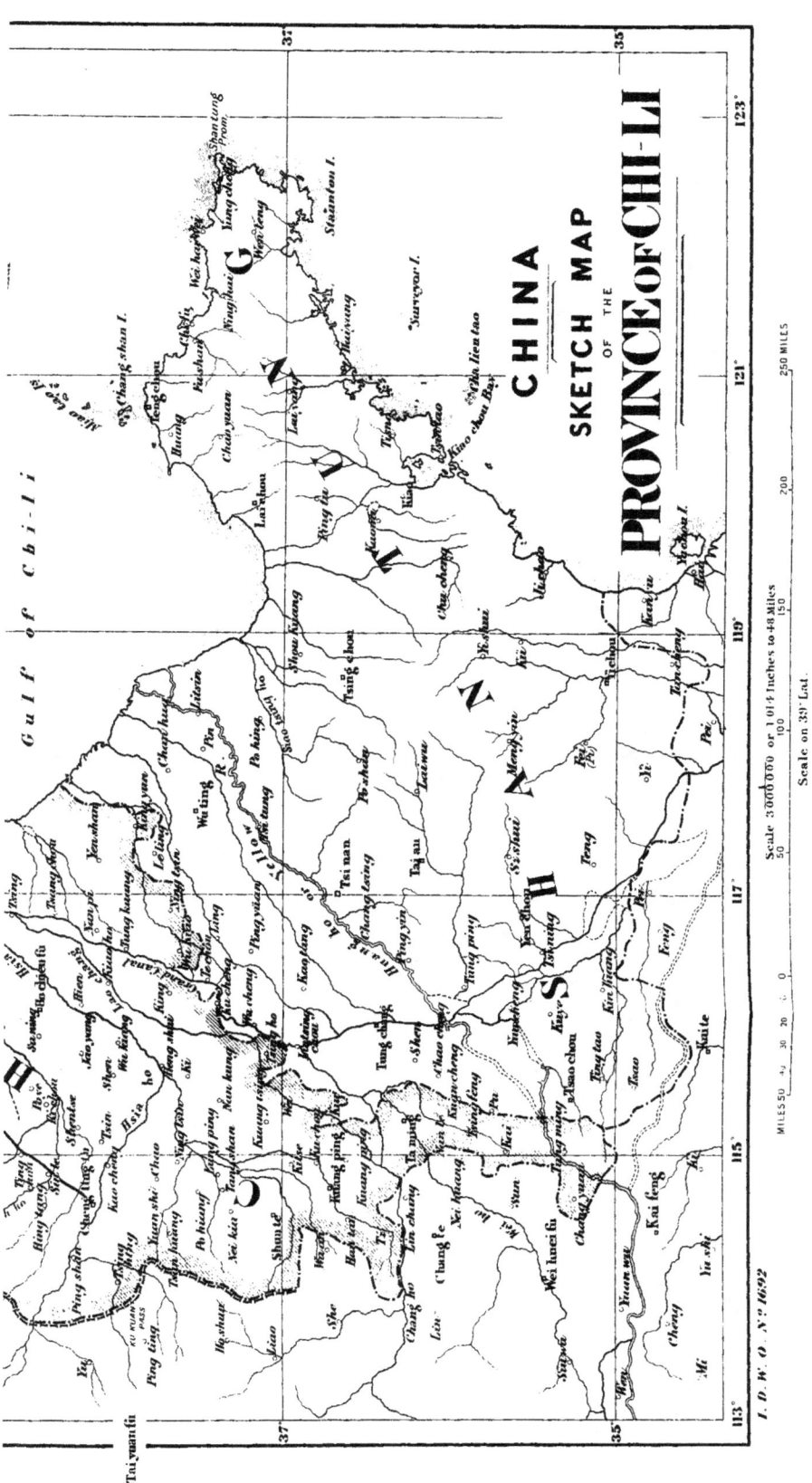

v

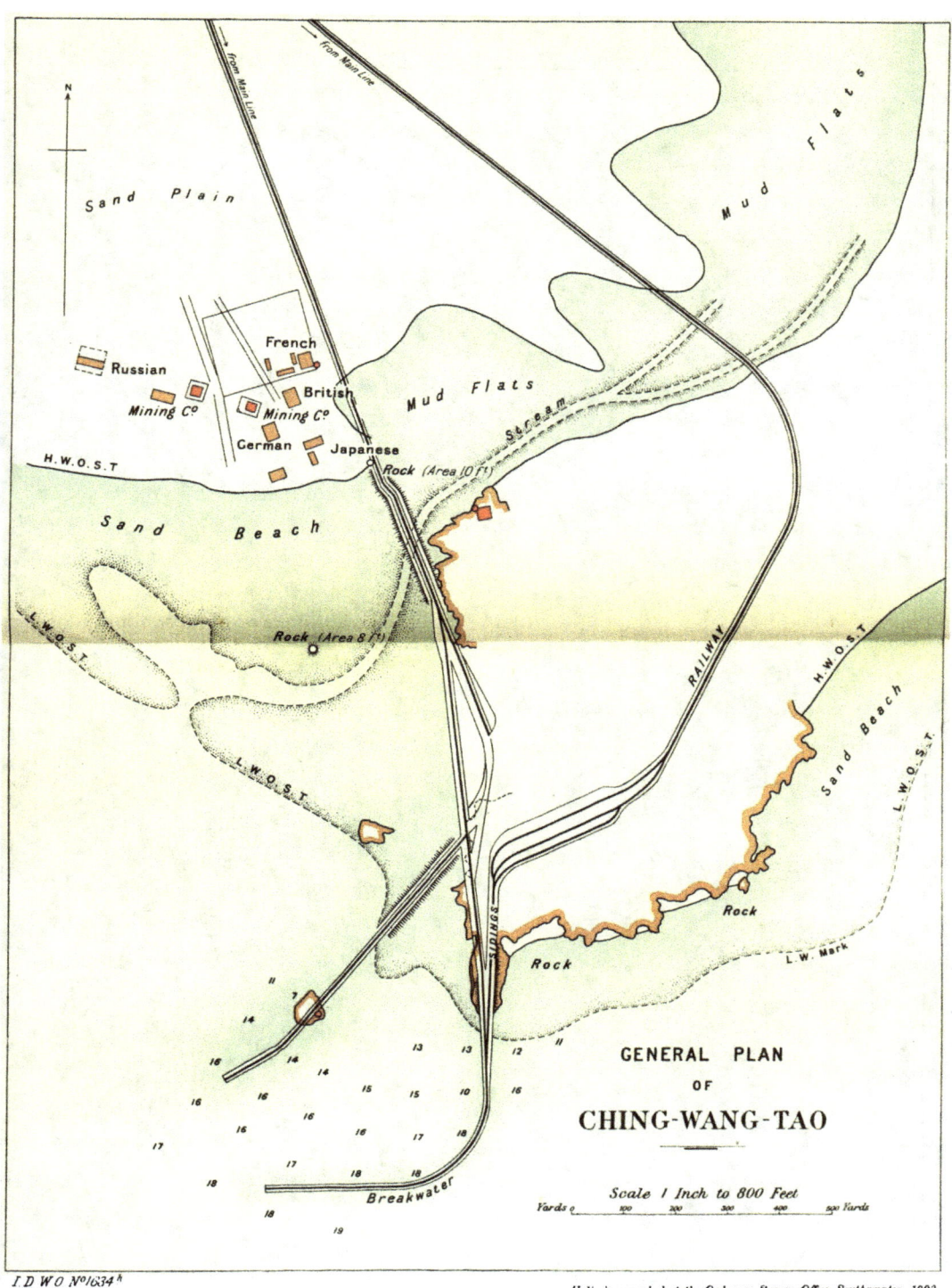

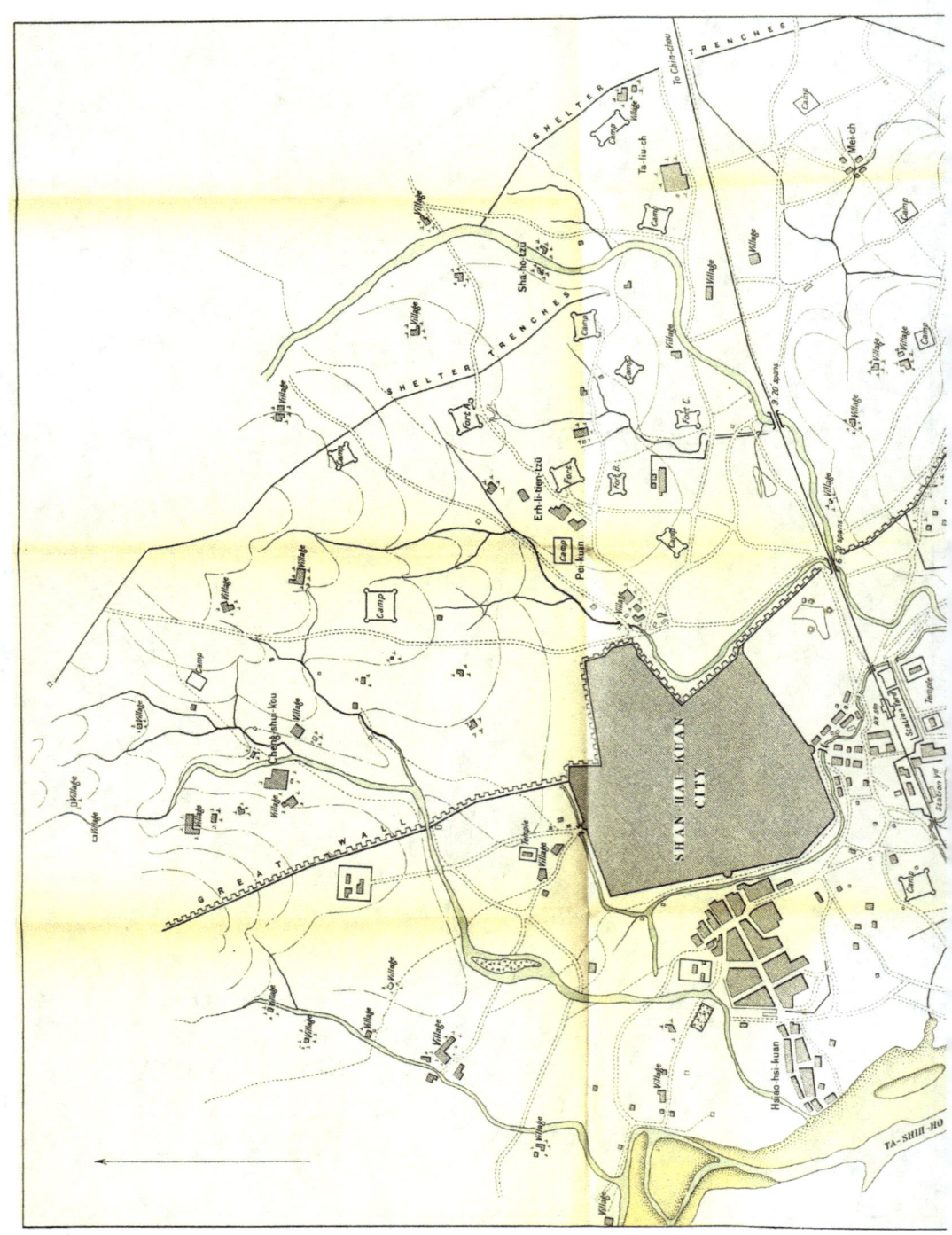

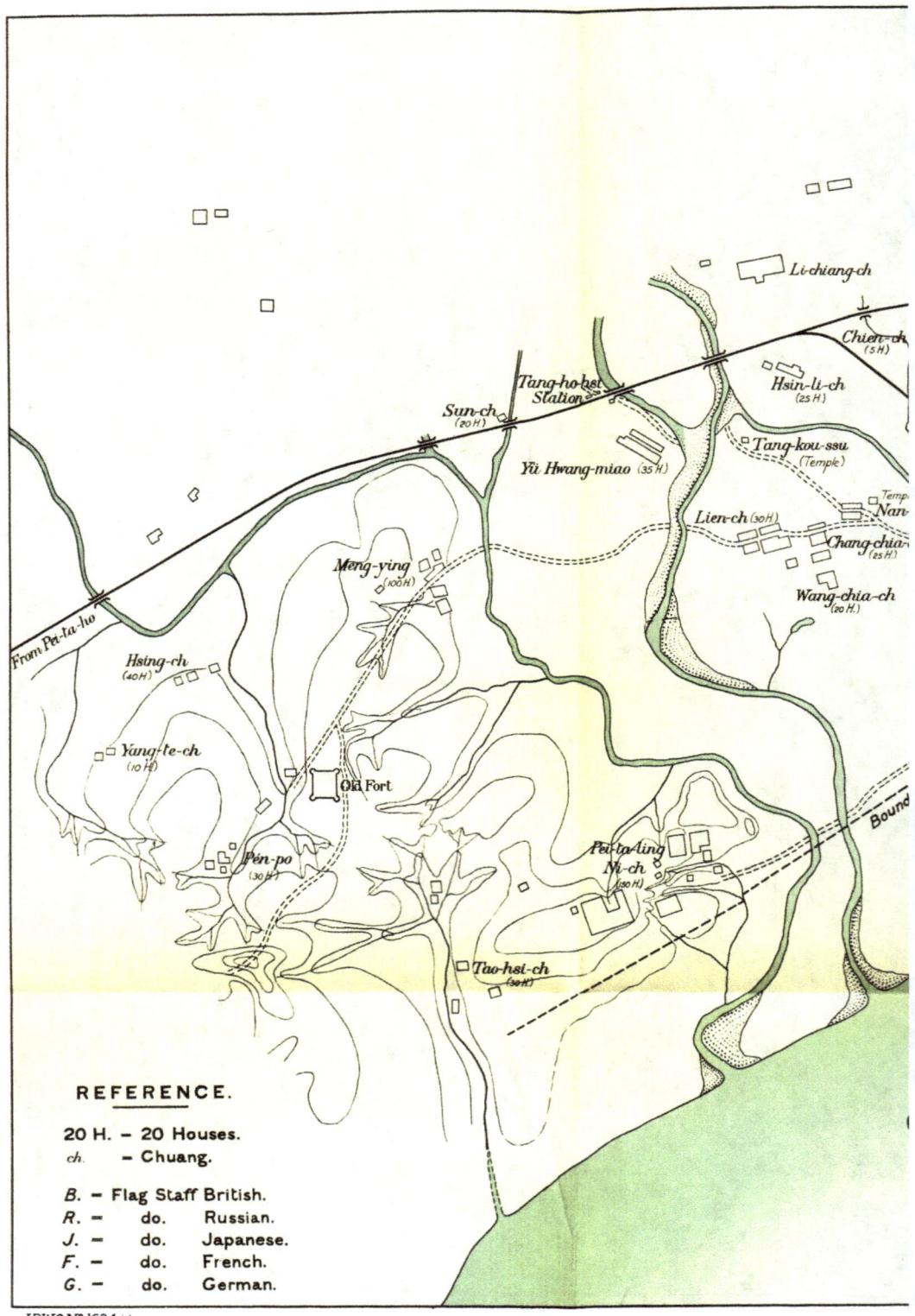

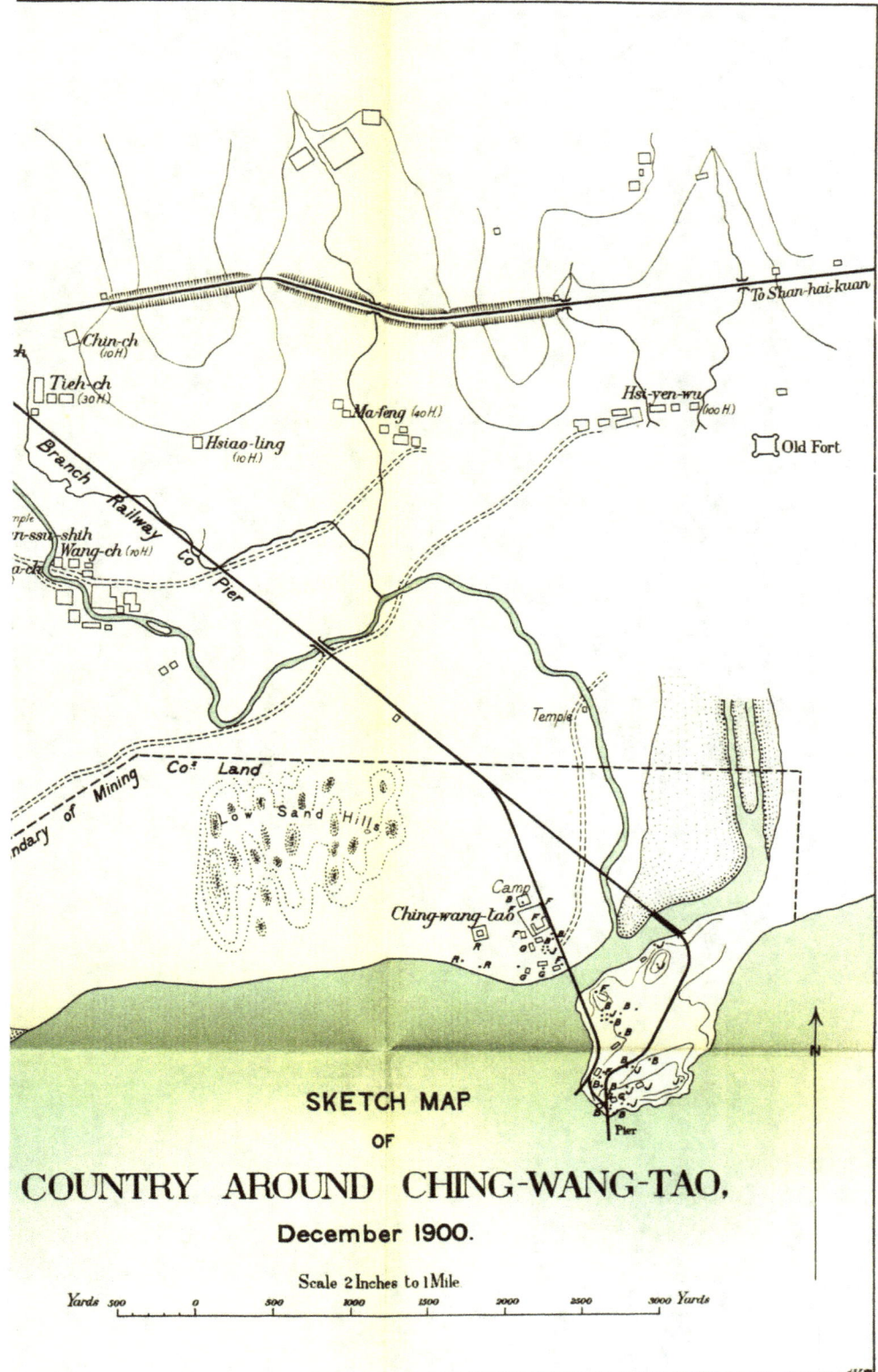

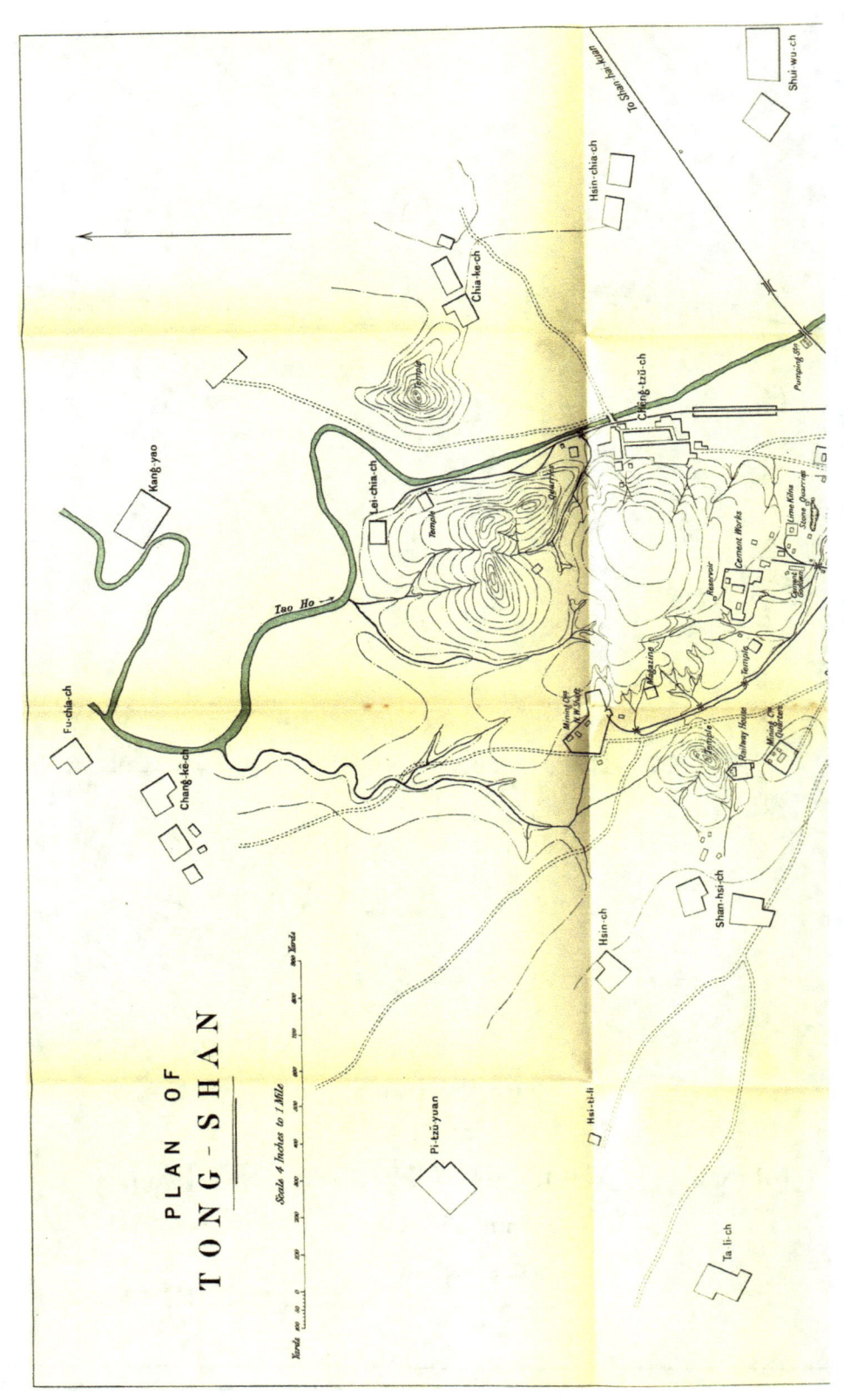

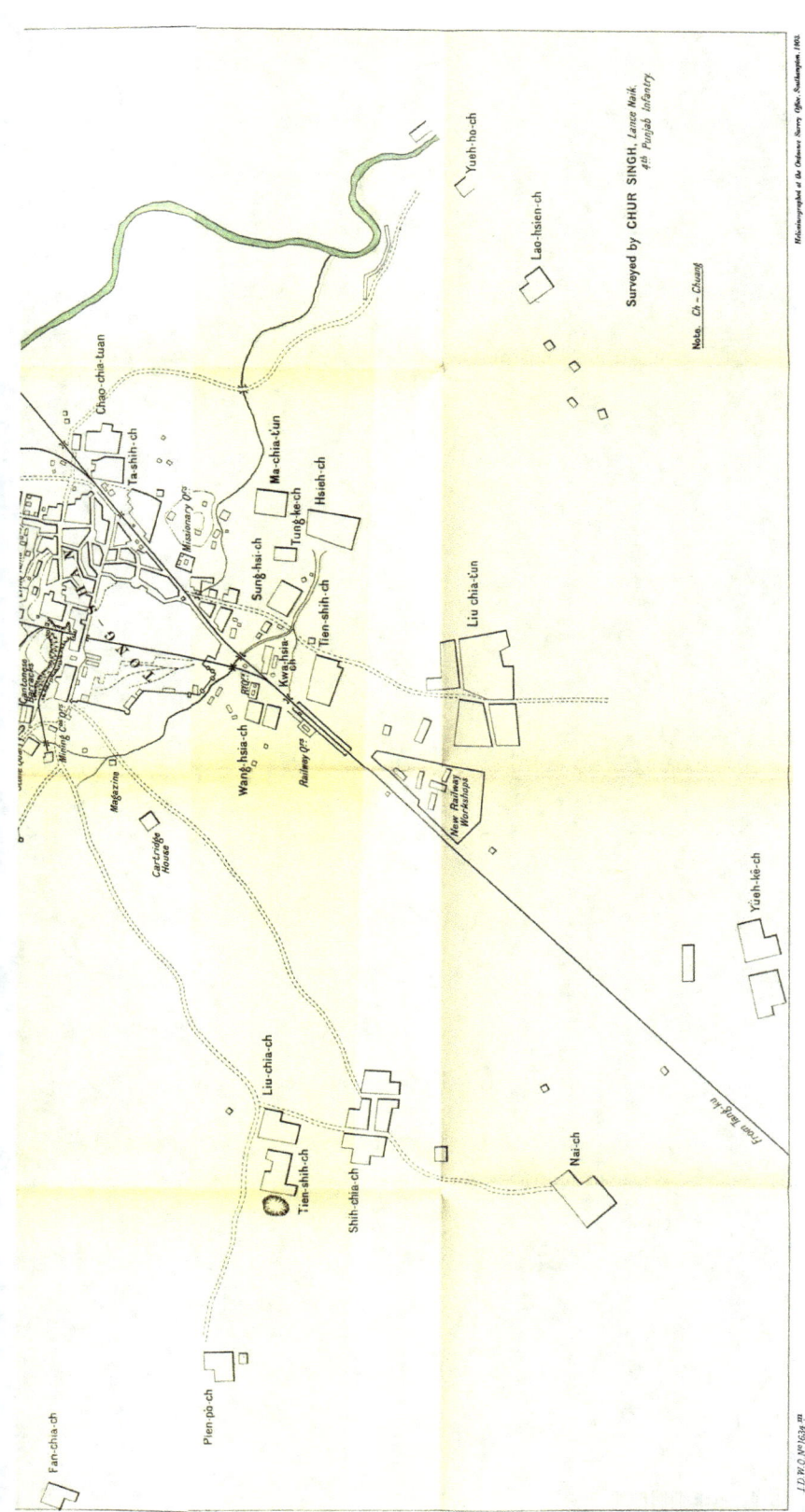

www.ingramcontent.com/pod-product-compliance
Lightning Source LLC
Chambersburg PA
CBHW071218290426
44108CB00013B/1211